GEOLOGY

OF

TENNESSEE,

BY

JAMES M. SAFFORD, A. M., Ph. D.,

STATE GEOLOGIST,

Professor of Natural Science in Cumberland University,
Lebanon, Tennessee.

BY AUTHORITY OF THE GENERAL ASSEMBLY.

NASHVILLE:
S. C. MERCER,............ ....PRINTER TO THE STATE.

1869.

PREFACE.

This Report, and the Map which accompanies it, embody the principal results of the geological surveys and researches made by myself in Tennessee, at intervals during the last twenty years. For six years of this period I acted under the authority of the State. For the remainder of the time, the surveys made, were on my personal account, and their results, in so far as they are here embraced, are a gratuitous contribution to the Geology of Tennessee.

What is presented in this volume is, with its merits and defects, essentially my own. The main part has been worked out laboriously in the field; and this without assistants, and with inadequate means. These circumstances constitute the only apology I offer for deficiences. The whole work has involved little, if any, less than 10,000 miles of travel.

The results of the labors of others, and especially, of my venerable predecessor, Dr. Troost, when available, have been freely used, and the proper credit given. To a number of my scientific cotemporaries, I am much indebted; their names are given in the course of the Report, and my obligations acknowledged.

To many friends in the State, I am also indebted for encouragement and assistance. To Col. S. D. Morgan, Dr. John B. Lindsley, of Nashville, Hon. Sam. Milligan, formerly of Greeneville, now of Washington, and Col. Wm. Bosson, of Murfreesboro', I am under especial obligations. These gentlemen, ever ready to advance any scientific investigation which, in their opinion, might redound to the interests of the State, deserve prominent niches as patrons of science in Tennessee.

The Report does not claim to be a complete presentation of the Geology of the State; it is rather an introduction to such a presentation, and, so far as it goes, will, I trust, be acceptable.

In 1831, the General Assembly took the first step towards

a geological survey of the State, by appointing Dr. Gerard Troost, then Professor of Chemistry, Mineralogy and Geology in the University of Nashville, to the position of State Geologist, on a meagre salary of five hundred dollars. Dr. Troost was continued in office until 1850. During this time, he made nine Reports, the first two of which, do not appear to have been published, or, if they were, I have never seen them. The most important Reports are the Third, Fourth, Fifth, Sixth and Seventh. These, though short, contain much valuable matter, and have been of essential service to the State The Fifth is the largest, and is an octavo pamphlet of seventy-five pages.

The Legislature, in February, 1854, passed an Act, creating again, the office of "Geologist and Mineralogist of the State," and a few days after, I was elected to fill the place. At the expiration of the first term, (two years,) I was re-elected to to the position, and again in 1858.

In 1856, I presented a preliminary Report, which was published under the title of "A Geological Reconnoissance of the State of Tennessee." This was a small volume of 164 pages. In February, 1860, it was thought desirable to publish a full Report on the Geology of the State, so far as it was practicable to do so, and the Report now presented, was commenced then. The work, however, had not proceeded far, when the war, with its ills, came upon us, and soon put a stop to it.

In March, 1868, the Legislature again authorized the preparation of the Report, and ordered it, when ready, to be printed.

After an eventful history, it is now presented to the General Assembly, and citizens of the State.

J. M. Safford.

Lebanon, Tenn., April 15, 1869.

NOTES ON THE MAP.

A great amount of labor has been bestowed upon the Map. Many topographical features are original, having been worked out by the author during the progress of the survey. It has been a point to håve the State and county boundaries as nearly correct, as possible. With a few exceptions, the railroads are from the actual surveys.* Aside from its Geology, the Map, so far as it goes, is the best geographical map of Tennessee yet published.

The section in the right-hand lower corner, is intended to illustrate the topography and the geology of the East Tennessee Valley, along the line M—N. It will correct the distorted dip of strata in the right-hand end of the principal section.

With reference to the Map as an Agricultural one, see page 525.

The engraver has, as a general thing, done his work well. A few omissions were observed, after it was too late to supply them. The names *Anderson* and *Clinton*, are wanting in Anderson County, though the boundaries of the county are given. *Maryville*, in Blount County, is also missing. These names, if desirable, can be supplied by those into whose hands copies of the Map may fall.

ROCKWOOD FURNACE IN ROANE COUNTY.

Since the last pages of this book were printed, I have received reliable information as to the furnace above mentioned. It appears that Roane County is but little behind Greene, (§ 1198.) Within fourteen months, the Rockwood Furnace, with all of its appurtenances, including a village of 500 inhabitants, has sprung up like magic, and is now in successful operation. The site of the furnace is near the base of Walden's Ridge, and about four miles from Kimbrough's Landing, on the Tennessee River. The ore used is the dyestone, which is obtained from beds in the Mountain Dyestone Range, mentioned on page 306. It is an interesting fact, that this is the first furnace which has made use of raw coal in the manuf cture of iron. The coal is obtained from the crest of Walden's Ridge, and is conveyed directly to the furnace, by a small railroad. Hot-blast is used, with steam as motive power. The production of the furnace, latterly, has been 84 tons of pig metal per week. This

* One of these exceptions, is the West Tennessee portion of the Northwestern Road. The line representing this road should pass through Huntingdon. It may be added, also, that an arm is now in course of construction from Huntingdon to Jackson.

extensive establishment has been constructed and put in operation at a cost of $150,000, by the "Roane Iron Company," under the efficient superintendence and management of Gen. John T. Wilder.

Before closing this preface, I must acknowledge my obligations to Leven S. Goodrich, formerly of Ætna Furnace, but now of Hurricane Mills, (P. O., Waverly,) Humphreys County. Mr. Goodrich is one of our best informed practical iron-masters, and a gentleman of scientific attainments. I am much indebted to him for assistance in researches made in Hickman County.

TABLE OF CONTENTS.

PART I.—Physical Geography.

PART II.—Geological Structure and Formations.

PART III.—The Minerals and Rocks of Special Use.

PART IV.—Soils and Agricultural Features; Climatic Tables.

PART FIRST.

PHYSICAL GEOGRAPHY OF TENNESSEE:

INTRODUCTORY.

1. Before considering the geological structure and formations of Tennessee, it becomes necessary to present a preliminary view of its physical geography. The configuration of the surface of the State is intimately connected with its rocky, or internal structure; it is, indeed, but the expression of this rocky structure, as found sculptured in valleys, plateaus, and ridges, by running water and by atmospheric agencies. The one becomes an important guide to the other. This will be made apparent many times in the course of the Report.

Attention is therefore directed, at the first, to the form, relief, general relations, natural divisions, and climatic features of the surface.

CHAPTER I.

THE STATE IN GENERAL.

BOUNDARIES, FORM, GENERAL SURFACE—GENERAL GEOGRAPHICAL RELATIONS: THE TENNESSEE AND NEW RIVER SLOPE—THE APPALACHIAN REGION—VARIETY AND CLASSIFICATION OF NATURAL FEATURES—THE GREAT NATURAL DIVISIONS OF THE STATE.—CLIMATE.

2. *Boundaries, Form, and General Surface.*—The State of Tennessee includes an area, that extends, in a belt-like form, from the Mississippi River directly eastward to one of the great ranges of the Alleghany, or Appalachian Mountains. The

high crest of this range* is, for the most part, its eastern boundary.

The Southern boundary of the State coincides mainly with the parallel of latitude 35° north; its northern limit is a broken line lying between the parallels 36° 29′ and 36° 41′. While the mean breadth of the State is but little over 109 miles, its mean length is about 385. In general outline, it has approximately the figure of a long rhomboid, and comprises an area of about 42000 square miles.

3. The *general surface* of the State, throwing out of view, for the time, some of the local geographical features,—the mountain ranges of the eastern portion, and the basins and valleys of the western,—coincides nearly with a great horizontal plane, having an elevation of about 900 feet above the sea. The surface, however, is to some extent a warped one, coinciding, at numerous points, with this plane, but at others, either rising above or sinking below it.

The upper or northeastern part of the great Valley of East Tennessee, for example, is, in general, a few hundred feet above, while its central and southern part at first coincides, and then very gradually falls below this plane. The highlands of Middle Tennessee, in some counties, as in Lawrence and Wayne, present a flat surface 100 feet higher, while in Montgomery and adjoining counties, the corresponding highlands are considerably lower. The ridge in West Tennessee, dividing the waters of the Tennessee and Mississippi Rivers, must, at some points, be nearly, if not quite, as high. West of this ridge, however, the general surface sloping off towards the Mississippi, falls considerably below the assumed plane, and may be regarded as terminating, at an average elevation not far from 400 feet, along the edge of the bluff-escarpment which faces the alluvial "bottom" of the great river.†

Upon the surface, as described, rest the mountains of the State, the most important of which are the Cumberland Mountain, or Table-land, and the great Unaka Chain; cut out of it,

* This great range or chain of mountains, will be described hereafter. It may be denominated the *Unaka Chain.*

† Tables presenting the elevations of numerous characteristic points will be given the second and third chapters.

and below it, are the great Basin in Middle Tennessee and the river valleys of this and the Western Division.

4. The entire State, with the exception of a very small area in the southeastern part adjacent to the Georgia line,* is drained by tributaries of the Ohio and Mississippi rivers, the most important of which are the Tennessee, the Cumberland, the Hatchee, and the Forked Deer. Referred to the beds of the principal rivers, the surface of the State is a long slope, which, (as characterized by the elevation of low water at the following points, namely: the State line on the French Broad, Knoxville, Nashville, and the Mississippi, at Fulton,) commences with an elevation of 1264 feet, and terminates with an elevation of about 200. Its fall is, therefore, in some degree, more than 1000 feet. About two-fifths of this is made on reaching Knoxville; four-fifths at Nashville, leaving but one-fifth for the remaining distance. The slope, therefore, descends less and less rapidly as we go westward. Along the northern boundary of the State the fall of this slope is greater than 1000 feet; along the southern boundary considerably less.

The view, however, before taken, of the general surface, in which it was referred to a horizontal plane 900 feet above the sea, is to be preferred, as it will best assist in making clear the physical features and geological structure of the State. In this, the high characteristic flat lands of Middle and West Tennessee are not lost sight of. The river-valleys of these divisions, moreover, are not, in general, characteristic of the face of the country; in the Valley of East Tennessee they are highly so, but there they conform sufficiently well to the plane.

5. *General Geographical Relations.*—Extending our view beyond the limits of the State, the general surface of Tennessee is but a part, although a large part, of a longer belt of surface generally sloping, which commencing along the crest of the Blue Ridge in North Carolina, terminates with the immediate Valley, or "Bottoms," of the Mississippi.

6. This is made apparent by regarding the valleys of the smaller rivers, namely, the Watauga, Nolichucky, French Broad, Big Pigeon, Little

* This area is an irregular segment of the State, drained by a portion of the Connasauga River, and by some of its tributaries. The Connasauga is a small stream, and lies mostly Georgia; it makes; however, a bend to the north, which reaches a few miles above the Tennessee line.

Tennessee, Hiwassee, and Ocoee, which, flowing from the southeast, empty into the Holston and the Tennessee. These rivers rise upon the northwestern side of the Blue Ridge, and flow, in a northwesterly direction, into the State of Tennessee, passing, without material deflection, the Unaka Chain, (§ 2, note,) in deep and grand mountain-cuts.

The two great ranges just mentioned are, in general, nearly parallel, the space between them being occupied by deep valleys and more or less isolated clusters or groups of mountains. It is a *remarkable fact*, that the Unaka Chain, although more massive than the other—the Blue Ridge—is intersected, and so directly, by all the streams enumerated above. It thus loses its importance as the summit of a great water-shed.

7. With these facts before us, it is plain that the general surface of the entire region, extending from the crest of the Blue Ridge through the western part of North Carolina and through Tennessee, a distance of about 430 miles, may be viewed as one. Starting with this crest, at a mean elevation of about 4500 feet above the sea, the general surface, or slope, falls rapidly to the foot of the Blue Ridge, reaching the valleys of the rivers in North Carolina at a level of from 2000 to 2500 feet; then, coincident with these mountain-hemmed valleys, it extends westward, falls with the rapids of the Unaka passes, and finally becomes the floor of the Valley of East Tennessee, where it has a mean elevation of 900 feet. From this valley on, it is the general surface of Tennessee, as already described; or it may be regarded as coinciding with the slope of the river-beds. (§§ 3 & 4.) To low water of the Mississippi, the entire fall is about 4300 feet.

Upon this general surface rests, not only the Cumberland Table-land, but the whole of the Unaka Chain, and the groups of mountains between the latter and the Blue Ridge, of which the most prominent is the pre-eminently high-peaked group of the Black Mountain.

8. The view just taken exhibits important relations sustained by the surface of Tennessee to that of the western part of North Carolina. But a still more extended and instructive view of the geographical relations of the State may be presented.

The Tennessee and New River Slope.—The great and long slope, which reaches from the southwestern part of New York through the western parts of Pennsylvania and Virginia, the whole of Kentucky and Tennessee, and parts of other States, to the Gulf, and which, facing the northwest, pours its waters into the Ohio and Mississippi Rivers, is divided transversely into three natural sections, or minor slopes. To the central and largest one of these our attention is here directed. This is a well defined area. Its southeastern limit is the high crest of that portion of the Blue Ridge which lies in North Carolina and in the southern part of Virginia. From this crest it descends, in a northwesterly direction, to the connected parts of the Ohio and Mississippi Rivers between Cincinnati and Memphis. The line between these cities, as traced by the rivers, is the northwestern boundary and foot of the slope. It includes within its limits, on the northeast, the valleys of the Great Kanawha and of New River, (which rivers, by the way, may be regarded as one,) and, on the southwest, those of the Hiwassee, the Tennessee, the Hatchee, and the Wolf. To the entire section I have given the name at the head of this paragraph.

9. The general direction in which the rivers flow, in other words, the general direction of drainage within this section, unlike that of those which adjoin it on the northeast and southwest, respectively, is to the northwest.* This is seen in the connected courses of New River, of the Great Kanawha, and even of the Ohio, from the mouth of the Kanawha to Cincinnati; it is seen, too, in the rivers of Kentucky, of Middle and West Tennessee, as well as in those which flow out of North Carolina into Tennessee.

To this northwesterly drainage, the upper part of New River, the portion of the Tennessee east of the Cumberland Tableland, and its Virginia tributaries, as well as a portion of the Cumberland River above Nashville, constitute apparent exceptions; these, however, as will be seen further on, may be consistently explained.

10. It is to be noted that the mountains in the western part of North Carolina present the culminating points, and the greatest masses of all the Appalachian Ridges. It is from this high belt—the Blue Ridge presenting the dividing line—that the Ohio and Atlantic waters flow away, the former to the northwest and the latter to the southeast; in these respective directions the rivers find their shortest and most rapid descent.

* It is, in fact, in this respect, unlike any other large section east of the Mississippi River.

The fall from the summit of the Blue Ridge, in a westerly direction, to the Mississippi—a distance of about 430 miles,—is as we have seen, (§ 7) approximately 4300 feet. To the Ohio, in the normal northwesterly direction of the slope, nearly the same fall is made in a distance less by, at least, 100 miles. These facts account for the unusual northwesterly tendency of drainage within the area under consideration.

11. This slope must not, however, except in a general sense, be regarded as continuous and unbroken—as having a uniformly descending surface. It is furrowed by valleys and ridges, or other elevated ranges, which run mostly from the northeast to the southwest, transversely to the direction of general drainage, but parallel to the Blue Ridge, to each other, and to the foot of the slope on the northwest. This is especially true of the southeastern, or upper part of the slope; here the valleys and ridges are very prominent, and well marked in direction; such are the Unaka Chain, the great Valley of Virginia and East Tennessee, with all its subordinate valleys and ridges, and the Cumberland Table-land. In the northwestern or lower part, they are far less prominent, yet even here they, or rather the general surface-features, show a tendency to run in parallel belts to the northeast or southwest.

12. These local features, it is plain, must interfere more or less, with direct drainage. The long, straight ridges, running horizontally along the face of the slope, intercept the stream; which, therefore, must either break through in deep *gaps*, or else, turned aside at right angles to their normal courses, must run in the valleys, to the northeast or southwest, until they find a passage through which they can escape. The one they do, perhaps, as frequently as the other. This will serve to explain the apparent exception before referred to. (§ 9.)

13. Of all the elevated ranges, the Cumberland Table-land is the most effectual barrier in the way of general drainage. By it the Tennessee River is deflected to the southwest, and is made to run many miles before being permitted to pass and flow on in its northwesterly course. The range permits the passage of New River, in Virginia, but at no other point, between its intersections with this and the Tennessee, does it present a complete water-gap.

14. The Valley of Virginia and East Tennessee, as we shall

see hereafter, is part of a great and complex trough, which extends each way beyond the limits of the slope. It is comparatively deep, and almost causes New River, on the one hand, to flow into the streams, which empty into the Atlantic, and the Tennessee, on the other, to flow into those which empty into the Gulf. The portion of the Valley between these rivers is divided into two very unequal subordinate slopes. The region dividing the waters of the two rivers is an elevated water-shed, the crest of which, on the Virginia and East Tennessee Railroad, is 2594 feet above the level of the sea. The New River, or northeastern side, is short, while the Tennessee, or southwestern side, is very long. On both sides, the ridges of the Valley deflect the tributaries to the northeast and southwest respectively. This is seen, on a great scale, in the long Virginia tributaries of the Tennessee.

15. The great Unaka Chain is remarkable, as before stated, (§ 6,) for not deflecting the North Carolina tributaries of the Tennessee. It does, however, throw the upper part of New River many miles to the northeast.

It may be added here, finally, that the Cumberland River above Nashville, is deflected to the southwest by a range of highlands, which, in general is parallel, and bears certain relations, to the better marked ranges just mentioned.

16. Such is the *slope* of which Tennessee is a part, and which, with its ridges and valleys trending to the northeast and southwest, and differing much in their geological character, as well as in their surface features, the State traverses. The belt or surface already mentioned, (§ 5,) extending from the Blue Ridge through Tennessee to the Mississippi, is a complete cross-section of this slope. Of this belt Tennessee is, by far, the larger part, and, owing to the direct easterly and westerly course of the State, the slope is traversed obliquely, making the cross-section an oblique one. Hence results the general obliquity of the State, with reference to natural features, which is so conspicuous upon maps of its surface.

17. The reference of the State to the area just considered enables us to understand much better than before its drainage and many of its surface-features. The question, however, arises, Whence come these belts, the long straight valleys, the

direct ridges and mountain ranges which stretch so independently across and beyond the more easterly parts of the State and of the slope? They must sustain important relations to some other natural geographical area or system. This leads me to notice briefly the following remarkable region or belt:

18. *The Appalachian Region.*—Upon examining any good map of the country between the Gulf of Mexico and the Hudson River, we will see a long continuous area or belt, from 50 to 100 miles in width, traversing, the eastern part of Pennsylvania, Maryland, Middle Virginia, East Tennessee, and the western part of North Carolina, remarkable for its long, parallel, straight, or gracefully curving mountains, ridges, and valleys. The general trend of this belt and its ridges is northeast and southwest; its rivers, too, and especially the smaller tributaries, generally conform to the same direction. This is a well developed portion of the Appalachian, or Alleghany region. The entire region, however, extends much beyond the area designated. It is in fact, a long, great *belt*, stretching for more than 1200 miles, from Gaspé, in Canada, through Vermont, the western part of Massachusetts, the eastern part of New York and the States mentioned, to Georgia and Alabama. This great belt throughout, is noted for its peculiar topography, its beautiful scenery, and its geological structure. The parallelism of its numerous valleys and ridges, and the remarkable and singular uniformity they preserve for long distances, both in direction and outline, are its most striking topographical features.

"While varying little in height, the ridges pursue a remarkably straight course, sometimes hardly diverging from a straight line for a distance of fifty or sixty miles; and one ridge succeeding latterly beyond another—all continuing the same general course in parallel lines, like the successive waves of the sea. As one curves round in a new direction, all curve with it. Thus the valleys between the ridges preserve a uniform width, and are as remarkable for their parallelism as are the hills which bound them."*

19. Many of the ridges of this region are well known mountains; the mountains of western New York, the Alleghanies, the Blue Ridge of Virginia and North Carolina, Clinch Mountain, the Unaka Chain of the latter State and Tennessee, the

* New American Cyclopedia, Art., Appalachian Mountains

eastern part of the Cumberland Table land, Walden's Ridge, Lookout, and the mountains of Georgia and Alabama, are examples. The valleys, which are often exceedingly beautiful, rich, and populous, have all special names; it would lead me, however, too far away to attempt to enumerate and describe here even the most important. The great valley of East Tennessee, with all its minor valleys and ridges, belongs to this region.

20. At its extreme ends the distinctive features of the Appalachian Region are gradually lost; in Alabama its rocks sink and disappear beneath beds of later formations.

Passing across its northwestern border, the ridges and valleys become less and less characteristic, losing their parallelism and their prominence, until, as Appalachian features, they are lost before reaching the great plains which lie to the northwest.*

21. The great belt just considered intersects, or rather supplies, the elevated and mountainous southeastern half of the slope to which Tennessee belongs. From it, come, therefore, the parallel ridges and valleys which make up the eastern part of the State; in other words, these are Appalachian features. A glance at the map accompanying this Report will show to some extent, their peculiar character.

22. It may be remarked finally, that Tennessee, especially its eastern portion, might be studied topographically from two points of view. If, in the first place, we take its river-system, or, in other words, its drainage, as the basis of surface-features, then we will be led to the northwest, (with, however, one great offset,) down the face of the slope as described; but, in the second place, if we make all-important the elevated belts and valleys, then, losing sight of the slope, we will be borne off at right-angles to the former direction, either to the southwest into Georgia and Alabama, or far to the northeast, through the Appalachian troughs. The correct understanding of the topography, however, will depend upon a proper combination of the two views.

*A low and broad "axis of elevation" (or bending up of the rocky strata) which runs through the central part of Tennessee and Kentucky, and the western part of Ohio, may be regarded as an outlying Appalachian feature. Along its course lie flat highlands, and, where greatly denuded, basins—the latter bounded by escarpments of highlands, all of which, with the axis itself, tend to run in a northeasterly and southwesterly direction. (See § 11.)

23. *Variety and Classification of Natural Features.*—Owing, for the most part, to the extent and varied nature of the country traversed by the State, one of its most prominent characteristics, with reference to natural features, is *great variety.* This is seen not only in the numerous divisions of its surface, but also in its geological formation and structure, as well as in its climatic and agricultural features. The number and diversity of its rocks, minerals and soils, are certainly not a little remarkable. Nearly all the important physical and geological features of the States around it are represented more or less—brought together as if by way of contrast—within its borders. Tennessee has, for example, on the one hand, some of the greatest ridges of the Appalachians, with their "bald" summits and ancient rocks; on the other, the low lands and cypress swamps and alluvial beds of the Mississippi; it has, also, well represented the singular parallel valleys and ridges of Middle Virginia; the high lands, the "barrens," and the rich limestone lands of Kentucky; the orange-colored sand hills, the cretaceous beds and cotton soils of North Mississippi. In climate, especially during the summer months, there are the same variety and contrast. The valley lands of upper East Tennessee have the summer of New Jersey and of Ohio; the low lands of Middle Tennessee, east of Nashville, that of the northern part of Georgia; while West Tennessee is warmed by the summer of the central parts of Georgia and South Carolina. And further to heighten the contrast, there is an extended line of high points just within the southeastern border of the State, which have the cool breezes, without the extremes, of a Canadian summer, and which, to some extent, are clothed with a Canadian flora.

24. The varied natural features, formations, and products of the State, such at least as will be treated of in this Report, may be grouped into four distinct classes, constituting as many general subjects, as follows:

(1.) The Leading Geographical Features, or the prominent natural divisions of the surface, such as great valleys, plateaus, and leading mountain ranges, with their external characteristics, including climate.

(2.) The Rocks, or Geological Formations, including the internal structure of the State.

(3.) The Minerals and Mineral Resources.

(4.) The Soils and Agricultural Features.

The first of these pertain to this Part of the Report. The others will be the subjects, respectively, of three succeeding Parts.

25. *Leading Geographical Features, or the Great Natural Divisions of Tennessee.* The State is divided into *eight* well defined natural divisions. These, though prominent and well marked, are not, I may add here, sufficiently known or appreciated as distinctive features. A knowledge of them is important in many ways. They have relations to the civil and political history of the State, aside from its geology, mineralogy, and agriculture, which make them well worthy of notice and study. Their special sanitary relations, too, are of great interest, for which reason they deserve the attention of medical men.

Several of these divisions have been already incidentally mentioned. They are all enumerated in the table below. In the next two chapters they will be described in some detail. The first forms the eastern border of the State; the others occur successively as we go westward.*

(1.) *The Unaka Chain.*—This name has been given to the great range of mountains that lies along the boundary line between Tennessee and North Carolina. (§ 2, note.)

(2.) *The Valley of East Tennessee.*—This division runs obliquely through the State, and constitutes one of its most populous and beautiful portions. It is bounded on the southeast by the Unaka Chain, and on the west, or northwest, by the eastern escarpment of the succeeding division.

(3.) *The Cumberland Table-land.*—The natural division thus named is usually known as the "Cumberland Mountain." It should be called the *Table-land.* It has a broad and generally level top, and stands in well defined and bold relief above the low lands on each side.

(4.) *The Highlands, or Highland Rim, of Middle Tennessee.*—The flat highlands of Middle Tennessee form an extensive and complete *Rim*, which encircles, terrace-like, a *Basin* of rich lowlands in the very centre of the State. The Rim lies next below, and west of, the Cumberland Table-land, and terminates

* These divisions are also indicated upon the map of the State accompanying this Report. This, and the general section upon the same sheet, should be consulted by the reader, in connection with the enumeration here given.

more than a hundred miles westward in the counties of Hardin, Wayne, Perry, Humphreys, and Stewart, breaking off in the high fringing ridges that bound the Valley of the Tennessee River on the east.

(5.) *The Central Basin.*—The Basin of rich lowlands mentioned above, encircled by the Rim, constitutes this division. It is the central part of Tennessee, furnishes the site for its capital, and is truly designated the garden-spot of the State.

(6.) *The Western Valley of the Tennessee River, or the Western Valley.*—This is the narrow, broken Valley of the Tennessee River in the western part of the State. It is bounded, on both sides, by high dividing ridges, whose spurs frequently run in close to the river.

(7.) *The Plateau, or Slope, of West Tennessee.*—This division includes the entire area between the dividing ridge west of the Tennessee River, and the low "Bottoms" of the Mississippi. It slopes towards the latter river, and terminates in a line of "Bluffs," or an escarpment, overlooking the bottoms.

(8.) *The Mississippi Bottoms, or Bottom.*—This, the last division, is a well marked feature. It embraces the Tennessee portion of the great alluvial and low plain through which the Mississippi flows.

26. *Climate.*—The learned Humboldt, in his Cosmos, says:*

"The expression *climate*, taken in its most general sense, signifies all those states and changes of the atmosphere which sensibly affect our organs: temperature, humidity, variation of barometric pressure, a calm state of the air or the effects of different winds, the amount of electric tension, the purity of the atmosphere or its admixture with more or less deleterious exhalations, and lastly, the degree of habitual transparency of the air and serenity of the sky, which has an important influence not only on the organic developments of plants and ripening of fruits, but also on the feelings and the whole mental disposition of man."

From this definition, it is seen, that to determine the climate of any region satisfactorily, in all its relations, is no small task. In fact, it can only be done after daily and varied observations, (bearing upon all the different features of climate,) have been made, at a number of characteristic points, for a long series of years.

* Col. Sabine's Translation, vol. i., p. 312.

27. Such extended observations are far from having been made in Tennessee. Enough has been done, however, to enable us to know, with a near approach to truth, the general features, and, to some extent, the local peculiarities of the climate of the State. At about a dozen points reliable observations, extending through periods respectively, of from a few months to ten years, have been made, for which we are indebted to the intelligence and industry of a number of private citizens, to the well directed efforts of the Smithsonian Institution, and to the officers of the Navy Yard formerly at Memphis.* The facts thus accumulated are, as far as they go, very valuable, and, for present purposes, may be regarded as giving good approximations, which, in connection with what has been done in the States around, will furnish much information in regard to the climate of Tennessee.

28. It is by no means proposed to enter fully into this subject, but simply to notice briefly, the leading features of climate, or those most commonly recognized, such as the averages and extremes of temperature, the length of period between frosts, the quantity and distribution of rain, and the character of the winds.

What may be said in this place will have reference to the State in general, with the exception of two of its natural divisions—the Unaka Chain of mountains and the Cumberland Table-land. These, owing to their elevation, have marked peculiarities of climate that require for them special notices. Some of the other great divisions, too, although, in this general view brought together, have, to a greater or less extent, peculiarities that will be spoken of when the divisions come to be considered separately.

29. The climate with which Tennessee is favored, is midway in character between that of a temperate and that of a tropical region; or rather, it combines the milder features of the two.

* For observations, the means and general results of which are, in part, given in this Report, and which have not hitherto been published, or at most but partially so, I am personally indebted to the kindness of Prof. W. M Stewart, of Glenwood, near Clarksville; Prof. A. P. Stewart, of Cumberland University, at Lebanon; Prof. A. H. Buchanan, of the same place; Mr. P. F. Tavel, of Nashville; the Messrs. Chas. T. and Wm. Bosson, of the Falls of Caney Fork, and Mr. B. Bentley, of Spring Grove, Cumberland county. To Rev. R. O. Currey, of Knoxville, I am also indebted for the use of observations made by Pres. Geo. Cooke and Prof. T. L. Griswold, formerly of East Tennessee University.

The means of temperature and quantities of rain for Nashville, previously to the year 1850, given in the following pages, have been derived from the observations made at the University of Nashville, by Prof. James Hamilton.

The observations made at Glenwood by Prof. W. M. Stewart, constitute the most complete and extended series yet made in Tennessee. This able observer has completed a series covering an entire *decade* of years. Had we, for the same decade, four or five such series—one for each of the most characteristic natural divisions of the State—a most interesting and useful comparative climatology could be made out for Tennessee.

Although subject to comparatively great extremes, in common with a large part of the Valley of the Mississippi, yet these extremes never reach the excessive cold of the northern States, nor the highest temperature of the tropics. Herbage is often green throughout the year, and cattle can generally graze, with but little interruption from cold or snow, during all the months of winter. Many shrubs, which in States further North, lose their leaves during winter, here, not unfrequently, retain them the year round. Light coats of snow sometimes cover the surface, but their stay is brief.

30. The *mean temperature of the year*, along the parallel of latitude running through the middle of the State, is not far from 57° in the Valley of East Tennessee, 58° in Middle, and 59°.5, or 60°, in West Tennessee. Between the first and last divisions there is, according to this, a difference in mean yearly temperature of 2°.5, or 3°. This is partly, but not wholly, due to difference in elevation. After correcting for this, it will still be found that a gradual increase in mean yearly heat occurs in passing westward through the State.

For points on the same meridian, a difference in latitude, north or south, forty or forty-five miles, diminishes, or increases, the yearly mean, about one degree. In West Tennessee, for example, in passing from the northern to the southern part of the State, the mean will range from 58°.5, or 59°, to 60°.5, or 61°.

The following table presents annual means derived from observations made at six stations.

*Annual means, in degrees and hundreths of a degree.**

	1851.	1852.	1853.	1854.	1855.	1856.	1857.	1858.	1859.	1860.	Average of Means.
Knoxville..	"	55.67	"	57.67	57.75	"	"	"	"	"	57.03
Lebanon...	57.43	58.10	"	"	"	"	"	"	"	"	57.76
Nashville..	"	"	"	"	59.83	57.77	57.05	59.16	58.52	"	58.47
Glenwood..	59.31	58.09	57.62	59.46	57.34	54.23	54.54	57.12	56.63	58.25	57.26
Falls of Caney Fork.	Period of 2 years, (1855 & 1856.)										58.48
Nashville..	" " 5 years, (1840 — 1844.)										58.44
Memphis...	" " 3 years, (1850 — 1852.)										60.80

*The following are the names of the observers, hours of observation, elevations above the sea, when known, etc.:

Knoxville.—1852, O. W. Morris, Deaf and Dumb Institute, elevation 960 feet.—1854 and

31. In reference to *seasons*, the means of spring and autumn do not differ materally from those of the year. Summer is the characteristic season; its mean heat, along the parallel traversing the middle of the State, is from about 74° (Valley of East Tennessee) to 77°.5 (West Tennessee.) Such, at least, it is, according to the limited data we possess. Were observations more extended, there is reason to believe a greater difference would appear between the summer temperatures of the extreme parts of the State.

As to winter, its average temperature, which is near 40°, is doubtless nearly uniform along the same parallel. The table below presents means of the two seasons just mentioned.

Mean Temperatures of Winter and Summer.

	1852.		1853.		1854.		1855.		Average.	
	Win.	Sum.	Win.	Sum.	Win.	Sum.	Win.	Sum.	Win.	Sum.
Knoxville....	39.28	70.87	....	....	37.76	75.85	38.40	74.09	38.48	73 60
Lebanon......	39.96	74.41	....	77.40	....	....	....	....	39.96	75.90
Glenwood....	40.11	73.92	38.62	75.51	40.12	77.75	37.37	74.29	39.05	75.37
Nashville.....	Observations of 5 years (1840–1844)...............								39.50	77.30
Memphis......	Observations of 3 years (1850–1852)...............								42.60	78.10

32. The *average of the yearly minimum temperatures* or of the extreme low temperatures, for the last ten years, is, in the northern part of Middle Tennessee, not far from 2°. The temperature, during winter, rarely falls below zero. In only five, out of the ten last winters, has it fallen below. The lowest degree reported is 13°.8 below zero, observed at Lebanon, January, 1852, by Professor A. P. Stewart.

1855, Pres. George Cooke and Prof. T. L. Griswold; 7 A. M., 2 P. M., and 9 P. M.; East Tennessee University; elevation nearly 1000.

Lebanon.—Prof. A. P. Stewart; from January to March, 1851, inclusive, sunrise, 9 A. M., 3 P. M., and 9 P. M., remainder of period, 6 A. M., 2 P. M., and 10 P. M.

Nashville.—1840 to 1844, Prof. James Hamilton, University of Nashville—1855 to 1859, inclusive, P. F. Tavel; sunrise, noon, and sunset.

Glenwood—near Clarksville; Prof. W. M. Stewart; from January, 1851, to January, 1853, sunrise, 9 A. M., 3 P. M., and 9 P. M.; for remainder of period, 7 A. M., 2 P. M., and 9 P. M., elevation 486.

Falls of Caney Fork.—Charles T. and Wm. Bosson; sunrise, noon, and sunset. The period of two years is complete, excepting January, 1855, which is not included.

Memphis.—Navy Yard; see Blodget's Climatology, page 46.

The latitude and longitude of the places given may be found by referring to the map accompanying this Report.

During the ten years mentioned, the highest of the yearly maximum temperatures reported, in the northern part of Middle Tennessee, is 100°, observed January, 1852, likewise at Lebanon. The *average of the maximum temperatures* is considerably lower than this, being about 94°.

33. From the above data, it is seen, that the *mean yearly range* of the thermometer, in this part of the State, is 92°; in the southern part it will be found to be less.

The data before me are not sufficient for the determination of a good approximation to the average yearly maximum and minimum temperatures of the Valley of East Tennessee. For points on the same parallel, the former would be probably about three degrees less than in the central part of the State.

34. The length of the *period between killing frosts*, is, especially to the farmer and gardener, an important element of climate. It is, to a great extent, the measure of the "growing" season. The following table, prepared by Prof. W. M. Stewart, will give correct information as to the approximate length of this period in the northern part of Middle Tennessee:

Tabular Statement of the occurrence of frost, from observations made at Glenwood, near Clarksville, Tennessee.

YEARS.	Last frost in spring.	First frost in autumn.	First skim ice.	Days free from frost.	Days free from killing frost.
1851	May 2d	Oct. 23d	Oct. 23d	173	173
1852	Mar. 23d	Oct. 15th	Nov. 8th	205	228
1853	Mar. 29th	Oct. 11th	Oct. 25th	195	210
1854	Apr. 18th	Oct. 19th	Nov. 5th	184	201
1855	Apr. 7th	Oct. 22d	Oct. 25th	187	200
1856	Apr. 23d	Oct. 16th	Oct. 18th	175	176
1857	Apr. 20th	Sept. 30th	Oct. 20th	162	181
1858	Apr. 25th	Oct. 9th	Nov. 14th	166	201
1859	Apr. 18th	Oct. 10th	Oct. 19th	174	182
1860	Apr. 2d	Sept. 21st	Oct. 12th	171	192
			Means	179.2	194.4

According to this table, the average length of the growing season is about 194 days. It is seen, too, that the last frost month of spring and the first of autumn, are pre-eminently April and October, months in which the farmer must be on the lookout for frost. From the third week in April, however, to the middle of October, it is hardly to be expected.

In the northern part of East Tennessee the growing season is doubtless a few days shorter. In the southern part of the State, and especially in the southwestern part, this period is twelve days, or two weeks, longer, than on the parallel of Glenwood; its length, therefore, will not be far from 208 days. This difference is of considerable importance to the cotton region of the State.

35. The *winds* act an important part in modifying climate, and therefore deserve a passing notice.

Tennessee belongs to a belt of North America, over which prevail two great systems of winds. The lower consists of currents flowing to the northeast and north; these are the southwesterly and southerly surface-winds of Tennessee. They come to us charged with warmth and moisture from the Gulf of Mexico, and give fertility and geniality of climate to the State. The upper system is one of northwesterly and northerly winds. These, dry and cool, flow, at a high elevation, above the fertilizing winds of the surface.

Such is the general circulation, were there no perturbing influences, each system would move on, in its normal direction, quietly, and without interfering with the other. But every rain, or change of temperature at the surface, is a disturbing cause tending to destroy the equilibrium and mingle the winds. Thus arises a conflict between the great systems, producing, to a greater or less extent, westerly winds, but often ending in the triumph of the northwest and upper system, and in the precipitation of a "Norther" upon the surface. Such a change is usually followed by a few days of cool, clear weather, when the southwest wind quietly resumes its course and position again.

36. From what has been said, it is seen that the regular winds of Tennessee are those from the south, southwest, west, northwest, north, and northeast, all of which belong to the general circulation, while those from the easterly and southeasterly directions, are due to abnormal influences.*

Such data as I have bearing upon the winds, are given below.

* For an able discussion of the subject of North American winds, illustrated by diagrams and maps, see Prof. Henry's articles in the Patent Office Agricultural Reports of 1855, 1856, and 1858, more especially the last. In these articles the distinguished secretary of the Smithsonian Institution gives an exposition of the general principles of climatology, which he applies especially to the climate of the United States. They are of great value, and well worthy of the attention of all interested in this subject. I here acknowledge my indebtedness to them.

The table is the result of the observations of Prof. W. M. Stewart, and presents the means of three years:

Tabular statement of Winds for the different seasons of the year.

Point from which, &c.	Spring.	Summer.	Autumn.	Winter.	Amount.	
N. E.	18	14	24	27	83	N. quadrant, 236.
N. N. E.	8	8	5	9	30	
N.	29	17	15	42	103	
N. N. W.	8	2	2	8	20	
N. W.	21	8	12	33	74	W. quadrant, 178.
W. N. W.	3	4	5	10	22	
W.	11	18	15	18	62	
W. S. W.	5	3	3	9	20	
S. W.	15	17	15	14	61	S. quadrant, 313.
S. S. W.	13	10	10	9	42	
S.	42	42	39	31	154	
S. S. E.	20	8	12	16	56	
S. E.	15	10	23	17	65	E. quadrant, 160.
E. S. E.	3	2	3	0	8	
E.	12	30	22	7	71	
E. N. E.	4	5	3	4	16	
Calm.	43	81	65	34	223	

From this it is seen, that, for the three years at Glenwood, the order of the winds, (grouping them in quadrants,) is, in point of frequency, as follows: First, the southerly winds, followed by the northerly; then the westerly, and finally the easterly.

37. At Knoxville, in East Tennessee, the order for the same number of years, is as follows:

(1) Westerly and southwesterly.
(2) Northerly and northeasterly.
(3) Southerly.
(4) Northwesterly.
(5) Easterly.
(6) Southeasterly.

These facts agree with the views expressed above. Although limited and insufficient, they clearly indicate, that, at the surface, the prevailing winds are from the south and west; that next to these, those from the north are most prevalent, and, finally, that easterly winds are the least so. The observations of a greater number of years would make this order more definite, but would not change it materially.

38. The quantity of *rain* which falls upon the surface of the State is not excessive, nor is it equal to that precipitated upon the States further South. In general, however, the supply

is amply sufficient. Temporary droughts do occasionally occur, especially during the summer season, and sometimes with serious consequences. That of 1860, felt so severely in Tennessee and in other Southern States, is an example. Such droughts however, are exceptional.

The following table presents the mean aggregate quantities of rain and snow (melted) precipitated at the places, and for the periods specified. The water is supposed to remain, for the different periods, where it fell in uniform sheets or strata, the vertical depth being, in each case, the measure of the quantity.

Quantities of Rain and melted Snow for the seasons and the year, in inches and hundredths of an inch. The years of observation are given under each Station.

	Knoxville, 1854–1855, two years.	Lebanon, Dec. '50, Aug. 1853, nearly three years.	Nashville, 1844-1849, five years.	Glenwood, 1851–1859, nine years.
Spring	10.12	10.55	15.04	12.28
Summer	15.45	9.57	14.47	9.74
Autumn	8.02	7.54	13.49	9.15
Winter	11.02	15.95	11.99	12.89
Annual	44.61	43.61	54.99	44.06

39. I close this notice with an extract from a recent work on the climatology of the United States.* The author is speaking of the Mississippi Valley and the Atlantic States.

"The principal feature of this area, as a whole, is its adaptation to a great range of vegetable and animal life. It [the climate] is extreme without being destructive, and it brings in tropical summer temperatures, and profusion of rain, with low winter temperatures, near to those of the extreme continental climates; and the result is a condition extremely favorable to the acclimation of tropical and semi-tropical plants and animals. This is the great advantage the area of the eastern United States and Mississippi Valley undoubtedly has over Western Europe, or the distinction, if not an advantage.

"The semi-tropical summer is, perhaps, the most noticeable feature of the measure of heat here. * * * * * * * At Baltimore, Cincinnati, and St. Louis, we have a mean of 75°; and over an immense area bordering the Gulf of Mexico, and reaching north, nearly to the 35th parallel,

* Climatology of the United States, &c., by Lorin Blodget, Philadelphia, 1857.

we have a mean temperature of 80° or more, which is considerably above that of many portions of the tropical seas of Central and South America. And this high temperature is associated with the peculiar features of the temperate climates in other respects, with equally distributed, yet abundant rains, and with the high curve of daily changes which belongs to the same districts. It is simply an excess of temperature and of humidity, engrafted on, without otherwise changing the characteristic laws elsewhere belonging to much lower temperatures. * * * * * * * If this measure of heat occurred without this great daily range, it would make the climate simply tropical; but, occurring under existing circumstances, it renders the country capable of great elasticity in the adaptation of vegetable and animal forms. Cotton, Indian corn, and the cane, find their natural climates here, but not elsewhere, in any considerable degree, beyond the tropics."

CHAPTER II.

THE NATURAL DIVISIONS OF THE STATE.

THE UNAKA CHAIN—THE VALLEY OF EAST TENNESSEE—THE CUMBERLAND TABLE-LAND.

40. The great physical features, or natural divisions of the State, that form the subject of this chapter, belong, with the exception of the western part of the Table-land, to the Appalachian Region. (§ 18.) With the same exception, they constitute that one of *the three political divisions* into which Tennessee is divided, known as *East Tennessee*. The remaining natural divisions will be considered in the succeeding chapters.

I.—The Unaka Chain.

41. *General Character.*—This is a long range of mountains, and the most massive of all the Alleghany, or Appalachian Ranges. Its high crest, as already stated, is, for the most part, the line dividing Tennessee and North Carolina. As here to be understood, this chain is not a single great ridge, but rather, especially on the Tennessee side, a long belt of parallel ridges, which vary at different points, counted across the chain, from two to four in number. One of these is the main axis; the others are subordinate and more or less broken, but all, in general, trending in the same direction. The range, or its main axis, is continuous lengthwise, excepting, principally, that it is intersected by the deep and rocky cuts of the tributaries of the Holston and Tennessee Rivers that flow out of North Carolina and the northeastern corner of Georgia.*

* The names of these tributaries have been already given. (See § 6.) In the cuts or *narrows*, as they are sometimes called, the steep mountain-slopes, or high rocky cliffs, frequently come down on both sides to the water's edge. The rivers in passing, form long and roaring rapids. A few years ago the cuts were impassable for travelers. But now good roads run through several of them. The most remarkable is the road up the Ocoee to the Ducktown Copper Mines. This passes through tortuous narrows for twelve or thirteen miles. It is but little above the water's edge and has been, nearly all the way, either cut out of solid cliffs, or dug out of the precipitous mountain side.

Formerly, most, or all of the travel between the Valley of East Tennessee and the

These divide it into sections; but the sections, abutting end to end, are merely links of the great chain.*

42. The Unaka Chain presents, in one of its longest sections —that between the deep cuts of the Big Pigeon and the Little Tennessee—numerous peaks but a few feet lower than the highest of the Black Mountains in North Carolina, and, without exception, the boldest and greatest mountain-mass east of the Mississippi. As a whole, it is the wildest feature in the physical geography of Tennessee; its geological formations are not found elsewhere in the State, and are important repositories of minerals; its botanical and agricultural characteristics are peculiar and well worthy of notice. For amateurs, its "bald" summits, its semi-arctic plants and balsam peaks, the magnificent scenery it affords; its roaring rapids and wild cascades; its game, and the "trout" of its cold streams, altogether, make it an elysium.

What I propose to say here, refers to the surface features of the chain. Its formations, minerals, and soils, will be discussed in the parts of the Report to which these subjects are respectively assigned.

43. *Extent and Relations; the Blue Ridge.*—Coming out of Virginia, the chain pursues a somewhat serpentine, though, in general, direct southwesterly course, along the Tennessee and North Carolina line, into Georgia. Its length, within the northern and southern limits of Tennessee is about 200 miles; it extends, however, a considerable distance each way beyond these limits. Its relations to the Blue Ridge, to the rivers of the western part of North Carolina, and, in general, to the

valleys of North Carolina passed over the mountains. But the cuts are now assuming much importance as the great, but narrow gate-ways between the former valleys and the southeast. Four have been surveyed with reference to the location of railroad lines through them. The Knoxville & Charleston Railroad, now under construction, runs through the cut of the little Tennessee.

* Several prominent portions of the chain, lying in different and distant counties, have the name *Unaka* applied locally to them. As it is desirable for greater convenience and for other reasons, that the entire range should, like the *Blue Ridge*, have a general and distinctive name, I have in this Report, borrowing the one above, denominated it the *Unaka Chain*.

Haywood, in his "Natural and Aboriginal History of Tennessee," (Nashville, 1823,) appears to use *Unaka* in the same general sense. He spells it *Unaca*, and says: "East Tennessee is divided from North Carolina by the Unaca or White Mountains—Unica, in the Cherokee language, signifying white."

Why they were called *White Mountains*, I cannot say. It may have been for the reason that, in winter, they are frequently capped with snow, and, in summer, with white clouds.

Tennessee and New River Slope, have already been noticed.* In Virginia, according to the best maps within my reach, the Unaka Chain and the Blue Ridge converge and finally unite; the former thus becomes a great branch of the latter.

44. The portion of the Unaka Chain within the limits of Tennessee—and to this portion our attention will be mostly confined—presents a strip; which, in breadth, will average about twelve or fourteen miles, varying, however, from two or three to twenty miles. Excluding the *coves*, confined within its ridges, it covers an area of not far from 2000 square miles.

45. Large parts, and generally the southeastern parts, of all the counties adjacent to the North Carolina line, are made up of the Unaka Ridges. These counties are Johnson, Carter, Washington, Greene, Cocke, Sevier, Blount, Monroe, and Polk. In Johnson the ridges lie in such a manner as to completely enclose the valleys, or rather *the great cove*, of this county. In Carter, too, they nearly enclose the valleys. Greene has less of its surface covered by the Unaka Ridges than any of the other counties mentioned.†

46. *Ridges and Outliers.*—It has been stated that the chain under consideration is a belt of parallel ridges. In general, it might be said, that the Tennessee portion is divided longitudinally into two ranges—one the high main axis, including its great spurs, the other a subordinate series or chain of outliers, mostly detached and lying along the base of the former, though generally separated by long coves. This typical character, however, does not always hold good, the greatest departure from it being northeast of the French Broad, or of the Big Pigeon. Some of the local features and principal ridges of the chain are pointed out below.

47. In the northeastern corner of the State, north of the Watauga River, in Johnson and Carter counties, the Unaka Chain is divided lengthwise into *three* leading ridges or mountains separated by wide and beautiful valleys. These ridges, seen from some points, appear to be parallel, but in reality they converge towards the northeast, the two most westerly

*See §§ 6, 7, 11, and 15.

† These counties may be named the *Unaka Counties*. Sullivan and McMinn have their eastern boundaries along the crests, respectively, of two western outliers of the chain, and have, therefore, but little of their surfaces with the Unaka area. For this reason they are not included in the above group.

coming together and blending in a common ridge, as they enter Virginia, which also, further to the northeast, unites with the most easterly and remaining one. (See Map.)

48. The most easterly, is the *Stone Mountain* Range, called also Iron Mountain.* This is a long bed of a few crowded ridges, along the highest of which the State line runs. It exends southward to the Watauga. *Forge Mountain,* a sandstone mountain, the southern end of which is a short distance east of Taylorsville, is one of its ridges. To the northeast, just within Virginia, the Stone Mountain culminates in the grand and conspicuous summit—the *White Top.* Other peaks, southwest of the White Top, are *Beech Summit, Cat Face, Slate Face,* &c.

49. The second, or middle ridge, is *Iron Mountain.* This is a long, heavy, straight ridge running through Johnson and Carter—a portion forming, for some distance, the boundary between the two counties. It is separated from Stone Mountain by the valley-lands of Johnson. It is cut through both by the Watauga and Big Doe Rivers, but nevertheless, continues as a well defined range to the southern part of Carter, where it gradually sinks away. South of the Watauga, it is separated from mountains on the east by a long, very narrow valley, the most important and widest part of which is *Doe River Cove,* in Carter.

50. The last and most westerly, is *Holston Mountain.* This is separated from Iron Mountain by a curious, very elevated basin of limited extent, called *Shady,* and by the large *Valley of Stony Creek.* It runs out boldly from its brother ridges into the "open country," and terminates abruptly a few miles north of Elizabethtown.

51. I may add here, too, as pertaining to this group, an isolated sandstone ridge called *Doe Mountain.* It rises up in the lower part of the Johnson County Valley, and divides the latter longitudinally into two portions, which, however, unite again around the southern end of the mountain. It commences near

*As on Mr. Rhea's Map. There is much confusion resulting from the indiscriminate use of local names by those living among, or in the vicinity of, the Unaka Ridges. Sometimes a well defined ridge has two or three different names. In many cases, the same name is applied to two or more distinct ridges, and sometimes when they are but a few miles apart. There are, for example, more than half a dozen "Iron Mountains" in the Unaka Chain, three of which, at least, are in Johnson and Carter, and which too, from some points, may all be seen at the same time. In selecting names, I have take those most used, except in cases where the use of such would lead to confusion.

Taylorsville and extends nearly to the Watauga. Towards its southern end, it is cut into by Doe Creek.

52. The eastern part of Carter, south of the Watauga Valley and east of the Iron Mountain Range, forms a region—a portion of the Unaka area—from 12 to 14 miles across, nearly square, or rhombic, in shape, and drained mostly by the tributaries of Doe River. This region is very rough, and is remarkable for the great mountains which bound it on the southeast and south, and for the *transverse direction* (more or less northwest and southeast) of several of its included ridges. Within it, on the upper waters of the Big Doe, lies an isolated group of mountain-hemmed valleys, called collectively *Crab Orchard.* This name I extend to the whole region specified. The following are some of its principal ranges and its limits:

53. On the north and west, this region is limited by a sandstone border, which may be called the *Flint Range.* This range is broken and not well defined. Starting from the State line below the Watauga, it may be regarded as running westward until near Iron Mountain, where, bending around to the southwest, it runs to the southern part of Carter parallel with the Iron Mountain, and separated from it by the narrow valley and Doe River Cove, mentioned above. (§49.) The range is intersected at several points, near to one another, by the main tributaries of Doe River just before they unite in Doe River Cove; the parts thus cut off from bold *knobs*, against which the ridges dividing the tributaries—the *transverse ridges,* by the way, referred to above—abut, and with which they unite.

54. Upon the east and south, the Crab Orchard region is bounded by the State line which here projects, in a great bend or angle, to the southeast. Leaving the Watauga the line pursues, at first, a straight course, passing over an interval of several miles in which the Unaka Chain is broken and loses, to some extent, its continuity. Towards the southern part of the region, however, it passes near and along the crests of several noble mountains—the *Humpbacks*, the *Big Yellows*, and the *Roan* —bending, at the same time, to the west, with the latter range. These mountains thus form a portion of the southeastern and southern border of Crab Orchard, overlooking the group of valleys—the local Crab Orchard—which lie at their northwestern base. (See Map.)

55. The *Roan,* though not having the highest peaks, is, in some respects, the grandest mountain of the Unaka Chain. It is high and massive, and has a chain or succession of beautiful *bald* places or "*balds,*"* which extends for several miles along its summit.

The greater part of the Big Yellow Mountain lies in North Carolina. Prof. Guyot, in speaking of the region between the Unaka Chain and the Blue Ridge, and of the clusters of high mountains within it, calls the Roan and the Grand Father, (the latter the highest part of the Blue Ridge and facing the Roan,) "the two great pillars on both sides of the Northgate to the high mountain region of North Carolina. * * * * That gate is almost closed by the Big Yellow Mountain."†

The State line, after running southwestward along the ridge of the Roan, for nearly, or quite, half a dozen miles, and when not far from its southwestern "bluff" end, (the mountain in this direction terminating very abruptly,) leaves it suddenly and runs north and west, over a connecting ridge, across to a *second Iron Mountain.* This leaves the Crab Orchard region, for the most part, to the northeast.

56. The Unaka Chain, in the extreme southern part of Carter County—in the region of *Limestone Cove*—is reduced to narrow limits. On account of the abrupt ending of the Roan, the Iron Mountain, just mentioned, lying several miles to the northwest, becomes the main range of the Unaka. The State line runs along its crest.

57. This *Iron Mountain* is a heavy ridge coming out of the Crab Orchard region. It runs in a southwesterly course, and is continuous with the eastern range of Washington County. It is but a few miles east of the disappearing and crowded ends of the Flint Range and of the first mentioned Iron Mountain, being separated from them by Limestone Cove, before referred to, which is a small, narrow valley on the head waters of Indian Creek.

58. In Washington County, the Unaka Mountains consist, in general, of two parallel subordinate beds, (§ 46,) which are separated by a long, straight valley, called *Greasy Cove.*

*So called by those living in the region of the Unaka and the Blue Ridge. The *balds,* in general, will be spoken of specially further on.

†Am. Jour. Sci., Nov., 1860.

59. The eastern bed may be designated the *Bald Mountain Range.* It runs to the southwest, continuing the State line, and has many great spurs and several prominent bald peaks. The Iron Mountain, of the southern part of Carter, may be regarded as forming a part of it. As it enters Washington County, the range rises up in a high, bold mountain, locally known as the *Unaka.* In the southern part of the county it swells up again and forms the *Great Bald,* well known in this section of the State for its elevation and the *bald* which crowns it.

60. The western bed may be called the *Buffalo and Rich Mountain Range.* Its northern end rises up right in the midst of the lowlands, at a point nearly opposite the bluff terminus of the Holston Mountain. (§ 50.) From this point it pursues a southwesterly course, parallel with the Bald Mountain Range, until it strikes the Greene County line. It passes entirely through Washington County, but is intersected by the Nolichucky, the northern part constituting *Buffalo and Cherokee Mountains,* and the southern, *Rich Mountain,* &c. It is really a double range, inclosing two small coves, the most important of which is *Bompass Cove,* extending southwestward from the Nolichucky.

61. Entering Greene County, we find the Unaka, within Tennessee, reduced suddenly to a single massive ridge. This is due to the large S-shaped bend that the State line makes along the southern boundary of Washington County. Soon after passing the Great Bald, the line, leaving the Bald Mountain Range, crosses over northward and westward, until it reaches the massive ridge mentioned. (See Map.) This is the conspicuous mountain lying to the southeast of Greeneville, and is in a line with the Buffalo and Rich Mountain Range of Washington.

In the Southern part of Greene two other well marked ranges occur.

62. The ridge, or mountain, lying to the southeast of Greeneville, belongs to what may be called the *Big Butt Range,* the northern end being well known as the "Big Butt." It starts up just within Washington, in a bold, high summit, presenting a bald, and partially separated by a gap from the Buffalo and Rich Mountain Range. It runs for more than half a dozen miles to the southwest, forming a straight, high mountain, pre-

senting, in its course, several bald places, and sending off short, but heavy, spurs. Further southward it sinks to a lower and less direct ridge, which, however, may be regarded as a portion of the same range. This portion continuing the State line, forms an elbow to the southeast, in which course it bends around near the Warm Springs, on the French Broad River, in North Carolina.

63. Before reaching the point where the last range loses its greater elevation, *Paint Mountain* rises up close upon, or forming, its western flank. This mountain soon becomes a distinct range running more directly southwestward to the French Broad, which it strikes at the "*Painted Rock*," forming with its rocks and its bluff end, the narrows, and the great mural escarpment and amphitheatre of solid sandstone, so well known to travelers on the French Broad.

Paint Creek, draining a very rough and rapidly descending valley, flows out from between this mountain and the southern part of the former range.

64. Northwest of Paint Mountain, and separated from it by a cove and a long valley, (*Peck's Trough*,) is an outlier, a long, straight ridge, called *Meadow Creek Mountain.* It first appears in the southern part of Greene, gradually swelling up from the lowlands, and runs in a southwesterly direction to the French Broad, in Cocke County.

65. After crossing the French Broad, there are in Cocke County, several subordinate ranges, continuations, to some extent, of those in Greene. The range which marks out the State line, is at first, for several miles, poorly defined, being very low and broken. Within six or seven miles, however, it rises rapidly, and soon becomes one of the greatest mountains of the Unakas.

66. Southwest of the Big Pigeon, the Unaka Chain throughout, may be divided generally, in accordance with the typical character, (§ 46,) into two parallel but unequal ranges. The *first,* which I will call the *Great Smoky,* is, in much of its extent, the State boundary. It is the greatest bed of mountains in Tennessee, having the highest peaks, and occupying with its high ridges, a large area. The *second* is a range, or chain, of prominent, isolated, and long mountains, all arranged lengthwise, nearly in the same line, and composed of the same

sandstones and conglomerates. They are all *outliers* skirting, at intervals, the northwestern base of the Smoky Range. They appear, in most cases, to rise up massively and independently, just within the southeastern edge of the East Tennessee Valley. The whole chain may be named, from one of its principal mountains, the Chilhowee Range.

The interval between the ranges is occupied by narrow valleys or coves, and numerous ridges and spurs. The ridges and spurs have, generally, a much lower elevation than the principal ranges; in a few cases, however, they become high, and conspicuous mountains.

67. The first range—the *Great Smoky*—has several local names. That of *Great Smoky*, as well as that of *Unaka*, is very generally applied to the more northeastern portions. In the southern part of Blount County, a portion is called the *Bald Mountain*, on account of the balds upon it. The section between the Little Tennessee and Hiwassee Rivers is often locally denominated *Unaka*. In Polk, south of the Ocoee, another portion is known as the *Frog Mountain*.

Along the State line, in Sevier and the eastern part of Blount, this range attains its greatest development. (§ 42.)

68. The general course of the Smoky Range is southwest. It makes, however, as may be seen by reference to the map, a great elbow, or angle, to the southeast in passing around the head waters of the Tellico River.

Within a few miles of the Hiwassee River, the State line leaves the course of the highest ridges and runs in a straight direction, nearly due south, to the Georgia boundary, a distance of about sixteen miles. This throws the range within Tennessee, and gives to the State, as it were, accidently, a most interesting triangular area—the *Ducktown Region*. This region is, physically, a portion of one of the mountain valleys, or basins of North Carolina and Georgia.

69. The second, the *Chilhowee Range*—that of the outliers—being a chain of detached mountains, has its parts more definitely named.

English's Mountain, lying lengthwise between Newport and Sevierville, is the first. It breaks up from the lowlands, three or four miles southwest of the former place, and is nearly a dozen miles in length.

70. *Chilhowee Mountain*, whose *bluff* end first appears five or six miles west of Sevierville, is the second. This mountain, coming out of Sevier County, runs through Blount and terminates at the Tennessee River. It is the longest and most important of the series. Little River, in Blount, cuts through it. The Montvale Springs are at a point of its northwestern base south of Maryville.

71. In Monroe County there are two short mountains in the Chilhowee line, lying between Play-Ball Creek and Tellico River. Taken together, they may be designated as the *Guide Mountain.*

72. Leaving the last mountain, and passing over an interval of eight or ten miles, the last of the chain rises up boldly from the valley, and runs on into Polk County, terminating at the Ocoee River. This outlier is called *Star's Mountain ;* next to Chilhowee, it is the greatest of the range. It is cut in two by the Hiwassee River.

73. *Elevation above the Sea.*—The general elevation of the Unaka Chain, along the Tennessee boundary, is doubtless greater than that of the part of the Blue Ridge, within the limits of North Carolina. It cannot be much, if any less than 5000 feet. One long section of the chain, that between the French Broad and the little Tennessee, has indeed, an average elevation much greater. Prof. Guyot, in speaking of this section, says :

"Though its highest summits are a few feet below the highest peaks of the Black Mountain, it presents on that extent of 65 miles, a continuous series of high peaks and an average elevation not to be found in any other district, and which give to it a greater importance in the geographical structure of that vast system of mountains. The gaps or depressions, never fall below 5000 feet, except towards the southwest and beyond Forney Ridge; and the number of peaks, the altitude of which exceeds 6000 feet, is indeed very large."*

* For the last ten years, Prof. Arnold Guyot, of Princeton, N. J., has devoted the greater parts of the summers to the study of the geography of the Alleghany, or Appalachian system, and to the measurement of its mountains. During four of these summers—those of 1856, '58, '59, and '60—he has, attended by assistants, given his attention to the mountains of North Carolina and to those of the Unaka Chain. It is to his able researches, in connection with the levels of the surveyed railroad lines, that pass through the valleys, or water gaps, of the chain, and to his kindness personally, that I am almost wholly indebted for the very satisfactory series of elevations presented in the following tables. (Am. Jour. Sci., Sept., 1857, and Nov., 1860.)

Mr. S. B. Buckley has given us valuable and interesting contributions bearing upon

The measurements hitherto made in the Unaka Chain have been almost entirely confined to its main axis. The general elevation, therefore, of the outliers upon the northwestern side, cannot be given with any accuracy. It may be estimated at about 2500 feet.

74. The following tables embrace the peaks and gaps that have been measured, with their heights in feet above tide-water. The heights of a number of points in the valleys and water-gaps immediately around the mountains, or in their vicinity, are also given for comparison.

(1.) The first table includes several high points of the Stone Mountain Range, (§ 48,) and of the neighboring valleys. Balsam Mountain is several miles northeast of White Top; both are in Virginia.

Balsam Mountain, Va.,	5,700 (about)	Guyot.
White Top. "	5,530	"
Cat Face Mountain, Tenn.,	4,913	Guyot.
State Gap, (Tenn. & N. C. line.)	3,400 (about)	"
Shull's Mill-pond, Main Watauga, N. C.,	2,917	R. R. Survey.
Taylorsville, Tenn.,	2,395	Guyot.
State Line, (Tenn. & N. C.,) in Watauga Valley,	2,131	R. R. Survey.

(2.) The following are prominent points upon the Yellow and Roan Range. (§ 55.)

Yellow, (above Brigg's house,)	5,158	Guyot.
Little Yellow, (highest,)	5,196	"
Roan, Cold Spring,	6,132	"
" Grassy Ridge Bald	6,230	"
" High Knob	6,306	"
" High Bluff	6,296	"
Toe River Ford, in N. C.	2,132	"
Brigg's house, foot of Roan, N. C.,	2,757	"

(3.) The following is the height of Bald Mountain, the only measured peak of the Bald Mountain Range, (§ 59,) so far as I know. The heights of Burnsville and Jonesborough, are added for comparison.

the elevation of the Great Smoky Range. He measured many points, along and near the State line in Cocke and Sevier Counties, which were afterwards measured by Prof. Guyot. Mr. B.'s heights are greater than Prof. Guyot's by quantities varying from 60 to 130 feet and more, mostly for the reason that the altitudes of the bases he started from were too great. (Jour. Sci., Mar., 1859.)

The lamented Dr. E. Mitchell, of Chapel Hill, N. C., and Prof. W. C. Kerr, of Davidson College, have likewise made measurements in the Unaka Chain. The former many years ago. (Jour. Sci., April, 1839.)

Bald Mountain........................5,550..........Kerr & Guyot.

Burnsville Court-House, N. C.......2,840............R. R. Survey.
Jonesborough, Tenn...................1,734......E. T. & Va. R. R.

(4.) I cannot give the exact height of the Big Butt Range. (§ 62.) The higher portion, however, is not much, if any, less than 5000 feet above the sea. Col. T. Johnson, of Greene County, who is interested in property upon this range, in a letter of March, 1859, says: "There are two high peaks near the *Cold Spring*" [a noted spring and summer retreat near the north end of the range] "which have the same height, and are from 5000 to 5500 feet above tide-water. There have been two measurements made, but neither, I think, is very reliable."

Adding, for comparison, the elevation of the depot at Greeneville, we have then:

Big Butt Range (highest point)....5,000 (?).........................

Greeneville (Depot).....................1,581......E. T. & Va. R. R.

(5.) The following table includes points of the Great Smoky Range between the French Broad and Little Tennessee. (§§ 67 & 73.) Most of them are on the State line. The elevation of a few points in the valleys and water-gaps are given as before:

Warm Springs, N. C....................1,326.3...Bench-mark R. R
" " Piazza of Hotel...1,335.....................Guyot.
Tennessee Line on the French Broad.,...........................1,264............R. R. Survey.
W. H. Campbell's house, head of Big Creek, tributary of the French Broad.......................3,287.........................Guyot.

Indian Grave Gap, (between Fr. Broad and Big Pigeon)..........4,288..................... "
Man Patch Gap, (do)................4,392..................... "
Bear-wallow Mt., (do)..............4,659..................... "
Bear-wallow Mt. Gap to Fine's Creek, (do).........................4,116 .... "
Luftee Knob, (on Tenn. Line at the corner of Haywood and Jackson, Counties, of N. C. The points below are between this and the gap of the Little Tennessee.)....................6,238*.................. "
Thermometer Knob....................6,157..................... "
Ravens Knob.............................6,230..................... "

*This elevation may not be correct within a few feet. Prof. G. states that he was interrupted when at this point by a storm.

Tricorner Knob	6,188	Guyot.
Mt. Guyot, (so named by Mr. Buckley, in Tenn.,)	6,636	"
Mt. Henry	6,373	"
Mt. Alexander	6,447	"
South Peak	6,299	"
The Three Brothers,—highest or central Peak	5,907	"
Thunder Knob	5,682	"
Laurel Peak	5,922	"
Reinhardt Gap	5,220	"
Top of Richland Ridge	5,492	"
Indian Gap	5,317	"
Peck's Peak	6,232	"
Mt. Ocona	6,135	"
Right-hand, or New Gap.	5,096	"
Mt. Mingus	5,694	"
Group of Bullhead in Tennessee:		
Central Peak, or Mt. LeConte	6,612	"
West Peak, or Mt. Curtis	6,568	"
North Peak, or Mt. Safford	6,535	"
Cross Knob	5,931	"
Neighbor	5,771	"
Master Knob	6,013	"
Tomahawk Gap	5,450	"
Alum Cave	4,971	"
Alum Cave Creek, junction with Little Pigeon River	3,848	"
Road Gap	5,271	"
Mt. Collins	6,188	"
Collin's Gap	5,720	"
Mount Love	6,443	"
Clingman's Dome	6,660	"
Mt. Buckley	6,599	"
Chimzey Knob	5,588	"
Big Stone Mountain	5,614	"
Big Cherry Gap	4,838	"
Corner Knob	5,246	"
Forney Ridge Peak	5,087	"
Snaky Mt.	5,195	"
Thunderhead Mt.	5,520	"
Eagletop	5,433	"
Spence Cabin	4,910	"
Turkey Knob	4,740	"
Opossum Gap	3,840	"
North Bald	4,711	"
The Great Bald's Central Peak	4,922	"

South Peak	4,708	Guyot.
Tennessee River at Hardin's	899	"
Chilhowee Mt., summit road to Montvale Springs	2,452	"
Montvale Springs, Tenn.	1,293	"

(6.) Between the Little Tennessee and the Hiwassee, we have the following elevations:

Hangover Knob, over	5,300	Guyot.
Haw Knob, over	5,300	"
Beaverdam, or Tellico Bald	4,266	"

(7.) South of the Hiwassee the average elevation of the chain is reduced to about 3400 or 3000 feet. Frog Mountain, south of the Ocoee, is a high portion of the chain. Prof. Guyot makes the elevation of its highest peak 4226 feet. The elevation of the Ducktown Copper Region, which lies to the east of Frog Mountain, is said to be about 2000 feet.

75. *The "Balds," Views, Balsam Peaks*, &c.—I have had occasion several times, to refer, incidentally, to the "balds" of the Unaka Range. Some further notice of them is required.

As a general thing, the Unaka Ridges are clothed with forests, the high, exposed summits, however, running up from 4000 to more than 6000 feet above tide-water, are frequently destitute of trees, owing to the cold climate of these heights. Such places are said to be *bald*, or are called the *balds*, and sometimes *balls*. They are treeless domes capping the great mountains.

These domes are, in some cases, nearly, or quite, a mile in diameter; sometimes a chain or succession of them, occurs along the summit of a ridge, giving, in fact, a more or less continuous bald for several miles. Such is the case upon the Roan. (§ 55.)

76. Although treeless, the balds are not wanting in verdure; supplied often with a good, though not deep, soil, they abound in grasses, ferns, and small shrubs,* several of which belong to a far more northern climate than is found in the valleys below. During the summer, the clouds, in which they are often buried, keep them moist, and supply with water the ice-cold springs which are frequently found around their edges, much to the comfort and relief of the mountain-climbers who visit them. In winter they are, much of the time, covered with snow.

* "Wild gooseberries," several species of huckleberries, and even strawberries, abound upon some of them, and are much esteemed for their rich flavor.

77. In ascending a mountain crowned with a bald, the changes which successively occur in the aspect of the trees and general growth, as we approach the bald, are curious and most interesting. Leaving the heavy forests on the slopes below, the oaks, beeches, and other trees, begin to diminish in size, and diminish more and more, as the bald is approached, until we find ourselves passing through strange, low groves of old looking dwarfs, often not much higher than one's head. Groves of stunted beeches, buckeyes, maples, oaks, with sometimes birches and patches of balsams, are found more or less, around all of them. On reaching the edge of the bald, the groves disappear, and the treeless summit is boldly spread out before the visitor; often, with the exception of occasional rocky masses here and there, as a great gently rolling meadow, and often, too, in the summer season, alive with "stock" of all kinds, feeding and fattening upon the rich herbage.

78. The balds, in themselves, are interesting, but when the great and magnificent views of the world below and around them are associated, they become in truth, sublime. They must be visited, to be appreciated. There is a fascination about them which cannot be told.

79. In general, the views on the one hand, to the east or southeast, in North Carolina, are made up in the distance of the broken heavy ranges and arms of the Blue Ridge. Near by, from nearly all the points, the spurs of the Unakas are seen running out from beneath one's feet, sometimes apparently interlocking, in much confusion, with those from the North Carolina ranges; often, however, the different sets are seen to be more or less parallel, and separated by beautiful valleys which look like garden spots deeply seated, and sometimes seemingly almost buried among the mountains.

80. On the other hand, to the west and north, in Tennessee, the view is different. There is not the same apparently unbounded ocean of mountain billows. In place of the rough ranges of the Blue Ridge, we have, in the distance, far below us, (combining the views from the different points along the Unakas,) the great Valley of East Tennessee, spreading out like a rich and checkered carpet, its inequalities, excepting a few heavy ridges to the north, being almost lost—its surface sinking down to a great plain, dotted all over with cultivated spots. In the extreme distance, especially from the central and more southern summits, the Cumberland Table-land is seen to the northwest, rising up dimly beyond the Great Valley, and bounding the view. From the more northern summits, the

Bay's Mountain group of ridges, and the Virginia ranges, the Clinch especially, which run their abrupt ends into Tennessee, appear in demi-relief, set in the midst of the Valley, and interpolated, as it were, between the Unaka and the Cumberland. (§ 95.)

At our feet the Tennessee Unakas are well seen. Great spurs run out from the main axis, at the base of which lie, very generally, long, narrow coves; just beyond which, again rise up long, straight mountain ridges—the outline of the chain (§ 46) trending with the main axis itself, to the northeast and southwest.

81. Many balds occur along the Unaka Chain. White Top, of the Stone Mountain Range, (§ 48,) has a conspicuous one, which can be seen from many and distant points. Other summits of the same range, have them. Those of the Roan, the Bald Mountain, and Big Butt ranges, have been referred to. (§§ 55,59 and 62.) Others occur along, or in the vicinity of the line in Cocke, Sevier, Blount, and Monroe.

Of all the balds, those of the Roan are doubtless the most extensive and beautiful. They are three or four in number, and lie in a chain six miles in length along the summit of the mountain. They are partially separated from each other by shallow depressions, or gaps, which abound more or less with groves of dwarfed trees such as generally surround the balds. (§ 77.) The largest lies at the southwestern end of the Roan. Dr. Mitchell appears to have had this one in mind when he wrote the following graphic notice of this mountain: "It is the most beautiful and will best repay the labor of ascending it, of all our high mountains. With the exception of a body of rocks, looking like the ruins of an old castle, near its southwestern extremity, the top of the Roan may be described as a vast meadow without a tree to obstruct the prospect; where a person may gallop his horse for a mile or two, with Carolina at his feet on one side, and Tennessee on the other, and a green ocean of mountains raised in tremendous billows immediately around him. It is the Elysium of the Southern botanist, as a number of plants are found growing in this cold and humid atmosphere, which are not seen again until we have gone some hundreds of miles further north. It is the pasture ground for the young horses of the whole country about it during the summer. We found the strawberry here in the greatest abundance and of the finest quality, in regard to both size and flavor, on the 30th of July."*

The bald of the Big Butt, in the neighborhood of the "Cold Spring," is easy of access, affords a magnificent view, (all the mountains and coves of

*Amer. Jour. Sci., 1839, Vol. XXXV. See also same Journal, 1842, Vol. XLII, for an interesting notice of the botany of this and other neighboring mountains, by Dr. Asa Gray.

Washington, to the northeast and east, among them the Great Bald, the towns of Jonesborough and Greeneville to the north and west, far down in the Valley, Bay's Mountain, &c., being in sight,) and will well compensate for the labor incident to a visit.

82. Those summits, or crests of considerable elevation, but not high nor exposed enough to be bald, are generally covered with a stunted open growth.

Some of the very highest points, in place of being bald, are dark with a heavy balsam and evergreen growth, through which it is sometimes impossible to pass. Such a dark, thick, sombre vegetation has given name to the Black Mountains of North Carolina; and some of the Tennessee peaks might well be denominated *Black* for the same reason. The following remarks refer, in part, to the "balsams" of the mountains of Cocke and Sevier counties:

"Most of the highest mountain tops are covered with the *Abies nigra* and *Abies Fraseri;* the former is the black spruce, and is erroneously called the balsam; the latter is the true balsam with blisters in its bark, from which balsam is collected. It attains a greater size than Pursh or Nuttall has given it. * * * * The black spruce appears to grow at a lower elevation than the balsam, but neither of them is often met with beneath a height of 4000 feet."*

83. Dr. Mitchell, who many years ago measured the peaks of the Black Mountain, and who, too, in after years, unfortunately lost his life while alone among their dark, cold summits, has left us the following notice of the laurel thickets and bear trails of this mountain. Similar thickets and trails occur upon some of the rough ridges of Tennessee.

"The ascent of the Black Mountain is very difficult, on account of the thick laurels which are so closely set, and their strong branches so interwoven, that a path cannot be forced by pushing them aside. The hunters have no method of advancing, when they happen to fall in with the worst of them, but that of crawling along their tops. The bear, in passing up and down the mountain, finds it wisest to keep the ridges; and, trampling down the young laurels as they spring up, breaking the limbs of the old ones, and pushing them aside, he forms, at last, a sort of burrow above ground through this bed of vegetation, along which he passes without difficulty."

84. *Climate.*—The cool, grassy balds, the high crests with open, stunted growth, the balsam summits and northern aspect

*S. B. Buckley, Amer. Journ. Sci., Vol. XXVII, 2d Series, p. 286.

of vegetation, which have been referred to, indicate the character of the climate on the tops of the higher Unaka ridges. In ascending these ridges no important changes are seen until near their tops. The same forests extend from the valleys a long way up the sides of the mountains. In the vicinity, however, of the higher crests and summits, and upon them, the aspect is very different. The changes in vegetation are especially striking. Many of the plants are sub-alpine in character, the equivalents of which must be sought for on the plains of Canada, several hundred miles to the north.

For the want of systematic observations upon the meteorology of the Unakas, no satisfactory statistics can be presented. All I propose to do is to estimate their mean temperature and other climatic features, using as data the averages obtained at Knoxville, the nearest point at which observations have been made. Knoxville occupies a position near the centre of the great valley of East Tennessee, but is within sight of some of the Unaka ridges.

85. It is well known that the greater the altitude of a place, the colder is its climate. The rate of decrease in temperature is one degree for about every 300 or 350 feet of elevation.

Prof. Guyot, in his excellent work on comparative Physical Geography, says:*

"An elevation of level of 350 feet, ... which is only that of many of our public edifices, is sufficient to diminish the mean temperature of a place by one degree of Fahrenheit; that is to say, the effect is the same as if the place were situated sixty miles further north. A few thousand feet of height, which are nothing to the mass of the globe, change entirely the aspect and character of a country. The excellent vineyards, bordering the banks of the Swiss lakes, become impossible at 1000 feet, at 500 even, above their present level; and the tillage, the occupations of the inhabitants, take here quite a different character. A thousand feet higher still, and the rigor of the climate no longer permits the fruit trees to flourish; the pastures are the only wealth of the mountaineer, for whom industry ceases to be a resource. Higher still, vegetation disappears, with it the animals, and soon, instead of the smiling pictures of the plain and the lower valleys, succeeds the spectacle of the majestic, but desolated regions of eternal ice and snow, where the sound and animation of life give place to the silence of death."

* The Earth and Man: Lectures on Comparative Physical Geography in its Relations to the History of Man, by Arnold Guyot. Boston, 1850.

I quote this passage for a double purpose; it contains practical illustrations for which we will have use hereafter.

86. Prof. Henry, in constructing the isothermal chart of the territory of the United States, which accompanies one of his instructive articles on Meteorology in the Patent Office Reports, has made an allowance for decreasing temperature of *one degree for every* 333 *feet of elevation, or three degrees for every* 1000 *feet.* This rate of decrease afforded him satisfactory and consistent results. It will be adopted in estimating the temperature of the high lands of Tennessee.

87. The mean annual temperature at Knoxville, so far as we can at present, determine it, is fifty-seven degrees, (§ 30,) and the height of the city, or rather of the points where the observations were made, is 1000 feet above the sea, or so near it, that this, for present purposes, may be taken as the height.

Many of the more elevated Unaka summits are from 4000 to 5000 feet higher than Knoxville, and some 5500, and a few even 5600 higher. The difference in temperature, must, therefore, be considerable. At the rate adopted, it is fifteen degrees for those points 5000 feet above Knoxville, or 6000 above the sea. This gives them a yearly mean of forty-two degrees, which is about that of the southern shore of Lake Superior, and of Quebec and Montreal.

88. The yearly mean of forty-two degrees belongs strictly to those points which have the same latitude of Knoxville, and are 6000 feet above the sea. A difference of latitude, in this region, of about forty-five miles, makes a difference in temperature of one degree. The elevation therefore, being the same, the mean, forty-five miles further north, will be forty-one degrees, and at the same distance south, forty-three degrees. It follows, also, that an elevation of 5666 feet above the sea, in the northern part of the Unaka Chain, will be equivalent, so far as it regards temperature; to one of 6000 feet on the parallel of Knoxville, and to one of 6333 forty-five miles further south.

Thus, finally, it is seen that, in *mean temperature* at least, these high local regions have a climate that is truly Canadian. But while the annual mean is that of Quebec, or of Montreal, the extremes of heat and cold are less than they are there; the winters being milder and the summers cooler.

89. As to *rain and moisture*, but little that is definite can be given. It is well known, however, that there is, in general, no lack of either. In the summer season, showers of rain frequently dash over these mountain tops, when scarcely a cloud is to be seen floating above the great Valley, to the west. The annual quantity of rain and melted snow at Knoxville, may, for the present, be taken at 44.5 inches, (§ 38.) That which falls upon the Unakas is greater than this. The moist westerly and southwesterly winds, when they strike, and flow up the mountain sides, lose a part of their sensible temperature, and, in consequence, may precipitate moisture, for the first time in their passage across the State, either simply as clouds enveloping and bedewing the summits, or as rain. During the winter, the highest crests and summits are, much of the time, white with snow.

The foregoing features of climate give the Unakas, for the most part, their agricultural characteristics; of these it is proposed to speak hereafter.

II.—The Valley of East Tennessee.

90. Leaving the mountains, we now descend to a great area, or Valley, fluted with scores of smaller valleys and ridges. Such are the relations of this area to the mountains on both sides, that it is well called, collectively, the Valley. It is one of the most beautiful and populous portions of the State. Within it is embraced nearly all the agricultural wealth which is usually accredited to the civil division we call *East Tennessee*. (§ 40.)

91. *Geographical Limits and Relations.*—The limits of this valley have been already briefly given in the table of the natural divisions. (§ 25.) As there said, it is bounded on the southeast by the Unaka Chain, and on the northwest, by the steep escarpments of the great Table-land next to be described.*

* The panoramic view, facing this page, presents the general appearance of the Valley of East Tennessee as seen from the point of Lookout Mountain near Chattanooga. In the extreme distance, upon the right, are seen some of the high ridges of the Unaka Chain, and near by, upon the left, the eastern escarpment of Walden's Ridge, (an arm of the Cumberland Table-land,) the wide valley lying between these mountain ranges. Some of the ridges included within the valley, are also seen. The conspicuous ridge east of Chattanooga, is Mission, or Missionary, Ridge. Further off, White Oak Mountain, parallel to the ridge, just mentioned, may be traced out.

To the northeast it is continuous with the Valley of Virginia; to the southwest it extends into Georgia and Alabama. It is, in reality, but a part of a long, great and complex trough that extends, at least from the Susquehanna, in Pennsylvania to the Coosa and Black Warrior rivers, in Alabama; and it is thus, too, I may add here, a portion of a great natural highway,—for such is this trough,—that Providence has opened between the North and the South, and which now is rapidly becoming available by iron tracks throughout its entire length. This trough, in its southwestern course, enters Tennessee obliquely with reference to its northern boundary, but, in crossing the State, turns with a graceful curve more southward, and passes the southern boundary at a much less acute angle. The Tennessee portion—the Valley under consideration—has, in the northern part of the State, (measured, for example, directly across from Meadow Creek Mountain, in Cocke county, to the Cumberland Gap on the State line, in Claiborne,) a width of about fifty-five miles. Towards the southern part of the State, however, its mountain walls converge and reduce its breadth. Measured across from Star's Mountain, in McMinn, to the foot of the Cumberland, in Rhea, it is only about thirty-four miles wide, and thus narrowed, it strikes the Georgia line.*

92. Altogether, with its outlying subordinate valleys and coves, the Valley of East Tennessee embraces the following counties and parts of counties: the whole of Hancock, Hawkins, Grainger, Union, Jefferson, Knox, Roane, Meigs, and Bradley, nearly all of Sullivan and McMinn; the parts, and in most cases, much the greater parts, of Carter, Johnson, Washington, Greene, Cocke, Sevier, Blount, Monroe, and Polk, not occupied by the Unaka Ridges; and finally, the parts of Claiborne, Anderson, Rhea, Hamilton, Bledsoe, Sequatchee, and Marion, not upon the Cumberland Table-land. The entire Valley, including its outlying valleys and coves, has an area of about 9200 square miles, considerably more than one-fifth of the area of the State.

93. *Component parts, the Ridges.*—The Valley of East Tennessee constitutes the largest and most interesting portion of

* I do not include here a remarkable and beautiful outlier—Sequatchee Valley—to be considered hereafter, which would increase the aggregate breadth.

that part of the Appalachian Region, (§ 18,) which lies within Tennessee. It has the Appalachian characteristics well developed. It is closely furrowed with parallel valleys and ridges, all trending to the northeast and southwest. Owing to this character, the surface in a transverse direction, that is to say, from the southeast to the northwest, is remarkably rolling. "Across the country" is here significant. The luckless traveler, whose route lies "across," unless happily favored with breaks and gaps in the ridges, prepares for "wave on wave succeeding." On the other hand, "up," or "down the country,"—to the northeast or southwest—is as equally significant of good level roads.

94. The ridges are very numerous, and differ more or less in height, sharpness of outline, agricultural and other features; while, at the same time, each one is remarkable for the uniformity of character it preserves from one end to the other—a distance, in some cases, of a hundred miles or more. The differences among them depend, for the most part, as will be seen hereafter, upon the differences in geological character. The most important are mentioned below.

95. In the first place, several, in the northern part of the Valley, are called *mountains*. Most of these are prominent ridges, which, coming out of Virginia, terminate abruptly, within the borders of Tennessee. They are arranged in three groups, one of which—the last noticed—belongs exclusively to Tennessee.

96. First, *the Powell's Mountain Group*.—This is a series of three great parallel ridges, which, coming from the northeast, and entering Tennessee, run through a corner of Hancock County, and terminate in the northeastern part of Claiborne. The remarks below refer to them as they occur in Tennessee, where they are, in fact, but little more than the ends of ridges. The first, on the northwest, is *Wallin's Ridge;* then, at the distance of about two miles, follows *Powell's Mountain*, the intermediate space being occupied by a lower ridge and a limestone valley. Powell's Mountain is succeeded by *Newman's Ridge*, the two being crowded closely together, with but a very narrow trough, or valley, between. These are high conspicuous ridges, but can hardly be designated as mountains.

97. Second, *the Clinch Mountain Group.*—*Clinch Mountain* is the most prominent of all the ranges included in the Valley. After pursuing a long course in Virginia, it crosses the Tennessee boundary and runs continuously for more than fifty-six miles, in a nearly straight line, to within sight of Knoxville, when it breaks off abruptly in a bold end. It has a sharp crest, and well defined outlines. In height, it will average not much, if any, less than 1000 feet above the level of the Holston. It is the boundary, in part, between the counties of Hancock and Hawkins, and between Union and Grainger.

98. Close along the southeastern base of Clinch Mountain, but separated from it by a narrow trough, or valley, (Poor Valley,) is, generally, a low sharp ridge. In Hawkins, however, on its southeastern side, there are several heavy ridges, the *Pine Mountain*, the *Stone Mountain*, and a curious outlier, the *Devil's Nose*, all of which, including Clinch Mountain, are crowded together, side by side, and constitute the group. *House Mountain*, an isolated, short, roof-like ridge, in Knox County, and a mile or two below the end of the Clinch, might also be included. This is a conspicuous object, and is seen from Knoxville, and from many other distant points.

99. Last, *the Bay's Mountain Group.*—This group lies wholly within Tennessee. It is a curious bed of half a dozen sharp, straight ridges, which, like those of the group just mentioned, are crowded laterally together, being separated only by very narrow trough-like valleys. The group itself is called, collectively, Bay's Mountain, and extends from the Holston, near Kingsport, to a point several miles below Bull's Gap, a distance of about forty miles.* Across its middle part, it is several miles through, and here the greatest number of ridges occur. Towards either end, the ridges one after another drop away, until, at the Holston and below Bull's Gap, the group terminates in single ranges. *Chimney Top* and *Fodder Stack*, are high, prominent points, capped with masses of sandstone, which belong to the most eastern ridge. The former affords, from its

*In Jefferson County, and even south of the French Broad, between Knox and Sevier counties, are ridges which are considered as continuations of Bay's Mountain, and take its name. They are, however, no part of Bay's Mountain proper. They are comparatively low, have a different geological structure, and no physical connection with it.

great sandstone "chimneys," a most beautiful and extended landscape view.

Bay's Mountain has points which are as high as the mean elevation of Clinch Mountain, or higher, yet its average height is considerably less.

100. Such are the "mountains" of the northeastern portion of the Valley. Owing to the presence of the first two groups, and of many intermediate ridges of less elevation, some of which will be mentioned, the region between Rogersville and Tazewell, by the way of Sneedville, is exceedingly rough or rolling. It is relieved, however, to some extent, by several fine limestone valleys lying imbedded between the parallel ridges.

101. The northern groups running out, the Valley far southward is without mountains. Its surface, it is true, is closely furrowed with ridges and valleys, but the former are comparatively low, and almost sink down into a common plain with the latter when seen in the great views obtained from the high summits of the Unakas. (§ 80.)

102. In the southern part of the Valley, however, is a single range which deserves to be mentioned here. This is the so-called *White Oak Mountain.**

This mountain first appears five or six miles below the Hiwassee River, near Georgetown. It runs in a direct course southwesterly to the Georgia line, and separates, in part, the counties of Bradley and Hamilton. It is a prominent range and a leading feature in this part of the Valley. Taylor's Ridge, in Georgia, is a continuation of White Oak Mountain.

103. In regard to the scores of ridges of less elevation, my remarks must be general. There are several different classes, or types, of these ridges—so far as their forms and outlines are concerned—features, by the way, depending in reality upon their geological characters.

104. In the first place, a large class is composed of those which are depressed, or rounded, along the summits or crests. These are generally limestone ridges, and often of great length. Most of them have a comparatively unbroken outline, others are more or less cut into a succession of dome-like knobs.

**Lookout Mountain*, which looms up abruptly and grandly just within the Valley, and near the Georgia line, is properly an outlier of the Cumberland Table-land, and is referred to that division.

Many of them are covered, to a greater or less extent, with sharp flinty gravel.

105. A second and large class, includes numerous ridges which are steep and sharp-crested. These owe their characteristic forms to the sandstone, and sometimes to the slaty layers which they contain. Though often occurring in groups, yet they more frequently, perhaps, alternate in position with those of the first class, and like them extend in length a great number of miles. Sometimes their sharp crests are notched by gaps, at short intervals, affording curious lines of pointed peaks. In such cases, they are frequently denominated *comby "ridges."*

106. Another class, and the last I shall mention here, includes a number of long and remarkable ranges of *"Red Knobs"* or *"Red Hills,"* traversing the southeastern part of the Valley. The knobs are separated from each other by deep gaps. They have generally a conical shape, sending up their peaks from 200 to 400 feet, and sometimes to a greater altitude, above the general level of the Valley. The soil upon them has a deep brownish red color, derived from the sandy ferruginous and calcareous rocks, of which, for the most part, they are composed. These curious hills dot out straight or gently curving ranges, remarkable for their length, and for their uniform appearance throughout.

107. For the purpose of presenting examples of the different classes, and, at the same time, of illustrating the surface-features of the Valley, which, indeed, is the main object desired, some of the most prominent ridges will be noticed. It will be best to speak of them in connection with the different sections of the Valley in which they occur.

108. The region west and north of Knoxville, is distinguished for its numerous parallel ridges, several of which are remarkable for their size, their directness, and length. The principal ones, in the order in which they successively occur, in going from Knoxville, are the *Black Oak*, *Copper*, and *Chestnut Ridges.* Copper Ridge runs from the Virginia line far down into Tennessee, and may be traced out for at least seventy-five miles. This, as well as the Black Oak and Chestnut Ridges, have a limestone basis, and, belong, with others, to the first class mentioned.

In addition to these, and in some cases, alternating with them, there are in this region many of the sharp crested ridges. Such are *Bull Run* and *Pine Ridges*. The ridge three miles west, or northwest of Knoxville, is also an example. In Hancock County several ridges of this kind occur; among them *Comby Ridge* is prominent.

109. The section of the Valley east of Bay's Mountain, and northeast of the French Broad River, including the counties of Sullivan, Washington, Greene, and part of Cocke, is in strong contrast, so far as *long* uniform ridges are concerned, with the one just mentioned. Here are no very long ranges like the Copper and Black Oak Ridges. The surface is furrowed, in common with all parts of the Valley, with ridges and valleys, running northeasterly or southwesterly; but the ridges are comparatively short, seldom running more than eight or ten miles, and their axes not always arranged consecutively in lines. The region may be said to be interruptedly furrowed or fluted.

110. Constituting one of the peculiarities of this section, are short and narrow *slate ridges*, which thrust their backs up here and there over its area.

Another feature is the occurrence, especially in Sullivan County, of *regions, or belts, of slaty knobs*. These knobs are crowded together without order, and, where most numerous, form wild labyrinths of conical hills, from which a stranger, once off the beaten track, might not easily extricate himself. The East Tennessee & Virginia Railroad, just north of the Watauga River, runs for about four miles through one of these "knobby regions."

111. Southwest of the last section, and east and south of Knoxville, as far down as the Little Tennessee River, there is another portion of the Valley, including the counties of Jefferson, Sevier, Blount, and parts of Cocke and Knox, in which the ridges are better defined than in the last, but not so well as in the adjacent section to the northwest. Many of the ridges belong to the first class. (§ 104.) Such is the so-called "*Bay's Mountain*," north of the French Broad A few have the sharply crested character, as the "*Bay's Mountain*," which lies south of the French Broad, and separates Knox County from Sevier.

112. It is here that the curious ranges of "Red Knobs," (§ 106,) are first seen. These constitute one of the most prominent topographical features of this region. They originate in Jefferson County and in the northern part of Blount, and extend to the southwest, for the most part, along the margins of two slaty belts traversing this part of the State. One of these ranges, which I mention as an example, originates in the vicinity of Strawberry Plains, and passes near Knoxville, its red prominent hills being just beyond the Holston; from this point it continues to the southwest, runs close by Athens, and reaches a point a few miles east of Cleveland. Here the Knobs cease to be prominent, but yet they can be seen, and the range they form traced on into Georgia.

113. The slaty belts just referred to, are often "knobby," forming, in fact, "knobby belts" like those of Sullivan. (§ 110.) One of these, several miles wide, traverses Sevier County. It originates in fact, in Greene, and traverses Cocke County before entering Sevier. It lies just to the west of Sevierville, strikes the end of Chilhowee Mountain, and then continues on down along the western side of this mountain, into Blount. This belt is noted for its conical hills, or "*knobs*," especially that portion of it in Sevier County.

114. The southern part of the Valley, the section south or southwest of the Little Tennessee, and of the Big Tennessee as far down as the mouth of Clinch River, is, in general, very uniformly fluted with ridges and valleys.

115. In the first place, the portion of this section west of the East Tennessee and Georgia Railroad, contains numerous long ridges, both sharp-crested and rounded, many of which, are continuations of those traversing the section west and north of Knoxville. White Oak Mountain, already mentioned, (§ 102,) occurs here. Missionary Ridge, east of Chattanooga, and prominent in the plate facing page 39, is one of the first class. (§ 104.)

116. North of Chattanooga and west of the Tennessee River, as far up, at least, as the mouth of the Hiwassee, is a strip, from four to six miles wide, which is broken and hilly. It is a *knobby region*, but of a different character from those before mentioned. Its knobs are more dome-like, and are covered

with flinty gravel. The rocks which compose them are not slate, but a magnesian limestone.

117. To the east of the railroad, in the second place, there is much uniformity in the direction and arrangement of subordinate parts. Here the ridges are principally rounded and flinty with a few conspicuous lines of red hills, all being continuations of the ranges from the northeast. The red hills of the Knoxville and Athens Range are very prominent in the northern part of this section. In addition to these, there are some narrow, knobby belts.

118. *Valleys and Coves.*—Such are the relations existing between the ridges and valleys of this great division, that much of what might be said here has been anticipated. The ridges mark out the valleys. Where the former are long and straight, and occur side by side, at short intervals, the latter will necessarily be long and narrow.

119. In the western half of the Valley,—that next to the Cumberland Table-land and reaching from Virginia to Georgia,—the subordinate valleys, as might be inferred from the character of the ridges, have the greatest longitudinal extent, and the greatest regularity in their arrangement. In fact they are remarkable for these features. There are several valleys or ranges of valleys here, which, although, perhaps not averaging more than one mile in width, run continuously through the State, a distance of more than 150 miles. They extend, moreover, each way beyond the limits of Tennessee.

120. These valleys may be easily traced out upon the Map. In one long range, which may be presented as an example, are found the towns of Tazewell, Clinton, Decatur and Georgetown; and I might add also, Ringgold, in Georgia.

121. Another range of valleys lying at the base of the Cumberland Table-land, or of Walden's Ridge, (as the eastern border of the Table-land is called,) may be here noticed. This range, with the exception of two or three short breaks in Roane and Campbell counties, is also continuous through the State. *Powell's Valley*, in Claiborne and Campbell counties, *Tennessee Valley*,* in Rhea and Hamilton, and *Lookout Valley*, in the southern part of the latter county, are among its well known

* Not of the Tennessee River

portions. This valley-range, however, does not come in direct contact with the base of the Table-land, being usually separated from it by a low, sharp ridge, and a very narrow and curious trough, often called the "*Back Valley*," the latter lying immediately at the base, and back of, the sharp ridge.

122. In the northeastern portion of the Valley, especially in Washington, Greene, and Cocke counties, the valleys partake of the nature of the ridges, and are comparatively short and broken. (§ 109.)

Southwest of this section, and especially south of the Hiwassee, there are again, long ridges and valleys succeeding each other laterally, with considerable regularity.

123. The valleys, in general, vary in width from a few hundred yards to several miles. Most of them are fertile and beautiful. Some of the narrow ones are not inviting, being cold and unproductive.

They are best classified in accordance with their geological characters. So far as may be necessary, they will be enumerated in connection with the descriptions of the formations with which they are associated.

124. My remarks, hitherto, have been confined to the subordinate valleys lying wholly and properly within the body of the great Valley. In addition to these, the *outlying valleys*, or *coves*, which are more or less interlocked with the ranges and arms of the Unaka and Cumberland, or are entirely surrounded by them, are to be noticed.

125. Beginning in the northeastern corner of the State, there is, at the first, one of the largest and most interesting coves in Tennessee, for such a cove, indeed, the valley-lands of Johnson County, taken together, form. The general outline and extent of this cove may be seen by reference to the map. Below Taylorsville, it is divided lengthwise by Doe Mountain; the parts, however, unite again around the mountain in the valley of the Watauga. (§ 51.) *Johnson County Cove*, as it may be called, is a more elevated body of valley-land than any other of equal extent in the State. Its average elevation is considerably more than 2000 feet above the sea, which is, at least, as high, if not higher, than the top of the Cumberland Table-land. It is well watered by the Watauga, and by Roane's Creek and its crystal

tributaries. Northward, it runs to a point not far above the Virginia line. It is entirely inclosed by mountains. On the east and south lies the Stone Mountain Range; (§ 48,) on the northwest, the Iron Mountain Range. (§ 49.) To enter or leave the cove, it is necessary, either to climb over the mountains, or to pass through the very narrow rocky gaps cut out by the water courses. The gaps most used are those formed respectively, by Doe River and the south fork of the Laurel; the former furnishing a pass to the southwest, and the latter to the northwest into Virginia.

126. Lying between, or rather, almost on the Holston and Iron Mountains, just before they unite near the Virginia line, is the curious basin called *Shady*. (§ 50.) This is also included in Johnson County. It is much higher than Johnson Cove, but is of limited extent. It is noted chiefly for its excellent iron. This little basin is so elevated that its flora partakes of a Canadian character. Within it flourish cranberries and northern coniferæ.

127. The two mountains which enclose Shady, diverge, as they pass to the southwest, and finally give between them a long, wide, and interesting area—the *Stony Creek Valley* of Carter County. (§ 50.)

128. In Washington County, between its two principal mountain ranges, is another long valley called *Greasy Cove*. (§ 58.) This has, perhaps, across its middle part, a width of about two miles. To the southwest it gradually becomes narrower and finally ends in a low gap upon the State line; to the northeast, however, it widens, and finally opens out boldly, opposite to the lower and larger end of the Stony Creek Valley. This valley and Greasy Cove, taken together, may indeed be regarded as one long fusiform cove nearly cut off from the Main Valley by the intervening Holston Mountain and the Buffalo and Rich Mountain Range which approach each other on the northwest. (§ 60.) These features, as well as the extent of the valleys, may be seen by reference to the Map.

129. *Limestone Cove*, in Carter, and *Bompass Cove*, in Washington County, have been already mentioned. (§§ 57 and 60.)

130. In Greene County, a cove of some importance lies between Paint and Meadow Creek Mountains. It runs down southwesterly, into a narrow valley, called *Peck's Trough*. (§ 64.)

131. South of the Big Pigeon, in Cocke County, several bands of limestone run to the southwest, back of English's Mountain, and taper off in long slender fingers which reach into Sevier. One of these fingers constitutes *Jones's Cove*, a narrow valley four or five miles south-east of English's Mountain.

In Sevier County, north-east of the Little Pigeon River, are other small coves, of which, however, it is not necessary to speak here.

132. In the southern part of Sevier, and in Blount County, there is a group of three large and very interesting coves. They lie completely imbedded among the mountains. The first two are surrounded by those ridges which occur in the space between the main Unaka Range and the outlier—Chilhowee Mountain; (§ 66;) the third lies immediately at the base of the main range. They all have nearly the same dimensions, ranging from five to six miles in length, and from one and-a-half to two miles in breadth. Their forms and relative positions may be seen upon the Map.

133. The first, *Wear's Cove*, is situated in the southern part of Sevier County. It is a beautiful and elevated region, walled in all around by high, rough ridges. Its bounding ridge on the southeast swells up to a conspicuous mountain, which is well seen from Sevierville, and from many other distant points. This cove has been settled very nearly sixty years, and now furnishes homes for about seventy families.

134. The second is *Tuckaleechee Cove*. This lies just within Blount County, and is separated from Wear's Cove by a narrow neck, or ridge, the two being about a mile apart. In leaving the latter we pass through a low gap, and then descend perhaps about 300 feet, into Tuckaleechee. This is the largest of the group. Little River flows through it, and in leaving it, cuts out a narrow pass through the mountain walls upon the west, thus forming the gateway of this imprisoned basin. Tuckaleechee has been settled about as long as Wear's cove, and now contains nearly one hundred families.

135. The last of the group is *Cade's Cove*. This is cut off from Tuckaleechee by a heavy ridge, which bifurcates towards the west, including between its branches, a little valley called "*El-dorado*."

Cade's Cove is highly elevated, being more than 700 feet above Tuckaleechee.* It lies, as I have said, at the base of the main Unaka Range, and only a few miles from the State line. Several fine "balds" occur upon this part of the range, (§ 81,) from which can be seen, not only the Cove below, but the mountains, lying west of the Cove, (Chilhowee being especially conspicuous,) and the great valley beyond the mountains, bounded by its western wall—the dim edge of the Cumberland Table-land.

Cade's Cove is remarkable for its rich bottoms and its meadow-like features. It is well watered by the tributaries of Abram's Creek. It contains at present about fifty families. It was partially settled about sixty years ago, but for many years it remained Indian territory.

136. *Miller's Cove* is a long narrow trough, immediately along the southeastern base of Chilhowee Mountain. It is situated partly in Sevier County, and partly in Blount. This cove has been settled about as long as those just mentioned, and contains, perhaps, thirty families.

137. In Blount and Monroe Counties, are several other small coves, several of which occur along the Little Tennessee River.

138. I have now noticed the principal valleys and coves associated with the Unaka ranges.† They have several characters in common, one of the most important of which is, that they all contain, or are based upon, limestone. After the general elevation of the whole Unaka region, it is doubtless, in part, to the removal of limestone, through the agency of water, (the hard slates, sandstones, and conglomerates, now forming the ridges being left,) that the existence of these troughs and basins, as such, among the mountains, is to be attributed. The discussion of this subject, however, belongs to another part of the Report.

139. We now pass across the Valley to the Cumberland Table-land. Here the aspect of things is very different. Instead

* In July, 1858, John Caldwell, Esq., of Jefferson County, was kind enough to accompany me through this group of coves. His knowledge of the country, and the researches he himself had made in this region, enabled him to render valuable assistance. With his help, and by means of a pocket level, the difference in the elevation of the two coves was approximately determined. We found it to be about 765 feet.

† The *Ducktown Region*, already spoken of, (§ 68,) is not included among the coves. It differs from them in its general relations, and especially in its geological character.

of a great bed of parallel ridges, including naturally, as it were, valleys and coves, we have an extended plateau, or table-land, the eastern border of which is nearly unbroken and continuous through the State. There are, however, two valleys, confined within the general limits of this table-land, which, although cut off from the main part of the Valley to the east, are, nevertheless, connected with it by their geological and physical features.

140. The first, and by far the largest, is the long and symmetrical *Sequatchee Valley*. The head of this valley is in the bosom of the Table-land, and nearly midway between the northern and southern boundaries of the State. From its head, it pursues a nearly straight southwesterly course, for about sixty miles, through the counties of Bledsoe, Sequatchee, and Marion, to the Alabama line. It is, in fact, a great trough sunk lengthwise in the body of the Table-land, dividing, or splitting, the latter from its middle part, southwestward, into two parallel but unequal portions or arms. All along, on both sides, it is bordered and overlooked by the high, steep, inner edges of these portions. These edges are from three to five miles apart, and, like great walls, mark out the limits of the long valley with singular definiteness.*

141. The arm of the Table-land that lies along the southeastern side of Sequatchee Valley, is a long and quite uniform belt, or table, from six to eight miles wide, running down into Georgia and Alabama. Near the Georgia line, however, it is much broken. In the first place, the Tennessee River, a few miles above the line, cuts completely through it, forming a deep, narrow and serpentine gorge.† Then again, partly upon the line, it is cut by Running Water Creek, not so deeply as before, but yet down to a low gap through which the Nashville and Chattanooga Railroad finds a passage. The belt, as a whole, separates Sequatchee from the main Valley to the east,

* The geographical features of Sequatchee Valley may be seen upon the Map of the State, accompanying this Report. To this the reader is referred.

† The point where the Tennessee cuts into this belt is well seen in the panoramic view facing page 40. Passing Chattanooga, the river makes a large bend—from its form called the *Moccasin Bend*—and then soon begins its passage through the mountain. It is in passing this that the river encounters those serious obstructions so well known to boatmen as the *Boiling Pot*, the *Skillet*, and the *Pan*.

and the narrow cuts, made by the Tennessee and by Running Water, are natural lines of communication between the two.

142. North of the Tennessee River, the above belt forms a part of *Walden's Ridge;* south of the river its broken portions constitute the *Raccoon Mountains.*

143. In a line with Sequatchee Valley, and a few miles northeast of its upper end, there is, I may add here, a curious little basin, sunk in the Table-land, called *Grassy Cove.* Still further to the northeast, in the same line, lies *Crab Orchard Gap.* Sequatchee Valley and Grassy Cove, likewise the latter and Crab Orchard Gap, are separated by high ridges.

144. The second valley, referred to above, is that of the *Elk Fork.** It lies in the northwestern part of Campbell County, in the northern part of the State. It is narrow, rough, and nearly straight. Originating near a point called *Elk Gap,* right in the midst of high ridges, it runs northeastward into Kentucky. Its southeastern side is well defined, all along, by a high, bold ridge, or crest, of the Cumberland Table-land, called *Pine Mountain,* which runs with the valley to the northeast. Its northwestern side, on the other hand, is irregular, being cut, or notched, by the ends of spurs from *Tellico Mountain,* another range of the Table-land. The valley may be regarded as lying between Pine and Tellico mountains. The bed of the Elk Fork has an average elevation of about 1200 feet above the sea.

145. *Elk Gap,* referred to, is a low pass, dividing the waters of the Cumberland River from those of the Tennessee, and connecting Elk Fork Valley with the valley of *Cove Creek.* These valleys originating at the same point, run off nearly at right angles to each other. The latter, however, is narrow and but little more than a straight, deep cut. It opens below into the southwestern end of Powell's Valley. (§ 121.)

146. The valleys of Cove Creek and of Elk Fork, are so situated with reference to each other, and to the local ridges of this part of the Cumberland Plateau, that they furnish a comparatively good route through the mountains for the Knoxville and Kentucky Railroad. They also completely detach within

* The Elk Fork is a tributary of the Clear Fork of Cumberland River.

the limits of Tennessee, a considerable part—a quadrilateral area or *block*—of the Cumberland *Table-land.*

147. *River System.*—The Valley of East Tennessee has an admirable system of rivers and water courses. Its rivers are, for the most part, wide and shallow, and consequently but moderately navigable; yet their waters are clear and beautiful, their smaller tributaries exceedingly numerous, and arranged with remarkable regularity. Crystal rills, flowing from thousands of bold springs, irrigate the land everywhere, and, with the larger mill-streams and the rivers, form a net-work of water courses, which, for completeness and elegance is, perhaps, not excelled.

148. The "*Big Tennessee*" and its proper prolongation, the Holston, (which, by the way, ought to be included whenever we speak of *The Tennessee,*) constitute the great stream into which all the other rivers pour their contents. The "Forks" of the Holston rise in Virginia. The *Clinch,* also, and its tributary, *Powell's* River, take their origin in the same State. All of these have, in general, a southwesterly course, and descend with a considerable fall.

149. At a point about half way through the Valley, the Holston becomes the Big Tennessee, which, after flowing a few miles to the northwest, and receiving the waters of the Clinch, takes a southwesterly course until near the Georgia line, in the vicinity of Chattanooga. At this point it makes its first attempt to break through the Cumberland Table-land and succeeds so far as to pass Walden's Ridge, (§ 141,) and to gain Sequatchee Valley. Here it is again sent off to the southwest, down the Sequatchee trough and its southwestern continuation, many miles into Alabama, where finally it escapes to the northwest through the southern broken portion of the Table-land.

150. The Tennessee and its Virginia tributaries thus follow, in general, the trend of the valley. Yet there is, at the same time, a well marked tendency westward, and even northwestward, for all the important offsets of the main stream, (the Tennessee and Holston,) of which there are three in the State, beside the great one in Alabama, are to the west and northwest. These throw the river into the extreme southwestern

corner of the Valley, and even into its most western outlier, the Sequatchee trough.

151. The tributary rivers which flow out of North Carolina, unlike those from Virginia, all pursue a westerly, and mostly a northwesterly, direction, until they unite with the Holston, or with the Big Tennessee.

152. There are thus two general directions in which the rivers of the Valley flow; one, to the northwest, corresponding to the direction of the general drainage pertaining to the great slope of which the State, as a whole, is a part; (§§ 9, 10;) the other, to the southwest, corresponding to the deflection of drainage caused by the intervention of the Cumberland Table-land, and by the Appalachian features of the Valley itself. (§§ 12, 13 and 11.)

153. The smaller tributaries—the "creeks"—have, generally, great uniformity in direction. Nearly every valley has its creek, flowing either to the northeast, or to the southwest, in conformity to the direction of the ridges. If they escape from one valley to another, they do so through narrow gaps in the ridges, and then only to be sent off again in a direction parallel to their former course. Some exceptions, however, there are, among which those that flow into the Tennessee from Walden's Ridge are the most important. Ooltawa, of Bradley and Hamilton, and Citico, of Monroe, might also be mentioned as important exceptions.

154. *Elevation above the Sea.*—The great Trough, extending from Pennsylvania to Alabama, including the Valley of East Tennessee, (§ 91,) is divided transversely, by the river systems, into natural sections or subordinate slopes. (§ 14.) Of these, none is better defined than that drained by the Tennessee River and its Virginia tributaries. The East Tennessee Valley constitutes the greater part of this, and it may give a better idea of the elevation and position of the Valley to consider it, at first, in connection with this entire slope.

155. The slope, or trough, has its many channeled head, in Virginia, from forty to sixty miles northeast of the Tennessee boundary, along a curved line running through the county of Tazewell, and through Mount Airy, between Smith and Wythe counties. This line is the crest of a water-shed dividing the

waters of the Tennessee on the southwest from those of New River on the northeast. The Virginia and Tennessee Railroad crosses "Mount Airy Ridge" at an elevation of 2594 feet above the sea. From this high region the slope extends in a southwesterly direction to the northern parts of Georgia and Alabama, a distance of about 300 miles.

156. The following tables give the heights, in feet, above tide-water, of many points in this area, most of which, however, are in the East Tennessee Valley. They have been derived mainly, from the railroad surveys.*

The points are arranged in lines, the first extending lengthwise through the Trough : the second is a limited line nearly parallel to a portion of the first, and connecting two of its points, Bristol, and a point near the railroad bridge over Lick Creek. The others are cross-sections. The places noted are in Tennessee, unless otherwise indicated.

(1.) The first series runs along the Virginia and Tennessee Railroad from Mount Airy Ridge to the Tennessee line; it is then continued along the East Tennessee and Virginia Railroad to Knoxville, and from this point, along the East Tennessee and Georgia Railroad to Dalton, Georgia. We thus have a complete longitudinal profile of the Valley of East Tennessee, and in fact of the entire subordinate slope to which it belongs.

Place	Height		
Mount Airy Ridge, Va.	2594	(Level of rails).	Va. & Tenn. R. R.
Marion, Va.	2129	"	" "
Seven Mile Ford, Va.	1976	"	" "
Holston River at Seven Mile Ford	1954	(Surfac of river)	" "
Glade Spring, Va.	2,078	(Level of rails)	Va & Ten. R. R.
Emory and Henry College, Va.	2,103	"	" "
Abingdon, Va.	2,071	"	" "
BRISTOL, *Va, and Tenn. Line*	1,678	"	" "
Holston River at Union	1,401	(Surface of River)	E. T. & Va. R. R.
Union	1,457	(Level of Rails)	" "
Summit between Holston and Watauga Rivers	1,606	"	" "
Carter	1,474	"	" "

* I am indebted for much valuable information, and for profiles, to Mr. Charles Williams, Chief Engineer of the Knoxville & Kentucky Railroad, and to Mr. R. C. Morris, Chief Engineer of the East Tennessee & Georgia Road, and its Cleveland and Chattanooga Branch. I am also indebted to the officers of the East Tennessee and Virginia Road for the altitudes along their line.

Watauga, at Carter.........	1,428	(Surface)	E. T. & Va. R. R.
Johnson's.........................	1,643	(Level of rails)	" "
Summit between Watauga and Nolichucky...	1,841	"	" "
Jonesborough.................	1,734	"	" "
Limestone........................	1,419	"	" "
Fullen's............................	1,489	"	" "
Greeneville (Depot).........	1,581	"	" "
Blue Spring..................	1,279	"	" "
Blue Spring Summit.......	1,368	"	" "
Lick Creek.....................	1,112	(Surface)	" "
Bull's Gap.......................	1,214	(Level of rails)	" "
Russelville........................	1,260	"	" "
Morristown....................	1,283	"	" "
Summit west of Morristown...................	1,352	"	" "
Mossy Creek..................	1,111	"	" "
New Market....................	1,057	"	" "
Strawberry Plains...........	906	"	" "
Holston, at Strawberry Plains....................	849	(Surface)	" "
McMillan's......................	868	(Level of rails	" "
KNOXVILLE, (*Depot*)........	898	(Grade)	E. Tenn. & Ga. R. R.
McClellan's Summit.........	992	"	" "
Knox County Line.........	882	"	" "
Lenoirs..........................	786	"	" "
Loudon..........................	814	"	" "
Tennessee River, at Loudon.......................	737	(Low water)	" "
Sweet Water Summit......	1023	(Grade) "	" "
Athens..........................	993	" "	" "
Hiwassee River.............	723	" "	" "
" "	684	(Low water)	" "
Cleveland.....................	878	(Grade)	" "
Summit in Tenn. *Dividing ridge between Tennessee and those flowing into the Gulf of Mexico..*	892	(Grade)	" "
STATE LINE, *Tenn. & Ga.*	837	"	" "
Dalton, Ga....................	771	"	" "

(2.) The following table includes the heights of certain points along one of the experimental lines of the East Tennessee and Virginia Railroad. It extends from Bristol through Blountville, crosses the Holston at Long Island, runs up the valley of Horse Creek, and then down that of Lick Creek, until it strikes the adopted line near the mouth of Gap Creek.

Bristol, Tenn. and Va. Line 1678 (Rails)........... Va. and Tenn. R. R.

Place	Height		Authority
Steele's Creek	1626	(Surface)	May's Survey.
Summit (3⅔ miles from Bristol)	1727	"	" "
Muddy Creek (near Blountville)	1560	"	" "
Summit (13 miles from Bristol	1773	"	" "
Holston River (upper end of Long Island)	1218	"	" "
Summit between Horse Cr. and Lick Cr.	1413	"	" "
Lick Cr. (13 miles from last Summit)	1192	"	" "
Summit (8½ miles further on)	1222	"	" "
Lick Cr. (5⅔ miles on)	1118	"	" "
Mouth of Gap Creek (near R. R. crossing of Lick Creek.	1113	"	" "

(3.) The following points occur along a line extending *across*, (indirectly,) from the Watauga Valley in N. C., through Johnson County, Tenn., to Abingdon and to the Saltworks, or Saltville, Va.

Place	Height	Authority
Headwaters of Linnville and Watauga rivers, west foot of Grandfather Mt., N. C.	4100	Guyot.
Shull's Mill-pond, Main Watauga, N. C.	2917	R. R. Survey.
STATE LINE, *Tenn. & N. C.* (Watauga Valley)	2131	R. R. Survey.
Taylorsville, Tenn.	2395	Guyot.
Holston, South Fork, Va., on the road to Abingdon	1778	"
Holston, Middle Fork, Va., id	1772	"
Abingdon, Va. (Depot)	2071	Va. & Tenn. R. R.
Saltworks, Va., Depot on the North Fork of Holston River	1712	" "

(4.) From the State line in the rocky gorge of the Little Tennessee River, through Knoxville to Kentucky, an interesting and entire cross-section is furnished. It is from the surveys of the Knoxville and Charleston, and the Knoxville and Kentucky railroads. It crosses nearly through the middle of the Valley.

STATE LINE, on the Little Tenn.*	1114	(Grade)	K. & C. R. R.	Survey.
Tenn. River near Harden's	900	"	"	"
Abram's Creek	872	"	"	"
" "	855	(Surface)	"	"
End of Chilhowee Mt.	870	(Grade)	"	"
Four-mile Creek†	825	"	"	"
" "	808	(Surface)	"	"
Dividing Ridge between Four-mile and Nine-mile Creeks	896	(Grade)	"	"
Dividing Ridge between Four-mile and Nine-mile Creeks	945	(Surface)	"	"
Nine-mile Creek, 30 miles from Knoxville	832	"	"	"
Nine-mile Creek, 26 miles from Knoxville	913	(Grade)	"	"
Nine-mile Creek, 26 miles from Knoxville	900	(Surface)	"	"
Dividing Ridge between the Tennessee and Little Rivers, 21 miles from Knoxville	1045	(Grade)	"	"
Dividing Ridge between the Tennessee and Little Rivers, 21 miles from Knoxville	1076	(Surface)	"	"
Pistol Cr., Mid. Fork (Maryville)	875	"	"	"
Pistol Cr. North Fork	835	"	"	"
Pistol Cr.	810	(Grade)	"	"
" "	790	(Surface)	"	"
Summit	870	"	"	"
Little River	802	(Grade)	"	"
" "	768	(Surface)	"	"
Summit	890	"	"	"
French Meadow Cr.	852	(Grade)	"	"
Summit, nearly 2 miles from Knoxville	936	"	"	"
Holston River	816	(Surface)	"	"

* For the elevation of the Tennessee line on the French Broad River, and the Warm Springs in North Carolina, see page 32.

† At a point, between Four-mile Creek and the "End of Chilhowee Mt.," the profile, from which these elevations were taken, suddenly drops, going toward Knoxville, fifty feet, the following note being attached: "Jostle of fifty feet from error in leveling." The profile is one deposited, according to law, in the office of the Secretary of State.

KNOXVILLE	900	"	K. & K. R. R. Survey.	
Black Oak Ride (Gap)	1106	(Grade)	"	"
Beaver Creek	982	(Surface)	"	"
Copper Ridge	1071	(Grade)		"
Bull Run	823	(Surface)	"	"
Chestnut Ridge	1038	(Grade)	"	"
Clinton	847	"	"	"
Clinch River, (Clinton)	791	(Surface)	"	"
Cane Creek	837	"	"	"
Coal Creek	855	"	"	"
Indian Grave Gap	1265	"	"	"
" " "	1188	(Grade)	"	"
Cove Creek	1041	(Surface)	"	"
Elk Gap	1702	"	"	"
" "	1620	(Grade)	"	"
State Line, (Tenn. & Ky.)	990	"	"	"

(5.) The following is another cross-section. It extends from Cleveland to Chattanooga, thence through the Running Water Gap of the Raccoon Mountains, across the Sequatchee Valley and by Stevenson, to the Tunnel of the Nashville and Chattanooga Railroad.

Cleveland	878	(Grade)	C. & C. Br. of E. T. & Ga. R. R.			
Candy's Creek	794	"	"	"	"	
Lea's Summit	913	"	"	"	"	
White Oak Mountain (Gap)	813	"	"	"	"	
Ooltawa Creek	790 ?	"	"	"	"	
Summit	912	"	"	"	"	
Chickamauga	682	"	"	"	"	
"	649	(Low Water)	"	"	"	
Tunnel	752	(Grade)	"	"	"	
Chattanooga*	675	"	"	"	"	
" Tenn. River	642	(Surface)	W. & A. R. R. (Ga. Road.)			
"	688	(Grade)	"	"	"	
"	676	"	N. & C. R. R.			
Lookout Creek	676	"		"	"	
Point near 6 miles from Chattanooga	676	"		"	"	

* The elevations pertaining to Chattanooga are derived from the several roads terminating at that place. The difference between the elevations given by the Cleveland and Georgia roads respectively, may result, in part at least, from the profiles not meeting at the same point.

The elevation given by the Nashville & Chattanooga road has been derived from the profile of this road carried through from Nashville; it is the height above low tide of Mobile Bay. When the elevations of points in Middle Tennessee are given, I will speak more particularly of this profile.

The heights 642 and 688 are from a profile on Bonner's Map of Georgia.

Running Water			......................N. & C. R. R.	
Summit.........	977	(Grade)	"	"
Running Water				
Summit... 1017		(Surface)	"	"
Whitesides............	868	(Grade)	"	"
Shell Mound.........	636	"	"	"
A Summit............	697	(Surface)	"	"
Tennessee River...	629	(High water	"	"
A Summit............	749	(Surface)	"	"
A point at, or near *Stevenson*†	630	"	"	"
Crow Creek Valley................	612	"	"	"
do do Low Water..........	598	"	"	"
Crow Creek Valley, 8 miles further on......	634	"	"	"
Crow Creek Valley, 9 miles further on......	674	(Surface)	"	"
TUNNEL*.............1153		(Grade)	"	"

(6.) The remaining table presents a cross-profile from "Cross Plains," (Dalton?) Ga., to Chattanooga, Tenn., along the Western & Atlantic Railroad. It is taken from Bonner's Map of Georgia.

Cross Plains, (Dalton) Ga...........	773................W. & A. R. R.		
Tunnel, Ga...............................	859................	"	"
SUMMIT OF RIDGE ABOVE TUNNEL. DIVIDING RIDGE *between Tenn. River waters and those flowing into the Gulf of Mexico*.........1082		"	"
TENNESSEE AND GEORGIA LINE...		"	"
Tenn. River, at Chattanooga......	642	"	"

† In a table of elevations of points along the Memphis and Charleston Railroad, published in one of the Reports of that road, the elevation of Stevenson is given at 602,80. On the N. & C. R. R. profile, from which the above heights were taken, it is not within my power to determine the exact point at which the two roads meet. The difference in the elevations may, in part, be due to this. I suspect, however, that 602,80 is below the true height of the Depot.

* At Montgomery's Gap, seven miles east of Winchester. In a report, made by John Edgar Thompson (1847) upon an experimental survey of the line of the N. & C. R. R., it is said: "The elevation of this Gap (Montgomery's) is 1365 feet above the Atlantic, and but 200 yards wide on top, with steep declivities on each side, admitting the passage of a railroad by means of a short tunnel 209 feet below its apex. . . . . At this point the road will attain an elevation of 1156 feet above the ocean, and pass through the mountain by a tunnel 2100 feet long." According to the profiles of the road the tunnel was made 2200 feet long.

157. From the tables, it is seen that the fall of the Holston and Tennessee River, from Saltville, (Table 3,) on the North Fork of Holston, Va., to Chattanooga, is approximatively 1040 feet. Of this fall very nearly one-half occurs in Virginia, in the valley of the North Fork, above Kingsport.

158. Confining ourselves to Tennessee, the general elevation and the southwesterly descent of the Valley of East Tennessee are best represented by the profile of its longer and central axis. This may be considered as extending from the Virginia line, near Kingsport, along the northwestern base of Bay's Mountain to Russellville, and then as being coincident with the East Tenn. and Va. Railroad, and with the East Tenn. and Ga. road as far down as the southern boundary of the State. Referred to this line, the Valley has an elevation (as determined by the river-surfaces) ranging, and running down, from about 1220 feet to 684 above the sea.

159. The following table exhibits the rate of descent. The heights are those of river surfaces. The *direct* distances between the points, and the differences in elevation, are given on the right.

Point	Height	Distance	Fall
Holston, at Long Island, above Kingsport,	1218 ft.		
		Dist. 85 miles.	Fall 369 ft.
Holston, at Strawberry Plains,	849		
		Dist. 16 "	Fall 33 "
Holston, at Knoxville,	816?		
		Dist. 28 "	Fall 79 "
Tennessee, at Loudon,	737		
		Dist. 40 "	Fall 53 "
Hiwassee, at Calhoun,	684		

160. From this it appears that the greater part of the descent (more than two-thirds) occurs before reaching Strawberry Plains.

161. Including the surface, along the axis of the Valley, the general elevation near the Virginia line, is, perhaps, 1300 or 1400 feet; towards Strawberry Plains it is less, and, from this point to the Georgia line, it may be taken at about 900 feet, or as ranging from 1000 down to 800.*

162. In addition to the southwesterly descent, the general

* In Jefferson County, along the line of the railroad, there is a high body of land, forming an interesting local plateau, which has an elevation of from 300 to 400 feet above the Holston, on the northwest.

plane of the Valley has, consistently with the northwesterly tendency of the rivers, (§§ 150, 151 and 152,) a decided slope to the northwest.

163. The following tables will give approximately the degree of inclination in this direction.

The heights (above the sea) of the mouths of the Clinch and Hiwassee rivers, respectively, have been determined by the rate of the fall of the Tennessee River between Loudon and Chattanooga. This is 0.805 feet per mile. The *direct* distances from point to point, and the differences in elevation, are given as in the last table.

	Place	Height	Distance	Fall
(1.)	Tenn. & N. C. Line, Watauga Valley,	2131*		
			Dist. 22 miles.	Fall 703 ft.
	Watauga, at Carter, E. T. & Va. R. R.,	1428		
			Dist. 17 "	Fall 210 "
	Holston, at Long Island,	1218		
(2.)	Tenn. & N. C. Line, French Broad,	1264*		
			Dist. 58 miles.	Fall 448 "
	Holston, at Knoxville,	816?		
			Dist. 16 "	Fall 25 "
	Clinch River, Clinton; K. & K. R. R.	791		
(3.)	Tenn. & N. C. Line, Little Tennessee,	1114*		
			Dist. 30 miles.	Fall 377 ft.
	Tennessee River, Loudon,	737		
			Dist. 14 "	Fall 18 "
	Mouth of Clinch,	719		
(4.)	Hiwassee, at Calhoun,	684		
			Dist. 16 miles.	Fall 27 ft.
	Mouth of Hiwassee,	669		

Reference may also be made to the table of heights (page 60) along the Western & Atlantic Railroad. Dalton has an elevation considerably above Chattanooga, and the Tunnel is more than 200 feet above the Tennessee at the latter place.

164. *Climate.*—In speaking of the climate of the State, in general, that of this division was necessarily included. I add but little more.

165. Knoxville is very near the centre of the Valley. Its higher portions are nearly 1000 feet above the sea; this, at any

* These are not the elevations of the river surfaces; they are all, however, within, perhaps, fifteen or twenty feet of those surfaces.

rate, without causing material error, may be taken as the height of the particular points at which the observations were made. The *mean annual temperature* here is 57°.03, or simply 57°, at least, according to the limited data we possess. (§ 30.)

166. In the upper part of the Valley, near the Virginia line, the annual mean, on account of greater elevation above the sea, and higher latitude, will be at least two degrees less ; while, upon the other hand, near the Georgia line, it will be as much greater. It will, therefore, range throughout the Valley from about 55° to 59°.

167. The *summer mean*, at Knoxville, which has been placed at 73°.6, (§ 31,) is about that of Philadelphia, Pa., as well as that of several points in Central Virginia, of Cincinnati, Louisville, Ky., Southern Indiana, and Central Illinois. It is, too, I may add here, that of the central part of Spain, and the northern part of Italy. The summer of the East Tennessee Valley, is, therefore, considering its valley-like character, and its low latitude, a comparatively cool one. This is mostly due to the considerable elevation of the region above the sea.

This lower summer temperature has its influence in giving to East Tennessee agricultural features, to some extent, different from those found elsewhere in the State.

168. It might be thought that the mountain ranges which bound the Valley on both sides, would materially affect its climate. This, however, is not the case. These ranges are happily, so situated as not to obstruct, to any considerable extent, the southwesterly and westerly winds, which, of all others, in an agricultural point of view, are most important. (§ 35.)

The great trough, of which the Valley is a part, is open towards the southwest, so that these winds, coming from the Gulf of Mexico, and charged with warmth and moisture, flow freely through it, imparting, during the spring and summer, fertility to all its parts. The mountain ranges, doubtless, change the direction of the winds, to some extent, and thus, make southwesterly and northeasterly winds more freqµent than they would be otherwise.

III.—The Cumberland Table-land.

169. *General Character.*—Leaving the Valley of East Tennessee, and passing westward, we meet next, with the elevated and wide-spreading plateau well known as *Cumberland Mountain*. This, in order, is the third great natural division of the State. (§ 25.) I have already, many times, called it the *Table-land.*

170. As a natural division, it is well defined, and, as to many things, has no lack of interest. As we will see hereafter, it is the great depository of all the stone-coal in Tennessee. Fruit-growers and horticulturists, notwithstanding its general agricultural character is not in the best repute, look to it as a field of promise; stock-raisers hope to make it a land of meadows and pastures; its cool summer nights, render it attractive during the hot months; and it bids fair, in a few years, to be the favorite summer resort of Southern men.

171. As yet, this portion of the State is, for the most part, but thinly settled. Over its wooded plains the deer is still chased, and, in some of its wild coves, the wolf and the black bear find hiding places. Nevertheless, it has upon its flat and elevated surface, a number of small villages,* and, upon its northern half especially, many tracts well covered with farms.

172. *Geographical Relations, Limits, and Area.*—Confining ourselves to Tennessee, this division is, in the main, a great table, or mountain-block, resting upon the general plane, to which the general surface of the State has been referred. (3.)

Its top is elevated above this plane, and above the low-lands on each side, from nine hundred to twelve hundred feet.†

173. Looking beyond the State, we find the Cumberland Table-land to be part of a long belt or high land extending from the southern part of New York, through Pennsylvania, Western Virginia, Eastern Kentucky and Tennessee, into Alabama, in which State it finally sinks away. This belt, in its entire

* Among them, are six county-towns.

† In the panoramic view facing this page, the western escarpment facing the Table-land, as it appears from its distant outliers—the Short Mountains—is seen. The view extends from Alabama through Tennessee, to within twenty miles of the Kentucky line, and embraces much of the western side. (See § 191.)

In the view opposite page 40, a portion of the eastern escarpment—that of the subdivisions Walden's Ridge and Raccoon Mountain—is prominent to the left of Chattanooga.

length, is intersected completely by only two streams, New River in Virginia, and the Tennessee in Alabama.* Its eastern escarpment presents, generally, a bold, steep face, and is known, in Pennsylvania and Virginia as the Alleghany Mountain.

484. The belt just mentioned, crosses Tennessee obliquely. The portion within the State—the Table-land we are considering—although much indented by valleys and coves, is nowhere completely cut in two by them. It could furnish a highway from Kentucky to Alabama, upon its flat top, along which a traveler might pass, without once descending, and even without discovering, at any time, his elevation. The engineers of the Nashville and Chattanooga Railroad, in their experimental surveys, could find within Tennessee, no low pass through one of the leading arms of the Table-land, and were therefore compelled either to ascend and go over, or else, by making a great deflection to the south in Alabama, go round it. The latter alternative they adopted.

The top of the Table-land, though comparatively flat, does not become monotonous to the traveler. Low ridges and shallow valleys, with crystal streams, are occasionally met with, and afford a pleasant variety, which relieves what would otherwise be the sameness of its "flat woods."

175. At almost all points, on both sides, the surface breaks off suddenly in sandstone cliffs and precipices, which are from 20 to 100, or even 200 feet high. These form all along the sides of the Table-land, a well defined margin or brow. From beneath this very frequently overhanging brow, the steep slopes of the sides commence, and run down to the low lands.

With the exception of the northeastern part of the division, the slopes below the cliffs rest mostly on limestone. The sandstone which appears in the cliffs caps the whole plateau, while limestone forms its base. The former gives sharpness of outline to its crested margin.

176. The eastern border of the Table-land is comparatively a nearly direct, or gracefully curving line. The indentations made by the streams, are, upon the map, hardly noticeable.

177. Along its western border, however, it is remarkably

* The portion between these rivers, is a marked feature of the Tennessee and New River slope. See Map of this slope facing page 5.

different. Here the Table-land is irregularly scalloped and notched by deep coves and valleys, separated from each other by long spurs jutting to the west. These deep indentations, from which, and in some cases, through which, flow the different branches of the Elk, Collins' River, the Caney Fork, Roaring River, and Obey's River,* give the western outline a very ragged and dissected appearance.

178. Along the Kentucky and Tennessee line, the Table-land is about seventy-one miles wide. It becomes narrower southward. Across it, along the southern boundary of the State, including Raccoon Mountain and Sequatchee Valley, it is fifty miles. Altogether, the division proper, covers an area of 5100 square miles—nearly one eighth of the State. It includes within its limits, the counties of Scott, Morgan, and Cumberland; the larger parts of Fentress, Van Buren, Bledsoe, Grundy, Sequatchee,† and Marion; considerable parts of Claiborne, Campbell, Anderson, Rhea, Hamilton, Overton, Putnam, White, and Franklin; and finally, small portions of Warren and Coffee.

179. *Parts, or Subdivisions, and Outliers.*—Unlike the great Valley to the east, the Cumberland Table-land is comparatively simple in structure and parts. (§ 139.) There are, however, two partially detached portions, certain ranges and groups of mountains bordering, or resting upon it, and a number of outliers which may be noticed.

The partially detached portions referred to have been already spoken of. One is the arm cut off by Sequatchee Valley; the other, the remarkable quadrilateral block detached by the Elk Fork and Cove Creek Valleys.‡

*In many of the coves and valleys referred to above at the base, and on the limestone or lower slope of the Table-land, are springs remarkable for their size and for the amount of water which they discharge. In quite a number of instances, these springs bring to the day, at once, large creeks, tributaries of the rivers mentioned. Some of them furnish excellent mill sites. Along the base of the eastern escarpment also, similar springs occur at intervals. These springs are the outlets of subterranean streams, many of which, doubtless, flow through long, and unexplored caves and passages in the great limestone bed upon which, the sandstone and shalecap of the Table-land rests. Not a little of the water which falls upon the surface of the Table-land is thus drained off.

† This county has been mentioned several times. It is proper to state however, that it has, at present, by a decision of the Supreme Court, no legal existence. It was made to include parts of Marion, Grundy, Bledsoe, and Hamilton, the most desirable portion of the county being in Sequatchee Valley.

‡ See §§ 140, 141, and 142; also § 145 and Map.

180. The northwestern side of the "block" just mentioned, rises in a high-crested ridge, or margin, forming the long, straight, and bold *Pine Mountain.* (§ 144.) This ridge runs to the northeast into Kentucky. Its northwestern face rises up steeply, to an average elevation, above Elk Fork Valley, of at least 1000 feet.

181. The southeastern and southwestern sides of the block (that is to say, the sides extending continuously in a line from Cumberland Gap to a point a few miles beyond Jacksboro', or to Wheeler's Cove, and then turning and running to Elk Gap) are both singularly and closely bordered by a steep and roof-like ridge, which, after running in a nearly direct line on one side, gracefully curves around, and runs along the other. (See Map.)

182. This "block" is, however, not the only part of the Table-land thus bordered by a high, roof-like ridge. There is, indeed, a tendency toward the formation, and isolation, of such a ridge most of the way along the eastern side of the Table-land, from the point where the Tennessee River cuts it, to the Virginia line. It is called, too, *Walden's Ridge*, nearly throughout this whole distance.

Immediately north of the Tennessee River the name Walden's Ridge is applied to the entire arm of the Table-land cut off by Sequatcheee Valley. Before this arm connects with the main body of the plateau, around the head of the valley mentioned, it takes the form of a shallow trough, the edges rising up in crested ridges. Above Sequatchee Valley, and in a line with it, the western edge becomes blended with, or rather constitutes the eastern side of, a range of mountains,* which rise above the general level of the Table-land, and may be regarded as resting upon it. At the same time, the eastern edge becomes more prominent, and soon alone takes the name of Walden's Ridge. It is more or less sharply crested, and appears like a ridge placed along on the margin of the Table-land.

183. Further north, above Emery River, this sharp ridge becomes entirely detached from the body of the Table-land,

*This is the *Crab Orchard Range*, soon to be spoken of. The southwestern mountain of this range is, itself, known as Walden's Ridge.

being separated from it by a deep and narrow valley, or line of valleys. From the Salt-works, in Anderson County, northeastward, this ridge is very prominent and characteristic; it runs many miles in a direct course, then curves beautifully around to the northwest, after which it again pursues a direct course until intersected by the valley of Cove Creek, near Col. R. D. Wheeler's, in Campbell, where it falls away. Here, however, it is very nearly continuous with the ridge of similar character of which I have spoken, (§ 181,) at the point where the latter curves. The portion of this first mentioned ridge from Cove Creek to Cumberland Gap may be considered as continuing the line of Walden's Ridge on to Virginia.*

184. These ridges, from the Emery to Virginia, are among the greatest curiosities of the whole Cumberland Table-land. Sharp, bold, and roof-like, mostly made up of vertical sheets of solid sandstone, they appear like a vast military work, designed to protect the main mountain from the encroachments of the Lowlanders. There are very few gaps in them. Those that do occur are water-gaps formed by creeks. To get at the foot of the mountain, though it may not be more than half a mile off, it is often necessary to ride half a dozen, to find a passage through these skirting ridges.

185. The northeastern portion of the division under consideration, presents other local features which remain to be mentioned. These consist of groups of high ridges, or mountains, which, rising above the general level of the Table land, appear, when seen from the west, to rest upon it.

186. First we have the *New River Group.* The head-waters of New River† flow from a group of mountain ridges, among which its tributaries are deeply sunk.

The range that divides these waters from those flowing into the Clinch, (see Map,) is one of the most important of these ridges, and is a conspicuous object to an observer in the great

* Walden's Ridge, above the Emery, must not be confounded with the "little" sharp ridge which is often found along its southeastern base, and to which reference has already been made. (§ 121.) The latter ridge pertains to the Valley of East Tennessee. Walden's Ridge, together with the narrow valleys which lie along its northwestern base, in Anderson, Campbell, and Claiborne counties, belong to the Table-land, having the same rocks, etc.

† This river is a tributary of the Cumberland River—a very different stream from New River, of Virginia.

Valley to the east. It forms, for many miles in Anderson and Campbell counties, the eastern escarpment of the main Table-land, or rather, it is the most eastern ridge of the group, the plateau-character of the division in this region, being to a great extent lost. It is called, for a good part of its length, *Cross Mountain*. *Tellico Mountain*, west of Elk Fork Valley, (§ 144,) may be regarded as a portion of the same range. They connect around the head of the above valley. The average elevation of Cross Mountain, above the sea, is, perhaps, not far from 2800 feet. (§ 194.) Along its southeastern and northeastern base runs the remarkable skirting, Walden's Ridge. (§ 183.)

187. Other elevated ridges occur in this group. They are all within that portion of the Table-land lying southeast of Huntsville, and between Jacksboro' and Montgomery.

188. Between Emery River and the head of Sequatchee Valley, and in a line with this valley, is a nearly straight range of mountains of some interest. It may be called the *Crab Orchard Range*, or *Group*. Originally the mountains of this range formed, doubtless, a continuous ridge. It is now cut into three unequal parts by two gaps—Crab Orchard and Grassy Cove gaps. (§ 143.) The southwestern mountain of this range is known locally as *Walden's Ridge*, a name, as we have seen, applied to several parts of the eastern side of the Table-land. The northeastern portion of the range is *Crab Orchard Mountain*. The highest parts of these mountains are but little, if any, less than 1000 feet above the general surface of the Table-land. The mountain between the two gaps is short and not as prominent as the others.

These mountains and gaps, together with Sequatchee Valley, all in the same line, will be shown hereafter to be curiously related.

189. There are but few outlying mountains belonging to the Table-land. The only one of importance, on the eastern side, is the grand *Lookout Mountain*, which starts up boldly just within the limits of Tennessee and runs into Georgia. This is a long, narrow mountain, closely related, geologically, to the Table-land. From its northern rocky point, the view facing page 40 was taken.

Two short, detached mountains, one in the southern part of Rhea County, the other, near Cumberland Gap, in Claiborne, both cut off by narrow valleys, are the remaining most conspicuous outliers on the eastern side.

190. Passing to the western side, we find, in the first place, several isolated and prominent peaks occurring at intervals along the base of the Table-land, and having nearly the height of the parent plateau. There are about half-a-dozen outliers of this class. Such, for example, are *Pilot Mountain,* in Warren, *Milk-sick Mountain,* in White, and *Pilot Knob,* in Overton.

In the latter county there is also a long, isolated ridge, west of the West Fork of Obey's River.

191. The most conspicuous, however, of the western outliers, are the *Short Mountains.*

These consist of two high ridges, separated but a little distance from each other. They form a small group, removed seventeen or eighteen miles from the Table-land. (See Map.) From many points along the entire western margin of the latter, this group may be seen. And on the other hand, from the southeastern end of the nearest ridge of the group, a great part of the western escarpment of the Table-land is presented in a beautiful and extended prospect; the great flat and wooded plain west of the plateau intervening.*

192. Thus far I have had reference to such outliers as have a height equal, or nearly equal, to that of the main Table-land. Along the western base of the northern half of this division, there is, however, another class of isolated ridges and "*little mountains,*" which are of sufficient importance to be mentioned. These are comparatively low, have flat tops, and generally form beautiful little plateaus. With them, too, must be included the "*benches,*" which, in this region, almost every-where run along the slopes of the Table-land, forming terraces along its sides, both around the spurs and back behind the coves.† All these plateaus and benches have the same height, about equal to half that of the Table-land. The ridges, or plateaus, are numerous, and some of them many miles long. Nearly all are known by local names; as, for instance, the *Hickory-nut Mountain,* near the Falls of Caney Fork, and the *Gum Spring Mountain,* to the northeast of the last.

*See plate facing page 66. In this view the centre of the picture is to the southeast.

†Those of my readers who have ascended the "Mountain" at Bon Air, can recall a good example of these terraces, the bench about half-way up, wide enough for a little farm, and furnishing a site for the toll gate, being one of them.

193. These flat-topped ridges, together with the benches, constitute a striking feature of this whole region. In the view from Short Mountain, (§ 191,) they are seen to the left, lying along in front of the main Table-land.

Along the base of the southern part of the Table-land, south of McMinnville, they do not appear to any important extent.

194. *Elevation above the Sea.*—The mean elevation of the Table-land is very nearly 2000 feet. Its *immediate* escarpments rise up steeply from the valleys and lower plains, to heights varying generally from 850 to 1000 feet. Below are the elevations of numerous points on both sides of the plateau:

(1.) Those pertaining to the eastern margin, are first presented.

The following were obtained, in 1854, from Mr. John G. Newlee, of Cumberland Gap:

Cumberland Gap	1,636 feet	R. R. Survey.
Pinnacle, near Gap	2,680 "	" "

(2.) The table below presents the elevation of points on the K. & Ky. Railroad, and on *Cross Mountain*, (§ 186,) opposite Jacksboro'. The Gap on Cross Mountain, is that through which the path passes, leading from Col. R. D. Wheeler's across to Beech Creek. Immediately below this gap, is the point of Beech Creek referred to. The heights pertaining to Cross Mountain and Beech Creek, were determined by means of a small pocket level, and are approximately correct. The elevation of points in the valleys, are given for comparison. (See page 61.)

Elk Gap	1,702	(Surface)	K. & Ky. R. R.
" "	1,602	"	" " "
Cross Mountain, Gap	2,875	(about)	
" " Point near Gap	3,370	(do.)	
Beech Creek	1,611	(do.)	
Cove Creek	1,041	(Surface)	K. & Ky. R. R.
" "	1,082	(Grade)	" " "

(3.) The heights of the Elk Fork Valley, and of the two high ranges on each side respectively, (§§ 144, 180, & 186,) may be indicated as follows:

Average of Bottom of Elk Fork Valley	1,200
Pine Mountain, general elevation, from	2,200 to 2,400
Tellico Mountain, points of summit ranging from	2,000 to 2,700

(4.) A. M. Lea, Esq., who, in 1837, by order of the General Assembly of Tennessee, made a preliminary survey of a route for a proposed "Central Railroad," measured the heights of the two sides of the Table-land as presented in a line running from a point near Sparta, across through Crab-Orchard Gap, (§§ 143 & 188,) to the eastern base on White's Creek.*

* Report of the Chief Engineer of the State of Tennessee, on the Surveys and Examinations for the Central Railroad, and for the Central Turnpike. Nashville, 1837.

Mr. Lea determined the total descent from a point in Crab-Orchard Gap, to the base in White's Creek Valley, to be 920 feet. From the base, to the Tennessee River, at White's Creek Shoals, he estimates the fall to be 90 feet, making the elevation of the point in the Gap, 1010, above the Teneseee River, which is about 1710 above the sea, the elevation of low water at the Shoals being approximately, 700 feet. This would give the higher plains of the Table-land, west of Crab-Orchard and Daddy's Creek, an elevation of at least 2000 feet above tide-water.

At the Gap, *Crab-Orchard Mountain* (§ 188) appears to rise nearly or quite, 1000 feet above the general elevation of the plateau, which makes its entire elevation not far from 3000 feet.

(5.) The highest part of the flat summit of *Lookout Mountain*—a point about half way between the hotel and the end of the mountain—is 1478 feet above the Nashville and Chattanooga Railroad, or (taking the elevaof the road here at 676 feet) 2154 feet above the sea.

(6.) A flat-topped ridge of the *Raccoon Mountains*, back of Whiteside Depot, on the N. & C. R. R., and above the uppermost coal banks, has an elevation above tide-water, of about 1900 feet.

(7.) Passing to the western side of the Table-land, we have, first, the following series of elevations along the *Sewanee Mining Company's Railroad.* This road connects with the Nashville and Chattanooga Railroad, near the western end of the tunnel, at Montgomery's Gap. (Page 62.) Running generally in a northeasterly direction, it ascends along the steep slope of the Table-land, and reaches the top of the latter, a little within six miles. From this point, the road runs over an open-wood and comparatively flat surface, thirteen miles further, to the coal banks near Tracy City.

The elevation of the junction of the Sewanee and N. & C. roads is taken at 1137 feet, which is sixteen feet below the grade of the tunnel.* The distances of points from the junction are given in miles.

Junction with N. & C. R. R.	1,137	(Grade)	S. M. Co's R. R.
Crossing above N. & C. R. R. at Tunnel	1,191	do.	" " "
Top of steep grade, 5.87 miles†	1,875	do.	" " "
do. do. do. do do.	1,883	(Surface)	" " "
Average of next mile†	1,875	(Grade)	" " "
Point, 8 miles†	1,955	do.	" " "
do. do.	1,964	(Surface)	" " "
Average next half mile	1,957	Grade)	" " "
Porter & Logan Coal Bank 8.7 miles	2,006	?	
Top of highest ridges in this vicinity	2,076	?	

* Owing to some difficulty in fixing on the N. & C. R. R. profile in my hands, the exact point at which the Sewanee road branches off, the difference—16 feet—may be too little or too great by a few feet—at the most, however, by not more than three or four. See section of the *Carboniferous Limestone* along the Sewanee road in the Second Part of this Report.

I take this opportunity to acknowledge my indebtedness, for profiles and other favors, to the kindness of Mr. G. S. Backus, and of Dr. J. C. Bebee, formerly engineers upon the Sewanee road, the former for many years Chief Engineer.

† This part of the road is within the grounds of the "*University of the South.*"

Point 9.6 miles	1,957	(Surface)	S. M. Co's R. R.		
" 13.1 miles	1,959	do.	"	"	"
General average between last two points	1,951	do.	"	"	"
Summer's, 14.4 miles	1,952	do.	"	"	"
Gizzard Creek, 17.1 miles	1,819	do.	"	"	"
East bank of Gizzard	1,887	do.	"	"	"
Tracy City, 18.2 miles	1,847	do.	"	"	"
Terminus of road, 19 miles	1,889	do.	"	"	"
Main Coal, Wooton Bank	1,922	(Hill side above terminus.)			
Tops of highest ridges in this vicinity	2,161				

(8.) The following are elevations of two well known points on the western margin of the Table-land. The first, *Ben Lomond*, is a circular mountain, lying nearly south of McMinnville, and terminating the ridge or arm of the main plateau which runs out between the waters of Collins' River and Hickory Creek. It has a flat, sandstone top, with an area equal to about one square mile.*

The second is the top of the Table-land just above *Bon Air*, and east of Sparta. The elevation given of this point, is approximate. Mr. Lea, to whose Report I have already referred, says: "In the vicinity of Sparta, the height of the crest of the mountain visible from its base, was ascertained to be 884 feet above the level of the 'barrens.'" This height is that of the immediate slope of the plateau. The elevation of the station of the Southwestern Railroad at Sparta, is 945 feet above low tide of Mobile Bay. How much above this the base of the Table-land below Bon Air is, I do not know. It is estimated to be at least 200 feet. We have, then,

Summit of Ben Lomond	1910.
" at Bon Air	2029?

195. *Views.*—The elevation of the Table-land is sufficient to enable an observer, standing upon either its eastern or western margin, to have extended and beautiful views of the country below.

From the eastern margin may be seen very satisfactorily, the great Valley of East Tennessee. The views extend quite across the Valley, and include in the distance, the high ridges of the Unaka Chain.†

The view from Lookout Mountain, to which I have several times referred, is one of the most beautiful and instructive in Tennessee. This

* I am indebted to Mr. E. F. Falconnet, formerly Chief Engineer of the Southwestern Railroad, and now of the Nashville & Northwestern Railroad, for the elevation of Ben Lomond above the McMinnville Depot, of the McM. & M. R. R. This elevation is 998 feet.

† Compare what has been said in reference to the views from the Unaka Mountains, § 80.

outlier (§ 189) is set at some distance from the Table-land, right in the great Valley, above which its summit has, too, a greater elevation than has, in general, the division to which it properly belongs. From its north-eastern end, the observer can look, without any obstruction, many miles up into the valley. (See plate, § 91.)

196. From the western margin, the views, looking west, though beautiful, are not equal to those obtained from the other side. They owe their interest, for the most part, to their extent. They all present a great, flat and wooded country, extending, with an apparently uniform level, as far as the eye can reach. This is their most important feature.* From many points, the isolated short Mountain Group (§ 191) can be seen, which serves to break the sameness of the view. In the northern part of the State, the outlying "little mountains," or low plateaus, (§ 192,) have the same effect. When with these a village or cultivated region and spurs from the table land are included, the views become most interesting. Those from Bon Air and Ben Lomond are of this kind. That seen from Sewanee, is also characteristic and highly pleasing.

197. *Climate.*—As indicative of the agreeableness of its climate in summer, it may be mentioned, that the Cumberland Table-land has been, for years, a favorite resort during the hot months. Hundreds of summer retreats, public and private, may be found upon its flat top, most of them located on, or not far back, from its sandstone edge. Much the larger number are temporary structures—log-cabins located at romantic and often wild points, near springs of crystal freestone, and not unfrequently of chalybeate water. Many of them, however, and the number is yearly increasing, are permanent and neat cottages. At several points, as at Beersheba, Lookout, and Bon Air, summer hotels have been erected; at these points, especially at the first two, there are, in addition, many elegant private cottages, altogether, forming attractive mountain villages. It will certainly not be many years before this beautiful plateau will become famous, as it ought, for the number and extent of such villages. The "University of the South" promises soon to cluster around it, upon a desirable portion of the Table-land, many summer villas of wealthy and intelligent

*The flat, wooded country referred to here, is well seen in the panoramic view taken from Short Mountain. See opposite page 65.

southern gentlemen. All this has been brought about by the agreeable summer temperature and the pure air of the Table-land, in connection with its pleasing, and, in the vicinity of its escarpments, its wild and grand topographical features.

I regret that it is not in my power to present the results of systematic observations for a series of years upon the climate of the Table-land. These are much desired. The thermometer has been observed at several points, but not with much system, for any great length of time.

198. During the summer of the year 1859, Benj. Bentley, Esq., of Spring Grove, upon the Table-land, in Cumberland County, and Prof. A. H. Buchanan, of Lebanon, made regular and systematic observations, at their respective residences, in order to furnish data for the comparison of the mean temperatures of the two places. The following tables contain the results:

(1.) *Mean Temperatures for the Summer of* 1859, *at Spring Grove, Cumberland County, Tenn.*

	June.	July.	August.	Summer.
6 A. M.	64.03	66.74	64.16	64.98
2 P. M.	78.46	83.71	77.00	79.72
9 P. M.	66.83	71.03	68.58	68.81
Mean.	69.77	73.82	69.91	71.17

(2.) *Mean Temperatures for the Summer of* 1859, *at Lebanon, Wilson County, Tenn.*

	June.	July.	August.	Summer.
6 A. M.	66.96	71.09	68.80	68.95
2 P. M.	80.55	85.87	80.42	82.28
9 P. M.	72.65	78.06	74.30	75.00
Mean.	73.38	78.34	74.50	75.41

(3.) *Extremes of Temperatures, or the Maxima and Minima, observed during Summer.*

	Maxima.	Minima.	Range.
Spring Grove.	July 19 & 21...93°	June 5...42°	51°
Lebanon	July 18 & 19...97°	June 5...46°	51°
Difference. ...	4°	4°	00

199. According to the first two tables, the summer mean, at Spring Grove, is 4.24 degrees less than at Lebanon. The former has, however, a lower latitude than the latter. Correcting for this, (§ 30,) or supposing the points to be on the same parallel, the difference in temperature becomes greater, and is equal to about 4.5 degrees. Observations taken at Nashville during the same summer, show very nearly the same result.

200. It would be interesting to compare the above summer mean of the Table-land with that of Knoxville, for the same season. Observations, however, so far as the writer knows, were not made at Knoxville during that period. The average summer heat of 1852, '54, and '55, at Knoxville, was, as we have seen, (§ 31,) 73.6 degrees, being 2.43 degrees greater than at Spring Grove, the latitude being nearly the same.

201. From these data we may assume, for the present, that the average summer temperature of the Table-land, in general, is from *two to three* degrees less, (comparing points on the same parallel,) than that of the Valley of East Tennessee, and from *four and a half to five* less than that of the Central Basin. (§ 25, (5.)). This difference in temperature is doubtless, in the main, due to difference in elevation. Those parts of the Table-land rising higher than the average elevation (as, for instance, the outlier, Lookout Mountain) will, of course, present greater contrasts.

202. The corresponding extremes of temperature, at Spring Grove and Lebanon, respectively, show nearly the same difference as the means; it is 4 degrees, or, for points on the same parallel, about 4.3 degrees.

203. It is further shown, by the tables, that *at night*, the temperature of the two places compared, present a greater contrast than at midday; the difference between the means of 9 P. M., is 6.19, while between those of 2 P. M., it is only 2.56 degrees. We may, therefore, conclude that, while midday on the Table-land is but 2.5 or 3 degrees cooler than in the Central Basin, the nights are as much as 6.5 or 7 degrees cooler. The means of Spring and Autumn, compared with those of the Basin, will be found, most likely, to differ by about half as much as those of the summer. Those of the winter will differ still less, there being, in this season, a greater approach to uniformity throughout the State.

204. The mean annual temperature of the Table-land, on the parallel passing through the middle of the State, may be placed at about 56 degrees; and ranging along a meridian, through the State, from 54 or 55, to 57 degrees.

205. Winds and rain have, doubtless, about the same character that they have in the central part of the State. The quantity of rain is, perhaps, a little greater.

It is to be hoped that some of the many intelligent gentlemen residing upon this beautiful plateau, will undertake to record systematic observations upon its climate. The "University of the South" will be expected, before long, to furnish, year after year, full and complete materials for the elucidation of the climate of its southern portion.

CHAPTER III.

THE NATURAL DIVISIONS OF THE STATE.—*Continued.*

THE HIGHLANDS, OR HIGHLAND RIM, OF MIDDLE TENNESSEE.—THE CENTRAL BASIN.—THE WESTERN TENNESSEE RIVER VALLEY.—THE WEST TENNESSEE SLOPE, OR PLAIN.—THE MISSISSIPPI BOTTOMS.

206. These, the remaining natural divisions of the State, are like the others, well defined. They differ from those described, in wanting that *marked* parallelism, and northeasterly and southwesterly direction of parts so characteristic of the latter. They show, nevertheless, in their general outlines, traces of these features. The divisions of the last chapter are mostly within the Appalachian Region proper; (§§ 40, 18;) hence the prominence of the features referred to. The divisions about to be considered, I have regarded as without this region, although in some of them, its peculiar geological structure, to some limited extent, exists, and has influenced, more or less, their formation, and the direction of their outlines. (§ 20, and note.)

207. In reference to general geological character, the divisions to be described may be divided into two groups.

The *first three,* constituting the *first group,* have (excepting the western border of the third) a rocky basis, their formations below the soil being always hard rocks, which are either limestones, silicious beds, or slates. These, too, with the exception of certain western parts included within the counties of Perry, Hardin, Decatur, Benton and Henry, belong to *the political division* of the State known as *Middle Tennessee.** The others

* The counties referred to are regarded *politically* as parts of West Tennessee. Perry, however, as well as the eastern part of Hardin, belong naturally to Middle Tennessee. The middle part of Hardin, and the eastern parts of Decatur, Benton and Henry, (but little of the latter, however,) are included within the limits of the third natural division, and of course, belong to the first, or *rocky group* mentioned.

constituting the *second group*, have a basis made up of beds of sand and laminated clays. They form, too, the greater part of *the political division, West Tennessee.*

IV. The Highlands, or Highland Rim, of Middle Tennessee.

208. *General Configuration, Limits and Area.*—The general surface of all Middle Tennessee, excluding the Cumberland Table-land, may be compared to an oval basin, or to a shallow plate, with a broad, flat rim. Murfreesboro' is near its center. In traveling from this point, in any direction, we pass from twenty to fifty miles, as the case may be, over rolling, blue limestone land; and, finally, ascending a more or less abrupt flinty "ridge," from three to five hundred feet high, find ourselves on an elevated plain. Such is the case, for instance, in going from Murfreesboro' to any of the following towns: Springfield, Lafayette, Smithville, Manchester, Tullahoma, Lawrenceburg, or Charlotte. In every instance, we pass over and leave the same limestone land, ascend the same flinty ridge, and reach the same flat plain. These elevated flat lands constitute the *Highlands,* or *Highland Rim,* to be considered; while the blue limestone area, below and within, is called the *Central Basin.* (§ 25, (4.)).

209. Could the reader be elevated 2000 or 3000 feet above Nashville, or rather above Murfreesboro', he would see, below and around him, the latter area—the Basin—oval in form, lying within the limits of Tennessee, yet reaching a little obliquely nearly across the State. He would see, too, further off, the Highland Rim, rising up first in bold walls—terrace-like—all around the Basin, and then extending off, in every direction, in great plains.

Far to the east and southeast, would be seen the western escarpment of the Cumberland Table-land, presenting the appearance, at this distance, of a long, straight, uniform bank or ridge, resting upon the Highlands, but in every other direction the eye would roam over the plains, with nothing to limit the view,

210. Commencing along the base of the Cumberland Table-land, the Highlands spread out westward, run around the northern and southern extremities of the Basin in narrow arms, and then wholly encompassing the latter, extend to the vicinity of the Tennessee River, where they break off, finally, in

long fingers, or ridges. The entire distance is not far from 120 miles. The whole region, from the western base of the Table-land to the breaks of the highlands, near the Tennessee, is, in fact, one great plain, out of the center of which by unknown agencies, the basin referred to has been excavated. This plain has an *average* elevation, as will be seen, (§ 220,) of from 900 to 1000 feet above the sea. Its northwestern part, however, is considerably below this.

211. Looking beyond the State, the Highlands have a much greater extent than that indicated above. They extend northward into Kentucky, forming the high plains of the southern part of that State, and southward, into Alabama. In the latter State, at the Muscle Shoals, the Tennessee River may be regarded as passing from off the Highlands.

212. The Highland Rim is the largest natural division of Tennessee. Its area is approximately 9,300 square miles, which is nearly two-ninths of the State. It includes the following counties and parts of counties: Robertson, Montgomery, Dickson, Hickman, Lewis, Lawrence, Wayne; the greater parts of Overton, Putnam, White, DeKalb, Warren, Coffee, Franklin, Perry, Humphreys, Stewart, Macon; considerable parts of Jackson, Cannon, Lincoln, Giles, Hardin, Williamson, Cheatham, Sumner; and small parts of Smith, Van Buren, Grundy, Bedford, Maury and Davidson.

213. *Continuity, Rivers, and Water-falls.*—The continuity of the Rim may be regarded as nearly complete, there being no wide or important valley to break it. The Cumberland, Duck, and Elk rivers, in their escape from the Basin, break through its western and southern sides, but they do so in narrow valleys, bounded on both sides by high hills. The Cumberland in entering the Basin, cuts the Rim in the same manner. The lower part of the Caney Fork has a deep and ragged valley—a narrow arm of the Basin—which runs up many miles into the Highlands, making next to the Cumberland, the most serious interruption, or gash upon the eastern side. (See Map.)

214. Many of the smaller streams, which flow from off the Rim, form beautiful water-falls from forty to one hundred feet high, as they pass down into the gorges, or valleys, which open into the Basin. This is more especially true of those streams—tributaries of the Cumberland, of Caney Fork, and of Duck and Elk Rivers—which flow from off the eastern side.

The accompanying plate presents one of these falls, and will serve to show their general features, as they are all very much alike.

215. The one presented is that of Fall Creek, a tributary of Caney Fork. This romantic water-fall is about two miles east of Smithville, in DeKalb County. In addition to the main fall, a cascade, from a greater height, is seen to the right, belonging to a much smaller and different stream. The waters of both streams meet at the bottom, in the same pool. The larger body of water falls ninety-three feet. The gorge below the falls is exceedingly wild and picturesque. Steep slopes rising from the narrow valley are surmounted by precipitous cliffs from one to two hundred feet in height, towering, in all, three hundred feet or more above the creek.*

Several other tributaries of Caney Fork, for instance, Falling Water, and also its branch, Taylor's Creek, furnish water-falls as interesting as that just mentioned.

216. *Subdivisions, the Barrens and Fertile Portions; "Sink-holes;" Summer Retreats.*—In reference mainly to agricultural features, this division may be divided into the "*barrens*" and the more *fertile portions*. Immediately around the Basin at many points, extensive tracts occur which are known by the significant name of "the barrens." In these, the soil is generally thin and greatly deficient in calcareous matter. They are, in great part, level and thinly wooded. At some points "shrub-oaks" occupy whole square miles. In these regions the valleys only, and the hill-sides along the streams are, at present, cultivated.

217. Further back, however, and beyond the barrens, limestone begins to be seen. The country is more rolling, and the soil becomes red and fertile. This red land is characteristic, and furnishes numerous fine agricultural regions. A wide belt of it runs along the western base of the Cumberland Table-land, within which are the towns of Livingston, Sparta, Mc-Minnville and Winchester. It occurs too, around the base of the Short Mountains. (§ 191.) In the counties which lie between the Basin and the Valley of the Tennessee River to the west, there is much of the same red land, especially in the

* This water-fall, and the region immediately around it, bears the name of *Cul-car-mac*—a name given to it several years ago, and suggestive of the names of the joint owners of the property at the time—the Hon. Wm. Cullom, Judge Ab. Caruthers, and Col. Wm. McClain.

The geological section presented at this place, will be given in the Second Part of the Report.

counties of Robertson, Montgomery, Dickson, Hickman, and Lawrence.

In approaching the western limits of this division, the red arable land gives place, more or less, to "barrens."

218. A traveler, in passing over the Highland Rim, and especially the fertile portions just spoken of, cannot fail to notice the great number of hopper-shaped cavities, or "*sinkholes*," with which the surface is indented. These constitute a characteristic feature of the limestone portions of this division. Sinkholes occur in all the limestone regions of Tennessee, but in none, excepting perhaps the limestone slopes of the Cumberland Table-land, so frequently, and of such large size, as in the regions under consideration.

These cavities are, across the top, from ten to one hundred (and even more) yards in diameter. Large fields are sometimes seen made up entirely of the slopes of a number of them. Their presence indicates the existence of underground streams and caverns; and it is, by the sinking or running of surface-water into these streams and caverns through fissures in the rocks, together with the caving in, and greater wear of the upper edges of the fissures, that the sinkholes have been formed. When the openings at their bottoms become stopped up with stiff mud, or otherwise, little lakes or ponds are formed. In Tennessee and Kentucky, they have been converted into artificial ponds by feeding hogs in them, the cobs from ears of corn, the offal and clay packed down by the tramping of the animals in time, closing up the fissures.

In some cases, these cavities slope down to a basin of cool water, connected directly with an underground stream, and in which sometimes small fish may be caught.

219. This division, especially the inner portion—that around the Basin—is noted for its sulphur and free-stone waters. The small streams of the barrens are generally beautifully clear. The springs that feed them furnish water nearly as pure as that from the clouds.

The "sulphur springs" are numerous, and are generally found around the slopes, or in the valleys.

The springs, the cool air, and retirement of the Highlands, although, in the main, less inviting than the corresponding features of the Table-land, (§ 197,) are, nevertheless, highly grateful, in July or August, to the invalid or visitor. A score of cool, and desirable summer retreats may be found, at different points, around and just outside the Basin, to which the inhabitants of the latter can escape from the hot sun and the cares of the city, or of the corn and cotton fields. (§ 223.)

220. *Elevation above the Sea.*—The general elevation of this division has been already spoken of, (§ 210.) It is nearly that of the horizontal plain, to which, in general, the surface of the State has been referred. (§ 3.) The following tables present more particular information.

As most of the railroad lines, from which the heights of characteristic points have been obtained, extend continuously from this division into the Basin, (the division next to be described,) or conversely from out the latter, upon the high plains of this, it has been thought best, in order not to break the lines, or profiles, to include also in these tables, the heights of points in the Basin. By this arrangement, in addition, the difference in the general elevation of the two divisions will be better exhibited. The names and the heights of points upon the Highlands, or Rim, are printed in Roman characters, and those within the basin, in *Italics*. This will serve to distinguish those of the respective divisions. The heights are in feet, and above low tide of Mobile Bay. (See note, p. 87.)

(1.) The points, the heights of which are given in the following series, are all upon the Highland Rim. They occur along the connected lines of the *McMinnville and Manchester* and the *Southwestern Railroads.** The first point, Tullahoma, is the junction of the McM. & M. R. R. with the Nashville and Chattanooga Road.

Tullahoma..........................	1070	(Grade)	McM. &	M. R.R.
Point 2, 5 miles from T., ...	1039	(Surface).....	"	"
" 4 " "	1067	do.	"	"
" 6 " "	992	do.	"	"
" 9 " "	1085	do.	"	"
Average of four miles, between points 7 and 11 miles from T.	1072	do.	"	"
Creek at Manchester, 12 miles.	996	do.	"	"
Point 13 miles from T., ...	1090	do.	"	"
" 15, 25 " "	1135	do.	"	"
" 20 " "	1124	do.	"	"
Average between last two points..........................	1114	do.	"	"
Point 21, 5 miles from T.........	1042	do.	"	"
" 24, 6 " "	1107	do.	"	"
" 28 " "	1037	do.	"	"
" 30 " "	1000	do.	"	"

* I am not quite certain that the profile of the McM. & M. line, used in determining the heights of the first part of this series, is, at all points, the same as that of the constructed road. It is possible that some changes in location may have been made. At the most, however, the changes have been small. It is the same at all important points, and, moreover, the profile used, is in itself complete.

The Southwestern Railroad is, as yet, in an unfinished condition. The Special data made use of in determining the heights along this line were obtained from a report made in 1858, by Mr. E. F. Falconnet, at that time Chief Engineer of the road.

Point 31 miles from T.,	957	do.	McM. & M. R. R.
Bottom of Hickory Creek	886	do.	" "
Summit	972	do.	" "
Barren Fork of Collins' River,	870	(Bottom)	" "
McMinnville, Depot	912	(Grade)	" "
" Depot	981	do.	S. W. R. R.
Bed of Collins' River	831		" "
Mud Creek Station	916		" "
Summit between Collins' River and Caney Fork	1006		" "
Bed of Caney Fork*	751		" "
Rock Island Station	906		" "
Summit near Gumspring Mt.	990		" "
Sparta Station	945		" "
Huddleston's, or Cookeville Sta.	1116		" "
Summit near Algood's	1150		" "
Marchbank's Summit	1162		" "
Summit between Spring Creek and Sulphur Lick	1139		" "
Livingston Station	966		" "

(2.) The following are points along an experimental line from Decherd, on the N. & C. R. R., to McMinnville. It connects with the McM. &. M. Road just before the latter crosses Hickory Creek. The distances are reckoned from Decherd:

Decherd, on N. & C. R. R	965
Summit, 4 miles	1053
Point, 7 miles	1023
Bottom of Elk River, 8 miles	950
Summit, 12 miles	1056
Bottom of Bradley's Cr., 12.5 miles	996
Point half-mile east of Hillsboro', 15 miles	1091
Point, 18 miles	1155
Point, 21 miles	1165
General elevation between last two points	1142
Head Spring of Hickory Cr., 21.3 miles	1113

* The Falls of Caney Fork are but a short distance below the point at which the railroad crosses the river. The water at these Falls descends impetuously in a series of rapids and cascades, falling altogether 94 feet, and furnishing great water power. The top of the Falls, at low water, is 391½ feet (389½ plus 2) above low water of the Cumberland at Nashville, or 756 feet above the sea. The following are elevations, above the sea, of several points in this vicinity. I am indebted to Mr. Wm. Bosson for information as to the heights of the first three above Nashville:

Foot of Falls	662 feet
Top of Falls	756 "
Surface in front of Judge Bosson's house	876 "
Average of general surface back from gorge of river, about	900 "
Top of Hickory-nut Mt., (§ 192,) about	1400 "

Point, 24 miles	1077
Bottom of Hickory Cr., 28.5 miles	972
Point, 30.6 miles	1027
Bottom of Hickory Cr., on McM. & M. R. R , 34.5 miles	886

(3.) The table following presents a long series running from the *Tunnel* on the N. & C. R. R., (page 62,) through Nashville to the *Kentucky State line*, on the Edgefield & Kentucky Railroad. It extends entirely across two opposite sides of the Highland Rim, as well as through the included Basin. Points within the latter are printed in *Italics*.* The distances are reckoned from Nashville.

TUNNEL	89 miles	1153	(Grade)	N. & C. R. R.
Cowan	87 "	973	"	" "
Summit	84.5 "	1036	(Surface)	" "
Wagner's Cr	82.2 "	944	"	" "
Decherd	82 "	965	(Grade)	" "
Elk River	78 "	865	(Surface)	" "
Point	72 "	1087	"	" "
Point	70 "	1097	"	" "
Tullahoma	69 "	1070	(Grade)	" "
Point	67 "	1079	(Surface)	" "
Average between points at 72 and 67 miles ("barrens,") about		1070	"	" "
Norman's Cr	62.2 *miles*	814	"	" "

* I take this opportunity of acknowledging my indebtedness, for profiles and maps pertaining to the different railroads in Middle Tennessee, and, in several cases, for personal assistance, to the kindness of Messrs. A. Anderson, Chief Engineer of Tenn. & Ala., Edg. & Ky., and Cen. Southern Railroads; J. H. Devereux, City Engineer of Nashville, and Resident Engineer of Tenn. & Ala. R. R.; G. Trafton, Assistant City Engineer of Nashville, and Assistant Engineer Tenn. and Ky. State line boundary; E. F. Falconnet, Chief Engineer of Nashville & N. W. R. R.; J. C. Wrenshall, of the L. & N. R. R.; W. F. Foster, Assistant Engineer in charge Cumb. R. Railroad Bridge; and R. C. Morris, Chief Engineer of Nash. & Chat. R. R., formerly of the East Tenn. & Ga, R. R.

To Mr. Devereux, I am under especial obligations. The heights above low tide, at Mobile, of the *base-lines* of all the railroads meeting at Nashville, and of the Cumberland River Railroad Bridge, were made out, for the most part, by him.

These base-lines were connected by means of the surveys of the Tennessee & Alabama Railroad, with the levels of the Mobile and Ohio road. As a check upon the results, it may be stated that the height of the Tunnel-grade, at Montgomery's Gap, on the N. & C. R. R., was found to be 1153 feet above low tide at Mobile, while, according to the levels brought from an opposite direction (from the Atlantic) it is 1156, a difference of only three feet. (See p. 62.)

The following table presents the heights of the base-lines mentioned above low tide at Mobile:

Base of Tenn. & Ala. Railroad	256.5 feet
" " Cumb. River R. R. Bridge	256.5 "
" " Edg. & Ky. Railroad	313.5 "
" " L. & N. "	351.25 "
" " N. & N. W. "	362.0 "
" " N. & C. "	366.5 "
" " Cen. Southern "	418.0 "

Place	Distance		Elevation		Road
Normandy	62	miles	834	(*Grade*)	N. & C. R. R.
Duck River	59.5	"	777	(*Surface*)	" "
Summit	56.5	"	864	"	" "
Garrison Fork	56	"	778	"	" "
Wartrace Creek	52.5	"	800	"	" "
Bell Buckle Summit	47	"	916	"	" "
Christmas Cr	41	"	695	"	" "
Stone's River	35	"	598	"	" "
Summit	33.5	"	643	"	" "
Murfreesboro' Depot	32	"	583	(*Grade*)	" "
Stone's River	30.5	"	538	(*Surface*)	" "
Top of banks of do	30.5	"	579	"	" "
Overall's Cr	25.5	"	513	"	" "
Summit	23	"	597	"	" "
Stewart's Cr	21.5	"	494	"	" "
A summit	17	"	599	"	" "
Hurricane Cr	15	"	539	"	" "
Summit	13	"	640	"	" "
Mill Creek	5	"	440	"	" "
Summit between Mill Cr. and Brown's Cr	2	"	541	"	" "
NASHVILLE—					
" *Depot*			435	(*Grade*)	" "
" *Depot*			438	"	L. & N. R. R.
" *Low water of Cumb. R.**			365		
" *High water of Cumb. R.**			422		
Edgefield Depot	0.5	*miles*	428	(*Grade*)	L. & N. R. R.
Summit	4	"	562	"	" "
Dry Creek	9.5	"	406	(*Bottom*)	" "
Junction	9.5	"	438	(*Grade*)	E. & Ky. R. R.
Summit	11.3	*miles*	517	(*Grade*)	" "
Goodlettsville	12.5	"	457	"	" "
Mansker's Cr	13.5	"	441	(*Surface*)	" "
" "	14.6	"	468	"	" "
Foot of "Ridge"	17	"	563	"	" "
Summit of "Ridge"	18.5	"	895	"	" "
" " "	18.6	"	877	(Grade)	" "
Point	22	"	822	"	" "
Point	25.3	"	748	"	" "
Springfield	29	"	659	"	" "
Sulphur Fork	30.5	"	570	"	" "
" "	30.5	"	512	(Surface)	" "
Point	32	"	672	(Grade)	" "

* According to low water of 1854 and high water of 1847, these heights were determined to be 364.5 and 421.5, respectively. For the sake of avoiding decimals, they are made as above.

Point 36	miles......	681	(Grade)	......E. & Ky. R. R.
Red River...................41.5	"	484	"	...... " "
" " 41.5	"	399	(Bottom)	...... " "
Point.........................45.5	"	592	(Grade)	...... " "
TENN. & KY. LINE....46.7	"	554	"	...... " "

(4.) The following are the heights (according to a profile kindly furnished me by Mr. J. C. Wrenshall) of characteristic points along the line of the Louisville & Nashville Railroad, from its junction with the Edgefield & Kentucky road, to the State line:

Junction.................... 9.5	*miles*......	438	(*Grade*)	....*L. & N. R. R.*
Mansker's Cr.............11.5	"	389	(*Bottom*)	.... " "
Summit......................13	"	528	(*Surface*)	.... " "
Drake's Cr.................15.5	"	449	"	.... " "
Summit.......................18	"	593	"	.... " "
W. Station Camp Cr...20.5	"	445	"	.... " "
Station Camp Cr........23.5	"	441	"	.... " "
Gallatin.....................26	"	528	"	.... " "
Summit.......................27	"	573	"	.... " "
E. Station Camp Cr. ...27,7	"	503	"	.... " "
Point, about foot of "Ridge,"................30.7	"	694	"	.... " "
Margin of Highlands.31.7	"	951	"	.... " "
Summit of grade at end of Tunnel..............32.3	"	833	(About)	.... " "
Valley, Drakes's Cr...33.4	"	800	(Surface)	.... " "
W. Fork " "...36.5	"	708	"	.... " "
Summit 39	"	853	"	.... " "
State Line.................45	"	755	"	.... " "

An experimental line from Gallatin, by the way of Bledsoe Creek towards Scottsville, in Kentucky, etc., presents a profile much like that of the surface passed over by the constructed road. By this route, the margin of the Highlands is reached about seventeen and a half miles from Gallatin, and has here an elevation of 1000 feet above the sea.

(5.) The following table presents the heights of characteristic points along the line of the Tennessee and Alabama Railroad from Nashville to Mount Pleasant, and, from the latter point, along a surveyed line across the Highlands to Hamburg, on the Tennessee River. By these lines the railroads of Middle Tennessee have been connected with the levels of the Mobile and Ohio road. As before, points within the Basin are printed in Italics. Those marked with an asterisk, thus (*), are within the *Western Valley of the Tennessee River*. (§ 25.) The distances given are the approximate distances of the points from Broad street in Nashville.

Place	Distance	Elevation	Kind	Authority
NASHVILLE, *old Terminus, Cherry St......*		469	(*Grade*)	......*Tenn. & Ala. R.R.*
Brown's Creek............	2.5 miles......	475	"	...... " "
Overton's Gap............	6 "	621	"	...... " "
Atkinson's Gap	9 "	737	"	...... " "
Little Harpeth River...	11.5 "	649	(*Bottom*)	.... " "
" " " ...	" "	668	(*Grade*)	...... " "
Summit..................	13.5 "	763	"	...... " "
Harpeth River...........	18.3 "	602	(*Bottom*)	...... " "
Franklin Depot.........	18.6 "	642	(*Grade*)	...... " "
Summit..................	23 "	759	"	...... " "
West Harpeth River.....	25 "	682	(*Bottom*)	...... " "
Summit, (Duck River Bridge)............	29 "	841	(*Grade*)	...... " "
Spring Hill Station ...*	31.5 "	770	"	...... " "
Carter's Creek..........	35 "	621	(*Bottom*)	...... R. R. Survey.
Duck River..............	42.5 "	528	"	...... " "
" *High Water......*	" "	571	....	" "
Summit	46 "	709	(*Surface*)	...... " "
Lick Creek..............	47.5 "	626	"	...... " "
Summit..................	49.5 "	707	"	...... " "
E. Branch of Bigby...	53 "	602	"	...... " "
Mt. Pleasant, Sugar Fork of Bigby........	54 "	625	"	...... " "
Bigby Creek.............	58 "	660	"	...... " "
Foot of Ridge...........	59.5 "	702	"	...... " "
Top of Ridge commencement of Highlands.	65 "	1019	"	...... " "
Top of Ridge, Tunnel.	" "	968	(Grade)	...... " "
Buffalo Creek.	71 "	802	(Surface)	...... " "
Point.....................	75.5 "	1035	"	...... " "
Br. of Little Buffalo..	79 "	862	(Bottom)	...... " "
Palo Alto P. O.........	82 "	1025	(Surface)	...... " "
Point.....................	92.5 "	1021	"	...... " "
Average elevation beteen the last two points, about......................		1000	"	...... " "
Point.....................	96.5 "	1069	"	...... " "
"	100.5 "	1087	"	...... " "
"	103.5 "	1056	"	...... " "
Point, between waters of Indian & Cypress Creeks....	113.5 "	973	"	...... " "

* From this point on to Mount Pleasant, the profile from which the heights were taken, is not, in the main, the actual profile of the road as finally located. It runs, however, very nearly over the same ground, so that the heights of corresponding points on the two will not differ essentially.

Point, between waters of Indian, Horse and Second Creeks	117.5 miles	902	(Surface)	R. R. Survey.
(*) Valley of Horse Cr. (off the Highlands	124.5 "	599	"	" "
(*) Bed of do.	137 "	425	"	" "
(*) Lick Cr. Summit.	139.5 "	616	"	" "
" " Tunnel.	" "	541	(Grade)	" "
(*) Tennessee River at Hamburgh	145 "			
" High Water		392		M. & O. R. R. Sur.
" Low Water		352		" "

(6.) The following are heights of points along the Central Southern Railroad. Two of these points, the first at Dodson's Gap, the other the summit of Madry's Hill, may be regarded as being upon the spurs of the Highlands. All the others are within the Basin. The distances are reckoned from Columbia.

Columbia Depot		657	(*Grade*)	*C. S. R. R.*
Point	1.6 miles	696	(*Surface*)	" "
Lytle's Creek	2.5 "	624	"	" "
Point	3.5 "	710	"	" "
"	6 "	624	"	" "
"	8.5 "	766	"	" "
Pleasant Grove	9.8 "	739	(*Grade*)	" "
Adam's Fork	12.7 "	693	(*Surface*)	" "
Elk Ridge, Dodson's Gap	15.8 "	937	"	" "
" "	" "	898	(*Grade*)	" "
Robertson's Fork	18.5 "	716	(*Surface*)	" "
Richland Creek	26.5 "	691	(*Grade*)	" "
Pulaski	33.5 "	648	"	" "
Richland Creek	39.5 "	630	"	" "
" "	" "	93	(*Surface*)	" "
Madry Hill	42.5 "	924	(Top)	" "
" " *Tunnel*	" "	736	(*Grade*)	" "
Elk River	46.5 "	598	"	" "
" "	" "	553	(*Surface*)	" "
Tenn. & Ala. Line	47.8 "	654.5	"	" "

(7.) Below we have a series along the portion of the Nashville and Northwestern Railroad that extends from Nashville to the Tennessee River. It presents a complete section of the Western side of the Highland Rim. The road, however, it must be remembered, following the valley of Harpeth

River, passes some distance in among the ridges and detached portions of the Highlands before it ascends and gets upon them. The place of ascent is then within the general limits of the division. The valley of the Harpeth may be regarded as a ramification of the Basin. The course and position of this river are such as to detach a small block of the Highlands from the main body of the division. (See Map.) In the table, as before, the points in Italics are within the Basin, and those marked with an asterisk, thus (*), within the Western Tennessee River Valley.

Nashville, Bridge, Summer Street		429.5	(*Grade.*)
Summit	3.2 *miles*	558	"
Richland Creek	5 "	449	"
Point	7.7 "	507	"
Summit	10.2 "	681	"
"	10.2 "	709	(*Surface.*)
Harpeth River	14 "	556	(*Grade.*)
" "	15.7 "	548	"
Point	20 "	573	"
Harpeth River	22 "	504	"
Kingston Station	25 "	506	"
Turnbull Creek	25 6 "	459	(*Bottom.*)
Sullivan Br.	26.7 "	473	"
Point	27 "	524	(*Grade*)
Top of Highlands	31 "	819	"
" "	31 "	841	(Surface.)
Point	34.8 "	842	(Grade)
"	37 "	754	"
"	39.2 "	862	"
"	39.2 "	885	(Surface.)
"	41.7 "	791	(Grade.)
Highest Point	45 "	915	"
" "	45 "	922	(Surface.)
Gordon's Branch	48 "	736	"
" "	48 "	795	(Grade.)
Point	50.5 "	839	"
"	50.5 "	854	(Surface.)
Hurricane Creek	54 "	626	"
" "	54 "	643	(Grade.)
Summit	57.5 "	837	"
(*) Point	61.7 "	632	"
(*) Trace Creek	64 "	575	(Surface.)
" "	64 "	587	(Grade.)
(*) Point	70 "	482	"
(*) Trace Creek	74.7 "	394	"
" "	74.7 "	374	(Surface.)
(*) Tennessee River	78 "	368	(Grade.)
" "	78 "	357	(High Water.)

(8.) Mr. Lea, from whose Report I have before quoted, (page 73,) gives us interesting information as to the elevation and general character of that portion of the Highland Rim lying between Perryville, on the Tennessee River, and Columbia; and of that part intersected by the deep and narrow valley of Duck River. He refers, also, to the fact that, all Middle Tennessee west of the Cumberland Table-land, may be regarded as an elevated plain, out of which has been excavated the great Central Basin, or, as he has it, the "basins" formed by the different rivers within the central part of the State—the group, or great basin, that these constitute, not being very clearly recognized. The following are remarks of his bearing upon these points. It will be recollected that Mr. Lea is speaking with reference to a route for a "Central Railroad."

"All that country lying between the western base of the Cumberland Mountain and the Tennessee River, may be regarded as a bench of the Mountain itself, and is elevated from seven to eight hundred feet above the Tennessee River. The geological formation of this region, being of the *secondary* order, the strata lie horizontally upon each other; and, at the depth of three to five hundred feet below the common surface, which is poor, gravelly and sandy, lies a stratum of limestone rock.* In various places the strata superior to this limestone are pretermitted, and exhibit the appearance of having been removed by some mechanical action; and thus, in many places, valleys or basins are formed, presenting all the richness incident to the horizontal limestone formations, of which the valley of Duck River is a remarkable instance. If you follow up Duck River from its mouth, for a distance of fifty miles, (measured in its general direction,) you will find it hemmed closely in by high and precipitous hills; but at the end of the fifty miles you emerge from the gorge, and enter upon a wide-spread and fertile valley, interspersed here and there with gently sloping hills, and presenting an appearance of unbounded wealth and beauty. But push your journey a few miles to either hand, across this valley, and you will find it surrounded by a high and rugged barrier, composed chiefly of sandstone; and, on ascending this barrier, you will find yourself upon the general level of the bench of Cumberland Mountain."

In this last statement, if Mr. Lea means that the valley of Duck River after leaving "the gorge"—say east of Columbia and within the counties of Maury, Marshall and Bedford—is limited on both sides by a high "sandstone" barrier, what he says needs some qualification. There is such a barrier on the

* I quote Mr. Lea's own words. Compare what is said of the geology of this region in the Second Part of this Report.

south side of the valley, separating it from the main and tributary valleys of Elk River. This is *Elk Ridge*, and will be noticed when I come to speak of the Basin. On the north side, however, there is no such barrier. The crest of the watershed separating the Duck River Valley from the subordinate valleys of the tributaries of the Cumberland is mostly a limestone ridge, which is much broken, and presents but very few points high enough to be capped with the stratum or formation, which Mr. Lea calls sandstone. Passing eastward, however, across the Basin, we find in Coffee County the valleys of the head-branches of Duck River, running up between spurs of the Highlands. (§ 214.)

After thus speaking of the valley of Duck River Mr. Lea refers to the "similar valleys or basins" of the Elk and Cumberland rivers, and of their tributaries, and then adds:

"It is a singular feature of the country, that these basins are generally at a considerable distance from the main river, and that there is a large body of high table-land along the Tennessee, which is only interrupted by the streams which drain these basins."

"When we cast our eyes on either side of Duck River, we find the minor streams, at every few miles, cutting chasms in the Table-land from three to five hundred feet deep, and thus presenting almost impassable gulfs. Perhaps there is not a more broken country in the world than that around about the lower part of Duck River."

"Having crossed the Tennessee, (at Perryville,) the route is very favorable up the valley of Cypress Creek, for a distance of seven miles, when it begins to run along the sides of the hills in order to ascend more rapidly than the natural rise of the valley. Rising about three miles, at the rate of sixty feet per mile, the road attains an extreme elevation of about 356 feet above high water in Tennessee River," (or about 730 above the sea,) "and passes the Buffalo Ridge at a gap one or two hundred feet below its general level." This makes the general level from 830 to 930 above tide water.

"Having passed the gap in the ridge, the road winds along on a bench of the mountain for about three and a-half miles, descending at the rate of sixty feet per mile." . . . . This part of the road will be very expensive, as it leads across many ravines in the side of the ridge, and requires high embankments, or bridges, to cross them. . . . . Still no other route has been found across the ridge at all competing with this in aggregate advantages.

"Passing Buffalo River without difficulty, the road runs on favorable ground up Hurricane Creek, about seven miles further, to the forks of the creek at Tom. Barber's, where the valley begins to rise more rapidly, but still continues smooth and open.

"From Tom. Barber's, the road rises sixty feet per mile, in the first mile, and 120 feet per mile for two miles further, when it attains the summit of the ridge, dividing the waters which fall into the Buffalo River from those which fall into Duck River, directly. This ridge has been appropriately named by Col. S. H. Long, after the lamented Lewis, the renowned traveler, who lies interred on its summit." (This is a flat-topped ridge, and its summit, the elevation of which is at least 1000 feet above the sea, may be regarded as a point of the top of the Highlands.)

"Having attained the summit of Lewis's Ridge, the road has a very favorable location for twenty-four miles along its crest, to the head of Big Bigby Creek, where it commences its descent with a deep cut, and then falls at the rate of sixty feet per mile, for five miles, along a rough and crooked ravine, before it attains the level of the flat grounds on the creek below the Factory.

"This division involves more difficulty than any other upon the whole route, except that over Cumberland Mountain."

221. The tables given in connection with the remarks made, will enable the reader to form a correct idea of the elevation of the entire Rim above tide-water. The height of its flat surface above the Basin, which it encloses, will be spoken of hereafter. The general level of the northwestern side of the Rim, that is to say, the part in the counties of Dickson, Robertson, Montgomery, Stewart, etc., the part, too, through which the Cumberland River breaks, is considerably lower than the part upon the opposite side in Franklin, Coffee, and Warren. Taking the Rim and Basin together, it may be said that the whole area dips (or the great dish is tilted) to the northwest. Passing beyond the limits of Tennessee, in North Alabama, the Highlands dip southward. These dips, or waves, conform generally, as will be seen hereafter, to the geological structure of the region.

222. It may be noticed, also, that the surface of the Rim, or Highlands, on the eastern and southeastern side, slopes gently at many points, eastward, toward the base of the Cumberland Table-land, so that the border of the division near the Basin has the greater elevation. At numerous points around the Basin, the high border or margin of the Rim is a dividing ridge between the low-bedded creeks of the former division, and the high-bedded ones of the latter.

223. *Climate.*—The features of climate already given, for the State in general, apply, in the main, to this large division. Owing to higher elevation, however, its mean temperature is a little less than that of the Basin. For points on the same par-

allel, the difference between the annual means is from one to two degrees; between the summer means, it is, doubtless, considerably greater. Immediately around and outside of the Basin, that is to say, upon the circular interior border of the Highlands, the difference in temperature is quite noticeable, especially in summer. For this reason, in connection with its freestone and sulphur springs, and its retired, open-wooded groves, this border, and in fact much of the division, has become noted for its summer retreats. (§ 219.)

224. We have climatological data from two points of this division, the Falls of Caney Fork and Glenwood. (See table, p. 14.) The latter point, the residence of Prof. W. M. Stewart, where he made (and is making) his excellent observations, is located upon the depressed portion of highland division, the elevation being here but 486 feet above the sea. This fact must be borne in mind should the Glenwood data be used in estimating the temperature, etc., of the higher and characteristic portions of the Highlands.

225. The observations made at the Falls may be compared with Mr. Tavel's at Nashville, since the hours of observation were, in both cases, about the same. According to these the annual mean temperature for 1855 and 1856, at Nashville, is 58°.80, and that, at the Falls, for the same years, (Jan., 1855 excepted,) is 58°.48. The former place has, however, a higher latitude than the latter. Allowing for this, the difference becomes nearly equal to one degree.

226. Between the summer means of the two places, and for the same years, the difference is much greater; it is, without correction for latitude, 3.33, the mean at Nashville being 77.99, while at the Falls it is but 74.66. Referring the points to the same parallel, it may be placed at four degrees.

V.—THE CENTRAL BASIN.

227. This unique division occupies the very centre of the State. It is truly the garden of Tennessee. Excepting great alluvial bottoms, it would be difficult to meet with a region of the same extent anywhere, possessing naturally the elements of prosperity and agricultural wealth in a greater degree. Although the fourth division in size, yet it is, at this time, the first in population, wealth, and political influence.

228. The description of the Basin, has necessarily been, in good part, anticipated in speaking of the Highland Rim encircling it. And here, it may be well to remark, that the latter division has been named with reference to the relation it sustains to the Basin. Aside from this relation, the name would not be appropriate. (§§ 25, 208 and 209.)

229. *Form, Outlines, and Area.**—The Basin has approximately the form of an ellipse. Its length, or greater diameter, is about 121 miles, and its average breadth, or shorter diameter, from 55 to 60. It lies within the limits of Tennessee, reaching, however, lengthwise, in a north-northeasterly and south-southwesterly direction, nearly across the State. At its extreme end, to the northeast, it has a narrow gateway, or outlet, into Kentucky, through the contracted and ascending valley of the Cumberland River. To the southwest, it has a similar outlet into Alabama, down the valley of the Elk. Besides these, the Basin has but two other outlets—a very narrow one to the west, through the gorge of Duck River, (p. 93,) and a more open one to the northwest, down the valley of the Cumberland.†

230. As to traveling and commercial intercourse, these gateways, or outlets, as such, (except, so far as river navigation is concerned, and that is confined to the Cumberland,) are of little service. The valleys that furnish them, are so narrow and broken, that none of the railroads, turnpikes, or other leading roads radiating from the capital of the State—whose site is very suitably within the Basin—pass through them. All these, when they reach the foot of the escarpment bounding the division, ascend at once, by steep grades, to the top of the Highlands or Rim. To get out of the Basin, is the first and most serious difficulty that the railroads running from Nash-

* The form, position, extent, etc., of this division, are well seen upon the large Map. To this the reader should, by no means, neglect to refer.

† The narrow outlets, or valleys, have already been referred to in connection with the continuity of the Rim. See §§ 213 and 214.

ville meet with.* To attain the margin of the Highlands they have a *direct* elevation of from 250 to 350 feet to overcome.

231. In tracing out the general outlines, or contour, of this division, we may commence with the "Ridge" in Sumner County.† This so-called ridge presents a steep face to the southeast, forming a well-marked portion of the northwestern side of the Basin. The general outline, or high edge of the Basin coinciding with the top of the Ridge, pursues at first, a general northeasterly course, then bending around to the east, it passes through the southern part of Macon County, into Jackson. Here it is cut by the valley of the Cumberland, presenting one of the outlets mentioned. (§ 229.) On the southeastern side of the Cumberland, it extends from Jackson County in a general southwesterly direction, passing approximately between Smith and Putnam; through the western part of DeKalb; through Cannon, east of Woodbury; on through the western parts of Coffee and Franklin, to the southern part of Lincoln south of the Elk. From this region, without quite reaching Alabama, the outline runs westward, gradually curving around to the northwest in Giles County, crossing in the meantime, Elk River, the narrow valley of which presents another of its outlets. From Giles, it runs in a northerly direction, through the western parts of Maury and Williamson; through Cheatham, and the western part of Davidson, to the "Ridge" in Sumner. In this last course, the remaining outlets of the Basin are presented in the valleys of the Duck and Cumberland Rivers.

232. The outlines of the Basin, in particular, are, at most points, rough, being broken more or less, by the fringing, or finger-like spurs which run from the Highlands within its general limits. These spurs, which are generally water-sheds between creeks, often retain, for several miles, the characteristic elevation of the Highlands.

* The Central Southern Railroad meets with two high spurs of the Highlands, namely, Elk Ridge (§ 233) and Madry Hill, before finally leaving the Basin. South of Elk River, the line continuing this road, gets upon the Alabama extension of the Highlands.

† The word ridge, as here applied, is in some degree, unfortunate. It must be recollected, that this ridge is the margin of highlands that extend off to the northwest, and constitute a portion of the Rim already described. It is true, that this margin is the dividing line between the waters of the Cumberland and those of Red River; but while the slope to the southeast is steep and sudden, that to the northwest is very gentle, and, in fact, out of the immediate beds of the streams, not noticeable to the traveler.

233. The most remarkable spur, is that known as "*Elk Ridge.*" This is, in fact, an almost unbroken, though narrow arm, running entirely across from one side of the Rim to the other, and cutting off, as a well-marked subdivision, the southern end of the Basin. In the main, it has about the elevation of the Highlands, and presents, in its course, but very few low gaps. It is the water-shed between Duck and Elk Rivers. Several branches run out from its southern side, separating the valleys of creeks in Giles and Lincoln Counties.

234. From another point of view, we may look upon the outlines of this division as being notched by the valleys opening into it. These valleys are narrow ramifications, or arms of the Basin. Most of the smaller streams from the Highlands, falling into the Basin, present, for a greater or less number of miles, before reaching the general outlines of the latter, deep and narrow valleys, or gorges. Passing up these gorges, we find them generally terminated abruptly by water-falls, or cascades. Here, too, they terminate as ramifications of the Basin. Above the water-falls, th valleys and streams pertain to the Highlands, or Rim. (§ 214.)

235. The outlets before spoken of, (§ 229,) are ramifications of the Basin but they extend entirely through the Rim. Next to these, the narrow valley of Caney Fork presents the longest and most important arm of the Basin, (§ 213,) ending, as such, with the noted falls of this stream. (Note, p. 86.)

Duck River presents, in the portion of its valley in Coffee County, a ramification comparatively short, which, at the "Old Stone Fort," near Manchester, bifurcates, each fork terminating very soon, with a beautiful water-fall.

The valley of Elk River, in Franklin County, and below Winchester, presents a narrow arm, of considerable length.

The lower part of the valley of Harpeth River, in Cheatham and Dickson Counties, is a ramification, which, with the valley of the Cumberland, entirely detaches a block of the Rim. These are the most important examples. (See Map.)

236. The following counties, wholly, or in part, lie within the Basin: all of Wilson, Rutherford, and Marshall; nearly all of Smith, Davidson, and Bedford; the greater parts of Sumner, Williamson, Maury, Giles, and Lincoln; large parts of Jackson, Cheatham, and Cannon; and, finally, small parts of Macon, DeKalb, Putnam, and Coffee.

The entire area of the division, is about 5450 square miles, which is more than one-eighth of the State.

237. *Subdivisions; Surface; " Cedar Glades."*—The Basin is comparatively simple in structure and parts. There is but one portion that may be regarded as a well-defined subdivision, and that is the southern end, cut off by Elk Ridge, to which reference has already been made. (§ 233.)

This subdivision embraces that portion of the valley of the Elk and its tributaries, lying in Giles and Lincoln Counties. The most important of the tributaries, is Richland Creek.

238. The remainder of the Basin might be divided into four sections, corresponding, respectively, to the valleys of Duck River, Harpeth, and its Forks, Stone's River, and the Cumberland. The ridges, however, that divide these, are, by no means, well defined, being at many points, low and broken, and hardly existing as continuous ridges.

239. Occasionally, aside from the ridges and spurs that have been mentioned, and within the body of the Basin, isolated peaks, and short ridges, or groups of these, are met with, which mount up to the level of the Rim.

In the main, however, the general surface of the Basin, is moderately rolling. Large and valuable tracts occur, which are nearly level, or but gently undulating. Excepting the " cedar glades," to be spoken of, there is very little waste land. The soil, based on impure, blue limestone, is generally of an excellent quality, and, in its native state, supported heavy forests, and, in many places, thick canebrakes.

240. The *cedar glades* constitute a characteristic surface-feature of the Basin. These are rocky places, generally flat, covered more or less, with red cedar, (*Juniperus Virginiana.*) They abound in many parts of the division.

241. A circular range of such glades is found in Rutherford County, enclosing a large area of fine, brownish-red lands. Murfreesboro' lies a short distance east of the center of this area.

In Wilson County, and along Duck River, in Bedford, Marshall, and Maury Counties, are many glades, covering large tracts.

The cedar timber of the glades is, or has been, of excellent quality. A vast amount of it has been cut for building purposes, cross-ties, fence rails, fire-wood, etc. Much of it has been carried out of the State. (§ 262.)

242. It has been suggested, that the Basin was once the bed of a lake. Without committing ourselves to such an opinion, it may, nevertheless, be well, as we pass, to regard the division from this point of view, as thereby our conception of it as a *basin* may be made clearer.

If the outlets mentioned, through which the Cumberland, Duck, and Elk Rivers escape, (§ 229,) were closed, by the filling up of the valleys, to the level of the highest points of the adjacent highlands, the back-waters of these rivers would accumulate, and finally, nearly fill the Basin, rising until high enough to run over the lowest part of the Rim.

There would thus be formed a large fresh-water lake, having the outlines, (§ 231,) form, and dimensions (§ 229) of this division.

243. The shores on opposite sides of this lake, would not differ very much in height—not more, generally, than from 100 to 200 feet. On the northwestern side, they would be lowest, being, however, nearly, or quite, 900 feet above the sea. Here the waters would first run over.

The margin of the lake, all around, to a greater or less extent, would be fringed by low headlands, and notched by narrow inlets, (§§ 232 and 234.) In its southern part, a group of narrow, and long islands would be seen. One line of these, arranged end to end, (Elk Ridge, § 233,) would extend from shore to shore, and partially cut off the extreme southern end of the lake. Islands, too, would be seen at different points, all around its margin. One of considerable size, or, perhaps a group, would appear in Cheatham County, corresponding to the Harpeth hills, between Harpeth and the Cumberland. (§ 235.) And here and there, within the body of the lake, sparcely scattered over its surface, small isolated islands, or groups of islands, would be met with. (§ 239.)

The water of the lake, would be deep in its northwestern part, especially over the bed of the Cumberland, and shallow in its eastern and southeastern parts. This would result from the tilting of the Basin and its Rim to the northwest, of which I have spoken. (§ 221.) At a point over Nashville, measured down to the track on the Railroad Bridge, the depth would be about 460 feet.

244. Judge Haywood, the author of a work already cited,* imperfectly recognized, the basin-like character of the part of Tennessee we are considering. He makes very properly, the "highlands, or ridges," west of Columbia, Franklin, and Nash ville, and north of the Cumberland, in Sumner and Macon, the western and northwestern limits of the basin-like area. On

* See note, page 21. The full title of this work is "The Natural and Aboriginal History of Tennessee, up to the First Settlements therein, by the White People, in the year 1768. By John Haywood, of the County of Davidson, in the State of Tennessee. Nashville: 1823."

This work is certainly one of the curiosities of the early science and literature of Tennessee. The author has left us, among many curious speculations and statements, much useful matter. He was among the first to notice many of the interesting minerals and some of the "geological phenomena" of the State. I shall have frequent occasion to refer to his work.

the other hand, however, he appears to regard the "Cumberland Mountains," as the eastern and southeastern side. The area, thus included, with a portion of Northern Alabama, is also, according to his view, divided into two subordinate basins by Duck River Ridge, to which ridge, he gives undue importance.

245. Our author, it will be seen, is wrong, in placing the greatly more elevated Cumberland Table-land, ("Mountains") in opposition to the western highlands mentioned. The latter have their opposite and corresponding equivalents in the highlands running through DeKalb, Cannon, Coffee, etc., the Basin proper, lying between. (§§ 208 and 231.)

The basin-like area has, therefore, by no means, the extent he would give it; and the subordinate basins, as he points them out, do not exist. The western escarpment of the Cumberland Table-land, excepting a few outliers, of which the Short Mountains (§ 191) are the most conspicuous, has nothing equally elevated, to face it, until we get far beyond the Mississippi River.

246. The following extracts will serve to indicate the views advanced by Judge Haywood:

"On the eastern side side of the rich lands of West [Middle] Tennessee, are the Cumberland Mountains, running northeast and southwest. On the western side of them are other parallel highlands, or ridges, at the distance of about one hundred and ten miles from the Cumberland Mountains. The traveler crosses the western ridge at Paradice's, going from Nashville to Clarksville; and at Robertson's, ten or twelve miles south of the former, in going from Nashville to Charlotte.

"In a northwardly direction, the ridge traverses the counties of Robertson, Sumner and Smith; and, approaching the Cumberland River, crosses the Kentucky line, ... and probably afterwards joins some spur of the Cumberland Mountains.

"Towards the south, it extends to the Duck River Ridge, which lies in the southern part of Dickson County; and also in the southern part of Williamson, and in the southern part of Rutherford, and through a part of Warren; and terminates west of Collin's River, near to a spur on the east side, which connects with the main mountain nearly west from Pikeville. . . . . .

"The country between the highlands and transverse ridges, of which there are others more to the south, ... as far as the Muscle Shoals, are the rich lands of West [Middle] Tennessee; the surface of which is everywhere covered with great numbers of limestone rocks. . . . .

That billows once rolled over this large plain, is too evident to admit of denial.* . . . . .

"The western ridge, before described, it is probable, was opposed, for some time after the recession of the waters below, to the passage of the Cumberland River and its tributaries, which were probably elongated after the waters withdrew. This opposition probably continued till the waters of *the lake*, made by the supplies of the Cumberland, rose high enough to find the lowest part of the ridge, and proceeded through that passage, continually widening, and sinking deeper, as the waters rushed over it, and carried off the constituent particles of the ridge, from the bottom and sides of the opening. The level of the water in the lake lowered in proportion, till coming to the falls, as we now see them, near the mouth of Big Harpeth and Sycamore Creek, the whole lake was finally carried off . . . .

"Similar remarks to those above made, apply to *the great lake*, once formed between the Duck River Ridge, on the one side, and the Cumberland Mountain on the other; extending as far as the Muscle Shoals, and connected by a transverse ridge, which served to dam up the waters, till a passage was made by the workings of the Tennessee, and the whole lake was carried off."

247. *Elevation above the sea; Depth.*—For reasons that have been stated, (§ 220,) the elevations of characteristic points within the Basin, have already been given.†

The margin of the Rim around the Basin—that is to say, the high edge of the Basin—has, with the exception of a small part to the northwest, a general elevation of more than 1000 feet; and the average of the part excepted, is but little less than 900. (§§ 221 and 222.)

248. From the margin, the steep slopes fall at once from 250 to 350 feet. (§ 230.) At some points, however, especially in Cannon and DeKalb Counties, the descent is greater. At Snow's Hill, the point where the Lebanon and Sparta Turnpike leaves the Basin and ascends to the top of the Rim, or Highlands, the fall is very nearly 500 feet. The average depth of the bottom of the Basin below its margin, is, perhaps, between 300 and 400 feet. The greatest depression is along the bed of the Cumberland. (§ 243.)

*These "billows" were those of *the deluge*, as our author would have it. It was his opinion, that the whole continent was flooded, at the time of the Noachian deluge, by a rush of waters from the South, and that afterwards these waters receded. "They carried with them to the northern regions, the equatorial and tropical plants, animals, weeds and trees, depositing them as far as the fiftieth degree of north latitude, where their remains are now every day found."

† See the tables on pages 87 to 92 inclusive. The *Italics* distinguish the points within the Basin.

249. *Climate.*—The climatological data, obtained at Nashville and Lebanon, that have been given in the first chapter, and the remarks founded thereon, apply, especially, to this division, as these places are within its limits. To these data and remarks the reader is referred.

I will add, however, that the summer of the Central Basin—the mean temperature of which may be placed at 76°.5, or 77°, (p. 15,) for the middle part, but ranging from about 75°.5 to 77°.5, in passing from the northern to the southern portions—is the same as that of Northern Georgia, and middle part of South Carolina.

The other seasons, however, are colder, than in the regions mentioned. A good portion of the Basin, as we shall see hereafter, is included in the cotton region.

VI.—The Western Valley of the Tennessee River, or the Western Valley.

250. *General Character.*—The Tennessee River, in its reflex course northward, from Alabama to Kentucky, flows through a comparatively narrow valley, remarkable for its broken and varied surface.

This area has, at many points, both in its main part and in its minor tributary valleys, tracts of excellent, alluvial, and valuable limestone land. Numerous landings, or shipping-points, are found within it along the river, which command, to a great extent, the trade, not only of the valley, but of several adjacent counties. Among many articles of export that might be mentioned, a special one is pig-iron, the product of numerous furnaces, some of which are within its limits.

251. The valley has, therefore, considerable agricultural and commercial importance. Nevertheless, in general, its bottoms are mostly narrow, and its surface rocky, abounding in "glades," and gravelly knobs and ridges. It has a much more limited agricultural value than we would look for in the valley of so large and beautiful a stream as the Tennessee.

In some of its geological features, as we will see hereafter, it is both unique and interesting.

252. *Geographical Relations and Limits; Area.*—This di-

vision separates the flat Highlands, or the western side of the Rim of Middle Tennessee from the elevated plain, or slope, of West Tennessee, next to be described. (Page 11.) The highlands, on both sides of the valley, are fringed by numerous spurs, many of which, run within two or three miles of the river, and some of them quite to it.

253. Between these spurs, the main valley sends out numerous ramifications—the narrow valleys of the tributaries of the Tennessee—many of which run back from ten to fifteen miles, and a few twenty, or twenty-five, before they terminate. Near their heads, many of them, those especially on the eastern side, branch off in closely hemmed gorges, which often terminate in cascades. In this, as well as in other respects, they are like the ramifications of the Central Basin. (§ 234.) The cascades, however, are, in general, by no means as prominent and interesting as those of the division referred to.

254. The creek-valleys of Hardin and Wayne Counties—for example, those of Indian and Hardin's Creeks—are among the longest ramifications. These valleys are serpentine and narrow, averaging, perhaps, not more than a mile in width, but at many points, very fertile. The land within them is generally occupied, and in a good state of cultivation. The spurs separating them are high, flat-topped arms of the Highlands. Such, in fact, are most of the spurs running into the Western Valley, especially on its eastern side.

255. Buffalo River presents, in Wayne and Perry Counties, a valley much like those just mentioned. This, with the lower part of the valley of Duck River, may be regarded as a ramification of this division, or perhaps, better alone, as a deep cut within the limits of the Highland Rim. It is separated from the Tennessee River by a long, well-defined arm of the Highlands. (See Map.)

256. The valley of the Big Sandy is a ramification of some importance. It will be convenient to refer the part northeast of Carroll County only to this division.

257. The Western Valley, as understood here, does not include the entire area drained by all the tributaries of the Tennessee, in this part of the State. Its *general* limits are the lines along which the highlands, on both sides, for the most part, break away. As thus limited, it has perhaps, an average width of not more than ten or eleven miles. Its area may be placed approximately, at 1,200 square miles—a small portion of the State.

The following parts of counties are included in the valley proper: the middle part of Hardin, the northeastern corner of Wayne, the western parts of Perry, Humphreys, and Stewart, and, finally, the eastern parts of Decatur, Benton, and Henry.

258. *Elevation above Tide-water; Slope and Depth.*—The high-water level of the Tennessee, may be taken as the bottom of this valley. This, at Hamburg, (page 91,) is 392 feet above the sea, and, at the point where the Nashville and Northwestern Railroad crosses the river, it is 357. (Page 92.)

The difference between these elevations—thirty-five feet—indicates the rate at which the valley slopes. According to this, it is a little more than one-third of a foot (0.38) per mile, by the river. It is to be noted, that the slope is towards the north, and in a direction nearly opposite to that in which the Mississippi River descends.

259. The depth of the valley, below the highlands that bound it on the east, may be taken in general, at about 500 feet. It ranges, however, from 400 to 600. The general depth, regarded from the highlands, on the west, is less. What it is, I am not able, for want of proper data, to state, with confidence. It cannot be, however, very far from 350, or 400 feet. At some points, these highlands are bold and high, and nearly equal in elevation, *apparently*, to those on the western side. (§ 3.)

The elevations of certain points, that properly pertain to this valley and its ramifications, have already been given.* It may be added, that the level of low-water in the Tennessee, is about forty feet below that of high-water. At its highest stages, the river overflows large areas of its bottoms.

260. "*Glades;*" *Artesian Wells.*—The *glades* of the Western Valley, like the "Cedar Glades" of the Central Basin, (§ 240,) constitute a characteristic feature. These are gravelly, and marly places, mostly naked, but presenting here and there patches of bushes, or shrubby cedars. They are sometimes several acres in extent, and occur usually upon hill-sides, but often entirely cover isolated and low knobs. The counties of Decatur, Perry, Hardin and Wayne, abound in them. They may be found, also, in the other counties of the valley.

261. These glades result from the disintegration of gray, and

* See the tables on pages 91 and 92. The points referred to are indicated thus (*).

sometimes reddish marly limestones, which contain, occasionally, interstratified, thin cherty layers. Their surfaces are made up of the debris from these rocks, and consist of marly matter, mixed with angular, calcareous, and flinty gravel. It is common for those upon hill-sides to present, at intervals, ledges of rock, forming two or three successive, more or less perfect, terraces. Fossil shells, crinoids, corals, and sponges, from the limestones, are found in comparative abundance, mixed with the debris, and have made this region of glades classic ground to palæontologists. Thousands of these fossils, have been collected by our foreign scientific friends, and carried to Europe, to say nothing of the numbers that have found their way into the cabinets of American Geologists, outside of Tennessee. Dr. G. Troost, my venerable predecessor, delighted in roaming over these glades, collecting, and studying its fossil treasures.

262. The glades under consideration, differ from those of the Central Basin in being, for the most part, destitute of trees, and in the marly character of the debris forming them. The glades of the Basin, are remarkable for the fine, large cedar trees, that grow in the crevices of the rocks. Their surfaces, too, are made up of hard, thin-bedded (sometimes thick-bedded) limestones, more or less broken into blocks, or course gravel, often mixed with soil, but with no marl.

263. It may be well to notice here, a third class of glades, belonging in common, to this and the succeeding division. These are found in Hardin, McNairy, and Henderson Counties, and are known as the "*bald hills,*" or "*bald places.*" They have long attracted attention, mostly on account of the great numbers of oyster-like shells, that are found strewed over their surfaces. Like the marly limestone glades, they are often destitute of vegetation, with the exception of occasional thickets.

264. These glades are not associated with any solid rocks, but result from the weathering of a peculiar formation, called "*green sand,*" and by some "*marl,*" that will be described hereafter. A meagre growth of grass, sometimes covers them. Where not relieved by this, they have a grayish, or ashen aspect.

The shells are always conspicuous, and many of them very large, and heavy, weighing sometimes, three or four pounds.

They all belong to extinct species. At some points, they have been collected by cart-loads, and burned into lime, a good quality of which they furnish.

Haywood, in his History, (§ 244,) did not fail to notice these shells. He says: "The country on the south side of the Tennessee, near where that river crosses the southern boundary line of this State, and for many miles to the northwest and south, is quite uneven, and exhibits the appearance of the ocean when agitated by a storm. To the south, in many places, are to be found immense banks of oyster-shells, some of which are petrified. And in many places, oyster-shells are to be found upon the surface of the earth. These shells are much larger than any live oyster now to be taken."

Upon another page, under the head of *Marine Apearances on the Surface*, he adds: "Between the Tennessee and Mississippi Rivers, is a ridge of oyster-shells, running in a northwardly and southwardly direction, and extending as far northwardly as the head-waters of the Forked Deer River, thirty or forty miles north of the southern boundary of the State of Tennessee. . . . . How much further north the bank extends, at present, is unknown to the writer. The ridge, or bank, is above the head of the rivers which run into the Tennessee, on the one side, and into the Mississippi, on the other."

265. The Artesian wells of this disvision, are worthy of notice. And, first, two such wells exist west of the Tennessee, but near enough to be overflowed by the back-water of the river, when at its highest stage. One of these is in the northern part of Hardin County, half-a-mile north of White Oak River, and about a mile and-a-half west of the Tennessee. The other is in the northern part of the State, in the bottom of the Big Sandy, and nine or ten miles from its mouth.

266. These wells were originally bored for salt-water. Both run down several hundred feet, but to what exact distance, I am not informed. From both of these borings, large streams of *sulphur-water* now flow out with considerable force. The amount of water discharged from the Big Sandy well, is greater than that from the other. The water of both is used, to some extent, by invalids.

267. It may be well to add, that numerous springs in this valley, in addition to the wells mentioned, furnish sulphur-water. A few have had improvements attached to them, and they have become the sites of pleasant watering-places, or summer retreats. Such are the "Hardin County Springs," two distinct, but neighboring establishments, situated near the Tennessee River, on its western side, and but little north of the Mississippi line. The more northern is known as the "White Sulphur;" the other as the "Red Sulphur."

268. "Bath Springs," in the southern part of Decatur, is another point well known for its sulphur-water. This place is about seven miles north-West of Clifton, on the road leading to Lexington and Jackson.

269. In the second place, we have, in this division, or rather in a region common to this and the succeeding division, many artesian wells, different in character from those mentioned. These are met with in McNairy, Henderson, and Hardin Counties. Wells of the same kind occur, too, south of the Tennessee line, in Mississippi. They have been bored through the formation ("green sand" that forms upon its out-cropping surface, the "bald hills" of which I have spoken, §§ 263, and 264,) for the purpose of obtaining good water, for domestic use. The depth of these wells, in Tennessee, varies from fifty to three hundred and fifty feet. The water rises in them to within a few feet of the top, rarely running over. For this reason, they may be said to be semi-artesian.

270. Ordinary wells, sunk in the green-sand, furnish, at many points, an impure water, too disagreeable to be used. By boring, however, entirely through this formation, water of good quality is obtained. In boring, a large auger, with a blade, or bit, five or six inches in diameter, is driven down through the mass until, finally, perforating a hard, gritty layer at the base of the latter, it reaches suddenly a bed of white, or gray quick-sand. As soon as this is done, the water rises. The perforation thus made, excepting a few feet at the top, needs no protection, the green-sand being compact enough to furnish a permanent wall.

The construction of buckets used in these wells, is peculiar. They are, in fact, mere tubes, made of tin, or wood, adapted to the bore of the well, being often three or four feet in length, and but a few inches in diameter. The closed end, or bottom, is provided with a valve, which opens upward, and admits the water freely as the bucket sinks, but closes, and retains it as the latter rises.

The success attending the boring of these wells, has, at some points in the green-sand regions, nearly, or quite doubled the price of land.

The general method of boring is much like that spoken of and illustrated in "Wailes' Agriculture and Geology of Mississippi,"* page 265.

271. *Climate.*—No climatological observations, so far as the writer knows, have been made within this division. Owing to its less elevation, it is, doubtless, to a small extent, warmer,

* Report on the Agriculture and Geology of Mississippi, embracing a Sketch of the Social and Natural History of the State; by B. L. C. Wailes, Geologist of Mississippi 1854.

especially in summer, than the Central Basin. In the main, however, its features of climate must be much like those of the division just mentioned.

VII.—The Plateau, or Slope, of West Tennessee.

272. This division, including all the uplands in West Tennessee, is one of the leading natural divisions of the State. In many of its physical features it is very different from the divisions we have considered. Here very few, or no regular strata of *hard rocks*, that is to say, of limestone, slate and sandstone,* like those we have in Middle Tennessee, are to be found. These disappear within the valley we have just left, and mostly in a great beveled slope facing the west. In their places, we find principally, great beds of sands associated, more or less, with clays and loams. (§ 207.)

273. The latter beds, along their eastern margin, abut against the hard rocks, or rather, like these, present a beveled slope—the counterpart of the one mentioned—that faces the east, and overlaps the former along its lower edge. It is between these slopes that the Western Valley of the Tennessee River, for the most part, lies.

274. The special geological character of this division gives to it a surface and an agricultural aspect very different from what is found elsewhere in the State. In entering it from the east, the traveler finds himself at once in a new country. The soil, at many points, is excellent; at others, thin and unproductive; generally it is mellow and good, susceptible either of the highest state of cultivation, or, in the hands of a careless farmer, on account of its very mellowness, of being soon made waste and worthless.

The entire area is to be regarded as a great plain or plateau, veined with peculiar river valleys, and sloping to the west. It might, in a more general point of view, be regarded as a part of the greater plateau lying in Kentucky, Tennessee, and Northern Mississippi; between the Valley of the Tennessee River on the one hand, and the bottoms of the Mississippi on the other.

* There are a few layers of limestone and sandstone occurring with the sands and clays of this division, but they are of very limited extent, and have only a local interest. In a general view, they are of no consequence. They will be specially noticed hereafter.

275. *Limits; the Eastern "Ridge," and the Mississippi Bluff.*—To speak more in detail, the plateau or slope, under consideration, includes and commences with the fringed edge of the highlands overlooking and limiting on the west, the valley last described. (§ 252.) Thence, more or less furrowed with river valleys, it extends to the west for an average distance of about 84 miles, when it abruptly terminates, falling off in the long and steep escarpment or *line of "bluffs,"* that overlook the great alluvial low plain, or the "*bottoms*" of the Mississippi.

276. The eastern limit is nearly coincident with the ridge dividing the waters of the Tennessee River from those flowing into the Mississippi. This ridge is the line along which the eastern side of the plateau begins to break up into fringing spurs. Running through the counties of Henry, Carroll, Henderson, and the eastern part of McNairy, it lies comparatively close, and parallel to the Tennessee, and thus throws the great body of the uplands in West Tennessee, on the Mississippi side of the water-shed. It is, therefore, nearly the eastern margin of the plateau. The division, however, extends eastward beyond this line, including the broken highlands, until the latter, for the most part, sink away and give place to the Valley of the Tennessee. The name *slope* or *Mississippi slope,* as well as plateau, may be given properly to this division, since the pre-eminently greater part forms a plain inclined toward the Mississippi.

277. The highlands that constitute the ridge just mentioned, and the eastern margin of the plateau, are, at many points, high and rough. They have already been spoken of with reference to their height, as compared with that of the general plain to which the surface of the State, as a whole, has been referred. (§ 3.) Their elevation above the Tennessee Valley has been estimated, in general, at from 350 to 400 feet, at some points being apparently considerably higher. (§ 259.)

278. In the middle and northern parts of McNairy County, and through Henderson, the ridges are high and bold, presenting many wild and picturesque regions. In the southern part of McNairy, along the line dividing the waters of the Tennessee from those flowing to the west, the ridges are more broken.

What Judge Haywood thought of this region—it being included in the "country" of which he speaks—may be seen in the quotation made on a previous page. (§ 264.)

279. The western escarpment of the plateau, or the line of "bluffs" in which it terminates, deserves especial notice. This constitutes a striking feature in the topography of the western part of the State. The escarpment, like the plateau, is cut by the river valleys into sections, but the sections run lengthwise nearly in the same line, and for present purposes, may be regarded as continuous. The whole line may be called the *Mississippi Bluff.* From its base the bottoms of the Mississippi extend to the west, while from its summit, the flat uplands extend eastward. Its steep face is greatly in contrast with the bottoms, one of the principal circumstances that give it interest.

280. Coming out of the State of Mississippi, the Bluff runs in a nearly direct course from Memphis through Tennessee, to and beyond Hickman, in Kentucky.

Within the limits of Tennessee, the Mississippi River now washes its base at four different points; one of which, however, in low water, is deserted and left inland. The highlands at these points, being conspicuous objects from the river, and relieving the continued sameness of its low banks, are familiar landmarks to boatmen, and have been called by them the "Chickasaw Bluffs." The first is at Fulton; the second, at Randolph; the third—no longer seen from the navigable channels—at "Old River," in the lower part of Tipton; the fourth, and last, is at Memphis—and hence the appropriate appellation of the "Bluff City."

281. The Bluff rises, at different points, from 50 to 180 feet above the bottoms. The average elevation is perhaps about 130 feet. Some of the highest points command extensive views of the wild, heavily timbered plains below. A view of this kind (the forests not concealing the Mississippi) is most beautiful. The writer has gazed upon this wild flat world, and its rolling, moving sea, with wonder and delight.

282. The view from the Bluff at Randolph, looking down the river, is among the best. It is not as wild as some, much of the bottom within sight being in cultivation. The presentation of the face of the Bluff and

of the river is, however, very fine. The portion of the Bluff at Memphis, as seen from the river, especially when low, is bold and interesting, but not so much so as that at Randolph, where the height of the Bluff is greater.

283. From the southern part of Kentucky, down at least half-way through Tennessee, the Bluff and the western margin of the plateau has been much cracked or fissured, by the well known earthquakes of 1811–12. At many points in Obion and Dyer counties, the Bluff has been greatly shattered. The traveler, in passing along its summit, frequently meets with "earth-cracks," or groups of these often several hundred yards long, and occasionally, traceable for half-a-mile or even a mile. The cracks or fissures, vary in width from two or three to twenty feet. Many of them originally were deep, but are now more or less filled up, and, in some cases, look like artificial canal beds, with a depth varying from three to fifteen feet. This is especially the case where the earth has sunk between two parallel fissures. Sunken belts of this kind, a hundred feet wide, are sometimes seen. The fissures often occur in complicated groups, the individual members of each group extending in the same general direction, and, in any given cross section, from two or three to fifty and more feet apart, but when followed out, separating in branches, and curiously interlocking with each other. The belts of earth between the fissures are often inclined at considerable and various angles to the general surface.

At many points within the region that has been thus disturbed, sand, fine gravel, and fragments of lignite ("coal") were "blown up" through the fissures, and are now found in little ridges or hillocks. The fine white sand of these hillocks is now sought for, at some points, for building purposes.

284. *Area and General Surface ; Rivers.*—The area of the entire division is approximately 8850 square miles, considerably more than one-fifth of the State. The counties and parts of counties included within its limits, are as follows: all of Weakley, Gibson, Carroll, Haywood, Madison, Henderson, Fayette and Hardeman; much the greater parts of Henry, McNairy, Shelby, Tipton and Lauderdale; and finally, large parts of Decatur, Benton, Dyer and Obion.

285. The parts of Henry, Benton, Decatur and McNairy, not included, are within the Western Tennessee Valley, (§ 257;) and the parts of Obion Dyer, Lauderdale, Tipton and Shelby, not in this division, pertain to the Mississippi bottoms.

286. The character of the eastern margin of the plateau has already been spoken of. (§§ 276 and 277.) Passing westward from the ridge, the surface, in general, becomes less broken, and soon presents, between the river valleys, extensive level

and gently rolling areas, the soil of which is, for the most part, mellow and fertile. Thus it continues many miles to the west.

287. Within twenty or twenty-five miles of the Bluff, however, although the division, as a plateau, extends on uniformly much the same, a different geological formation, and, to some extent a different soil, are met with. These are confined to the western side of the Plateau. They form a belt contiguous to the Bluff that runs through the State. The superior formation of this portion of the Plateau, is a great bed of light-yellowish ashen earth, or a fine silicious loam, furnishing a strong and fertile soil. It may not be too much to assert, that Obion and Dyer, the uplands of which belong to this belt, are naturally the richest counties in the State. Here, at any rate, may be seen a growth of great poplars, walnuts, beeches, white-oaks, &c., unsurpassed, I am sure, by any thing elsewhere in Tennessee. The heavy timber has, to a considerable extent, retarded the settling of these lands.

288. So far as the soil, (including subsoil,) and surface-formation—that is to say, the formation or stratified bed next below the soil—are concerned, the belt just referred to is a well-marked, and the most important subdivision of the Plateau. Other less extensive subdivisions might have been mentioned. These are presented in the "green-sand" regions of McNairy and Henderson counties, (§§ 263–4,) and in the marly and clayey districts or belts of Hardeman, Madison, Carroll and Henry. All these will be particularly spoken of hereafter.

Excepting the subdivisions above, and the immediate river-valleys, or bottoms, the Plateau every-where presents much the same soil and geological character. The former is seen in the railroad cuts, in the freshly washed banks of streams, and wherever penetrated, to rest upon beds of orange and yellow sands, often brightly colored, and containing occasionally local beds of clay.

289. The entire division, as a plateau, is comparatively simple in its general features. Its form is nearly rhombic. The river-valleys cut it into subordinate sections, but these, as such, are of little importance.

290. The rivers are ,in some respects, peculiar. Nearly all of them pursue a northwesterly course,* until they intersect or nearly reach the Bluff—that is to say, the western escarpment

* See page 5, where the direction of the rivers is spoken of in connection with the great Slope, of which the State is a part.

of the Plateau,(§ 289,)—when they turn in the bottoms of the Mississippi, to the southwest. They are long and sluggish, and have wide flat bottoms, filled with heavy timber. The Bald Cypress, (*Taxodium distichum,*) with its curious *knees*, is very common. The immediate valleys are generally from 100 to 200 feet deep, averaging however, nearly 200. The bottoms generally lie upon both sides of the streams. To render roads across them passable at all times, it has been found necessary, generally, to throw up "levees," or embankments, upon which the road may run. These levees are sometimes from one to two miles long.

291. *Elevation above the Sea.*—The tables following, present such special data, bearing upon the elevation of this division, as I have in my possssion. The materials are not as complete as desirable. In reference to the eastern and higher portion of the Plateau they are especially deficient.

(1.) The first table presents the heights, in feet, of the stations of the Memphis and Charleston Railroad, above Mobile Bay. It has been taken from the "Seventh Annual Report of the Directors" (1857) of this road. The entire series has been copied, although but a portion is in Tennessee. The stations from Chawalla to Memphis, inclusive, pertain to the division under consideration. At Grand Junction and La Grange, the road is fairly upon the Plateau. The distances are reckoned from Memphis. The elevations of high and low water at Memphis are added:

Stevenson	Ala.	271.0	miles	602.80
Bellefonte	"	259.0	"	639.19
Scott's Mills	"	254.0	"	651.84
Larkin's	"	247.7	"	620.45
Woodville	"	237.3	"	600.68
Paint Rock	"	232.9	"	595.68
Brownsboro'	"	223.3	"	630.76
HUNTSVILLE	"	211.6	"	612.14
Madison	"	202.5	"	573.13
Moore's	"	192.5	"	601.32
Decatur	"	188.0	"	572.89
Trinity	"	182.0	"	633.61
Hillsboro'	"	176.5	"	598.61
Courtland	"	168.5	"	560.21
Jonesboro'	"	163.0	"	560.41
Leighton	"	155.5	"	562.71
Tuscumbia	"	145.0	"	468.25
Barton	"	133.3	"	497.79
Dickson	"	126.6	"	487.71

Iuka	Miss.	114.8	"	554.85
Burns	"	107.3	"	463.10
Glendale	"	99.0	"	494.61
Corinth	"	92.8	"	434.12
Chawalla	Tenn.	83.7	"	408.61
Pocahontas	"	74.4	"	394.31
Middleton	"	69.3	"	407.13
Saulsbury	"	57.6	"	535.51
Grand Junction	"	52.0	"	574.91
La Grange	"	49.0	"	530.74
Moscow	"	39.0	"	351.74
Lafayette	"	30.9	"	315.54
Collierville	"	23.8	"	378.54
Germantown	"	14.5	"	377.89
Buntyn	"	5.5	"	303.54
MEMPHIS	"	0.0	"	245.44
High water of the Mississippi at Memphis				220.44
Low water " " "				170.44 ?

(2.) The following elevations have been determined by the experimental surveys of the engineers of the Mobile and Ohio Railroad. They are copied from the Report of the "Proceedings of the Second Annual Meeting of Stockholders," 1850. The elevations are in feet above "low tide at Mobile :"

Snake Creek Summit, N. E. of Purdy	542	Grade,	583	Surface
Huggins' Creek Summit, N. W. "	505.5	"	520.5	"
Jackson Summit, between South and Middle Forks of Forked Deer River	487.5	"	499.5	"
Middle Fork of Forked Deer	337	"	332	"
Cane Creek Summit, between Middle and North Forks of Forked Deer	390.5	"	400.5	"
North Fork of Forked Deer	304	"	310	"
Four-mile Summit, between Obion River and North Fork of Forked Deer	375.5	"	402.5	"
Obion River	287	"	282	"
State line Summit, Tenn. and Ky	427	"	447	"

Mississippi River, at mouth of the Ohio, low water	276.5
" " " " high water	320
" " at Columbus low water	269.5
" " " high water	308.5

(3.) The table following includes the elevations above Mobile Bay of a number of points on "The Mississippi Central and Tennessee Railroad." They were made out from data kindly furnished me by Mr. E. Laas, an engineer upon this road.

Wolf River, Mississippi	394
Mississippi and Tennessee Line	465

Grand Junction	574.91
Middleburg	537
Bolivar	430
Hatchee River	332
Medon	420
"Divide," between Forked Deer and Hatchee rivers	520
South Fork of Forked Deer	335
Jackson	459

In addition, it may be mentioned that the Bluff at Memphis, in front of the Gayoso Hotel, for example, has an elevation of about 100 feet above low water of the Mississippi, or 270 feet above Mobile Bay. At Randolph it is about 185 feet above low water of the Mississippi, and 378 above Mobile Bay, estimating low water at the river here at 193 feet above the latter level.

(4.) In 1839, by order of the General Assembly of the State, C. W. Nance, Esq., of Nashville, surveyed "a route for a Canal from the Tennessee to Hatchee River."* The lowest point of the ridge dividing the waters of the two rivers, was determined by this survey. It is in the southern part of McNairy County, between the head waters of Lick and Muddy creeks, the latter a tributary of Cypress. The route selected commences about two miles above Hamburg, on the Tennessee River, passes over the point mentioned, and terminates on the Hatchee, and at its junction with the Tuscumbia. The level of low water in the Hatchee, at the end of the line, proved to be the same as that of low water in the Tennessee at the beginning. The summit, or the low point of the ridge, was found to be 166 feet above this level. At the point of beginning, which is at the head of "Big Bend Shoals," the low water mark is about 354 feet above Mobile Bay, giving the summit an elevation above the same base, of 520 feet.

According to the levels and estimates of Mr. Nance, "the summit of the ridge at Purdy is 60 feet higher," or 580 feet above Mobile Bay.

292. From the data presented, we may assume that the elevation of the plateau, or of its top-surface, is, in the southeastern part of the division, between 500 and 600 feet above the sea, and that, in the central and northern part, from Jackson, northward, along the Mobile and Ohio Railroad, it becomes less, ranging from 400 to 500 feet. It also appears that, in going toward Memphis the elevation is reduced to a level considerably below 400.†

* "Report upon the Survey of the Route for the Tennessee and Hatchee Canal; by C. W. Nance, Civil Engineer. Nashville, 1840."

† It must be recollected that the data furnished by railroad lines are frequently not altogether characteristic of the general elevation of the country through which the roads pass. These lines often run from one valley over a "summit" into another.

293. The Bluff doubtless has a mean elevation of about 400 feet. In the vicinity of Memphis, its height above the sea, as well as above the river, for a well-marked portion, is less than usual. At Randolph it has nearly an average height above the Mississippi; but as we go northward, from this point, its height, with reference to the level of the sea, becomes greater, conforming in general, to the rise of the bed and bottoms of the river.

294. As to the elevation of the highlands along the eastern side of the Plateau in McNairy, Henderson and Carroll, it may be added to what has been said, (§§ 276–8,) that here the division has its highest part The tops of the most elevated ridges can hardly be less than 700 feet above the sea, and some of them, perhaps, not less than 800. Snake Creek Summit, a point on one of the experimental lines of the Mobile and Ohio Railroad, and referable to this range of highlands, has an elevation of 583 feet. [Page 115, (2).] Having been selected as a suitable point for the passage of a railroad line, it is probably lower than other points in the same vicinity.

295. *Climate.*—The principal climatal features of this division, like those of the East Tennessee Valley and the Central Basin, are presented in the general and comparative view of the climate of the State already given. (§§ 30, 31, etc.) To this, the reader is referred. It may be well to remark, that of all the leading natural divisions, this, doubtless, has the highest yearly and summer temperatures. The differences amount, at the most, to a few degrees only, nevertheless, they are sufficient to lengthen the growing season, and so to modify the climate, as to throw a large part of the division into the cotton producing region.

The heights of the summits, or of the points most elevated, are in a district having a general plateau character, most characteristic of its elevation, and even these are often too low.

VIII.—The Mississippi Bottoms, or Bottom.

296. We have now reached in our course westward, the last natural division of the State. Entering this, we leave behind all the uplands of Tennessee, and find ourselves upon a low and great alluvial plain, which, at many points, is below high-water level of the Mississippi. The division is well characterized. It embraces all the bottom-lands of the Mississippi within Tennessee. It differs much, in its general features, from any other large section of the State. The bottoms of the Tennessee River in the Western Valley, and of the rivers within the division just described, present features to some extent similar, but they are comparatively on a small scale, and imperfectly foreshadow what is found here.

297. Much of the area to be considered is covered with swamps and lakes; much, too, is wild and dark with heavy forests, even yet the retreat of deer and other wild animals. Other portions, confined for the most part, to a belt bordering the river, are in a good state of cultivation. The undeveloped agricultural resources of the division, as a whole, are great, and, in proportion to its area, may make it some day, when its lands shall have been reclaimed, the wealthiest part of the State.

298. *General Relations; The Great Valley-Plain of the Mississippi.*—This division is the Tennessee portion of the great alluvial plain lying within the immediate valley of the Mississippi.

This magnificent valley-plain (or bottom-valley) is altogether, including the delta of the river, which is but the extension of the plain into the Gulf of Mexico, about 600 miles long. Mr. G. W. R Bayley, a Civil Engineer of Louisiana, thus defines its limits:

"The head, or the alluvial plain, or delta, of the Mississippi, may be assumed as occurring where rock *in situ* forms both shores, or at a point some thirty miles above the mouth of the Ohio, known as 'The Chains.' The entire alluvion, extending thence to the sea, comprises an area of about 40,000 square miles, and presents a front upon the Gulf of Mexico of 260 miles, 85 miles north, and 175 miles west of the river's mouth." (*The Mississippian.*)

Sir Charles Lyell, who has devoted much time to the study of the "valley-plain" and delta of the Mississippi, says of the former:

"It is very variable in width from east to west, being near its northern extremity, or at the mouth of the Ohio, 50 miles wide, at Memphis, 30, at the mouth of White River, 80, and contracting again further south, as at Grand Gulf, to 33 miles." (*Lyell's Second Visit to the United States.*)

299. Taking high-water level as that of the great plain, the latter attains, at the mouth of the Ohio, an elevation of 320 feet above the Gulf.* Considering the distance, the slope seaward is, therefore, very gradual.

300. The valley-plain proper is bounded on the east and west respectively, by two ranges of highlands, approximately parallel, and rising from 50 to 200 feet above the plain. These highlands generally present steep slopes, or faces toward the plain, but preserve, for the most part, their elevation in the opposite direction, extending off as table-lands. The eastern range, called in general the *Mississippi Bluff*, has already been referred to, mostly with reference to the part occurring in Tennessee. (§§ 279 and 280.)

301. The section of the plain, lying between the parallels of latitude that bound West Tennessee on the north and south respectively, the part also, with which we at present are most interested, is limited on the East by the Bluff, as stated, and on the west, in Arkansas, by Crowley's Ridge.† This ridge forms "the divide between the waters of the St. Francis and White rivers." It is the counterpart of the Bluff in Tennessee, and a portion of the western range of highlands bounding the great valley-plain.

The plain between these limits has, at Memphis, as already mentioned, a width of 30 miles. On the parallel of the northern boundary of West Tennessee it is wider, being here 45 miles across.

*According to the elevation of high water at Cairo, determined by the surveys of the Mobile and Ohio Railroad, see page 116.

†See First and Second Reports of a Geological Reconnoisance of Arkansas, made during the years 1857, '58, '59 and '60; by David Dale Owen. First Report, page 19, and second Report, p. 413.

302. Through this area, the Mississippi winds in its tortuous course. The general direction of the river is now such as to throw the greater part of the plain into Arkansas. Toward the south the river hugs the Tennessee highlands, striking them at several points, and forming the Chickasaw Bluffs already mentioned. (§ 280.)

303. The section of valley-plain designated, like all of its portions, abounds in bayous, lakes, and heavily timbered swamps. Some of the lakes are crescent-shaped, and are manifestly old river-bends. The Mississippi has probably, during past ages, occupied successively all parts of the area. At one day it may have washed the base, or portions of the base, of Crowley's Ridge.

304. The valley-plain, as a whole, is itself of great antiquity. It has apparently, however, been washed out of another more ancient and extensive alluvial plain, the remains of which are seen, at a higher elevation, in the slopes and cliffs of the highlands on each side, (as for example, in the bluffs of Tennessee, and in the slopes of Crowley's Ridge, in Arkansas.) These highlands have a corresponding elevation. They present, too, along their opposing faces, the same vertical succession of formations. The strata of loam, gravel, sand and clay, whose edges now crop out upon their slopes, once extended across from side to side in continuous layers, forming the more ancient and higher plain. It has been the work of the river to carve out of this greater plain its great valley of "bottoms." The eastern Bluff and the western Ridge are, at this day, the limits of its lateral movements, and remain, moreover, as monuments of the great changes that have occurred.*

305. It is the opinion of Sir Charles Lyell, that an extensive region, including the valley-plain of the Mississippi, has been subjected to a great oscillation of level. This at first depressed the region, or rather the more inland portion of it, about 200 feet below its present level, and then restored it again to its former position. During the first part of this oscillation, and at the period of greatest depression, the materials of strata, the remnants of which are now seen in the bluffs and slopes of the highlands, were deposited during overflows, very much as

* See section of the Bluff and of the valley plain in the Second Part of this Report.

alluvial matter is now. But when the movement was reversed and the region was slowly upraised, the river carved out its valley "through the horizontal and unconsolidated strata as they rose, sweeping away the greater portion of them, and leaving mere fragments, in the shape of terraces, skirting" the newly-formed alluvial plain, "as monuments" of the changes in level.*

According to this view, the water of the river, at the period of greatest depression, covered during overflows, a much greater area than that now occupied by the valley-plain.

306. *Area; Reelfoot Lake.*—The portion of the great valley-plain within the limits of Tennessee, constituting the division we are considering, has an area approximately of 900 square miles. It is, therefore, the smallest of the eight natural divisions into which the State is divided. The greater part of this area is in the northern part of the State, the Mississippi inclining towards the highlands in the southern part. (§ 302.)

307. The western and large parts of Obion, Dyer and Lauderdale counties, lie within the bottoms, and therefore belong to this division. Small parts of Tipton and Shelby, more of the latter, however, than the former, are also included. To this western tier of counties the division is confined. The eastern and larger parts of all these counties consist, for the most part, of uplands, and are embraced within the limits of the West Tennessee Plateau. (§ 284.)

The river, by striking the highlands at the different Chickasaw Bluffs, cuts the division into several unequal sections, which, however, as such, are of little consequence.

308. The bayous and lakes of this division, and of the section of the valley-plain of which it is a part, have been referred to. (§§ 297 and 303.) One of the latter, Reelfoot Lake, in Obion County, deserves notice. This lake had no existence previously to the "Shakes" of 1811–12. Its origin appears to have been due to the filling up of the old channel of Reelfoot Creek during the convulsions of that period. This dammed up the water, that before ran without obstruction into the Mississippi, until it overflowed a large area, and formed the lake as we now find it.

The waste-water of the lake now escapes southward, into Obion River, with a fall, according to information given me by an intelligent citizen of

* Lyell's Second Visit to the United States, Vol. II, Chapter XXXIV, and Manual of Geology, 5th Edition, pp. 121 and 122.

Dyer County, of "at least forty feet." In its course it passes through several smaller lakes. The northern end of the lake projects a short distance into Kentucky. Its length is about eighteen miles. Its width varies from three-fourths of a mile to three miles.

309. When seen by the writer, a few years ago, there was much dead timber standing in the water around its shallow margin. This was cypress, ash, mulberry, beech, etc., but mostly cypress.

From different points of the Bluff, running, as it does, near the eastern side of the lake, (§ 280,) beautiful and extensive views of the wooded bottoms, and of the lake encircled by them, may be obtained. And when the latter is concealed by the forests, its outlines may often be distinctly traced out by the lines of dead cypress trunks and branches. The First Volume of the Report of the Kentucky Geological Survey (p. 117) favors us with a view of this lake, taken from a point in Tennessee.

The region of Reelfoot has, for many years, been a favorite resort for fishermen and hunters.

310. *The Earthquakes of* 1811–12.—I have before referred to some of the effects produced by these earthquakes. (§ 283.) As they were felt, to a greater or less extent throughout Tennessee, it may be well to add a few remarks with reference to them.

The region around New Madrid, on the Mississippi River, was the center of their most violent action. They were felt over a large area. Their effects in West Tennessee have been spoken of. (§ 283.) In Middle Tennessee they were sensible enough to cause considerable alarm. In South Carolina, too, they were observed. Humboldt, in his Cosmos, mentions these earthquakes as presenting one of the rare instances of tremblings felt almost every hour for months together, at a distance far from any volcano.

311. The violent earthquake that destroyed in March, 1812, the city of Caraccas, in South America, appears to have had some connection with the shocks felt at the same time in the Valley of the Mississippi. Lyell says: "It is possible that these two points are parts of one subterranean volcanic region." In Carraccas "the surface undulated like a boiling liquid, and terrific sounds were heard underground. The whole city, with its splendid churches, was, in an instant, a heap of ruins, under which 10,000 of the inhabitants were buried."

312. An account of the earthquakes of New Madrid may be found in Lyell's Principles of Geology, Chapter XXVIII, (8th Ed.) Judge Haywood also presents us with a description published in 1823, a portion of which, as his work (note 100,) is out of print, I here reproduce.

"The earthquakes of 1811 commenced on the 16th of December, half past two o'clock in the morning, and have been felt at intervals up to 1819, and as late as July, 1822. For two or three months the shocks were frequent, almost every day. Then they gradually decreased in frequency, and took place at longer intervals, which continued to lengthen until they finally ceased. In May, 1817, in Tennessee, they had come to be several months apart, and were but just perceptible.

"The next day but one, before the first earthquake, was darkened from morning to night by thick fog; and divers persons perceived a sulphureous scent. The wind ceased, and there was a dead calm, without the least breath of air, on the day of the earthquake. The like calm preceded all the shocks. A dull and heavy obscuration of the atmosphere also usually preceded them. The effluvia which caused the dimness of the day, seemed to be neither cloud nor smoke, yet resembling both. It was too light for clouds, and too thin for common smoke, and of a lighter cast. It seldom terminated in condensation, as Tennessee vapors usually do."

"In the time of the earthquakes, lights were seen in the night, sometimes westwardly, like the light of the sun before it is closed by the darkness of the night; but shooting much further toward the east, and continuing much longer than the light of the sun after setting. And sometimes in the night, the heavens would seem to be tinged with a reddish color, supposed to be the effect of invisible effluvia issuing through the pores of the earth, and collecting above us like smoke in the spring, which rises from log-heaps and brush-heaps, and shows itself like light at a distance."

"In the time of the earthquake, a murmuring noise, like that of fire disturbed by the blowing of a bellows, issued from the pores of the earth. A distant rumbling was heard, almost without intermission, and sometimes seemed to be in the air. Explosions, like the discharge of a cannon at a few miles distance, were heard; and at night flashes of lightning seemed sometimes to break from the earth."

"In some places west of the Mississippi, a troublesome warmth of the earth was perceptible to the naked feet."

"The motions of the earth were undulating. The parts agitated quivered like the flesh of a beef just killed. The motions in Tennessee progressed from west to east, and were sometimes, though seldom, perpendicular; resembling a house raised and suddenly let fall to the ground. When the shocks came on, the stones on the surface of the earth were agitated by a tremulous motion, like eggs in a frying-pan, altogether made a noise similar to that of the wheels of a wagon in a pebbly road. The ponds of water, where there was no wind, had a troubled surface the whole day preceding any great shock."

"The frightened horses ran snorting in the fields, the hogs squealed; the dogs barked; and the fowls descended from their roosts. In the time of the shocks, many persons experienced a nauseating sickness at the stomach, and a trembling of the knees."

"The first shocks, which were the most violent, had these effects. The water in the Mississippi near New Madrid, rose in a few minutes, twelve or fourteen feet, and then fell like a tide. Some lakes were elevated, and the bottom raised above the common surface of the earth in the neighborhood, and still remain so. The country near New Madrid was everywhere broken up in furrows six or eight feet wide, and as many deep."

"In many places in West Tennessee, old sulphur springs have commenced running again, which, some years before, were dried up. And in some places, new springs of sulphureous water broke out of the earth and still continue to run."

"The earth in the western parts of West Tennessee opened in several places, and white sand issued from the aperture. Near New Madrid hot water of a dark color and of a strong sulphureous smell, issued from the holes. Where the white sand was thrown up, it lay around the hole in a circular form. In some places, there issued from the earth something like wind from the tube of a bellows, passing through burning coal. In the Chickasaw country it cast up hillocks of white sand of the size of potatoe hills. These are all through the Chickasaw country."

"The agitations above exceeded those immediately upon the surface. On the west side of the Mississippi, trees were, in many places, split from the roots upward. In some instances the trees were broken off; the tops fell to the ground, and the trunks were left standing."

"Spouts of water, three or four inches in diameter, sprang from the Mississippi, and ascended to a great height. In some parts of the Mississippi the river was swallowed up, for some minutes, by the seeming descent of the water into some great opening of the earth at the bottom of the river. Boats with their crews were ingulfed, and never more heard of."

313. *Elevation above the Sea.*—The general surface of this division of the State, must coincide very nearly with the high water level of the Mississippi. (§ 299.) Referrred to this level, its elevation, on the northern boundary of the State, may be placed approximately, at 295 feet above the Gulf, and on the southern boundary below Memphis, at about 215, the fall in this distance being, therefore, 80 feet. The division presents a belt along the river, that has in general, an elevation a little greater than other portions.

314. *Climate.*—It would be interesting to know the peculiarities of climate that belong to this division. Its low elevation, the presence of the great river, numerous bayous, swamps and lakes, with their vapors and fogs, must give rise to peculiar features, not a little in contrast with those of the plateau to the east. In the absence of the proper data, however, nothing that is very satisfactory can be given. So far as temperature is concerned, this division is, doubtless, the warmest region in the State.

PART SECOND.

GEOLOGICAL STRUCTURE AND FORMATIONS

OF TENNESSEE.

315. In the First Part of this Report, the surface features of Tennessee have been considered. We come now, to the great rock-beds, or formations, the outcrops of which make up the surface, and the aggregate, or mass of which constitute the deep foundations of our valleys, plains, hills, and mountains.

It is proposed in this Part, to enumerate and describe the formations which occur in Tennessee, to treat of them as to their lithological character, their extent, their fossils, the minerals they hold, and the soils they yield. We will be led to consider, also, the relations the formations sustain to each other, their relative positions, the foldings and displacements they have in common, undergone, and generally, the part they play, as elements in the rocky structure of the State. It is important that the Geological Structure of the State should be known and understood. Information of this kind, in addition to other important but less practical considerations, explains many of the apparent anomalies which often present difficulties to the miner; it enables us to trace out, with facility and precision, beds of coal, iron ore, etc., and guides us, often, to the very spot where they may be found; it aids in determining the extent, position, and range, of veins and mineral deposits, and points out the most economical plan of reaching and securing their contents; it is, in fine, indispensable to the successful development of any mineral region.

A knowledge of the formations, and of the areas within which they respectively outcrop, is essential, also, to the proper appreciation of the agricultural capacities of the State. A geological map, is a map of the soils, and their classification must be based upon the classification of the formations. The soils, (excepting alluvial bottoms,) are derived from the rocks which underlie them; and to these rocks, they owe, for the most part, their characteristics. This connection, is practically recognized by the farmer, when he talks of "sandstone soil," "limestone soil," "slate soil," &c., and his talk is more or less to the point, in proportion, as his acquaintance with the rocks, is more or less extended. This subject will be resumed hereafter.

CHAPTER IV.

THE GENERAL CHARACTER OF THE FORMATIONS; THEIR ORIGIN; THE CHANGES THEY HAVE BEEN MADE TO UNDERGO; HOW THEY ENTER INTO THE STRUCTURE OF THE STATE.

THE ROCKS STRATIFIED—FORMATIONS, AND THEIR CHARACTERISTICS—USE OF THE FOSSILS THEY CONTAIN—EXTENT OF FORMATIONS—ORIGIN OF THE OLDER FORMATIONS—ORIGIN OF THE SANDS AND CLAYS IN WEST TENNESSEE—DENUDATION IN MIDDLE AND WEST TENNESSEE—THE FOLDING, DISLOCATION AND DENUDATION OF STRATA IN EAST TENNESSEE—THE SEQUATCHEE FOLD—ELK FORK DISLOCATION; EASTERN SLOPE OF THE TABLELAND—CONSIDERATION OF THE FOLDING, &c., IN EAST TENNESSEE CONTINUED—FOLDS, UPLIFTS, AND FAULTS IN MIDDLE TENNESSEE.

316. *The Occurrence of the Rocks in Layers and Strata.*—It may be said, generally, that all the rocks *in Tennessee*, including the sands and clays of the Western Division, are disposed or arranged in layers and strata.* For this reason, they are said to be *stratified*. The strata are of various thicknesses, from that of thin leaves, as in the case of many States, to that of beds fifty or a hundred feet through.

317. The only rocks in Tennessee, not stratified, are masses, constituting certain *mineral veins* and *volcanic* dikes. But these

* A *Stratum* of rock may consist of many *layers*; the latter, is a subdivision of the former. A stratum is a bed of rock including all the layers of the same kind, that lie together.

are so limited, comparatively, that they need not be regarded in considering the rocky structure of the State.

The different classes of veins will be spoken of, hereafter. Those of one class, with the dikes, are fissures intersecting the strata, filled with mineral or rocky matter. In veins, this matter has been precipitated from water; in dikes, it has been injected as melted rock, by volcanic agencies. The veins have been formed, in narrow fissures, comparatively; the dikes are often wide, presenting great vertical walls of *granite*, *trap*, and other igneous rocks. A few of the latter are found in the crystaline rocks, along our North Carolina border. The most conspicuous that I have seen, are in Johnson and Carter Counties, but nowhere, are they of much importance.

317*a*. The mineral veins vary in thickness from one inch or less, to a score or more of feet. Small veins are common in limestone rocks. They often contain ores of lead and zinc, but rarely in sufficient quantity to be of value. The important veins will be noticed in the Third Part of this Report.

318. *Formations, and their Characteristics.*—We often meet with a series of strata, that appear to have been formed successively, in the same period, under conditions more or less the same, and consequently, presenting certain common characteristics. Such series, it has been agreed to call, *Formations*. Our Tennessee rocks are thus grouped in this report, into *thirteen formations*, a table of which is given in the next chapter.

319. As an example, the *sandstones, slates*, and *coal*, which form the upper part of the Cumberland Mountain, or table-land, (§ 169,) are grouped in a *formation* called the *Coal Measures*, with the following, among other common characteristics: *First*, coal is found at intervals, throughout the series; *secondly*, the strata are parallel; *thirdly*, the same, or closely related, *fossils*, such as, different species of petrified shells, corals, scales and teeth of fishes, leaves, branches and trunks of trees, occur, imbedded, more or less, in the rocks, from the top to the bottom of the series. *Characters* similar to these, unite the strata of all the formations.

The character last mentioned, we must refer to more particularly, on account of its great importance in designating with precision, the group to which local and isolated beds of rock belong.

320. *Fossils and their Use.*—With the exception of the first, all the formations adopted, contain *fossils* or petrifactions of

some sort; in fact, certain limestones are mostly made up of them.

"The dust we tread upon was once alive!"

They are, generally, parts of petrified plants, shells, corals, crustaceous animals; sometimes, the teeth and bones of fishes, and even of quadrupeds. With but few exceptions, they are the remains of animals and plants, whose species, or kinds, do not exist at present, upon the globe. The part of Geology which treats of them is called *Paleontology*.

321. Now, every formation has, in great part, its own species of fossils. *Most of those found in one do not occur in any other.* Upon this fact depends the great utility of fossils. They furnish, when known well enough to be recognized, unmistakable evidence of the geological position; and hence the general character, of the formation in which they occur. By means of them, for example, it is often easy for a geologist, traveling in a country wholly unexplored, to know certainly when he is in the midst of a coal-region, without having seen a trace of coal. The shells in the limestone, the fossil branch or trunk in the sandstones, the leaf-impressions in the slates, he recognizes at once as those belonging to the rocks associated with and including the beds of coal; they can belong nowhere else in the geological series, and better evidence often of the presence of coal-bearing rocks is not required.

322. *Extent of the Formations.*—The formations are generally of wonderful extent. The great rocky and comparatively very thin sheets, one upon another, often spread over thousands of square miles. A few examples will illustrate this.

323. One of our formations is a *black slate*, or *shale*, not at any point in Tennessee much over a hundred feet in thickness. This formation is found in the western part of the State, cropping out along the hills on both sides of the Tennessee River. Going eastward, it appears again all around the slopes of the Central Basin; runs under the Cumberland Table-land, and issues from beneath the mountain in the Sequatchee Valley; thence it runs under Walden's Ridge and Lookout Mountain, and rëappears at the base of the Cumberland, all along its eastern slope, with but few interruptions, from Georgia to Virginia. We find it, too, as far east as the narrow valley which

lies along the eastern base of Clinch Mountain, as well as in the vicinity of Montvale Springs, in Monroe. It thus extends, though comparatively very thin, almost from one end of the State to the other, always occupying the same relative position with reference to the formations above and below. But this is not all; this "*black slate*" reaches beyond Tennessee, extending northward to the Lakes and southward far into Alabama. I have seen it well developed at Blount Springs in the latter State, presenting the same appearance that it does at many points in both Middle and East Tennessee.

The formation next above the one mentioned—which is a very different rock—is nearly as extensive. And so it is with many of them.

324. The stratified sands and clays of the Western District—which are also called, technically, *rocks*, although for the most part unconsolidated—spread out southward to great extent, and are found represented in Mississippi and Alabama, some even in the Atlantic States as far north as New Jersey.

325. The formations, however, though in a general way of great extent, are not continuous and unbroken; they have been cut more or less into great patches, or sections, by the action of water in the excavation of basins and valleys; in East Tennessee they have in addition, been *folded* and *displaced* by great disturbing forces.

326. In one period of the Earth's history nearly all the rocky formations of Tennessee were *continuous* and comparatively *horizontal* over the whole State, West Tennessee and the valley-plain of the Mississippi not excepted. The *sands* and *clays* of West Tennessee are later formations and have never reached east of the Tennessee River, to any considerable extent. They rest in a great deep trough cut out of the older solid strata. This trough, with one of its rocky sides far over in Arkansas and the other on the east washed by the Tennessee River, holds, not only the sands and clays referred to, but also the bottom-plain of the Mississippi through which the great river winds its way. (§ 296.)

327. *Origin of the Older Formations.*—Most of the strata of these formations contain the remains of marine animals and

plants abundantly. This fact, together with others which it is unnecessary to mention here, indicates their origin, and compels us to believe that they were formed, at a much lower level than they now have, beneath the surface of an almost world-wide ocean. That such an ocean did exist, covering not only the area occupied by Tennessee, but the larger part of America, there can be but little question.

328. The rocks we are considering are the consolidated sediments which, in layer after lawyer, accumulated at the bottom of the Ancient Ocean. The material was in part the washings of the land that then existed, in part the remains of dead marine animals and plants, and in part chemical precipitations from the waters. The matter brought from the lands was not at all times the same; at one time it was argillaceous mud which ultimately became slate; then, it was sand for a sandstone, or gravel for a conglomerate; then again, calcareous matter for a limestone, or it was two or all of these in varying proportions, giving rise in the end to mixed rocks. In all these sediments the remains of life, shells, corals, and other hard parts of animals and plants became entombed, all hardening into rock.

329. Thus the formations were built up successively in the order in which we now find them, each the product and representative of a certain long period—being, in fact, a *stony record* —tables of stone recording the kind and condition of marine life, the physical condition of the Ocean, and to a certain extent of the lands at the time.

They have been elevated to their present inland position by the upheaval of the land, the sea, at the same time, retiring.

330. The strata of the last of our older formations—the *Coal Measures*—were deposited, under conditions, in some respects, different from those attending the deposition of the strata of the others. In the rocks of this formation, we find the remains, not only of marine, but also of fresh water and land life. The land had become more extended—it covered a larger area. The ocean had grown shallow—that part, at least, covering the submerged portion of North America—its bottom had become subject to slow, alternate elevation and depression,

giving sometimes land and sometimes sea.* When land existed, beds of vegetable matter accumulated, either in vast swamps, or otherwise; when the sea prevailed, these beds were flooded, and covered with layers of mud and sand.

Thus, alternately, may have been formed the strata which have since become the coal, shale and sandstone of our Coal Measures.

331. *Origin of the Sands and Clays of West Tennessee.*—The formations peculiar to West Tennessee, were formed long after the others had been raised from their mother ocean. Nevertheless, the materials of these, too, were deposited from water.

The Atlantic, at one time, owing to the lower level which the Southern States once had, appears to have covered a wide strip of country next to the seaboard, from Virginia around to Texas, and to have extended an arm up the Mississippi basin, nearly as far as the mouth of the Ohio. Almost the whole of West Tennessee, and a great extent of country beyond the Mississippi, were thus covered. (§ 326.)

Then it was that most of the *sands* and *clays* were deposited; then, too, the shell fish, the remains of which now constitute the great "shell-banks" of McNairy and adjoining counties, lived and flourished in their sea-water home. (§§ 263–4.)

332. Subsequently, by the gradual upheaval of the land, and the consequent retiring of the sea, the width of this arm was contracted until it covered but a third of the district. And now the fresh water from the North began to prevail, and soon expelled that of the sea, or in other words, the Mississippi, wide and lake-like, at first began its career; the arm of the sea becomes the river.

Then were deposited, over the whole area covered by the

* It may appear strange to some, that we speak so freely of the *elevation* and depression of land. It is, nevertheless, in perfect accordance with what is now occurring. Although our own coasts are, at this time, stable—although no changes in the relative level of land and sea have been observed with reference to *them*, for the last three hundred years—yet no reason can be assigned, why, long before, they might not have occurred.

It is certainly true, that just such movements are *now* going on at many points upon the globe. It has been demonstrated that six hundred miles of the west coast of Greenland has been slowly sinking, for the last four centuries, and that what was once dry land, is now sea-bottom. On the other hand, parts of Sweden are experiencing a contrary movement. Many like examples of *upheaval* and *subsidence*, known to have taken place, or to be taking place, might be mentioned.

fresh water, the strata of sand, lignite, gravel, clay and loam, which are to be seen in the Mississippi Bluff. (§ 279.)

333. By still further upheaval, these strata, too, were elevated above the waters, the Mississippi was drawn into narrow limits, and, with increased velocity and greater power, commenced the work of carving out or excavating from the sandy and loamy strata just formed, the present Valley, many miles wide, in which are the low "bottoms" and the ever-changing channel of the river.

Remnants of the strata cut away, crop out along the "Bluff," and run back eastward, to the second range of counties parallel with the Mississippi.

The *bottoms* have been formed, removed, and formed again, time after time, during the progress of the excavation of the Valley, and are still subject to similar changes.

334. *The Denudation of the Formations of Middle and West Tennessee.*—The cutting and washing away, or, as geologists express it, the *denudation* of certain strata by the Mississippi, has just been referred to. The *older rocks*, at many points, show the effects of such cutting and removal on a stupendous scale. (§ 325.) The agent has been water, but when and how it acted, to effect these results, it is not always easy to determine. Many of the small valleys have been cut out by the streams which flow through them, but there are no *existing* causes to which can be referred the excavation of the great rocky basins of Tennessee, and of the adjoining States. Much, doubtless, has been done by oceanic currents, just before, or during, the time of the upheaval of the formations.

335. The denudation of the formations in *Middle* and *West Tennessee*, is more easily understood than that of those farther east. In the former divisions, the rocks are approximately horizontal; but in East Tennessee they have been folded, or *wrinkled, on a grand scale*, and in many cases, dislocated and thrown upon their edges, on account of which, the geological structure of this part of the State is complicated, and the action of denuding agencies less simple.

336. The Central Basin of Middle Tennessee, (§ 227,) is a fine example of denudation. It has been dug out of the strata of six of the formations. Originally, when continuous, the strata

rose up in a slightly elevated *dome*, the summit of which was over the central part of Rutherford County. Taking the formation of the flat highlands around the Basin as the topmost of the dome, the amount of matter removed at this point, could not have been less, in vertical thickness, than 1300 feet.

337. Throughout this Basin, remnants of the Strata have been left in the hills and ridges; these remnants always occurring in a certain order, building up the hills, and giving to them a like geological structure. All sides of the Basin present the out-cropping edges of the same strata in the same order. That the hills have a like structure, results, necessarily, from the nature of the case, the Basin having been scooped from horizontal strata, and the hills and ridges being simply portions left by the denuding agencies.

338. What these agencies were, is a question of interest. The simplest theory is, that the work has been done by running water, aided, more or less, by frost. The waters of the Cumberland, Duck, and Elk Rivers, are *now* at work, washing down the hill sides, and deepening the lower areas; and it is not improbable, that the same waters commenced the excavation of the Basin, each branch, creek, and rill, doing its part of the work. This, of course, has required long ages of time, during which, the streams have been constantly changing and deepening their channels, and their immediate local valleys. The Basin is the aggregate result of the work of all the streams, small and great.

339. In the First Part of this Report, I have spoken of the narrow, deep valleys, or gorges, through which many of the streams flow as they enter the Basin on its eastern side. (pp. 82 and 83.) The water-falls spoken of, are at the heads of these gorges. The deep valleys have been cut out, doubtless, by the streams which now run through them.

In each, the cutting has extended as far up as the "falls;" and here, the work is still going on, the falls receding year after year, more or less. The recession of these falls and cascades is exceedingly slow, but not the less real. The water and sand wear away the rock to some extent, but most of the work is accomplished by undermining. The series of strata over which the water falls, presents, at top, hard flinty layers, but below, shale and limestone. The latter strata yield to the action of water, and are removed, undermining the flinty beds, and causing detached masses of them, to fall at intervals.

340. The removal of shale below the upper hard layers, very often forms along the sides of these gorges, and especially near the cascades, and sometimes under them, sheltered places called locally, "rockhouses" Where the upper flinty layers project out boldly, the rockhouses are of considerable size. Their most interesting feature is, that, in them, are often found *native alum* and *copperas*. These salts form incrustations on the crumbling surface of the shale, and also lumps or irregular masses, on the floors of the rockhouses.

341. The Western Valley, (p. 104,) is another interesting example of denudation. Here, the Tennessee and its local tributaries, have washed a rough and broken valley, out of very much the same strata, cut into, in the formation of the Central Basin.

342. But these examples become small affairs when we come to consider the vast denudation which preceded, and which swept away the formations, above those out of which the Basin and Valley mentioned, were excavated.

The two great formations of the Cumberland Table-land, (p. 66,)—the *Coal Measures* above, and the *Mountain Limestone* below—once spreading out westward, covered the whole of Middle and West Tennessee, and connected toward the northwest, in Kentucky, with the same formations. But now—taking the uppermost formation first—of this great expanse of Coal Measures, with the exception of the extensive remnant left in the Table-land, and a few inconsiderable fragments or outliers associated with it, nothing now remains in Tennessee; by far the greater part, has been swept away, perhaps, before the denuding power of submarine rivers.

343. So too, the Mountain Limestone has, to a great extent, disappeared. Patches of it remain here and there, in the hills and ridges near the western side of the Table-land. But west of these, from the entire area of Middle Tennessee, it has been almost wholly removed.

344. *The Folding, Dislocation and denudation of Strata in East Tennessee.*—I have already referred to the folded or wrinkled, and dislocated condition of the strata in East Tennessee. (§ 334.)

These features are due to great disturbance, and need elucidation.

The strata of the western side of the Cumberland Table-land, though much cut up by the action of water, are, approximately horizontal, which position they retain, with a few local exceptions, more than half way across the Table-land. Approaching the eastern limit of this division, however, we meet with indications of a remarkable action. The strata begin to lose their horizontal position ; they are more or less inclined, or in technical language, they *dip*, and otherwise, exhibit clear evidences of having been *crowded up in long straight folds.* Proceeding eastward, into the valley of East Tennessee, the evidences of this folding, become more marked. Not only, have the strata been folded, but, in many cases, in efforts to form folds, they have been split into long ribbon-like masses, or blocks, which, yielding to the force producing the action, have been crowded, one upon another, like thick slates or tiles on a roof, the edge of one overlapping the opposing edge of the other. (See §§ 360 and 444.) The folds, the ribbon-masses, and the lines of junction, all run lengthwise, to the northeast and the southwest.

345. To conceive the better of the force concerned, and the effects produced, let us go back to the time when the formations of East Tennessee were horizontal. If, now, we suppose, a vast force to be applied along the southeastern edge of these horizontal formations, and to act in a northwesterly direction, the strata, if not able to resist, would yield and rise up, like thick cloth, in great wrinkles or folds, or else, lacking the proper degree of flexibility, would break along lines of least resistance, in long parallel bands or ribbons, which would be crowded together, the edge of one overlaping the adjacent edge of the other. In this way, indeed, have the formations been acted upon, and such the folds and dislocations produced.*

Examples of these folds and dislocations are given below.

346. In passing eastward across the Table-land, the first important fold of the strata met with is in a line with *Crab Orchard Mountain* (§ 188) and *Sequatchee Valley.* (§ 140.) Crab Orchard Mountain is nothing more nor less, than the nearly *unbroken back* of *one end* of this first great fold. The mountain, though a ridge several miles long, presents but a very small part of the fold. In the highest part of the mountain the fold rises up a thousand feet above the level of the Table-land, the

*The lines along which dislocation and lapping have occurred, are called *faults.*

strata arching over in a striking manner. (See section on the map.) Sequatchee Valley, though a great trough in the bosom of the Table-land and so different from the mountain, is intimately related to the same fold. To this indeed, as a fundamental cause, they both alike owe their existence.

It remains to trace out this grand flexure, and to speak of it in more detail. I have designated it throughout as

347. *The Sequatchee Fold.*—It commences near the Emery River, in Morgan County, and running in a direct course to the southwest, forms the Crab Orchard Mountain and all the high points between it and the head of Sequatchee Valley.

348. At "Crab Orchard House" it is intersected by a gap, which gives a pass for the Sparta and Kingston road, and exposes the *Mountain Limestone elevated by the fold* above the general level of the Table-land.* A few miles further southwest there is another break and depression, called *Grassy Cove*, which also exposes the limestone. This cove is a curious basin surrounded by mountains. Its existence is due to the denudation of a section of the fold. Between this cove and Sequatchee Valley is a high mountain.

349. Proceeding southwesterly we find the fold following the long and straight Sequatchee Valley from one end to the other, (§ 140,) and continuing in the same direction, to the Alabama line. Remarkable as it may appear, the valley has been cut out along the back of this great flexure. This portion of the fold appears to have been rent open along its summit; water has thus had access to the limestone below, and by its denuding power has excavated the valley.

In the Crab Orchard portion the hard cap rocks were not thus rent, the softer strata in consequence, were protected and the fold left nearly intact in a mountain ridge.

350. The following diagram will throw light upon the character of the fold we are considering. It is a section of the formations and country from a point eight miles north of Jasper, in Marion County, to the eastern base of Lookout Mountain, its length being about twenty miles. There are several

* The two great formations of the Cumberland Table-land are the *Coal Measures* and the *Mountain Limestone*. The first is every where the cap formation of the Table-land, the latter is beneath it. (§175.) The *fold* brings up the limestone above the general level, and at the point mentioned it is uncovered by the superior formation and exposed.

points illustrated by this section, to which reference will be made hereafter. What concerns us *mostly* now, is the portion representing Sequatchee Valley and its formations.

SECTION ACROSS SEQUATCHEE VALLEY, &c., TO LOOKOUT MOUNTAIN.

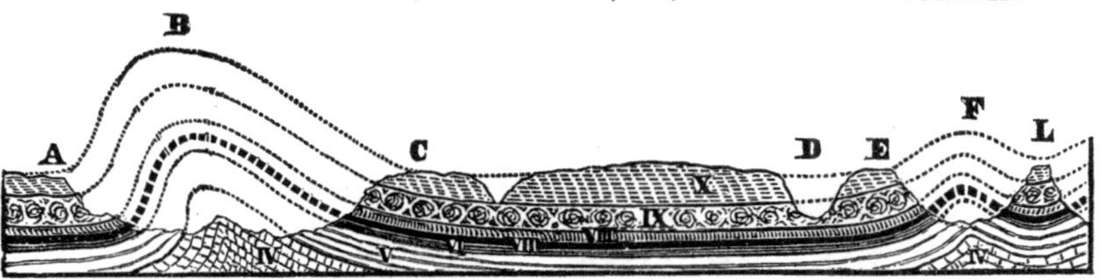

The following are the formations represented: IV, Knox Dolomite, 2, c; V, Trenton and Nashville, 3 and 4; VI, Dyestone Group, 5, c; VII, Black Shale, 7; VIII, Siliceous, 8, a; IX, Mountain Limestone, 8, b; X, Coal Measures, 9. See Chapter V.

The bands between the lines represent the formations; these are numbered in accordance with the tables in the next chapter. The shaded portions between the unbroken lines are the formations as now found; the blank portions between broken lines the parts of formations removed by denudation. Two restored folds are represented—the larger A B C the Sequatchee Fold; the smaller E F L that of the valley of Lookout Creek. The depression in the shaded part, between A and C, is Sequatchee Valley. A is the edge of the Table-land on the northwest side of the valley; C, the edge on the opposite side. The portion of the Table-land between C and D is *Walden's Ridge.* (§182.) D, narrow valley of the Tennessee River; the section crosses a few miles above Kelly's Ferry. E, portion of Raccoon Mountain. Depression between E and L, Lookout Valley. L, Lookout Mountain.

In this section the Sequatchee Fold is well represented; its summit B, was greatly elevated above the level of the Table-land. The amount of matter removed has been enormous. No attempt has been made to represent the rents made, doubtless, in the strata when elevated. The imagination of the reader can supply these.

It is essential to state, however, that, in the region of Jasper and *southward* the strata have been *fractured* along the northwestern side of the fold, and, in consequence, have been more or less thrown out of the positions they would have, had the flexure been regular as represented in the diagram.

351. The following cut, taken from Lyell's Elementary Geology, will be useful in illustrating the structure of Sequatchee Valley, as well as that of

other valleys and ridges in East Tennessee. The cut was intended originally to exhibit the structure of the Swiss Juras, but it will answer as well for some of our mountains and valleys.

a, b, c, d, e, Great rocky layers, or formations, which by lateral pressure have been crowded up into the folds A, B, and C. Both B and C are unbroken and undenuded, forming long straight ridges. A, however, has been fractured and denuded along its summit; thus a trough or valley has been formed along the line of elevation.

The structure of Sequatchee Valley resembles that of the trough A. The former valley has, however, been subjected to greater and deeper denudation. In the cut, the valley between B and C has a geological structure very different from that at A; it is a trough between two great folds. Many of our East Tennessee valleys have a similar structure.

352. Before presenting the above illustrations we had traced out the Sequatchee Fold to the Alabama line. It does not stop here. It extends on a long way into Alabama. In fact, the greater part of it is in this State, its southwestern end being near the junction of the two Warriors within forty miles of Tuscaloosa. The whole length of the fold, commencing at the Emery, in Tennessee, and extending to the junction mentioned, is about 225 miles. And for this whole distance, in longitudinal direction, it is straight, or at most, curving, as we enter Alabama, a little to the west.

353. The fold, including its geographical and geological features, is beautifully symmetrical. It terminates at both ends in mountain ridges, these ridges sinking away with the two extremities of the fold. The denuded part (Sequatchee Valley being the northeastern end) is a canoe-shaped, beautiful trough, in which are small, characteristic ridges and valleys. This trough has a rim of Coal Measures all around it. Its

length is about 160 miles, a little more than 60 of this being in Tennessee; its greatest width is from five to six miles. It has a fault along the middle part of its western side, the displacement bringing the Knox strata in contact with the Lower Carboniferous rocks.

The Tennessee River bears symmetrical relations to this trough. This stream, soon after leaving Chattanooga, breaks through the mountains into the trough, and then, turning to the southwest, flows in it for more than 50 miles. At Guntersville, Ala., the river again changes its course, cuts through the mountain barriers, and escapes to the northwest. (§ 149.)

The town of Pikeville is near the northeastern end of the trough, and Blount Springs, in Alabama, near its southwestern.*

Were this the proper place, I might add much more with reference to this most interesting fold and range. I have, myself, traversed it, and stood upon its terminal mountain at each end, traced out its formations and studied their changes, and I desire to add that, in the investigation of but few special fields have I had more pleasure, or have I met with more to point me to the great Creator, whose work it is.

354. *The Elk Fork Dislocation.*—This is an example of a broken fold, resulting in a *dislocation* or *fault.* In going eastward, across the Table-land near the Kentucky line, the first noteworthy disturbance of the strata met with, is seen in the Valley of the Elk Fork, a tributary of the Clear Fork of Cumberland River. This valley is narrow, and deeply set in the Table-land. Its head is at "Elk Gap," in the very midst of high mountains, and at a point about eleven miles a little north of west from Jacksboro; from this point it extends northeastward, into Kentucky. (See § 144.)

On the next page is a cross section that this valley presents at one point. The section shows the relative positions of the mountains bounding the valley, the formations outcropping in it, and the great *fault*, on one side of which, the lower formations have been forced up many feet out of place.

* The following towns are also within it: Blountville, Warrenton, Guntersville, Belle fonte, Stevenson and Bridgeport, Ala., and Jasper and Dunlap, Tennessee.

Horizontal scale 4000 *feet to the inch.*
Vertical *do* 2000 *do. do. do.*

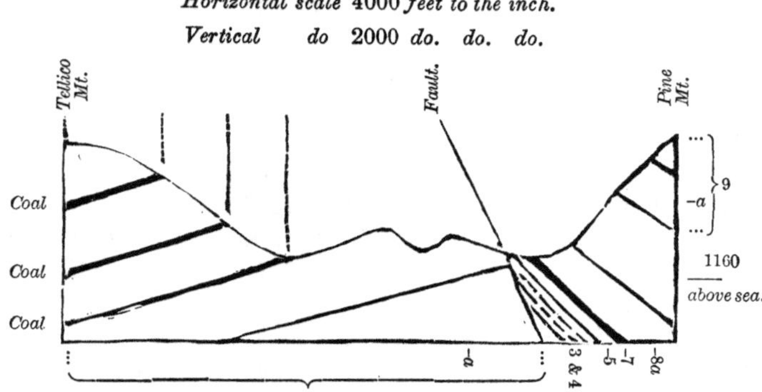

On the right is *Pine Mountain*, a high, straight ridge, (§180,) running parallel with the course of the valley; in fact, the valley and the ridge owe their existence to the same ultimate cause—the special elevation and dislocation we are considering.

The place of the *Fault* is indicated. The lowest formation appearing at the surface on the right hand side of the fault, has been raised between 2000 and 3000 feet. Its counterpart on the left, is that distance below the surface. Great as this displacement is, there are some in East Tennessee exceeding it. Faults are by no means rare east of the Table-land, some of which are more than a hundred miles in length.

The Elk Fork elevation is about in a line with the Sequatchee Fold, but forms no part of it; the two are separated by a great area of undisturbed horizontal rocks.

355. The Valley of *Cove Creek*, (§§ 145 and 146,) has a geological structure similar to that of Elk Fork, but the fault has not displaced the formations to so great an extent. It has, on its northeastern side, corresponding to Pine Mountain, a sharp roof-like ridge, which is mostly made up of sandstones, highly inclined. This remarkable ridge, as it escapes from the narrow valley, curves around to the northeast and skirts the mountain into Virginia. (§ 181.)

356. The fault of the Elk Fork Valley (extending, however, beyond the valley proper, into Kentucky) and that of Cove Creek, cut off, as I have before stated, (§ 146,) a large block o the Table-land. To the lateral movement of this great mass, by a vast power acting in a westerly direction, is to be attrib-

uted the partial elevation and the fracture of the strata in the valleys, as well as the upturning of the rocks in Pine Mountain.

357. The Sequatchee fold, and the broken folds just mentioned, are the only *great* disturbances of the kind that I have observed within the area of the Table-land. At a number of other points, as, for instance, near the Davis coal bank, in Cumberland County, disturbances have been observed, but they are comparatively local. These local uplifts and breaks are exceptional, but they foreshadow the greater ones further east, where folds and faults are the rule.

358. *The Crested Slope of the Eastern side of the Table-land.*—The eastern margin of the Table-land is composed, generally, of the upturned edges of the formations. The strata are horizontal back, but approaching the margin, they bend, more or less, upward, and form the sharp crest which so distinctly defines the Table-land on the east. The sandstones of the *Coal Measures* generally form the crest of the margin, while the *Mountain Limestone*, the *Silicious Group* and the *Niagara*-formations to be noticed further on—outcrop along its slope and base. In some few cases, great blocks of the *Coal Measures* have been detached and thrown over the crest, and now rest against the slope, or lie flat in the valley. Such fragmentary masses yield coal at several points, as at Kimbro's, and at points in the "Tennessee Valley" further south.

In the northern part of the State, the crest formed by the upturned edges of the strata becomes, in great part, detached from the body of the mountain back, and forms a sharp skirting ridge, of which I have already spoken. (§§ 182 and 183.)

359. *Consideration of the Folding, etc., in general, Resumed.*—The fact has been referred to, that, passing from the margin of the Table-land, eastward, the folds and faults become great, and occur in rapid succession. (§§ 344 and 345.) Having reviewed the features of several special examples, we go back to the consideration of the subject more in general.

Entering the *Valley of East Tennessee*, we get truly into the *region of disturbance.* This Valley and the Unaka division, constitute a part of Tennessee in which folds and dislocations and, in consequence, *dipping strata,* are the rule. Here the faults and the *position* of the rocks, together with the more or less destructible nature of the latter, have determined the physical characteristics of the surface. (§§ 93 and 94; also 18 and 19.) They have given *direction* and *form* to the scores of minor valleys and ridges, which make up the *fluted* area of the Great Valley, as well as to the subordinate ranges and deep coves of the Unaka division.

360. The following general section, (and in part ideal,) from the Table-land across the valley to Unaka Range will illustrate the present arrangement of the formations and the movements to which they have been subjected. (Compare real sections §§ 350, 354, 444, &c.)

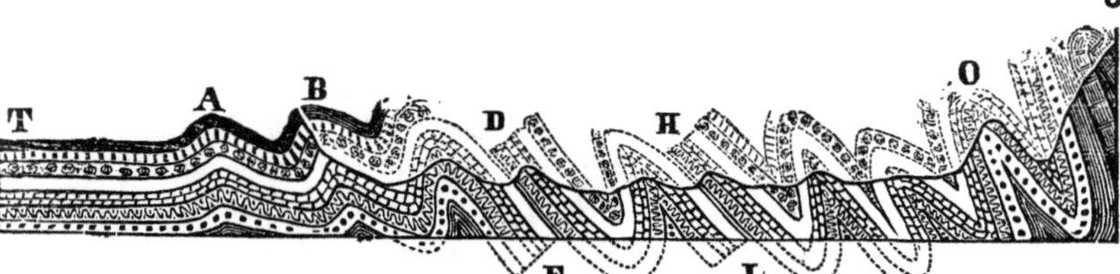

The vertical scale of this section, it must be recollected, is much greater than the horizontal. The number of folds and faults is less, too, than would be found in an actual section.

T, A, B, is the Table-land. At T the formations represented by the differently shaded bands, are horizontal; at A they rise in a moderate fold, as at Crab Orchard Mountain, (§ 346;) at B is a more abrupt fold, and partly denuded. At this point the valley commences. U, principal Unaka Range.

The valley lies between B and U; its present surface is represented by the line dividing the light and heavy-shaded portions. The folding of the formations and their dislocations explain themselves. At D, E, and H, L, are dislocations. D and E were once united, the formations being continuous; but in the great movement they were broken, and the edge D pressed up and over E. This will serve as an example of a *fault.*

The light-shaded portions above the line representing the surface of the valley are parts of folds, &c., supposed to have been removed by denudation.

361. One feature illustrated by this section is, the folding of the rocks, and the great scale upon which it has been done. The great flexures thus formed differ in magnitude; most of those of the Table-land are moderate in elevation; many of

those of the valley and of the Unakas are thrown up and over to the *northwest* in enormous plaits.

In addition to the greater folds, multitudes of subordinate ones occur in the strata. Thus the formations are often extensively corrugated as they rise in the great flexures.

362. Another feature illustrated is the dislocation of the formations. Two dislocations, or *faults*, are introduced. The displacements in many faults are very great, in some cases amounting to five or six thousand feet, or even more. Thus the two edges of a broken stratum may be separated more than a mile in vertical, or nearly vertical, distance. One edge may form the crest of a mountain, while the other is a mile below, buried beneath a valley.

The physical and geological characteristics of East Tennessee are now easily accounted for.

1st. A striking one is the *parallelism* of valleys and ridges. (§ 93.) The direction of these conforms to that of the folds and dislocations. The strata, thrown up edgewise, and cropping out in bands of unequal hardness, have given direction to denudation. Along the lines of rocks easily removed by water, such as blue limestones and soft shales, the *valleys* have been washed out; but along those of sandstones, hard slates and flinty limestones, *ridges* have been left. All the *mountain* ridges within the valley are, at least, capped off with hard *sandstones*, which have protected the softer rocks below. To these protecting sandstones the ridges owe their existence. A number of them, including Clinch and Powell's Mountains, have a great sheet of sandstone, forming one slope from top to bottom, and protecting the softer rocks seen on the other slope. (See also §§ 103, 104, and on.) The sharp-crested, and "comby" ridges, (§ 105,) have a *thin* sheet of hard material, sandstone or slates; this, when broken down at intervals, give rise to the notched or comby structure. The red and slaty knobs (§§ 106, 110, 112, and 113) are accounted for much in the same way. Some of the layers are hard, and have resisted denudation more or less, but being thin, have not been able to form continuous ridges.

2d. The occasional vertical position, and the more general dipping of the rocks to the southeast, is accounted for. By the crowding of the folds *over* to the north-west, and the subsequent denudation of their summits, the strata have necessarily been left dipping, as we now find them.* It is, too, a necessary result of the overlapping of the formations along the lines of fracture and dislocation, urged as they have been from the southeast.

3d. The frequent recurrence of the same formation, or rather of the same *series* of formations, seen in crossing East Tennessee, is accounted for. This, also, is a necessary result of the peculiar structure developed. In traversing the edges of the formations, from the southeast to the northwest, a very great variety of such series is observed.

In the first place, crossing the denuded *summit* of a *fold*, we pass successively from newer to older formations, until we reach the turning line, or axis; then the order is reversed. Representing the formations by numbers, and the axes of folds by a dot, the series thus passed over will be indicated by combinations like the following: 8, 7, 6, 5, 4, 3, 2,· 2, 3, 4, 5, 6, 7, 8; 6, 5, 4, 3, 2,· 2, 3, 4, 5, 6, 7; 7, 6, 5,· 5, 6, 7, 8, etc.

In crossing a *trough*, or concave flexure between two folds, the order is likewise reversed, but the upper or newer formations are nearest the axis, as follows: 1, 2, 3, 4,· 4, 3, 2; 4, 5, 6,· 6, 5, 4, 3, etc., etc.

If we traverse a *dislocation*, a *part* or the whole of the series is repeated in the *same* order. Representing the line of displacement by a hyphen, such series may be thus indicated: 7, 6, 5, 4, - 7; 6, 5, 4; 9, 8, 7, 6, 5, 4, - 6, 5, 4; 4, 3, - 6, 7, 5, 4, 4, etc., etc. Combinations of these different classes, in great variety, are presented in nature.

363. *Folds, or Uplifts, and Faults in Middle Tennessee.*—It has been stated that the formations are *approximately* horizontal in Middle Tennessee. (§ 335.) The word approximately was properly used, since, in tracing out the formations, they are often seen to sink and rise in gentle local undulations, and moreover, are found to have a general, though small, inclination or dip in some direction or other. Yet, notwithstanding this, when we compare their position with that of their counterparts in East Tennessee we can almost say they are horizontal.

* When the *summit* of a fold is cut by the surface, the rocks on each side may dip in opposite directions, etc., etc.

But there are exceptions to this general approximate horizontal position in the formations of the Middle Division. I have met with localities here in which are presented, though on a small scale comparatively, the folding and faulting and high inclination of strata so characteristic of East Tennessee.

364. The most interesting of these localities is in the region of Cumberland City, a small town on the Cumberland River, in Stewart County. This town is on the side of an elliptical area, or basin, containing six or seven square miles, and surrounded by hills. The river cuts through the northern end of the basin. Wells Creek enters it on the south, and flows through it to the river. From this circumstance I have named it the *Wells Creek Basin.* Within this area the strata are highly inclined. We have here indeed, a very considerable upheaval of the formations. The strata were lifted in a high dome, the top of which has been worn and washed away. The elevation was so great as to bring to the light, through the subsequent denudation, certain low strata (upper part of Form. 2, c) no where else to be seen in Middle Tennessee.* These strata occupy the central part, and a large part, of the Basin. They dip at high angles and, at some points, are even vertical, forming low "hog-back" ridges. Outcropping around the strata of Form. 2, c, are those of the higher formations, each group appearing successively in order, the rocks dipping away from the centre of the Basin. The hard rocks of the *siliceous* (8, a) form the encircling hills, and, with the *Mountain Limestone* above, (8, b,) constitute the formation of the whole country outside.

365. The disturbance, however, has not been confined to the area of the Basin; it has extended to the strata beyond its limits. This is seen in the bluffs on the river, both above and below Cumberland City. In these, the strata show small and great folds, fractures, dislocations, and inclinations at all angles, all, however, so far as seen, being confined to the rocks of the Lower Carboniferous. Coming up the river, the first bluff in which these disturbances are seen to have occurred is the one several miles be-

* When I first saw these rocks I recognized them at once as East Tennessee *acquaintances*, but was greatly surprised to meet with them here, a point where, of all other points in Middle Tennessee, I least expected to find them, as in all this country one of the higher formations, the *Lower Carboniferous*, is brought down to the level of the Cumberland River. By the uplift the top of Form. 2, c, has been thrust up through the Lower Carboniferous, as well as through all the intervening beds, the elevation of the lowest strata being not less than 2500 feet.

low Cumberland City, known to river-men as the *Checkered-house* bluff. In the upper part of this, the strata are boldly bent and faulted.

366. Another area of disturbance is in the upper part of the valley of Flynn's Creek, in Jackson County. This area is limited in extent, and has comparatively little importance, yet the formations are greatly disturbed. The rocks are seen to dip at high angles, and are occasionally almost vertical. The valley is narrow, and the hills on each side high. In their normal position the *siliceous* (8, a) is at the top of the series of formations, and the *Black Shale* (7) next below. In several places both are brought down, by great folds and faults, to the bottom of the valley, and, at one point, may be seen abutting against the Nashville Formation. One fault shows a displacement of a thousand feet. The lines of disturbance run nearly north and south.

367. But, by far the most important elevation of the strata in Middle Tennessee was the wide dome, the decapitation and denudation of which have given us the *Central Basin.* (pp. 81 and 97.) This can hardly be considered a local disturbance; it covers too great an area. The strata were not folded abruptly, nor broken and displaced; they were elevated not more than six or seven hundred feet in a dome, whose cross-section is about a hundred miles in length. The highest part of this was over a point not far from Murfreesboro', in Rutherford County. From above this point, as stated before, (§ 336,) not less than 1300 feet of rock have been removed. Here the lowest strata of the Central Basin are to be seen, and, with the exception of Formation 2, exposed in the Wells Creek Basin, (§ 364,) the lowest in Tennessee west of the Cumberland Table-land. From this central point the strata dip at a low angle in every direction, but less in the northeasterly and southwesterly than in other directions. In passing from the central area of the Basin, in any course to its rim, we cross in succession, the formations seen in this part of the State. (§ 208.) These outcrop approximately in concentric bands. The formation of the rim is the same as that of the hills which encircle the comparatively small Wells Creek Basin.

368. This dome like elevation of Middle Tennessee is sometimes associated with a similar elevation of the strata further

north, within an area divided among the States of Kentucky, Ohio and Indiana. The City of Cincinnati is about the centre of this area. The elevation in Tennessee, and that in the Cincinnati area, doubtless occurred at the same time, and are *perhaps* parts of a single line, or axis, of elevation extending from Tennessee to Ohio. The elevation, however, was greater in the Cincinnati and Tennessee parts than in the intermediate portion. This line of elevation is sometimes called the *Cincinnati axis*. (p. 8, *note.*)

CHAPTER V.

ENUMERATION AND SEQUENCE OF FORMATIONS IN TENNESSEE.

FORMATIONS NUMBERED AND TABULATED—COMPARATIVE TOPOGRAPHICAL AND STRUCTURAL IMPORTANCE—THE COMPLETE SERIES ESTABLISHED BY GEOLOGISTS—UNABRIDGED TABLE OF TENNESSEE FORMATIONS.

369. *The Formations Numbered and Concisely Tabulated.*— The rocks of Tennessee are, in this Report, grouped into *Thirteen Principal Formations.* (§ 318.) Most of these are natural, and may be considered as established; others are provisional, and may be changed. A number of them include *minor groups* of more or less importance, and to these, also, as as matter of convenience, the name *Formation* will sometimes be applied. The main groups, commencing with the lowest in the series, are numbered consecutively, from 1 to 13; and their subdivisions are designated by adding letters to these numbers.

On this and the next page, is a table giving the names of the formations, and the order in which they occur. It is to be read from the bottom, upward, 1 being the lowest formation and 13 the topmost.

ABRIDGED TABLE OF TENNESSEE FORMATIONS.

13.	**Alluvium,** - - -	(*Most recent and topmost.*)
12.	**Bluff Group,** - - - -	POST TERTIARY.
	12, *b*. BLUFF LOAM, - -	" "
	12, *a*. BLUFF GRAVEL, - -	" "
11.	**Tertiary Group,** - - -	TERTIARY.
	11, *c*. BLUFF LIGNITE, (*provisional,*)	" " ?
	11, *b*. ORANGE SAND, (or *La Grange Group,*) - -	" "
	11, *a*. PORTER'S CREEK GROUP, (*provisional,*) - -	" " ?

10. **Cretaceous,** - - - -	CRETACEOUS.
10, *c.* RIPLEY GROUP, (*provisional,*) -	"
10, *b.* GREEN SAND, (*Shell bed,*) -	"
10, *a.* COFFEE SAND, - - -	"
9. **Coal Measures,** - -	- CARBONIFEROUS.
8. **Lower Carboniferous,** - -	"
8, *b.* MOUNTAIN LIMESTONE, -	"
8, *a.* SILICEOUS, - - -	"
7. **Black Shale,** - - -	DEVONIAN.
6. **Lower Helderberg,** - -	UPPER SILURIAN.
5. **Niagara,** - - - - -	" "
5, *d.* MENISCUS LIMESTONE, (*Sneedville Limestone,*) -	" "
5, *c.* DYESTONE GROUP, - -	" "
5, *b.* WHITE OAK MT. SANDSTONES, - - -	" "
5, *a.* CLINCH MT. SANDSTONE, (*Medina,*) - -	" "
4. **Nashville,** or **Nash,** - -	LOWER SILURIAN.
3. **Trenton,** or **Lebanon,** - -	" "
2. **Potsdam,** - - - - -	" "
2, *c.* KNOX, or KNOXVILLE, -	" "
2, *c'''.* KNOX DOLOMITE, -	" "
2, *c''.* KNOX SHALE, - -	" "
2, *c'.* KNOX SANDSTONE, -	" "
2, *b.* CHILHOWEE SANDSTONE, (*Potsdam proper,*) - -	" "
2, *a.* OCOEE GROUP, (*Eozoic,*) -	" "
1. **Metamorphic,** (*Eozoic.*) (*Oldest and Lowest,*) - - - -	" "

370. *Comparative Topographical and Structural Importance of the Formations.*—It must not be inferred that groups of the same rank in the table, are of equal importance in their relations to the topography and rocky structure of the State. This is far from being the case. Several of them have very little importance of this kind. The *Black Shale*, for instance, though a wide-spreading formation, and, in other respects, one full of interest, contributes little to the topography, or to the rocky mass of the State. Again, any one, even of the subgroups 2, *a*, 2, *b* and 2, *c*, has more topographical importance than have the groups 5, *d*, (excluding 5*a*,) 6 and 7 together. The in-

terest attached to the formations in making up the surface of the State, or as elements in its structure, is, in a measure, proportionate to their respective thicknesses. There are, however, other characters to be considered, as, for instance, hardness and durability.

371. In thickness, as will be seen further on, the leading formations differ much. While the Potsdam (2) is many thousand feet thick, most of the others are not as many hundred, and some of them do not reach one hundred. It is to be remarked, however, that several of those, which, in Tennessee, are thin, increase in thickness when traced into other States.

372. *The Thinning out of Formations in Tennessee.*—The formations occurring in the States of New York and Pennsylvania, present quite a complete series, which is often referred to as a standard, by American geologists. Several of the numbers of this series, though very thick in the States mentioned, grow thinner when traced southward, and finally, thin out, and disappear before reaching Tennessee. Others, extending further south or southwest, have their *feather edges* in Tennessee; as, for instance, the *Lower Helderberg*, and, to a certain extent, the *Black Shale*, as well as the sub-group of the Niagara—the *Clinch Mountain Sandstone.* The Tennessee series is, therefore, less complete than the northern. Not only are some of the formations wholly absent, but others are reduced to very thin beds.

373. But further: certain Alabama and Mississippi formations run out in Tennessee, as well as some of the northern ones. This is true of the sub-groups of the *Cretaceous*, which, in the States mentioned, are very heavy, but in Tennessee, thin out and disappear.

This absence and thinning out of formations, is one of the geological peculiarities of Tennessee,

374. *The Complete Series of Formations as established by Geologists.*—In order to be able to compare the Tennessee series with the general one made out by geologists, I give the latter as found in Dr. Dana's most excellent Text-Book, and what the author says in explanation.

But first, the reader must bear in mind that the strata were formed in succession, and that each stratum, more or less loaded with organic remains, is part of a record of the changes, both physical and organic, that were going on during a certain portion of past time. (§§ 327 to 329, inclusive.) The strata are thus the leaves of a great book, in which may be read the *history* of changes in the oceans and lands, in the atmosphere and climate, in plants and animals; the history, in a word, of the earth's physical and organic progress. The formations may be regarded as chapters in the history, each containing the record of a period, or part of a period. By careful study of the whole series of formations, especially with reference to organic remains, it is found that the history is divided into several distinct *parts*, (groups of formations,) each the record of a great *age*, embracing several periods. Corresponding to these parts, we have as many ages. In Dana's own words, the following have been ascertained :*

"(1.) There was, *first*, an age, or division of time, when there was *no life* on the globe; or, if any existed, this was true only in the latter part of the age, and the life was probably of the very simplest kind.

(2.) There was next an age, when *Shells, Mollusks, Corals, Crinoids* and *Trilobites*, abounded in the oceans, when the continents were almost all beneath the salt waters, and when there was, as far as has been ascertained, no terrestrial life.

(3.) There was next an age, when, besides Shells, Corals, Crinoids, Trilobites and Worms, there were *Fishes* in the waters, and when the lands, though yet small, began to be covered with vegetation.

(4.) There was next an age, when the continents were at many successive times largely dry or marshy land, and the land was densely overgrown with *trees, shrubs* and *smaller plants*, of the remains of which plants, the great coal-beds were made. In animal life, there were, besides the kinds already mentioned, various *Amphibians* and some other *Reptiles* of inferior tribes.

(5.) There was next an age, when *Reptiles* were exceedingly abundant, far outnumbering and exceeding in variety, and many, also, in size, and even in rank, those of the present day.

(6.) There was next an age, when the Reptiles had dwindled, and *Mammals* or *Quadrupeds* were in great numbers over the continents; and the size of these Quadrupeds, like that of the Reptiles in the preceding age, was far greater than the size of modern species.

(7.) After this came *Man*, and the progress of life here ended.

The above-mentioned ages in the progress of life and the earth's history, have received the following names:

*Text-book of Geology, pp. 63–66.

Ages.		*American Periods.*	*Tennessee Divisions.*
Carboniferous Age, or Age of Coal Plants.		15 Permian.	....
		14 Carboniferous, or Coal Measures.	9 Coal Measures.
		13 Sub-carboniferous.	8 Lower Carboniferous.
Devonian Age, or Age of Fishes.		12 Catskill.	....
		11 Chemung.	....
		10 Hamilton.	7 Black Shale.
		9 Corniferous.	.... ?
		8 Oriskany.	....
Silurian Age, or Age of Mollusks.	Upper.	7 Lower Helderberg.	6 Lower Helderberg.
		6 Salina.	....
		5 Niagara.	5 Niagara.
	Lower.	4 Hudson.	4 Nashville.
		3 Trenton.	3 Trenton.
		2 Potsdam, or Primordial.	2 Potsdam.
Azoic.		1 Azoic.	1 Metamorphic.

Ages.	*Periods.*	*Tennessee Divisions.*
AGE OF MAN.		13 Alluvium, and
AGE OF MAMMALS, OR CENOZOIC TIME.	Post-tertiary.	12 Bluff Group.
	Tertiary.	11 Tertiary.
AGE OF REPTILES, OR MESOZOIC TIME.	Cretaceous.	10 Cretaceous.
	Jurassic.	....
	Triassic.	....

NOTE.—This section is the same as that in the Text-book, with the exception of the right hand column, which has been introduced in order to show the Tennessee Divisions.

1. AZOIC TIME OR AGE.—The name is from the Greek *a*, *not* or *without*, and *zoe*, *life*.
2. AGE OF MOLLUSKS, or the SILURIAN AGE.
3. AGE OF FISHES, or the DEVONIAN AGE.
4. AGE OF COAL-PLANTS, or the CARBONIFEROUS AGE.
5. AGE OF REPTILES, or the REPTILIAN AGE.
6. AGE OF MAMMALS, or the MAMMALIAN AGE.
7. AGE OF MAN.

The first of these ages—the *Azoic*—stands apart as the preparatory time for the commencement of the systems of life. The next three ages were alike in many respects, especially in the air of antiquity pervading the tribes that then lived, the shells, crinoids, corals, fishes, coal-plants, and reptiles belonging to tribes that are now wholly or nearly extinct. The era of these ages has, therefore, been appropriately called *Paleozoic time*, the word *Paleozoic*, coming from the Greek *palaios*, *ancient*, and *zoe*, *life*.

The next age was ushered in after the extinction of many of the Paleozoic tribes, and its own peculiar life approximated more to that of the existing world. Yet it was still made up wholly of extinct species, and the most prominent of the tribes and genera disappeared before, or at is close. This age corresponds to *Medieval* time in geological history, and is called *Mesozoic time*, from the Greek *mesos*, *middle*, and *zoe*, *life*.

The next age was decidedly modern in the aspect of its species, the higher as well as lower, although only a few of those of its later epochs survive into the age of Man. It is called *Cenozoic time*, from the Greek *kainos*, *recent*, and *zoe*, *life*, (the *ai* of the Greek words always becoming *e* in English, as, for example, in *ether*, from the Greek *aither*.)

The following are, then, the grand divisions of geological time, adopted :

I. AZOIC TIME.

II. PALEOZOIC TIME, including (1) The Age of Mollusks, or Silurian ; (2) The Age of Fishes, or Devonian; (3) The Age of Coal-plants, or Carboniferous.

III. MESOZOIC TIME, including the Reptilian Age.

IV. CENOZOIC TIME, including the Mammalian Age.

V. The AGE OF MIND, or the Human Era.

The foregoing section represents the successive formations of the globe, arranged in the order of time, with the subdivisions corresponding to the Ages and Periods.

The various strata in the formations of an age, are very diversified in character, limestones being overlaid abruptly by sandstones, conglomerates or shales, or either of these last, by limestones; and each may be very different from the following in its fossils. These abrupt transitions in the strata are proofs that there were great changes, at times, in the conditions of the region where the strata were formed; and the transitions in the kinds of fossils are evidence of great destruction, at intervals, in the life of the seas. Such transitions, therefore, naturally divide off the ages into smaller portions of time, or *periods*, as they are called. By transitions similar in kind, but not so great, *periods* may often be subdivided into still smaller parts or *epochs*.

In the preceding section, Azoic is at the bottom, on the left; above it, there are the names *Silurian*, *Devonian*, and so on; and the names of the Periods, *Potsdam*, *Trenton*, etc., dividing off these Ages, on the right.

The names of the Periods in the first part of the section (those of the *Paleozoic*) are derived from the names of American rocks. The names in the other parts are mostly European, as the series of rocks it contains (those of *Mesozoic* and *Cenozoic* time) are more complete in Europe than in America.

375. The section given is Dana's, with the exception of the right hand column. In this I have introduced the names of

the leading Tennessee divisions, or formations, as given in the table on page 150. These, so far as they go, correspond to Dana's periods. It will be seen that *eight* of the spaces in the Tennessee column are blank. These are the geological horizons, which, though well developed elsewhere, are not represented in Tennessee. (§§ 372–3.)

376. It will be seen that the blank opposite the *Corniferous* period is marked doubtful. I have seen, at a few points, a *thin local limestone* containing corals, which may prove to be a member of this formation. The evidence, however, is by no means satisfactory, and, for the present, the bed is included in the formation next below.

377. *The Black Shale* is all that represents the Hamilton Period. In New York, the strata pertaining to this have a maximum thickness of 1200 feet. In Tennessee, its upper part alone is represented by the Black Shale, with a thickness rarely reaching 100 feet. In New York, this upper part is called the *Genesee Shale.*

Excepting the Hamilton, and those followed by a blank, all the remaining periods are well represented in Tennessee.

378. *Unabridged Table of Tennessee Formations.*—Below is presented an unabridged tabular view of the formations and their divisions, as found in Tennessee. It is an expansion of the Table given on page 150. Important localities are also mentioned, and, in some instances, topographical relations.

The Table begins with the lowest group, and ascends through the series.

Tabular View of Tennessee Formations.

1. **Metamorphic.**

Characters.—Altered rocks—Azoic or Eozoic in part, mountain-making.

Thickness many thousand feet.

Examples.—The talcose slates, in part, of Beech Mountain and Slate Face, in Johnson County. Gneissoid rocks of Stone Mountain.

The syenitic gneiss of Roan Mountain.

The gneiss and mica slate of the Great Bald, in Washington.

The talcose slates and hornblendic beds of Ducktown.

2. **Potsdam.** LOWER SILURIAN,

Embraces three great sub-groups,
2,*a*. *Ocoee conglomerate and slates,*
2,*b*. *Chilhowee sandstone,* and
2,*c*. *Knox Group.*

2,*a*. OCOEE.

Char.—Semi-metamorphic, Eozoic; mountain-making.
Thickness, 10,000 feet ?

Ex.—The conglomerates and slates of the Ocoee River.

Semi-talcose slates and conglomerates of Monroe County.

Conglomerate and slates of the Little Tennessee River.

Slates of the West Fork of Little Pigeon, in Sevier County.

Conglomerates and slates of the Smoky Mountain, in Sevier County.

Conglomerates and slates on the French Broad, in the eastern part of Cocke County.

Rocks of the Big Butt, in Greene County.

Conglomerate of the Laurel Gap of Iron Mountain, in Johnson County.

2,*b*. CHILHOWEE SANDSTONE.

Char.—Sandstones and sandy shales; mountain-making.
Thickness, 2000 feet. (§ 482.)

Ex.—Sandstones and sandy shales of Chilhowee Mountain, and of all the great outliers of the Unaka range, including Holston and Iron Mountains; Cherokee and Buffalo Mountains; Paint Mountain; English's Mountain; Chilhowee, Guide, and Star's Mountains, etc.

2,*c*. KNOX GROUP.

A triple Formation, in ascending order, as follows:
2,*c′*. *Knox Sandstone,*
2,*c″*. *Knox Shale,* and
2,*c‴*. *Knox Dolomite.*

2,*c′*. KNOX SANDSTONE.

Char.—Hard sandstones and shales, of different colors—strata often charged with sea-weeds.

Contains, at some points, interpolated layers of dolomite.

The sandstones make sharp-crested and "comby" ridges. (§ 105.)

Thickness, 800 to 1000 feet. (§ 516.)

Ex.—The rocks of Comby Ridge, in Hancock and Grainger

Counties; of Webb s Ridge, in Knox, and Poor Valley Ridge, in Grainger; of Beaver, Bull Run, and Pine Ridges, crossed in going from Knoxville to Clinton; of Piny Ridge, between Clinton and Walden's Ridge; of Bays Mountain forming the southeast boundary of Knox County; of the Ridge west of Rogersville, etc.

2,c″. KNOX SHALE.

Char.—Variegated shales, containing, occasionally, layers of blue oolitic dolomite and limestone—these, at points, fossiliferous. Valley-making.

Thickness, 1500 to 2000 feet. (§ 524.)

Ex.—The rocks of Poor Valley, in Knox County; of Hinds' Valley, west of Black Oak Ridge; of Bull Run Valley, and of Wolf Valley—the latter west of Chestnut Ridge; of Walker's Valley, in which Cleveland is located, and of Mouse Creek and Candy's Creek Valleys; of the Valleys of the two Chestna Creeks; of Carter's, and of Stanley Valley, in Hawkins; of the Valley of Richland Creek, in Grainger, etc.

2,c‴. KNOX DOLOMITE.

Char.—A great series of heavy-bedded dolomites and limestones, mostly the former. Lowest strata, blue oolitic, and often fossiliferous; strata next above, dark gray and granular; upper strata, light gray. Upper part contains layers of chert. Ridge-making. (§ 104.)

Thickness, 4000 feet. (§ 541.)

Ex.—The strata of Knoxville; these belong to the upper part.

The rocks of Black Oak, Copper, and Chestnut Ridges, between Knoxville and Clinch River.

The rocks of Missionary Ridge east of Chattanooga, and of many other ridges in East Tennessee.

The rocks, in part, of Tazewell, Kingston and Chattanooga; the rocks of Blountville, Jonesboro' and Greeneville; of Dandridge and Maryville; in part of Newport and Athens; of New Market, Loudon, Pikeville, Benton, etc.

The rocks of the central area of the Wells' Creek Basin, in Stewart County, Middle Tennessee, etc., etc.

3. **Trenton,** or **Lebanon.**

Char.—Blue and dove-colored limestones, thick and thin-bedded. Highly fossiliferous.

In East Tennessee, including the Nashville strata, generally valley-making; also (the upper shale part) making knobby belts.

In Middle Tennessee (with the Nashville formation) the mass out of which the Central Basin has, for the most part, been excavated.

Thickness, in East Tennessee, *including the Nashville rocks*, 2500 (?) feet.

Thickness, in Middle Tennessee, *not including Nashville*, 500 feet.

Ex.—In East Tennessee, *including Nashville rocks:* The Maclurea blue limestone of Kingsport, in Sullivan; of Strawberry Plains, of Lenoirs, etc.; the variegated marbles of Hawkins, Knox and other counties; the iron-limestone of the red knobs in Knox, Blount, Monroe, McMinn and Bradley; the shales of Lick Creek, in Greene; and of the knobby regions of Sullivan, Cocke, Sevier, etc; the rocks of a number of fine valley-ranges between the Holston and the East Tennessee and Georgia Railroad on the southeast, and the Cumberland Table-land on the northwest; the rocks, in part of Tazewell, Jacksboro', Clinton, Greeneville, Newport, Washington, Athens; those of Sevierville, Decatur, Georgetown, etc.

In Middle Tennessee, *not including the Nashville rocks:* The rocks of Lebanon, Murfreesboro', Shelbyville, Lewisburg; Campbellville, in Giles; Duck River Bluffs, at Columbia; Woodbury, in Cannon; Liberty, in Smith, etc.

4. **Nashville,** or **Nash.**

Char.—In East Tennessee, in part shales; in Middle Tennessee, mostly limestone. All fossiliferous, limestones highly so.

In East Tennessee, as above stated, *with the Trenton*, valley-making; the shale, in the southeastern part of the valley, making knobby belts.

In Middle Tennessee, *with the Trenton*, the rocks, for the most part, of the Central Basin.

Thickness, in East Tennessee, see under Trenton.

Thickness, in Middle Tennessee, 500 feet.

Ex.—For examples in East Tennessee, see under Trenton.

In Middle Tennessee, *the rocks of Nashville*, Gallatin, Hartsville, Gainesboro'; the rocks of the hills about Carthage, (the lowest rocks being Trenton;) the rocks of Fayetteville, Pulaski, Mt. Pleasant, Franklin; the upper rocks of Columbia, etc.; the hydraulic limestone of Clifton, and of other points in the western valley of the Tennessee River; the *orthis* and *cyrtodonta* beds of the Central Basin, etc.

5. **Niagara Group,**

Includes several formations, in ascending order, as follows:

5,*a*. *Clinch Mountain Sandstone,*
5,*b*. *White Oak Mountain Sandstones,*
5,*c*. *Dyestone Group*, and
5,*d*. *Meniscus Limestone.*

5,*a*. CLINCH MOUNTAIN SANDSTONE.

Char.—A sandstone, mostly white or gray, overlying red shales; confined to East Tennessee. The sandstone mountain-making.

Thickness: Shale, 400; Sandstone, 300, (?).

Ex.—The sandstones and red shale of *Clinch Mountain*, of House Mountain, of the Devil's Nose, in Hawkins, of the ridges of the Bays Mountain group north of Bull's Gap, including Chimney Top and Fodder Stack, of Powell's Mountain and of Lone Mountain, in Claiborne and Union.

5,*b*. WHITE OAK MOUNTAIN SANDSTONES.

Char.—Variegated sandstones, with some shales; rocks often, red or brown, fossiliferous, more or less equivalent to the last. Confined to East Tennessee. These sandstones often abound in crinoidal buttons.

Thickness, 500 feet.

Ex.—Sandstones of the gaps in White Oak Mountain, and generally of the mountain itself. (In Georgia, in gap of Taylor's Ridge, at Ringgold. Taylor's Ridge and White Oak Mountain are the same range.)

5,*c*. DYESTONE GROUP.

Char.—Variegated shales, with thin, smooth sandstones at some points. An East Tennessee formation.

Contains beds of fossiliferous iron ore, called locally *dyestone.*

Thickness, from 100 to 300 feet.

Ex.—The shales and dyestone bands in the small ridges, the range of which skirts the eastern base of the Cumberland Table; the variegated shales along the eastern base of Powell's and Lone Mountains; the shales and ore in the ridge lying on the east, or southeast side, of Big Valley, in Union and Anderson Counties; the shales and ore of Half-moon Island and vicinity; of the small ridge skirting the base of Lookout Mountain, etc.

5,*d*. MENISCUS LIMESTONE.

Char.—In the western valley of the Tennessee River, fossiliferous limestone; gray, above; and variegated, below.

In the Central Basin, gray limestone.

The Sneedville (East Tennessee) limestone may be placed here.

Thickness: 150 feet in East Tennessee, and 200 feet in Middle Tennessee.

Ex.—For the greater part, the limestone of the glades in Perry, Decatur, Wayne and Hardin Counties; the gray limestone below the Black Shale, in Giles, and parts of Lincoln; the marble of the Big Sandy, in Henry County; the limestones below the Black Shale, at Centreville; the rocks of Savannah, in Hardin County, etc.

In East Tennessee, limestone on the southwest side of Sneedville; the bluish and light gray limestone in the valley between Powell's Mountain and Newman's Ridge. A bed of fossiliferous limestone, the age of which is not fully settled, lying along the eastern base of Lone Mountain, in Claiborne and Union Counties, may belong here.

6. **Lower Helderberg.**

Char.—Highly fossiliferous bluish limestone, with sometimes shale.

For the most part occurring in the Western Valley of the Tennessee River.

Thickness, maximum, 100 feet ?

Ex.—The limestone below the Black Shale, at Linden, in Perry County, and at several other points below this, on Buffalo River; the limestone seen in the heads of the hollows about Decaturville; the bluff on Big Sandy, in Henry County, at Esq. John Williams's Mill, and other bluffs below, on the same stream; in the southern part of the State, the limestone and chert of the White Sulphur Springs, in Hardin County; the upper beds of limestone in the valleys of Indian and other creeks, etc. Portion of the limestone in the first bluff below Cumberland City, on the Cumberland River.

7. **Black Shale.**

Char.—Black bituminous shale, containing, more or less, iron pyrites, in grains and nodules. A very persistent bed.

Thickness, maximum, about 100 feet.

Ex.—In East Tennessee: The black shale, one mile west of Montvale Springs; the black shale, along the eastern base of Clinch Mountain; the black shale, of Sneedville;

that along the eastern base of Powell's Mountain; that in the ridge next east of Big Valley, in Union; that east of White Oak Mountain: the black shale in the small ridges skirting the eastern base of the Cumberland Table-land; that on each side of the Sequatchee Valley.

In Middle Tennessee: The black shale, generally high on the hills, within and around the sides of the Central Basin; the black shale, of Henry, Stewart, and of the other counties, including the Western Valley of the Tennessee.

8. Lower Carboniferous.

Has two divisions, as follows:

8,*a*. *Siliceous* below, and

8,*b*. *Mountain Limestone* above.

8,*a*. THE SILICEOUS, OR THE SILICEOUS GROUP.

Char.—Limestone, often siliceous, the strata generally interstratified with layers of chert. In some regions, beds of shale occur.

The division is made to include the *Lithostrotion beds* as its upper part.

Ridge-making, in East Tennessee; plateau-making, in Middle Tennessee.

Thickness, from 300 to 550 feet.

Ex.—In East Tennessee: The sandstone and sandy shales of the ridge next west of Montvale Springs; the crinoidal chert layers on the east side of White Oak Mountain; sandstone and sandy shales of Pine Mountain, and of parts of Stone Mountain, east of Clinch Mountain, in Hawkins; siliceous shale, on the west slope of Newman's Ridge; the beds of crinoidal chert, in nearly all of the dyestone ridges between the Tennessee and Clinch Rivers, on the southeast, and the Cumberland Table-land, on the northwest; the crinoidal chert of the small skirting ridge generally seen at the base of the Table-land; the chert of the skirting ridges on each side of Lookout Mountain; the chert bed at the foot of the mountain, on the east side of Sequatchee Valley, and, in some parts, on the western side.

In Middle Tennessee: The group of rocks making the great plateaus of the *Highlands*, or *Highland Rim*, of Middle Tennessee, (see page 81,) and making, too, the crests of the slopes bounding the Central Basin, and the Western Valley, (pp. 97–101;) the cap rock of Elk Ridge, and its ramifications in the southern end of the Central

Basin, and of the highest ridges and knobs in other parts of the Basin.

On the rocks of the upper part, are the towns of Livingston, Cookville, Sparta, McMinnville, Winchester, Lawrenceburg, Charlotte, Dover, Clarksville, and Springfield.

On the rocks of the middle and lower parts, are Smithville Manchester, Tullahoma, Waynesboro', Newburg, Linden, Camden, and Lafayette.

8,*b*. MOUNTAIN LIMESTONE.

Char.—Mostly limestone; includes one bed of sandstone, and several beds of shale.

Starting below the sandstone crests, forms very generally, the slopes of the Cumberland Table-land.

Thickness, from 300 to 700 feet.

Ex.—The limestone and shales of Montvale Springs, in Blount County, (its extreme southeastern presentation.)

The limestone belt next east, or southeast, of Pine Mountain, in Hawkins County.

The limestone of the ridge, commencing east, or northeast of Sneedville; that of Newman's Ridge.

The limestone of the valley range, east of White Oak Mountain.

The limestone and shales of the middle and upper portions of the steep slopes of the Cumberland Table-land on all sides.

The limestone and shales of Crab Orchard Mountain, and of Grassy Cove and vicinity.

The middle and upper limestones of the slopes of the Short Mountain, in Cannon County.

9. **Coal Measures.**

Char.—A series of sandstones, shales, and *stone-coal* interstratified.

The sandstone plateau-making, and when tilted, ridge, or mountain-making.

The series the cap-formation of the Cumberland Tableland.

Thickness, from 200 to 2500 feet.

Ex.—The flat top of the Cumberland Table-land.

The sandstones and shales forming the cap of the two Short Mountains, in Cannon County.

The sandstones and shales of the outliers in Overton and Fentress, among them, Double Top Mountain, of the latter county; Pilot Knob, near Old Monroe, etc.

The conglomerates, sandstones, and shales of the top of Lookout Mountain; of Walden's Ridge, Raccoon Mountain, etc.

The following towns are on the Coal Measures: Jamestown, in Fentress; Huntsville, in Scott; Crossville, in Cumberland; Spencer, in Van Buren; and Altamont, in Grundy.

10. **Cretaceous,**

Has been divided as below:

10,*a*. *Coffee Sand*,

10,*b*. *Green sand, or Shell bed*, and

10,*c*. *Ripley Group*.

10,*a*. COFFEE SAND.

Char.—A series made up of beds of gray and dark sands (when not weathered,) interspersed more or less, with clay seams. Contains occasionally, a bed of laminated clay.

Contains leaves, fragments of wood, etc., more or less converted into *lignite*.

A West Tennessee formation.

Thickness, 200 feet ?

Ex.—The sands of the bluffs on the Tennessee River, at Coffee. Crump's and Pittsburg Landings, respectively.

Most of the stratified sand-beds in Hardin and Decatur counties.

Decaturville is in part upon the outcropping edge of this formation.

10,*b*. GREEN SAND, or SHELL BED.

Char.—A clayey sand, more or less calcareous, and containing *green grains* throughout, and mica scales. Highly fossiliferous. Also a West Tennessee formation.

Thickness, 200 to 350.

Ex.—The strata of the "Bald Hills" three miles northwest of Monterey, in McNairy County.

Exposures, two and three miles east of Purdy.

Cuts of the Memphis and Charleston Railroad, south of Purdy, near the Tennessee and Mississippi line.

The bed passed through in boring the Artesian wells of McNairy. (§ 269.)

The green sand bored through in the valley of Beech River, in Henderson County.

In general, the sand bed, which, at its outcrops, strews the surface with the large oyster-like shells, in McNairy and Henderson.

10,*c*. RIPLEY GROUP. (*Provisional.*)

Char.—Stratified sands, laminated more or less with clayey leaves.

Occasionally beds of darkslaty clay.

Contains a bed of impure limestone, and a sand bed with green grains.

Not found in the State east of Tennessee River.

Thickness, 400 or 500 feet. ?

Ex.—The stratified sands in the vicinity of Pocahontas, in Hardeman County.

The Turritella Limestone, of Muddy Creek, in Hardeman, and the bed of green sand in the same vicinity.

The strata outcropping around Purdy, in McNairy, and Lexington, in Henderson; Camden, in Benton, is at its eastern limit.

The strata of the upper part of the Big Sandy Valley.

11. **Tertiary Group,**

Embraces the following divisions:

11,*a*. *Porter's Creek Group,*
11,*b*. *Orange sand*, and
11,*c*. *Bluff Lignite.*

11,*a*. PORTER'S CREEK GROUP. (*Provisional.*)

Char.—Sands and Laminated clays. West Tennessee.

Thickness, 200 or 300? feet.

Ex.—The laminated clays on Porter's Creek, near Middleton, in Hardeman; and on the Memphis and Charleston Railroad, for seven or eight miles west of the place mentioned.

The "Soapstone" beds in the eastern part of Hardeman, between Bolivar and Purdy.

The laminated clay-beds at Huntingdon and Paris.

11,*b*. ORANGE SAND, (or *La Grange Group.*)

Char.—Mostly made up of beds of sand, the strata often orange and yellow, sometimes red, white, etc. Presents occasionally, beds of clay, white and variegated. Middle area of West Tennessee.

Thickness, 600 feet.?

Ex.—The sands and clays of the ravines about La Grange.

Strata of numerous cuts on the Memphis and Charleston Railroad, and on other railroads.

Strata of Somerville, Bolivar, Jackson, Brownsville, Trenton and Dresden; Huntingdon and Paris are about on the eastern limit of this group.

11,*c*. BLUFF LIGNITE. (*Provisional.*)

Char.—Laminated sands and clays, with well marked beds of Lignite.

Pertains to the middle and lower parts of the Mississippi Bluff, (§ 279,) through the State.

Thickness, 150? feet.

Ex.—Strata below the gravel at "Old River," Randolph and Fulton—well exposed at numerous points in the Mississippi Bluff.

Laminated beds and Lignite below the gravel at Ra leigh, in Shelby County, and on Coal Creek, in Lauderdale.

12. Post Tertiary.

Presents two formations, as follows:

12,*a*. *Bluff Gravel*, and

12,*b*. *Bluff Loam.*

12,*a*. BLUFF GRAVEL.

Char.—A persistent bed of sand and *gravel*, appearing along the face of the Mississippi Bluff, from Kentucky to Mississippi.

Thickness, from 10 to 50 feet.

Ex.—The gravel bed of the bluffs at Randolph and Fulton.

The gravel in the lower part of the Bluff at Memphis.

The gravel in the section at Raleigh.

The gravel bed in the Bluff along the east side of Reelfoot Lake, in Obion.

12,*b*. BLUFF LOAM.

Char.—A remarkable bed of light, ashen, buff-colored earth—a fine silicious loam, more or less calcareous. Caps the Mississippi Bluff at all points.

Thickness, from 30 to 100 feet.

Ex.—The city of Memphis is built upon it; seen in the cuts made about the city, as well as in the upper part of the Bluff.

Tne following towns are located upon it: Covington, Ripley, Dyersburg and Troy, and in addition to the county towns, Raleigh and Portersville.

13. Alluvium.

In this are grouped, (*provisionally*,)

13,*a*. *The Gravel of the Western Iron-ore Region, or simpler, the Ore-region Gravel.*

13,*b*. *The Gravel bordering the rivers of East Tennessee, or the Eastern Gravel.*

13,*c*. *The alluvial beds of the river bottoms, and especially of the Mississippi.*

13,*a*. THE ORE-REGION GRAVEL.

Char.—West of Nashville, *on the highlands* crossed in going to the Tennessee River, are often seen beds of gravel. These occupy high and low points, especially the former. This gravel is seen on both sides of the Tennessee River, and often many miles from it; it occurs, too, on the rolling lands outside of the bottoms, in the valley itself.

13,*b*. THE EASTERN GRAVEL.

Char., etc.—Bordering the rivers of East Tennessee, and running back several miles from them, are almost universally beds of gravel. This gravel is often coarse, and consists of rounded pebbles—the water-worn fragments of the rocks of the mountains through which the rivers flow.

13,*c*. THE ALLUVIAL BEDS OF THE RIVERS.

All the rivers have bottoms made up of beds of sand, or clay, or both. The rivers have formed, and are forming, these beds.

The bottom of the Mississippi is a great area, constituting a division of the State. (§ 296.)

Beds of gravel, too, belong to this alluvial group. The sand-bars of the rivers show much gravel, fine and coarse.

On the next page is a table exhibiting at one view, the probable equivalents of the older, or paleozoic rocks, as named and described in different countries and States. It will be useful for reference. This table has been taken from the Report on the Geology of Canada, for 1863. The Tennessee column has been changed so as to agree with the classification adopted in the work.

TABLE PRO V LENTS AMONG THE PALÆOZOIC ROCKS OF GREAT BRITAIN AND NORTH AMERICA.

	I. Great Britain.	II. Western Canada.	III. Eastern Canada.	IV. New York.	V. Pennsylvania.		VI. Tennessee.
Carboniferous.	Carboniferous series.	....	.... Bonaventure formation.	....	XIII. XII. XI. X.	Seral. Umbral. Vespertine.	IX. Coal Measures. VIII*b*. Mountain limestone. VIII*a*. Siliceous.
Devonian.	Upper Devonian. Middle Devonian. Lower Devonian.	.... Chemung and Portage group. Hamilton formation. Corniferous formation. Oriskany formation.	Gaspe sandstones, and Famine River limestones.	Catskill group. Chemung group. Portage group. Genesee slates. Hamilton group. Upper Helderberg group. { Onondaga and Corniferous limestones. Schoharie grit. Cauda-galli grit. Oriskany sandstone.	IX. VIII. VII.	Ponent. Vergent. Cadent. Post merid'nal. Meridional.	VII. Black shale. ....?
Upper Silurian.	Ludlow Group.	.... Water limestone. Onondaga formation.	Limestones of Gaspe and the Bay of Chaleurs.	Lower Helderberg gr. { Upper Pantamerus, Encrinal, Delthyris, Pentamerus, and Tentaculite limestones. Water-line group. Onondaga salt group.	VI.	Pre-merid'nal. Scalent.	VI. Lower Helderberg.
Middle Silurian.	Wenlock limestones. Upper Llandovery rocks. Lower Llandovery rocks.	Guelph formation. Anticosti group. { Niagara formation. Clinton formation. Medina formation.	Limestones of the Chatte River.	.... Niagara limestone. Clinton group. Medina sandstone. Oneida conglomerate.	V. IV.	Surgent. Levant.	V. Niagara.
Lower Silurian.	Caradoc or Bala Group. Upper Llandeilo rocks. Lower Llandeilo rocks. Lingula flags.	Hudson River gr. { Hudson River formation, and Utica formation. Trenton group. { Trenton formation. Black River and Birdseye formation. Chazy formation. Calciferous formation. Potsdam sandstone.	.... Hudson River and Trenton groups probably wanting. .... Quebec Group. Potsdam group.	Hudson River gr. { H'ds'n Riv'r shales, or Loraine shales. Utica Slate. Trenton, Black River, and Birdseye limestones. Chazy limestone. Calciferous sandstone. Potsdam sandstone.	III. II. I.	Matinal. Auroral. Primal.	IV. Nashville. III. Trenton. II. Potsdam.

CHAPTER VI.

THE METAMORPHIC GROUP; FORMATION I.

CRYSTALLINE ROCKS IN EASTERN PART OF STATE—THE METAMORPHIC CONDITION—GEOGRAPHICAL POSITION, EXTENT AND RANGE—VARIETIES, AND GENERAL DISTRIBUTION—DIP AND RELATIONS TO STRATA, OF OTHER GROUPS—USEFUL PRODUCTS, MINES AND MINERALS—AGRICULTURAL FEATURES.

379. In the last chapter, general tables of the formations were given. I now propose to describe each group, in as much detail as may be desirable. The lowest, or oldest, in the series, will be considered first, and is the subject of this chapter; the others, will be taken up successively, in ascending order, and will be treated of in succeeding chapters.

In describing a formation, reference will, in general, be made to its *geographical position, extent and range;* its *topography;* its *lithological character;* its *fossils*, its *useful ores, minerals and rocks;* its *agricultural features*, and to such other characters and relations belonging to it, as circumstances may make desirable.

380. *Crystalline Rocks in the Eastern Part of the State; the Metamorphic Condition.*—In the extreme eastern part of the State, and forming some of the highest mountains of the Unaka Chain, (§ 41,) are certain rocks, composed for the most part, of the same mineral constituents that make up granite. These rocks are crystalline in structure, occur in stratified beds, and belong mostly to the varieties called by geologists, *gneiss*, (a term equivalent in meaning, to *stratified granite,*) *talcose slate, and mica slate.* They are *altered*, or, in technical language, *metamorphic* rocks. They were once common sandstones, conglomerates, shales, &c., but have lost their original character, and have become crystalline, through the agency of subterranean heat, or, in other words, through the *steaming* or *baking*, to which they have been subjected.

381. A portion of the strata under consideration, can be traced out, to unaltered beds. The original strata, from which they have been derived,

are, thereby, known. As these will be described hereafter, it might be thought, that their metamorphosed, or altered parts, ought to be noticed then. It must, however, be recollected, that all of our metamorphic rocks, cannot be, as yet, referred back, satisfactorily, to known, unaltered beds; and that, in addition, those which can be, are so thoroughly changed as to be essentially different from their originals. At the same time, they are much the same in kind and form, when taken together, a natural group, which, for practical purposes, it would be inconvenient to break up. It has been thought best, therefore, to include all these rocks—those which have been thoroughly altered, and are truly metamorphic—in one group.

It may, however, be desirable, when speaking hereafter, of the unaltered beds, to notice whenever there may be occasion, how far they have contributed to this group.

382. *Geographical Position; Extent and Range.*—The metaphoric rocks, are wholly confined to East Tennessee. With the exception of two very limited strips, to be mentioned hereafter, they occur in detached areas or sections, immediately along the North Carolina line. (See Map.) These sections, however, are only detached within the limits of Tennessee; they are parts of a continuous and extensive belt of rocks which runs from Virginia to Georgia, having its western limit, alternately, in North Carolina and in Tennessee.

To the west of this belt, and in contact with it, are great beds of conglomerate and slates, and occasionally, of sandstone and limestone.

383. The line separating the rocks just mentioned, from those under consideration, or, in other words, the western limit of the Metamorphic Group, is, sometimes well defined, often, however, but poorly, the rocks gradually losing their crystalline characters, and running insensibly into the adjacent conglomerates and slates. In general direction, the line of separation conforms to the Appalachian, northeastern, and southwestern trend, (§ 18,)—the direction in which the mountain ridges of this portion of the State, for the most part, run.

Such too, is the general course of the boundary line which separates us from North Carolina. This was fixed, in the main, along the range of the highest mountains, west of the Blue Ridge. This range is the principal axis of the Unaka Chain, (§ 41,) which, therefore, not only divides the States, but, is, *approximatively*, as was pointed out by Troost, the western limit of truly metamorphic rocks.

384. The limited and isolated patches of gneiss, mica slate, and allied rocks, that we have in Tennessee, may almost be said to be ours, accidentally, being mere sections cut off from the main North Carolina belt, by the meanderings of the State line, and belonging, *physically*, to our sister State. Nevertheless, we welcome them, adding, as they do, an interesting member to our geological series, and bearing with them, ores for our miners, and majestic grass-covered mountains for our herdsmen.

385. It remains to trace out more in detail our metamorphic areas. Commencing in Johnson County, at the extreme northeastern corner of the State, the conspicuous White Top Mountain, being our starting point, with its neighbors, the Beech Mountain, Slate Face, &c., (§ 48,) in our track, we find the group represented, (if represented at all,) by a narrow strip, adjacent to the North Carolina line, scarcely within the State, and not well marked at that, the rocks being, apparently, not more than the half-baked layers of the group next to be described. The rocks here, are, in great part, a pale, greenish talcose slates, often abounding in small, rough masses, or knots of quartz, which are, perhaps, remains of pebbles. These slates, might be referred to the Ocoee Group.

386. Progressing southwestward, along the line, however, we find the metamorphic character well defined. Opposite Taylorsville, the county town of Johnson, the group, consisting mostly of gneissoid rocks, spreads out, and becomes several miles wide, reaching to within about three miles of the town. The group is here, at one point, in direct contact with a band of magnesian limestone. Eastward, at the State line, it forms Stone Mountain.

387. In a southeastern direction from Taylorsville, at the distance of a little more than four miles, a narrow band of gneissoid rocks, with greenstone, is met with. This is separated from the main belt by conglomerate, the latter, being not far from a mile wide. After the conglomerate, going southeastward, the gneiss sets in again, and continues up the mountain four or five miles, to the State line.

388. The western limit of the group, in this county, has a nearly direct southwest course. The State line, however, southeast of Taylorsville, makes an elbow eastward, which throws a considerable area of these rocks into Tennessee. In the southern part of the county, the boundary line returns, and, where it crosses the Watauga River, very nearly coincides

with the western limit of the group. The Johnson County portion of our metamorphic rocks, is thus nearly, but not quite, detached.

389. Soon after crossing the Watauga, the rocks of the group extend out rapidly westward, until their western limit in Carter County, (measured along the waters of the Big Doe,) is about fourteen miles from the State line. Here is the greatest width of metamorphic rocks in the State. The area they thus form, is one of much interest.

It includes the group of mountain-hemmed valleys called Crab Orchard. (§ 52.) It has, along its eastern and southern boundary, the Noble Mountains, the Humps, the Big Yellows, and the Roan. (§§ 54 and 55.) Its rocks and minerals, too, are matters of interest, and will be referred to.

390. The State line between the "bluff" of the Roan (§ 55,) and Iron Mountain to the west, is the southern boundary of the metamorphic area. In its course from the Watauga River to Iron Mountain, the State line, forming a great bend, and approaching closely the sandstones and limestones of Limestone Cove, (§ 57,) almost detaches a metamorphic section for Carter, as we have seen it nearly does for Johnson.

391. East of Limestone Cove, the Metamorphic Group has a width of not more than two miles. From this point, it continues in a belt, from three to six miles wide, running in a nearly southwest course, through Washington County, into North Carolina. This portion forms two high and noble mountains, both on the State line, the so-called Unaka, partly in Carter, and the Great Bald, in the southeastern part of Washington. (§ 59.) Soon after leaving the Bald, the State line turns round to the north and west again, and runs a dozen miles or, more, before it resumes its normal direction. It thus forms a great S-shaped bend. (See Map.) This throws the Metamorphic Group wholly within North Carolina, where it remains for many miles, not entering Tennessee again until it passes the French Broad River.

392. The belt of metamorphic rocks, reaching from the northeastern corner of the State through Johnson and Carter Counties, to the extreme southern part of Washington, is the most extensive in Tennessee. It is nearly cut into three detached sections, as we have seen, by the windings of the State line. Its entire length is nearly seventy miles.

393. In Cocke County, near the headwaters of Big Creek, the Metamorphic Group appears again on the mountains of the

line. To follow the group, or rather its western limit, continuously, through North Carolina, let us return to the southern part of Washington. From this point, after leaving Tennessee, it runs southwestward, nearly coinciding with the course of the Laurel, a tributary of the French Broad. A few miles above the Warm Springs, it crosses the French Broad, soon wheels around to the west, all adjacent formations doing the same, and runs to the Tennessee line. Thus, at the point designated above, in Cocke County, the true gneissoid rocks are thrown again upon our boundary, and, for a few miles, within the State. It is only, however, for a short distance comparatively; they soon pass back again into North Carolina.

394. From this region, southwestward a long distance, on down to the headwaters of Tellico River, in Monroe County, there are no important areas of metamorphic rocks, the high mountains of the State line being composed, in the main, of the group next to be described—the Great Conglomerate, and its slates.

395. In passing around the headwaters of Tellico River, the State line throws out an elbow to the southeast, which projects out far enough to have its apex crossed by the metamorphic rocks. This gives another area of these rocks.

396. A few miles further on, in the vicinity of the Hiwassee River, the metamorphic rocks, mostly mica and talcose slates, again enter the State and run across its southeastern corner into Georgia. The area thus formed is one of great interest, and is well known as that in which the Ducktown Copper Mines occur. Five or six miles north of the Hiwassee, the State line, instead of following the highest dividing ridges, takes a straight course, nearly southward, to the Georgia line. (§ 68.) Had the boundary been marked out along what may be regarded as its natural route, the Ducktown region would have been thrown into North Carolina. The area thus, we may say accidentally, given us, lies in Polk County, is triangular in form, has a base along the Georgia line about nine miles in length, and includes altogether, about sixty square miles.

397. Such are our principal metamorphic areas, the most extensive and important being respectively at the northeast and southeast corners of the State. All mentioned are segments of

the North Carolina belt. Together, they occupy comparatively, as may be best appreciated by referring to the Map, a very small part of the State.

As to *thickness*, it is difficult to make an approximation to the truth. It is certain that the volume of the group is great. A mile in thickness may be a small estimate.

398. We have before referred to two limited strips as exceptions, occurring, as they do, entirely detached from the metamorphic group proper. These strips are limited in extent, and are mainly interesting on account of the singular positions they respectively occupy.

The first occurs in Johnson County, about three miles west of Taylorsville, and five or six miles west of the gneissoid rocks, and separated from them by formations not at all metamorphosed. The strip is narrow, but a few rods wide, and is made up of gneissic rocks, which are included between highly-inclined layers of conglomerate on the one hand, and of calcareous slates upon the other—all lying at the base of Iron Mountain.

399. The other strip is of more interest, though, perhaps, not as well characterized as to its metamorphic condition. It is located near Clinch River, on the west side, in Union County. It is from fifty to one hundred feet wide; includes a bed of comparatively homogeneous, bluish or greenish, shale, but is mostly made up of a soft, dark-greenish gray shale, abounding in smoky scales of mica, and in grains of magnetite. Good cabinet specimens of magnetite, often in crystals, and fine masses of grayish-white compact chorite, are found in the shale, and scattered about upon the surface. The strip lies in a line of great dislocation, running in a northeasterly and southwesterly direction. It separates the gray magnesian limestone of the Knox Group, (2,*c*,) upon the southeast, from lower carboniferous strata, upon the northwest.

It is possible that other metamorphic strips may be found in this or neighboring counties. I have occasionally been told of the finding of mica, etc., at different points. In some cases, it has been turned up by the plough. As yet, however, no other areas of metamorphic character than those mentioned, have been observed. If they exist at all, they are certainly of very limited extent, and unimportant.

400. *Varieties, and their General Distribution.*—As already stated, our metamorphic rocks are, in good part, *gneiss* and *mica slate*—rocks which, like granite, are generally aggregates, or mixtures, of three distinct minerals—*quartz*, *feldspar* and *mica*. It must be mentioned, however, that many of them are *syenitic;* that is, they contain the mineral *hornblende* in place of mica. Such rocks are syenitic, or hornblendic, gneiss. In addition to these, chloritic slates are also met with.

401. East and southeast of Taylorsville, in *Johnson County*, where the group is well defined, the rocks are generally gneiss, which is here mostly composed of quartz and feldspar, (often reddish,) with but little mica. They are, for the most part, thick-bedded, sometimes slaty.

402. The large area in *Carter*, mentioned above, (§ 389)—the Crab Orchard region—contains several varieties of gneissoid rocks. These are mostly quartzose and feldspathic, mica not being abundant. At some points, a slaty gray quartzose and hornblendic rock occurs for the most part. The rocks of the Roan Mountain are, in good part, a gray, rather slaty, gneiss, much of it syenitic. In some parts of this region, however, gneiss with mica, is found.

403. In the southern part of *Carter*, east of Limestone Cove, gneiss again prevails; mica slates, however, and, to a limited extent, talcose slates, also occur. Here, too, the gneiss is occasionally more or less syenitic. Such, also, in brief, are the characters of the metamorphic group through *Washington County*.

404. In *Cocke County*, the group, as mentioned above, appears again. (§ 393.) In this section, the rocks are "a granite," (gneiss,) which is composed of quartz, reddish feldspar, a few small spangles of black mica and chloritic talc, which belongs to the *protogine* of the French geologists."* In one portion of this county, near the point at which the group enters the State, a rock has been observed abounding in greenish granular epidote, being in fact, a kind of epidote gneiss. Pebbles of this material frequently occur along some of the small streams, in the northeastern part of the county.

405. Passing to the southern part of the State, and taking the Ducktown region, in *Polk County*, as an example, we find the rocks mostly talcose chloritic and mica slates. Interstratified with these, beds of hornblendic rock are met with.

Such, in general, are our metamorphic rocks. It will be seen that, with the exception of the region last mentioned, gneiss (which is sometimes syenitic) is the prevailing rock.

406. *Trap*, or *Greenstone dikes*, are occasionally found intersecting the metamorphic strata; they are apparently most numerous in the large area

* Troost; Fifth Report.

of Carter. Here, too, are bands of granite-like materials, which most likely are of volcanic origin. Volcanic rocks, however, as a general thing, are not abundant or conspicuous within the limits of Tennessee. A few dikes have been observed in the Ocoee Group.

Veins of quartz are frequently seen, interstratified with (rarely intersecting) the metamorphic strata. In the Ducktown region they are quite numerous.

407. *Dip and Relations to Strata of other Groups.*—The metamorphic beds, together with those of other groups that are adjacent or neighboring, all appear to follow the same law of dip and strike. The *dip* (or inclination of the beds) is, in the main, at a high angle to the southeast, the *strike* (or direction of their edges along the surface) being northeast and southwest. I have not been able to satisfy myself as to the want of conformableness in the beds of this group, or in these and beds of adjacent groups taken together. They all apparently belong to the same system of upheavals—have been crowded upon their edges by the same forces, and during the same period. At some points there appear to be exceptions, the beds of this group coming abruptly against others not metamorphic, as in Johnson, where the gneiss comes in contact with limestone. (§ 386.) Other similar cases occur. But these unconformable junctions are naturally referable to *local* fractures and displacements. Such displacements are common in Tennessee, even among members of the same group. Moreover, this unconformableness is local, and not the rule; it is generally true that the metamorphic beds run so gradually into adjacent unaltered ones, that it is difficult, within certain limits, to trace out a line of separation.

408. With reference to age, I have no reason for believing that this group, within Tennessee, includes the metamorphosed beds of any formation of more recent date, than the Ocoee Conglomerate and Slates. A portion of the beds are certainly referable to the Ocoee Group; the remainder, although conformable, may be older, and most likely are.

There are sections which show clearly the change of the conglomerate, and its associated rocks, into gneiss and mica, and other slates. In approaching, for instance, the Ducktown region, from the west, the pebbles of the conglomerate gradually lose their forms, becoming more and more, small, shapeless masses of quartz, and yet discernible, even when the gneissoid or complete metamorphic character is seen. In the northern part of the State, at many points, the passage of the Ocoee beds into gneiss, is gradual and apparent. A considerable part, indeed, of our metamorphic rocks, can be, I think, thus referred to these beds. The question as to the greater age of other parts, is not so easily settled, and must remain open for the present. I know of no sufficient reason for referring any of these rocks to the Huronian or Laurentian series of Canada.

409. *Useful Rocks, Mines and Minerals.*—It is proposed simply to mention here the useful purposes to which some of the rocks under consideration, have been, and may be, applied, and to give a catalogue of the minerals which occur, and have been observed within the limits of the Group. Further details will be found in Part Third of this Report, where the useful rocky material, the ores and minerals of all the formations, are specially and systematically considered.

410. Valuable quarries of *building materials* might be opened in some of the beds of this Group, especially in the more northern counties, where syenetic gneiss is found. I have frequently seen in Johnson, Carter and Washington, beds of gneiss, both gray and flesh colored, from which handsome and durable blocks might easily be quarried. Beds suitable for such purposes, occur, too, in Cocke County, and might be found among the mica beds of Polk. It is to be regretted, that such localities are nowhere intersected by any of our railroads, for, otherwise, we might have *Tennessee* "granite" for our public edifices. As it is, the blocks, if quarried, would have to be hauled twenty-five or thirty miles, even from the most convenient localities, before they could reach a railroad. But this difficulty will, doubtless, be overcome at no distant day.

411. At several points the hard quartzose gneiss has afforded tolerably good *millstones*. In Johnson County, a few miles east of Taylorsville, stones have been cut out of such material, and have answered a good purpose, especially for grinding corn. In Carter, on Little Doe River, about twelve miles from Elizabethton, a syenitic gneiss, or granite, was formerly worked into millstones, some of which were of large size, and were, at one time, highly esteemed, both for grinding corn and wheat. Of late years, however, they have not been manufactured, owing to the introduction of foreign buhr-stone.

White quartz rock, too, from veins in this Group, has been cut into millstones, which have been used with very satisfactory results.

412. The most interesting *mineral regions* within the limits of the Group, are those of Ducktown, in Polk County, and of Crab Orchard, in Carter; the first, very near the extreme southeastern corner of the State, on the Ocoee River, has attracted much attention on account of its "*Copper Mines;*" the second, although by no means having the importance of the first, is interesting as a locality of *Magnetic Oxide of Iron*, (*magnetite.*)

413. The *Copper Mines* will be spoken of hereafter, in sufficient detail. The following are the principal *ores* and *minerals* they afford:

Ores and Minerals of the Copper Mines.

1. *Copper Pyrites*, an important ore.
2. *Iron Pyrites*, occurs with the last, abundantly.
3. *Magnetic Pyrites*, associated with 1 and 2 in quantity.
4. *Copper Glance*, in small quantity.
5. *Zinc Blende*, " " "
6. *Galena*, " " "
7. *Orthoclase*,
8. *Albite*,
9. *Tremolite*,
10. *Actinolite*,
11. *Diallage*,
12. *Zoisite*,
13. *Calcite*,
14. *Quartz*,
15. *Rutile*,

(7–15) } Associated with the preceding ores in greater or less quantity, many of them are found in well developed and beautiful crystals.

16. *Garnets*, plentiful in some slates.
17. *Allophane.*
18. *Alisonite*; rare.
19. *Bornite.*
20. *Red Copper*, a rich ore.
21. *Chalcotrichite*, unimportant.
22. *Malachite*, a rich ore.
23. *Azurite*; rare.
24. *Copperas.*
25. *Blue Stone*, valuable.
26. "*Black Oxide*," a name applied to a mixture of oxides and sulphides of copper and iron. It is of great value as an ore.

27. *Native Copper*, not in quantity.
28. *Harrisite*, rare.
29. *Rahtite*, a doubtful mineral.
30. *Limonite*, ("*Gossan*,") abundant.

The minerals last enumerated, commencing with No. 17, may be called secondary minerals, as they have been derived by oxidation, and other chemical processes, from the ores at the head of the list.

414. In *Crab Orchard*, (§ 389,) the following minerals occur:

1. *Magnetite*, in workable quantity.
2. *Pyroxene*, (Sahlite,) crystalline associated with magnetite.
3. *Hornblende*, and
4. *Epidote*, associated also with magnetite.

415. Other minerals and localities, are as follows: *Specular Iron*, occasionally in small plates or masses in gneissoid rocks, in Washington, and other counties; *Molybdenite*, occasionally in scales, in Washington; *Epidote* in gneiss, or granite, forming a kind of epidote gneiss abundant in Cocke County.

In § 399, I have mentioned the occurrence of *magnetite* and *chlorite* in the curious metaphoric or semi-metaphoric strip in Union County.

416. *Agricultural Features.*—The rocks of this group form, for the most part, in Tennessee, high, rough mountains, attached to which, we do not expect to find much agricultural interest. These mountains are generally cold and rocky, with a thin, sandy soil. Nevertheless, on the tops of some of the highest ranges, are extensive tracts, which, in summer, are covered with grass, and then are common pasture grounds for the "stock" of the farmers in the valleys. At this season the cool temperature is agreeable, and herd and herdsmen enjoy it.

417. I have already spoken of the *Balds* of the Unakas. (See pages 33–36.) Some of the most noted, those of the Roan, and that of the Great Bald, in Washington County, belong to metamorphic mountains. The soils of these places are often prairie-like, black and rich. On some of the wooded slopes, also, are tracts of considerable fertility, upon which may be found growing, the beech, walnut, wild cherry and poplar.

418. It is rare to meet with a settler located upon these mountains. The summer is too short, and the winter is too

severe. The "settlements" are in the narrow valleys at the bases of the mountains, where the winds are cut off, and spring is early. These valleys sometimes present along the streams, strips of rich, sandy bottoms, which well repay labor, in yielding corn, wheat, rye, potatoes, etc. Crab Orchard, in Carter County, is a group of such valleys, (§ 52,) and the only group on metamorphic rocks, the middle or northern part of the State. (§ 389.)

419. In the Ducktown Basin are also numerous valleys dotted with small farms. The Ocoee, especially, has a number of rich, sandy bottoms. The Ducktown region, including Turtletown, is, indeed, by far the most important agricultural, as well as mineral, area, the metamorphic rocks present.

420. Excepting the alluvial flats of the mountain-hemmed valleys, the agricultural features of the metamorphic group are, upon the whole, of limited interest. Its soils, compared with those of the great limestone formations, take an inferior place. The mountains will be, for the most part, grazing ground for cattle, and, for this purpose, they doubtless have a future.

CHAPTER VII.

THE POTSDAM GROUP; SERIES II.

420, *a*. This group includes three great subdivisions, each of which, may be regarded, as a Formation. They are as follows, in ascending order:

2, *a*. *The Ocoee Conglomerate and Slates.*

2, *b*. *The Chilhowee Sandstone*, and

2, *c*. *The Knox Group of Shales; Dolomites, and Limestones.*

The equivalents of these, in other States, and in Canada, are given in the tables, in chapter V. The table on page 169, presents the synonymes in one view.

421. The group corresponds to Dana's *Potsdam Period*, and, in the above arrangement, my purpose has been to follow him. It is not easy to separate, lithologically, the *Ocoee sub-group* from the *Chilhowee*, as they often run into each other. The distinction between the latter and the *Knox* is much more apparent.

Perhaps a better arrangement would have been, to throw the *Ocoee* and *Chilhowee* together, as the *Potsdam*, the *Knox* remaining as an individual group. We may, hereafter, find *Paradoxides* in the slates of the Ocoee, and a fauna, which will justify us in separating it from the Chilhowee permanently. But, be the grouping what it may, in this Report the sub-divisions above will be treated of as separate formations, so that there can be no misunderstanding. Each sub-division will be the subject of a section.

422. *Formations of the Unakas.*—Before considering the subdivisions, or formations above, specifically, it will be well to state that the first two—the Ocoee and Chilhowee Formations, in conjunction with the Metamorphic Group already described—embrace all the rocks of the Unaka ridges. These are, emphatically, mountain-making formations. The Metamorphic, with the Ocoee, build up the greater more easterly range with its subordinate parts; (§§ 46, 66;) the Chilhowee sandstone makes the bold isolated outliers which so singularly skirt, in a long broken line from Virginia to Georgia, the base of the

greater range. The former are the formations of White Top, Stone Mountain, the Roan, the Great Bald, the Big Butt, the Great Smoky, the Frog, &c. The latter is the formation of the Holston, the Buffalo, the Meadow Creek, the Chilhowee, the Star's Mountain, and a number of others which are links in this outlying chain.

Section I.

THE OCOEE CONGLOMERATE AND SLATES; FORMATION 2,*a*. SECTION ON THE OCOEE RIVER—EXTENT AND TOPOGRAPHY—CROSS SECTIONS; LITHOLOGICAL AND OTHER CHARACTERS; (*a*) TELLICO SECTION; (*b*) LITTLE TENNESSEE SECTION; (*c*) SECTION OF THE VALLEY OF EAST TENNESSEE; (*d*) LITTLE PIGEON SECTION; (*e*) THE GROUP ON BIG PIGEON; (*f*) FRENCH BROAD SECTION; (*g*) BIG BUTT; (*h*) GREASY COVE SECTION; (*i*) JOHNSON COVE SECTION—USEFUL ROCKS AND MINERALS—AGRICULTURAL FEATURES.

423. *The Section on the Ocoee River.*—It has been stated as a remarkable fact, (§§ 6, 41, and note, p. 21,) that the Unaka Chain, though higher and more massive than the Blue Ridge, in North Carolina, is intersected by the tributaries of the Holston and Tennessee Rivers, that rise upon the western slope of the latter ridge.

In passing the Unakas the tributaries flow through narrow rock-bound valleys, or gorges. The Ocoee is one of the tributary streams, and its gorge is the longest and grandest of all. In its tortuous course, the gorge is twelve or thirteen miles long, and is cut through the strata of the Ocoee Group. The belt of these rocks presented here, has a direct width of about twelve miles. The strata, from one end of the gorge to the other, are generally highly inclined, and, on both sides of the river, rise up from the water's edge in precipitous cliffs. There are but few bottoms in the whole distance, and these are very narrow—not wider than is necessary for the wagon road which has been constructed along the stream. Although, in general, the strata are highly inclined, with a dip to the southeast, yet they occur at all angles, and are frequently presented in great flexures, or are broken in faults.

424. In the route from Cleveland to the Copper Mines, we first pass over several wide belts of dolomite limestones and shales, (belonging mostly to

the Knox Formation) to the southern extremity of Star's Mountain. (See the section.) Passing around this extremity, and traveling for a few miles up the valley lying along the eastern base of the mountain mentioned, we at length turn eastward, and enter the great gorge of the Ocoee. Traveling through this, and making a considerable ascent at the same time, we finally reach the metamorphic rocks, and the elevated basin of the Ducktown region. A few miles further on, and the mines are in sight.

425. The section presented in the *gorge* of the Ocoee, is a very interesting one. The strata are well displayed. They are, in general, coarse gray conglomerates, talcose, chlorite and clay slates repeatedly interstratified, all having a semi-metamorphic aspect. The slates predominate, and of these, the greenish and light bluish gray, or the chloritic and talcose varieties, are the most abundant. At one point, more than half way through the gorge, at a place called *Mundic Bluff*, the slates are filled with beautiful cubes of pyrites, some of which are an inch through. At other points, weathered slates contain cubical cavities, from which the pyrites have disappeared.

426. The middle part of the section presents little conglomerate, but in the upper part, it abounds. Along the road, it will be seen exclusively for half-a-mile, or more; then, again, in great beds, alternating repeatedly with chloritic and clay slates. The lower part of the gorge has several heavy bands of conglomerate.

427. The conglomerate is sometimes coarse, the pebbles being as large as hen's eggs, or larger. Generally, however, they are smaller. Occasionally the rock becomes a sandstone. The pebbles are quartz and feldspar, mainly, generally rounded, but sometimes more or less angular. In addition to these, fragments of clay slate, and other varieties of slate, are often seen in the rock. The conglomerate usually contains more or less chloritic and talcose matter in its interstices.

Veins of quartz are occasionally seen in the cliffs of the Ocoee. They are often interpolated in the strata, so as to be conformable, but sometimes occur as fissure veins, especially the smaller ones. But very few exceed a foot in maximum thickness.

428. The following diagram exhibits the general section of the formations from Cleveland to the State line beyond Ducktown, and will serve to show the extent and the position of the Ocoee sub-group in this region.

The section is made along a straight line, running from Cleveland

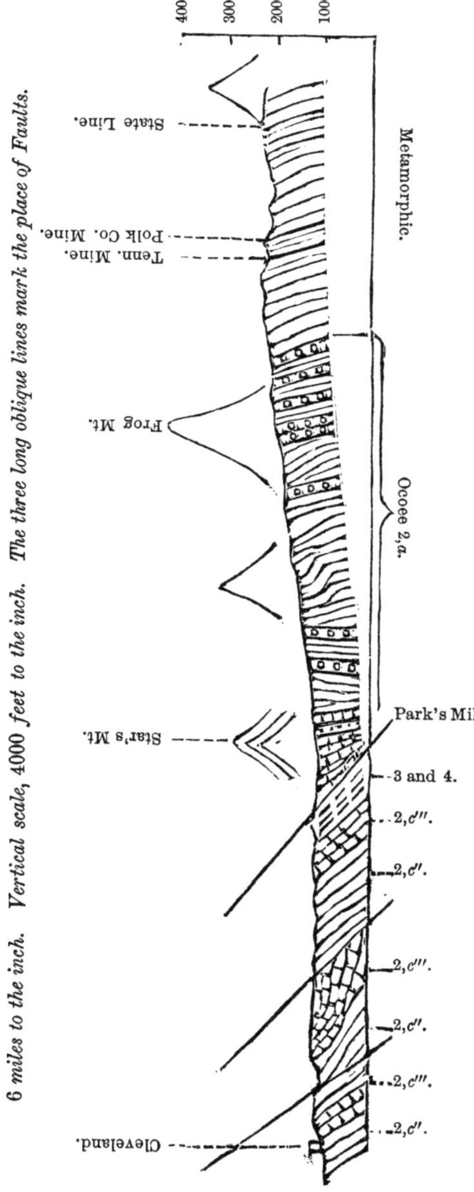

6 miles to the inch. Vertical scale, 4000 feet to the inch. The three long oblique lines mark the place of Faults.

through the gap at Park's Mill, on the Ocoee, and the Tennessee Mine, in Ducktown, to the North Carolina boundary. Observations made in the gorge of the Ocoee are referred to this line.

429. The rocks passed over from Cleveland to Star's Mountain, or to Park's Mill, have been mentioned. (§ 424.) In addition, it may be noticed, that one band of 3 and 4, (Trenton and Nashville rocks,) is intersected.

430. At the mill, a nearly vertical ledge of whitish quartzose sandstone, (Chilhowee sandstone, 2,*b*,) is met with. This ledge is all that is here seen of the great formation, which, further to the northeast, makes the massive Star's Mountain. At this point, there has been great displacement. Nearly all the sandstone is gone, and all the lower part of the Knox; and, moreover, some of the dolomite of the upper Knox has been thrown to the east of the sandstone ledge. Immediately east of this displacement, the Ocoee rocks begin, and continue through the belt of rough mountains to the Ducktown metamorphic basin.

431. *Extent and Topography of the Ocoee Formation.*—The strata of the Ocoee gorge, as given above, may be taken as types of the whole formation. This section presents, better, perhaps, than any other in the State, the general character of the formation, and, for that reason, has been more particularly noticed. The thickness of the Ocoee Formation is not known. It may be more than 10,000 feet.

It will be observed, (see Map,) that the great body of these rocks lie between the French Broad River and the Georgia line. Between these limits, they make a massive mountainous belt.

432. Northeast of the French Broad, we have several important belts, but no great continuous one, like that to the southwest. Of those to the northeast, that of the Big Butt Range, (§ 62,) is the most massive. In Johnson County, several belts are seen; one lying along the southeastern side of Iron Mountain; another, at the extreme northeastern corner of the State, adjacent to the strata forming Beech Summit, Cat Face, and Slate Face Peaks, on the State line; and another, southeast of Taylorsville.

433. The Ocoee Group, is, usually, adjacent, on its southeastern side, to the metamorphic rocks. Where this is not the case, and a later formation intervenes, it has been thrown out of place by a fault and dislocation. The relation the group sustains to the metamorphic beds, has been spoken of already. (§ 408.) On the western side, no fault interfering, it is bounded by the Chilhowee rocks, from which its strata are separated, often, by no well marked horizon. (§ 421.)

434. Some of the highest mountains of the Unaka Chain, as for instance, the Great Smoky, in Sevier County, the Balds, in Monroe, and the Big Frog, in Polk, together with others in the northern part of the State, already mentioned, are formed of strata of the Ocoee Formation. It is truly, as already stated, a mountain-making formation. (§ 422.)

435. Nevertheless, when the conglomerates are absent, it gives, often, especially in Sevier, Blount, and Monroe Counties, elevated plateau-like regions, and high valleys of some interest in an agricultural way. (§ 437.)

In Blount and Sevier Counties, its strata enclose the interesting coves described in the First Part of this Report, (§§ 133–135,) but these do not properly belong to this formation. They are based, mostly, on the rocks of the Knox Formation, and owe their origin to the fact that great patches of the Knox strata, were, during the period of disturbance, (§ 344,) cut off, and entangled among the Ocoee beds. These patches of softer rocks, by subsequent denudation, have been hollowed out into the coves, as we now find them.

436. *Cross Sections; Lithological, and other Characters, (a.)*— The section presented in the gorge of the Ocoee has been given. Passing northeastward, *that, from the old Tellico Iron Works in Monroe County, southward to the State line, may be noticed.* The old works are located on Tellico River, just within the edge of the Ocoee Group, a belt of Knox dolomites and shales, lying but a little distance to the northwest, about the Furnace, and commencing below at the edge of the Knox, the rocks are mostly, pale greenish or bluish, semi-talcose slates, containing, occasionally, bands of sandstone and conglomerate. Some of these slates are fissile, and might furnish roofing slates. Passing from the Furnace, southeastward, the same rocks continue for about two miles, and, within this distance, rise up into a considerable mountain, over which the North Carolina road passes. Ascending the Tellico River, from the Furnace into the gorge through which the river passes the above mountain, the slates, including at intervals, bands of sandstone and conglomerate, are well seen. At the upper rapids, three-fourths of a mile from the Furnace, the conglomerate is well characterized.

437. Crossing the mountain, we reach an elevated and wide belt of mountain country, almost wholly made up of slates. This belt, viewed from high points, appears like a wide, shallow trough, lying between the great mountains on the line, and the mountain, or range, just crossed, the rocks of which we have considered.* The width of the belt is from four to five miles. It extends, longitudinally, to the northeast and southwest, nearly as far as the eye can reach. In a direct line, we enter it about two miles from the Iron Works. It includes the gold region of Coqua, or Coca Creek, a circumstance which attaches much interest to it as a metaliferous region.

* I have spoken of this mountain as a single range; it consists, really, of two ranges near together, with no great depression between. The site of Tellico Iron Works, is at the western base of the double range.

438. The slates of this belt, dip, as usual, to the southeast, at varying angles, but generally, with steep inclinations. They are talcose and chloritic slates; of pale blue and greenish colors, much like those about the Tellico works. Many of them present a silvery aspect, and a semi-micaceous appearance. In crossing the country, veins of quartz are frequently met with, intercolated between the layers of slate. Among these, some are gold-bearing, the special consideration of which belongs to the Third Part of this Report.

439. Passing to the southeast, beyond the belt just considered, and reaching the foot of the mountain on the line, we again come up with conglomerates and slates. Beyond, in North Carolina, these are succeeded by the metamorphic strata.

440. (*b.*) The *Section of the Ocoee Group presented along the Little Tennessee* from the end of Chilhowee Mountain to the State line, is now to be considered.

This section shows more conglomerate, alternating with the slates, than the last. It also exhibits, entangled in Ocoee strata, several patches and bands of limestone, or dolomite. Several of these are extensive enough to have formed by denudation, coves of some interest, the river intersecting them: Chilhowee and Tallassee Coves, are the principal ones. The limestones and dolomites of Tallassee, the uppermost cove, show, by fossils, that they belong to the lower part of the Nashville Formation, (the Nash,) and the upper part of the Knox. The other bands of limestone, belong, perhaps, to the Knox. But it is uncertain. From their relations to the conglomerate, one would almost be ready to locate them in the Ocoee Group. And to this we would be more inclined, were it not for the fossiliferous character of the Tallassee rocks.

A few layers of limestone are met with, which are made up of angular fragments and pebbles of calcareous matter forming breccias and calcareous pudding-stones. Some of these, have been worked as marble.

441. Chilhowee Mountain, and with it, for the most part, its special group of sandstones, runs out, before quite reaching the Tennessee River. On the river, in a line with the mountain, therefore, the Chilhowee sandstones are absent. There is, here, much displacement of the formations. A band of conglomerate forming a considerable ridge, is seen on the northwest side of the point of Chilhowee. It is too, separated from the greater body of conglomerate, by a narrow band of Nash rocks.

442. Passing the range of Chilhowee Mountain, and traveling the road up the river, we intersect, for the first three miles, heavy beds of conglomerate and slates interstratified. Much of the conglomerate is very coarse. In the first mile, a narrow band of breccia limestone is seen. In the fourth mile, Chilhowee Cove is entered. This is, for the most part, surrounded by slates.

From the cove mentioned, to Tallassee, the road does not run directly across the strata. The belt of rocks intersected is between two and three miles wide. They are, mainly, pale greenish talcose slates, and contain but few beds of conglomerate. A second bed of breccia limestone is seen in this division.

443. Passing the limestones of Tallassee Cove, slates and conglomerates appear again, and continue to be the rocks on to the State line, a direct distance of about seven miles. The line runs on the top of a mountain ridge, and as we approach this, the relative amount of conglomerate increases, becoming finally greater in volume than the slates.*

The slates and conglomerates have the same general character that they have on the Ocoee. Of the slates, the pale greenish, or bluish, predominate. About half-way between Tallassee and the State line, a considerable bod of clay slate is seen. All the way between these points, veins of quartz are occasionally met with.

444. (*c.*) I introduce on the next page, *a section taken directly across the middle and narrowest part of the Valley of East Tennessee.* It was constructed for the purpose of illustrating the geological peculiarities of the Great Valley. It extends from the Cumberland Table-land, in a southeasterly direction, to the mountain on the North Carolina line, striking the latter in the region of the two Balds a few miles to the northeast of the Little Tennessee River. The Ocoee Group is seen in this section, at its southeastern end. The relation it sustains to the Chilhowee sandstone, and to the other formations, will be observed.

445. The length of the section is 52 miles. Eight great faults are crossed. (§§ 344, 359, 360.) The places of these are indicated by the oblique lines reaching above the surface. It is to be observed that no great flexures

* In the mountain gorges, near the line, are frequently observed great isolated blocks of conglomerate, as large as good-sized cabins. These the mountain-men call "graybacks," a name reminding one of the old *graywacke*. These graybacks have rolled from above, into the gorges.

occur. This is the most crowded part of the Valley. The incipient folds were split open longitudinally, and the southwestern side of each heaved up and over the northwestern. The older formation is on the southeastern side of a fault. In passing from one fault, in a southeasterly direction, to another, the successive formations are met with in ascending order until the second fault is reached; passing this, an older formation occurs again, to be followed, as before, by newer ones. The formations are thus arranged by the faults into successive series, the series being much alike, in fact, to a great extent, repetitions of the same thing. In the section there are eight of these series between Walden's Ridge and Chilhowee Mountain.

The formations mostly concerned in these repetitions, remain to be described. In connection with them, there will be frequent occasion to refer again to this section.

446. The section shows how Ocoee strata may occur along the northwestern base of a Chilhowee sandstone mountain. Several of these mountains have a strip of Ocoee rocks in this position. To this, however, we will refer, when we come to speak of the Chilhowee sandstones.

447. (*d.*) In *the route from Sevierville up the West Fork of the Little Pigeon, to the State line,* the rocks are well displayed. The road runs to the southeast and across the strata.

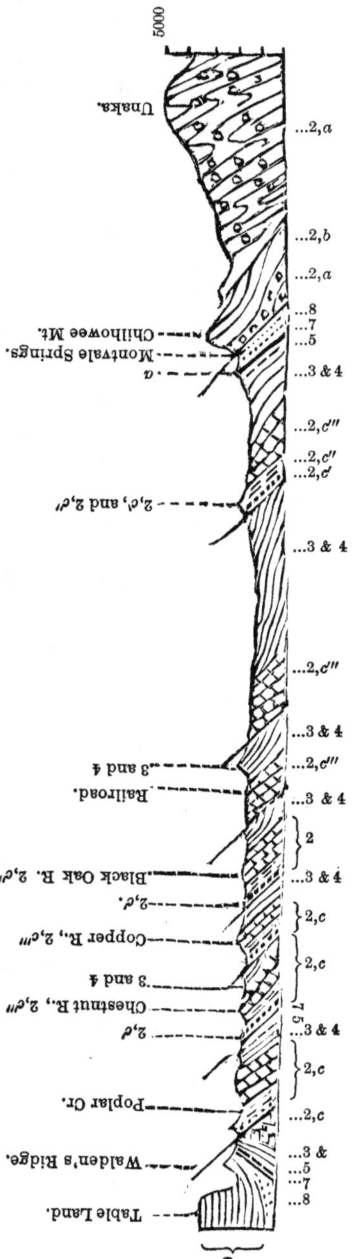

Sevierville is located on the *Graptolite Shale*. Leaving this point and proceeding on our route to the southeast, this shale continues for nearly two miles, when a band of Trenton limestone, with fossils, is encountered. This limestone is the top of a fold, and is soon followed by the shale. The latter, however, does not continue far. In half a mile after its first appearance, the limestone comes to the surface the second time, and is then followed by Knox limestones and dolomites, which are traveled over for the next mile and a half. Four miles from Sevierville, the Trenton re-appears, and is followed by the Graptolite Shale.

448. At six miles, and following the shale mentioned, a series of slates commence, which have a semi-metamorphic aspect. They are clay and talcose, or semi-talcose, and blue slates. Further on, they become more marked as talcose slates, of pale bluish and greenish colors. They dip generally at high angles, and are the rocks along the road as far as to the fifteenth mile, when they begin to be interstratified with bands of conglomerate. The belt is about nine miles wide. They enclose, occasionally, harder layers, approaching sandstone in texture, and, near the southeastern side of the belt, several bands of clay, or roofing slates.

449. Passing the fifteenth mile, the slates continue much the same, excepting that they are interstratified with bands of conglomerate. We have now reached the base of the great mountains of the State line. (§ 434.) From the fifteenth mile (the distance being estimated directly) to the line, is about eight miles. In the ascent, the alternating slates and conglomerates are crossed all the way. The bands of conglomerate are massive, and its "graybacks" fill the mountain ravines. (§ 443, note.) Reaching the summit, no true metamorphic rocks are seen, these being beyond, in North Carolina.

450. The slates of these mountains are often silvery, or semi-micaceous in appearance. At points they are dark bluish, and contain much pyrites, which, in sheltered places under the rocks, decomposes and forms, with alumina and magnesia, from the decomposing rocks, alum and Epsom salt. There is a noted locality of this kind on the side of one of the great ridges near the line of our section, called *Alum Cave*.

451. The section presented by these mountains, is much like

that between Tallassee Cove, on the Little Tennessee, and the State line. (§ 443.) Veins of quartz occur at intervals in it.

452. I have placed the western limit of the Ocoee Group at the point six miles from Sevierville. (§ 448.) Some of the slates included, may, however, belong to superior formations, as, for instance, to the *Graptolite Shale.* Further investigations are required to settle the question. For the present, the change in the character of the slates, together with the fact that, along this line of division, following the strike of the rocks, two or three miles to the northeast, (E. N. E.,) a band of characteristic coarse conglomerate occurs, justifies the arrangement adopted.

453. At a point on the Big East Fork of Little Pigeon, from seven to eight miles from Sevierville, the line of division, as adopted, between the Graptolite shale and the Ocoee slate, crosses this stream. East of this line is the band of conglomerate spoken of. The conglomerate is half a mile, or more, wide, includes two or three narrow belts of slate, and forms a sharp, conspicuous ridge. Beyond this ridge, to the east, are found the same talcose slates that occur in the line of section on the West Fork.

454. Below the ridge, on the west, is slate, or shale, for one mile, some of it certainly Graptolite Shale; then comes the Trenton, with *Leptæna sericea,* and other fossils, and then the Knox. This corresponds to the parallel part of the West Fork section.

455. It will be observed that the West Fork section of the Ocoee rocks, interpolating the conglomerate ridge of the Big East Fork, is like the Tellico section, in having a wide belt of slates between the two ranges of mixed rocks, conglomerates as well as slates, the greater range on the southeast, and the less on the northwest. The same feature, though not so well marked, is seen on the Ocoee River.

The Little Tennessee section differs in presenting bands of limestone and dolomite.

456. (*e.*) Advancing northeastward, *to the waters of the Big Pigeon,* in Cocke County, we find the conglomerates and slates of the Ocoee Group, in great part, giving way to the strata of superior formation. The great belt we have been considering becomes very much narrowed. It widens, to some extent, in the valley of the French Broad, but north of this, its strata are reduced to comparatively narrow, and more or less detached

strips. As a consequence of this, the northeasterly counties along the North Carolina border have not great areas of mountain country, like Sevier, Monroe and Polk.

457. (*f*) *Newport*, the county seat of Cocke, is located immediately on the junction of the *Nash Graptolite Shale* and the *Trenton*. The latter rocks form here a comparatively narrow band. *Passing these, and traveling up the French Broad River*, a great section of Knox limestones and dolomites is seen. These Knox rocks extend up the river to a point about six miles (five direct) from Newport. The prevailing color is blue, though many layers are gray. In this section are several minor flexures and faults. (See section on the map.)

458. Succeeding these, we next cross a belt of Knox red shales, more or less calcareous, the belt being narrow on the road, but reaching one fourth of a mile in width, at a point not far off to the northeast.

459. Following the shales is a fine display of Chilhowee sandstones, which are the rocks for about one-fourth of a mile, or more. The first part of the mass is gray quartzose sandstone, some of it with green grains; the second part whitish and quartzose. Some of the layers contain *Scolithus linearis*.

460. Passing the sandstones, we meet with the Ocoee Group, and for eight miles (seven direct) travel upon it. The Group, here, is mostly shale or slate, the bands of conglomerate occurring at intervals. At one point a few layers of dolomite are seen.

The first shales met with, are more or less sandy, and have not so much the usual metamorphic aspect. The country, too, is comparatively open. The shales of the eastern part of the belt, however, present the semi-metamorphic appearance, are greenish talcose, and weather, at some points, to a chestnut brown. With the conglomerates they form a mountainous region.

461. After the Ocoee, the Chilhowee sandstones re-appear and continue, for several miles, up the river to the State line at the "Painted Rock." Just below Painted Rock, the river makes a short horse-shoe bend as it passes in a deep gorge through the sandstones. On the north side, the strata are nearly horizontal, and are piled up in a magnificent section, exposing a thousand feet of rocks. (§ 63.)

462. In North Carolina, a short distance beyond the line, the Ocoee Group sets in again, and is the formation to within a mile of the Warm Springs. Then follows a Knox belt. The Springs are located on Knox dolomite, and the belt to which it

belongs runs westward into Tennessee, terminating just within the line. Beyond the Springs follow Chilhowee sandstones, then Ocoee rocks, and finally, gneiss.

463. The *Valley of Paint Creek*, a stream which empties into the French Broad at Painted Rock, is within Tennessee, and lies between two Chilhowee sandstone ranges, Paint Mountain on the northwest, and the line range on the east. (§ 63.) The rocks of this mountain-valley belong to the Ocoee Group, and are talcose slates, with dark clay, or roofing slates, and a few bands of conglomerate.

464. (*g*) The *Big Butt*, so conspicuous from Greeneville, (§ 62,) is, as to its principal range, made up of the conglomerates and slates of the Ocoee Group. The latter are pale greenish, mostly, but include some purple slates. Much of the conglomerate is coarse; pebbles, as large as pigeon's eggs, are abundant, but they are often larger. The general appearance of these rocks recall portions of the Ocoee River section.

465. Along the northwestern base of the mountain, and terminating its spurs in a line of knobs, is a belt of Chilhowee sandstones. The belt is not massive enough to have formed an independent mountain.

466. It may be remarked here, that several strata of hard reddish ferruginous sandstone were observed on one of the spurs. At one point, on one of these strata, iron ore has been obtained, the ore resulting, doubtless, from the weathering of the red rock.

466½. (*h*) The diagram given further on, (§ 490,) represents, in a general way, the arrangement of the rocks about *Bumpass and Greasy Coves, in Washington County.* In this section, the outcrop of the Ocoee Group, (II.,) presents no large areas like those it gives in Sevier and the other southern Unaka Counties.

Between II. and IV., on the left of the section, which numbers correspond respectively to 2,*a* and 2,*c* of the classification adopted, is a great fault, presenting another instance of the kind of displacement occurring along the western bases of most of the Chilhowee Sandstone Mountains. (§ 446.)

467. From this region, towards the Virginia line, strips of Ocoee rocks are found, as before mentioned, (§ 432,) but the group in general, in this part of the State, is, by no means so important, topographically, as a mountain-maker, or otherwise, as the Chilhowee sandstones, or as the gneissoid rocks.

468. (*i.*) Approaching the Virginia line, however, the group shows itself in considerable masses, and forms, in part, the great ridge between Tennessee and North Carolina. This ridge is the northern part of the Stone Mountain range, (§§ 47 and 48,) the more southern part of which is wholly metamorphic.

468½. In the First Part of this Report, I have spoken of the *Johnson County Cove,* (§ 125,) in which name I proposed to include all the valley-lands of Johnson. These lands lie together, in a long trough, and are completely surrounded by great mountains. The route out of this trough, or cove, to the northwest, into Virginia, is through a gorge in Iron Mountain, (§ 49,) the same through which the South Fork of Laurel runs. In this gorge, a fine section of rocks is exhibited. I have constructed a section running through this gorge, and extending, in a southeasterly course, across the upper end of the Johnson Cove, to the North Carolina line. The gorge lies both in Virginia and Tennessee, so that the northwest end of the section is in Virginia.

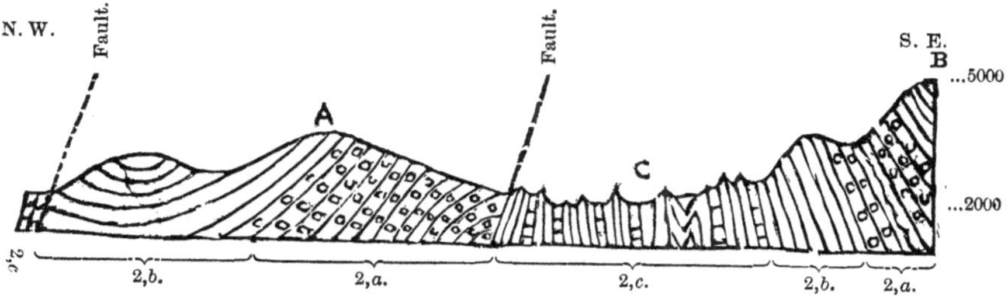

468¾. The length of this section is eight miles, and its vertical scale is 5000 feet to the inch. A, is Iron Mountain; B, the Stone Mountain Range, on the North Carolina line, the point being 5000 feet above the sea; C, is the Cove between, commencing at the left end of the section. The first formation is Knox dolomite, dipping as represented; then comes a great mass of Chilhowee sandstones, nearly horizontal, and separated from the Knox by a fault; next follows a great volume of conglomerate. The conglomerate is cut off by a fault, and is then followed by Knox strata—hard, red shales, with dolomite, but mostly the former—which occupy the cove.

469. Crossing these, we reach the foot of the mountain, and, in ascending, pass over a heavy belt of Chilhowee sandstones, and then two massive

belts of conglomerate, separated by a narrow belt of pale greenish talcose slates; after the conglomerate, slates come in again, and continue to the summit.

Many of the slates mentioned, contain small knots of quartz. Those on the summit run so gradually into the truly metamorphic rocks, that it is not easy to draw the line of separation. (§ 385.)

470. The belt of conglomerate in Iron Mountain, at A, is, together with the sandstones, grandly exposed in the gorge of the mountain. According to my measurement, the *direct* thickness of the conglomerate alone, at this point, is 6600 feet. As to whether this is the true thickness, we cannot be certain, though in this case, I believe, it is a near approximation. In a region like this, are minor faults and displacements, which render measurements uncertain.

This conglomerate is often coarse; the pebbles are quartz, feldspar, and slate, but mainly quartz. They are held in a siliceous and talcose matrix. The rock, when freshly broken, has often a pale greenish color. This belt contains no slate.

471. Near its western side, the belt holds two trap dikes. No truly metamorphic rocks were observed. The metamorphic strip, on the side of Iron Mountain, opposite Taylorsville, spoken of in chapter sixth, (§ 398,) appears to go with this belt of conglomerate, its place being between the latter and the Knox on the east.

472. *Useful Rocks and Minerals.*—At a number of points, the slates of this group are fissile enough to yield roofing-slates, as near Tellico Iron Works. (§ 436.) Other localities are on the Ocoee River, and on the West and Big East Forks of Little Pigeon, in Sevier County. But, beside these, there are numerous localities within the areas occupied by the Ocoee Group, where the strata present the features of roofing-slates, and are well worthy of a trial. To be good for this purpose, they must contain no pyrites; must split easily, with smooth surfaces, into thin plates; must not readily absorb water, and ought to be firm and tough.

473. Those slates which contain pyrites—a mineral composed of iron and sulphur, and often decomposing easily—can be used for making alum, sulphur, sulphuric acid, copperas, and, when magnesia is present, epsom salts. A noted instance of the

natural formation of alum and epsom salts is furnished in Alum Cove, in Sevier County, a locality of which I have already spoken. (§ 450.) This is an open place, under a shelving rock —such a place as in this country is often called a *rockhouse.* The slates around and above this contain much pyrites, in fine particles, and even in rough layers. They also contain reniform masses of dark gray sandstone and conglomerate. The salts are formed above, and are brought down by trickling streams of water. There was a wagon load of each of the salts on the floor of the cave, when visited by the writer—the epsom salts being at one end, and the alum at the other. Fine cabinet specimens could be obtained, white and pure, a cubic foot in volume.*

474. Pyritiferous slates of this kind, are frequently met with, and their presence is often indicated by a line of iron ore on the surface. The slates at Mundic Bluff, on the Ocoee, have been mentioned. (§ 425.)

475. It is in this formation that the most important gold-bearing quartz veins of the State are found. Gold can be, and in fact the most of it has been, washed out of the gravel and sand found in the beds of the streams, occurring in the region of the veins; but it originally came from these veins. The quartz has crumbled down with the adjacent rocks, and liberated the gold, which, with the rocky fragments, has been washed into the streams. There are several regions in McMinn, Monroe, and Blount, where gold has been found. In the Third Part of the Report, the facts bearing on the occurrence and yield of gold in Tennessee, will be more fully presented.

476. I have spoken of the conglomerate and breccia limestones found in association with the Ocoee rocks. Such occur on the Little Tennessee River, and in other regions. (§ 440.) These are interesting as supplying frequently a beautiful marble. The fragments making up the rock have different colors,

* This cove, or rather "rockhouse," I visited, in company with Dr. B. C. Jillson, in the summer of 1855. After walking twelve miles, or more, over the rough mountains of this region, our guide led us to the cave, where we remained for the night. Although in August, our elevation was so great that we suffered with cold, and had but little rest. This cave is not easily accessible, a circumstance which accounts for the fact that the alum and "salts" had not been carried off. Since that time, the war has been upon us, and both may have disappeared. They are, however, constantly forming.

and a block, having no hard pebbles or places in it, can be polished, and will then present an agreeable checkered or blotched appearance.

477. *Agricultural Features.*—These are, in the main, much like those of the Metamorphic Group. (pp. 180–81). Like that, the Ocoee Group has its great mountains, on many of which are open woods, and even bald places, suitable for grazing. Other mountains of the group are covered with balsam, spruce, and small evergreens, so thickly set as to form a mass of wild vegetation, almost impenetrable. (§ 82.) From my own observations, I feel safe in saying that the open-wooded, or the grazing mountains, are far more numerous than the others. Such points and ridges, as are covered with balsam and its associates, are very high. The lower ridges are nearly all open and easily accessible, presenting free and desirable "ranges" for cattle, well appreciated by "stock raisers."

478. The high valleys and plateaus of this Group, (§ 435), present many areas which can be, and are, cultivated. The elevation makes such places well adapted to the growth of fruit.

Section II.

THE CHILHOWEE SANDSTONE; FORMATION, 2,*b*.

LITHOLOGICAL CHARACTER; FOSSILS; THICKNESS—TOPOGRAPHICAL RELATIONS—SECTIONS; (*a*) LAUREL SECTION; (*b*) IRON MOUNTAIN SECTION; (*c*) BOMPASS AND GREASY COVE SECTION; (*d*) PAINTED ROCK; (*e*) CHILHOWEE MOUNTAIN; (*f*) HIWASSEE GAP—MINERALS AND USEFUL ROCKS—AGRICULTURAL FEATURES.

479. Following the Ocoee Group, in ascending order, is a series of sandstones constituting the *Chilhowee Formation.* I have given this name to these sandstones for the reason that they are finely displayed in the well-known and conspicuous Chilhowee Mountain. (§ 70.) It has been stated that the rocks of this formation are not always easily separated from those of the Ocoee series. (§ 421.) In the main, the distinction is well marked, for the characteristic rocks of one are sandstones, often including whitish quartzose beds, while those of the other are dark, coarse conglomerates, and semi-metamorphic slates.

480. *Lithological Character; Fossils; Thickness.*—The lithological character has been, in part, given. It is a great group

of heavy-bedded sandstones, often dark, but generally weathering to a grayish white, and containing great beds of whitish quartzose sandstone, or quartzite. Interstratified with the heavy-bedded rocks are, at some points, sandy shales, and thin flags, often containing scales of mica. Some of the sandstones are coarse and approach fine conglomerate. It may be mentioned, too, that not unfrequently the strata have green grains (glauconite) disseminated through them.

481. The sandstones of this Group very often show the worm-holes, and the sandy rods within them, belonging to Hall's species *scolithus linearis*. It is the exception not to meet with them. In addition to these, the surfaces of the strata sometimes show impressions of fucoids. No other fossils, that I know of, have been found in this horizon of Tennessee.

482. This formation is by no means as thick as the Ocoee series; yet it has volume enough to form conspicuous mountain ridges. It is not easy to determine its thickness; its maximum is not less, however, than 2,000 feet, and it may be considerably more. The sections to be given will aid us in estimating the thickness.

483. *Topographical Relations.*—The Chilhowee is the third, and the last of the Unaka Formations. As stated, it is the formation of the great outliers. (§ 422). Of the mountains mentioned under "Unaka Chain," (pages 22 to 28,) the following are, for the most part, made of these rocks:

Forge Mountain..............................§ 28...*Johnson County.*
Iron Mountain..............................§ 49...*Johnson and Carter.*
Holston Mountain..............................§ 50...*Johnson, Carter and Sullivan.*
Doe Mountain..............................§ 51...*Johnson.*
Flint Range..............................§ 53...*Johnson and Carter.*
Buffalo and Cherokee Mountains......§ 60... *Washington.*
Rich Mountain..............................§ 60... *Washington.*
Paint Mountain..............................§ 63...*Greene.*
Meadow Creek Mountain................§ 64...*Greene and Cocke.*
English's Mountain........................§ 69...*Cocke and Sevier.*
Chilhowee Mountain......................§ 70...*Sevier and Blount.*
Guide Mountain..............................§ 71...*Monroe.*
Star's Mountain..............................§ 72...*McMinn and Polk.*

There are a few others, but these are the principal ones. Most of them are remarkable for their isolated positions, and for the bold and abrupt manner in which they rise up from the valleys or low lands.

484. At the ends of these mountains, the sandstones, which form them, are suddenly and curiously cut off and wholly disappear. The mountains, and their rocks of course, lie generally, immediately on the southeast side of a fault. The sandstones broken in wide blades appear to have been thrust up endwise, to the northwest, through the overlying formations. The displacement is, in some cases, very great. In the case of Chilhowee Mountain, (see section, page 190,) the sandstones, or rather Ocoee conglomerates, have been brought up and abutted against *carboniferous limestone.*

485. The mountains of the formation have elevations varying from less than 1,000 to 2,000 feet above their bases They have but very few or no great spurs. These, when they exist, are short.

486. *Sections.—(a)* I will first notice the Chilhowee sandstones of the Laurel or Johnson Cove; section already given on page 190. Here is a great presentation of these sandstones. The direct thickness cannot be much, if any less, than 2000 feet. This estimate is based upon a partial measurement.

The strata are mostly heavy-bedded gray sandstones, often quartzose. The uppermost beds are sandy shales.

487. It will be observed that these rocks form on the left of the section, a shallow depression. We have in this depression the commencement, or apex, of a great V-shaped synclinal valley, or trough, that extends, widening as it goes, to the southwest and nearly to the Watauga River. It is a trough of Chilhowee sandstones, the northwestern edge of which is Holston Mountain, and the southeastern, Iron Mountain. (See Map.) It is one of the best marked synclinals in East Tennessee. The sandstones of its two edges are thrown up within the lines respectively, of two great faults, one at the northwestern base of the Holston, the other at the southeastern base of Iron Mountain. In the Holston the rocks dip to the southeast, in Iron Mountain to the northwest.

488. This trough of Chilhowee sandstones holds within it the hard variegated shales, and the dolomites of the overlying

Knox Group. High in its angle is the basin called Shady; its lower, wider portion is the Stony Creek Valley.

The elevation of the edges of the sandstone is sufficiently great to bring up more or less of the conglomerate, especially on the southeastern side.

489. (*b*) The Iron Mountain just spoken of, is intersected in Carter County by Doe River. In the Gap is a good section of the Chilhowee strata.

Below I give the section and the results of measurement made by myself. The thickness in each case, is direct. The strata dip to the northwest in angles varying from 36° to 55°. The series commences at the fault on the southeastern side of the mountain, and advances to the northwest, or, in other words, it is given in ascending order. The rocks on the southeastern side of the fault, are Knox Shales.

Sandstones with fine conglomerate; some of the sandstones hard and quartzose	472	feet.
Heavy gray quartzose rock mostly	60	"
Sandstones with conglomerate, dark and even bedded	44	"
Heavy gray quartzose sandstone, with unimportant layers of fine conglomerate	60	"
Sandstones not well seen	180	"
Heavy bedded quartzose sandstones	38	"
Sandstones and fine conglomerate with two quartzose bands	275	"
Thin sandstones and sandy shales	320	"
Quartzose sandstone	40	"
Thick and thin bedded sandstones, generally dark colored, occasionally sandy shales, but little fine conglomerate	1,720	"
Quartzose sandstone	40	"
Sandstones and sandy shales	370	"
Quartzose sandstones	35	"
Sandstones and sandy shales	250	"
Quartzose sandstones	10	"
Sandstones and shales as above	70	"
Quartzose sandstone	55	"
	4,039	feet.

The last bed above is followed by Knox Shales, which continue on to Elizabethton and beyond. The conglomerate given in the section, is simply coarse sandstone. It is probable that the great aggregate thickness of the strata is due in part to recurrence by faulting and displacement.

490. (*c*) The following is a general section through Bompass and Greasy Cove, in Washington County. It is not intended

to be accurate in detail. It presents the general arrangement of the formations along a line running, in a northwesterly and southeasterly course, near the intersection of the Buffalo and Rich Mountain Range, by the Nolichucky River. (§ 60.)

SECTION ACROSS BOMPASS AND GREASY COVE, IN WASHINGTON.

(*Length eight miles.*)

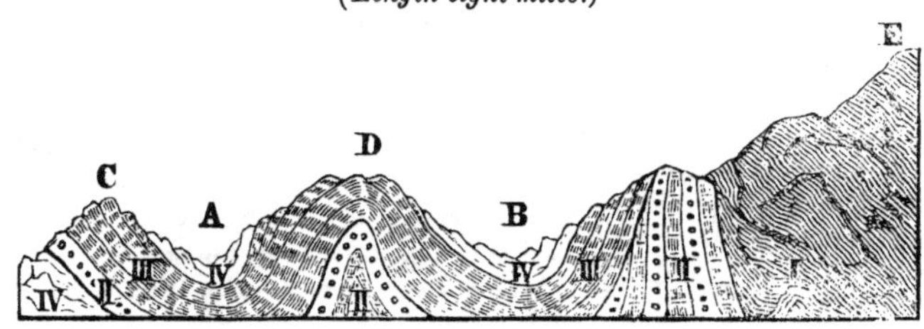

A, Bompass Cove. B, Greasy Cove. D, Rich Mountain. E, Summit of the main Mountain and the North Carolina Line.

I. Metamorphic; II. Ocoee Conglomerates and Slates; III. Chilhowee Sandstones; IV. Knox Shales, Dolomites and Limestones.

Between II. and IV, on the left, is a fault. On the northwest side of this, are Knox Dolomites and Limestones.

The Chilhowee rocks of this section are dark sandstones and and sandy shales, with lighter bands of quartzose sandstones. Two or three of the latter are conspicuous in the vicinity of the Iron works at the northwestern end of the section. Some of the shales are fine, and have a semi-metamorphic appearance.

491. (*d*) A grand section of the rocks under review, are seen on the French Broad River at and below the "Painted Rock." In the great amphitheater that the river and the cliffs form here, not less than a thousand feet of sandstones are seen. (§§ 63 and 461.) They are heavy bedded layers, hard and quartzose often containing *scolithus*, and are interstratified with thin sandy flags and shales. In a portion of the section the rocks are nearly horizontal. Many of the sandstones are dark colored; some contain green points. The shales show scales of mica. On the top of Paint Mountain the weathered strata might be taken for the sandstones and sandy shales of the Coal Measures. On many of the mountains, in fact, enumerated on page 199, the rocks have such an aspect.

492. (*e*) The section on page 190 crosses Chilhowee Mountain,

which is represented at one point in the diagram. The sandstones, as well as the Ocoee conglomerates, are seen to be the rocks of the mountain. The sandstones have the same features here that they have in the mountains further north.

493. (*f*) Star's Mountain is cut in two by the Hiwassee River; in the gap thus formed is a fine exhibition of Chilhowee sandstones. The strata are nearly horizontal and show great thickness. They include some fine conglomerate.

494. It is not necessary to give more examples. The truth is, the lithological features of this formation are much the same in all of its presentations, from Virginia to Georgia.

495. *Minerals and Useful Rocks.*—I have not met with any minerals of special interest in this formation.

It abounds in excellent building material. Many of its sandstones are in smooth layers of suitable thickness, and could be quarried easily. The hard quartzose rocks are not desirable for such purposes, but they are interstratified with beds having a more open sandy texture, which can be worked. Even the harder rocks, when partially weathered, become often pretty good freestone. At some points, good flags might be obtained.

496. *Agricultural Features.*—This formation is confined to mountain ridges, and the areas suitable for cultivation it presents, are very limited. On the tops of some of its mountains are small areas which can be cultivated. The soil of these is frequently quite strong, and makes good garden spots. But it is as pasture ground mainly that these Chilhowee Mountains have any special agricultural interest; and, in this respect, they are much like the other Unaka ridges, of which I have spoken. They have none of the characteristic bald places of the latter. (§§ 416 and 477.)

SECTION III.

THE KNOX, OR KNOXVILLE GROUP; FORMATION, 2,*c*.

THE KNOXVILLE AND WEBB'S RIDGE SECTION, PRELIMINARY; SUBDIVISIONS; GEOGRAPHICAL DISTRIBUTION, BELTS AND FAULTS; SYNCLINALS AND ANTICLINALS.

2*c*′. KNOX SANDSTONE; LITHOLOGICAL CHARACTER; TOPOGRAPHY; MINERALS.

2c″. KNOX SHALE; LITHOLOGICAL CHARACTER; PALEONTOLOGY; VALLEYS; AGRICULTURAL FEATURES.

2c‴. KNOX DOLOMITE; LITHOLOGICAL CHARACTER; PALEONTOLOGY; TOPOGRAPHY; USEFUL ROCKS AND MINERALS; AGRICULTURAL FEATURES.

497. This great series of sandstones and shales, dolomites and limestones, forms, by its outcrops, the greater part of the surface of the East Tennessee Valley. With the exception of a single spot in Stewart County, (§ 364,) its strata are confined to East Tennessee.

The city of Knoxville is located on a ridge made up of its limestones and dolomites; and this circumstance, together with the fact that the threefold typical character of the series is well developed in Knox County, has induced me to name it the *Knoxville*, or the *Knox Group*.

498. *The Knoxville and Webb's Ridge Section; Preliminary.*— Before entering fully into the consideration of the Group, let us first notice the following section. This section commences at Webb's (or Rosebury's) Ridge, nearly three miles northwest from Knoxville, and extends to the Holston River. It is about three miles in length, and was taken along Second Creek. In this are seen the three subdivisions of the Group.

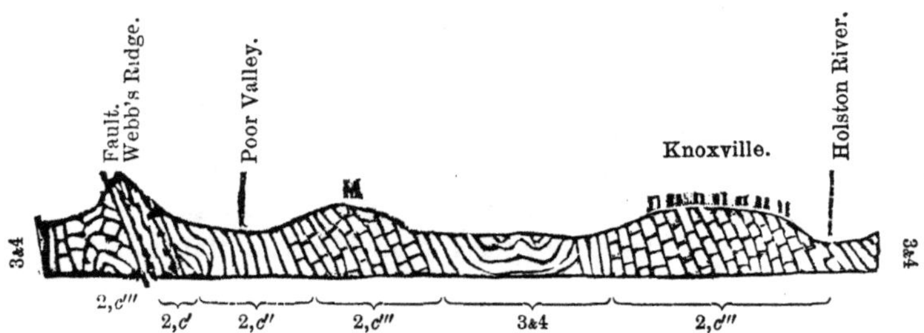

499. Commencing at the fault on the left and proceeding towards Knoxville, we have first, in Webb's Ridge, a series of hard, brown, greenish and gray shales, and thin sandstones, interstratified with which are several layers of hard, dark gray sandstone, the whole being 540 feet thick. The hard strata have given origin to the ridge.

500. This series is followed, in Poor Valley, by soft variegated shales. These were, originally, more calcareous than now.

They include, occasionally, thin bands of limestone, which is often oolitic and sometimes fossilferous. Owing to local folds and displacements, it is next to impossible to ascertain the true thickness of these shales. As an approximation 1,500 feet may be taken ; it may be much more. It will be observed that the soft shales lie in a depression between ridges. They have yielded to denuding agencies more readily than the rocks of the ridges, and hence the valley.

501. Next follows a very heavy series of dolomites and limestones. These strata are in the ridge M, and occur, in ascending order, as below:

(*a*) Limestone and Dolomite, mostly blue, but some of the upper strata dark gray and sparry; the blue is partly compact and partly oolitic; the lower part is interstratified with shale, thus running into the shale division below; fossiliferous; entire thickness	650 feet.
(*b*) Dolomite, mostly dark gray and sparry, heavy bedded; contains more or less chert throughout, some of which approaches sandstone; upper part includes gray dolomite; thickness	1,870 "
(*c*) Chert	4 "
(*d*) Dolomite and Limestone, mostly light gray sparry dolomite, with more or less chert throughout; upper part interstratified with blue layers which are fossiliferous; thickness	980 "
Entire thickness	3,504 feet.

502. These rocks make up the ridge M, and are followed on the east by the Trenton series. The ridge owes its existence, in good part, to the chert contained in the dolomites and limestones. This chert in a clear section, such as is seen along the stream in the gap of the ridge, makes but little show comparatively. On the top and sides of the ridge, however, it is very abundant; the surface is covered with its loose angular fragments, so much so as to suggest the name, Flint Ridge.

The Knoxville Ridge is composed of the dolomites that we find in M. Between these ridges the rocks belong to the Trenton and Nashville formations, and will be spoken of in another place.

503. The part of the section between the fault on the left and the eastern, or southeastern, base of the ridge M, is to be taken as typical of the Knox Group. It is seen that the group in the section has a threefold character; its lower division is

characterized by the presence of hard shales and sandstones; its second division by softer shales; and its uppermost, and greatest, by massive dolomites and limestones, containing more or less chert.

504. *Subdivisions.*—In accordance with this, the Group, in general, has been divided, in ascending order, as follows:

2,c′. Knox Sandstone.
2,c″. Knox Shale, and
2,c‴. Knox Dolomite.

505. Each of the above divisions has its especial topography. The first builds up sharp roof-like, or when notched, saw-like ridges. In the typical section Webb's Ridge is one of the roof-like class. The second division is valley-making, and the third gives us a broad, rounded, and generally cherty ridge, like M, and the Knoxville Ridge in the section. These characteristic ridges exist only where the strata dip at a considerable angle. (Compare §§ 103, 104, and on.)

506. The threefold character of the Group is well marked west and south of Knoxville, both as to rocks and topography. In the northeastern part of the Valley, however, as in Sullivan, Greene, Washington, Johnson and Carter, it is not so prominent; the shales of the lower divisions become more calcareous, and often include beds of dolomite and limestone; the topography, too, is different. (See §§ 108 and 109.)

507. The two lower divisions, when exposed in any part of the Valley, show, occasionally, beds of dolomite and limestone, one of the circumstances uniting the three divisions; but in Sullivan, Greene, etc., the rocks mentioned, become more abundant, comparatively, and more mixed with shale. We may, indeed, say that the *Knox Group*, in the northeastern part of the State, is a great series of calcareous rocks, (limestones and dolomites,) the upper part free from shaly admixture; the rocks of the middle and lower parts frequently interstratified with bands of shale, and often striped with thin seams of it; while, at the bottom, the shales predominate, are harder, and sometimes hold sandstones which are variegated, and occasionally jaspery.

508. *Geographical Distribution; Belts and Faults.*—It is not necessary to enumerate here the areas in which the Knox strata outcrop. The map has been prepared for the purpose of showing them, and reference must be made to it. Attention

is called, however, to the occurrence of the Group in long belts or ribbons. There is a most remarkable set of these west of Knoxville. Some of the ribbons run entirely across the State, and, indeed, beyond its limits, in both directions, carrying with them the characteristic ridges and valleys of the Group. (Compare §§ 93, 94 and 108.) The diagram on page 190, presents sections of these ribbons. The spaces between the consecutive faults, as represented in this diagram, are mostly filled up with Knox strata—the northwest and middle portions of each being occupied by them. The southeast sides are usually Trenton and Nashville strata, though sometimes embracing the Niagara, Black Shale and the Siliceous.

509. The ribbons are bounded by the faults. They are long belts of strata, having a northeastern and southwestern trend, that have been split off, tilted and crowded together, the edge of one overlapping the adjacent edge of the other, like slates on a roof. (See also §§ 344 and 359.)

510. A *typical* general section of one of these ribbons, commencing at the fault on the northwest, and ending with that on the southeast, is as follows;

(*a*) Following the fault is a sharp ridge, holding the hard layers of the subdivision, the *Knox Sandstone*. The plane of the fault is often included in the ridge as stated below.

(*b*) Next a Knox Shale valley.

(*c*) Then follows a wide Knox Dolomite cherty ridge.

(*e*) A wide blue limestone (Trenton and Nashville) valley. As we pass into this valley from the chert ridge, the strata are seen to dip at a less angle than further back.

(*f*) Here follows, in many cases, the second fault, cutting off the formations. If such is not the case, the Dyestone Group (Niagara) may come in and terminate the series, or this may be followed by the Black Shale and the Siliceous Group. When this latter formation, the Siliceous, ends the series, its hard chert rocks are brought in contact with the sandstones of the lowest Knox division; in this case both chert and sandstone make the crested ridge, the fault-plane cutting the ridge longitudinally.

The second fault occasionally cuts off a part, or all, of the Trenton and Nashville strata, in which case, the upper Knox terminates the series.

511. The formations just mentioned, the Dyestone, Black Shale and Siliceous Group, are not usually heavy, and are often found with the Knox Sandstone in, or near, the same sharp ridge.

Section from Cumberland Gap (A) to Sneedville, (F) in Hancock County, 25½ miles.

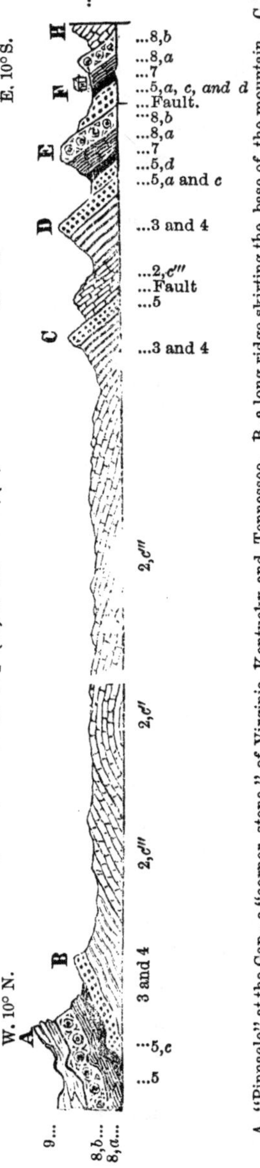

A, "Pinnacle" at the Gap—a "corner stone," of Virginia, Kentucky and Tennessee. B, a long ridge skirting the base of the mountain. C, Wallin's Ridge. D, Powell's Mountain. E, Newman's Ridge. F, Sneedville. H, "Combys" Ridge. See Powell's Mountain Group, § 96. The formations are numbered in accordance with the tables in chapter V.

512. The section here given, may be compared with the diagram on page 204. The correspondence is seen at once, as far as the two ridges and the intervening valley on the left are concerned. The Knoxville fault is a local one, and soon disappears, the valley between Knoxville and M being a synclinal one.

The typical section is illustrated, also, several times in succession, in the diagram on page 190.

513. *Synclinals and Anticlinals.*—In the region of Powell's River, and lying in the counties of Claiborne, Union, and Campbell, is a broad belt of the Knox Group. It is a well-defined, gently curving arch, or anticlinal, the axis having a northeasterly trend. The annexed section illustrates its features, as well as the relations the Group itself sustains to the other formations. The elevation at some points along Powell's River, is sufficient to bring up the top part of the shale member.

514. Most of the valleys of East Tennessee lie in the outcrops of imbricated formations, like Poor Valley, in the section on page 190, or like the valleys between the mountains C D and D E, in this section. The ridges, too, have a corresponding relation to the strata. This results from the fact that, faulting and imbrication are the rule. (§ 359.) It follows that true synclinal or anticlinal valleys and ridges, are not ordinarily to be looked for.

515. A second important anticlinal exhibiting Knox strata, is that of the Sequatchee Trough. (See Map, and the section on page 139.) An interesting synclinal, holding the rocks of the Group, has been noticed on page 200.

2,c′. KNOX SANDSTONE.

516. *Lithological Character.*—The general features of this division have been given. Its principal rocks are hard shales, and thin sandstones, heavier sandstones being interstratified with these. The heavier sandstones are fine or coarse grained, sometimes quartzose. They occasionally abound in green grains. Eastward and southward the heavier beds cease to be conspicuous.

In the section of Webb's Ridge. (§ 499,) the hard, dark, gray sandstone referred to, occurs six times in beds from three to ten feet thick, and weathers into a buff, softer material. In general, the included layers vary much in appearance. As before stated, (§ 507,) beds of dolomite are met with in the division.

The thickness of these rocks cannot be much less than 800 or 1000 feet. In Webb's Ridge, where they are in less force than at many other points, the thickness is 540 feet.

517. The strata are often ripple-marked, and sometimes covered with fucoidal impressions and ridges. Aside from fucoids, I have not met with any fossils in these rocks.

518. In the northeastern counties, Johnson, Carter, Washington, etc., the division becomes more cálcareous. (§ 507.)

In these, and in the other mountain counties further south, we sometimes meet with layers of jaspery rock in this horizon, especially when in the vicinity of a Chilhowee sandstone mountain. I have seen beautiful specimens of jasper and chalcedony in these beds.

519. It may be mentioned as a prominent feature of this division and of the Knox Shale overlying it, that they present shales and sandstones of many different colors. The rocks are pale green, brown, and red, chestnut-colored, buff, gray and other colors. Brownish red, greenish and buff, are, perhaps, the prevailing tints. The colors are often bright, and notably agreeable.

520. *Topography.*—The sharp-crested ridge, as stated, is the

characteristic topographical feature of the Knox sandstone when its layers are tilted. (§§ 505 and 510.) *Webb's Ridge* has been spoken of. Other examples are *Beaver*, *Bull Run*, and *Pine Ridges*, crossed successively in going from Knoxville to Clinton; *Piny*, between Clinton and Walden's Ridge; another is *Comby*, in Hancock and Grainger; another in Grainger skirts the eastern base of Clinch Mountain, the northern extension, in reality, of Webb's Ridge, (§ 530;) the ridge immediately west of Rogersville is an example; of this class, too, is the so called *Bays Mountain*,* forming the southeastern boundary of Knox County. These are a few among the most prominent.

The location of most of these ridges is indicated upon the Map. Their normal places in the great rocky ribbons split off by the faults, have been given. (§ 510.) They are not known by the same name throughout. The same local name is applied in some cases, to parts of very different ranges. *Pine*, or *Piny*, is very commonly given to them for the reason that they are often covered with pines.

The ridges are not high, their elevation rarely exceeding 400 feet, and being generally under this.

521. *Minerals.*—Many of the iron-ore (limonite) deposits of the eastern mountain counties rest upon the rocks of this and the succeeding Knox divisions. Of these deposits I will speak hereafter.

In Carter County, seven miles above Elizabethton, on the west side of Stony Creek, is a layer of massive hematite, from one to two feet in thickness. The locality is known as the Cannon bank. The iron-ore is regularly stratified, rests on a thin bed of conglomerate holding small pebbles, and has sandy shales above. The group of rocks appears to belong to the lower part of the division under consideration. It may, however, belong to the upper part of the Chilhowee Formation.

The occurrence of jasper and chalcedony in this division, has already been mentioned. (§ 518.)

2,*c''*. KNOX SHALE.

522. This, the second division of the Knox Group, is the formation of numerous subordinate valleys in the great Val-

* This ridge has no connection with the Bays Mountain between Greene and Hawkins. (See note p. 43).

ley of East Tennessee. It is eminently the valley-making portion of the group, especially in the north-western, western, and southern portions of this section of the State. It is a formation of great interest in an agricultural way. In connection with the blue limestones of the lower part of the overlying division, it promises an interesting paleontological field.

The general topographical and structural relations of the division have been given, and it will not be necessary to dwell upon them here. (§§ 503 to 512.)

523. *Lithological Character; Thickness.*—Variegated shales are the characteristic rocks of this division.* (§ 519.) Interstratified with these, at intervals, are thin layers of blue limestone, which is often oolitic. These rocks yield the finest specimens of oolitic limestone to be found in the State; the spherules are often as large as the o's on this page, and sometimes larger. The calcareous bands in the lower part of the division are not numerous; toward the top, they generally become more abundant, increasing as we ascend, until finally the shales disappear, and the blue oolitic limestone and dolomites are the only rocks. In this way, the shale division runs into the uppermost one.

524. In the northeastern part of the State the shales, as a division, are not well characterized. As already stated, (§ 507,) they are much mixed with beds of limestone and dolomites, and lose, in good part, their distinctive features. Moreover, in this region there is little oolite rock. A portion of the shale appears to be replaced by a blue limestone containing thin clayey seams, which give the surface, especially when weathered, a striped appearance.† This striped rock, occurs, too, further south, its place being at the top of the shale.

The thickness of the Knox Shale is not easily determined. What is said in reference to the thickness of the strata in Poor Valley, on page 204, applies generally. We may place it as an approximation at 1500 or 2000 feet.

525. *Paleontology.*—At many points the blue limestones, interpolated in the shales of this division, contain fossils, some-

*These, in many valleys, were, perhaps, much more calcareous than they are now, They present the appearance, more or less, of leached material.

†This, in my notes, is designated "Blue banded limestone." Some of it is, doubt less, dolomite.

times abundantly. They occur both in compact and oolitic layers. Toward the top of the divison, and in the blue rocks of the succeeding division, they are seen at many points. The shales themselves, are occasionally fossiliferous. (See, also, § 558.) The forms are certainly of an ancient type. Those given on this page recall Dr. Owen's species of the "*Lower Sandstone of the Upper Mississippi.*" In fact, one of them may be identical with his *Lonchocephalus Chippewaensis.**

526. The opportunity has not been presented of working out satisfactorily, the fossils of this geological horizon. The following have been described. See Appendix A.

(1.) *Crepicephalus similis;* Safford.
(2.) " *Roanensis;* "
(3.) " *Tennesseensis;* "
(4.) *Lonchocephalus fecundus;* Safford.
(5.) *Agnostus arcanus;* "
(6.) *Lingula prima?* Conrad.

Nos. 1, 2, 4 and 5, occur in a Knox Shale Valley, four and a half miles east of Kingston, on the road to Knoxville. The rock is a thin band of trilobitic limestone, almost, wholly made up of fragments of *Lonchocephalus fecundus.* The others, Nos. 3 & 6, were found in a belt of shale, at a point about a mile and a quarter north of Rogersville. The generic names are after Owen, and are used provisionally.†

It might be mentioned here, that my *C. similis* is much like Mr. Billings' *Bathyurus Cordai*, of the Quebec Group. (*Paleozoic Fossils*, Vol. I., p. 412.) The difference, according to this distinguished paleontologist, who has seen my specimen and has compared it with his, is in the marginal rim of the front of the head, that of his, being more convex on top.

527. *Valleys; Agricultural Features.*—In the section between Knoxville and Clinton, the Knox Shale gives the following valleys, namely, *Poor Valley*, already mentioned; (§ 500;) *Hinds' Valley*, lying west of Black Oak Ridge; *Bull Run Valley*, west of Copper Ridge; and *Wolf Valley*, west of Chestnut Ridge. Between Clinton and Walden's Ridge, is still another.

Some of these, are sections of long valley-ranges, which reach from Virginia to Georgia. (§§ 119 and 508.) That, for

* Geological Survey of Wisconsin, Iowa and Minnesota, page 576, Tab. I and I, A.

† The description of these Species were written in 1860, and have not been revised.

example, of which the Bull Run Valley is a portion, extends, on the one hand, into Virginia, and, on the other, into Georgia. In the southern part of the State, the valleys of Roger's and Candy's Creeks, tributaries of the Hiwassee, are sections of this range. So, also, is most of the valley of Big War Creek, to the northeast, towards Virginia. And still further north, Powell's River runs for a number of miles in it.

528. The range, of which Hinds' Valley is a section, is, also, a long one. Its northern end, is not far from the southern extremity of Clinch Mountain, and its southern is in Georgia. South Mouse Creek, in Bradley County, is in this range.

529. All of the valleys west of Cleveland, to within less than a mile of White Oak Mountain, are Knox Shale Valleys, and this group extends far into Georgia. The shale valley, (Dogwood Valley,) in which Tunnel Hill Depot is situated, belongs here.

About half way between White Oak Mountain and Missionary Ridge, is another wide range. This becomes narrow northward. Kingston is partly located upon it.

530. Midway between Charleston and Benton, a wide belt of the shales is crossed. The two Chestua Creeks are in this belt. Madisonville is located in it. The valley of Dumpling Creek in Sevier and Jefferson Counties, is about its northern termination.

Poor Valley, of the section on page 204, extends, or rather, its range extends, many miles northeastward. It lies on the southeast side of House and Clinch Mountains, from which it is separated by a very narrow valley and a ridge, the latter being the continuation of Webb's Ridge, of the same section. The range in front of Clinch Mountain, becomes a fine rich valley, that of Richland Creek. The town of Rutledge, and Bean's Station are in it.

Rogersville is in one of the Knox Shale valleys. Northward, the range divides into three valleys, Carter's and Stanley valleys being two of them. The range widens out above Rogersville, and is divided by the interpolation of Knox Dolomite ridges. The valleys show more or less limestone with the shales, and are desirable and rich. (See also, § 549.)

531. The agricultural features of the Knox Shale valleys, are, as may be inferred from what has been said, quite varied. Generally, when wide, and not too rough, they present choice farming areas. Some of the most desirable and best improved farming regions, are in the valley-ranges pertaining to this division. The layers of limestone, interstratified with the shales, as well as the calcareous matter often found in the shales themselves, contribute much to the strength and favorable condition of the soil. The native growth is mainly made up of different species of oak, with which are often found poplar, dogwood, occasionally walnut, &c. In some regions, yellow pine is not uncommon.

532. Some of the valleys fall below the character given. Several, indeed, have the name "Poor Valley" fixed upon them, as that through which the section in § 498 runs. These valleys are generally narrow, and owe their bad name to local causes.

They are hilly, or contain shale ridges, with but little soil upon them; or else, the soil is thin, with the shales beneath, thoroughly leached and deprived of their calcareous matter. These valleys, however, have portions which come up to the standard, and present the sites of excellent farms. The Richland Creek portion of the Poor Valley range illustrates this.

533. In the northeastern part of East Tennessee, in the counties of Cocke, Greene, Jefferson, Hawkins, Washington, Sullivan, Carter, and Johnson, where the subdivisions of the *Knox Group* are not so well marked, (§ 506,) are many valleys, the rocks of which are alternating bands of dolomite, or limestone and shale. These are, generally, good agricultural belts, and have been in cultivation many years.

534. The soils of the Knox Shales are clayey, but mellowed, more or less, by the debris of thin sandy layers, and by calcareous matter. They are well adapted to the cultivation of small grain, and to the making of meadows.

Some of the iron-ore banks, are, in part, located upon the Knox Shale, but the division has not the interest attached to it, as a mineral-bearer, that belongs to the superior member of the Knox Group.

2, *c'''*. KNOX DOLOMITE.

535. This division is the most massive formation of calcareous strata in Tennessee. In the Eastern Valley, it is very conspicu-

ous, and is the formation of many ridges and valleys. In Middle Tennessee, it does not appear, except, at one remarkable spot, already mentioned. (§ 364.)

536. *Lithological Character; Thickness.*—The section in § 501, presents the general lithological character of this division in the southern part of the East Tennessee Valley, as well as in that portion west of the Holston.

537. The chert in the upper part, is to be noticed, inasmuch as it has supplied the gray, flinty gravel which, so extensively covers the ridges and Knobs of this formation. This chert very generally has minute rhombohedral cavities interspersed through it, a character by which it may be distinguished from similar material in other formations.* The thicker layers are at a number of points, as stated further on, worked into millstones. (See also, §§ 502, 505, and 510, (*c*).) Thin beds of sandstone occur, locally, in the middle and upper parts of this division.

538. Passing to the northeastern part of the valley, we find the gray sparry dolomite less heavy, and the chert less abundant, and the middle and lower portions in good part, made up of blue rocks, with argillaceous seams. The lower part in this region, contains very little oolitic limestone. (See § 507.)

539. In the larger part of the valley, and especially in the portions mentioned in § 536, the upper strata of this division include beds of dull variegated dolomite, which is, at some points, worked as marble, and, in many places, used as a building material. It is a light gray, rather fine-grained rock, variegated with brownish red clouds. At some points, there is between one and two hundred feet of this. Some of it is argillaceous, and weathers to shaly material. Some fossiliferous beds are associated with it. Its upper part runs into Trenton limestones.

* I first observed these cavities many years ago. They present a character which has been of much use. At many points, loose chert is abundant on the surface, when the strata are entirely concealed. Among the dislocations of East Tennessee, it often becomes a question as to whether the rocks belong to the division under consideration, or to the Siliceous Group, the chert of the two being much alike. The presence of the cavities, I have, so far, found characteristic of the Knox chert. They are the empty moulds of crystals of dolomite, once filling them. In rocks freshly quarried, showing chert, the crystals are seen. The chert of the Siliceous Group, is, generally, characerized by the presence of large crinoidal buttons.

540. The gray dolomites of this division often contain fine sand as an impurity. Sometimes, in weathering, especially beneath the soil, they become encrusted with a coat of powdery sand. Weathered surfaces, exposed to the air, often present a hacked appearance, quite different from anything seen on the exposed surfaces of blue limestone.

541. The thickness of this division of the Knox Group, is not far from 4000 feet. It may be less, or more, than this; at any rate this is the nearest approximation I can, at present, make. Taking the aggregate thickness of the first and second divisions at 3000, (§§ 516 and 524,) the entire thickness of the group will be 7000 feet. This, most likely, is a maximum.

542. *Paleontology.*—The lower limestones of this division, are, at some points, quite fossiliferous. Fragments of trilobites are abundant; orthes, and other genera of brachiopods, have been observed. The species, however, have not been worked out. It is an inviting field, and it is to be hoped that its treasures may soon be exhumed. The middle, and larger portion, including the dark and light gray sparry dolomites, rarely show fossils. The uppermost portion, especially the blue layers, contain them, but in general, not abundantly. In this horizon, forms resembling *Pleurotomaria calcifera*, *P. calyx*, and *P. docens*, have been observed at a number of points. The latter, *P. docens*, has been identified.

543. *Topography.*—The Knox Dolomite has been stated to be ridge-making, (§ 505,) and it has been so represented in sections. (§§ 444, 498, &c.) This is eminently so wherever the strata are tilted at a considerable angle, which, by the way, is generally the case.

The following are some of the ridges pertaining to this division, a number of which are remarkable for their length. They are the rounded ridges spoken of in the First Part of this Report, (§ 104,) and are as follows:

(*a*) Intersected in going west from Knoxville:
Black Oak, Copper and Chestnut Ridges; a second *Black Oak* lies west of Clinton.

(*b*) In the eastern part of Claiborne:
Wallin's Ridge.

(*c*) In Sullivan and Greene Counties:
A ridge, running through these counties; in the former, known as *Chestnut Ridge*, and in the latter, as *Big Ridge.*

(*d*) East of Chattanooga:
The war-renowned *Missionary Ridge.*

(*e*) Running through the middle of the East Tennessee Valley:
The *Knoxville and Athens Ridge;* this, in its southern extension, lies just to the east of Charleston.

There are several of these ridges between Cleveland and Benton. The latter place is located on one of them. Benton, Maryville, and Dandridge, are situated on the same Knox Dolomite range, or ridge. An ill-defined ridge extends from Greeneville to Newport, the former place being on its southeastern side, and the latter on its northwestern. Another, of like character, reaches from Russellville to Virginia, running between Rogersville and the Holston.

Just west of Washington, in Rhea County, is a wide ridge of Knox Dolomites, which runs parallel with the eastern escarpment of the Cumberland Table-land. West of Decatur, is one, which, in its northern extension, lies on the east side of Kingston.

544. These ridges are, more or less, covered with angular gray chert. A number of them are very conspicuous, and well known.

In addition to these, are several important ranges which can hardly be called ridges. One is the belt, forming, for the most part, the wide anti-clinal of Claiborne, Union, and Campbell Counties, a section of which is given in the diagram on page 208. Another is the belt forming the middle part of *Sequatchee Valley.* (§ 349.) In both of these, the Knox dolomites are raised to a considerable elevation, especially in the former; and they would form (as in fact they appear to be, when seen from distant high points) continuous heavy ridges, were it not for the rivers which flow longitudinally through them. Powell's River and its tributaries, cut deeply into the Claiborne and Campbell anti-clinal, dissecting, tortuously and transversely, the would-be ridge. Sequatchee River cuts the range through which it flows, into a belt of knobs.

545. The way these rivers (Powell's and Sequatchee) wind along on the backs of the two anti-clinals, respectively, is curious and noteworthy. The streams have no valleys of consequence. Powell's River flows in a very tortuous course, and is bounded generally, while on the axis of the anti-clinal, by rough hills, often four and five hundred feet high, closely hugging the stream, and presenting at nearly all points, either on one side or the other, bold picturesque bluffs. Opposite the bluffs, are small, rich bottoms, or slopes, which, on account of their fertility, are generally in cultivation.

Sequatchee River presents similar features, though not on so large a scale.

Both of the belts mentioned, lie between well-defined blue limestone (Trenton and Nashville) valleys. It is remarkable that the rivers should have cut their beds through the high ridges rather than through one or the other of the valleys.

546. The upper part of the Knox Dolomite, where approximately horizontal and abounding in chert, presents belts of country remarkable for being made up of isolated hills, or "knobs." Such areas are known as "*The Knobs*." One of these belts has been mentioned; (§ 116;) it lies north of Chattanooga, and reaches northward toward Washington, west of which place it is a tolerably well-defined ridge. (§ 543.) Immediately east of Missionary Ridge and west of Savannah Valley, (the valley skirting the western base of White Oak Mountain,) are ranges of cherty knobs belonging to this formation. Northward, these become ridges.

547. Most of the ridges mentioned, are, as I have said, cherty. On many of them, the chert is mostly confined to the southeast side, the northwest being comparatively free of it, for the reason that the lower blue limestones, oolitic or otherwise, outcrop on this side.* Sometimes, the blue rocks of the northwest slope are separated from the gray strata by a narrow local valley, having the bearing of the ridge. In this case, the range becomes double—one part, more or less, cherty; the other, comparatively, without chert. The latter usually presents rich fertile land. Copper Ridge, in the northern part of the State, is thus, in several regions, divided into two subordinate ranges.

548. The *Richland Knobs*, the range of which lies east of Rutledge, are made up of the blue limestones and dolomites of the lower part of this division. They are rich, and in cultivation. To the east of these, come in the gray cherty rocks.

549. Between two and three miles, northwest of Morristown, commences the range of *Boatman's Ridge*. This is a long and tolerably wide belt, and is the same as the range, already mentioned, lying between Rogersville and the Holston. (§ 543.) On its southeastern side, are the gray, cherty

* It may be stated here, also, that the northwest slope is often steeper than the southeast, the dip of the rocks becoming greater as we approach the Knox Shale valleys. This is true, especially, of Copper Ridge.

dolomites, and on its northwestern, blue calcareous rocks, which include, in some parts, as west of Morristown, some of the shales of the Shale Division. West of Boatman's Ridge, on the road from Morristown to Bean's Station, is a narrow Knox Shale valley, which is the southern end of the Rogersville, or Carter Valley, Range. From May's, on the Holston, to Bean's Station, the geological section through Boatman's Ridge, &c., is repeated.

550. The rocks of this division, when horizontal, or nearly so, form plateaus, or valleys, unless, in some way the chert becomes predominant, when "knobby regions," usually are found. (§ 546.)

The wide anti-clinal of Claiborne and Campbell, (§ 544.) may be regarded as a plateau, and the deep bed of Powell's River as a cañon winding through it.

551. There is an interesting plateau of this formation in Jefferson County, between the Holston and the so-called Bay's Mountain, and extending from the vicinity of New Market to Russellville; these towns, and Morristown, being upon it. This area is from 300 to 400 feet above the Holston, and presents some excellent and extensive farming regions. A portion is called the New Market Valley, and is noted for its fertility.

The rocks of this plateau, are at many points, but little inclined. They are, in reality, at the northern disappearing end of a synclinal trough. Below New Market, the synclinal character is more apparent, and but a short distance southwest of this place, commences an important range of Trenton and Nashville rocks. These lie in the synclinal, and on the rocks we are considering.

552. The interesting mountain-hemmed coves, noticed in the First Part of this Report, (§§ 132 to 138,) present areas for the most part of Knox dolomites and limestones. Associated with these, however, there are, at a few points, Trenton and Nashville limestones and shales. Some Knox shales also occur. The rocks of the coves are not unfrequently, nearly or quite, horizontal. They are patches of the great calcareous formations which became entangled, by the folding and faulting to which all the strata in common were subjected, in the mountain masses of the Ocoee and Potsdam Formations. Doubtless, these coves, or basins, were once filled to the tops of the surrounding ridges, with calcareous matter. Water has removed this, and excavated the coves.

553. The exceptional spot, in *Middle Tennessee*, showing outcropping Knox Dolomite, has been noticed. (§ 364.) It may be added, that the part of the basin holding these rocks, rises up (regarding the area generally) in a wide, low dome—a feature consistent with the ridge-making character of the same rocks in East Tennessee. The dome shows upon the surface, in isolated pieces, the characteristic chert of the division. Its agricultural features are good, and the basin in general, is highly valued as a farming region. The dome has a depression all around it—a ring of valleys, in which outcrop the Trenton, Nashville and Niagara rocks.

554. *Useful Rocks and Minerals.*—The following is intended to be, for the most part, simply an enumeration of the rocks and minerals of this formation, which are, or can be, put to practical use. The systematic notice of them belongs to the Third Part of the Report.

The upper portion of the division at very many points, contains beds of a variegated rock, which answers an excellent purpose as a building stone. Its surface presents a gray ground, mottled with reddish brown clouds. This rock has been referred to in § 539. There is a quarry in it at Chattanooga, and the pillars which support the roof of the passenger depot at that place, are built of it. The rock occurs in separable layers of convenient thickness. It is sometimes called a marble, but its colors are rather dull to be much valued as a marble. The material is limestone, more or less dolomitic and argillaceous. It has a wide range occurring in the horizon mentioned as far north as Claiborne County.

Other varieties of building material can be obtained from different portions of this formation.

555. Many of the dark blue layers of this division are, at many points, profusely intersected by small reticulating veins of calcite. This is the case often, where a layer of limestone or dolomite, lies in the compressed angle of a local flexure, the rock having been more or less cracked in the bending. These vein-marked rocks will, at numerous localities, yield a handsome marble, and they are well worthy the attention of those who are interested in such matters. The limestones are sometimes very dark, and their polished surfaces, showing the

reticulating white veins, would be beautiful. Such rocks may be found at nearly all points where the blue layers have been much wrinkled. I have observed them in the vicinity of Jonesboro', Greeneville, Newport, on the Pigeons, in Sevier, in McMinn, Polk, etc.

556. Dark limestones, without veins, forming a good black, or nearly black, marble, are not uncommon, and are associated, more or less, with the preceding; they are the same, in fact, without the veins. Black marbles of this kind from East Tennessee, form the bases of the columns in the Senate Chamber at Nashville.

557. In addition to the above, there are *conglomerate and breccia* limestones and dolomites in East Tennessee, some of which deserve attention. These belong to the different divisions of the Knox Group, in fact, some may belong to the Ocoee Group. (§ 440.) These rocks, when free from siliceous points and masses, can be made to present an agreeable surface. The fragments making up the masses are generally of different shades of color, and the polished surfaces of the breccias resemble mosaic work. Marbles of this sort are found on the Little Tennessee, south of Chilhowee Mountain. I have observed them in Greene, Cocke, Sevier, and, in fact, in all the Unaka counties. On the Little Tennessee, and in Monroe County, some of it has been wrought.

558. In McMinn County, at one point in North Chestua Valley, is a bed of variegated crinoidal limestone, from which marble slabs have been sawn. This rock is interpolated in the Knox Shale, such being the formation of this range. (§ 530.) The point is interesting as a locality of *fossiliferous rock* in the shale.

559. The *chert* so characteristic of the upper part of the Knox Dolomite is manufactured, at several points, into excellent mill-stones. Layers of it, having a suitable cellular structure, occur in Claiborne, Jefferson, Knox, and other counties. It is generally the weathered outcropping portion of these layers that is used. After getting a certain depth, the cavities are found to be more or less filled with crystals of dolomite and other matter.

560. In several counties, among them Jefferson, McMinn, Polk, &c., layers of tough hornstone occur in the blue limestone. These being inclosed in tilted strata outcrop along a line, in some cases, for several miles. Dotted along on such outcrops, in the counties mentioned, are old half-filled pits—ancient "diggins"—originally made by the Indians for the purpose of procuring flint. They are in fact, old *flint mines*. Large trees now grow in these pits.

561. Many *Iron ore* banks are located on the Knox Group. In considering these banks, it is best to take the sub-divisions of the Group together. The special notice, however, will be found in the Third Part of the Report. There are two species of iron ore associated, more or less directly, with the rocks of this Group; these are *limonite* and *hematite*.

562. The first of these, *limonite*, (sometimes called brown iron ore,) is a hydrous oxide of iron, and is of very general occurrence. This ore results from the decomposition of ferruginous minerals, such as pyrite, carbonate of iron, etc., contained in the rocks. Any of the strata of the Knox Group, which contain compounds of iron, such, for instance, as the dark gray dolomites, or the red and green shales, will, when disintegrating under certain conditions, yield limonite. For this reason, more or less of it is to be seen in all regions where such rocks outcrop. It is only, however, at certain localities that the ore accumulates in sufficient quantity to be of practical value. When such a locality is met with it is called a *bank*.

563. Banks of limonite occur in all the mountain counties from Johnson to Polk. Ore from most of them has been made into iron for many years. The ore is found in isolated masses, in bunches, irregular layers in a matrix of clay, sand, chert and debris of the disintegrated strata, all or part, variously mingled.

For some reason, not well understood, the valuable deposits of limonite are most numerous in the coves and valleys of the Knox Group, near or among the mountain ridges of the Unaka belt. Small unimportant deposits of ore are occasionally met with on all the Knox Dolomite ridges.

564. The other species of ore, *hematite*, is found at one point in a regular bed, and has been already mentioned. (§ 521.) At another locality, Sharp's Bank, in Sullivan County, it occurs

in a vein-like, nearly vertical mass. Much ore has been taken out, and the opening made, is, at one point, forty feet across. This part, however, is wider than the rest of the vein, and includes a columnar mass of rock, or, as the miner would say, a "horse." This mass of ore is associated with light gray dolomite, of the uppermost part of the Knox Group. The rocks dip at a high angle. The hematite most likely dips with them, not being a true vein intersecting the strata.

Other localities of this ore exist in Sullivan County. Hand specimens of *magnetite* (loadstone) are sometimes found at these localities.

565. *Iron Pyrites* is often found in the rocks of the Knox Group. It is a mineral met with, for that matter, in nearly all formations. In the Knox Group it is found associated, pretty generally, with *galena* and *blende*, at the localities of these minerals. A few miles south of Greeneville, in one of the valleys of Greene County, is a heavy body of pyrites in layers more or less mixed with shaly limestones. At the time of my visit the excavation previously made, in search of something better than this mineral, was partly filled with water, so that the character of the deposit could not be made out fully. Much pyrites had been thrown out. The locality deserves attention. At other points, in the same valley, beds of pyrites are found.

566. *Galena* occurs at numerous localities in the Knox Dolomite. It presents itself in true veins, as at the Caldwell Mine, on Powell's River, in Union County, in isolated grains and small lumps, from the size of a pea to that of an orange, or larger, interspersed sparsely through the whole mass of certain beds of dolomite; and in bunches, or deposits, consisting of local accumulations of grains and masses of galena in the rock, mostly as a matrix, as the lead mine in Bompass Cove, in Washington County.

567. The most interesting example of a bed of dolomite, containing scattered grains and lumps of galena, that I have met with, lies in the southwestern part of Claiborne County, near Powell's River. The portion of the bed examined, and seen to contain ore throughout, is about six miles long and two miles wide, and lies between Slate and Camp Creeks, on the hills more or less elevated above the river. Most likely, however, the lead-bearing portion extends beyond these limits. The horizon of the bed in the Knox series is in the upper part of (*b*) in the section. (§ 501.)

The ore occurs in buttons from the size of buckshot to that of a walnut, but occasionally large enough to weigh several pounds. The masses are sparsely scattered through the rock, so much so that its separation is impracticable. At points, where the masses are more abundant than usual the hunters have been in the habit of digging in the soil near the rock, or in the clay filling crevices, for pieces of ore which, in time, have become detached. Frequently their labor is rewarded by the discovery of several pounds of ore, supplying them well with the lead they need.

568. *Cerussite* (carbonate of lead) is found in small gray pieces at a point on the road from Greeneville to the Warm Springs in the valley between Paint and Meadow Creek Mountains. It is dug out of the soil, and is derived, doubtless, by alteration, from galena contained in the rocks of the vicinity. At a number of the galena localities the same mineral may be found.

569. The following ores of zinc, are found at numerous localities in the Knox Group:

(*a*) *Blende*—sulphide of zinc, associated with galena at many localities;

(*b*) *Smithsonite*—carbonate of zinc; and

(*c*) *Calamine*—hydrous silicate of zinc; the two last associated at Stiner's zinc mine, on Powell's River, in Union County; at the Mossy Creek mine, and at several other points, to be mentioned hereafter.

570. *Black Oxide of Manganese* is of very general occurrence in regions where iron ore is found. Pieces are not uncommon on the Knox chert ridges. In Jones' Valley, in Cocke County, and on Boatman's Ridge, between Morristown and Bean's Station, considerable masses of it have been observed. Localities at which hand specimens can be found, are very numerous.

571. In addition to the minerals mentioned, the following also occur in the rocks of the Knox Group:

(*a*) *Heavy Spar* (*barite*)—found in veins, as at a point twelve miles from Greeneville, on the road to Chimney Top, etc.; also associated with galena at a number of points, forming, in the main, the găngue of the ore.

(*b*) *Flour Spar* (*fluorite*)—associated with the preceding in lead veins, etc.

(*c*) *Calcite* (*carbonate of lime*)—in crystalline masses and in crystals, associated as the last, and common in small veins—a very common mineral.

(*d*) *Dolomite* (*carbonate of lime and magnesia*)—occurs in crystals in the cavities of chert, and of the bedded rocks; also, in veins associated with the minerals mentioned above.

(*e*) *Quartz*—in crystals, in the cavities of chert, etc.

572. *Agricultural Features.*—The Knox Dolomite presents some of the best farming regions in East Tennessee. This division, and the Knox Shale, taken together, are the most important formations of this section of the State, so far as agricultural interests are concerned. They present a much greater number of acres of good arable land than all of the other formations combined. In this, the East Tennessee Valley differs widely from the Central Basin. (§ 227, and on.) In the latter the soils overlie, and are derived from the blue limestones of formations next to be described, namely, the *Trenton* and *Nashville Groups.* In the Basin, no strata of the Knox Group are seen at the surface.

573. In East Tennessee there are long valley-ranges, as will be seen, of excellent lands based on the Trenton and Nashville rocks, but the aggregate area they give is far less than that presented by the Knox Dolomites and shale.

574. In noticing the topography of the Knox Dolomite, reference has, several times, been made to agricultural features. (§§ 547, 548, 551, 553.) It may be stated, generally, that, where chert-gravel is not too thick upon the surface, the lands of this formation are good, many of them excellent. The southeastern slopes of many of the characteristic ridges, (§ 543,) like that of Copper Ridge, are well adapted to farming purposes. These slopes run gradually into the valleys, where the blue Trenton and Nashville limestone lands are found. The northeast sides of these ridges are often free from chert and richer; (§ 547;) but they have the disadvantage of being steeper and more broken, besides having a northern exposure.*

575. The principal formations of the northeastern part of the State, (excluding the mountains,) are, as we have seen, Knox dolomites and shales. Upon these are based many ridges and valleys, which, however, are not marked like those

* The northern exposure would be an advantage in some cases. It would be better for fruit, grass, etc.

west of Knoxville. Many of the valleys contain dolomitic rocks and shales interstratified. These are generally good farming belts. In fact, the whole section is a superior one, as to its agricultural features. It has, too, been longer in cultivation than any other portion of the State.

576. The coves referred to in § 552, are, for the most part, desirable farming regions. Cade's Cove is noted as a grass producing area. The coves, generally, are well suited to small grain, grass and fruit. The same remark will apply to all the coves and valleys among, or in the vicinity of, the Unaka Ridges. These coves and valleys deserve more consideration than they have received. They have peculiar attractions. Their elevation, and the presence of mountains around them, make them cool, and, in the summer, delightful. Their very isolation would make them, to some minds, all the more desirable.

CHAPTER VIII.

THE TRENTON AND NASHVILLE GROUPS; FORMATIONS III AND IV.

577. Succeeding the dolomites of the *Knox Group*, we have, both in East and Middle Tennessee, beds of blue, highly fossiliferous, limestones, equivalent, in general, to beds, which, in New York, are referred to the Chazy, Black River, and Trenton Formations. In East Tennessee it is generally an easy matter to know when, in traversing the country, we pass from the rocks of the upper Knox to those of the Trenton. There is some admixture of gray and blue strata in the horizon of junction, but the compact gray (or variegated gray) strata, and the gray chert on one side, and the blue limestone (often knotty and fragile) on the other, are quite in contrast. On the one side, too, rises the ridge—on the other is the valley. This is a lithological and topographical contrast; as to fossils, there is more or less blending.

578. The blue limestones referred to above, constitute a group which retains its general features tolerably well throughout both Middle and East Tennessee. But not so with the overlying and remaining beds of the Lower Silurian Formations. These, in East Tennessee, present a different aspect from what they do in Middle Tennessee. Moreover, they present differences in the Eastern Valley itself, being on the northwest side mainly limestones, and on the southeast, shales. Again, in certain regions, or belts, of the valley, they include several interpolated and interesting beds of special character, making, altogether, a series quite heterogeneous.

In the Basin of Middle Tennessee the entire series of Trenton and Nashville rocks is much the same from bottom to top, being mainly different varieties of *blue limestone*.

579. I will notice first the Trenton and Nashville Series, as presented in East Tennessee Valley, and after that, pass to the consideration of the same rocks in Middle Tennessee. The Central Basin (p. 97) has some claims to be be considered, first,

for the reason that it has become in Tennessee, typical ground, so far as these rocks are concerned, a fact due to the undisturbed condition and fine development of the strata, and to the greater study given to its fossil species. In the *Basin*, the strata are, without difficulty, grouped into the two divisions which I have named *Trenton* and *Nashville*. In the *Eastern Valley*, they are not, in this Report, thus systematically grouped, but are considered together as the *Trenton and Nashville Series*. Notwithstanding the claims of the Basin, it will be more in accordance with the order adopted, to commence with the formations of the Eastern Valley.

SECTION I.

THE TRENTON AND NASHVILLE SERIES IN THE VALLEY OF EAST TENNESSEE.

GENERAL CHARACTERS;—SECTIONS NEAR KNOXVILLE—INTERPOLATED BEDS. **A**, THE BLUE OR MACLUREA LIMESTONE—LITHOLOGICAL CHARACTER, THICKNESS—TOPOGRAPHY, EXTENT AND RANGE—PALÆONTOLOGY, AGE: (1) THE RED AND GRAY MARBLE—EXTENT AND RANGE, THE RED BELT;—(2) THE IRON LIMESTONE—LITHOLOGICAL AND OTHER CHARACTERS—EXTENT AND RANGE—THE RED KNOBS;—(3) OTHER SPECIAL BEDS—DIVISION NEXT ABOVE IRON-LIMESTONE, AND THE CRINOID BED—THE UPPER MARBLE—THE BROWN SHALE. **B**, THE UPPER MEMBER OF THE SERIES;—(*a*) THE SHALE (EASTERN)—THE GRAY BELT, ITS TOPOGRAPHY—AREAS OF SHALE, SYNCLINALS—LITHOLOGICAL CHARACTER; GRAPTOLITES;—(*b*) LIMESTONE AND SHALE (WESTERN)—TOPOGRAPHY, AREAS—LITHOLOGICAL AND OTHER CHARACTERS; TRANSITION BEDS; APPENDIX;—USEFUL ROCK AND MINERALS;—AGRICULTURAL FEATURES.

580. *General Characters.*—The Trenton and Nashville rocks in East Tennessee, may, *in general*, be described as follows: They are first a stratum of blue limestone, more or less argillaceous, from 200 to 600 feet thick, (§ 590;) then above this a great body of sky-blue calcareous and often sandy shales, weathering yellowish gray, or buff, and containing occasionally thin flaggy limestones, and at some points, thin sandstones.

We thus divide the series into two members, the *Blue Lime-*

stone and the *Shale*. The latter has a maximum thickness of about 2000 feet.

581. The upper member, as thus characterized, pertains properly to the middle and southeastern portions of the Valley, supposing the latter to be divided longitudinally. In going to the northwest, towards the Cumberland Table-land, in any part of the Valley, the shale becomes more and more calcareous, approaching the condition the same strata present in Middle Tennessee.

582. I have given above, let it be noted, *general* features. There are special features, as before remarked, of much interest and importance. In the middle portion of the Valley the *Shale* contains interpolated or local beds of *marble*, and of a *hard, sandy, iron-limestone*. One bed of marble lies at or near the base of the shale; the iron-limestones and another bed of marble, are interstratified with layers at higher levels.

583. These interpolated beds are mostly confined to the middle portion of the Valley. Their longer dimensions have approximately, the direction of the trend of the ridges, a characteristic, by the way, of other beds to be mentioned, and one that is interesting as to its bearing on the early history of Appalachian movement.

And here it may be added, generally, that lithological changes in *most of the formations of the Valley* occur much more rapidly in going "across the country," that is to say, to the northwest or southeast, than in traversing it in a longitudinal, or northeast and southwest direction.

584. *Sections in the vicinity of Knoxville—The Interpolated Beds.*—If a section across the strata, on a line between Rogersville and Greeneville, were taken, a portion of it would present the Trenton and Nashville Series in its twofold character of *blue limestone* and *shale*, (§ 580,) the latter constituting much the larger, and by far the more conspicuous part of the whole. Intersecting, however, the same series on the southeast side of Knoxville, or say, more generally, on the southeast side of the ridge Knoxville is located upon, (§ 543, (*e*,)) the section loses its simple character, and becomes varied by the presence of the interpolated or local beds just spoken of.

585. I present on the next page a section across the belt of

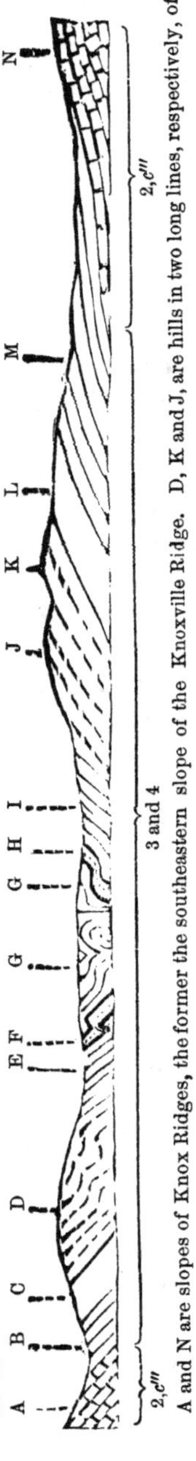

A and N are slopes of Knox Ridges, the former the southeastern slope of the Knoxville Ridge. D, K and J, are hills in two long lines, respectively, of remarkable red knobs.

Trenton and Nashville rocks, which lies next east, or southeast, of Knoxville. The section was taken a few miles northeast of Knoxville; the line of it runs to the northwest and southeast near the mouth of the French Broad River.

586. The following is the series of beds and formations, presented in the section in descending order:

(7.) *Calcareous Shale*, (G, G,) with occasionally thin, flaggy limestones and a few layers of hard, sandy limestone; contains *Leptæna sericea*, *Strophomena alternata* and *S. filitexta.* This and the shales below are sky-blue, weathering yellowish gray, or buff. Owing to, folds thickness uncertain, say in feet, 400?

(6.) *Red Marble*, (F, H,) fossiliferous, variegated, mostly red marble, with gray and greenish layers; folded and thickness doubtful, say........................... 300?

(5.) *Calcareous Shale*, (E, I,) with more or less flaggy, fossiliferous limestone; thickness doubtful, as above, say...... 500?

(4.) *Iron-limestone*, (D, J, K,) a hard, sandy, very ferruginous limestone, weathering to a porous, dark brown, sandy *skeleton;* fossiliferous, among the species *Asaphus platycephalus* common. Thickness from 200 to 300 feet......... 250

(3.) *Calcareous Shale* containing interstratified beds of iron-limestone, as well as of blue, flaggy limestones. (The division above (4) might be included in this, as the upper member.)............ 400

(2.) *Red and Gray Marble*, (C, L,) coralline, grayish white, and variegated......... 380

(1.) *Blue Limestone*, (B, M,) argillaceous, fossiliferous; contains *Maclurea magna*, and is followed below by rocks of the Knox Group................................. 500

587. The Knoxville Ridge has a belt of Trenton and Nashville rocks on its northwest side, also. The general section on

page 204, crosses this. It lies between the ridge M, and that on which the city is located. Commencing with a bed of reddish brown shales in this valley, and proceeding in a northwesterly direction to the base of the ridge, M, the series of strata in this belt is approximately, in descending order, as follows:

(6.) *Brownish-red Shale;* a more or less calcareous rock, weathering into shale; contains some grayish layers more calcareous. This bed is crossed on a Clinton road before reaching the Knoxville Cemetery gate; it occurs in several folds. Thickness uncertain, say (in feet)........................ 300?

(5.) *Calcareous Shale*, with occasionally thin, flaggy, fossiliferous limestones. The shales are sky-blue, weathering buff and yellowish gray. They measure across their outcrop 1700 feet; allowing for dip, plications, etc., their thickness may be *estimated* at..1000?

(4.) *Iron-Limestone*, like No. 4 in last section, about................ 100

(3.) *Calcareous Shale*, sky-blue, weathering buff........................ 320

(2,*c*.) *Variegated Marble*.. 375

(2,*b*.) *Blue Limestone* like No. 1, below.................................. 136

(2,*a*.) *Variegated Marble*.. 35

(1.) *Blue Limestone*, same as No. 1 of last section, and resting on strata of the Knox Group.. 510

588. In passing from the belt of Trenton and Nashville rocks on the southeast side of Knoxville, to that on the northwest, the two being separated by a dolomite ridge, considerable change occurs in the strata. This may be seen by comparing the two sections just given. The *Iron Limestone*, for example, on the northwest has lost its prominence. On the southeast it has volume enough to form high hills; (the red hills seen across the river from Knoxville;) on the northwest it gives no marked topographical feature.* In the belts still further northwest it soon thins out and is not seen. This is in harmony with statement made in (§ 583.)

589. Another difference in the sections, is the presence of the bed of *Brownish-red Shale* in one, (the northwestern,) and its absence in the other, unless, indeed, the Red Marble of the eastern section, is synchronous, the marble, being the product

* It may be mentioned here, that this band of Iron Limestone on the northwest of Knoxville, becomes heavier when traced "down the country" to the southwest. It soon begins to form characteristic red knobs, and ultimately makes a conspicuous line of them.

of a local, encrinal, and coralline colony. Fragments of corals, and the buttons and plates of crinoids, in quantity, mixed with red marly mud, would harden into such rock.

With these remarks, we pass to the special consideration of the Strata.

A.—The Blue, or Maclurea Limestone.

590. This is the lower Blue Limestone Member of the Trenton and Nashville Series, spoken of in §§ 580 and 584; it is, too, the lowest bed in the two sections on page 230. I propose to call it the *Maclurea Limestone*, for the reason, that the large and conspicuous fossil shell, *Maclurea Magna*, is found in it, and, at some points, very abundantly, as at Kingsport, in Sullivan County.

591. *Lithological Character; Thickness.*—The geological position of this formation, is next above the Knox Dolomite. (§ 535.) It is, generally, a blue, more or less, argillaceous limestone. In the central part of the valley, it is often knotty, and breaks up, more or less, in lumps, in weathering. In some regions, as in the northern part of Jefferson, and in the vicinity of Bull's Gap, it breaks in small blocks, and has been designated, the "*Block Limestone.*" In this same region, too, it is rich in fragments of trilobites, *Asaphus*, *Ampyx*, *and Illaenus.*

592. In the northeastern counties, Greene, Washington, Carter, and Sullivan, the formation presents, generally, a more compact limestone, and is greatly reduced in thickness. At Greeneville, for instance, it is not more than 120 feet thick. It lies just southeast of this town, in a clear section, between the Shale and the Knox Dolomite.* It is, at this point, a blue limestone, some of the layers of which, are blackish blue, and much intersected by small veins of calcite. Masses of the latter might be selected, from which beautiful marble slabs could be sawn.

593. In Washington, and in Sullivan east of Blountsville, as well as northeastward in Virginia, the Maclurea Limestone

*Immediately southeast of Greeneville, the line of a long *Shale* ridge passes. This ridge is narrow, tolerably sharp, and is made by the lower part of the Trenton and Nashville Shale. Along the base of this ridge, and, at some points, on both sides of the Shale, the Maclurea Limestone is seen.

presents very much the character that it does at Greeneville. At some points, it is reduced to a thickness of fifty feet.

594. Going southwestward from Greene County, the formation, wherever it outcrops, is much the same as at Greeneville. It is so at Newport, which town is located upon it and the overlying shale. (§ 457.) A few miles east of Sevierville, on both of the forks of the Little Pigeon, its blue layers are seen separating the gray dolomites and the shale. (§§ 447 and 453.) The rocks here, show, to some extent, the knotty structure.

595. A short distance east of Benton, in Polk County, the formation is intersected. It lies at the western base of a shale and sandstone ridge. Below the shale, is, first, a bed of blue argillaceous, flaggy limestone, containing Maclurea; then succeeds a blue, compact, fossiliferous limestone, which is followed by Knox Strata. The formation is heavier in this region than further north.

596. On the northwest side of the valley, that is to say, on the side next to the Cumberland Table-land, the Maclurea Limestone is not distinguished from the overlying part of the Trenton and Nashville Series, by any well marked lithological characters. As before stated, the entire series begins, here, to exhibit Middle Tennessee features, (§ 581,) and is much the same throughout.

597. The maximum thickness of the Maclurea Limestone is about 600 feet, and, as stated, its minimum, (in the northeastern corner of the State,) is 50. At no point in an unbroken section, presenting the two contiguous formations, have I seen this group absent.

598. *Topography; Extent and Range.*—These limestones are, usually, valley-making, and, in connection with the other and overlying rocks of the Trenton and Nashville Series, have, especially in the northwestern half of the valley, yielded to denuding agencies, and formed many fine valley-ranges. (See §§ 649 and 650.) In some of these ranges, the Maclurea Limestones, when highly tilted,* present themselves in low rounded ridges, along which the strata outcrop in parallel lines, forming glady places, often with a growth of red cedar.

* In which position, like shales, they are more commonly found, than are the solid, heavy bedded strata.

599. In the Trenton and Nashville Valleys, pertaining to the great and long ribbons, into which the formations have been faulted, and which are intersected in going from Knoxville to the Cumberland Table-land, (§§ 508 and 510,) the place of the Maclurea Limestone is on the northwest side of each valley, and next to the ridge-making Knox Dolomite. In the valleys lying along the base of the Table-land, as for instance, Powell's Valley in Claiborne and Campbell, and Tennessee Valley in Rhea and Hamilton, the place of the formation is on the southeast side, the formations occurring successively in ascending order in going to the northwest.

600. The great *anticlinal* ranges, like that of Claiborne, Union and Campbell, and that of Sequatchee Valley,* (§ 514,) when presenting a central belt of Knox Strata, have this belt bordered on both sides by Maclurea Limestones. And, so too, a *synclinal* range of Trenton and Nashville Strata, will show a border of Maclurea Limestones on both sides. This is, for the most part, true of the great range, (the Gray Belt, § 640,) which extends from Kingsport on the Holston, quite through the State. Its border throughout, on the northwest side, is made up of these limestones; on the southeast side, they are, at some points, engulfed in local faults, though at most points, appearing in place.

601. In some regions where the strata dip but little, considerable areas are underlaid by the Maclurea Limestone. Such an area is crossed by the section on page 230, at M, or between L and N. The argillaceous crumbling limestones form a glady belt, abounding in red cedars. Such places recall forcibly the great cedar glades of the Central Basin, (§ 240,) which, by the way, are located on certain flaggy layers of the same formation.

The area above extends a number of miles southwestward, and is brought up on the end of an anticlinal point, as may be seen by referring to the map. The road from Knoxville to Sevierville crosses this outcrop of Maclurea Limestone, which, along this line, is, perhaps two miles wide. It contracts, how-

*In reference to the anticlinal of Sequatchee Valley, it must be stated, that in the middle and southern part of the valley, the anticlinal fold is faulted on the northwest side, and, in some parts, the Maclurea Limestone, and, indeed, the whole Trenton and Nashville Series, is engulfed.

ever, rapidly, and further to the southwest, disappears beneath the higher beds—the marble, shales, and iron-limestone.

602. In the region of Strawberry Plains,* above and below, along certain lines, there is much of this rock. The running out of the synclinal mentioned in § 551, brings it up. It occurs, for the most part, in bands between the dolomites of the Knox Group and the overlying marbles, etc. There are, also, similar anticlinal and synclinal points in Jefferson, Greene, and other counties, which cause this formation to outcrop in belts and areas more or less extended.

603. *Palæontology; Age.*—The fossils of the Maclurea Limestone have not, as yet, been thoroughly studied. It is at some points quite rich in species, many of which are new forms. The following are some that have been observed:

1. *Maclurea magna, Lesueur.* This is an abundant and characteristic fossil in this formation. It is found at numerous localities in the Valley, in fact, we may say, wherever the bed outcrops. Among the localities, the following may be mentioned : the western base of the ridge next east of Benton, in Polk County; the blue limestone on the east side of the railroad, at Lenoir's in Roane County; the outcrops of the formation around Knoxville; the blue limestone at Kingsport, in Sullivan, etc.

The locality at Kingsport is a noted one; the rocks are so full of the shells, and casts of this species, that they attract much attention.

2. *Rhynconella plena*, Hall. This species is abundant in the blue limestone at Lenoir's.
3. *Leptaena sericea*, Sowerby. In Sevier County, a few miles east of Sevierville, at the junction of this formation with the upper division—the shale—of the Trenton and Nashville series. (§ 594.)
4. *Orthis bellarugosa*, Conrad. Near Benton, in Polk County, associated with *Maclurea magna.*
5. *Strophomena incrassata*, Hall. East of Benton, same locality as the last.
6. *Orthoceras pertinax*, Billings. Collected at Lenoir's, in association with *Rhynconella plena* and *Maclurea magna.*
7. *Illaenus latidorsata?* Hall. In the "block limestone," White Horn Creek, Jefferson County. (§ 591.)
8. *Asaphus canalis*, Conrad. "Block limestone," same locality as last, and other localities.
9. *Ampyx Jillsoni*, Safford. "Block limestone," east side of Bull's Gap.

* The Depot at Strawberry Plains is built of the Maclurea Limestone.

604. The above species are found in the middle and southeastern portions of the valley (dividing the latter longitudinally) in which the *Maclurea Limestone* is a distinct lithological group. Approaching the Cumberland Table-land, the lower portion of the *Series* (taking the Trenton and Nashville Groups together) presents many of the forms to be enumerated hereafter, as belonging to the Trenton Formation in Middle Tennessee.

In the list above, 1, 2 and 6 are *Chazy*, or *Black River* forms, or both; 5 and 8 are *Chazy*, but also *Trenton* and *Hudson River;* 4 is *Trenton*, and 3 is *Trenton* and *Hudson River*. The formation is doubtless about equivalent to the Chazy and Black River rocks, of New York and Canada, rocks that we include, with Dana, in the Trenton Group, or Period.

(1.) THE RED AND GRAY MARBLE.

605. This (the first interpolated bed, § 582) is represented in the section (C, L,) on page 230, as resting upon the limestone just described. It is also given in the table on page 231. In the latter the bed is duplicated. This may be due to a fault and displacement, or the marble, 2,*a*, may be in its natural position—interpolated between strata of the Maclurea Limestone. For several miles to the northeast, on this range, the same arrangement is observed.

606. *Lithological Character.*—This bed is one of great interest on account of the valuable marble for ornamental and building purposes, it can supply. In the section, page 230, it is 380 feet thick. The bed is, in general, a variegated crinoidal and coralline limestone. Its colors are grayish white, and brownish red; sometimes pinkish red, or even greenish. The latter colors, however, are not common. The most esteemed variety has, when polished, a bright ground of brownish red colors, mottled more or less freely, with white or gray spots, or fleecy clouds. These clouds and spots, in that of first quality, are well defined, and, to the naked eye, show little of their fossiliferous character. The whitish spots are due, for the most part, to the presence of corals, with small cells like *Chaetetes* or *Stenopora.*

607. At some points, much of the bed becomes grayish

white, without admixture of red. It is then called "white marble," (in reality, grayish white,) and is esteemed for tombstones, monuments, floors, ornamental gate posts, as a building material, and for other purposes.

A few miles northeast of Knoxville, and near the line of the section on page 230, is a valuable quarry, of the gray variety.* The section of the entire bed, at this point, commencing at the bottom and ascending, is as follows:

1st.	Variegated, with gray and red, so as to be more or less flesh-colored	55 feet
2d.	Grayish-white, no red	95 "
3d.	More or less reddish, especially upper part	230 "

The quarry is in the middle, or 2d portion, which is here, the most valuable.

Marble of much the same quality is found at the mouth of the French Broad River. This belongs to the bed, L, in the section just referred to. The Williams quarry is in the belt represented at C, in the same section.

608. *Sloan's quarry* is located on a ridge, nearly two miles north of Knoxville, and near the East Tennessee and Virginia Railroad. It is on the duplicated range spoken of in § 605. This range runs parallel with the Knox Dolomite belt, forming the ridge, M, in the section on page 204, from which it is separated by Maclurea Limestone, At this quarry, the section is much the same as that in § 586.

The variegated variety has, for the most part, been obtained here, and the locality is interesting, as being that from which most of the marble in the State Capitol, at Nashville, was taken.

609. Hawkins County has, so far, supplied the most desirable marble from this formation. That used in ornamenting the Capitol, at Washington, is from Hawkins. The best display of Tennessee marble to be seen anywhere, is at the National Capitol. As an ornamental rock, that of Hawkins County is, of its class, unsurpassed. The authorities at Washington caused an extensive quarry to be opened at the point

* This quarry, when I visited it last, in August, 1858, was owned by Col. John Williams, and it may be held by him now. It was sold, in the bed, to the quarry-men, at the rate of eight cents per cubic foot.

where the marble range of the county strikes the Holston River. The supply is unlimited. The rock is of the most desirable variegated variety.

610. *Extent and Range; the Red Belt.*—By referring to the Map, it will be seen that an important area of Trenton and Nashville rocks, originates a little south, or west, of New Market, and runs through the Valley, to Georgia.* Its widest part is southeast of Knoxville. It will be seen, also, that the Knoxville Ridge, or rather, the formation which makes it, rises a few miles to the northeast of the city, and splits off an arm of this area, the arm running out before reaching Athens; and again, that another arm, though much shorter, is split off by a dolomite range commencing several miles east of Knoxville, and running northeastward.† Taking this area, with its arms, we may, as it is desirable to have a name, call it the *Red Belt*, of the Trenton and Nashville Series.

611. In this *Red Belt*, as above described, the marble-bed we are considering, is pretty generally found in place. Its position, with reference to the other formations, is as represented in the section on page 230, the Maclurea Limestone separating it from the Knox Dolomite. It exists in greatest force in Knox County, its maximum thickness being not far from 400 feet. It is found in the vicinity of Strawberry Plains, and has been traced southward through the western parts of Blount and Monroe, the eastern part of Roane, to McMinn.

612. In the belt of the Trenton and Nashville Series, lying next west of the one just considered—that immediately west of Webb's Ridge and Clinch Mountain—the marble is, again, observed, but it is not as heavy, and, at intervals, is absent. In the northern part of the valley, west of Copper Ridge, a narrow band occurs, but west of this, it is not seen.

613. In Hawkins County, the marble is part of a comparatively short belt of Trenton and Nashville rocks, lying west of

* There is, however, one break in this range. On the road from Cleveland to Ducktown, at the point of the range intersected, the Trenton and Nashville Series is entirely wanting, the upper part of the Knox Group appearing on the surface. A little to the north of this, however, the rocks are seen, the "red hills," one of the great features of this range, being conspicuous.

† The last mentioned dolomite range is the one at N, in the section on page 230.

Rogersville, but separated from the town, by a conspicuous ridge. This belt is cut off at each end by one of the great faults. It is, however, sixteen or seventeen miles long, the marble lying on the southwest side, and running nearly through its whole length. As in the vicinity of Knoxville, the marble bed is separated from the Knox Dolomites, by the Maclurea blue limestones. It is from fifty, to two or three hundred feet in thickness. The government quarry, (§ 609,) is near the southwestern end of the range.

Southeast of the Red Belt and the Hawkins Range, the marble is not observed, or, at most, exists only in traces.

614. Originally, when continuous, this rock occupied a long belt-like area, reaching from the northern part of McMinn County, to the Virginia line north of Rogersville. It had the general trend of the present country. Although a hundred and twenty miles long, it was, perhaps, not anywhere, twenty wide. Early in Appalachian movements, this bed appears to have rested in a shallow trough, and, in this, the coral and crinoidal animals may have flourished and died, one generation after another, each leaving their calcareous remains, and contributing to the mass which is now a solid rock, noted for its use and beauty. (See § 583.) In the succeeding part of the Report, this bed will be further considered.

(2.) THE IRON-LIMESTONE.

615. From Knoxville, across the Holston, there may be seen, a line of high hills. These are covered, more or less, with a deep red soil, and belong to a remarkable line of red knobs which runs far down the valley. This line is one of the ranges spoken of in the First Part of the Report. (§§ 106 and 112.) These red hills owe their topographical features, and their red soils, primarily, to a highly ferruginous, sandy, fossiliferous limestone, to which I have given the name at the head of this section. This rock occurs in strata of various thicknesses, and is interstratified with calcareous shale and flaggy limestones.

616. *Lithological and Other Characters.*—Under the name *Iron-limestone*, I include not only, the characteristic ferruginous rock, but, also, the shales and the limestones associated with it. The group includes divisions 3 and 4, of the table on page 230. The maximum thickness is about 700 feet.

617. The characteristic rock, is a hard, dark gray, or dark bluish gray, iron-colored limestone. As stated, it is highly fer-

ruginous, giving the soil, in decomposing, its strong, red color, and even yielding, at some points, oxide, rich enough to be called ore. Its powder is light gray, mottled with red. The iron, doubtless, exists, for the most part, in the rock, in the form of carbonate. In addition to the ferruginous matter present, it is generally well loaded with sandy impurity, a circumstance also contributing to its peculiar character. Its hardness is due to the sand present. At a few points, I have observed small pea-like pebbles in some of its layers, making it a conglomerate; but this is rare.

When the rock is thoroughly weathered, it becomes a light, spongy, dark brown, sandy mass, and such masses are strewed over the areas in which it outcrops.*

618. Were it not for this sandy impurity, certain layers of the iron-rock might be used as an iron-ore. It is an interesting question, as to whether science or experience, will ever bring forward practicable methods for the separation of iron from such a rock as this. To do it, would, indeed, be a great achievement, and would add vastly to the mineral wealth of the world. There are other rocks in Tennessee which are equally ferruginous, as, for instance, the White Oak Mountain Sandstones, to be described. Like this, many of them are deeply red with iron. The aggregate amount of metal such rocks contain, is very great.

619. When the iron-rock is exposed to the action of water, as in a bluff on a river, a laminar structure is often made apparent, the laminæ, from half an inch to an inch, or more, in thickness, and separated by softer plates, being brought out in relief. Such exposures often exhibit cross-stratification, a fact indicating the formations of the beds in running water. These features may be seen in the bluffs at the mouth of the Little Tennessee, opposite Lenoir's, and on the Holston, at other points.

620. The Iron-limestone *as a group*, includes divisions 3 and 4, on page 230, the entire thickness being 650 feet. In more detail, the section is as follows, numbered in ascending order:

8. Iron-limestone proper	250 feet
7. Blue, flaggy limestone, with some shales	155 "
6. Iron-limestone	6 "
5. Blue, flaggy limestone	22 "

*The rock is, at some points, very fossiliferous, fragments of trilobites and crinoidal buttons being especially conspicuous. These give some of its layers a marble-like aspect. Other layers, at times, present an oolitic structure, but these features are subordinate to the general character above given.

4. Iron-limestone	45 feet
3. Shale, lower part interstratified with Iron-limestone	117 "
2. Iron-limestone	52 "
1. Shale, (resting on the marble-bed)	3 "
	650

621. Another section, about a mile southwest of the last, is as follows:

5. Iron-limestone, top not seen	175 feet
4. Shales with flaggy Iron-limestone	88 "
3. Shale?	224 "
2. Iron-limestone	33 "
1. Shale, (resting on the marble-bed)	30 "

622. Much of the Iron-limestone of these sections, is thin-bedded and flaggy, and such, for the most part, is the general character of the rock. The surfaces of its layers often show ripple-marks, another circumstance indicating its formation in a current of water.

The *blue* flags, also ripple-marked, sometimes graduate into the iron-rock, while, on the other hand, they as often run into shales. The shales have very frequently a bright buff color, but sometimes are grayish-yellow. They are the weathered outcrops of blue calcareous and argillaceous strata.

The flags are used extensively, for curbing and paving purposes, in Knoxville. There is a point from which they are obtained, near Williams' marble quarry. A mile and a half, or two miles above Knoxville, the Holston River intersects the range. The flags are quarried on a hill-side, near the river, and conveniently boated down.

623. There is a good presentation of the rocks of this group in the cuts of the Knoxville and Charleston Railroad, beyond the Holston, and immediately opposite Knoxville. The first cut presents mostly shale, with, however, two beds of iron-rock; the next, together with the hill-sides, gives a great display of the iron-rock, the mass being not less than 200 feet thick; and there is still a third cut in which the rock is seen. The mass of the second cut is generally thin-bedded; some of for the layers are of good thickness for building purposes. Stone for the construction of the railroad culverts, were quarried from them. Some of the layers are quite crinoidal, and inclined to be red and gray, approaching marble in appearance.

624. All of the rocks of the group are more or less fossiliferous, especially the blue flags and the iron-rock. The fossils have not been systematically studied, but enough is known to justify the reference of this bed, as well as the marble-bed below, to the *Trenton*.

There is a shaly limestone in this group, found in the red hills east of Chatata Valley, in Bradley County, which is remarkably filled with *Orthocerata* and allied genera. The bed is eight or ten feet thick. A *Lituites* is found here much like *L. undatus*, Conrad. Most of the species are, perhaps, new.

625. *Extent and Range; The Iron-limestone* is mainly confined to the *Red Belt* of the *Trenton and Nashville Series*. (§ 610.) I have thus named this belt on account of its red hills and the iron-limestone which makes and colors them. The maximum volume of the group is in Knox County. It diminishes in thickness going southwestward, and runs out in Chatata Valley in Bradley. It becomes also, less important northeastward, and disappears in the region of Strawberry Plains. Outside of the *Red Belt*, to the north, or northeast, it does not appear in any of the areas occupied by the Trenton and Nashville rocks.

To the southeast, however, in Blount County, there is a strip of it making a line of red knobs in front of Chilhowee Mountain. It is here in a range of Trenton and Nashville rocks, which extends, in a southwesterly direction, nearly to the Hiwassee River. Within this the iron-rock first appears near the northeastern end of Chilhowee Mountain, and extends with the range of rocks to the vicinity of the river. In front of the north end of Star's Mountain, the Iron-rock, nearly horizontal, occupies a belt three or four miles wide.

626. On the northwest side of Knoxville the rock occurs, but much reduced in volume, as we have seen (§§ 587 and 588.)* In the Trenton and Nashville ranges still further northwest, as stated, it has thinned out, or, at most, but mere traces of it are to be found.

From what has been said, the extent of the *Iron-limestone*, when continuous, and unbroken by Appalachian movements, can, in part, at least, be made out. It did not extend as far

*The Trenton and Nashville belt referred to in § 587, is one of the arms of the *Red Belt* described in § 610.

northward as the marble-bed below it. Its western limit was much the same as that of the marble, while its extent southwestward and southeastward, was greater. Its longer dimension was in the direction of the general trend of the Valley, in that respect agreeing with the marble, (§614.)

627. The upper iron-rock bed of the group, appears to have been the most persistent. The lower ones run out and e place to shales. Thus, in the section in § 587, we have 320 feet of shales next above the marble. So, in McMinn and Bradley Counties, there is a heavy bed of shales and thin limestones, between the Maclurea Limestone and the iron-rock stratum.

628. "*The Red Knobs.*"—These have been referred to several times. (§§ 106, 112 and 615.) The outcrops of the iron-limestones, especially when the rocks are tilted and in considerable volume, generally present ridges, or lines of knobs.

The hard rocks, not yielding to the action of the weather, or to disintegrating agencies, like other neighboring beds, have been left in elevated crests and peaks. In some cases, a single bed or plate of hard rock, has given origin to a ridge, first, by itself resisting the wear and tear of the weather, and secondly, by *protecting*, from such action, softer material below it.

A ridge formed by a comparatively thin stratum of rock, is, generally, found cut up into a line of knobs, for the reason that the *protecting* plate, being thin, is easily fissured, and each fissure originates a gap.

629. The most conspicuous, and longest line of red knobs, is that passing near Knoxville, on the southeast side. This has been sufficiently described. (§§ 112, 615.)

Another, is found in the Trenton and Nashville belt, immediately west of the Knoxville Ridge. Traces of it are seen opposite the city; it becomes more marked southwestward; is represented by low, red hills, near, and to the southeast of Loudon, but soon runs out when traced further southwestward.

A line is, generally, to be found on the southwest side of the *Red Belt.* (§ 610.) This coalesces with the main line in the southern part of McMinn and in Bradley. Another line of knobs runs near the mouth of the French Broad River.

In addition to these, one in front of Chilhowee Mountain has been spoken of. (§ 625.)

630. The Red Belt is, in general, a synclinal trough. Where wide, as in Knox County, the strata, in the central portion, run in moderate waves, and are, in places, approximately horizontal. This, in certain sections, brings the iron-rock, (as well as the other special beds,) several times to the surface. Thus, in crossing the belt along the Knoxville and Maryville road, quite a number of areas are crossed, in which the iron-rock outcrops. It usually alternates with a calcareous shale, weathering buff. Some of the iron-rock, along this route, is oolitic.

(3.) OTHER SPECIAL BEDS ABOVE THE IRON-LIMESTONE.

631. *The Division above the Iron-rock, and its lower part, the Crinoid Bed.*—In the section §§ 585 and 586, the last division is succeeded, in ascending order, by a heavy series of calcareous strata, mostly, weathering to a buff shale, but containing, more or less, flaggy, blue limestone. The thickness of the series is uncertain. It is given in the section, as 500? The corresponding horizon, in the section on page 231, has it 1000? It may be placed at about 800.

632. The lower part of the division, is in the line of the section, (§ 585,) a group of shaly limestones about 100 feet thick, which is well filled with shells and crinoids. This group rests upon the *Iron-limestone.* I have named it the *Crinoid Bed.* Among the species occurring in this bed, the following were seen ; *Orthis Bellarugosa?* Conrad. *Strophomena incrassata,* Hall. *Asaphus canalis,* Conrad. Several new species of *Orthis* occur, as well as new forms of *Paleocrinus, Rhodocrinus, Hybocrinus,* and *Carabocrinus.*

The abundance of crinoidal remains, not only in this bed, but, also, in many of the strata, between this and the *Maclurea Limestone,* is a noteworthy circumstance.

633. *The Upper Marble.*—Succeeding the division last noticed, is another bed of variegated marble. This is a reddish-brown rock, with white or gray, rarely greenish, clouds and bands. Like the lower marble, (§ 605,) it is coralline and crinoidal. It resembles the lower bed, but is not as valuable. Its maximum thickness has been estimated at about 300 feet. It can be traced, southwestward, through Knox, the western parts of

Blount and Monroe, and through McMinn into Bradley.* It generally, presents itself in two parallel bands, occupying a place within the two principal lines of red knobs, pertaining to the Red Belt. (§§ 610, 630.) In the section from Athens to the southeast, across the belt mentioned, one range of this marble is intersected about a mile from the town. This section, also, shows the two ranges of the red knobs.

634. Outside of the Red Belt, this bed, at least as marble, is not in noteworthy volume. A trace of it may be seen, occasionally, in the first Trenton and Nashville ranges, northwest of Knoxville.

In the section from the government marble quarry in Hawkins, across the valley, in a northwesterly direction to Short Mountain, a marble is intersected, which may be referred to this bed.

635. *The Brown Shale.*—In the table on page 231, we have in the place of the Red Marble of the preceding table, a bed of brownish-red shales, and this we take to be synchronous with the marble. To this I have already referred. (§ 589.) The marble itself, when traced to the southwest, is, at intervals, much like this shale; at some points the bed is shale and marble, mixed. The beds of the two sections will be regarded as one.

636. West and northwest of Knoxville, the *Brown Shale* rarely presents a marble-like aspect, and is but little fossiliferous. It occurs in all, or nearly all, of the valleys of the Trenton and Nashville Formations lying between Knoxville and the Cumberland Table-land. It usually presents itself in long belts, which run longitudinally with the valleys. Its strata dip at all angles; and when the inclination is considerable, which is more frequently the case than otherwise, it forms long, low, "hog-back" ridges.

These ridges are sometimes nearly destitute of soil, the strata outcropping in parallel bands. A growth of red cedar is frequently met with upon them.

* There is a bed of gray, crinoidal marble a few feet below the iron-rock of the red hills in the northern part of Bradley, which may be a local stratum, referable to the Iron-limestone Group. It is separated from an iron-rock, by the orthoceratite bed, mentioned in § 624.

637. In § 634, I have spoken of a marble between the Government quarry and Short Mountain, in Hawkins County. Seven or eight miles to the northeast, this marble appears to be represented by a belt of the Brown Shale at the southeastern base of the Devil's Nose.

The valley-ranges intersected west of Knoxville, and containing Trenton and Nashville rocks, show the Brown Shale far to the southwest. In Roane and Meigs counties, some of the more compact layers, clouded with dove-colored bands, are regarded as marble. It has been used in making the foundation of the Court-house in Kingston.

Northeast and east of the Red Belt, this formation has not been observed.

638. The Brown Shale is, when freshly quarried, a compact, brownish-red, calcareous rock. As ordinarily seen, it is weathered into shale The compact rock from the range west of Knoxville, has been used for making hydraulic lime, which has answered a good purpose.

This completes the consideration of the beds given in the sections on pages 230 and 231, with the exception of the calcareous shale above the Red Marble in the first, which is referred to the general division to be described.

B. The Upper Member of the Trenton and Nashville Series.

639. I include in this, all of the strata of the series above the *Maclurea Limestone.* (§ 509. This embraces, of course, the interpolated beds already described. This classification is the same as that given on page 228. The upper member is there designated as the *Shale.* It must be borne in mind, however, that while the division is shale in the southeastern part of the Valley, it becomes mostly limestone in the northwestern. (§ 581.)

It will be well to consider this formation under two separate heads, these referring respectively to its different presentations in the southeastern and northwestern portions of the Valley.

(a) *The Shale,* (Eastern.)

640. *The Gray Belt; its Topography.*—Before speaking of the lithological and other features of the *Shale*, I will notice a very important area in which it is found, and to which it gives character.

If the reader will take the map, and direct his attention to the Valley of East Tennessee, among the belts of Trenton and Nashville rocks, he will observe a large, club-shaped one commencing north of Kingsport, on the Virginia line, and extending nearly to the Hiwassee River. This is the largest area of these rocks in East Tennessee, the *Red Belt* (§ 610) being the next in extent. And as we have found it convenient to have a name for the latter, so it will be of service to christen this. We will denominate it the *Gray Belt*, from the prevalence of earthy gray rocks and knobs.

The boundaries, form, and range, of the *Gray Belt*, are best appreciated by a reference to the map.

641. The most characteristic topographical feature of this area, is the presence of isolated knobs. Many portions of it are spoken of, locally, as "*The Knobs.*" The knobs are conical hills of all heights, from 100 to 500 feet. Sometimes they are more or less elongated, forming short ridges. In certain regions, they are closely set, making a wild country traversed by narrow, labyrinthine, but rich and fertile valleys.* Knobby portions occur in Hawkins and Greene, on both sides of Bays Mountains, also in Cocke, Sevier, Blount, Monroe and McMinn. In Sevier County, around the northern end of Chilhowee Mountain, the knobby feature is very bold.

642. The prevailing knobs are, as stated, earthy gray, and in this respect, in contrast with the characteristic knobs of the Red Belt. The lower end of the Gray Belt, however, has some of the red knobs, owing to the presence of the strip of *iron-rock* mentioned in § 625.

643. It is to be observed that the northern wide part of the belt embraces the mountain ridges to which the collective name of *Bay's Mountain Group* has been given. (p. 43.) These ridges are capped with a formation—the *Clinch Mountain Sandstone*—which is not included in the Trenton and Nashville Series. The topographical feature presented in this group, must be considered apart from those which are characteristic of the *Gray Belt* in general.

* Some of these regions when viewed from high points, look like *mammoth potato patches*, the hills, however, not in very regular rows.

644. *Areas of the Shale; Synclinals.*—The *Gray Belt* just described, is the most important and marked area of this shale. East of it, in Sullivan, Carter, Washington and Greene counties, are other areas, but they are comparatively very limited. Those in Sullivan, and in the western part of Carter, are the most important. Their number and extent can be seen upon the Map. They are all characteristically knobby belts. (§ 110.)

In Washington and Greene, the lower beds of the *Shale* are presented in very narrow "*black slate ridges.*" (§ 110.) One of these ridges (that passing immediately back of Greeneville) has been spoken of. (§ 592 and note.) It may be taken as a type of the rest. The *Shale* rests in a compressed trough of *Maclurea Limestone.*

The shale and sandstone of the ridge east of Benton, in Polk County, referred to in § 595, may be mentioned here. The rocks are shales below with a sandstone above. This ridge borders a fault. (See section page 185.) The formation is that numbered 3 and 4.

In addition to the areas mentioned, the *Red Belt* may be regarded as containing this *Shale.* It is the great matrix holding the interpolated beds. Here, however, the formation is more calcareous, and presents, more or less, flaggy limestone.

645. In most of the belts and areas mentioned, including the *Gray Belt*, the *Shale* is held in synclinal troughs and rests upon the *Maclurea Limestone.* Some of the troughs are locally faulted on their eastern side, as, for example, the Gray Belt in the section on page 190. See, also, § 600. It is remarkable that these wide synclinal waves are found on the side of the Valley next to the great mountains.

644. *Lithological Character; Graptolites.*—The formation is, in general, a great body of sky-blue calcareous shales, more or less sandy, weathering to a yellowish-gray color, as stated in § 580. In addition to the characters given the base of the formation, in the eastern border counties, (including Sullivan,) as far down as Blount, is a fine dark or black shale, becoming, in places, 100 or 150 feet thick. This often appears as a margin along the limits of the *Shale* followed below by the *Maclurea Limestone.* The black shale is prominent in the "slate ridges" spo-

ken of. (§ 644.) It abounds, very generally, in *graptolites*.* The *graptolites* are, however, not confined to this lower stratum; they run up into the main body of the *Shale*, and are found at numerous localities. I have sometimes denominated the formation the *Graptolite Shale*. These fossils have not, as yet, been studied. Some of them will, doubtless, prove to be new species.

645. In the middle and upper parts of the *Shale*, especially east of Bay's Mountains and southward in the *Gray Belt*, plates of a hard calcareous sandstone are met with, to which the knobs owe, in part, their origin, very much as the red knobs owe theirs to the iron-rock. (§ 628.)

This sandstone has the color of the shales with which it is associated.

646. The following is a section of the *Shale* from Bull's Gap† westward to White Horn Creek, a distance of nearly one mile. The rocks dip southeastward at an average rate of 30 or 40 degrees; the dip, however, ranging from 5° to 90°. Immediately at the Gap, the strata form a synclinal axis, dipping to the northwest after passing it.

(3) *Reddish-brown Calcareous Shale*. This constitutes the base of the ridge at the Gap. The top not seen. Above it, on the surface, are detached masses of grayish-white sandstone—*Clinch Mountain Sandstone*. The shale and sandstone are referred to the same formation, (5,*a*.)
Thickness of the shale seen........................ 80 feet.

(2)
- *Calcareous Shale*, or argillaceous pale brownish, bluish, or rarely greenish, limestone, weathering to shale...112 feet.
- *Sky-blue Calcareous Shale, and thin blue flaggy Limestones*.. 77 feet.
- *Sky-blue Calcareous Shale*, with occasionally flaggy limestones. Has a few layers of calcareous sandstone..933 feet.
- *Sky-blue Calcareous Shale*, weathering grayish buff..860 feet.

* These are fossils, which, in the shales, are long and narrow, and have the form of blades of grass, excepting that they have saw-like edges.

† Bull's Gap is at the northeast corner of Jefferson County, and is the point at which the East Tennessee and Virginia Railroad passes the middle ridge of the Bay's Mountain Group. (§ 99.)

(1) *Maclurea Limestone*, in thin layers, with shaly seams, and breaking into blocks—"Block Limestone," (§ 591,) contains *Trilobites*, and other fossils.

Thickness seen..................................200 feet.

647. Division (2) is the *Shale*. Its thickness here is 1982 feet. This is near the maximum, which has been placed at 2000. (§ 580.) The flaggy limestones show that we are advancing westward, or rather, northwestward, the formation becoming more calcareous.

This section may be compared with that on page 230. The principal difference is in the absence in this, of the marbles and iron limestones. The blue limestones in both, are fossiliferous.

(b) *Limestone and Shale*. (Western.)

648. The lithological changes that occur in the upper portion of the *Trenton and Nashville Series*, in going from the southeastern portion of the Valley to the northwestern, have been already given. (§§ 578, 581, 596, and 639.)

The difference in topographical features presented by these rocks in the two portions, is also quite marked, and will be noticed.

649. *Topography; Areas.* West of the *Red Belt*, (§ 610,) and the Holston River, this division and the *Maclurea Limestone*, are best considered together. In fact, it is not always easy to separate them, as they form a natural group. (§ 596.) I have spoken of them collectively as the *Series*, and will continue to do so.

In the part of the Valley we are now considering, these rocks outcrop in long ribbon-like areas, making one class of the remarkable valley-ranges mentioned in the First Part of this Report. (§§ 119, 120, 121.) The special topographical features of the eastern knobby belts, are, in general, lost in these ranges. There are, however, a few exceptional areas, which are more or less knobby. The Hawkins Belt, in part, and the wide area at the south end of Clinch Mountain, both mentioned below, are examples.

650. The western valley-ranges of this *Series* are enumerated on the next page. Most of them have been referred to. The reader will be aided in tracing them out, by having the Map before him.

(1.) The *Hawkins Belt*, west of Rogersville. This supplies one of the beds of marble. (§ 613.) The area is short, being cut off by the long fault, lying on the east side of the *Clinch Mountain* region.

(2.) *Beaver Creek Range*. This lies next northwest of *Clinch Mountain*, and, further south, includes the valley of *Beaver Creek*. It has Copper Ridge on its northwest side. This range widens out in a local area around the south end of *Clinch Mountain*, and also around *House Mountain*. (§ 98.) Going southwestward, it then bifurcates; the eastern arm runs west of *Webb's Ridge*, and, further down, forms a part of *Grassy Valley*, in Knox County; the western is the *Beaver Creek Valley*. Both arms run out between the Tennessee and Hiwassee Rivers.

(3.) *Raccoon Valley Range*. This belt is known in Knox and Anderson Counties, as *Raccoon Valley*. It extends northeastward to Virginia. The mouth of Indian Creek, in Grainger, is in it, as well as a portion of Clinch River, in Hancock. It forms a wide valley at the point intersected by the Tennessee River, but, like the arms of the last range, runs out before reaching the Hiwassee.

(4.) *Hickory Valley Range*. This is known, in the northern part of Union County, as *Hickory Valley*. It lies immediately west of *Powell's Mountain*, in Claiborne and Hancock, as well as west of *Lone Mountain*, in Grainger and Union. It widens out locally, around the south end of Powell's Mountain. From its point of intersection with Clinch River, it runs southwestward toward Maynardville. Still further southwestward, it runs out at least as a valley-range of the *Trenton and Nashville Series*.

(5.) *Big Valley Range*. The portion of this, in Anderson and Union Counties, is known as the *Big Valley*. The range has been instanced, on a previous page, as an example of the long valleys in this section of East Tennessee. (See § 120.) It is there spoken of as continuous. There is, however, one break in it, made by a local uplift of the rocks of the Knox Group. This break is in Claiborne County. This range includes *Savannah Valley*, in the southern part of East Tennessee and west of White Oak Mountain. At the northern end of the Mountain just mentioned, the rocks of the *Series* spread out in a wide local area. Over a good part of it, the rocks are nearly horizontal.

(6.) *Washington Range*. A short range, running next west of the iron-ore ridges in the region of *Half-moon Island*. Washington, in Rhea County, is located upon it.

(7.) *Chattanooga Range*. A part of the Valley south of Chattanooga and east of Lookout Mountain, is underlaid by the rocks of this Series.

(8.) The *Mountain Range*. This important belt is so called, for the reason that it skirts the eastern base of the Cumberland Table-land, with but few breaks (due to local faults,) from Virginia to Georgia. The range is noticed in § 121, to which the reader is referred. In Hamilton County, its strata form a well-defined, anti-clinal axis, to which the valley of Lookout Creek belongs. (See section on page 139, at F.)

(9.) The *Elk Range.* The valley of the *Elk Fork* is, for the most part, made up of other formations. It contains, however, a narrow strip of Trenton rocks, brought to the light, as shown in the section on page 142.

(10.) The *Sequatchee Ranges.* On both sides of *Sequatchee Valley*, are minor valley-ranges, in which these rocks outcrop. (See section on page 139; also § 600, and note.)

651. When a mountain bounds one of these Trenton and Nashville ranges, on either side, the upper strata of the *Series* are usually found at a greater or less elevation, on the slope facing the range. This is especially true of those mountains, which, like the *Clinch*, are made up of an inclined plate of *Niagara Sandstone*, (5,*a.*) This formation,* when present, is next above the *Trenton and Nashville Series.* In the mountains which it makes, the tilted sandstone forms one slope, and presents its outcropping edge at the summit. This exposes the edges of the softer strata of the underlying formation on the other slope. These are, however, protected from washing and denudation, by the hard plate of rock overlying them. (Compare § 628.) *Clinch*, *Powell's* and *Lone Mountains* (the latter that of Grainger and Union Counties) present the upper strata of the *Trenton and Nashville Series,* on their western slopes. Some of the Bay's Mountain ridges are like these; others, have the sandstone on the west, the underlying rocks outcropping on the eastern, or rather southeastern, side. Some isolated peaks, or short mountains, like *Chimney Top* and *Fodder Stack*, (§ 99,) and like *Devil's Nose* and *House Mountain*, (§ 98,) have a bed of sandstone on top, while outcropping on the slopes all around, are the strata of the underlying formation. In the southern part of the Valley, White Oak Mountain has the rocks of the *Series* under consideration, on its western side, and outcropping around its northern end.

652. It must be observed that the upper layers of the *Knox Dolomite* are often found either on one side or the other of the above valley-ranges. They contribute, also, in some regions, to the area of the range. The side of the valley-range, in which the junction of the two formations occurs, is generally the northwestern. In the *Mountain Valley Range*, (§ 650, (8,)) the reverse is the case. I have already spoken of the position of

* This formation includes a bed of red shale below the sandstone, which, in common with the Trenton and Nashville rocks below, is protected by the sandstone proper.

the *Maclurea Limestone*, (§§ 599 and 600,) and to this the reader is referred. The upper member of the Series will, of course, follow in ascending order. (See sections on pages 189 and 208, and remarks upon them.)

653. *Lithological, and other Characters.*—The entire Series is limestone and shale. The lower part, mainly blue limestone; the upper part, though more calcareous than the same member in the *Red* and *Gray belts*, (§ 610 and 640,) is less so than the equivalent rocks in the *Central Basin*, (§ 227.) The uppermost beds of the Series are, very generally, shale and shaly limestone. In descending Clinch Mountain, on the northwest side, for instance, we find below the white hard sandstone, first, a bed of brownish-red shale, (included in a group with the sandstone,) then several hundred feet of sky-blue shale, running down into thin-bedded blue limestone. These upper beds contain, at many points, Nashville fossils. Below the beds mentioned, occur other beds of shale, one of which has been considered important enough to be noticed, (§§ 635, 636.)

The thickness of the Trenton and Nashville Series diminishes a few hundred feet, going westward.

654. *Transition Beds; Appendix.*—At the top of the Nashville Formation, in the western part of the Valley, are, at certain localities, rocks, which appear to be beds of passage from the formation mentioned, to the *Dyestone Group*, described below. In the next chapter, a section, taken on the Nashville and Chattanooga Railroad, just above Lookout Station, and near the Georgia line, will be presented, in which these beds will be given. They contain such fossils as *Orthis testudinaria, O. bellarugosa? Strophomena planoconvexa, S. tenuistriata, Leptæna Sericea, Atrypa marginalis*, &c.

655. *Useful Rocks and Minerals.*—The *Trenton* and *Nashville Series* affords, in East Tennessee, several beds of *rock-material* susceptible of practical application. Among them, the *marbles* stand prominent. The geological relations, and general features of these, have been given. See pages 232, 236, 244, and 246. It likewise supplies *flags*, (§ 622,) and other building material, in addition to the marble. Certain layers of *iron-limestone*, (§ 623,) and many beds of blue limestone, in the different belts of the Series, yield building stone, of excellent

quality. It contains, too, no lack of rock for making excellent lime; the gray marbles, among many beds which might be mentioned, are well adapted to this purpose. The *Brown Shale* affords material for *hydraulei lime,* (§ 638.) These useful products will be further noticed in the Third Part of the Report.

656. *Calcite* in small veins is quite common in the *Maclurea Limestone.* Such veins occur, also, in the *Shale* in the south-eastern part of the Valley. Some of the veins in the Shale contain, imbedded in the calcite, isolated, and often beautiful crystals of *Quartz*, as on Boyd's Creek, east of Brabson's Store, in the western part of Sevier County, in the region of Bull's Gap, and at points between that and Dandridge, in the vicinity of Warrensburg, in Greene County, and at other localities. They are also observed in Greene County, on the surface overlying the *Maclurea Limestone*, and in small veins, at a point half-a-mile north of the road from Greeneville towards Chimney Top Mountain. At some localities, these crystals are quite abundant on the ground, their facets sparkling in the sunshine like diamonds. They were all, doubtless, originally imbedded in the veins of calcite. Small, isolated crystals of *Gypsum* are found in the soil over the shale, at a number of points east of the Bay's Mountain Group. Veins of *Heavy Spar*, (*Barite*,) also occur. At the quartz locality, near the Greeneville and Chimney Top road, a vein of this, of the fetid crystalline variety, is found. Masses on the surface indicate a vein a foot or more thick.

657. *Iron-ore* is found as *Limonite* on the surface, and in deposits in the soil overlying these rocks, at many points, but not constituting extensive banks. The ore results from the decomposition of *Pyrites* found locally in bunches in the shales.

Near the Benton and Madisonville road, about eleven miles from the latter place, and in McMinn County, is a heavy bed of *Fossil Iron-ore*, known as Hill's Bank. The ore resembles very much the *Dyestone* of the *Niagara Period.* It lies, however, between the *Maclurea Limestone* and the *Trenton and Nashville Shale*, and may belong to the *Series* embracing these. It contains flattened, oolitic grains and crinoidal buttons, but no recognizable fossils were seen. The bed may be traced for nearly half-a-mile, and at some points, is fifty or sixty feet wide. See, also, remarks on the Iron-limestone as an ore. (§ 618.)

658. *Agricultural Features.*—The strata of the *Trenton and Nashville Series* form the basis of much of the best arable land in East Tennessee. They are the rocks of many rich and beautiful valleys. The long ranges enumerated in § 650, the *Beaver Creek Range*, the *Raccoon Valley Range*, the *Hickory Valley Range*, the *Big Valley* and *Mountain Ranges*, the *Sequatchee Ranges*, and others, are just so many long lines of farming regions, susceptible of high cultivation. They are now more or less improved, presenting some among the most desirable agricultural sections in the State; but there is room for greater improvement and a higher state of cultivation. The resources of these valleys, of such natural beauty with their rills and watercourses, (§ 147,) their invigorating and healthy air, have not reached their full development. This, however, they will do, and perhaps, at no distant day.

The soils of the valleys are usually strong, being derived from calcareous rocks, more or less argillaceous, and are well adapted to the production of small grain, corn, grass and fruit. In nearly all cases, the valleys belonging to the ranges mentioned, have, on one side or the other, a gently sloping ridge facing the valley. The slope can often be cultivated nearly to the summit. Thus, the farmer can have upland and low land, and arrange his fields with reference to special and varied purposes. These slopes are underlaid by the magnesian limestone formation, (*Knox Dolomite*,) and generally have a productive, strong soil.

659. In the southeastern portion of the Valley, as in the *Gray Belt*, (§ 640,) the agricultural features of this *Series* are quite different. There the *Shale*, together with its peculiar topography, determines the agricultural capabilities. In the *Knobby Regions*, the arable lands do not lie in large bodies, but the narrow winding valleys and the hill-sides are rich, and often present a heavy growth of large white oaks, poplars and hickories. At many points these lands are in cultivation, and in passing through "*The Knobs*" of some sections, the traveler meets, at almost every turn, with a cabin and a miniature farm. Such areas have been denominated, with some force, "The Poor Man's Rich Country."

660. To the knobby regions of the *Red Belt*, (§ 610,) the same remarks are applicable. These, however, are by no means, so extensive as those of the other.

The *Shale*, however, presents us with some valleys of con. siderable extent like that, for instance, of Lick Creek, in Greene County. The soils of these are not as strong, generally, as those of the limestone areas, but many of them are productive and well adapted to the production of wheat, grass, etc.

In the *Red Belt* the valleys are better defined, and contain many very desirable farming sections.

Section III.

THE TRENTON AND NASHVILLE SERIES IN MIDDLE TENNESSEE.

661. Leaving Sequatchee Valley, and passing westward, there are no more outcrops of the rocks of the *Trenton and Nashville Series* until we enter the *Central Basin* of Middle Tennessee. This Basin, second to no natural division of the State in importance and interest, has been described so far as its topographical and structural relations are concerned. The reader is referred to pages 97—104, 134—136, and 148, as well as to the section in Chapter X. See, also, Map.

662. We are now in a field of very different character from that of the great *Valley of East Tennessee.* Within the *Basin,* the direction and form of the subordinate valleys have *comparatively* little to do with the rocks. There is no marked northeast and southwest trend; there are no long and straight valley-ranges; no undeviating ridge-lines a score, or *seven-score,* miles in length; no lines of bold, red knobs; and, finally, no bounding mountain-ranges, grouping, and comparatively sinking, the minor parallel valleys and ridges, and all else, into one great, fluted, long, and beautiful *Valley.*

In East Tennessee the geology of the country is intimately connected with the topography, and one cannot be properly studied without keeping in mind the other.

663. In the *Central Basin,* the rocks are horizontal, or nearly so, and, below the formation of *siliceous* strata which make the *crest* surrounding and overlooking the oval area, are approxi-

mately homogeneous in lithological character. If we exclude the formation making the crest, and confine ourselves to the homogeneous rocks, or in other words, to the *Series* under consideration, the connection between the strata and the topography is only occasionally manifested. If, however, that be included, the connection becomes general, and is seen in this, that the hard *siliceous* rocks have resisted denudation giving us the crest and the outlines of the Basin, and also in the fact that they have remained to form the cap and protecting rock of the higher included ridges.

664. In the Basin the rocks of the *Trenton and Nashville Series* are mainly blue limestone throughout. The beds of these differ, more or less, in certain particulars to be mentioned. Occasionally a limited bed of shale is met with, and some beds of red and gray limestones occur, but these are exceptional. The entire *Series* is about 1000 feet thick, and is equally divided between the *Trenton* and *Nashville* formations. (§ 577.) The bottom is not seen, the *Knox Dolomite* not coming to the surface at any point.* The top, on the eastern side of the Basin, is in contact with the *Black Shale*, all intervening formations being absent. On the western side, it is generally separated from the *Shale* by *Niagara*, and sometimes *Lower Helderberg rocks*, but not always.

665. The section on a following page, in Chapter X, shows how these rocks are brought to the surface, and the relations they sustain to the other formations. The strata are presented as they occur along the line of the Nashville and Chattanooga Railroad, from Tullahoma to Nashville, and along the Edgefield and Kentucky Railroad, from Nashville to the summit of the steep grade above Baker's Station. The entire line is a continuous one, and runs completely across the Basin. The geological, as well as the topographical features, of the Basin, as a whole, are also illustrated by the section.

666. The *Series* under consideration is a *natural group*, and though each of its members has many species of its own, yet

* The only region in Tennessee, west of the Cumberland Table-land, in which I have seen the *Knox Dolomite* is the *Wells Creek Basin*. (p. 147.) How thick the *Trenton and Nashville Series* may be here, I have not had the opportunity of ascertaining. There is, however, no reason for thinking that it is thicker than 1000 feet, indeed, I doubt if it reaches this. So far as can be ascertained, these rocks grow less in volume in that direction.

there are quite a number of forms uniting the two. It is divided, both on lithological and paleontological grounds, into its two *sub-groups.*

A.—The Trenton, or Lebanon; Formation III.

GEOGRAPHICAL RELATIONS—THE BEDS OF THE FORMATION. (1) THE CENTRAL LIMESTONE—(2) PIERCE LIMESTONE—(3) THE RIDLEY LIMESTONE—(4) THE GLADE LIMESTONE—(5) CARTER'S CREEK LIMESTONE. AGRICULTURAL FEATURES, USEFUL ROCKS AND MINERALS OF THE TRENTON.

667. *Geographical Relations.*—The outcrop of the rocks included in this formation, occur over a considerable area, nearly half that of the Central Basin. Their strata may be regarded in general, as forming *the bottom* of the Basin, the strata and the bottom, however, being slightly tilted to the west. (§ 221.) The rocks outcrop at a higher elevation on the east side than on the west, and sink below the level of the rivers, at, or near, Nashville, Franklin, and Columbia, respectively. Nearly all of Wilson, Rutherford, Bedford and Marshall counties are within the outcrop of the Trenton Formation. The area of outcrop includes, also, parts of all the counties, excepting Franklin, contiguous to the section embracing those mentioned. On the map, a line is traced out separating the *Trenton* areas from those of the *Nashville Formation.*

This formation is one of great interest, especially from an agricultural point of view. The soils it yields are among the best. To the paleontologist it is an inviting field, its strata presenting a rich fossil flora.

668. *The Beds of the Formation.*—The *Trenton Formation* is made up of several beds, each characterized by special features. Arranged in their natural order, they are as follows :

(5) *Carter's Creek Limestone.* (*Topmost.*) A heavy-bedded, light blue, or dove-colored, limestone, the upper part often gray; contains *Stromatapora rugosa, Columnaria alveolata, Tetradium columnare, Petraia profunda, Strophomena filitexta, Rhynchonella recurvirostra, Orthoceras Bigsbyi, O. Huronense, Pleurotomaria lapicida. etc.* The thickness of the stratum is from 50 to 100 feet.

(4) *The Glade Limestone.* A stratum of light-blue, thin-bedded, or flaggy, limestones. Pre-eminently the bed of the great "*Cedar Glades*" of the Central Basin. Contains *Stropho-*

mena incrassata, S. filitexta, Orthis deflecta, O. perveta, O. tricenaria, Rhynchonella orientalis, Cyrtodonta obtusa, Trochonema umbilicata, Orthoceras rapax, Illaenus Americanus, Leperditia fabulites, etc. Maximum thickness 120 feet.

(3) *The Ridley Limestone.* Next below is this stratum—a group of heavy-bedded, light blue, or dove colored, limestones. Some of its fossils are as follows: *Orthoceras anceps, Stromatapora rugosa, Columnaria alveolata, Orthis bellarugosa, Camerella varians, Rhynchonella Ridleyana, etc.* The maximum thickness observed is 95 feet.

(2) *Pierce Limestone.* A group of thin-bedded, flaggy limestones, with generally a heavy-bedded layer near the base. These rocks are highly fossiliferous and abound in *Bryozoa.* Among the fossils are *Orthis Stonensis, Rhynchonella Ridleyana, Dalmanites Troosti, etc.* The group has a maximum thickness of 27 feet.

(1) *Central Limestone.* An important group of thick-bedded, cherty limestones, of a light blue, or dove color. Contains *Salterella Billingsi,* and *Leperditia fabulites* in abundance; also *Cyrtoceras Stonense, Trochonema umbilicata?, Helicotoma Tennesseensis, H. declivis, Rhynchonella altilis, etc.*

This bed is the bottom-rock of the *Central Basin,* and presents in its heaviest exposures a thickness of about 100 feet.

669. It will be seen that the above limestones are all light-blue, or dove-colored, and that the groups are alternately thick and thin-bedded. It may also be mentioned here, that the thick-bedded groups are frequently *cherty,* though the two upper ones are much less so than the lower one. In accordance with our usual order, the lowest bed will be considered first.

670. (1) *The Central Limestone.*—As stated, this is an important body of limestones, and it is mostly so on account of its agricultural relations. Excepting the strata of the comparatively small *Well's Creek Basin,* (§§ 364, 553,) these rocks are the lowest in Tennessee west of the *Cumberland Table-land.* How they are brought to the surface, is shown in the section referred to in §665. Their outcrop occupies an approximately circular area around Murfreesboro, in Rutherford County. I have given the name above to the group, for the reason that it is thus presented in the very center of the State.

671. Murfreesboro is located upon these rocks. In going towards Nashville, from Murfreesboro, they appear at the sur-

face, with the exception of a few high points, as far, nearly, as Smyrna. Going south on the Chattanooga road, they are seen as far as Christiana and Christmas Creek. In this distance, however, several of the more elevated portions of the country crossed hold higher beds, and of these, mainly the *Ridley Limestone.* Towards Woodbury, they outcrop for a distance of three or three and-a-half miles. And finally, on the Lebanon road, the layers of the *Central Limestone* are exposed as far as Stone's River. These rocks thus occupy (excepting the hills and the low ridges, of which there are no great number) a circular area, having a diameter of from twelve to fifteen miles. Murfreesboro is about half-way between the center of this area and its eastern side.

672. I will add here, that, in Rutherford County, the overlying beds form, in succession, by their outcrops, concentric rings or circular belts around the area just mentioned.* This is especially true of the *Ridley* and *Glade* beds. The latter gives a very marked ring, made so by the *cedars* which so generally grow upon it. The *Cedar Ring* is crossed by the Chattanooga Railroad, about half way between Murfreesboro and Nashville, and is nearly or quite four miles wide. It encircles the outcrops of both the *Central* and the *Ridley* beds, in one large basin-like area of splendid country, nearly twenty miles across.

673. The lithological character of the *Central Limestone*, has been, in good part, already given. Its upper part, contains much black flint or chert, in thin layers and in nodules, the black color being due to the presence of a compound of iron. The decomposition of the flints, which is constantly going on, liberates the iron in the form of oxide, and this imparts a characteristic brownish-red, or chocolate color to the soil.

The limestones of the bed, are very generally fetid. At some points on Bradley's Creek, an upper layer is found, which is finely and beautifully laminated.

674. On the next page, is a section taken on Stone's River, at Pierce's mill, the point at which the Murfreesboro and Lebanon Turnpike crosses. It is one of a series of sections to be given, running up through the beds of the Trenton Formation.

* This must be taken in a general sense. The ridges break up, more or less, the symmetry of these circular belts, yet, in no great degree.

(3) *Ridley Limestone*, forms the top part of the bluff, opposite the mill; thick-bedded, light blue limestone, containing *Orthoceras anceps*, *Columnaria alveolata*, *Stromatopora rugosa*, and an other fossil sponge not described, and characteristic of the bed. Thickness 23 feet seen.

(2) *Pierce Limestone*, made up of the following rocks, in all 27 feet:

(*c*.) Thin-bedded layers, mostly, with smooth surfaces, and separated by thin, argillaceous, or shaly seams, very fossilliferous, contains *Bryoza*, &c. Thickness 19 feet.

(*b*.) Coarse, thick-bedded limestone—4 feet.

(*a*.) flaggy limestones, like the upper portion, (*c*.)—4 feet thick.

(1) *Central Limestone*, at th base of the bluff, very cherty, heavy-bedded, contains *Saltarella Billingsi*, *Orthoceras Bigsbyi*, *Leperditia fabulites*, *Helicotoma Tennesseensis*, *H. declivis*, and other species. At Pierce's Mill, but little of this bed is seen. Descending the river, however, its strata are observed to rise, until in a bluff half a mile below the mill, they are 70 feet thick.

675. The best known fossils, that occur in the Central Limestone, are given in the catalogue of species, at the end of this chapter. (See column C.) One of the most abundant species, is, *Salterella Billingsi*. Its beautiful thorn-like forms occur by thousands at some localities. *Leperditia fabulites* is, also, very abundant. The species mentioned, together with *Helicotoma Tennesseensis, and H. declivis*, occur at nearly all localities, and, in this association, are characteristic.

676. (2) *Pierce Limestone.*—This group has been so named on account of its fine exposure in the section at Pierce's Mill. It has been sufficiently characterized in § 668, and in the section just given. The group has no especial importance, excepting as a horizon of reference and of division. It is observed at many points in Rutherford, lying between the Central and the Ridley beds. In thickness, it is variable, often less than that given. At some points it is all flaggy limestone, the thick layer being absent.

677. (3) The *Ridley Limestone.*—The description of this has also been, in good part, anticipated. At Judge Ridley's Mill, near Old Jefferson, there is a good exposure of the rocks of this bed, and hence the name *Ridley*. The bed occupies the low grounds of this vicinity. At the mill, the thin limestones of the Pierce Bed are below it. *Orthoceras anceps*, and the characteristic sponge spoken of in § 674, (3,) are quite abundant in these rocks.

678. The following is a section taken at Las Casas, in the northeastern part of Rutherford, and not far from the Wilson County line. It was taken on the side of a rocky ridge. The entire *Ridley Bed* is presented in it.

(4) *The Glade Limestone.* This *caps* the ridge. The rocks are thin-bedded limestones, containing characteristic fossils.

(3) *Ridley Limestone.* Thick-bedded, dove colored, limestone, presenting the general characters of the bed. There were observed here *Columnaria alveolata, Stromatopora rugosa, Tetradium fibratum,* among other fossils. Thickness 95 feet.

(2) *Pierce Limestone.* at the base of the ridge, and followed below towards the creek, by the *Central Limestone.*

679. The *Ridley Limestone* outcrops, in general, around the circular area of the *Central Limestone* in Rutherford. (§ 672.) Its belt is from half-a-mile to six miles in breadth.

The bed, however, occurs locally, on the higher grounds within the area mentioned. It is, also, sometimes made the surface-rock by local depressions in the strata.

680. Outside of Rutherford County this bed is but seldom seen. At a few points in some of the other counties in which the *Glade Limestone* is extensively presented, the top part of this bed is exposed by the removal of the overlying rocks. But such exposures are of limited extent, and are generally in low places, as, for instance, in the lower part of certain bluffs on the Cumberland River, between Wilson and Sumner. The bed, too, may be looked for in the lower parts of the bluffs on Duck River, between Columbia and Shelbyville.

681. (4) The *Glade Limestone.*—The outcrops of the rocks of this bed embrace large areas in the *Central Basin.* It is a group of much interest. Its rocks are, as has been stated, (§ 668,) thin, flaggy, fossiliferous, dove-colored limestones. The areas in which the group appears on the surface, abound in bare, or nearly bare, rocky places, called *glades.* Upon these, is, very generally, a growth of *red cedar*, the trees finding root in the crevices of the rocks. (§§ 240 241.) The cedars are not, however, confined to the bare places; they thrive and attain a large size where the soil of the group is deeper. The *glades* and the *cedars* almost always indicate the presence of these rocks beneath.

682. The principal areas presenting these rocks, are in Wilson, Rutherford, Bedford, and Marshall, and they extend west-

ward, more or less, into Maury, Williamson, and Davidson. These areas, also, are the cedar regions of Middle Tennessee. Reference has been made to the *cedar ring* encircling the outcrops of the Central and Ridley beds in Rutherford, in § 672.

The towns of *Lebanon*, *Shelbyville*, and *Columbia*, in part, are located upon this group. At all of these places, its rocks, presenting the same assemblage of fossils, are well exposed.

683. In 1851, the author contributed to the *American Journal of Science and Arts*, (Vol. XII, Second Series, p. 352,) a paper accompanied with a plate, on the "*Silurean Basin of Middle Tennessee*," &c. On the plate, the portions of the Basin especially abounding in cedars, are indicated. There are seen to be three principal areas, namely: one in Wilson, in which Lebanon is located; the circular belt in Rutherford, and finally, the Duck River Valley, between Columbia and Shelbyville.

684. The section below, taken near Readyville, in the eastern part of Rutherford, presents the bed of the *Glade Limestone* entire.

(5) *Carter's Creek Limestone.*—The rocks of this bed form the top of the hill, are thick bedded, and have a thickness of 50 feet.

(4) *Glade Limestone.*—Thin bedded, flaggy limestone, presenting the usual features of the group; contains a heavy bedded layer, about three feet thick, near the middle, and another near the base. Entire thickness, 118 feet.

(3) *Ridley Limestone.*—This constitutes the base of the section, and forms a bluff running down to the level of the water. It has an exposure of 35 feet.

685. The flags of the glade bed, have, sometimes, thin clayey, or shaly seams between them, but not always, being separable without such seams. The surfaces of the flags are often, covered with *Bryozoa*, *Orthes*, fragments of *Trilobites*, and individuals of *Leperditia fabulites*. The individuals of the last mentioned species, are especially abundant.

686. (5) *The Carter's Creek Limestone.*—This is the uppermost division of the *Trenton Formation*. Its rocks are prominently exposed on *Carter's Creek* in Maury County, and hence, the name given to it. It is, here, a whitish gray rock, heavy bedded, and is quarried for building purposes, and for making lime. It contains some chert, and the characteristic fossils of the division.

This rock shows itself at many points along the railroad, between Columbia and Carter's Station. It often presents in the bluffs, a castellated appearance, rising up in curious peaks or turrets, and attracting the attention of the traveler.

687. The rocks of the *Carter's Creek* division, *in general*, are, as stated in § 668, light blue, or dove-colored, heavy bedded limestones. In Maury County, the upper part is gray, as we have seen. At many points, at the very top of the group, are a few feet of thin bedded limestones, separated by thin, clayey partings, and, sometimes, by a layer of clay, a foot or more thick. These thin limestones, contain a group of fossils, recalling that of the *Glade Bed.*

688. As in the Ridley division, so in this, the limestones contain, occasionally, layers of chert or flint, but, as stated before, in less quantity than those presented in the *Central Limestone.**

The following group of fossils, is characteristic of the *Carter's Creek* division; *Orthoceras Bigsbyi*, *Stromatopora rugosa*, *Petraia profunda*, *Tetradium columnare*, *Columnaria alveolata*, and *C. Carterensis*. Individuals of these species, when found associated, determine, at once, the division.

The cedars of the *Glade Bed*, sometimes, extend over the rocks of this.

689. The following is a section, taken at the bluff, just below Cole's Ferry, on the Cumberland River. The point is between Lebanon and Gallatin. The section, so far as the division, under consideration, is concerned, is a complete one. and brings us up to the lower member of the *Nashville Formation.*

NASH. (1) *Orthis Bed*, represented by a few of its lowest sandy layers. This bed is the lowest member of the formation next described.

TRENTON. (5) *Carter's Cheek Limestone.* In the main, light blue, heavy bedded limestone, containing the usual fossils, and, otherwise, having the common characters of the division. The upper ten feet, is, mostly, thin bedded, and contains *Tetradium fibratum*, the cell-tubes in long stringy groups. The presence of *T. fibratum* in this, is, by the way, not usual in this horizon. Entire thickness 95 feet.

(4) *Glade Limestone.* All thin-bedded, excepting one heavy bedded layer eight feet thick, and 27 feet from the top. Entire thickness down to low water, 74 feet.

* It may be remarked here, that in all of the thick bedded divisions, the fossils are, generally, siliceous, while, as generally, in the thin bedded ones, they are calcareous.

690. At *Columbia*, a good section is to be seen. It includes both *Trenton* and *Nashville* rocks. The *Carter's Creek Limestone* is not as heavy as it is further north, and, moreover, differs in having a lighter color. The following, is the section.

NASHVILLE.

(2) *Middle Member*. A series of blue, highly fossiliferous limestones, running up to the top of "*Mount Parnassus*." This division includes, here, about 200 feet of limestone, contains *Orthis lynx*, *O. occidentalis*, *Columnaria stellata*, *Ambonychia radiata*, *&c*. The upper layers are made up of small corals, *Stenopora*, *Constellaria*, and others. Specimens may be gathered on the top of the hill about the old fort, by the peck.

These rocks resemble those around the Capitol at Nashville. Just above the *Orthis bed*, at the base of this member, are layers, packed with individuals of *Strophomena alternata*.

(1) *Orthis Bed*, or *Lowest Member*. This is a group of blue, siliceous, and sandy limestones, some layers of which, are literally made up of individuals of *Orthis testudinaria*. The rock weathers into sandy masses and shales. The shells are generally silicified and the liberated ones are abundant on the surface. Towards the top, the bed is laminated, with, occasionally, cross stratification, characters showing the formation of this portion in a current. Thickness 60 feet.

TRENTON.

(5) *Carter's Creek Limestone*. Heavy bedded, light dove colored limestones below, and gray above. The rock is quarried for building purposes. Has the characteristic group of fossils, and contains some chert. This rock is exposed at the top of the bluff, at the old cemetery. Thickness about Columbia, from 50 to 60 feet.

(4) *Glade Limestone*. Well exposed in the bluff below the cemetery, and about the bridge. Thin bedded limestones with the usual fossils of this division. The greatest thickness seen above low water, is 80 feet.

691. The *Carter's Creek Limestone* occupies, in general, areas around those of the Glade Bed. It is also present in the hills and ridges occurring within the Glade areas. South of *Elk Ridge*, there are but few places where it comes to the surface, the limestones of the valleys, in that section of the *Central Basin*, (§§ 233, 237,) belonging, mainly, to the *Nashville Formation*. This division of the *Trenton*, however, does appear in the valley of Richland creek in Giles County. From Lyn-

ville, on down, to within five or six miles of Pulaski, its gray rocks are well seen at many points near the creeks. Campbellville is also located upon its rocks. A patch of it exists west of Pulaski; another, in the valley of the Elk, opposite upper Elkton.

692. A few miles below Columbia, the division sinks below the river; it is, then, only seen, occasionally, in patches, being brought to the surface on the backs of local waves. One of these patches occurs near Hampshire, another on Snow Creek, near Santa Fe, &c.

693. In Smith County, along the creeks between New Middleton and Carthage, as on Mulherrin, are exposures of the *Carter's Creek Limestone.* So, also, on Smith's Fork, in De Kalb and Smith, etc.

Liberty in De Kalb, Statesville in Wilson, Woodbury in Cannon, and *Columbia,* (in part.) in Maury, are located upon the rocks of this division. At Nashville, they come to the surface above the water-works, and are seen in the lower parts of the hills about Mt. Olivet. In the region of Mill Creek, on the Murfreesboro turnpike, are good exposures.

694. *Agricultural Features, Useful Rocks* and *Minerals of the Trenton.*—The *Central Basin,* has been denominated the garden of Tennessee. (§ 227.) Its lands, in general, are of first rate quality, strong and fertile, adapted to the raising of almost any thing that the climate will admit of. Cotton, corn, tobacco, small grain, and grasses, find congenial conditions in the soils of the basin, and flourish well. The area is the counterpart of the "Blue Grass Region" of Kentucky; it is the Blue Grass Region of Middle Tennessee. The rocks—the bases of the soils—are much the same in both.

695. The lands of the Basin fall naturally, into two divisions, the two being underlaid respectively, by the *Trenton* and *Nashville* Formations. To one group of lands, we may give the name *Trenton,* to the other, *Nashville.*

The soils derived from the Trenton rocks, are, as a general thing, more clayey than those from Nashville beds, the latter, containing more sandy, or siliceous matter. This difference, results from the difference in the composition of the limestones belonging to the respective formations, the one contains more argillaceous, and the other, more siliceous matter.

696. The fine country encircled by the *cedar ring* in Rutherford, has been referred to. (§ 672.) These red lands, are no-

ted for their productiveness, and constitute one of our most important cotton regions. The *Central Limestone* of the *Trenton*, very generally, has an excellent soil upon it. The sand formed by the disintegration of the black chert, helps to make the soil mellow, and the red oxide of iron, acts a part, as a chemical agent, to make it more fertile.

The *Ridley Limestone*, as to its agricultural presentations, may be classed with the *Central*. It does not contain as much chert, but, otherwise, in lithological character, the two are similar.

697. The *Glade Limestone* gives a strong, rather stiff subsoil, which has a fertile loam on top. Its lands are wheat, and grass lands. The great physical feature of this division is presented in its *cedar glades*. These originally covered, or, at least, the cedars grew, upon the greater part of its outcrop.

The better portions of the area are now in cultivation. Many of the rocky glades are still covered with cedar,

The *Carter's Creek* division is, also, the basis of a good soil, nearly equal to that of the *Central Limestone*. It has not the characteristic red color of the latter, but contains, more or less, fine, sandy chert. Its outcrop is often presented in rocky ledges, or hill-sides, with little soil.

698. Stone, for building purposes, is obtained from all the heavy bedded divisions of the Trenton. The upper part of the Carter's Creek division, however, supplies a superior article. This whitish gray limestone, already spoken of in § 686, is quarried extensively in Maury County. It is conveniently located along the line of the railroad, and could be shipped to Nashville, or other points. Its nearly white color, its texture, and occurrence in layers of suitable thickness, make it desirable. Some layers contain chert; these must be refused. The lime this rock makes is very white.

699. The *Glade Bed* is the source of a supply of limestone flags. Many of these have a smooth surface, and if such alone, be used, make an excellent pavement. They are, however, too often put down with rough ones. Many pavements, are made of flags from this division, in Lebanon. Large flags, a yard across, and from two to four inches in thickness, can be obtained without much trouble. Flags can be found at all the extensive presentations of the rocks of the *Glade Bed*.

700. Such minerals as *Calcite*, *Barite*, *Fluorite*, *Galenite*. (*galena*,) *Sphalcrite*, (*zinc blende*,) *Quartz*, *Pyrite*, (*pyrites*,) and tarry *Petroleums*, or *Pittasphalts*, have been observed in the Trenton, in Middle Tennessee. The tarry petroleums occur, occasionally, in all the heavy bedded divisions filling small cavities, which are usually lined with crystals of *calcite*. I have seen them in the vicinity of Lebanon, in the *Carter's Creek Limestone*. The *Central*, and *Ridley Limestones* contain such cavities, and the rocks themselves, are notably fetid.

Galenite, (lead ore,) occurs in small veins, at numerous points, with *Calcite*, *barite*, &c. There are veins of this sort in every county, but too small to be of value.

701. In Smith County, on Mulherrin Creek, is a considerable vein, running vertically through the *Carter's Creek Limestone*. This has been traced for several miles, and is, at points, a foot or more wide. It contains, mainly, *barite*, (heavy spar,) with *calcite*, and *fluorite*. In this gangue are bunches of lead ore, with, occasionally, some *zinc blende*. A shaft or two, has been sunk on this vein, near the Trousdale's Ferry and Lebanon road, and much *barite* thrown out, but with no special developments otherwise.

On Smith's Fork in De Kalb, is a vein, containing considerable *fluorite*, and some *galenite*, with lead.

B.—The Nashville; Formation IV.

DIVISIONS OF LOWER SILUREAN, NAMES AND EQUIVALENCY—(1) ORTHIS BED—(2 & 3) MIDDLE AND UPPER MEMBERS OF NASHVILLE:—ROCKS OF SPECIAL USE, AND MINERALS OF THE NASHVILLE FORMATION—CATALOGUE OF FOSSILS.

702. In the *Columbia* section, in § 690, the *junction* of the *Trenton* and *Nashville* formations is given.

The passage from one to the other, is well marked and abrupt. This is well seen at Columbia, and at all other points in the *Central Basin*, (§ 227,) where this rock-horizon is accessible. The Trenton ends with light colored, heavy bedded limestones, (immediately at the top, often thin bedded, with clayey seams, §687,) and the Nashville begins with a siliceous, blue, calcareous rock, weathering, often, into thin earthy, buff, sandy masses, and sometimes, into shales.

703. *Divisions of Lower Silurean, Names and Equivalency.*—The division of the *Lower Silurean* rocks of Middle Tennessee, into the two formations

adopted in this work, I made in 1851, in the paper referred to in § 683. In that paper, they were named, respectively, the *Stones River*, and *Nashville* groups. At that time, and in 1856, when the *Reconnoissance* was published, I hesitated as to the equivalency of the lowest member of the *Nashville Group*, (the *Orthis Bed*, to be described,) sometimes regarding it as *Upper Trenton*, and sometimes, as *Hudson River*. In the *Reconnoissance*, I wrote it *Upper Trenton*. This hesitation grew out of the extension of the *Trenton* species, upward, into the bed.

704. Notwithstanding this, the division was, or rather is, a natural one, and the two groups are equivalent, respectively, to the *Trenton* and *Hudson River* formations, as understood by American geologists. The name, *Stones River* has been dropped, but *Nashville* has been retained, and it embraced the same rocks in 1851, that it does now. It is true that *Trenton* species do run up into the lowest member, but so they do into the upper members, and are found in association with many *Hudson River* forms.*

705. But we have, in the *Orthis Bed*, the very characteristic species *Ambonychia radiata*, and *Cyrtolites ornatus*, both commencing here, and running up through the upper members. In addition, the bed holds *Rhynchonella modesta*, and *R. capax*, which, like the last, first appear in this bed and continue through the formation. (See note.)

On such grounds, we make the bed in question, *Hudson River*, and fix the equivalency of the entire *Nashville Formation*.

The lithological features of the beds concerned, so far as they can have any bearing, also place the plane of division, immediately below the Orthis Bed.

706. *Divisions of the Nashville Formation*. These are as follows:

(3) *Upper Member*, embracing about 200 feet of layers.
(2) *Middle Member*, embracing about as much as that above.
(1) *Orthis Bed*. The lowest division, having a thickness of from 50 to 70 feet. (§ 710.)

The *Orthis Bed* is a well marked division. The others will be considered together, as they constitute, naturally, a single group, and have only been separated, for more convenient reference.

707. (1) *The Orthis Bed*.—This division is one of considerable interest. Its place in the series, is shown in the *Columbia* section. (§ 690.) It is, in general, a siliceous, often shaly, calcareous rock. When freshly quarried it is blue. In its weathered condition, it often presents the appearance of a mixed

* The fact is, such forms are *Orthis lynx*, *O. Occidentalis*, *Rynchonella modesta*, and *R. capax*, are, at least, in Middle Tennessee, characteristic species of the Hudson (Nashville) Period. And the last three are so in Canada. See *Geology of Canada*, pp. 944 and 945.

bed of fine, thin, earthy, yellowish sandstones and shales. The weathered, detached blocks of the thin, flaggy layers, generally show a blue nucleus, when broken.

708. It is, frequently, especially in its western and southwestern presentations, a group of smoothly laminated flags, interstratified with shaly seams. Such is its typical character on the Tennessee River, in Hardin and Wayne counties, where its flags are burnt and ground into *hydraulic cement.* When wet, in the bottom of a creek, it looks much like the *Black Shale*, (Form. VII.,) and has been mistaken for it.* At Franklin, on the banks of the Harpeth, below the bridge, the bed may be seen, presenting its interstratified flag and shale character. On the Nashville and Lebanon Turnpike, immediately east of Mill Creek, at the foot of the hill on Wm. Nichol's place, it is well exposed, showing the same laminated condition. At this point, its flags have been exposed to the weather in a stone fence, for several years, and exhibit a tendency in the rock to break up in small pieces. At many points about Columbia, and in Maury County, it exhibits the same features as at Franklin.

709. In the more northern and eastern parts of the *Central Basin*, the bed frequently presents, with impure limestones, more or less shale, and, sometimes calcareous sandstóne, or even a layer of cherty material. Almost at all points, throughout Middle Tennessee, where this division comes to the surface, it is seen to contain vast numbers of individuals of *Orthis testudinaria.* These are frequently silicified, and, in some regions, form compact flinty layers of adhering shells, as about Mount Pleasant, and at other points in Maury County.†

710. The thickness of the Orthis Bed, in the Basin, is from 50 to 60 feet. Southwestward, it appears to be thicker. Along the Tennessee River, in Hardin, Wayne and other counties, are many exposures, but I have never seen the bottom of the bed in any that have come under my observation. At Clifton, the bed shows a thickness of 70 feet above low water.

711. This bed has already been presented in one section, that taken at Columbia. (§ 690.) Below is the Clifton Sec-

* As for instace, a bed of it in Hardin County, in the rear of Savannah, on Horse Creek,

† A figure (8) of a small specimen of one of these shells, is given in the group, on a following page.

tion. It includes the strata seen at the landing, as well as the hydraulic rock at the cement works.

NIAGARA.

Brownish red, and gray limestone. The topmost rock at the landing, contains large crinoidal stems, and abounds in individuals of several species of *Orthoceras.* This forms the upper, and main part of the bluff, down as far as Carrollville. In some of the high bluffs below Clifton, it is 95 feet thick. At Clifton, its base is elevated, and the rock, traced up the river, soon runs out.

NASHVILLE.

Calcareous Shale, bluish, or greenish, contains *Leptœna sericea, Strophomena alternata,* and *Rynchonella capax.* Thickness 15 feet.

Blue Limestone, in rough layers, somewhat sandy; contains *Strophomena alternata, S. tenuistriata, Rynchonella capax, R. dentata, Cyclonema bilix, Columnaria stellata, Tetradium fibratum,* &c. Thickness 23 feet.

Orthis Bed. The *Hydraulic limestone*; a thin, and smooth bedded, fine, blue, impure limestone, breaking, more or less, with conchoidal fracture. The flags are separated by shaly matter; and have a thickness, generally, of from 2, to 4 or 5 inches.

Contains *Orthis testudinaria, Rynchonella modesta, Lingutœ, Trilobites,* &c.

This forms the bluff at the cement works, the rocks sinking towards Clifton. Thickness down to low water, 70 feet.

The section above, has interesting features about it, aside from the Orthis Bed, to which reference will be made hereafter.

712. In the Central Basin, the bed under consideration outcrops in areas outside of those of the upper Trenton beds. In addition, it caps many of the low ridges and the limited local plateaus within those areas. It is, in a certain degree, a plateau-making stratum, a character due to its siliceous, and hence, weathering-resisting nature.

713. In Maury, Williamson, Davidson and Sumner, it is the basis of much splendid land. In Maury, especially between Columbia and Mount Pleasant, it underlies a country, much of which is unsurpassed. In general, when the beds of the creeks are in it, or but little below it, and the country devoid of high ridges, the lands overlying it are among the most desirable of the State. The soil it yields is argillaceous and calcareous, mellowed by the siliceous, or fine, sandy impurity of the rock.

714. Franklin, Columbia, in part, and Mount Pleasant, are located upon the Orthis bed. At Nashville, it rises to the surface east of the engine house of the water-works, and still further east, is the shaly rock of Mount Olivet. On the Murfreesboro turnpike, it is seen in the hills after passing Brown's Creek, and hundreds of its little *orthes* may be gathered along the road. At the wire bridge, the bed lies at the bottom of the river, and is only visible at low water.

715. The *Trenton* beds, with the exception of the *Wells' Creek* area, (§ 364,) are confined to the Central Basin. This is not the case with the Nashville beds. The latter appear, also, as we have seen, near the Tennessee River, in Hardin, and Wayne counties, or, in other words, in the *Western Valley.* (§ 708.) The outcrop of the Nashville rocks in this division of the State, is, however, very limited. It occurs in a number of separate areas, or patches, mostly confined to the bed of the Tennessee River, and the beds of some of its tributary creeks. By the local waving of the strata, the rocks are, alternately, above and below the water level of the streams. These exposures occur in the part of the Valley between the mouth of Cedar Creek, in the southern part of Perry, and Savannah.

716. Of the Nashville strata, in this region, the Orthis Bed, or the hydraulic rock, is, by far, the most conspicuous. Along the Tennessee, between the points mentioned, it is seen at the base of several of the bluffs. In these, it is overlaid, (with the other Nashville beds,) by variegated, red, and gray limestones, which often present a high, bold front. Its dark band resting on the water, is quite in contrast with the variegated and brighter ones above.

717. Exposures of the hydraulic rock occur, as stated, on Horse Creek, east of Savannah; also, on Indian, Hardins, and Beech creeks. On the upper part of the latter creek, not more than four miles from Waynesboro, is a patch of it, and others are met with on the same stream, in going down towards its mouth. It occurs, also, on the west side of the Tennessee River. About half a mile south of Saltillo Landing, in Hardin County, on a small stream, is a considerable bluff of it. At Saltillo, however, on the river, it does not appear, the lowest rock in the bluff being the variegated limestone.

718. This bed is interesting as a source of hydraulic cement. Its flags were burnt for this purpose, in Hardin county, twenty years ago. About the beginning of the war, Mr. G. A. Pillow and others, had completed arrangements for the manufac-

ture of cement on a large scale, and had actually commenced operations. The works were quite extensive and substantial, and located on the bluff a short distance above the landing at Clifton. Since the war, the works have been repaired, and put in operation again.

719. The cement manufactured, is of lighter color than the Louisville cement, and of good quality. In 1861, Mr. Pillow sent me a barrel, of that first manufactured, for trial. The barrel was put away in my cellar, and, owing to the troubles which soon came upon us, was left there without being opened. In the meantime, during a very rainy season, water rose in the cellar, and the cement got thoroughly wet. It soon hardened, the hoops and staves fell away, and the cement was left in a solid cylindrical mass—a good cast of the barrel which held it. I have also seen, in the Tennessee River, barrel-shaped masses of the hardened cement, from lots originally lost by the sinking of steamboats.

Some of the exposures of this rock in the Central Basin, as at Franklin and at other points mentioned, present material that it would be well to test practically.

720. The *fossils* of this bed are given in a catalogue at the end of the chapter. Its paleontological relations have been discussed in §§ 703–705, and to these paragraphs, and the catalogue, the reader is referred.

721. (2 & 3.) *The Middle and Upper Members of the Nashville.*—In paragraph 506, the Nashville Formation has been divided into three members, the lowest of which, the Orthis Bed, we have considered. The remaining members, are here thrown together, as, in general features, they are much the same.

These members constitute a group of rather dark blue, highly fossiliferous, often roughly bedded, impure limestones, with a maximum thickness of about 400 feet.* The group occasionally includes shaly, calcareous beds; but these are local. The limestones often contain shaly laminæ, and, in weathering, yield rough, thin, flaggy masses, whose surfaces are often thick with fossils.

722. The greatest thickness of the group is in the northern, and northeastern parts of the Basin, in Wilson, DeKalb, Smith, &c. In the southern, and southeastern counties of the Basin

*I have, on previous pages, placed the maximum thickness of the Trenton and Nashville Series, in Middle Tennessee, in round numbers, at 1000 feet. The sections thus ar measured, would make it something less, and between 900 and 1000.

it is considerably reduced; while, in the western valley, as shown in the Clifton section, where it is only 38 feet, (§ 711,) the group is so much reduced as to be of little or no importance.

723. These rocks outcrop within the Basin, outside of the areas of the Trenton rocks, and of the Orthis Bed. They make many fine agricultural sections. In addition, their outcrop forms, in general, on all sides, half the slope of the escarpments bounding the Basin. They are the limestone rocks of the rich valleys and hills of Jackson; of the rich hills of Smith, DeKalb, and the eastern part of Wilson; of the western parts of Cannon, and Coffee; the rocks of the rich slopes of Elk Ridge, and of all of its ramifications; those of the hills in the western parts of Maury, Williamson, Davidson, and Sumner. Owing to the dip of the strata, these rocks are brought low on the western side of the Basin, and, hence, underlie, and make, in connection with the Orthis Bed, (§ 713,) in Sumner, Davidson, Williamson and Maury, much fine rolling land, and many choice valleys. In the section south of Elk Ridge, in Giles and Lincoln counties, (§ 237,) all the valleys, (throwing out of them a few areas, in which Trenton rocks outcrop, and to which reference has been made,) are based on these rocks; and, so too, are the slopes of the ridges, at least half way up. The valleys of this section are rich, and many of them beautiful.

724. The rocks of the Nashville Formation, as a whole, yield, by disintegration, the best native soil, (excluding, always, alluvial bottoms,) in the State. This is due to the character of the impurities in the limestone, it being a proper combination of clay and fine sand; and, also, in a measure, I may add, to the organic matter in the rock. Something is due, likewise, to the form the limestone assumes in weathering. I have already spoken of the lands of the Basin, in general, and have compared, briefly, the Trenton and Nashville soils. (See §§ 694 and 695.)

725. Reference has already been made, indirectly, to the paleontology of this part of the Nashville Formation. (§§ 703, 704, 705.) It teems with fossils. Many of its layers are simply beds of corals. Others are made up of sponges. Others again, especially towards the top, are wholly shells, the most common, being *Orthis lynx*, and *Strophomena alternata*. Certain horizons abound in *Cyrtodontæ*, others in *Merchisoniæ*, and others in *Rynchonellæ*. In the catalogue at the end of the chap-

ter, (§ 224,) the best known species, not only of the rocks we are now considering, but of all the *Lower Silurian* strata in Middle Tennessee, are given; and to this the reader is referred.

TRENTON AND NASHVILLE FOSSILS.

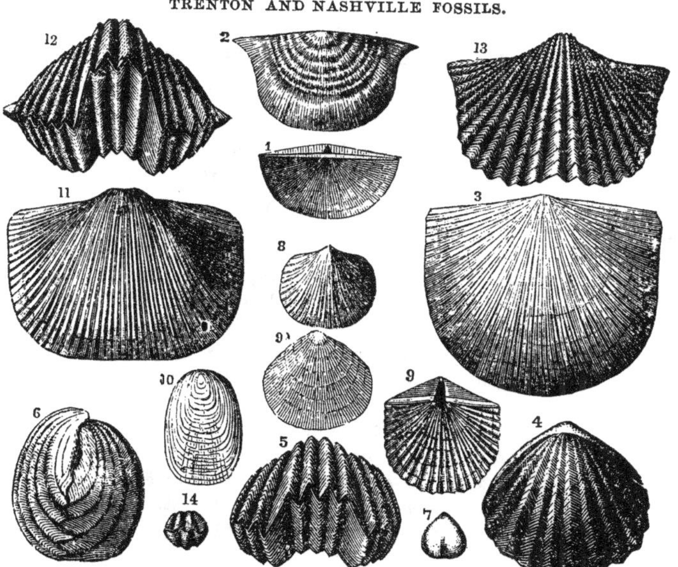

1. *Leptœna sericea.* 2. *Strophomena tenuistriata.* 3. *Strophomena alternata.* 4, 5, 6. *Rynchonella capax.* 7, 14. *Rynchonella bisulcata.* 8. *Orthis testudinaria.* 9. *Orthis tricenaria.* 11. *Orthis occidentalis.* 12, 13. *Orthis lynx.* 9. *Obolus filosus.* 10. *Lingula quadrata.*

On this page is presented a group of the figures of certain shells, which are characteristic of the Trenton and Nashville formations taken together. Familiarity with these and other associated forms, will enable the observer to know when he is on rocks of this geological horizon. (§ 320–1.) Of the species figured, *Orthis lynx*, *O. occidentalis* and *Rynchonella capax,* are confined to the *Nashville Formation,* and their associates may be seen in the catalogue. (See note under § 704.) *Orthis testudinaria* occurs in both, but is rare, excepting in the Orthis Bed of the Nashville, where, as we have seen, it is found in vast numbers. *Leptœna sericea,* also, appears in both the Trenton and Nashville formations. *Orthis tricenaria,* I have only seen in Trenton rocks in Tennessee. *Strophomena alternata* is in both, but is very rare in the Trenton, and very abundant in the Nashville, and so much so as to be characteristic. *Strophomena tenuistriata*, (*rugosa*,) I have only seen in the Nashville. The remaining species are unknown to me as Tennessee forms.

726. Thus far, the general characters only of the Middle and Upper members of the Nashville Formation have been given. There are, in some counties, local beds presenting special features, which remain to be noticed. More of these occur in Davidson County than elsewhere. Below is a section of the rocks at Nashville, in which the local beds of the region are presented. The section commences in the river beneath the wire bridge, and ascends to the top of Capitol Hill.

(6.) *College Hill Limestone.* When freshly quarried, a dark blue, highly fossiliferous, coarsely crystalline and roughly stratified limestone, with more or less of its laminæ shaly. The mass weathers, generally, into rough, flaggy limestones, and shaly matter, interstratified, often liberating multitudes of fossils—especially small corals.

Some of the layers of this limestone are wholly made up of corals and shells. *Stenoporæ*, *Constellaria antheloidea*, *Tetradium fibratum*, *Columnaria stellata*, *Stromatopora pustulosa*, *Strophomena alternata*, *Orthis lynx*, *O. occidentalis*, and others, are abundantly represented by individuals. *Bellerophon Troosti*, species of *Cyrtodonta*, *Ambonychia radiata* occur, and, in fact, nearly all the forms given in column M of the catalogue following. This division is well seen on *College Hill*, and in the upper part of the bluff at the *Reservoir*. There is, also, a fine presentation of it on *Capitol Hill*, around the Capitol. Its lowest layers are at the top of the bluff at the *Wire Bridge*.

These rocks pertain to the highest stratum in the vicinity of Nashville. The division, as here presented, may be taken with the upper division, ((2) Middle Member,) of the Columbia Section, (§ 690,) as typical of the *Nashville Formation* in general.

This division, at *Capitol Hill*, measures 120 feet.

(5.) *Cyrtodonta Bed.* Immediately below the College Hill Limestone, is a remarkable bed of coarsely crystalline, ashen gray, or light yellowish gray limestone, in great part, made up of valves of species of *Cyrtodonta*, individuals of *Bellerophon Lindsleyi*, and *B. Troosti*. (See Pl. G.) Of the *Cyrtodontæ*, *C. Saffordi* (Pl. F.) is especially abundant.

This bed is best developed in the bluff at the Wire Bridge. It is here, ten or eleven feet thick, and forms one solid layer. The shells are silicified, and pretty generally have their edges rounded and worn, as if they had been rolled in currents of water, or by waves.

The bed is seen again at the *Engine House* of the Water-works, where it is six feet thick. In tracing it beyond the Engine House, it very soon runs out, and is replaced by a compact, dove-colored limestone, like No. 3, below.

Descending the hill on the west side of the Capitol, it is also seen, but it is, for the most part, replaced by the compact limestone spoken of. It is well exposed at other low points about the city, and has been traced, in some directions, a mile or two beyond the city limits. This rock has been used for building purposes, to some extent, and for making corner posts. Maximum thickness, 11 feet.

(4.) *Bed of Limestone* of the common type; much like the College Hill Limestone, coarsely crystalline, fossiliferous, &c. It occurs below No. 5, on the west side of the Capitol. In the bluff at the Wire Bridge, it is 23 feet thick. In the bluff above the Engine House of the Water-works, it measures 28 feet.

(3.) *Dove Limestones.* This is a group of three layers, for the most part. The upper layer is a light dove-colored, compact limestone, 4 feet thick, breaking with conchoidal fracture, containing strings (mostly vertical) of crystalline matter, which show points on a horizontal surface. (Birdseye.) The middle layer is, mainly, the common dark blue crystalline limestone, (2 feet.) The lowest layer, (4 feet,) is mostly like the upper, but more or less mixed with blue layers. Such is the group as seen at the foot of *Gay Street*, in a quarry on the river bank. This group presents itself at many points, in and around the City. It is conveniently studied at the quarry mentioned, at the foot of Gay Street. At the end of the bluff beyond the Water-works, it may also be seen, and is here ten or eleven feet thick. The group may also be seen in the region of the Penitentiary, and of the old State quarry, overlying the rock of that quarry. It appears at many points in Davidson County, outside of Nashville. The layers are generally of desirable thickness, and are quarried at numerous points in and about the city, for building and other purposes.

The group contains a number of species. Detached *siphuncles* of *Orthoceras Bigsbyi*, and of an allied species, are numerous at some points, especially in the middle layer. *Tetradium*, *Bellerophon*, *Murchisonia*, *Pleurotomaria*, and other genera are represented. It is in this group, that *Leperditia Morgani* is found. Thickness, 11 feet.

(2.) *Capitol Limestone.* This bed supplied the rock to build the *Capitol*, and was formerly well exposed in the old State quarry west, and in sight of the building. It is limestone; but has the appearance of a laminated sandstone. It is, in fact, a consolidated bed of calcareous sand, the sand being the comminuted fragments of shells and corals. Originally, the mass was drifted in running water, and arranged in laminæ. As we find the rock now, it is, when quarried, a massive, bluish gray, granular limestone, with a well marked lamellar structure. When cut and ground smooth, a block of it, presented edgewise, shows well, the laminar character Such a surface is bluish gray, plentifully banded with darker lines. The Capitol is a splendid presentation of this rock as a building material.

The rock often contains rolled fragments of the beaded siphuncles of species of *Orthoceras*. Some specimens of these, are seen in the faces of the blocks in the walls of the Capitol. It exhibits, also, examples of cross stratification, another evidence of the current-action to which it was originally subjected. The mass contains some little siliceous matter, mostly in grains, and in small fragments of silicified shells, so that they do not interfere, materially, with the working of the rock. It is easily quarried, and can be obtained in blocks of any desirable size. In its natural exposures it exfoliates in laminæ by long weathering.

The bed, pretty generally, underlies the city; has been quarried at the foot of Gay Street, on the river; is near the water, under the Wire Bridge; and appears beyond the Water-works, where it has also been quarried, and is 20 feet thick. The lamellar structure of this bed runs into the one just below, to some extent, and it is not always easy to draw a line of separation. Below the Wire Bridge, my measurements make the thickness of the bed 25 feet.

(1.) The *Orthis Bed* underlies the last, and is the lowest member of the Nashville Formation. It is in the water below the Wire Bridge, but rises in going down the river, and may be studied in the bluff below the Railroad Bridge. It may be seen, too, and its *Orthis* gathered, at the first mile-stone on the Murfreesboro turnpike. It rises at the end of the bluff, beyond the Water-works; and still further east, as at Mount Olivet, it may be seen resting on the *Carter's Creek Limestone*—the upper member of the Trenton Formation. It has, however, been described, and its thickness given.

727. The *Capitol Limestone* (No. 2, above,) is pretty generally represented in the Basin, outside of Nashville and Davidson County, wherever its proper horizon is presented. It is generally not as good a building material as in Davidson, but is, more or less, laminated and current-formed. The whole area

of Middle Tennessee appears to have been swept over by a current, at the closing of the epoch of the *Orthis Bed*. As far south as Upper Elkton, in Giles County, I have seen this bed well characterized. It here also takes the place, for the most part, of the Orthis Bed, the *Carter's Creek Limestone*, on the opposite side of the river, and about a mile from Elkton, coming up from beneath it, with but little intervening rock.

728. The *Dove Limestone*, (No. 3,) also, is frequently seen in different parts of the Basin, though by no means as persistent as the other bed. At Elkton, it is well exhibited in place, resting on the laminated bed.

It is well, perhaps, to note, that there are, at some localities, other layers of this variety of rock, (Birdseye,) occupying horizons, different from that of No. 3. They are, however, local, and need no especial mention. The *Cyrtodonta Bed* east of the Water-works at Nashville, is, as we have seen, replaced by similar limestone.

729. In order to exhibit the relation the Nashville Formation sustains to the overlying groups, I present below, two sections, taken, respectively, on opposite sides of the *Central Basin*. The first is the section at *Snow's Hill*, in DeKalb County, a few miles east of Liberty, the point at which the Lebanon and Sparta road leaves the *Basin*, and ascends upon the *Highlands*. (p. 81.) It brings us up to the *Black Shale* and the *Lower Carboniferous* formations.

LOW. CARBONIFEROUS.

(*c*.) THE SILICEOUS. (*Formation* 8,*a*.)

Topmost. A leached mass of earthy, buff siliceous shales, containing interstratified layers of chert, or flint, (many of them heavy.) The mass, more or less dotted with small, siliceous geodes, or hollow concretions. At the bottom 3 or 4 feet of grayish, argillaceous shale.

Thickness of the whole,.............................. 140 feet.

DEVONIAN.

(*b*.) THE BLACK SHALE. (*Formation* 7.)

A thin, fissile, black, or bluish-black, rather tough, bituminous shale. A foot of the shale at the top, contains kidney-shaped nodules.

Thickness,.. 45 feet.

LOWER SILURIAN.

(*a*.) THE NASHVILLE. (*Formation* 4.)

This immediately follows the *Black Shale* in descending order. It is a great series of limestones, containing many fossils, and having the general characters already given as belonging to the formation. At the base of the hill is the current-formed bed spoken of above.

Entire thickness to the bottom of the hill, ... 303 feet.

730. Leaving the foot of Snow's Hill, and passing down the valley towards Liberty, the Orthis Bed is soon intersected, and the upper member of the Trenton Formation, met with.

The entire absence of formations 5 and 6, in this section, the Black Shale resting immediately upon the Nashville, is to be noted, as well as the high position of the shale.

731. In passing across the Basin, to the point presenting the section below, a high peak is met with—*Mount Lindsley*—which is topped off with the Black Shale and the Siliceous Formation. This peak is about a mile from Greenwood Seminary, and about five miles from Lebanon. It rises 500 feet above the general surface of the country, and presents a section very much like that of Snow's Hill. The Shale and the Nashville are still in contact. The siliceous rocks of this peak contain carboniferous fossils.

732. Below is the section of formations presented along the *steep grade* of the Edgefield and Kentucky Railroad. The foot of this grade is at Baker's Station, on or near the line between Davidson and Robertson counties. By this grade the railroad ascends from the Basin to the Highlands. (§ 230.)

LOW. CARBONIFEROUS.	(*d.*) SILICEOUS. (*Formation* 8,*a.*) *Upper part,* soil and leached shaly matter, with some layers of chert; contains, also, some beds of fossiliferous limestone. *Middle part,* bluish silico-calcareous rock, weathering to shale; contains small siliceous geodes. *Lower part,* shales bluish above, and pea-green below. Two feet from the base of this is a layer of ferruginous and argillo-calcareous rock, a foot and-a-half thick, containing carboniferous fossils. Entire thickness, ...	268 feet.
DEVONIAN.	(*c.*) BLACK SHALE. (*Formation* 7.) Black shale like that in the Snow's Hill section; contains *Lingulæ.* The upper foot of this contains the kidney-shaped nodules, or the *kidneys,*—argillaceous bodies, very fetid,..	28 feet.

UPPER SILURIAN.

(*b*.) NIAGARA. (*Formation* 5,*d*.)

Gray limestone; much of it sparry and crinoidal; some layers argillaceous and light bluish; contains *Caryocrinus ornatus*, and species of *Eucalyptocrinus* within eight feet of the Black Shale. The lower 20 feet doubtful as to age.

The foot of the steep grade is 39 feet above the base of this group.

Entire thickness, ... 81 feet.

LOWER SILURIAN.

(*a*.) NASHVILLE. (*Formation* 4.)

The top of this is seen some distance below Baker's Station.

The upper layer is red, very ferruginous limestone, or *dyestone;* is fossiliferous, and 8 feet thick. Below this are the usual Nashville layers, highly fossiliferous.

733. Two points are to be observed in comparing this section with that of Snow's Hill: the first, that one of the missing formations is present, and that the Black Shale no longer rests on Nashville rocks; the other, that the Shale is low in the hills, and the Nashville at their base. This is in accordance with the fact already stated, that the strata of the Basin dip to the west. (Compare section in chapter X.)

734. The Nashville Formation sinks below the Cumberland River before reaching Harpeth Shoals; below Duck River, at the mouth of Bear Creek, several miles beyond Centreville, in Hickman County; and below the Elk, in Alabama, before reaching the Tennessee River. (§ 229.) It re-appears locally, as we have seen, in the southern part of the Western Valley, and in the Well's Creek Basin. (§ 364.)

735. *Rocks of Special Use, and the Minerals of the Nashville Formation.*—The agricultural features of this formation have already been spoken of. Its beds supplying rock-material for building purposes, have also been noticed. (See especially § 726.) In addition to the beds noticed, there are many solid layers of the formation which may be, and are, used in masonry. There is, in fact, no lack of material of this sort. But there is, on the other hand, much that is not durable, as the rocks in the walls of some old buildings about Nashville will testify. There is not a little room for discrimination. The *natural outcrop* of a bed proposed to be used in masonry ought

to be examined. The action the weather has upon a rock, is generally a good test of its durability. If it crumble easily, under the weather, and, especially, into a multitude of small corals and shells, it ought to be avoided.

Layers pure enough for making lime, can be found in most any part of the formation.

The *hydraulic limestone* of the Orthis Bed has been noticed. The thin, smooth, laminar rocks, found at some localities in this bed, are good *flags*.

736. In the section last given, a red, ferruginous limestone occurs. It is called *dyestone* by those living in the vicinity, and is used for dyeing purposes. The bed is here eight feet thick. Some of it appears to be rich enough to be used as an iron-ore. A few miles south, or southwest, of this point, in Davidson County, this, or a similar bed of red, calcareous rock, rich in iron, occurs. The hills containing it are of a deep red color. This rock resembles, in some respects, the *dyestone* of East Tennessee. It rests upon rocks of the Nashville Formation, to which it is referred. Its fossils, however, although having a Lower Silurian aspect, have not been carefully studied; and it may be found necessary hereafter to include it in the Niagara Group, of which, in this region, it would then form the base. These remarks apply especially to the rock represented in the section. Another dyestone layer occurs on the waters of Harpeth River, in the southwestern part of Davidson.

737. A bed of brownish red, coralline *marble*, occurs in this formation, on the waters of Elk River, in Franklin County, seven or eight miles west of Winchester. The bed is quite extensive, and was formerly worked, to a limited extent, at the county-seat. Other beds, some of them gray, are found in Franklin.

738. On Leiper's Creek, at the *Oil Spring*, in Maury County, and about half a mile below the Williamson line, is another bed of *marble*. This is a gray crinoidal, and coralline rock, spotted with red, and having a flesh-colored appearance. Associated with it are other layers, with red, gray, and green colors. Slabs cut from these rocks, and polished, present a handsome appearance. The main bed is ten feet thick, and quite massive. This marble is at the top of the Nashville Formation, and is followed, in ascending order, by the Niagara, which is here,

50 feet thick; and this, again, by the Black Shale, (8 feet,) above which is about 60 feet of the rocks of the Siliceous Formation.

739. In Sumner County, a few miles north of Hartsville, immediately below the Black Shale, is a bed, from which *millstones* were formerly extensively manufactured. This bed is a mass of shells, closely packed, and silicified. The bed is several feet thick, and contains Nashville species.

The shells are so packed as to make the rock, in due degree, cellular. The weathered portions, near the outcrop, are preferred, for the reason that, within, the spaces between the shells are filled with calcareous matter, which, by exposure, is leached out. (§ 559.) The millstones manufactured here, were highly esteemed. I do not know that any have been made of late years.

740. The following is a list of minerals occurring in the Nashville Formation. A number of them are given in Troost's enumeration of the minerals of Davidson County. (7th Rep., p. 8.) The most of them occur in all the counties in which the formation exists, and are most frequently met with in railroad cuts, and at points where the rocks are quarried.

1. *Calcite*, (carbonate of lime;) common in small veins, and in crystals in small cavities of the limestone.
2. *Siderite*, (carbonate of iron;) in part, the dyestone rock noticed in § 736.
3. *Dolomite*, (carbonate of lime and magnesia;) occurs in cavities.
4. *Celestite*, (sulphate of strontia;) in small veins and cavities, associated with *barite*. In crystals in a small vein at Nashville, and in limestone seven miles from Nashville, on the Nolensville road. (Troost.)
5. *Barite*, (sulphate of baryta;) in many small veins associated with *galenite*, and in cavities alone, or with other minerals; Haysboro', near Nashville, is an important locality.
6. *Gypsum*, (hydrous sulphate of lime;) common at many points in cavities; fibrous, massive, and crystalline.
7. *Anhydrite*, (anhydrous sulphate of lime;) occurs, occasionally, in limestone, as above.
8. *Galenite*, (galena, sulphide of lead;) found in veins, mostly small and unimportant. Haysboro' an exception.
9. *Sphalerite*, (blende, sulphide of zinc;) found in small quantity, associated with the last.

10. *Fluorite*, (fluoride of lime;) in veins with *barite* and *calcite*, or alone in cavities.

11. *Pyrite*, (iron pyrites, sulphide of iron;) in small quantity, frequently seen in limestone.

12. *Quartz*; in a variety of forms; in crystals lining cavities, &c.

13. *Hematite*, (red oxide of iron;) abundant, in ochreous condition, in the soil overlying dyestone. (§ 736.)

14. *Petroleum*, This oozes, and has been doing so for many years, from the Nashville Formation at a number of points; at the Oil Spring on Leiper's Creek, in Maury County, the petroleum coming out of the marble; (§ 738;) at a point near the Cumberland River, on Mill Creek in Jackson County; and at several points on Obey's River, in Overton County.

15. *Pittasphalt*, (mineral tar;) often in the cavities in the limestone, the cavities being frequently lined with crystals of calcite; in a narrow fissure on Wm. Watkins' place, two miles north of Mount Pleasant in Maury County.

16. *Asphaltum*, (mineral pitch;) occurs like the last, in cavities and fissures.

741. *Catalogue of Fossils found in the Trenton and Nashville Formations.*—The following species are known by the author to occur in the Trenton and Nashville rocks of Middle Tennessee. In addition to these, there are many forms not made out, most of which, doubtless, are new. Much care has been taken in identifying the described species. Figures and descriptions have not been wholly relied on. With but very few exceptions, the fossils have been compared directly with New York or Canada specimens, and have been under the eye either of Prof. James Hall or of Mr. E. Billings. To these distinguished paleontologists I am under obligations for many favors.

A few of the new species are named for the first time, some of which are accompanied with a brief descriptive note. Full descriptions will be given hereafter. See, also, Appendix A. The table has the general form of that in the "Geology of Canada," p. 936.

The letters stand for the subdivisions of the formations as follows:

1st. TRENTON; C., *Central Limestone;* P., *Pierce Bed;* R., *Ridley Limestone;* G., *Glade Limestone;* Cr., *Carter's Creek Limestone.*

2d. NASHVILLE; O., *Orthis Bed;* M., *Middle Nashville;* U., *Upper Nashville.*

CATALOGUE OF TRENTON AND NASHVILLE SPECIES OCCURRING IN THE CENTRAL BASIN.

	Genera and Species.	Authors and Notes.	Trenton.					Nashville.		
			C.	P.	R.	G.	Cr.	O.	M.	U.
	PLANTÆ.									
	Buthotrephis?									
1	B. cæspetosa,	Hall, 3d Reg. Rep.	...	...	...	*				
	AMORPHOZOA.									
	Stromatopora.									
2	S. rugosa,	Hall's Sp.	*	...	*	*	*			
3	— pustulosa,	Safford. (n. sp.) Differs in having conical pimple-like elevations on its surface, otherwise much like *rugosa*	...	...	...	...	...	...	*	*
	ZOOPHYTA.									
	Stenopora.	*Chœtetes.*								
4	S. fibrosa,	Goldfuss.	*	*	*	*	*	*	*	*
5	— petropolitana,	Pander.	...	...	...	*	...		*	*
6	— Libana,	Safford. Like *fibrosa* but with cell-tubes much larger.	...	...	...	*				
7	— ramosa,	D'Orbigny's sp.	...	...	...	...	...	...	*	*
8	— frondosa,	"	...	...	...	...	...	...	*	*
	Constellaria.									
9	C. antheloidea,	Hall's sp.	...	...	...	...	...	...	*	*
	Tetradium.									
10	T. fibratum,	Safford.	...	...	*	...	*	...	*	*
11	— columnare,	Hall's sp.	...	...	...	...	*			
	Columnaria.									
12	C. alveolata,	Goldfuss.	...	...	*	...	*			
13	-- stellata,	*Favistella stellata*, Hall. I do not think this the same as *alveolata*.	...	...	...	...	...	...	*	*
14	— Carterensis,	Safford, (n. sp.) Hemispherical masses, tubes five and six sided, about one line in diameter.	...	...	...	...	*			
	Petraia.									
15	P. profunda,	Hall's sp.	...	...	...	*	*			
	CRINOIDEÆ.									
	Cleiocrinus.									
16	C. Libanus,	Safford. (n. sp.)	...	...	...	*				
	Dendocrinus.									
17	D. modestus,	Safford. (n. sp.)	...	...	...	*				

	Genera and Species.	Authors and Notes.	Trenton. C.	P.	R.	G.	Cr.	Nashville. O.	M.	U.
	Glyptocrinus.									
18	G. Libanus,	Safford. (n. sp.)	...	...	...	*				
	Palæocrinus.									
19	P. sulcatus,	Safford. Allied to *P. striatus*. Billings	...	*						
	ATERIADÆ.									
	Petraster.									
20	P. ? antiqua,	Troost's Sp.; 5th Rep., pp. 11 and 58	...	...	...	...	...	...	*	...
	BRYOZOA.									
	Ptilodictya.									
21	P. acuta?	Hall's sp.	...	*	...	*				
22	— symmetra,	Safford. (n. sp.)	...	*	...	*				
23	— explicans,	" (")	...	...	...	*				
24	— multiramis,	" (")	...	...	...	*				
25	—? Libana,	" (") A simple ribbon-like species, from three to five inches long, and from seven to eleven lines wide	...	...	...	*	[illegible]			
	Retepora.									
26	R. fenestrata,	Hall. 3d Reg. Rep.	...	*	...	*				
	Graptolithus.									
27	G. amplexicaule,	Hall.	...	...	...	*				
	BRACHIOPODA.									
	Leptæna.									
28	L. sericea,	Sowerby.	...	...	...	*	...	...	*	*
	Strophomena.									
29	S. alternata,	Conrad.	...	*	...	...	...	*	*	*
30	— incrassata,	Hall,	...	*	*	*				
31	— filitexta,	"	...	*	...	*	*			
32	— planumbona,	"	...	...	...	...	...	..	*	*
33	— planoconvexa,	"	...	...	...	...	...	...	*	*
34	— tenuistriata,	Sowerby.	...	...	...	...	...	...	*	
	Orthis.									
35	O lynx,	Eichwald.	...	...	...	...	...	*	*	*
36	— occidentalis,	Hall.	...	...	...	...	...	...	*	*
37	— pectinella?	Conrad.	...	...	...	...	...	...	*	...
38	— testudinaria,	Dalman.		*			...	*	*	*
39	— deflecta,	Conrad. *Lep. deflecta* Pal. N. Y., Vol. I, p. 113.	...	...	*	*	*			
40	— perverta,	Conrad.	...	*	...	*				
41	— subæquata,	"	...	...	...	*	...	*		
42	— Stonensis,	Safford. (n. sp.) Resembling the last in form, but the fine radiating ridges thrown into groups by stronger ones, much as in *S. alternata*.	...	*						

	Genera and Species.	Authors and Notes.	Trenton.					Nashville.		
			C.	P.	K.	G.	Cr.	O.	M.	U.
43	— bellarugosa,	Conrad.	...	...		✲	*			
44	— tricenaria,	"	...	...	*	✲				
	SKENIDIUM.									
45	S. Halli,	Safford. (n. sp.) 12th Reg. Rep. p. 70. This is the Tennessee species spoken of in the above Rep.	...	...	...	✲				
	RHYNCHONELLA.									
46	R. capax,	Conrad. *R. increbescens*, pars	...	...	...	...	...	✲	*	✲
47	— modesta,	Say,	...	...	...	...	...	✲	*	*
48	— recurvirostra,	Hall.	...	...	...	✲	✲			
49	— Ridleyana,	Safford. (n. sp.)	...	*	*					
50	— altilis,	Hall.	✲							
51	— orientalis,	Billings.	...	...	...	✲				
52	— dentata,	Hall.	...	...	...	...	...	...	✲	
	TRIPLESIA.	*Camerella*, Billings.								
53	T. varians ?	More globose than the Canada specimens.	...	...	*	*	...			
54	— extans,	Hall.	...	...	...	...	...	...	*	
	CONCHIFERA.									
	AVICULA.									
55	A. demissa,	Conrad.	...	...	...	...	...	...	✲	
	AMBONYCHIA.									
56	A. radiata,	Hall.	...	...	...	...	...	✲	*	*
57	— maxima,	Safford. (n. sp.) From three to five inches long.	...	...	...	...	...	...	✲	
58	— Swanana,	Safford. (n. sp.)	...	...	...	...	...	...	...	*
	CRYTODONTA.	*Palæarca*, Hall.								
59	C. Hayniana,	Safford. (n. sp.) Pl. F. Fig. 1.	...	...	...	...	...	...	*	
60	— Saffordi,	Hall. sp. 12th Reg. Rep. p. 11. This Rep. Pl. F. Fig. 2.	...	...	...	...	...	...	*	
61	— obtusa,	Hall.	...	...	...	✲				
62	— ventricosa?	"	...	...	...	✲				
63	— Canadensis,	Billings.	...	...	*	✲				
64	— amygdalina,	Hall.	...	...	...	✲	*			
65	— Normanensis,	Safford. (n. sp.)	..	...	...	...	*			
66	— Winchelli,	" (") Pl. E. Fig. 2.	...	...	...	...	...	*	✲	
67	— Gantii,	" (") Pl. E. Fig. 1.	...	...	...	...	...	*		
	CTENODONTA.	*Tellinomya*, Hall.								
68	C. nasuta,	Hall.	✲	...	...	✲	✲			
69	— contracta,	Salter.	✲	...	...	...	*			
70	— Logani ?	"	*							
71	— Hartsvillensis,	Safford. (n. sp.) Pl. F. Fig. 3.	...	...	...	...	...	...	✲	

	Genera and Species.	Authors and Notes.	Trenton.					Nashville.		
			C.	P.	R.	G.	Cr.	O.	M.	U.
	Modiolopsis.									
72	M. modiolaris,	Conrad.	...	...	...	...	...	*	*	
	GASTEROPODA.									
	Holopea.									
73	H. obliqua,	Hall.	*	...	...	*				
	Cyclonema.									
74	C. bilix,	Conrad.	...	...	...	...	...	...	*	*
	Subulites.									
75	S. subfusiformis,	Hall.	...	...	..	...	...	...	*	
76	— vittata,	"	...	...	...	*	*			
77	— elongata,	Conrad.	...	...	...	*				
	Eunema.									
78	E. prisca,	Billings.	*							
	Helicotoma.									
79	H. Tennesseensis,	Safford. (n. sp.)	*	...	...	...	*			
80	— declivis,	" (")	*							
	Maclurea.									
81	M. magna,	Lesueur.	*	...	...	*				
	Trochonema.									
82	T. umbilicata,	Hall's sp. The individuals found in *Bed C.* may belong to a distinct species.	*	...	...	*	*			
	Pleurotomaria.									
83	P. subconica,	Hall.	*	...	...	*	*			
84	— Americana,	Billings.	*	...	...	*	*			
85	— rotuloides ?	Hall.	...	...	...	...	*			
86	— lapicida,	Salter.	...	...	...	*	*			
87	— Progne,	Billings.	...	...	...	...	...	...	*	
88	— staminea ?	Hall.	...	...	...	*				
	Murchisonia.									
89	M. ventricosa,	Hall.	...	...	...	*	*			
90	— gracilis,	"	...	...	...	*	*			
91	— Sumnerensis,	Safford. (n. sp.) Pl. G. Fig. 1.	...	...	...	...	...	...	*	*
92	— bicincta,	Hall.	*	*	*	*	*	*	*	*
93	— serrulata,	Salter.	...	...	...	...	*			
94	— aspera?	Billings.	...	...	...	*				
95	— Bowdeni,	Safford. (n. sp.) Pl. G. Fig. 2.	...	...	...	...	...	...	*	*
	HETEROPODA.									
	Crytolites.									
96	C. ornatus,	Conrad.	...	...	...	...	...	*	*	*
97	— compressus,	"	...	...	...	*				

	Genera and Species.	Authors and Notes.	Trenton.					Nashville.		
			C.	P.	R.	G.	Cr.	O.	M.	U.
98	— cristatus,	Safford. (n. sp.) Surface without waves or imbrications.							✲	*
	BELLEROPHON.	*Bucania*, Hall in part.								
99	B. bidorsatus,	Hall,	✲	...	...	✲	*			
100	— expansus,	"	...	...	...	*				
101	— punctifrons,	Emmons.	...	...	...	...	...	✲		
102	— Lindsleyi,	Safford. (n. sp.) Pl. G. Fig. 4.	...	...	...	...	...	...	✲	
103	— Troosti,	Pl. G. Fig. 3.	...	...	...	...	...	..	✲	
	CARINAROPSIS.									
104	C. carinata,	Hall.	...	...	...	...	...	✲	✲	
	PTEROPODA.									
	CLIODERMA.									
105	C. Saffordi,	Hall. 14th Reg. Rep.	...	...	...	*	✲			
	CONULARIA.									
106	C. Gattingeri,	Safford. This may be *C. Trentonensis*, which it much resembles. A specimen found in excavating the cellar of Dr. Gattinger's house, in Nashville, is greatly larger than any of the figures of *Trentonensis* that I have seen. The original was about ten inches long.	...	...	...	...	...	...	✲	
107	— Trentonensis ?	Hall.	...	...	...	...	...	...	...	✲
	SALTERELLA.	*Billings. Pal. Foss. p.* 17.								
108	S. Billingsi,	Safford. (n. sp.) From one and a half to two inches long, straight, large end of longest specimens about one-sixth of an inch in diameter, tapering to a point, striated longitudinally, cross-section circular. A beautiful and abundant species; at least three cones, one within the other.	*	...	...	✲				
	CEPHALOPODA.									
	ORTHOCERAS.									
109	O. bilineatum,	Hall.	...	...	...	...	...	...	✲	
110	— fusiforme,	"	✲	...	...	✲				
111	— multicameratum ?	"	...	...	...	...	...	...	✲	*
112	— strigatum,	"	...	...	...	...	...	...	*	✲
113	— amplicameratum,	"	...	...	...	...	...	...	*	
114	— decrescens,	Billings.	...	...	...	✲	*			
115	— pertinax,	"	...	...	...	*	*	*		
116	— Allumettense,	"	...	...	...	...	✲			
117	— Huronense,	"	...	...	...	...	✲			
118	— rapax,	"	...	...	...	✲	...	✲		
119	— Bigsbyi,	Stokes.	✲	✲	*	✲	*		✲	
120	— anceps,	Hall.	*	...	*	✲				

	Genera and Species.	Authors and Notes.	Trenton. C.	P.	R.	G.	Cr.	Nashville. O.	M.	U.
121	— capitolinum,	Safford. (n. sp.) Intermediate in character between *Bigsbyi* and *anceps*. Plate G. 3, Fig. 1.	...	...	...	...	...	...	*	
122	— Foxense,	Safford. (n. sp.)	...	...	...	*	✲			
	Cyrtoceras.									
123	C. Bondi,	Safford. (n. sp.) Pl. G. 3, Fig. 3.	✲	...	...	...	✲			
124	— constrictum,	Hall.	...	...	...	✲				
125	— " ?	"	...	...	...	...	...	..	✲	
126	— macrostomum,	"	...	...	...	...	...	...	✲	
127	—? Stonense,	Safford. (n. sp.) Pl. G. 3, Fig. 2.	✲							
128	— Massiense,	" " Pl. G. 3, Fig. 4.	...	...	...	...	...	...	✲	
	Lituites.									
129	L. undatus,	Conrad.	...	...	...	✲				
	Trocholites.									
130	T. ammonius,	Conrad.	...	...	...	*				
	CRUSTACEA.									
	Asaphus.									
131	A. Barrandi ?	Hall. Foster and Whitney's Rep. Part 2d, p. 210.	...	...	...	*				
132	— canalis,	Conrad.	...	...	...	*	✲		✲	
	Calymene.									
133	C. Blumenbachii,	Brongniart. *C. senaria.*	...	...	...	*	...	...	✲	*
	Cheirurus.									
134	C. pleurexanthemus,	Green.	*	...	...	*				
	Encrinurus,									
135	E. excedrinus,	Safford. (n. sp.	...	...	...	*				
	Illaenus.									
136	I. Americanus,	Billings.	...	...	...	✲				
137	— ovatus,	Conrad.	...	...	...	✲				
	Lichas.									
138	L. Trentonensis,	Conrad.	...	...	...	...	...	...	✲	
	Phacops.									
139	P. callicephalus,	Hall.	...	...		✲				
	Dalmanites.									
140	D. Troosti,	Safford. (n. sp.)	✲	*						
	ENTOMOSTRACA.									
	Leperditia.									
141	L. fabulitus,	Conrad. Very abundant.	*	...	...	*	✲			
142	— capax,	Safford. (n. sp.)	...	...	...	...	...	...	*	*
143	— Morgani,	" "							*	

CHAPTER IX.

THE NIAGARA AND LOWER HELDERBERG GROUPS; FORMATIONS V AND VI; UPPER SILURIAN.

742. In this chapter, the *Upper Silurian* beds, as developed in Tennessee, are described. These, taken together, form a group which is very heterogeneous in lithological and other characters, and which, moreover, is of limited volume compared with what it becomes when followed northward into the States of Pennsylvania and New York. It is a collection, to some extent, of the feather-edges and the outlying patches, or of the odds and ends of disappearing, or reappearing, formations. (§ 372.)

743. The *Upper Silurian* group, as here treated, embraces sandstones, limestones, shales, all of many colors, and beds of iron-ore. The minor formations composing it, have always occupied areas more or less local, never having been continuous, and State-wide, as we have reason to think the great limestone formations already described, once were.

744. In some parts of the State, in horizons in which we would naturally look for these rocks, and where underlying and overlying formations are present, not a bed is found to represent the group. In the belt of country skirting the western base of the Cumberland Table-land, this is notably the case, and in every ravine deep enough, the outcropping rocks show it to be so. Along the eastern escarpment of the Central Basin, (p. 98,) from the Kentucky nearly to the Alabama line, the Black Shale, as seen in the Snow's Hill section, (§ 729,) and in the sections of the Basin on the Map, and in chapter X, rests on the Nashville Formation, without any intervening rock.

745. On the western escarpment, this is also the case at a few points, but generally a Niagara bed has appeared to separate the two, bearing above it, here and there, a *trace*

Lower Helderberg. The Niagara and Helderberg strata are *unconformable* to the Nashville, and never covered the dome of the Basin. (§ 367.)

The two groups—the Niagara and the Lower Helderberg—will be considered respectively, in separate sections.

Section I.

THE NIAGARA GROUP, OR PERIOD; FORMATION V.

746. The subdivisions of this group are, in descending order, as follows:

5,*d.* *The Meniscus Limestone;* uppermost.
5,*c.* *The Dyestone Group, or Subgroup.*
5,*b.* *White Oak Mountain Sandstone.*
5,*a.* *Clinch Mountain Sandstone,* at the base.

The lowest three are East Tennessee formations. The *Meniscus Limestone* is represented in this division of the State, but it is preëminently a formation of the Western Valley, (§ 104.) These formations represent the *Medina*, *Clinton*, and *Niagara epochs* of the New York nomenclature, and are all embraced in Dana's *Niagara Period.*

(5,*a.*) The Clinch Mountain Sandstone.

747. The characteristic rock of this formation, is a white, or grayish-white, hard *sandstone*, having a maximum thickness of at least 400 feet.* It is typically presented in *Clinch Mountain*, the boldest and greatest mountain within the limits of the East Tennessee Valley. (§ 97.) The sandstone lies in a great sheet, on the eastern slope of the mountain. It is a heavy-bedded rock; contains rarely a layer of shale; frequently presents on its exposed surfaces multitudes of fucoids; and has some of its beds profusely pierced with rods, filling the holes of a species of *Scolithus.* Layers, twenty inches thick, have

* In the Table of Formations, on page 161, the thickness of this sandstone is given doubtfully at 300 feet. Its maximum is, however, more than this, and may even exceed considerably that given above. No opportunity has been presented of measuring it where present in greatest volume.

been observed, with rods in abundance, running through them.* The surfaces of the layers are also often ripple-marked. The rock is generally fine grained, but sometimes coarse enough to constitute a conglomerate, with pebbles as large as peas.

748. In its more western presentation, as in Powell's Mountain, in Hancock and Claiborne Counties, it graduates upward into brown and red sandstones, some of which are highly ferruginous. These red sandstone, however, will be referred to the *White Oak Mountain Group.*

749. But, in addition to the white sandstone, the Clinch Mountain Formation is made to include, *provisionally*, an underlying heavy stratum of *red calcareous shale.* The sandstone, at all points, rests upon this shale. In one section, that of the *Nose*, in Hawkins, the shale measured 400 feet. This stratum has already been incidentally referred to in the Bull's Gap and White Horn section, on page 249.

750. Below are presented several sections, which will enable the reader to understand the relations the Clinch Mountain Group sustains to the other Niagara divisions, as well as the relations the Niagara, as a whole, sustains to the other great formations. The sections will also be of service for future reference.

751. The *Nose* referred to above, is the short isolated mountain known as the *Devil's Nose*, and mentioned on page 43. The *white sandstone* caps the mountain; the *red shale*, and the underlying Nashville beds, outcrop around its slopes. The following is a section taken on its eastern slope:

(3.) Clinch Mountain Group.

(*b.*) *Sandstone;* white, or whitish-gray; mostly fine-grained and hard; some layers fine conglomerate; about 200 feet thick.

This rock caps the Nose, and is a remnant of the base of a synclinal fold.

(*a.*) *Shale;* brownish-red calcareous rock, weathering into shale; upper part inclined to be sandy; thickness, 400 feet.

* The species concerned, is most likely Hall's *Scolithus verticalis* of the Medina Sandstone. The rods are much like those of *S. linearis* of the Chilhowee (*Potsdam* Sandstone, (§ 481,) and if the two formations were brought together by a fault and displacement, it would be difficult to distinguish between them by means of these fossils.

(2.) TRENTON AND NASHVILLE.

(*e.*) *Buff Shales*, weathered; lower part containing thin limestones; several hundred feet.

(*d.*) Bands of *Reddish Calcareous Shale*, near the foot of the mountain. (§§ 635, 637.)

(*c.*) *Flaggy Blue Limestone;* some layers containing, plentifully, individuals of a species of *Receptaculites;* several hundred feet.

(*b.*) Marble. (§§ 605, 613.)

(*a.*) Maclurea Limestone. (p. 232.)

(1.) KNOX GROUP.

752. The diagram on page 208 represents a section which intersects many of the formations, and among them, all the members of the Niagara Group, if we regard the red sandstone referred to in § 748, as belonging to the White Oak Mountain division. The Niagara divisions are not separated in the diagram, the group being represented as a whole.

The places of the occurrence of the group are indicated by the dotted belts, and, also, by being numbered 5, either with or without letters.*

753. The points C, D, and E, of the diagram, are ridges of the *Powell's Mountain Group*, (p. 42.) The following section, commencing at a gap in D, (*Mulberry Gap*,) and extending through Sneedville, to H, the east end of the diagram, presents the formations of two of them. It may be observed here, that the dip given to the strata in the part of diagram, from C to F, is too great. It is generally considerably less than 45°.

(15) *Knox Sandstone*, making *Comby Ridge*, (§§ 108, 520.)

— *Fault*..

(14) *Mountain Limestone*, in ridge a short distance east of Sneedville.

(13) *Siliceous Group*, in same ridge, as above.

(12) *Black Shale*; heavy presentation; Sneedville is located upon it.

(11) *Meniscus Limestone*, with shale, contains *Halysites catenulata* and other fossils. Not as heavy as at the eastern base of Powell's Mountain.

(10) *Dyestone Group*, repetition of 5 below, and commencing a new *series*. (p. 146.) This forms the eastern slope of *Newman's Ridge*. It must be noted, however, that at some points sandstones of 4, below, and even of 3, occur, cut off with the Dyestone rocks by the fault.

— *Fault*..

(9) *Mountain Limestone*, on Newman's Ridge, and upper part of western slope.

* There is an error as to one figure; the first 5 at the west end of the diagram should be 7.

(8) *Siliceous Group*, heavy, much shale, lower part of west slope of Newman's Ridge.

(7) *Black Shale*, heavy presentation, outcrops in a narrow trough or valley, between the two mountains. Big Sycamore Creek runs in the southwestern part of this trough.

(6) *Meniscus Limestone*, bluish; upper part light gray; lower part inclined to be sandy; all fossiliferous. Thickness, 145 feet.

(5) *Dyestone Group*, Shales and thin sandstones, brown, red, gray and greenish, with a band of Dyestone ore. Some layers ripple-marked. The group quite fossiliferous; contains *Bellerophon trilobata, Strophomena corrugata, Calymene Clintoni? Beyrichia lata, etc.* Thickness, 325 feet.

(4) *White Oak Mountain Sandstone;* brown and red sandstones, with some fine conglomerate, much of both very ferruginous. This, and the white sandstone below, make the eastern slope, and the crest of Powell's Mountain. Thickness uncertain, say 100 feet.

(3) *Clinch Sandstone*, light gray; contains some fine conglomerate. Thickness doubtful, but much below maximum, say 100 feet.

(2) *Clinch Shale*, reddish argillaceous limestone or calcareous shale, beneath the last, under the crest of the mountain on west side.

(1) *Trenton and Nashville Series;* outcrops on the lower part of western slope of Powell's Mountain, and makes the valley west of the mountain, in the southwest part of which flows Little Sycamore. The entire valley may be called *Little Sycamore Valley.*

754. A section will be given below, illustrating the occurrence of formations in the region of *Cumberland Gap*, the region to which the west end of the diagram on page 208 pertains; and, in order to have an *entire section* from the Gap to Comby Ridge, it may be well to introduce here a section supplying the intermediate part. These sections, taken in connection with the diagram, will illustrate, not only features belonging to the Niagara beds, but, also, the geological character of much of the country in Hancock and Claiborne counties.

(6) *Knox Dolomite*, forming a heavy, cherty ridge, becoming very wide and high east of Tazewell, (Wallin's Ridge.) This formation follows in order, the Trenton and Nashville Series (1) of the last section and the ridge mentioned lies next west of the valley in which the rocks of that series outcrop.

— *Fault*..

(5) *Dyestone Group*, as in last section; contains a layer of iron-ore one foot thick.

(4) *White Oak Mountain Sandstone*, not as heavy as in last section.

(3) *Clinch Mountain Group*, including the Sandstone and the Shale; the former becoming thin and losing its importance.

This group, with the Dyestone and the White Oak Mountain groups above, forms a sharp ridge along this line of section, which is separated from that of the Knox Dolomite above, by a very narrow valley, and which, too, with the formations which make it, runs out before reaching a point opposite Tazewell.

(2) *Trenton and Nashville Series*, follows the Shale of the Clinch Group, and the sharp ridge mentioned, just as the same rocks (1) in the last section follow the Shale and Powell's Mountain.

The series, moreover, presents a valley similar to the Little Sycamore Valley. Tazewell is located in it. East of the latter place, this Series follows the Knox Dolomite of Wallin's Ridge, the fault separating the two.

(1) *Knox Dolomite;* this succeeds the last in the great anticlinal of Claiborne, Union and Campbell. (§ 513.)

755. Passing the axis of the anticlinal just mentioned, the order in which the formations occur is reversed. From this axis *eastward*, we pass from older formations to newer, until a fault is met with, which throws us abruptly back to some one of the lower formations as a new starting point. Advancing, however, the formations we meet with occur in the same succession as before, until a second fault is encountered, and another starting point presented, and so on. (See page 146.) To meet with the formations of Cumberland Gap, in ascending order, our course from the axis of the anticlinal must be *westward*.

756. The following is a section of the rocks in the vicinity of *Cumberland Gap*. The point A, in the diagram on page 208, is a bold, conspicuous cliff of sandstone, called the *Pinnacle*. The elevation of this is given on page 73. Its rocks are the uppermost of the section.

The formations are presented as in the foregoing sections, in their natural order, and numbered in accordance, that is, from below, upward. The lowest formation rests directly upon No. 1 of the last section.

(7) *Base of Coal Measures;* hard sandstone forming the Pinnacle.

(6) *Mountain Limestone;* a heavy bed, but not measured.

(5) *Siliceous Group;* a heavy stratum of bluish, or greenish, more or less calcareous, shale; 15 or 20 feet of which, at top, contains characteristic layers of chert. Some iron-nodules and a few unimportant layers of brown shale are seen. Thickness, 520 feet.

(4) *Black Shale;* at the base of the mountain.

(3) *Dyestone Group;* in upper part shales with thin sandstones, the shales mostly greenish, followed below by a valuable bed of ore from 24 to 30 inches thick. Below this, shales with some heavy layers of fine-grained sandstone, which may represent the Clinch Mountain sandstone; if so, the latter formation has not quite disappeared.

This group makes *Poor Valley Ridge*, a low ridge skirting the base of the mountain for many miles to the southwest.

(2) *Clinch Red Shale*, not exposed.

(1) *Trenton and Nashville Series*, making the long and interesting *Powell's Valley*, and resting upon the Knox Dolomite, No. 1, of the preceding section.

757. In the sections given, the Clinch Sandstone is either on the top, or, as a great tilted plate, forms one of the slopes of a mountain. It makes the cap of the Nose, (§ 751.) In connection with some of the red sandstones of overlying formations, it makes the eastern slopes, and the crests of Newman's Ridge, and of Powell's Mountain. In fact, the mountains mentioned owe their existence, as such, to these sandstones. Had the latter been shales, or limestones, like those of Little Sycamore Valley, the whole region, long since, would have been without mountains.

How hard plates of rock, like these sandstones, are mountain-making and mountain-saving, has been explained. (See §§ 362 and 628.)

758. The Clinch Sandstone has given us, either alone or with other formations, three distinct groups of mountains, as follows:

1. *The Powell's Mountain Group*, the geology of which we have just considered. (See also § 96.)

   In this group ought to be included the *Lone Mountain*, of Claiborne* and Union Counties, which is in a line with Powell's Mountain, the opposing ends of the two being about four miles apart. These mountains are the same geologically. The White Oak red sandstones, however, are prominent, and the Clinch Sandstone less so, in Lone Mountain, than in Powell's.

2. *The Clinch Group*, (See § 97.) I have spoken of the occurrence of the *Sandstone* in the main *Clinch Mountain* itself, in § 747, and of its presentation on the *Nose*, in § 751. It also makes, in part, *Stone Mountain* of this group. *House Mountain*

* *Claiborne* and Union, not *Grainger* and Union, as appears on pages 251 and 252.

is an outlier, and very much, in all respects, like the Nose. It is capped in the same manner, and the slopes of the two present the same formations.

Pine Mountain is made by the hard rocks of the *Siliceous Group*, and so is *Stone Mountain*, in part.

In this region, the red sandstones of the *White Oak Mountain Group* do not occur in any noteworthy force.

2. *The Bay's Mountain Group.* (See § 99, and also § 648.) In this group, the Clinch Sandstone alone is the mountain-making layer. In a section across the middle of the group, the strata are seen to be arranged in a series of synclinal and anticlinal waves. The first range met with on the southeast side is broken, and includes the prominent points, *Chimney Top* and *Fodder Stack*, both of which are capped off with sandstone like the Nose, in Hawkins. The next range has also a high point, *Stone Mountain*, capped as the others. Then follows a pair of mountains, with a smaller ridge between, and in the double valley thus formed, rests a low double-synclinal trough of sandstone, a section of which is like the letter **W**, with the inner part reduced in size. After this, come four or five synclinals and anticlinals of sandstone, forming ridges that are not as high as those on the eastern side.

759. The last presentation of the *Clinch Sandstone*, going southward, is in House Mountain. This is about thirteen miles northeast of Knoxville. The greatest development of the Sandstone is in Clinch Mountain. West of this, it loses volume, and is much reduced in the Powell's Mountain Group. It does not reach the Cumberland Table-land, unless, indeed, the sandstone which helps to form Poor Valley Ridge, (§ 756, (3,)) near Cumberland Gap, and southward, in Claiborne, is its feather-edge. Eastward, it is last seen in the Bay's Mountain Group, on the summits of Chimney Top and Fodder Stack. It passes to the northeast out of the State, and extends through Virginia and Pennsylvania into New York, where it has long been known as a part of the *Medina Sandstone*.

760. The *Clinch Red Shale* is prominently seen involved with the Sandstone in the anticlinals and synclinals of the Bay's Mountain Group. Its place is below the Sandstone. The beds of the latter, at some points, however, have been observed to contain some shale, but in small quantity.

The Shale has a wider extension eastward and southward than the Sandstone. It occurs beneath the Dyestone Group, at the base of Poor Valley Ridge, in Claiborne, and of Walden's Ridge, in Campbell.

In the southern part of the State, it has not been made out satisfactorily as a distinct bed.

761. At many localities, the Clinch Sandstone could supply excellent building material. It is often well bedded for quarrying, and its light gray color, and its texture, would make it popular. As yet, no railroad touches it at any point.

(5,*b*.) WHITE OAK MOUNTAIN SANDSTONE.

762. Starting up south of the Hiwassee River, and running in a southwesterly course, the line of which is east of Chattanooga about fourteen miles, is a nearly straight ridge, that reaches far into Georgia. This, in Tennessee, is called *White Oak Mountain*, and in Georgia, *Taylor's Ridge*. (§ 102.) It is, for the most part, made up of a heavy group of variegated alternating sandstones and shales, to which I have given the name above.

763. The *sandstones* are mostly fine-grained, thin, and even-bedded, sometimes thick-bedded, fossiliferous, generally, reddish-brown, but also greenish gray, buff, and of other colors. Their surfaces often abound in crinoidal buttons. Some of the layers are highly ferruginous, making an iron-rock, to which the remarks in § 618 are applicable. Many beds can be used for building purposes with advantage. The depot at Ringgold, in Georgia, is built of this rock, as well as certain culverts on the line of the railroad.

764. The *shales*, of reddish-brown, pale green, and other colors, alternate in beds of various thicknesses with the sandstones, and generally constitute the greater part of the volume of the group.

765. The rocks of this group resemble, more or less, those of the two lower divisions of the Knox Group. (§§ 499, 519 and 523.) At certain points, the rocks of the two groups are thrown together. In such cases, the fossils of the White Oak beds enable the observer to separate them without difficulty.

765. It is in White Oak Mountain, and Taylor's Ridge, that this formation appears in greatest volume. It must be, at

least, 600 feet thick in the gap at Ringgold, and, perhaps, considerably more. In Tennessee, its maximum may be placed at 500.

The lateral extent of the formation, at least in Tennessee, is very limited. It is not observed, either east or west of the belt, including White Oak and its spurs.

766. In the northern part of the State, certain beds of ferruginous brown-red sandstone and fine conglomerate have been referred to this formation. These occur in the Powell's Mountain Group, and are presented in the sections in §§ 753 and 754. The occurrence of the formation in Lone Mountain is also spoken of in § 758. As in the White Oak Mountain region, so here, these rocks are confined to a comparatively narrow belt, not appearing outside of the area including the ridges of the Powell's Mountain Group.

767. Along the line from Lone Mountain to the north end of White Oak, there are no especial presentations of the rocks of this formation. Traces occur at intervals, in the Dyestone ridge, which lies in this range. There is a considerable ridge in the line, just north of the Hiwassee River, which may contain some of the lowest layers, and a curious amphitheatre of hills just south of this river, the highest points of which may show them.

768. This amphitheatre, or circle of hills, is isolated, and more than a mile in diameter. It rests in a wide area of rocks, belonging to the Trenon and Nashville Series. This area is due to the lateral extension of Savannah Valley caused by the running out of White Oak Mountain. The amphitheatre is an outlier of the latter mountain, and is separated from it by an interval of from three to four miles. In the area around it the rocks are nearly horizontal.

769. Just south of Georgetown, which is located in the area mentioned, the north end of White Oak appears, not as a sharp ridge, but more as the end of a long plateau. This end is nearly two miles wide; its strata outcrops in nearly horizontal layers, and the rocks of the formation under consideration, appear at the top in very feeble force. But southward, the rocks of the mountain become tilted, with dips of from 25° to 35°. The sandstones and shales increase rapidly in volume, and

the mountain becomes a well defined ridge, highest and boldest in Georgia.

770. This formation presents another example of a stratum following, for long distances, the trend of the valley, with but little lateral extension, (See §§ 582 and 583.)

771. The northern presentation of the group in the Powell's Mountain region is of minor importance, so far as volume is concerned. The relations, however, of these rocks to the Clinch Sandstone, are there seen. The two groups in this region overlap, the red White Oak sandstones being on top. In the southern part of the State the Clinch Sandstone, as we have stated, is wanting.

772. The *White Oak Mountain Sandstone,* as I have described it, ought, perhaps, to be regarded as a *provisional* group. Its ferruginous, variegated rocks naturally associate it with the *Dyestone Group* next above it, and doubtless its paleontological characters unite it with that. I have, however, thought best for the present, mostly on account of its great and special development in White Oak Mountain and in Taylor's Ridge, to keep it separate.

773. Below is a section of the formations as they are presented in the gap of White Oak Mountain, through which the Chattanooga and Cleveland Railroad runs. It may be well to state that, in approaching White Oak Mountain from the east, along the line of the railroad, a *fault* is met with at a point about two and a third miles from the foot of the main mountain. Passing this, the road intersects, at once, an *outlying and local ridge,* made up of the sandstones and shales of both the White Oak and Dyestone formations, and in which, too, a band of iron-ore occurs of from one to three feet thick. The rocks of this ridge dip to the southeast, and are the overturned southeastern side of a synclinal trough, of which White Oak Mountain, itself, is the greater northwestern side. Between the ridge and the mountain is a *cove,* into which outcrops *Carboniferous limestones,* (*Mountain Limestone,*) the beds of which, at many points, are horizontal.

It may be added here, that, to the southeast of the *fault* spoken of, the country, for many miles, is underlaid by strata of the Knox Group.

774. The section is arranged in ascending order, the formations being so numbered. The topmost bed is on the cove side of the mountain, the lowest on the western. The strata dip to the southeast at an average rate of about 28°.

(5) *Siliceous Group.* At top, rough, cherty layers running beneath the *Carboniferous* limestones of the cove, about 20 feet seen, upper part concealed.
Greenish shale, 30 feet.
Gray crinoidal limestone, crinoidal buttons, large, 15 feet.
Greenish shale, 8 feet.
Thickness in all,.. 73 feet.

(4) *Black Shale*............ .... 20 feet.

(3) *Dyestone Group.* Red and greenish shales mostly, alternating with thin, even-bedded, fine-grained sandstones, and containing dyestone ore,...................................... 200 feet.

(2) *White Oak Mountain Sandstone.* A heavy series of shales and sandstones, of reddish-brown, green, gray and buff colors, the reddish-brown and green most common. The sandstone, thick and thin-bedded; one hard brown layer near the base, eight feet thick. This series graduates into that above.
Thickness in all,.. 420 feet.

(1) *Transition Beds,* passing down into Nashville rocks.
Alternating greenish shale and shaly, blue, fossiliferous limestone, 130 feet. Below this, reddish, argillaceous limestone, weathering into shale; variegated with greenish bands, 152 feet.
Thickness in all.............................. .... 282 feet.

(5,*c.*) THE DYESTONE GROUP.

775. This group is neither great in volume, nor of much importance, as to topographical or agricultural relations. Nevertheless, it is highly interesting as a repository, or matrix, of iron-ore. The group is confined to East Tennessee. It is a series of variegated shales and thin sandstones, for the most part, the rocks presenting a variety of colors, among which, red, brown and green, are predominant. It holds from one to three or more layers of fossiliferous iron-rock, which is generally available as an iron-ore. Much of the mass either is, or

has been, quite calcareous. At some points, thin beds of limestone occur with the shales; at others, the mass is pretty thoroughly leached so far as its outcrop is concerned, and, indeed, for many feet within.

776. The sandstones are generally fine-grained, thin, and smoothly bedded. Sometimes thick, heavy layers occur. Occasionally they appear to be wholly absent. This is especially the case at some points in the southern part of the State, in Hamilton County, and in Sequatchee Valley, the group being mostly shales and limestone, with but little sandstone.

777. The *iron-ore* (often called *dyestone*, being sometimes used as such, and hence the name of the group) is in stratified layers. It is highly fossiliferous, abounding in casts of crinoidal buttons, small corals and *bryozoa*. It contains, also, shells and fragments of trilobites. In addition, the ore abounds in small, flattened, *oolitic* bodies, in consequence of which it is called both *oolitic* and *lenticular* ore. Fragments long exposed on the surface, have, externally, a dark brown, or reddish-brown, appearance, but the ore when freshly quarried, has a more or less bright reddish, and at certain points, nearly a scarlet, color. At some localities it is more or less calcareous, while at others it appears to be thoroughly leached. It is highly esteemed as an iron-ore, and is the main dependence of all the furnaces and forges in the western part of the Valley.

778. A number of sections have been given, in which the Dyestone Group is represented, and from which its characters and its relations to other formations can be learned.

See paragraphs 753, 754, 756 and 774. The cuts on pages 139, 142, 190 and 208, may also be referred to. In those on pages 142 and 190, the place of the group is indicated by the figure 5, and in that on page 208, by 5,*c*.

779. Below is a section taken on the Nashville and Chattanooga Railroad, above Lookout Station. The locality is on or very near the Tennessee and Georgia line, and embraces the places known as Love's and Cross's Hollows. In this region the *Siliceous Group*, the *Black Shale*, and the *Dyestone Group* outcrop, from beneath overlying strata, near the base of one of the spurs of Raccoon Mountain. The strata dip to the northwest at a low angle, running under the mountain. This local-

ity corresponds to a point near the right hand base of the mountain, E, in the diagram on page 139. The range of formations intersected, skirts, for a long distance, the eastern base, not only of Raccoon Mountain, but also of Walden's Ridge, north of Tennessee River. (§§ 141, 142.)

The formations are numbered in ascending order.

(4) *Siliceous Group.* Gray crinoidal limestone charged with layers of chert. Contains *Agaricocrinus.* Seen at base about... 100 feet.

(3) *Black Shale*, with a bituminous sandstone at base, averaging about one foot in thickness.
In all... 12 feet.

(2) *Dyestone Group.*

i. Greenish shale, 22 feet.

h. Dyestone ore, with shale interstratified; one foot and a half.

g. Fine sandstone, somewhat ferruginous, in part inclining to be shaly. Contains individuals of *Pentamerus oblongus;* six feet.

f. Greenish shale, with occasionally thin seams of ferruginous layers, approaching dyestone; some layers more or less calcareous; 67 feet.

e. Calcareous dyestone, alternating with shale; fresh, the dyestone has the aspect of deep red limestone, is fossiliferous, and much of it oolitic, weathers into a rather open iron-ore; one layer, 12 inches thick. In all, 4 feet.

d. Greenish shale, much like *f*, above; contains one or two thin seams of calcareous dyestone; in its lower part, are *Strophomena profunda?* *S. depressa, Orthis elegantula?* &c.; 21 feet.

c. Dyestone, calcareous; 6 inches.

b. Shale and thin limestones alternating; 14 feet.

a. Dyestone, like *c*, above; contains *Leptæna sericea, Strophomena depressa, Orthocerata,* &c.; three to six inches.

Thickness of entire group................................ 136½ ft.

(1) *Transition Beds.* An alternation of thin limestones and shales; freshly quarried, the whole mass is blue, thin limestones predominating.

This, together with the corresponding mass in section § 774, ought perhaps, to be included in the *Upper Silurian,* although Nashville fossils begin to appear. The bed has been referred to in § 654, and some of the fossils given. *Strophomena tenuistriata* of that list, is doubtless *S. depressa*, *Atrypa marginalis* is quite common.

Thickness.. 112 feet.

Below this reddish limestones come in, and well marked Nashville rocks are met with.

780. The entire absence in the above section, of the red sandstones of the White Oak Mountain Formation, is to be noted. The Dyestone Group itself, lacks its thin sandstones, only one bed of the latter appearing, and that near the top. The group is seen, moreover, to be quite calcareous at this point, as it is pretty generally in this portion of the State.

781. In the section, in § 753, the thickness of the Dyestone Group, on the east side of Powell's Mountain, is 325 feet; in the White Oak Mountain section, (§ 774,) it is placed at 200 feet, and in the section above, at 136½. The *transition beds*, however, in the last section, might very well be included in the group, as well as about 100 feet of layers below them, making in all nearly 350. But these so-called transition beds occur in the section of § 774, with the great White Oak Group of red sandstones interpolated between them and division 3, of the section. Including, then, divisions 1, 2, and 3, in the Dyestone Group, the latter becomes, in White Oak Mountain, 900 feet thick—a great development of *Clinton* (*Medina*, in part?) rocks. (See also § 772.)

In addition to the fossils enumerated in § 753, and the section above, as pertaining to this group, *Atrypa hemispherica*, (Sowerby,) has been observed on the east side of Powell's Mountain, in abundance.

782. *The Outcrops of the Dyestone Group; the Dyestone Ridges.*—The Dyestone Group, (the rocks dipping more or less,) outcrops, in the western portion of the Valley—that next to the Table-land—in quite a number of long narrow belts, which, like the belts of the other formations, run in northeasterly and southwesterly courses. These outcrops, or belts, are generally found either on one or the other slope of long, narrow, characteristic ridges, which the hard layers of the group help to make, and which we designate as *Dyestone Ridges*. Sometimes, the ridge is wanting on a portion of a bed of outcrop, but such instances are exceptional.

783. In a few instances, the ridge is wholly made up of the rocks of the Dyestone Group, but generally, the heavy cherty layers of the *Siliceous Group* constitute the most important element in their structure. In fact, we have a *trio* of forma-

tions, ordinarily going together, and making up these ridges. These are, the *Dyestone Group*, the *Black Shale*, and the *Siliceous Group*, the latter occurring as a heavy bed of hard cherty layers. The first and last are the weathering-resisting formations, and the *Black Shale* between is protected, more or less, by one or the other, as the case may be. The hard rocks of the trio, taken together, form no very great volume, and make usually nothing more than a moderate ridge.

When a heavy sandstone formation is interpolated beneath the Dyestone Group, like the Clinch Sandstone, or the White Oak red group, then a Mountain results, and both Dyestone and Siliceous Formations are subordinate. Thus it is, for the most part, in the Powell's Mountain Group, and in White Oak.

784. Below, the Dyestone Ridges, or ranges, are enumerated. The iron-ore outcrops usually on the sides of these, but is sometimes found at the summits. It ought to be observed, also, that these ridges not only give us the outcropping ranges of the Dyestone Group, but also many of those of the *Black Shale*, and of the *Siliceous Group*.

We commence with the ridge which lies at the foot of the eastern slope of the Cumberland Table-land.

785. (1) *The Mountain Dyestone Ridge and Range.*—On page 251, in the table of *valley-ranges* in which Trenton and Nashville rocks outcrop, I have there mentioned the *Mountain Range*. This valley-range, as stated, skirts the base of the Table-land almost continuously from Virginia to Georgia. It is also stated, on page 49, that this range does not come in direct contact with the base of the Table-land, being generally separated therefrom by a low, sharp ridge, and by a very narrow, curious trough, often called "*Back Valley*," the latter lying back of the sharp ridge. This sharp ridge is the Dyestone Ridge under consideration. It is formed by the outcropping of the trio of formations spoken of above, the *Dyestone*, *Black Shale* and *Siliceous*, as they rise to the surface from beneath the Carboniferous strata of the Table-land.

The west end of the diagram on page 208, illustrates how these formations outcrop on the surface. At B is the *Dyestone Ridge*, the Black Shale (erroneously numbered 5 instead of 7) and the Siliceous Group at this point being no part of it. The diagrams on pages 139 and 190 give sections of the formations occurring in the range, or along the line of this Dyestone Ridge, although the ridge being at these points small, is not represented. In that on page 139, its place is near the eastern base of the spur E. (See, also, § 779.) In the one on page 190 it is near the base of the eastern slope of Walden's Ridge.

786. The Mountain Dyestone Ridge comes into Tennessee from Virginia. From the vicinity of Cumberland Gap, where it is called *Poor Valley Ridge*, (the Back Valley being here, "*Poor Valley*,") it reaches southwestward, skirting the Table-land closely, with but few interruptions, to the Georgia line, a distance of nearly 160 miles. (See Map.) Its best defined portions have usually local names. One of these I have mentioned; another in Rhea County is *Shin-bone Ridge*.

In some parts of its line, as in the southern portion of Campbell County, and along the eastern base of Walden's Ridge, in Anderson, it is poorly developed, yet traceable, and the formations present. At a few points, the principal one being the vicinity of the Salt-works, in Anderson, the range, including both ridge and formations, is ingulfed in local faults, and thus interrupted. At other points, and especially in the vicinity of the Little Emery, in Roane County, it is duplicated by local folds or faults.

787. One or more beds of iron-ore outcrop in this ridge, or in the range when the former is not well developed, throughout its whole length. Generally there is but one important bed which varies in thickness from a few inches to two or three feet, swelling out occasionally, however, to six or eight feet. At some localities several different beds occur. In § 756 the bed of ore as found at Cumberland Gap, is mentioned.

788. (2) *Lookout Dgestone Ridges.*—Lookout Mountain, which starts up so boldly near Chattanooga, and runs southwestward, into Georgia and Alabama, (§ 189,) rests in a synclinal trough. Its position and geological relations are seen in the diagram on page 139 at L. The trio of formations, the Dyestone, Black Shale, and Siliceous, (VI, VII, and VIII of the diagram,) are seen to outcrop on both sides of the mountain, near its base, and their outcrops, though not thus represented in the figure, make skirting ridges. Lookout, nearly throughout, from Chattanooga to Gadsden, Alabama, is bordered on each side by a Dyestone ridge.

789. These ridges extend northward, some distance beyond the end of Lookout Mountain, and are intersected in passing from Chattanooga to Walden's Ridge. Traces of one or both of them, may be observed nearly as far up as the Rhea County line.

North of Chattanooga, in addition to the two Lookout ridges spoken of, are two or three short dyestone ridges, made by local folds. The lower end of one of these forms the high hill on the West side of Chattanooga, a fine section of which is seen in the bluff at the brewery.

Layers of ore are found in all of these ridges. The Lookout ridges in Georgia and Alabama are especially interesting as depositories of ore.

790. (3) *Half-moon Island Range.*—Lying in Roane, Rhea, and Meigs, and a little east of the mouth of White's Creek, is a local synclinal several miles in length, made up of the trio of formations, the Dyestone, Black Shale and Siliceous. (See Map.) The Siliceous Group occupies the axis, the other formations outcropping on each side. This synclinal supplies excellent and extensive beds of ore.

The ore outcrops in two lines, which, across the middle part of the synclinal, are nearly a mile apart. The western line runs through *Half-moon Island*, in the Tennessee River, at one end of which is an ore quarry, which, for years, supplied Eagle Furnace, as well as other furnaces, and several forges. For a mile, running through this island, the ore will average four feet, and at a point or two, swells out to twenty feet in direct thickness. The ore is highly esteemed, and makes excellent soft iron.

Immediately west of this ore belt is a strip of Trenton and Nashville rocks, appertaining to the Washington Valley range. (p. 251.)

791. It may be mentioned here, that, at Post Oak Springs, in Roane County, a limited patch of the Dyestone Group, showing some iron-ore, occurs. This point is in an interesting little cove surrounded by ridges, which may be called *Brown's Cove*. It contains an isolated patch of Nashville, Dyestone, and Black shale rocks. On the west of it is a Knox Dolomite cherty ridge, and on the east, Knox Sandstone ranges.

792. *Big Valley, and White Oak Mountain Dyestone Range.*—This is an important, though broken range. The line of it runs from Virginia to Georgia. It lies immediately on the eastern side of the equally long *valley-range* to which I have given the name, on page 251, of Big Valley range. In the range under consideration, the Dyestone Group appears in a ridge or mountain, generally associated with the Black Shale and Siliceous Group.

To the east of this ridge or mountain, as the case may be, follows one of the great faults of East Tennessee. This sometimes cuts off the Siliceous Group, and with it, occasionally, the Black Shale, and even the Dyestone Group itself. (§ 510.)

793. Commencing at the Virginia line, the first portion of the range is in Wallin's Ridge, in Hancock and Claiborne counties. Its place in the diagram on page 208 is at C. It is also seen in the section in § 754, and at the point represented, it contains a bed of ore one foot thick. This portion is, perhaps, about ten miles long, being cut off by the fault before reaching a point opposite Tazewell.

794. The second portion begins with the re-appearance of the range near the mouth of Big Barren Creek, in the southern part of Claiborne, and extends through Union and Anderson, passing east of Clinton, into Roane. In this portion, the ore outcrops at numerous points, ranging from a few inches to three or four feet in thickness. It has also been worked extensively, especially that of Union and Claiborne counties, both in furnaces and forges. In this part, the ore-bed at some points, is multlplied and greatly increased in quantity, by local folds in the rocks, there being, sometimes, three or four parallel bands in the place of one.

795. East, or southeast, of Kingston, a few miles, and near the Tennessee River, a third portion of this range begins. Near the river, on both sides, it shows considerable ore. On the south side of the river, back of Col. Welcker's, on the ridge, are outcrops several feet thick. From this region the range extends, with more or less interruption, in a southeasterly direction, towards White Oak Mountain.

796. The Dyestone Group, bearing with it considerable ore, is found on the eastern slope of White Oak Mountain, as far as the Georgia line, and I might add, much beyond. It is also found in the outlying ridge east of the mountain, to which reference has been made in § 773. In this outlier, as stated, is a bed of ore from one to three feet thick.

The section in § 774 embraces the Dyestone Group of White Oak Mountain.

797. (5) The Dyestone Formation in Wallin's Ridge has been noticed as a portion of the last described range. It remains to mention the other belts of this formation in the Powell's Mountain Group. (§ 96.)

798. The first in order, is that of Powell's Mountain and of Lone Mountain, the two being in the same line. They both have the Dyestone Formation on their eastern sides, the formation in each case containing beds of iron-ore. The place of the formation in Powell's Mountain, is at the eastern base of D, in the diagram, page 208. It is also (5) in the section in § 753.

799. The second, following, is the belt on the eastern side of Newman's Ridge, and seen at (10) in the section of paragraph of 753. There is some dyestone ore in this belt, but its presentation is not equal to what it is generally, in the more western ranges.

800. East of range (4)—the Big Valley and White Oak range—the Dyestone Formation, excepting the belts in the Powell's Mountain Group just mentioned, is rarely seen. Some traces of it appear to exist on the east side of Clinch Mountain, but they appertain, doubtless, to the feather edge of the formation; moreover, they are often absent, the Black Shale resting directly on the Clinch Sandstone.

In the southern part of the State, east of the range, not only the Dyestone Formation, but the Black Shale and the Siliceous Group, as well, are cut off by the great faults. (See diagram on page 190.)

801. There is, however, at least one interesting exception to this remark, and that occurs in front of Chilhowee Mountain. Along a good part of the western base of this mountain, is a great fault, by means of which the *Carboniferous Limestone* is brought in immediate contact with the lower part of the *Chilhowee (Potsdam) Sandstone*, or even the upper part of the *Ocoee Conglomerate*, involving a vertical displacement of the strata of more than 10,000 feet. In the diagram on page 190, the place of the fault is shown by the location of Montvale Springs, which are nearly upon it. A section at this place, from the fault westward, through the ridge *a*, is as follows:

— *Fault.*

(3) *Carboniferous Limestone.*

(*b*) *Mountain Limestone.* First a stratum of shaly limestone, containing many characteristic fossils.

Then, thin-bedded and soft sandstones.

Followed by a space in which the rocks are not seen.

The above rocks form a narrow valley in which the Hotel and Springs are located.

(*a*) *Siliceous Group.* Thin-bedded, dark-gray sandstones, with some sandy shale, several hundred feet. Forms in the main, the ridge *a*, of the diagram.

(2) *Black Shale,* well characterized; 25 or 30 feet thick; underlaid with whitish and reddish clay, mixed with more or less sand, 8 or 10 feet thick.

(1) *Dyestone Group?* Reddish-brown, sandy shale, at least 100 feet, and followed below by the shales of the Trenton and Nashville Series.

802. This section is interesting not only on account of its relations to the fault, but as affording the most southeasterly presentations we have of several of the higher formations.

As to the Dyestone Group, it is not altogether certain that the reddish sandy shales belong to this group. I was informed, however, that dyestone iron-ore occurs at a few points along the range. The fact did not come under my own observation.

803. The Fossil Ore mentioned in § 657, may be placed in this enumeration, as it may prove to be a member of the Dyestone Formation. It is an important range. The ore from it has been used on a small scale, for making iron. The ore is abundant, and will doubless be extensively worked some day.

804. The enumeration of the Dyestone ridges and ranges, was commenced with the *Mountain Range*, that skirting the eastern base of the Table-land, (§ 785,) and from this we proceeded eastward. But west of this, also, in both Elk Fork (§ 144) and Sequatchee (§ 140) Valleys, the Dyestone Group outcrops.

The diagram on page 142 illustrates the geological structure of the Valley of the Elk Fork. Formation 5 is the Dyestone Group, and the figure explains how it is brought to the surface. Its outcrop extends longitudinally through a good part of the valley, and presents an excellent bed of ore, having a nearly uniform thickness of three feet. The dip of this ore-bed at some points, is much less than that indicated in the diagram, thus making the ore easily accessible over wide belts. In addition, by local folding the outcrop of ore in some parts of the valley is multiplied, several parallel bands appearing at the surface.

805. In Sequatchee Valley the Dyestone Group appears in place near the base of the mountain all around, excepting in certain parts on the west side, where this, with other formations, are cut off by a fault. The diagram on page 139 gives a section of the Valley between A and C, and illustrates how the formations, and among them the one under consideration, outcrop. The fault, however, does not appear in this figure. (Compare § 600 and note.) The Dyestone Group is not heavily presented in Sequatchee Valley. At the head of the Valley, above Pikeville, considerable dyestone ore is found, and it is presented in limited quantity at all points between this and the Alabama line, wherever the formation to which it belongs outcrops.

806. In the Elk Fork and Sequatchee Valleys are the last presentations of the Dyestone Group, as we have limited it.

On the west side of the Table-land, this, and all the Niagara divisions, are absent at the first re-appearance of the Black Shale. (§ 744.)

(5,*d*.) The Meniscus Limestone.

807. The *Meniscus Limestone* is the uppermost of the formations grouped in this Report, under the name *Niagara*. As already stated, (§ 746,) it is eminently the formation of the *Western Valley*, or rather, it should be stated, of one large section of this valley. The topographical features and outlines of this area have been given in the First Part of the Report. (See pages 104–109.) In the Western Valley, the *Meniscus* Limestone presents two subdivisions, the upper one of which contains a *lens*, or *meniscus-shaped* fossil *Sponge*, to which Roemer, in a work that will be referred to hereafter, has given the name *Astræospongia meniscus*, and which also is figured on plate H, at the end of this volume. This fossil occurring abundantly, and being very characteristic, especially of the upper

member mentioned, I have given the name *Meniscus* to the formation. The bed is doubtless equivalent to rocks of the Niagara epoch in New York. It is desirable, however, when a formation is so far removed from the type, to have a local name for it.

808. In East Tennessee, the formation is represented by the the limestone, (Sneedville Limestone,) occurring in the Powell's Mountain Group, and lying next above the Dyestone shales. Several belts of this limestone are presented, two of which have already been noticed; one in the valley between Powell's Mountain and Newman's Ridge, and the other at the eastern base of the latter ridge. These are given in the section in § 753 to which the reader is referred.

In addition to these belts, there is a considerable presentation of the limestone at the south end of Newman's Ridge. Along the eastern base of Lone Mountain, in Claiborne and Union counties, a bed of limestone occurs, at least 100 feet thick, which, perhaps, is to be referred to this formation, although it is succeeded above by Dyestone layers, an arrangement, however, which may have been brought about by a local fault.

Outside of the region of the Powell's Mountain Group the formation is generally wanting in East Tennessee.

At one point about four miles southeast of the Saltworks in Anderson County, and in the line of the Big Valley Dyestone range, I have seen a local cherty bed, pretty well charged with corals, and in contact with the Black Shale. This I referred to the formation under consideration. It is the only bed of the kind I have met with.

809. We now pass westward, over a large section of the State in which no rocks of the Meniscus Limestone occur, and it is not until we reach the western slopes of the Central Basin (p. 97) that they are met with again. (See §§ 732, 733, also 744, 745.)

Here the formation is generally seen in place between the Black Shale and the Nashville rocks, but not in full force. Passing, however, still further to the west or southwest, it reappears from beneath overlying rocks in its maximum development, and outcrops over wide areas in the southern part of the Western Valley, in Perry, Decatur, Wayne and Hardin counties.

810. Upon entering the Central Basin from the east, the feather-edge of the Meniscus Limestone is met with on the northern side, in Macon County, and on the southern, in Lincoln, and in the southwestern part of Bedford. In the western part of Lincoln, and in Giles, the ridges usually present the formation on their slopes in a bed occupying a place between the Black Shale and the Nashville rocks, and from two or three to fifty, or occasionally more, feet in thickness. In the high hills which immediately encircle Pulaski, and which are capped with rocks of the Siliceous Group, neither the Meniscus Limestone nor the Black Shale are usually well presented. But a few miles east, on the Fayetteville road, are good exposures.

It is not proposed, however, to mention specially the outcrops of this formation and the areas it occupies. These, indeed, are best determined and appreciated by reference to the Map.

811. The formation consists of thick-bedded crystalline and fine-grained limestones, more or less argillaceous, and often weathering into shale. Most of the limestones are sparry and crinoidal. Many of them contain green points. The series is divided into two nearly equal members, the *Sponge-bearing Bed* above, and the *Variegated Bed* below, each about 100 feet in thickness. The lower bed is an alternation of gray, red, and mottled layers, the crinoidal portions sometimes making a fair marble. Much of the mass tends to crumble into shale. The limestones of the upper bed are light gray, and light-bluish gray, and, as in the lower bed, much of it weathers into shaly matter. On the hill sides layers of this limestone frequently outcrop in two or three successive ledges, separated by intervals of shale. Thin layers of chert often occur, interstratified with the limestone, or embedded in it.

212. It is the upper member of the Meniscus Formation, for the most part, that appears on the slopes of the Central Basin; the Variegated Bed presents itself mainly in the Western Valley and in its ramifications. (§ 253.)

813. On pages 106 and 107 I have spoken of the *glades* of the Western Valley. Both members of the formation help to make these glades. The *fossils*, however, come mostly from the upper, or *Sponge-bearing Bed.* The Variegated Bed is fos-

siliferous, many of its layers are crinoidal, as I have stated, and at many localities, it is very rich, especially in its lower part, in individuals of a number of species of *Orthocerata*, but it presents no such varied fossil fauna as does the bed above it.

814. Dr. Ferdinand Roemer has presented us with a Monograph on the *Silurean Fauna of Western Tennessee*,* which we welcome with pleasure, as a handsome contribution to the paleontology of the State. It is really, so far as it goes, a monograph of the fauna (excepting one or two species) of the Sponge-bearing Bed mentioned above. There are, however, many species in the bed which are not given in the work, most of which are undescribed. The species of new corals, especially, are quite numerous. The crinoids collected by Troost on the glades of Perry and Decatur counties, are nearly all, in fact all, that I have seen, from this bed. It is to be regretted that the Doctor's work was not published long since. As it is, there is so much uncertainty connected with his names that they cannot, in most cases, be used with any satisfaction.

815. At the end of this section is appended a catalogue of fossils occurring in the Meniscus Limestone. It includes the described species, or, at least, such as I have had the means of identifying. The most of these occur in all the counties in which the formation outcrops, in Hardin, Wayne, Perry, Decatur, Benton, Henry, Hickman, Lewis, etc. Some of them are almost always present, and very characteristic. Among such are *Caryocrinus ornatus*, *Pentatrematites Reinwardtii* and a minute crinoid, which has never been properly made out and figured, that I am aware of, named by Troost *Haplocrinus hemispihericus*. I have rarely failed to find this in the outcrops of the formation in the counties mentioned. It is alone sufficient to fix the horizon of a layer. The sponges are also of common occurrence, especially the one from which the formations takes its name. This is quite as useful as the little crinoid. *Cyathophyllum Shumardi*, *Petraia Waynensis*, species of *Eucalyptocrinus*, *Calceola Tennesseensis*, and *Lampterocrinus Tennesseensis*, are common and characteristic forms.

* Die Silurische Fauna Des Westlichen Tennessee; Eine Palæontologische Monographie von Dr. Ferdinand Roemer; Breslau, 1860.

816. Below is presented a group of figures* representing some of the fossils, which, in the State of New York, are found in the Niagara Formation, the equivalent of our Meniscus Bed. Most of these have not been, as yet, observed in Tennessee. *Strophomena rugosa* (Fig. 11) is quite a common species, and what is unusual, is found in several geological horizons outside of the one we are considering.

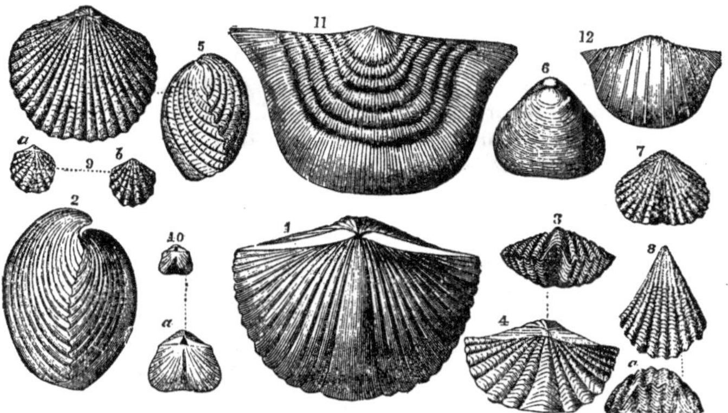

Figs. 1, 2, *Spirifer Niagarensis*.
" 3, 4, " *sulcatus*.
Fig. 5, *Atrypa nodostriata*.
" 6, *Merista nitida*.
" 7, *Pentamerus interplicatus*.
Fig. 8, *Rhynchonella cuneata*.
" 9, *Leptocœlia disparilis*.
" 10, *Orthis biloba*.
" 11, *Strophomena rugosa*.
" 12, *Leptæna transversalis*.

817. I have, on a previous page, (see § 711,) given a section of the rocks seen in the bluff at and above Clifton, on the Tennessee River, in the northwestern part of Wayne County. The base of the Meniscus Limestone in this section, rests upon strata of the Nashville Formation. The junction is well seen, not only at Clifton, but for several miles below that place, along the eastern bank of the Tennessee River.

Below I give a general section of the formations in this part of Wayne County. The successive beds outcrop along a line commencing at the level of low water at Clifton, and terminating nearly four miles back, at the top and on the end of one of the spurs that jut out from the high lands further east. (§ 252.) This region is the most favorable for studying the entire Meniscus Formation that has come under my observa-

* Taken from Dana's Manual of Geology, page 241.

tion. The strata are presented in the section in their natural order, and are to be read from the bottom, upward.

(5) *Siliceous Group.* (Form. 8,*a.*)
Caps the ridge overlooking the valley of Eagle Creek; strata mostly concealed; loose, cherty masses scattered over the surface, and containing Carboniferous fossils... 53 feet.

(4) *Black Shale Group.* (Form. 7.)
(*b.*) Proper *black shale*, mostly replaced by *bluish and greenish siliceous shale*, (weathered) Eight feet at the base, interstratified with thin, smooth, fine-grained sandstones, containing individuals of *Lingula subspatulata?* 42 feet.
(*a.*) *Fine-grained sandstone*, highly charged with the same *Lingula* as above, 8 feet.
Entire thickness of the group........................ 50 feet.

(3) *Lower Helderberg.* (Form. 6.)
Gray crinoidal limestone, fossils obscure at this point. This particular bed may belong below; it occupies, however, the horizon of well-marked Lower Helderberg rocks in the vicinity... 25 feet.

(2) *Meniscus Limestone.* (Form. 5,*d.*)
(*b.*) *Sponge-bearing Bed;* gray, crinoidal, and argillaceous limestones, many of them glade-forming, highly fossiliferous, containing sparsely thin layers of chert. 90 feet.
(*a.*) *Variegated Bed;* gray, red, and mottled limestones, interstratified; many layers argillaceous; Orthocerata abundant in its lower part. Clifton is located in part upon it. 96 feet.
Entire thickness of the formation,.................. 186 feet.

(1) *Nashville Formation.* (Form. 4.)
See section in paragraph 711.

818. Sections similar to this, but rarely showing the base of Nashville rocks, may be found in the northern part of Hardin County, near the Tennessee River, and also on Hardin's, Indian, and Horse Creeks, and on some of their principal tributaries. There are many good exposures of the formation on these large creeks. At many of them the Helderberg rocks are absent, and the Black Shale Group rests directly on the Meniscus Limestone.

819. On the upper part of Birdsong Creek, in Benton, and also on Big Sandy, in the southeastern part of Henry, sections

including the Variegated Bed, can be obtained. Good presentations occur on Duck River, in Hickman, as well as on Cane and other creeks of the same county. The upper part of the valley of Buffalo River, in Lewis and Wayne, afford many good sections.

820. In the northern part of Sumner County, at the point where the Gallatin and Glasgow Turnpike ascends the ridge and leaves the Basin, the *Meniscus Limestone* is present in considerable volume, there being about 120 feet of it. The rocks are gray, and bluish-gray, crinoidal and argillaceous limestones. The middle portion and the lower part of the upper portion, abounds in individuals of *Pentamerus oblongus* associated with *Caryocrinus ornatus*, and other Niagara forms.

821. Below is a section of the formations as they are presented in the bluff at Montgomery's Mill, in Hickmán County, on Piney River, near its mouth.

(4) *Gravel-bed* on top of the ridge.

(3) *Siliceous Group.*

(*b.*) A heavy bed of compact, gray, metal-ringing limestone; some of its upper and lower layers contain flinty burs, averaging size of filberts; rarely showing cherty bands. This mass is wholly made up of *finely* comminuted crinoidal remains. It is mostly concealed at the top of the ridge above the mill, but at Esquire Curl's, about a mile distant, (where it is 125 feet thick, is capped with alternating layers of shale and chert, and rests directly upon the Black Shale,) it is well exposed. 135 feet.

(*a.*) A group of heavy cherty layers with shales and limestone. 45 feet.

Thickness in all,.. 177 feet.

(2) *Black Shale Group.*

(*c.*) Layer of "kidneys" (§ 732) half a foot.

(*b.*) Black Shale, very fetid, 8 feet.

(*a.*) Fine-grained sandstone, 6 to 12 inches.

Entire thickness,.. 9 feet.

(1) *Meniscus Formation.*

(*c.*) Mostly compact, gray, sparry limestone, with a few feet of shaly limestone at top. Some bands are tinged with red, 30 feet.

(*b.*) Marly limestone, loaded with fossils and yielding them readily. Contains several species of *Eucalyptocrinus*, *Caryocrinus ornatus*, *Platyostoma Niagarensis*, *Rhynchonella Tennesseensis*, *Spirifer macropleurus*, etc., 4 feet.

(*a.*) Gray limestones, inclining to be marly; at base thin, gray, sparry layers, some few with red tinge; runs down to water. 44 feet.

Thickness of entire formation,......... .... 78 feet.

822. *Rocks of Special Use, Minerals, and Agricultural Features of the Meniscus Limestone.*—As already stated, some of the variegated crinoidal layers of this formation are a fair *marble*, and, indeed, they have been worked as such, at a number of points. Quarries have been opened on Big Sandy, in the southern part of Henry County, in a region where a local but wide dome or swell in the strata, brings the Variegated Bed to the surface. Localities of the same rock occur on Birdsong Creek, in Benton County. In the more southern counties, Perry, Decatur, Wayne and Hardin, where the Variegated Bed has its greatest presentation, numerous localities occur, and many of them immediately on the Tennessee River. This rock, though a fair marble, is not equal to the best of Hawkins County.

Building material of good quality, is found at many points in this formation, and frequently on the river, thus admitting of easy transportation.

823. After passing the solid rocks of the Western Valley, and getting upon the sands and clays of West Tennessee, it becomes an important object to find material for making *lime*. The Meniscus and Lower Helderberg limestones are the ones drawn upon for this purpose. Along the line of their last appearance, are many points where the rock is burnt into lime to be sold and carried westward.

824. *Galenite* (lead-ore) is found occasionally within the area of this formation in small veins, but I know of no locality worthy of special notice. A small vein is said to cross Cane Creek, in the southwestern part of Hickman County. It could not be seen at the time of my visit. Near Montgomery's Mill, the locality of the section just given, pieces of galenite have been picked up, but no vein found.

825. On the glades of the Meniscus Limestone are very generally found isolated cubes, and cubo-octahedrons of *pyrite* (iron-pyrites.) The specimens are often interesting. Compound forms, and symmetrical groups of crystals, from the size of a walnut to that of one's fist, are often met with.

826. The limestone of this formation, like the Trenton and Nashville limestones in the Basin, afford, occasionally, cavities containing *petroleum*. At Montgomery's Mill, on Piney River, and from rocks at the very base of the section given above, is a crevice, from which a black looking petroleum has been oozing ever since 1830. It was first observed in blasting out the foundation for the mill. Since that time it has frequently been gathered for medicinal purposes. The oil is, perhaps, deeply seated, and may come from Nashville rocks which are not far below. A boring has recently been made at this point, but with what success I am not informed.

827. The topographical, as well as, to some extent, the agricultural features of the Western Valley have been given in the First Part of the Report. (Pages 104–110.) As a whole, the area is rough, but it contains numerous rich and well cultivated minor valleys. The large creeks in Hardin County, present long strips of good land based on the limestones of this division. So, too, with the creeks in Wayne, Decatur, Perry and Hickman. The upper part of Buffalo, with its tributaries, of Cane Creek, and of Duck River, below Centerville, the lower parts of Piney River and Beaver Dam, portions of the creeks in Benton, with many others in the counties mentioned, have lands underlaid by the Meniscus limestones, which, together with the alluvial flats along the streams, present sites for multitudes of productive and very desirable farms.

828. Below, is the catalogue referred to in § 815. No species has been admitted but such as I know, or have good reason to think, belong to the Meniscus or Niagara horizon. With the exception of a very few, I have them all in my cabinet, having collected them myself. The catalogue includes *all* of Roemer's species with but two exceptions. One of these is *Orthis biloba*, which was overlooked. The other, *Strophomena euglypha*, Hall's *Strophodonta punctulifera*, was purposely omitted, as I have never seen it outside of the Lower Helder-

berg horizon. I might add that several of the *trilobites* are doubtful as to specific relations.

1. *Astylospongia præmorsa*, Goldfuss, (sp.,) Monograph, page 8
2. *Astylospongia stellatim-sulcata*, Roemer, " " 11
3. *Astylospongia inciso-lobata*, " " " 11
4. *Palæomanon cratera*, " " " 13
5. *Astylospongia imbricato-articulata* " " " 12
6. *Astræospongia meniscus*, " " " 14
7. *Stenopora fibrosa*, Goldfuss, (sp.,)
   (calamopora fibrosa) " " 20
8. *Thecostegites hemisphæricus* Roemer, " " 25
9. *Thecia Swinderenana*, Goldfuss, " " 26
10. *Heliolites interstincta*, Linn., (sp.,) " " 23
11. *Plasmopora follis*, Edwards and Haime, " " 24
12. *Halysites catenularia*, Linn., (sp.,) " " 25
13. *Favosites favosa*, Goldfuss, (sp.,)
    (calamopora favosa.) " " 18
14. *Favosites Gothlandica*, Goldfuss, (sp.,)
    Calamopora Gothlandica.) " " 18
15. *Favosites Forbesi*, Ed. and H., var. *discoidea*,
    (Calamopora Gothlandica var. discoidea)" " 19
16. *Favosites Niagarensis*, Hall,
    (Calamopora Gothlandica var., etc.,) " " 19
17. *Favosites cristata*, Edwards and Haime,
    (Calamopora cristata) " " 20
18. *Cyathophyllum Shumardi*, Edwards & Haime, " " 27
19. *Petraia Waynensis*, Safford. This Volume, pl. H., Fig. 2
20. *Petraia Fanningana*, " " " " " " 3
21. *Aulopora repens*, Walch and Knorr, Monograph, page 28
22. *Alveolites repens*, Hisinger, " " 22
23. *Cladopora reticulata*, Hall, Pal. N. Y. Vol. II, p. 141.
24. *Fenestella acuticosta*, Roemer, Monograph, page 30
25. *Caryocrinus ornatus*, Say " " 33
26. *Apiocystites Anna*, Safford,
    Much like Hall's *A. elegans*, (Pal. Vol. II, p. 243,) but the pectinated apertures are on the edges of the plates, and those of each pair close together. The markings on the body plates mostly fine sharp ridges.
27. *Pentatrematites Reinwardtii*, Troost, (sp.,) Monograph, p. 60

28. *Saccocrinus speciosus*, Hall, Monograph, page 42
29. *Platycrinus Tennesseensis*, Roemer, " " 35
30. *Lampterocrinus Tennesseensis*, Roemer, " " 37
31. *Cytocrinus lævis* " " " 46
32. *Eucalyptocrinus cœlatus*, Hall;
    I doubt as to this being Hall's species " " 48
33. *Eucalyptocrinus ramifer*, Roemer, " " 51
34. *Coccocrinus bacca*, " " " 51
35. *Synbathocrinus Tennesseensis*, Roemer, " " 55
36. *Porteriocrinus pisiformis*, " " " 54
37. *Cystocrinus Tennesseensis*, " " " 56
38. *Haplocrinus hemisphericus*, Troost;
    (See § 815.)
39. *Calceola Tennesseensis*, Roemer,
    (The same as *C. Americana*, Safford, Amer. Jour. Sci. II, Vol. XXIX, p. 248.) Monograph, page 73
40. *Strophomena rugosa*, Dalman, (sp.,)
    (S. depressa,) " " 65
41. *Streptorhyncus subplanus*, Conrad,
    (Strophomena pecten,) " " 67
42. *Orthis fissiplica*, Roemer, " " 64
43. *Orthis hybrida*, Sowerby, " " 63
44. *Orthis elegantula*, Dalman, " " 62
45. *Spirifer crispus*, Hisinger, Pal. N. Y., Vol. II, p. 262
46. *Spirifer macropleurus*, Conrad.
    (S. Niagarensis var. oligoptycha,) Monograph, page 68
47. *Atrypa reticularis*, Linn., " " 69
48. *Atrypa marginalis*, Dalman, " " 69
49. *Pentamerus oblongus*, Murchison, (§ 820,) Silurian System.
50. *Pentamerus Littoni?* Hall.
    Hall refers this to the *Lower Helderberg*, but if it be the species I think it is, its horizon is in the upper part of the *Meniscus* (*Niagara*) *Formation*. I have seen it at a number of localities; Pal. N. Y., Val. III, page 262.
51. *Pentamerus galeatus*, Dalm.
    This is a Lower Helderberg species; but it also occurs in the topmost part of the *Meniscus Limestone*, Monograph, page 73
52. *Athyris tumida*, Dalman, " " 70

53. *Rhynchonella Wilsoni*, Sowerby, " " 71
54. *Rhynchonella Tenneeseensis*, Roemer, " " 72
55. *Platyostoma Niagarensis*, Hall, " " 75
56. *Platyceras Niagarensis*, Hall,
(Acroculia Niagarensis) " " 76
57. *Cyclonema Tennesseensis*, Roemer;
(Turbo Tennesseensis) " " 77
58. *Orthoceras annulatum*, Sowerby, " " 78
59. *Ceraurus bimucronatus*, Murchison, " " 80
60. *Sphærexochus mirus*, Beyrich, " " 81
61. *Dalmania caudata*, Brongniart, " " 82
62. *Calymene Blumenbachii*, Brongniart, " " 79
63. *Bumastus Barriensis*, Murchison, " " 83

SECTION II.

LOWER HELDERBERG; FORMATION VI.

829. This formation does not appear to occur in East Tennessee. The portion of the State to which it appertains is the Western Valley, (§ 250,) and a narrow belt of country adjoining this on the east.

830. It is a series of light-blue limestones, often shaly, highly fossiliferous, frequently containing cherty layers, especially in its upper part, and having a maximum thickness, so far as yet observed, of 70 feet.

831. The formation has been met with in greatest volume, for the most part, in its most westerly exposures, as, for instance, in the vicinity of the White Sulphur Springs, in the southern part of Hardin County, and within a considerable area in Henry County, commencing at the mouth of Big Sandy, and extending up the valley of that stream five or six miles. In the southern part of Benton, as well as in Decatur, it is also seen well developed at a number of points.

832. The areas and points referred to, lie in a narrow strip of country, running across the State, and contiguous to the Tennessee River on its west side, in which the strata of all the older formations, from the *Nash-*

ville to the *Siliceous*, inclusive, are, as a single group, suddenly beveled off, and made to give place to the sand, clay, and gravel beds of West Tennessee, the latter overlapping and abutting against the former. (See §§ 272 and 326.)

In this belt any one of the older formations may come in contact with the later and unconsolidated beds of the west, a circumstance depending upon the comparative elevation of the formation, and its local topography.

833. In the strip mentioned, many clear exposures have been observed, presenting sections of the Helderberg Limestone from 50 to 70 feet thick, and in some cases without either the top or the bottom of the formation being seen. It will be safe to place its maximum thickness at 100 feet.

834. Passing eastward from the Tennessee River, the formation is found (by the study of the sections exposed in the deep valleys cut in the Highlands by the streams,) to grow thinner, and to become more or less fiagmentary until it disappears, for the most part, before reaching the Central Basin. Doubtful traces exist in the sections on the west side of the Basin, (§ 744,) but they are rare and hardly note-worthy.

835. Along the valley of Duck River, the formation scarcely reaches Hickman County. In the valleys of Indian and Hardin's creeks, in Hardin and Wayne counties, it occurs locally in thin beds, but is generally wanting. In the upper part of the valley of Buffalo, in Wayne and Lewis, it is absent; but in the lower part of this valley, in Perry, and at a few points in Humphreys, the formation is well presented, and loaded with fossils. It is seen below the Black Shale at the foot of the hill at Linden. Three miles below Beardstown, on Buffalo, it measured 30 feet in a section showing both the Black Shale above and the Meniscus Bed below. Twomiles above the mouth of Buffalo, by a local swell in the strata, it is brought up, and is exposed in a bluff, showing a thickness of 50 feet.

There is also a good presentation of Helderberg rocks in the Wells Creek Basin, in Stewart County. (§§ 364, 553.)

836. The formation at most points, is rich in fossils. A group of some of those commonly occurring is figured on the next page. All the species represented are found in the rocks of the formation in the State of New York,* and most of them in the same

* The formation is well developed in the *Helderberg* Mountains, south of Albany, in New York, and hence the name given to it.

horizon in Tennessee. Two, *Spirifer macropleurus* and *Pentamerus galeatus*, occur with us, both in the Helderberg and Meniscus formations. In the latter, *Pentamerus galeatus* is found at the top of the group, while *S. macropleurus* occurs sometimes at a lower level. (§ 821.) The individuals of both species are usually of a smaller size in the Meniscus Formation than in the Helderberg. *Merista ? sulcata*, *Strophomena radiata*, and *Pentamerus pseudo-galeatus* have not, as yet, been identified as Tennessee forms.

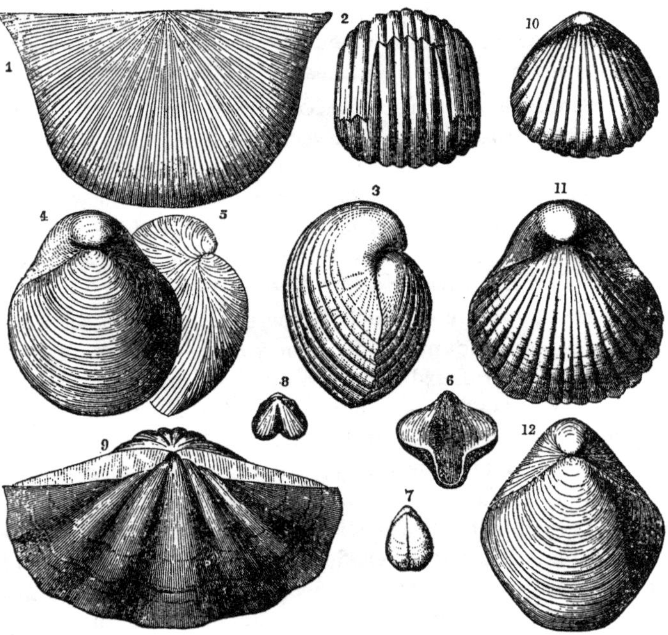

1. *Strophomena radiata.*
2, 10. *Rhynchonella ventricosa.*
3, 11. *Pentamerus galeatus.*
4, 5. *Pentamerus pseudo-galeatus.*
6. *Eatonia singularis.*
7. *Merista ? sulcata.*
8. *Orthis varica,*
9. *Spirifer macropleurus.*
12. *Merista lævis.*

837. Below is given a list of such species, from among those collected by the author from the Helderberg rocks of Tennessee, as have been identified with described forms. Before presenting this list, however, it will be well to call attention to some of the principal localities, and to their character.

838. There are two classes of these localities. The first includes a number occurring at points where no other rocks, below the Black Shale, but those belonging to the Helderberg Formation, are present. The second includes certain localities at which the junction of the Helderberg with the underlying Meniscus (Niagara) limestones is seen, and at which, too, it is frequently difficult to point out the plane of separation. The lithological character is much the same, and the two formations, in some regions, appear to run into each other. Certain beds occupying the horizon of junction, do contain, more or less, both Helderberg and Niagara species. I have designated the localities by capital letters, and it has always been made a point to mark every specimen collected with the letter of its locality.

Below are the localities, each with its letter, which present, below the Black Shale when occurring, Helderberg rocks alone:

839. (A) A locality in Henry county, on Big Sandy, about five miles above its mouth, at Williams' Mill. About fifty feet of bluish limestone are exposed; all shaly, excepting a few layers of gray limestone at top. On the surface above the limestone, are loose, angular, flinty masses, containing the fossils of the rock below, and derived from cherty layers not seen. The bluff is capped with a bed of orange-colored sand and gravel belonging to the later formations.

840. (B) A locality similar to the last, on a tributary of Birdsong Creek, in the southern part of Benton County.

841. (W) White Sulphur Springs, near the Tennessee river, in the southern part of Hardin County. The establishment is located upon the upper part of the Helderberg rocks, and from them the sulphur water of the springs issues. Masses of chert, containing the fossils of the formation, are found abundantly on the surface. About a mile from the Springs, on the opposite side of the river, is a bluff, two or more miles in length, at the base of which the Helderberg rocks are exposed. The following is a section at a point opposite the springs:

(4) Top of hill above the bluff capped with *sand and gravel*, in good part cemented into a *ferruginous conglomerate.*

(3) *Siliceous Group* (Form. 8,*a*.)

(*b*) A leached mass, consisting of cherty layers, with chalky-looking shale between, 10 to 12 feet.

(*a*) Fine-grained, sky-blue, calcareo-siliceous rock, ("water-lime",) weathering into siliceous shale, 65 feet.

Entire thickness,.................................... 75 feet.

(2) *Black Shale Group.* (Form. 7.)

Nearly wanting at this point; represented by a fetid sandstone, with slaty seams.................................. 3 feet.

(1) *Helderberg Limestone.* (Form. 6.)
Bluish limestone, abounding in cherty nodules and layers, and running down to the water's edge ; all fossiliferous. The limestone has, at its top and base, thick-bedded layers.. 63 feet.

842. (F) On Buffalo river, in Perry county.

843. At the following localities both Helderberg and Meniscus (Niagara) rocks are seen, or else there is presented a bed of limestone immediately below the Black Shale horizon, and above the Meniscus layers, having, in paleontological features, a more or less mixed character.

844. (C) A locality near Esq. A. B. Gant's, on Indian Creek, in Wayne County, fourteen miles from Waynesboro, and twenty-two from Savannah.* The fossils in column C of the list, are from this locality, and from limestones within 20 feet of the Black Shale rocks. The section at the particular point is as follows:

(4) *Black Shale Group*, represented by its lowest member—the sandstone.

(3) A layer of gray limestone, containing the fossils of column C, which are silicified.. 10 feet.

(2) *Space*, rocks not seen.. 8 feet.

(1) Argillaceous limestone at the foot of the hill, which may be referable to the Meniscus Formation.................... 5 feet.

845. I introduce here a general section of the formations as they occur in the valley of Indian Creek, in the vicinity of Esq. Gant's, and of Cravens' Mills, a short distance below.

(4) *Siliceous Group.*
Caps the hills on both sides of the valley; not well seen at top, but its liberated cherty fossiliferous masses are plentifully scattered over the surface; occasionally a specimen of *Lithostrotion Canadense* is met with; lower part, a bed of heavy, cherty layers, interstratified with limestone and shale.
Thickness, from a few feet to.............................. 250.

(3) *Black Shale Group.*
(*b*) Fine, blue, calcareo-siliceous rock, weathering into shale, and alternating, especially in its lower part, with thin, fine-grained sandstones; abounds in the lingulæ of the group; maximum thickness about 60 feet.

* I take this opportunity of expressing my thanks to my friend and former pupil, A. B. Gant, Jr., now living in Texas, for valuable assistance rendered me in my investigations on Indian and Eagle creeks. Mr. Gant has discovered several most interesting localities of fossils in both Wayne and Hardin counties.

(*a*) Fine-grained, bituminous sandstone, contains lingulæ, and generally forms a ledge, more or less prominent, along the slopes, 8 to 12 feet.
Thickness entire.. 70 feet.

(2) *Helderberg Limestone.*
Does not differ essentially, in lithological character, from the rocks below; eastward, runs out; same as 3, in last section; thickness variable; maximum about 35 feet.

(1) *Meniscus Limestone.*[1]
From 4 to 6 feet at top; rock compact, forming a ledge, as at Craven's Mills.
Next below, sparry, crinoidal limestone; some of it thin-bedded; all more or less inclined to crumble and form gravelly places; contains *Astræospongia meniscus*, *Caryocrinus ornatus*, *&c.* Including the rock of the ledge, it is the Sponge-bearing member, with a maximum thickness of 65 feet.
Below this, again, are about 20 feet of the Variegated Bed, red and gray limestones alternating, which takes us to the bottom of the creek. These rocks are well seen at Craven's Mill.
Thickness entire,.. 85 feet.

846. Two and a half miles west of Esq. Gant's, is a bed (m) 25 feet thick, well filled with *Niagara* corals, and separated from the base of the Black Shale Group by 10 feet of gray limestone.

847. (S) A locality in Hardin county, at Col. Smith's, nine miles from Savannah, on the Waynesboro road. The fossils come from a bed about 20 feet thick.

848. (D) Bath Springs, in the southern part of Decatur county. These fossils are from a bed twenty feet thick, followed below by a hard limestone, three feet in thickness, forming a ledge. Below the ledge are eighteen feet of shaly limestone, containing *A. meniscus*, *&c.* This is underlaid by variegated limestones at the bottom of the hill.

849. In the table a column is appropriated on the right, to each of the localities mentioned. The arrangement will enable the reader to see the range of the species, and the better to appreciate how they are associated. The age of the rocks at the localities C, S, and D, respectively, is debatable. It may be found desirable, upon further investigation, to refer these beds to the Niagara horizon.

I take this opportunity of acknowledging the kindness of Prof. James Hall, in aiding me, personally, in the determination of many of the fossils in the following list. And I must add here, that his great work on the

Paleontology of New York, and indeed I might say, on the Paleontology of America, has been the foundation of the most that has been done towards the making out of the Paleozoic formations of Tennessee.

HELDERBERG FOSSILS OCCURRING IN TENNESSEE.

	NAMES OF SPECIES AND REMARKS.	A	B	W	F	C	S	D
1	Anisophyllum Agassizi, Edwards and Haime, ...	...	...	...	...	...	*	*
2	Favosites Gothlandica, Goldfuss, ...	*	...	*				
3	Favosites Niagarensis, Hall, ...	...	...	*	*			
4	Apiocystites Anna, Safford. This is given in the catalogue of Meniscus (Niagara) species, but ought to be included here, as it occurs in D, at Bath Springs.	...	...	...	...	...	...	*
5	Leptæna concava, Hall.	*						
6	Strophomena rugosa, Hisinger, ...	*	*	*	*	*	*	*
7	Strophodonta punctulifera, Conrad, ...	*	*	*				
8	Strophodonta Beckii, Hall, ...	...	...	*				
9	Strophodonta varistriata, Conrad ; var. arrata, Hall, ...	*						
10	Orthis varica, Hall, ...	*						
11	Orthis oblata, Hall, ...	*	*	*	*	*		
12	Orthis subcarinata. Hall, ...	*						
13	Orthis eminens, Hall, ...	*						
14	Orthis elegantula, Dalman, ...	...	...	...	...	*	*	*
15	Orthis Halli, Safford ; a fine species, with prominent striæ, much like those of *O. fissiplica*, Roemer, and a form recalling the Trenton *O. deflecta*, but having a narrower cardinal area ; is also like *O. fasciata*, Hall, ...	*						
16	Spirifer perlamellosus. Hall, ...	*	*	...	*			
17	Spirifer cyclopterus, Hall, ...	*	...	*	*			
18	Spirifer macropleuris, Conrad, ...	*	*	...	*			
19	Spirifer Saffordi, Hall, ...	...	...	...	...	*	...	*
20	Spirifer tenuistriata, cannot locate it, ...							
21	Trematospira simplex, Hall, ...	...	...	...	...	*		
22	Nucleospira ventricosa, Hall, ...	...	...	...	...	*		
23	Nucleospira concentrica, Hall, ...	...	...	...	...	...	*	*
24	Rhynchospira globosa, Hall, ...	*	...	...	...	...	...	*
25	Rhynchospira formosa, Hall, ...	*	...	...	*	*	*	*
26	Leptocœlia, (undes.)	*	..	..	..	*		
28	Rhynchonella Wilsoni, Sowerby, ...	*	*	...	...	...	*	*
27	Rhynchonella mutabilis, Hall, ...	*	...	*	*	*		
29	Rhynchonella Tennesseensis, Rœmer, ...	...	...	...	...	*	*	*
30	Rhynchonella ventricosa, Hall, ...	*						
31	Atrypa reticularis, Linn, ...	*	*	*	*	*	*	*
32	Merista lævis, Vanuxem, ...	*	*	...	*			
33	Merista (Athyris) tumida, Dalman, ...	...	...	...	*	...	...	*
34	Camarium Meeki, Hall, Decatur County, ...							
35	Eatonia singularis, Hall, ...	*	...	...	*			
36	Pentamerus galeatus, Dalman, ...	*	*	...	...	...	*	*
37	Pentamerus Verneuili, Hall, ...	*	...	...	*	...	*	*
38	Platyostoma ventricosa, Conrad, ...	...	...	...	*			
39	Platyceras tenuiliratum, Hall, ...	*	...	...	...	...	...	*
40	Phacops Hudsonicus, Hall, ...	*						
41	Dolmania micrurus, Green, ...	*	..	*				
42	Dalmania nasutus, Conrad.	*						

850. There is nothing special to add with reference to the agricultural features of the formation. In connection with the Meniscus Limestone, it presents some desirable farming areas. It might have been included with the Meniscus Formation, when speaking, in a previous paragraph, of the agricultural features of the latter.

So far as I know, it does not contain any minerals of importance.

CHAPTER X.

THE BLACK SHALE; FORMATION VII.

851. This formation is sometimes denominated the *Black Shale.* Although comparatively very thin it is, on soveral accounts, one of the most interesting formations in the State. It is wonderfully persistent, appearing in place, with rare exceptions, wherever its horizon is presented at the surface. It outcrops on that old *gulf shore*, the western beveled slope of the older formations of which we have spoken, (§ 832,) and it appears at the other end of the State, under the brow of Chilhowee Mountain. (§ 801.) It is the geologist's plane of reference, as well as puzzle, the would-be coal digger's *ignis fatuus*, a source of mineral waters, the alum and coperas maker's stock, an oil-schist and a pyroschist.

852. The characteristic and principal mass of this formation is a nearly black, bituminous, rather tough shale, or slate, which can frequently be obtained in plates a yard or more across. This shale contains, very generally, grains and nodules of *pyrite* scattered through its mass. At some localities, the pyrite occurs most abundantly in certain layers of the formation, as, for instance, at the top or bottom. The presence of bituminous matter is also characteristic. The shale generally contains so much of this as to be readily ignited, and to burn for a while with considerable energy when in large heaps, or when fragments of it are thrown upon glowing coals. For this reason it is sometimes called a *pyrochist.* It does not, however, like stone coal, burn to ashes. The bulk, after burning, is the same as before, their being little else consumed beside a small per centage of bituminous matter. It loses, however, its color, by the process, the mass becoming reddish gray. It is often taken as an indication of stone coal, and, in Tennessee, thousands of dollars, and a vast deal of enterprise, have been wasted, in drifting into it.

853. The shale yields by distillation in close vessels, from one to fifteen, or even twenty per cent. of oily matter allied to petroloum, and can be used as a source of oils for illuminating, lubricating, and other purposes.

854. West of the Cumberland Table-land, in most of the counties, the formation does not consist alone of the characteristic Black Shale. The latter has here, at its top, a thin layer of argillaceous, very fetid, concretionary bodies, which I have sometimes called *kidneys*, a name which has already been used with reference to them. These bodies are round, oval, kidney-shaped, and usually more or less flattened. They vary in size from that of a peach-stone to thick, cake-like masses two feet across, and occur packed, often closely, with bluish shale, in a layer from two to twelve inches thick. The kidneys vary in size with the thickness of the layer. These bodies have been mentioned in the sections given respectively in paragraphs 729, 732 and 821.

855. In addition to the kidneys at its top, the shale has immediately below it, very generally, a dark-gray, bituminous, fetid *sandstone*, usually fine-grained, and from a few inches to 15 feet in thickness. In Wayne, Hardin, and in the southwestern part of Lewis, this sandstone is often thick enough to be quite conspicuous, forming ledges along the slopes of the hills, and sometimes small local plateaus.

856. In the counties mentioned, it is frequently the only representative of the group, the kidneys and the Black Shale being absent or replaced by it. Thus it is on Green River, below Waynesboro', where the sandstone is from ten to fifteen feet thick, with the blue shale of the Siliceous Group above, and the Meniscus Limestone immediately below. In the section, also, near the White Sulphur Springs, in Hardin County, (§ 841,) the sandstone, for the most part, represents the group. On Indian Creek, in the region of Esquire Gant's and Craven's Mills, (§ 845,) the Black Shale appears to be represented by an alternation of blue shales and thin, fine sandstones, resting upon the lower member. (See also, § 817.)

857. North and east of Wayne, Hardin and Lewis, the sandstone below the Black Shale is not as thick, in fact, it very often measures but the fraction of a foot. At Montgomery's Mill, (§ 821,) it hardly reaches twelve inches, and at numerous other points it is but three or four.

The sandstone is seen in place on the eastern side of the Cumberland Table-land in the section on the Chattanooga Railroad, above Lookout Station. (§ 779.)

858. This rock, in addition to the *Lingula* of the shale, frequently contains multitudes of individuals of a minute globular spiral shell, which has not been studied. It also shows occasionally, fragmentary remains of plants, and certain curious bodies not understood.

859. The following section presents the Black Shale Formation in its triple character. It was taken in Wayne County at T. A. White's Mill, on Buffalo River, a point a few miles below the mouth of Green River. The section also shows the total absence of Helderberg rocks at this locality, which, by the way, is the case on Buffalo and Green Rivers, east and south, respectively, from the region of the mill. The character of the Siliceous Group above the Black Shale, is also illustrated to some extent.

(4) A thin bed of *Gravel* (water-worn pebbles) on top, with some loose, angular chert. The gravel is found at the top of all the high ridges in this region. Specimens of *Lithostrotion Canadense* (not water-worn) are also found loose on the surface.

(3) *Siliceous Group.*
Rocks concealed, surface covered with small, angular, cherty masses, 199 feet to top of ridge.
Bluish shale with layers of chert, 15 feet.
Bluish shale, 24 feet.
In all, ... 238 feet.

(2) *Black Shale Group.*
(*c.*) Layer of kidneys, 6 inches.
(*b.*) Black Shale, 2 feet.
(*a.*) Sandstone, at top thin bedded, surfaces abounding in *Lingulæ*, 9 feet.
In all, ... 11½ feet.

(1) *Meniscus Limestone.* (Niagara.)
Gray, mostly crinoidal limestone; contains the characteristic *Haplocrinus hemisphericus* immediately below the sandstone; thickness down to the water, ... 67 feet.

860. The Black Shale Group is, as the sections already given indicate, of variable thickness. Its maximum is in the East Tennessee Valley where it is often 100 feet, and at some localities more.

In Middle Tennessee, including certain bluish shales, as in the Indian Creek section, (§ 845,) its thickness rises as high as

70 feet. Excluding these, it rarely reaches 50. The *Black Shale,* itself, is of all thicknesses, below 50, averaging, perhaps, about 25 feet. In some parts of Wayne and Hardin counties, it is as we have seen, entirely wanting.

Including the sandstone, however, or taking the *group,* I have never found it absent from its proper horizon but at one point, and that is at the foot of the "big hill," five miles from Mount Pleasant, on the Waynesboro' road. Here the siliceous cherty layers, rest directly on Nashville rocks, all intervening formations being absent. Very soon, however, to the right and left, both the Black Shale and the Meniscus Limestone, come in.

861. The Black Shale Group is usually characterized by the presence of a *lingula* which is doubtless *L. subspatulata* of Meek and Worthen. (Geol. of Illinois, Vol. III, p. 437.) Their figure is that of a large sized specimen. In addition to this, there appears to be another species. A *discina* also occurs in the black shale. I have also met with a species of *chonetes,* as well as beautiful specimens of wood converted into pyrites. The fossiliferous character of the sandstone has been spoken of above. (§ 858.)

862. The lateral extent of the Black Shale has been referred to in § 323. In the Valley of East Tennessee it is often associated with the Dyestone and Siliceous groups in the Dyestone Ridges, forming, with them, the *trio* of which I have spoken, (§ 783.) It is, however, frequently wanting in these ridges, being, with the Siliceous Group, cut off by the faults. (Compare §§ 509-511.) The extreme southeasterly outcrop of the Black Shale is near Montvale Springs. (See § 801.) There is a long outcrop of it at the southeastern base of Clinch Mountain, forming Poor Valley.

863. In Hawkins county, to the southeast of the mountain mentioned, the great fault, which, in Tennessee at least, lies not far from the base of Clinch, throughout its whole length, bends in a bow considerably to the east, allowing the presence of an interesting synclinal trough, several miles wide, holding Lower Carboniferous strata. On the northeast side of this synclinal, the Black Shale comes up, and forms the outcrop in Poor Valley. On the southeast side, the formation outcrops in a curving and broken line, running not far from the western and northern base of the Devil's Nose.

864. At a point on this outcrop of the Black Shale, about six miles in a

northwesterly direction from Rogersville, a shaft was sunk, a number of years ago, for copper. The copper was not found, as might have been anticipated, but the shaft soon became filled with strong alum-water, and is now a medicinal well of considerable reputation.

865. Linear outcrops of the Black Shale skirt the Dyestone rocks in Powell's Mountain, Newman's Ridge, and in White Oak Mountain. Sneedville, as we have seen, is located upon it. (See §§ 753-774.) As to its occurrence in the Dyestone Ridges, and its manner of outcrop in East Tennessee, from beneath the Carboniferous limestones of the Table-land, including Lookout Mountain and Walden's Ridge, see §§ 756, 779, 785–791, and the diagrams on pages 139, 142, 190, 208, as well as the Map.

866. In Middle Tennessee, the Black Shale outcrops all around on the slopes of the Central Basin, and on the slopes of the high ridges within it. It is brought down lower in the hills on the west side of the Basin than it is on the other, and even sinks below the level of the Cumberland and Duck rivers, before re-appearing in the Western Valley. It forms, by its outcrop, one of the concentric rings around the central area of the Wells Creek Basin. (§§ 364, 553.) Its position in relation to other formations in Middle Tennessee, has been illustrated in a number of sections, to which reference may be made. See §§ 729, 732, 831, and the Map.

867. The diagram on next page presents a section running quite across the Central Basin, from Tullahoma, through Murfreesboro' and Nashville, to the summit of the steep grade above Baker's Station, on the Edgefield and Kentucky Railroad. (§ 732.) It illustrates both the geological and topographical features of the Basin. The section has already been referred to several times, and is especially spoken of in § 665. It exhibits clearly the position the Black Shale Group holds on each side of the Basin, as well as the relation it sustains to the other formations.

868. It may be well to add here, that the diagram illustrates what has been said in § 336, and especially in § 367, as to the elevation of the strata in Middle Tennessee in a *dome*. In § 336 the summit of the dome is stated to have been, before denudation, over the *central* part of Rutherford; it was rather over the *southern* part of this county. See, also, §§ 208 and 209.

869. *Minerals of the Black Shale, and what it may be made to*

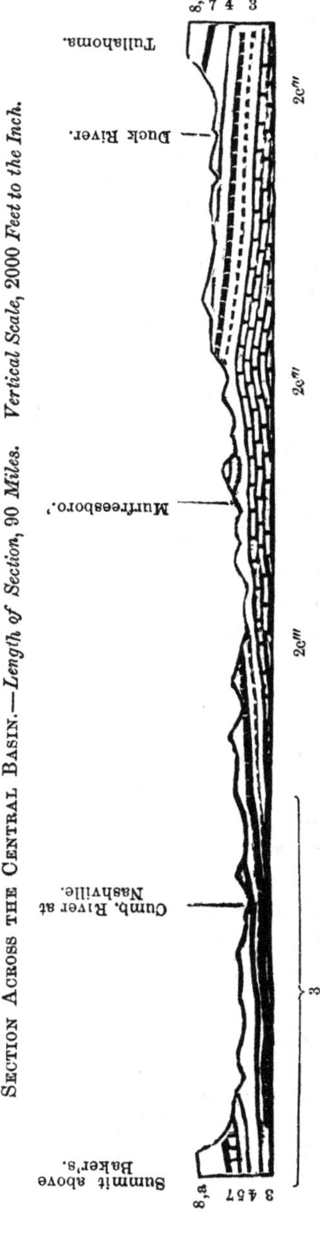

SECTION ACROSS THE CENTRAL BASIN.—*Length of Section*, 90 *Miles*. *Vertical Scale*, 2000 *Feet to the Inch.*

2c'''. *Knox Dolomite*, not seen at the surface within the Basin. 3, *Trenton*; in this the *double broken line* represents the *Glade Limestone*, the blank space above it the *Carter's Creek Limestone*, that below, the *Ridley*; the *single broken line* is the *Pierce Limestone*, and the blank space below it the *Central*, resting upon the Knoxville Dolomite. 4. *Nashville Formation* in contact above with the *Black Shale* on the right, and with the *Meniscus* (*Niagara*) on the left. 5. *Meniscus Formation* (Niagara) wanting on the right; between the Nashville and the Black Shale on the left. 7. *Black Shale Group*, the heavy black line of each end of the diagram. and lying next below 8,a. 8.a. *Siliceous Group* the cap-rock of the *Highlands* around the Basin.

yield. The principal minerals occurring in connection with the Black Shale, are as follows:

(1) *Pyrite*, (Sulphuret of Iron,) already mentioned (§ 852.)

(2) *Bitumen*, (Asphaltum.) The shale is impregnated with it, (§ 852.) Also occurs, rarely pure, in thin seams, from the eighth of an inch to an inch in thickness. The bitumen of these shales is hardly an asphaltum, being *generally*, perhaps, more like the bitumen of cannel coal.

(3) *Petroleum*, oozes from the formation at a few points in the valley of Obey's River, in Overton County.

(4) *Copperas*, in efflorescences and incrustations on the shales in sheltered places—"rock houses." Localities very numerous, and in all the counties in which the formation outcrops to any considerable extent. This mineral comes from the decomposition of the pyrite in the shale.

(5) *Alum*, both iron and potash alum; the first most abundant. This mineral occurs, like the last, in efflorescences and incrus-

tations in the "rock houses," and quite abundantly. In many of these places, are cart loads of material, made up of earth, crumbling shale, copperas and alum. The localities are, perhaps, the most numerous in Jackson, Overton, Putnam, DeKalb, Cannon, Coffee, Franklin, Lincoln and Giles counties.

870. The Black Shale might be used profitably at many points, in the vicinity of the railroads, for the manufacture of both copperas and alum. The pyrite in the rock contains both sulphur and iron, and when moist and exposed to the air, spontaneously changes into copperas. When this change takes place in contact with shale, as it generally does, both copperas and alum are formed. The shale contains alumina, one of the essential ingredients of alum, and the pyrite, for the most part, supplies the others. This produces an iron alum, but the addition of potash would convert it into common alum.* It is not proposed to give the details of the process by which the substances mentioned may be manufactured from the shale. Any one interested in this matter can find these in Ure's Dictionary of Arts, Manufactures and Mines, and in works on Chemical Technology. It is very certain that alum and copperas could be manufactured from this shale, on a large scale, in Tennessee, under very favorable conditions as to material and its accessibility.

871. Were it not for the presence of pyrite, which, in decomposing, disintegrates the shale, the formation would be a source of roofing slate, and would afford, also, smooth and very large flags; but the mineral that makes it an alum and copperas-producing rock, unfits it for these purposes. For the same reason it is worthless as a building material. Stone-fences, or walls, built of it, last but a few years. They crumble down into heaps of shaly stuff, which, when protected from the rains, is well mixed with copperas and alum. A notable instance of the worthlessness of this rock as a building material, is seen at Blount Springs, in Alabama. At that place, a number of years ago, several cottages, for the accommodation of guests, were built of it. In 1866, the writer was there, and the *slate cottages*

* Many of the "rock houses" have been frequented by Indians and hunters, some of them, perhaps, regularly inhabited. This has been the means of bringing ashes, and hence potash, into them, to which, perhaps, the formation of small quantities of common alum are due.

had crumbled into just such heaps as those mentioned, and, where sheltered, were ready for the alum maker.

872. An interesting circumstance connected with the Black Shale is, that it can be made, as stated in § 853, to yield *oils*, suitable for illuminating, lubricating, and other purposes, by distilling it in close vessels. The bituminous (or hydro-carbonaceous) matter in the shale (§ 852) is decomposed by the heat, and converted into the oils, which are distilled over and condensed in suitable vessels. The richest of the shales will produce from thirty to forty gallons of oil to the ton, but ordinarily they yield much less than this.

From this it is seen that the Black Shale is a source of supply of "coal oil," as the fluid in use is called in parts of Tennessee, to fall back upon when the petroleum wells are exhausted.

873. Below is an extract taken from the Report on the Geology of Canada, (1863, p. 784,) giving an account of the production of oil from bituminous shales in that country. The shales in Bosanquet, mentioned in the latter part of the extract, are, most likely, synchronous with those of the Tennessee Black Shale:

In 1859, works for obtaining these oils were erected on the locality of this shale, near the town of Collingwood. Twenty-four longitudinal cast-iron retorts were set in two ranges, and heated by means of wood; of which twenty-five cords are said to have been required weekly. The shale, broken into small fragments, was heated for two or three hours; from eight to ten charges being distilled in twenty-four hours. In this way, it is said, from thirty to thirty-six tons of shale were distilled daily, and made to yield 250 gallons of crude oil, corresponding to about three per cent. of the rock. By a farther continuance of the heat, a small additional proportion of oil was obtained from the shale; but it was found more economical to withdraw the charge after two hours and a half. The bed of shale available for the purpose, adjoins the works, and was furnished, ready broken, at twenty cents the ton. The cost of crude oil from the shale, was stated by the manufacturers to be fourteen cents the gallon. When rectified and deodorized, it gave from forty to fifty per cent. of burning oil, and from twenty to twenty-five per cent. of pitch and waste, the remaining being a heavy oil, fitted for lubricating purposes. After two or three unsuccessful trials, and the repeated destruction of the works by fire, they were at last, in 1860, got into successful operation, and a ready market was found for the oils. Data are, however, wanting to show whether the enterprise was remunerative; and it was after some time abandoned, partly, it is probable, on account of the competition of the petrolium of Enniskillen, which was about that time brought into market in large quantities, and at a very low price. Should it, however, at any time, be found advantageous to renew the experiment of distilling the bituminous shales of this formation, those of Collingwood offer very favorable conditions, from their accessible position, and also from the ready means of transport afforded both by the lake and the railway.

The shales of the Devonian series in Bosanquet, are not less rich in combustible materials than those of Collingwood. An experiment made on a small scale, gave 4.2 per cent. of oil, which is equal to about ten gallons to the ton of shale. The specimen was obtained from Cape Ipperwash, where a section of twelve or fourteen feet of the shale is exposed. They here contain so much organic matter, that the broken shale, which forms the shingle of the beach, is said, when set on fire, to continue burning for a considerable time. Large portions have been thus burned, and have assumed a reddish color. These shales are also seen in Warwick and Brooke.

873a. The Black Shale is the source of hundreds of "Sulphur Springs." The so-called sulphur-water is water impregnated with sulphureted hydrogen gas, one of the substances resulting from the decomposition of the pyrite (sulphide of iron) contained in the shale. The sulphur-water of White's Creek Springs, in Davidson county, of the Epperson and Red Sulphur Springs, in Macon, Winchester Springs, in Franklin, Elkmont Springs, in Giles, and of many other more or less frequented places, both in Middle and East Tennessee, flows from this formation.

The alum well, located in the Black Shale in Hawkins County, has been mentioned. (§ 864).

CHAPTER XI.

LOWER CARBONIFEROUS; FORMATION VIII.

874. We now reach, in our upward progress, a great group of strata intervening between the Black Shale, just described, and the Coal Measures. This group is mostly limestone; in addition, it contains beds of shale, a few sandstones, and, in its lower part especially, heavy layers of chert. Its maximum thickness is about 1200 feet.

875. It has been found convenient to divide this formation into two groups, as follows:

8,b. *Mountain Limestone*, the greater and upper portion, the greatest presentation of which is on the slopes of the Cumberland Table-land.

8,a. *Siliceous Group*, of which cherty limestones, calcareo-siliceous rocks, and heavy layers of solid chert, are quite characteristic; forms, often, ridges in the Eastern Valley, and plateaus (the Highlands) in Middle Tennessee.

This division is the most useful that can be made, so far, at least, as the consideration of the topographical and agricultural features of the State are concerned. Each member will be the subject of a section.

SECTION I.

THE SILICEOUS GROUP. (8,a.)

LOWER, OR PROTEAN MEMBER—UPPER, OR LITHOSTROTION BED; ST. LOUIS LIMESTONE—USEFUL ROCKS, MINERALS, AGRICULTURAL FEATURES.

876. The name "*Siliceous Stratum*," was used by Troost in his Reports, and was intended to embrace about the same rocks as are here described. The epithet, *Siliceous*, refers to the fact that the formation contains, very generally, or is in good part made up of, siliceous material in some form

or other. This material may be chert, fine sandstone, silico-calcareous rocks, or siliceous shale.

877. The Siliceous *Group* includes the two following members, the lithological characters of which, as observed in Middle Tennessee, are briefly given.

(b) *Lithostrotion, or Coral, Bed;* this, the upper part, is cherty limestone, fossiliferous, often crinoidal, sometimes siliceous and argillaceous, and everywhere characterized by a large coral, known to geologists as *Lithostrotion Canadense.* The bed is the equivalent of the *St. Louis Limestone* of the Missouri geologists, and has a maximum thickness of about 250 feet.

(a) *The Lower, or Protean Member;* a series of strata, silico-calcareous in the main; often limestone; often sky-blue, silico-calcareous, and sometimes argillaceous, rock, weathering into shale; the series containing, as a characteristic feature, especially in its middle and lower portions, heavy layers of chert, ranging in thickness from an inch to two feet, and alternating with the other rocks of the member. In addition, the series holds layers, and locally heavy beds, of crinoidal limestones.

The strata, very generally, excepting the purer limestones, are sparsely dotted with small concretions, usually siliceous. At a few points, well-formed geodes, lined inside with quartz crystals, occur of considerable size. Thickness, in general, from 250 to 300 feet, but falling, in the southern part of the State, below this.

878. (a) *Lower, or Protean Member.*—I have, above, briefly characterized the two members of the Group as they are presented west of the Cumberland Table-land.

The lithological features of the *Lithostrotion Bed* are comparatively constant. But not so with the *Lower Member.* In some sections the layers of chert in this are wanting, as at Paradico's Hill, on the Clarksville road, in the northwestern part of Davidson county, (§ 246,) where the mass is siliceous and argillaceous limestone, containing small calcareous and siliceous concretions, and running down into bluish shale.* See, also, § 732. Again, on Obey River, in Overton county, near the Kentucky line, the rock is of such a character as almost wholly

* In 1846, Dr. D. D. Owen and Dr. J. G. Norwood made the following section at this point (Researches among the Protozoic and Carboniferous Rocks of Central Kentucky, &c., p. 4.)

(4) At top; soil, siliceous beds, and nodules.................................. 77 feet.
(3) Fine siliceous rock, with segregations of impure limestone............ 29 feet.
(2) Impure argillaceous limestone, with calcareous concretions, and beds of water-limestone, passing downwards into bluish gray argillaceous shale..178 feet.
(1) Top of *Black Shale* at the foot of the hill, and at a vertical distance below the summit of...284 feet.

to weather into shale. These instances are, however, exceptional. The chert-layers are generally present, and outcrop in the upper parts, and at the tops of the hills on all sides of the Central Basin. They cap, too, the highest hills and ridges within it. As presented around the Basin, the Lower Member of the Siliceous Group is often a leached mass of chert-layers, alternating with sandy shale.

879. In the southern part of the State, at certain points, the member is cherty, crinoidal limestone, resembling the Lithostrotion Bed above. In fact, going southward, the lower member becomes thin, and below Huntsville, on the anticlinals of Alabama, the two members, in my opinion, become one bed, characterized throughout by *Lithostrotion Canadense*.*

880. It may be well to mention here, some of the local beds occurring in the *Lower Member* of the Siliceous Group in Middle Tennessee.

Layers of gray *crinoidal limestone* occur at many points; sometimes these become beds from ten to fifty, or more, feet in thickness. They are either pure or impure limestone. Such beds furnish the crinoids of White's Creek, in Davidson county, and at other points.

881. In Hickman county, on Piny River, and extending northwesterly to the valleys of Sugar, Tumbling, and other creeks, in Humphreys, is a bed of current-formed, metal-ringing, bluish gray limestone, made up of grains of comminuted shells. It occupies a position on, or near the Black Shale, and has a maximum thickness of not less than 150 feet, though its thickness is generally much less. The bed occurs near the top of the bluff at Montgomery's Mill, and represents the Siliceous Group in the section presented at that place. (See § 821.) The entire bed is sufficiently well characterized in what is said of it in the section referred to. The bed is seen at Vernon, on Piny. It contributes not a little to the agricultural value of the Piny River Valley.

882. In the *Checkered-house* bluff on the Cumberland River, in Stewart County, mentioned in § 365, the layers of rock are separable into two groups; the upper, including gray and crinoidal limestone, with more or less chert in nodules, and from 200 to 250 feet in thickness, is the Lithostrotion Bed; the lower is a bed of calcareous rock, full of *burry* chert, a thickness of 150 feet of which is exposed in the bluff. The upper portion of the latter rock, aside from the abundance of the burs, is something like the metal-ringing limestone mentioned in the last paragraph. The thickness of this rock is, perhaps, considerably more than 150 feet. It occurs at a number of points in Stewart County, and lies not very far above the Black Shale.

* A little below Gadsden, in Alabama, I have seen a number of specimens of this coral in an outcrop of the Siliceous chert, very near the Black Shale.

883. In the counties of Wayne, Lewis, Hickman, Humphreys, and in the western parts of Williamson and Maury, the base of the Siliceous Group often presents itself as a pale blue, fetid, calcareo-siliceous shale, alternating in layers, more or less, with chert. At some points the chert layers are numerous, making half, or more than half, the mass; then, again, they are wanting through considerable vertical distances, so as to leave beds of shale, without chert, from ten to fifty feet in thickness. At a few points beds of this shale occur from 60 to 100 feet in thickness, as at Col. Cooper's, on Swan Creek, in Lewis County, where it is nearly or quite 100 feet, and without chert. The shale is seen in Green River, at Waynesboro', measuring, a little below the town, 40 feet. It is also shown in the section at White's Mill, on Buffalo. (§ 859.) It occurs, however, at numerous localities. The shale at Paradice's Hill, (§ 878, note,) may be referred to it. I have said that it is fetid; it has often, however, an agreeable and remarkable aromatic odor.

This shale is mainly interesting from the fact that it contains a fauna which has not been much studied, and in which species of *Trilobites*, *Conularia*, *Atrypa*, *Discina*, *Lingula*, *Chonetes*, *Leda*, *Pleurotomaria*, and of other genera, occur.

884. In much of the region between the Central Basin and the Western Valley, especially in Lewis, Wayne, Perry, Hickman, Dickson and Humphreys counties, the Lower Member of the Siliceous Group often presents itself, as a stratified, *leached mass* of soft, pale-yellowish, or orange-gray, porous *sandstone*, which can be easily sawn or cut with an axe. Many exposures, sometimes great bluffs, of this material, occur at intervals along the water courses, the original rock having lost its calcareous part and its sky-blue color by weathering.

It is a common circumstance, in traveling through the region mentioned, to meet with a farm-house having a neat chimney built out of square blocks of this sandstone. As a building material it will answer well for many purposes. Entire houses might be constructed out of it. After exposure it becomes harder than when first quarried. The manner of working this sandstone, and the uses made of it, recall, although a very different rock, the "*rotten limestone*" of Mississippi and Alabama.

885. The "*chalk*," of Wayne, and of other counties, may be mentioned in connection with the sandstone above. The rocks of the formation, and more especially the chert, instead of presenting their weathered masses in the form of a soft sandstone, often afford considerable beds of a harsh, pulverulent, white, stratified substance, locally called *chalk*. About three miles south of Waynesboro' is the mouth of a tributary of Green River, which is known as *Chalk Creek*, so named on account of the occurrence of the chalky substance in its bed and along its banks. The "chalk" is seen for three or four miles along this stream. On, beyond this valley, and about nine miles from Waynesboro, on Fall Branch, a tributary of Indian Creek, an exposure of 30 feet of it was observed. It also occurs in the heads of the hollows leading down into the valley of Beech Creek, and in similar positions on the waters of many other creeks.

As presented in the banks of the streams, it is an alternation of soft and harder layers, mostly white, some of it yellowish. It is mainly siliceous, and layers occur showing the transition from chert to "chalk." Occasionally a thin layer of plastic clay occurs with the others. The material frequently resembles *kaolin*, and has been mistaken for it. It occurs in great quantities, and doubtless will be put to some useful purpose. If the opportunity be presented, it will be investigated with reference to its economic relations.

886. This Lower, or Protean, Member of the Siliceous Group, is, in general, equivalent to the divisions of the Lower Carboniferous Limestone lying below the St. Louis Limestone. It is, perhaps, more especially the equivalent of the Keokuk Limestone; it contains, however, some Burlington forms. Below are some of the species occurring in this member. It was my intention to give, so far as possible, a full list of all the Lower Carboniferous species that have been met with in Tennessee, but want of time prevents it. The White's Creek Crinoids, of Troost, are from this formation, but few of them, however, are included here.*

(1) *Spirifer imbrex*, Hall. Occurs *immediately* above the Black Shale below Huggins's Mill, near Manchester, in Coffee County, associated with *Productus semireticulatus;* also in the same horizon at White's Creek Springs, and near Col. Robinson's, on the Middle Fork of Cold Water, in Lincoln County.

(2) *Spirifer subæqualis?* Hall. Sumner County, Louisville and Nashville Railroad Tunnel.

(3) *Spirifer tenuicostatus*, Hall? Same locality as the last.

(4) *Spirifer suborbicularis*, Hall. Tunnel of Louisville and Nashville Railroad; and also Col. Robinson's, in Lincoln County.

(5) *Spirifer subcuspidatus*, Hall. Hawkins County, East Tennessee.

(6) *Spirifer lineatus,* Martin. (*S. pseudolineatus*, Hall.) Many localities.

(7) *Orthis Michelini*, L'Eveille. White's Creek; Col. Robinson's, Middle Fork of Cold Water, Lincoln County.

(8) *Platyceras equilatera?* Hall. Falls of Caney Fork, below Col. Bosson's house.

(9) *Granatocrinus granulatus*, Roemer. (*G. cidariformis*, Troost.) Middle Fork of Cold Water, Lincoln County.

(10) *Agaricocrinus Americanus*, Roemer. (*A. tuberosus*, Troost.) Cannon County, near Woodbury; White's Creek Springs.

* On most of the specimens of the species enumerated, I have had the benefit of the opinions of Prof. James Hall, A. H. Worthen, and Prof. A. Winchell, and to these savans I express my obligations.

(11) *Actinocrinus conicus*, Cassedy and Lyon. (*conocrinus tuberculosus*, Troost.) White's Creek Springs; Cannon County associated with the last.

(12) *Actinocrinus Nashvillæ*, Troost. White's Creek; Ridge in Sumner County.

(13) *Actinocrinus* (*Batocrinus*) *magnificus*, Cassedy and Lyon. White's Creek.

(14) *Actinocrinus* (*Dorycrinus*) *Gouldi*, Hall. Ridge Sumner County.

(15) *Cyathocrinus stellatus*, Hall. White's Creek Springs.

(16) *Forbesiocrinus Meeki*, Hall. Same locality as the last.

(17) *Forbesiocrinus Saffordi*, Hall. Near White's Creek Springs, in Davidson County.

(18) *Icthiocrinis tiaræformis*, Troost. White's Creek Springs.

887. Most of the above species, occurring out of Tennessee, are Keokuk forms. *Spirifer imbrex* and *Orthis Michelini* are found in the Burlington Limestone. *Spirifer subæqualis*, and *S. tenuicostatus* are Warsaw forms, and the latter also Keokuk. (See table at the end of this chapter.)

888. (b) *Upper Lithostrotion Bed; St. Louis Limestone.*—Some of the general features of this member of the Siliceous Group, as it is presented in Middle Tennessee, have been given in § 877. The *chert* of these rocks is quite characteristic as well as the large corals.

It occurs, for the most part, in nodular or lenticular, though often rough, masses, and not in extensive layers, like the chert or flint of the lower siliceous. Moreover, it is usually highly fossiliferous, abounding in lace-like *bryozoa*. Whenever the rocks of the Lithostrotion Bed are present, the surface is strewed, more or less, with loose, half-decomposed masses of chert, from which fossils may be obtained. The soil overlying it is generally red, made so by oxide of iron liberated in the decomposition of the cherty masses. And here, I am inclined to think, we have a clue to the source of the iron accumulated in the ore-banks of our western iron-region.

889. There is no considerable area in Middle Tennessee, presenting the lower rocks of the Siliceous Group, in which, upon the highest points, as upon the ridges, traces, at least, of the Lithostrotion Bed are not to be found. It is a very common circumstance, in traveling on the Highlands, to meet with the large coral (always silicified) and the chert characterizing the

formation. Even in the areas where all the limestone has been leached away, some of these are often left to tell of its former presence.

(Fig. 1.) (Fig. 2.)

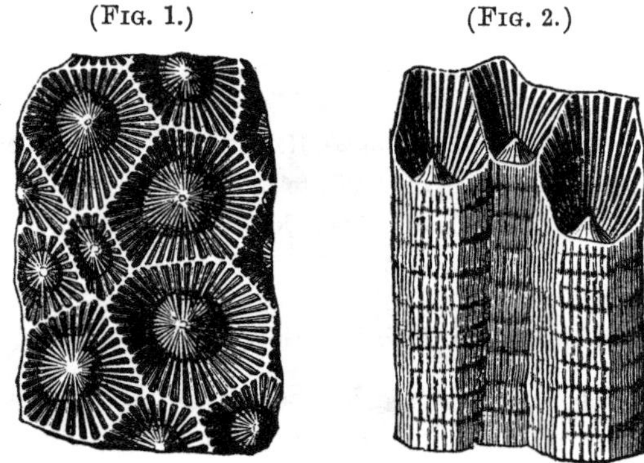

Lithostrotion Canadense.

The above cuts are representations of the large coral to which reference is so frequently made in this section. Fig. 1 is a view from above, showing the cup-like ends of the prisms; fig. 2 is a lateral view.

(Taken from Dana's Manual.)

890. This bed may be regarded as covering an area nearly co-extensive with that of the Highlands of Middle Tennessee (page 81,) although, at many points, but a few of its lowest layers are present. At some, all is gone, as I have stated, but remnants of its cherty parts. Where absent, or nearly so, the Lower Siliceous being at the surface, the country is generally poor, and such regions constitute the "barrens." (See § 216.) Where, however, the Lithostrotion Bed is present, in some volume, the soil is red and the lands are generally rich. In the areas spoken of in § 217, it is this formation which gives the lands their character.

891. An interesting topographical feature, more nearly connected with this formation than any other, is presented in the "sink-holes" which everywhere occur within the areas underlaid by it. See § 218.

892. The following places are located upon the Lithostrotion Bed: Springfield, Clarksville, Charlotte, Dover, Lawrenceburg, Winchester, McMinnville, Sparta, Smithville, Cookville and Livingston. Waverly, Centreville, Linden and Waynesboro' are upon strata of the Lower Member of the Siliceous Group; while Newberg and Manchester occupy an inter-

mediate position. Camden, in Benton, is located on the siliceous group, on the line of its western abrupt termination.

893. The most marked area underlaid by these rocks, is the belt spoken of in § 217, lying along the western base of the Cumberland Table-land. The rocks of the bed generally outcrop, in considerable volume at the base of the Table land on its west side, extending more or less upward on its slopes. Another marked area is found in the counties of Robertson, Montgomery and Stewart, north of the Cumberland River. The fertile red lands of this area give us our most important tobacco region. In it may be included the plains of Southern Kentucky, much of which are based on the same formation.

894. It may be well to introduce here a section of the rocks at Clarksville, in further illustration of the character of the Lithostrotion Bed. The section was taken near the mouth of Red River, at a time, however, when the Cumberland was tolerably high, and covered the lowest layers. (Compare § 882.)

(7) *Rocks at the top* of the hills covered with soil; loose, fossiliferous, cherty masses, with occasionally a specimen of *L. Canadense* strewed over the surface.................. 30 feet.

(6) *Bluish limestone*, siliceous, moderately cherty, contains small concretionary cavities........................... 15 feet.

(5) *Limestone*, not cherty, contains a small *Granatocrinus*...... 20 feet.

(4) *Limestone*, mostly like No. 6; contains *L. Canadense*....... 32 feet.

(3) *Limestone*, like that above, with plates and spines of species of *Archæocidaris* abundant, fragments and plates of *Melonites multipora*, in its lower part *Pentremites obliquatus?* etc.. 48 feet.

(2) *Limestone*, light-bluish, massive, crinoidal, semi-oolitic, without chert; some of the layers abound in plates of *Melonites;* thirty feet measured down to the high water at the time, say... 40 feet.

(1) Below the last, as seen at other times, the limestone is thin-bedded and cherty, containing, occasionally, crinoidal layers; seen in the bed of the river about Clarksville, say.. 30 feet.

895. The beds above are all fossiliferous. Among the species occurring are *Spirifer lineatus, S tenuicostatus, S. subcardiiformis, Hemipronites crenistria, Pentremites conoideus*, the small, undescribed *Zaphrentis*, mentioned in the list below, plates of species of *Melonites*, more or less, in all the beds, etc.

896. The following are a few of the species occurring in the Lithostrotion, or St. Louis, Limestone of Tennessee. It is my purpose to give a more complete list on some future occasion. The fossils are generally silicified.

(1) *Lithostrotion Canadense*, Castelnau. Found at nearly all points with the rocks of the formation.

(2) *Lithostrotion proliferum*, Hall. Clarksville and Cowan; not as common as the last.

(3) *Zaphrentis spinulifera*, Hall. Many localities.

(4) *Zaphrentis*, undes? a small species, from a half to three-fourths of an inch in length, having short spines on its surface, occurs abundantly at Clarksville, Charlotte, Estill Springs, and also, as Mr. Worthen informs me, at Spurgen Hill, Indiana.

(5) *Pentremites conoideus*, Hall. Clarksville, Iron Mountain Furnace, Charlotte, Cowan, &c.

(6) *Pentremites obliquatus?* Roemer. (See plate I, Fig. 2 a, b, c, d.) Its horizon is given in the Clarksville section above.

(7) *Dicchorinus simplex*, Shumard. Charlotte, and at other points. Dr. Troost's specimens of "*Doliolocrinus ovalis*," the same as this, were not found at Sparta, Tenn., but came from a point a few miles north of Scottsville, in Kentucky. Sparta, however, might be a locality.

(8) *Melonites multipora*, Owen. Clarksville, Charlotte; and other points.

(9) *Melonites Stewartii*, Safford. Differs from *M. Multipora* in having fewer rows of plates in the interambulacral spaces; the latter also rise in more rounded ridges. Other points of difference are also presented. See plate I, Fig. 1, a, b, c, d. The precise locality of this fossil is not known to me; it is, however, from Middle Tennessee, and I have reason to think, from the Lithostrotion Bed. I take pleasure in dedicating this species to my distinguished friend, Prof. Wm. M. Stewart, of Clarksville.

(10) *Spirifer tenuicostatus*, Hall. Clarksville, Tunnel of the L. and N. Railroad, in Sumner county, Charlotte, Cowan, etc.

(11) *Spirifer subcardiiformis*, Hall. Clarksville.

(12) *Spirifer Keokuk*, Hall? Cowan, and other points; may be a new species.

(13) *Spirifer Leidyi*, Norwood and Pratten. Clarksville, Charlotte, Cowan, Sparta, &c.

(14) *Spirifer spinosus*, Norwood and Pratten. Same localities as last.

(15) *Spirifer lineatus*, Martin. At many points.

(16) *Hemipronites* (*Streptorhyncus*) *crenistria*. At many localities.

(17) *Retzia vera*, Hall. Sparta, Cowan, &c.

(18) *Rhynchonella mutata*, Hall. Sparta.

(19) *Productus pileiformis*, McChesney. Clarksville and Cowan.

(20) *Productus punctatus*, Martin. Clarksville, Charlotte, etc.

(21) *Conularia Missouriensis*, Swallow. Sparta, and vicinity of Clarksville. A fine specimen of this was presented to me by Prof. W. M. Stewart.

897. Many of the above species are characteristic forms of the St. Louis Limestone; others, in the Northwestern States, are found in horizons either above or below this.

898. *Consideration of Siliceous Group in General Resumed.*—As yet, I have, for the most part, considered this Group with reference to its two members in Middle Tennessee. It will now be taken as a whole. So far as its presentation in East Tennessee is concerned, no division is practicable.

899. The group is one of great extent in Middle Tennessee. A greater or less thickness of its strata constitutes, at all points, the cap-rock of the natural division of the State, described in the First Part of this Report as the *Highlands* or *Highland Rim* of Middle Tennessee. (See pages 81–96.) The area of the Siliceous Group is the same as that of the Highlands, and both have the same limits. To the siliceous material of the former is to be attributed the present existence of the latter, as a plateau, or collection of plateaus. This material makes the strata of the Group weather-resisting, and hence, when they are horizontal, or approximately so, plateau-making. The Group is, in fact, a hard crust, which, although elevated, has had power to resist, to a considerable extent, denuding agencies.

900. The *Central Basin* is a large oval area in which this *crust* has been broken through, undermined, and removed. (§§ 208, 209 and 867.) Beneath the crust the strata are comparatively soft, yield to the action of water, and, where uncovered, wash away. In this way not only has the Central Basin been formed, with its ramifications, like those of the

Caney Fork and Duck River, (§§ 234, 235,) but also the Western Valley and its branches. (§250–256.) See, also, the Map.

901. The mutual relations of the Lower and Lithostrotion beds, as to the proportional parts of the Highlands they underlie, have been referred to in §§ 889 and 890. Among the areas underlaid by Lithostrotion rocks, certain special ones are mentioned in § 893.

902. In the *Valley of East Tennessee*, the Siliceous Group, outside of its topographical relations, has very little interest attached to it. It does not present itself here as the cap-rock of a plateau, for the reason that its strata, like those of the other formations, are very generally tilted, or inclined at a considerable angle to the horizon. It is here, like certain other groups, *ridge-making*, and for reasons that have been given. (See remarks under the Iron Limestone, § 628.)

903. In this part of the State it is often associated with the two underlying formations of the Black Shale and the Dyestone Group, in the *Dyestone Ridges*, the three making the *trio* mentioned on a previous page. (See § 783, and also, § 862.)

The formation occurs at nearly all of the presentations of the Black Shale, with which it is in contact, either on one side or the other. It is seen in the ridge immediately west of Montvale Springs, at which point it is mostly sandstone. (§ 801 and *a*, in diagram, p. 190.) It occurs along the eastern base of Clinch Mountain, and generally forms a ridge, the Black Shale lying between it and the mountain. In Hawkins it outcrops on both sides of the synclinal spoken of in § 863, the outcrop on the Clinch Mountain side forming *Pine Mountain;* further south, and about opposite Rice's, both outcrops contribute to form *Stone Mountain.* (§ 758(2).)

904. In Hancock County are two principal outcropping lines of it. These are crossed by the section in § 753; one lies in the ridge starting up northeast of Sneedville; the other is on the northwest side of Newman's Ridge. (See, also, diagram on page 208.) The Siliceous Group is also seen in the Cumberland Gap section, in § 756, as well as in the diagram just referred to. It occurs in most of the Dyestone Ridges as already stated. (See §§ 358, 782 to 801, also diagrams pages 139 and 142.)

As to the difference between the chert of the Siliceous Group and that of the Knox Dolomite, see § 537.

905. *Rocks of Special Use, Minerals, and Agricultural Features of the Siliceous Group.*—In paragraph 884 I have spoken of the *soft sandstone* resulting from the leaching of certain rocks in that Group. Considering the wide extent of country in which this is found, the ease with which it is worked, and the uses to which it may be applied, this sandstone becomes a matter of considerable interest. It may be added that, occasionally, a layer of it occurs fine enough to be used as a *polishing powder*, like tripoli; much of it might be used for scouring purposes, in the place of Bristol brick.

The siliceous, chalky material, of Wayne, has been mentioned in § 885.

906. Much of the Group is too rough and cherty to be used for building purposes, nevertheless it contains, especially in its upper portion, many layers of limestone of compact structure, without chert, and well-bedded for quarrying. Some such layers, exposed along the Cumberland River, are oolitic, of a light gray color, and are a desirable building stone.

907. Near the heads of several of the small valleys in Stewart County, are deposits of fire clay, of considerable interest. One of these, situated on the Cumberland Iron Works property, and near the "Morgan Bank," has furnished material for fire-brick for many years. The bed is in a flat bottom, near the head of a small valley. It is grayish-white, lies in a compact stratum beneath a superficial layer of gravel from three to five feet thick. It is well exposed in two or three pits, some of which have been sunk in the clay five or six feet without reaching the bottom. The bed is quite extensive doubtless, and may underlie several acres. The clay has been in use at the furnaces, and was used at the old rolling mill for many years. Mixed with fine gravel, it makes an excellent fire-brick. It has been in demand at other points. Much of it has been shipped down the river to Hillman's Works, in Kentucky.

908. A bed of clay situated like this, and similar to it, though not as extensive, was seen about four miles southwest of Cumberland City, in Stewart County. Highly esteemed fire-brick have been made from this, also, and used in the furnaces.

909. These beds are located in valleys of the Siliceous Group. The material in them comes from the decomposition of silico-argillaceous layers,

and has been brought to these places by water, and deposited. Doubtless, other beds, in addition to those known, may be found at spots where the conditions are similar.

910. It is upon this formation that most of the *Iron Ore banks* of the Western Iron Region of Tennessee rests. The *ore* itself is, doubtless, of a much more recent age than the underlying rocks, and perhaps is synchronous with the bed of *water-worn* gravel, which appears almost everywhere on the ridges within the ore region.

911. The *matrix* of the ore in the banks is made up, in good part, of the *ruins* of the Siliceous Group, angular, half-decomposed chert and clay; to these, is sometimes added, near the top of the banks, water-worn gravel. This mass, generally located on the top of a ridge, is often a hundred feet deep. The ore appears to have been introduced into it by water, or, at least, to have been precipitated within it from water.

912. I have been much inclined to think that the principal and original source of the ore has been the ferruginous chert of the Lithostrotion Bed. (§ 888.) It has iron enough to color the soil characteristically red. The banks are centres, at which, through the agency of chalybeate waters, drawing their iron from the decomposing chert, the ore has accumulated. The consideration of these ore-banks, however, properly goes with the description of the gravel-bed mentioned.

913. The only successful borings made in Tennessee for *petroleum*, as yet, are in this formation, and these are in a region of limited area on Spring Creek, in the southern part of Overton County.

Three borings within 150 yards of each other, obtained oil at a very moderate depth—from 22 to 52 feet. The supply was not lasting, however, and the borings were made deeper. The *Newman Well* has been the most productive, and has yielded many barrels of oil. What its condition is now, I know not. In this region the Black Shale is about 200 feet below the surface. The Siliceous Group above it is made up of alternating layers of limestone and chert. The body of oil appears to have been in the latter formation, but its source may have been deeper.

914. On the West Fork of Obey, a short distance north of the crossing of the Livingston and Jamestown road, is a group

of *oil springs* in this formation which are quite promising. The oil comes to the surface near the water's edge. No boring has been made at this point. Other springs occur on this stream.

Some petroleum has also been found on Jones Creek, in Dickson County.

915. *Quartz geodes* of some size and interest, are found in the rocks of this formation at several localities. Among these, may be mentioned a point on the ridge east of Chestnut Mound, and near the Putnam and Smith County line; another a few miles east of Woodbury, on the McMinnville road. At both localities interesting specimens may be found lined inside with crystals of quartz. At that near Woodbury, the geodes afford sometimes rhombohedral crystals with mere traces of modifying planes. (—1.)

916. At Alisonia, in Franklin County, fine specimens of native sulphur have been obtained in these rocks. In some specimens, the sulphur is in beautiful crystals. Native sulphur is frequently met with in the lower part of the formation, and sometimes fills small siliceous geodes.

917. The agricultural features of the Siliceous Group have been referred to several times, and need not be dwelt upon now. What is said in §§ 216 and 217, in reference to the agricultural features of the Highlands, applies, of course, here. See, also, §§ 890 and 893.

Section II.

THE MOUNTAIN LIMESTONE. (8,b.)

918. This is a heavy body of limestone, constituting, for the most part, the base of the Cumberland Table-land. Its strata outcrop on the slopes of this great plateau, from beneath the overlying sandstones and conglomerates, on all sides, (§ 175.) Its boldest and most important presentation is on the western slope. It generally appears on the eastern side, but its outcrop, owing to the disturbed condition of the rocks in this part of the State, (§ 344,) is not uniform, either as to height above the valleys, or as to the

manner or position in which the strata are presented at the surface. At a few points on this side the formation does not appear at all, being ingulfed by local faults, and the strata of the Coal Measures being in the valleys. Such is the case in the region of the Saltworks, in Anderson County, and at a point below Kimbrough's, in Roane County. The outcrops of this limestone, not connected with the Table-land, will be noticed below.

919. The *Mountain Limestone* is a heavy group of limestones and shales, the latter constituting, in the aggregate, about one-fourth of the mass. In addition to these, the strata include a a *sandstone*, which, in the more northern counties, is from 40 to 50 feet thick. The group has its maximum thickness in the southern part of the State, where it is about 720 feet. Going northward, its volume becomes less, until, near the Kentucky line, it is reduced to 400 feet.

920. Several sections will be given below, in which are presented the strata of the Mountain Limestone. Two of these present not only this formation, but the entire *Lower Carboniferous Series*, from the Black Shale to the Coal Measures.

In these sections the lithological features of the Mountain Limestone are given in detail. The beds may be grouped and characterized, in general, as follows:

(f.) At top, next below Coal Measures, very generally a stratum of *crinoidal limestone*, sometimes with more or less shale above, and from 4 to 70 feet in thickness. (§ 960.)

(e.) *Variegated Shales and Marl*, with occasionally a layer of limestone, from 50 to 130 feet.

(d.) *Argillaceous Limestone*, usually interstratified with more or less shale, which is sometimes variegated; the limestone is a light bluish-gray, fine-grained rock, ("lithographic limestone," or a mud-stone,) breaking with conchoidal fracture, and crumbling under the weather. It occasionally includes layers of blue fossiliferous and other limestones, (as No. 6, of the Spring Creek Section, and Nos. 17 and 18, of the Sewanee Section.) From 60 to 150 feet thick.

(c.) *Blue Fossiliferous Limestones* mainly, some beds oolitic, some argillaceous, with occasionally a layer of shale, from 90 to 170 feet.

(b.) *Sandstone*, fine-grained, often flaggy, caps, and gives character to the benches and plateaus mentioned in §§ 192 and 193. In White and Overton Counties, it is from 40 to 50 feet thick; in the Sewanee Section it is poorly represented by about 8 feet of sandstone, more or less calcareous. This sandstone has not been observed on the eastern side of the Table-land. In Alabama, south of the Tennessee River in the anticlinal valleys, it becomes a heavy formation.

(a.) *Limestones*, with a few beds of shale; fossiliferous; beds often oolitic; occasionally argillaceous; from 160 to 270 feet.

The sections below give, not only lithological details, but also, to a limited extent, paleontological features.

921. (1.) The first presents the entire thickness of the *Lower Carboniferous Limestone*, near the head of Spring Creek, in Overton and Putnam Counties. It embraces all the strata, from the Black Shale to the Coal Measures. It is a combination of two sections; the lower one begins below with the Nashville Formation, in the boring of the "*Jackson Oil Well*," which is located about three-fourths of a mile from the *Newman Well*, (§ 913,) at the foot of the "first bench" of the Table-land, (§ 192,) on Spring Creek, (or rather, near this creek, on its tributary, Hurricane,) and ascends to the sandstone at the top of the bench; the second, or upper one, commences with this sandstone, at Esq. Cooper's, between three and four miles south of the locality of the first, and ascends with the Walton Road to the top of the mountain. The strata of the Coal Series were not measured.

	Stratum	Thickness
COAL MEASURES.	(3) *Sandstone*, on a high point south of the road. Thickness?	
	(2) *Shales*, a heavy bed, with clay iron-stones. This, with the sandstones, was estimated to be	130 feet.
	(1) *Sandstone*, upper part thin-bedded or shaly,	120 feet.
	In all	250 feet?
MOUNTAIN LIMESTONE.	(10) *Blue Limestone*,	4 feet.
	(9) *Variegated Shale*, brown, gray and green,	12 feet.
	(8) *Shale and Marl*, mostly gray, with some brown and green at top; at intervals some thin layers harder than others,	40 feet.
	(7) *Argillaceous Limestone*, dull bluish gray, breaking with conchoidal fracture; has cavities containing *dolomite*,	27 feet.
	(6) *Blue Limestone*, fossiliferous,	22 feet.
	(5) *Argillaceous Limestone*, resembling 7, above, but more compact, and somewhat fossiliferous,	20 feet.
	(4) Blue Limestones,	85 feet.
	(3) Shales,	6 feet.
	(2) SANDSTONE, fine-grained, more or less flaggy,	48 feet.
	(1) Blue Limestone, fossiliferous,	168 feet.
	Entire thickness,	432 feet.

LITHOSTROTION BED. *Upper Siliceous.*

(2) *Cherty Limestone,* limestone not seen; chert abundant on the surface,......128 feet.

(1) *Limestone,* impure, of water-lime aspect, lower part containing sparry blue layers; contains *Lithostrotion Canadense,*...... 75 feet.

In all,......203 feet.

PROTEAN BED. *Lower Siliceous.*

Sandstone, fine-grained, seen at a number of points in Overton and Putnam,...... 8 feet.

Limestone, blue, fetid, rather coarse, fossiliferous and crinoidal, seen,...... 45 feet.

Rocks penetrated by the boring of the Jackson Well: many layers chert,......216 feet.

In all,......269 feet.

BLACK SHALE, resting on the Nashville Formation,...... 28 feet.

922. The two following sections combined, give the series of Lower Carboniferous strata, as found in White County, complete, from the Black Shale to the Coal Measures. The first and uppermost is a section of the slope of the mountain, or Table-land, taken at a point from four to five miles east of Sparta, and running up to Bon Air. It includes the *sandstone* of the *Mountain Limestone* division.

The latter, or second section, was taken in the vicinity of the Falls of Caney Fork, and extends from an outcrop of the Black Shale, in the river below the Falls, upward, to the sandstone capping Hickory-nut Mountain, and the same, geologically, as that mentioned above. The diagram below illustrates how the two sections are related:

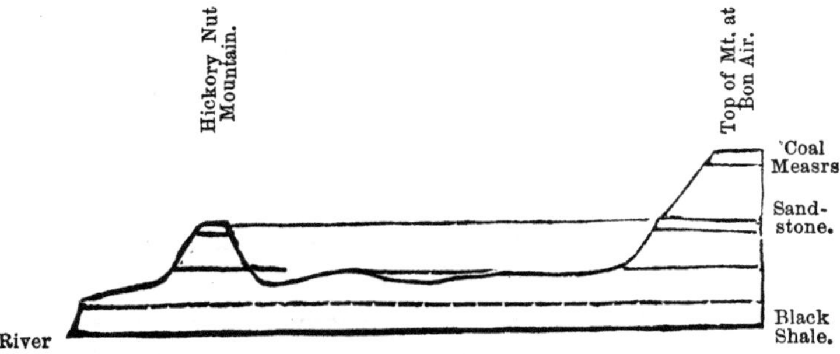

The heavy line at the bottom is the *Black Shale*; the *Coal Measures* cap the Mountain, or Table-land, at Bon Air; the *sandstone* uniting the sections, occupies, on the right, an intermediate position, and is seen to cap Hickory-nut Mountain on the left. The space between the Black Shale and the Coal Measures is all Siliceous Group and Mountain Limestone.

923. This will be designated as the *Bon Air Section.*

COAL MEASURES.

(2) *Conglomerate*, capping the mountain at Bon Air...... 90 feet.

(1) *Shales*, with three or four thin seams of *Coal*,.........102 feet.

In all,...192 feet.

MOUNTAIN LIMESTONE. FORM, 8,b.

(8) *Limestone*, bluish, crinoidal, contains *Archimides Swallovana*, some layers oolitic,......................... 40 feet.

(7) *Variegated Shales and Marls*, green, brown and gray; thin, harder layers at intervals; about the middle of the mass is a layer of shale full of *Athyris ambigua*, and also containing *spirifer bisulcatus*........100 feet.

(6) *Shale or Marl*, with two or three beds of impure fossiliferous limestone and some cherty layers at top, 15 feet.

(5) *Limestone*, hard, blue, fossiliferous, weathering brown; contains cavities holding *barite*,............ 7 feet.

(4) *Shale and Limestone* in alternating layers; upper part mostly shale, lower part mostly limestone; shales variegated, mostly greenish, some brown; limestone, bluish gray, fine-grained, argillaceous, breaking with conchoidal fracture, non-fossiliferous; at the base a cherty layer,......................... 63 feet.

(3) *Limestone*, blue, fossiliferous, with occasionally a thin layer of shale; much of it oolitic; contains *Pentremites Godonii* and *P. pyriformis*, *Agassizocrinus*, &c.; has an argillaceous local layer in its middle part, about five feet thick, with a band of breccia marble above; at base, shale five or six feet,......123 feet.

(2) SANDSTONE, fine-grained, and at some points flaggy, forms a bench around the mountain. (See note under § 192,)... 40 feet.

(1) *Limestone*, in alternating, oolitic, sparry, crinoidal, and fine-grained, argillaceous layers; two or three thin layers cherty; contains the same *Pentremites* as above, also *Agassizocrinus dactyliformis*, *Aspidodus crenulatus*, *Zaphrentis spinulifera*, etc.; lower fifty feet of rock not seen,.......................................213 feet.

In all,...601 feet.

LITHOSTROTION BED, or *St. Louis Limestone*, (*Upper Siliceous*,) at the base of the mountain; rocks mostly concealed, but surface covered with decomposing, fossiliferous, cherty masses, and among them specimens of *Lithostrotion Canadense;* thickness from the lowest point accessible, ...100 feet.

924. Below is the section in the region of the Falls of Caney Fork. We may call it the *Hickory-nut Mountain Section.*

MT. LIMESTONE.

(2) SANDSTONE, at top of Hickory-nut Mountain; same as 2 (*Mountain Limestone*) of last section,.......... 40 feet.

(1) *Limestone.* (See Bon Air Section above.)..................215 feet.

In all.. 255 feet.

LITHOSTROTION BED, or *St. Louis Limestone,* (*Upper Siliceous;*) cherty limestone, containing *Lithostrotion Canadense;* chert, for the most part, in nodular masses, and much of it highly fossiliferous,...................................... 244 feet.

PROTEAN BED. (*Lower Siliceous.*)

(5) *Limestone* at the general level of the country above the valley of Caney Fork, more or less cherty,... 100 feet.

(4) *Limestone,* bluish, crinoidal, without chert,............. 30 feet.

(3) *Rock* weathering into shale,................................ 20 feet.

(2) *Limestone and Chert;* crinoidal limestone interstratified with heavy, rough layers of chert,............... 68 feet.

(1) *Limestone and Chert;* near the base mostly layers of chert, separated by thin seams of crinoidal limestone, above siliceous limestone, with more or less chert, and abounding in large crinoidal stems,..... 57 feet.

BLACK SHALE, seen at top 15 feet, below not seen; in all down to the river,.. 36 feet.

925. The following is a section of the Lower Carboniferous Limestone in Franklin County, as presented along the Chattanooga and Sewanee Railroad, from Cowan to the *brow* of the mountain. We will call it the *Sewanee Section.* (See page 74, (7.))

COAL MEASURES.

(4) *Sandstone,* forms a bluff along the mountain at this point,.. 52 feet.

(3) *Shale* with a thin seam of coal,.............................. 14 feet.

(2) *Sandstone,* rather thin-bedded, at the base a ferruginous, shaly layer, containing fossil *nuts, calamites,* etc.,..25 to 30 feet.

(1) *Local bed* of sandy, ferruginous shale, and a hard, sandy, heavy ferruginous rock, below this bluish and brownish shale,.. 12 feet.

In all,.. 108 feet.

MOUNTAIN LIMESTONE.

(21) *Limestone and Shale;* rocks not well exposed; three feet of crinoidal limestone seen at the top; below this, variegated, brown and red shales, doubtless, with some limestone,.. 85 feet.

(20) *Limestone,* blue and light-blue, the latter oolitic..... 32 feet.

(19) *Shale and Limestone* in alternating beds; shale greenish, bluish-gray, and brownish, and most abundant; limestone fine-grained, argillaceous, gives conchoidal fracture, breaks into angular pieces on exposure. This division is much like 4, (*Mountain Limestone,*) of the Bon Air Section. The old Bowers' road crosses the railroad track on this,.. 70 feet.

(18) *Limestone,* rough, hard, rather thin-bedded, dark-gray, with sometimes a brownish tinge; has cavities lined with chalcedonic quartz, and some filled with gypsum; includes a few layers of shale,...... 25 feet.

(17) *Limestone,* blue, fossiliferous, some of it oolitic; *Pentremites pyriformis, Spirifer bisulcatus,* etc.,......... 21 feet.

(16) *Limestone and Shale,* like 19, above; the most of it thick-bedded limestone; decomposes easily, like that referred to above, both forming glady places along the sides of the mountain,........................ 35 feet.

(15) *Limestone,* heavy-bedded; lower part abounds in cavities, some filled with gypsum,...................... 55 feet.

(14) *Limestone,* dove-colored, argillaceous, weathers in rough layers, contains cavities lined with crystals; eight feet of the middle part rather even-bedded, with a line of small chert nodules in one layer... 28 feet.

(13) *Limestone,* mostly oolitic, heavy-bedded and light-bluish, fossiliferous; near the base *Archimedes Pentremites,* etc.,.. 50 feet.

(12) *Shales and Limestone* alternating; above argillaceous limestone, weathering to shale, containing cavities lined with crystals of *quartz* and of *calcite* (8 feet;) below this blue, compact, fossiliferous limestone; (6 feet;) then a limestone weathering to a dirty drab, (4 feet;) argillaceous dove-colored limestone, (3 feet ;) blue fossiliferous limestone, (3 feet,).. 26 feet.

(11) *Shale,* greenish and bluish,.................................. 12 feet.

(10) SANDSTONE, fine-grained, micaceous and calcareous, 8 feet.

(9) *Shale;* contains a few layers of limestone, one in its middle part three feet thick and oolitic; fossiliferous,.. 31 feet.

MOUNTAIN LIMESTONE.—*Continued.*

(8) *Limestone*, (13 E,) thick-bedded, lower part dark-blue and sparry; upper, light bluish-gray and oolitic; at top, a foot or two of thin limestones and shales abounding in *Archimedes;* the whole mass very fossiliferous; (see list of species,)........................ 13 feet.

(7) *Greenish Shale*, with a bed of limestone three feet thick four feet from the bottom; mass fossiliferous, contains *Astraea* (*Palastræa*) *carbonaria?*........ 27 feet.

(6) *Limestone*, mostly dove-colored, some layers compact without fossils, others sparry, with them; at top is a layer of bluish-gray oolitic limestone, five feet thick, which forms the ceiling of the Nashville and Chattanooga Railroad Tunnel at its western end; the Tunnel enters the mountain from the west in this bed.. 32 feet.

(5) *Limestone*, knotty and argillaceous, weathers into knotty lumps and shale; lower layers contain *Archimedes*,.. 9 feet.

(4) *Limestone*, mostly thick-bedded, much of it oolitic and light-colored, some crinoidal, other beds compact argillaceous; contains the common *Pentremites*... 70 feet.

(3) *Limestone*, blue, thin-bedded, with cherty seams; contains *Archimedes* and *Pentremites*,...................... 8 feet.

(2) *Limestone*, beautiful bed of gray limestone, with but a trace of blue,.. 20 feet.

(1) *Limestone*, alternating beds of gray oolitic, and dove-colored, or blue, argillaceous limestones,............ 57 feet.

Entire thickness,.. 704 feet.

LITHOSTROTION BED, or *St. Louis Limestone.*

Cherty Limestone, very fossiliferous, down to the creek at Cowan, about.. 110 feet.

926. I add here, for comparison, a section of the strata exposed in Monte Sana, near Huntsville, Alabama. It was taken by A. H. Worthen, now Director of the Geological Survey of Illinois, and first published in Prof. Hall's Report on the Geology of Iowa. (Vol. I, Part I, page 114.)

It appears here with some changes, having been revised recently by Mr. Worthen. I am requested to state that the thickness of the different strata were only estimated.

COAL MEASURES.

Ferruginous sandstone,.. 30 feet.

Slate and impure coal.. 4 feet.

Group	Strata	Thickness
CHESTER GROUP.	Light bluish-gray limestone, containing teeth of *Aspidodus crenulatus*, N. & W., *Pentremites Godonii*, and *Archimedes*,	50 feet.
	Shaly limestone, somewhat cherty, containing *Spirifer bisulcatus*, and *Terebratula ambigua*, mostly hidden under a covered slope,	100 to 120 feet.
	Compact bluish-gray limestone, semi-oolitic in part, containing *Pentremites Godonii*, *P. pyriformis*, and *Archimedes*,	250 feet.
	Ferruginous sandstone with fossil plants,	10 to 15 feet.
	Compact gray limestone, with *Pentremites* and *Archimedes* in abundance, *Zeacrinus*, two or three species, *Agassizocrinus conicus*, *Productus elegans*, *P. semireticulatus*, etc.,	200 feet.
	Decomposing cherty layers,	4 feet.
ST. LOUIS GROUP.	Gray, cherty limestones, with some highly oolitic beds, containing *Lithostrotion Canadense*, *L. proliferum*, *Spirifer striatus?* and joints of crinoidea, with *Productus ovatus?* and *P. semireticulatus*, etc.,	150 to 200 feet.
KEOKUK?	Dark bluish-gray, siliceous rock, weathering to shale in some localities, with a few fossil shells scarcely determinable,	100 feet.

927. *Paleontology of the Mountain Limestone.*—A number of the species occurring in these rocks have been given in the sections, and their horizons exhibited. The cuts below represent two of the forms; these are both common and characteristic.

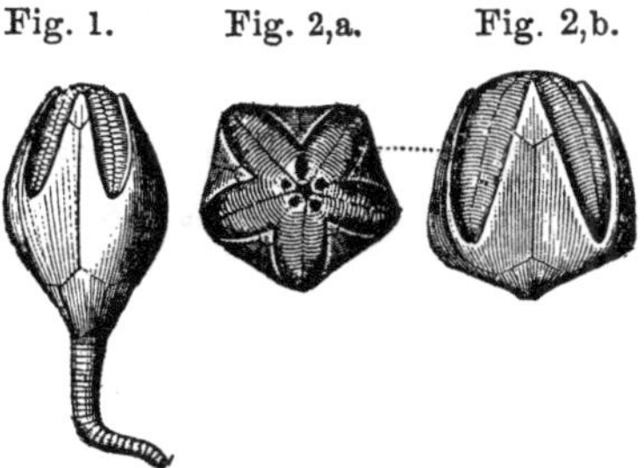

Fig. 1, *Pentremites pyriformis;* Fig. 2,*a* and 2,*b*, *Pentremites Godonii* (*florealis.*)

In the following list, a few of the species of the Mountain Limestone, including those of the sections, are presented: (§ 886.)

(1) *Astræa (Palastræa) carbonaria?* McCoy. My specimens are doubtfully referred to McCoy's species. The fossil, in fine specimens, is found in No. 7, of the Sewanee Section. (§ 925.) It also occurs at Crab Orchard, in Cumberland County, and back of Stevenson, Alabama.

(2) *Zaphrentis spinulifera*, Hall. In both (a) and (c,) § 920. Associated with the last at the localities mentioned.

(3) *Archimedes Swallovana*, Hall. Occurs at intervals, pretty well through the entire group.

(4) *Pentremites Godonii*, DeFrance. Occurs in both the upper and lower parts of the formation, like the last.

(5) *Pentremites pyriformis*, Say. Cosmopolitan, like 3 and 4.

Between one and two miles north of Cowan, in Franklin County, and on the end of a spur running out from the Table-land, is a rich locality of *pentremites*, and other fossils. The bed in which they occur is shaly, and has about the horzon of the shales in the vicinity of the Nashville and Chattanooga Railroad Tunnel.

(6) *Pentremites obesus*, Lyon. Lower part of No. 6, Sewanee Section. (§ 925.)

(7) *Dichocrinus sex-lobatus?* Shumard. Pentremital locality mentioned under No. 5.

(8) *Agassizocrinus dactyliformis*, Troost. No. 1, Bon Air Section, (§ 923;) Pentremital locality near Cowan, and other horizons and localities.

(9) *Spirifer bisulcatus*, Sowerby. (S. increbescens, Hall.) Bon Air Section, No. 7; Sewanee Section, No. 17, and at many other points.

(10) *Spirifer spinosus*, Norwood and Pratten. Top of bed No. 4, Sewanee Section, and just below Tunnel.

(11) *Spirifer Leidyi*, Norwood and Pratten. No. 5, Sewanee Section; Montvale Springs, in Blount County.

(12) *Spirifer lineatus*, Martin, (*S. pseudo-lineatus*, Hall. Nos. 5 and 8, Sewanee Section, and many other localities, including Montvale Springs.

(13) *Spirifer Keokuk*, Hall? No. 8, Sewanee Section, and No. 1, Bon Air Section. (See § 349 (12).)

(14) *Spiriferina Kelloggi*, Swallow. Nos. 5, 7 and 8, Sewanee Section.

(15) *Hemipronites (Stretorhyncus) crenistria*. No. 8, Sewanee Section, and other localities.

(16) *Athyris ambigua*, Sowerby. (*A. subquadrata*, Hall.) Nos. 3 and 7, Bon Air Section; Nos. 7 and 8, Sewanee Section.

(17) *Terebratula trinuclea*, Hall. No. 5, Sewanee Section.

(18) *Rhynchonella explanata?* McChesney. No. 5, Sewanee Section.

(19) *Athyris Royissii*, L'Eveille. (*A. sublamellosa*, Hall. Pentremital locality near Cowan, and at many other points.

(20) *Productus semireticulatus*, Martin. Cosmopolitan.

(21) *Productus Cora.* Cosmopolitan, like the last. Both of these occur below, in the Siliceous Group.

(22) *Productus pileiformis*, McChesney. Bed No. 8, Sewanee Section.

(23) *Productus longispinus.* No. 8, Sewanee Section.

(24) *Productus elegans*, Norwood and Pratten. Same locality and horizon as the last.

(25) *Productus punctatus*, Martin. No. 8, Sewanee Section, and other points.

(26) *Aspidodus crenulatus*, Newb. and Worthen. Bed 20, Sewanee Section, and, *perhaps*, upper part of No. 1, Bon Air Section.

(27) *Claydodus magnificus*, Tuomey. No. 8 of the Sewanee Section, and at a lower horizon of the same section.

928. Many of the above species are characteristic of the *Kaskaskia* (or Chester) Limestone, of the Northwestern States, and very nearly all of them occur in that formation. The *Mountain Limestone* of this State, is, therefore, its equivalent. The *Warsaw Limestone* is not distinguished here as a separate Bed. (See the *table* at the end of this chapter.)

929. In paragraph 918, the occurrence of the Mountain Limestone on the slopes of the Cumberland Table-land has been spoken of. The Table-land, as there referred to, includes its out-liers. On some of these the presentation of the strata of the formation is high and bold, as, for instance, around the end of *Lookout Mountain*, near Chattanooga, (§ 189,) and of *Ben Lomond*, near McMinnville, (page 75.) Other out-liers, on the slopes of which these rocks outcrop, are *Pilot Mountain*, in Warren, *Milk-sick Mountain*, in White, and *Pilot Knob*, and others, in Overton, as well as the *Short Mountains*, in Cannon, (§§ 190 and 191.) The "*little mountains*," spoken of in § 192, are capped with the sandstone of this formation, and have a structure like that of Hickory-nut Mountain, a section of which has been given. (See §§ 922 and 924.) Of this class is the long flat-topped and much notched ridge in Overton, which reaches

out so far from the mountain region to the northwest, between the waters of Roaring and Obey's rivers.

930. In East Tennessee there are but few outliers proper, of the Table-land. A *trace* of the synclinal, in which Lookout Mountain rests, appears to extend up as far as the Rhea County line, presenting a strip of Mountain Limestone on the east side of the Tennessee Valley, (§ 121.)

Lone Mountain, in the southern part of Rhea, is an outlier, having Carboniferous Limestone around it.

Attention may be called here, to the outcrop of this Limestone at the western base of *Pine Mountain*, on the southeast side of the Elk Fork Valley, §§ 180, 354. In the diagram on page 142, the *unnumbered space* below 9 on the right, is 8,b, or the *Mountain Limestone.*) Attention, also, is directed to the manner of its outcrop in Sequatchee and Lookout Valleys, (diagram, p. 139 and Map.) With reference to the exposure of this formation at Crab Orchard and Grassy Cove in Cumberland County, see page 138.

931. It remains to notice the belts of *Mountain Limestone* which occur, disconnected with the Table-land. There are several of these in East Tennessee, as follows:

(1) The *Montvale Belt*, in Blount County. This has been noticed in § 801. The strip runs for several miles in front of Chilhowee Mountain.

(2) The *Hawkins Belt*, held in the synclinal described in § 863. The strip of country lying immediately southeast of *Pine Mountain* is underlaid by this formation. This is a belt of considerable extent.

(3) *A narrow belt* in the ridge east of Sneedville, (§ 753.)

(4) In *Newman's Ridge*, at its crest and on its western slope, (§ 753.)

(5) A long belt, sometimes a mile wide, at the eastern base of White Oak Mountain, in the southern part of East Tennessee, (§§ 773 and 774.)

932. *Minerals, Rocks of Special Use, and Agricultural Features of the Mountain Limestone.*—A number of the layers of this formation contain geodes and cavities affording, often, beautiful crystals. The following minerals have been observed. (See sections.)

1. *Dolomite*, in cavities.
2. *Barite*, (*Heavy Spar*,) also in cavities.
3. *Quartz*, in many forms; in geodes lined with chalcedony.
4. *Gypsum*, in cavities or geodes; sometimes in balls of considerable size, as white and flesh-colored *Alabaster*.

(5) *Epsomite*, (*Epsom Salt*,) in considerable abundance in many of the caves in the limestones of the Table-land, as those on the Gulf of Caney Fork, in White County, and on the East Fork of Obey, in Overton and Fen-

tress. At many of them the salt could be prepared for market by the barrel.

(6) *Nitre*, in many caves along the slopes of the Table-land. These caves yielded, during the first part of this century, a very large amount of nitre, and at that time the most available part of the nitre-earth they contained, was worked over. The mineral most abundant in the earth is, doubtless, *nitrocalcite*.

(7) *Galenite*, (*Lead Ore*,) occasionally met with in limited quantity, in small veins.

(8) *Petroleum* occurs in this formation in the deep and narrow valley of the Big South Fork of the Cumberland River, in the old Beaty Salt Well, near the Tennessee line, in Kentucky.

933. Many of the limestones of this formation could be used with advantage for building purposes. Some of the oolitic limestones, and those, too, that are accessible by means of the Nashville and Chattanooga Railroad, are a beautiful, grayish white, and durable building material.

The *argillaceous limestone* mentioned in § 920 (d) has been used in masonry, but it is a comparatively worthless material, as the history of the abutments of the Running Water Bridge, on the N. & C. road, which are built of it, demonstrates.

934. The sandstone of the formation (§ 920 (b)) often presents itself, especially in Overton and White, as good flags. It would also supply, at many points, easily quarried and desirable building stone.

935. The Mountain Limestone, unlike the Trenton, Nashville, and several other formations, outcrops in no very extended fla or rolling areas, and therefore its agricultural value is comparatively limited. But on the slopes of the mountains it often underlies a strong, rich soil, which supports, frequently, heavy forests of the finest timber, large poplars, walnuts, white oaks, etc. Many small but rich farms are located upon it. Such places are well adapted to the raising of fruit.

With reference to the large springs issuing from the limestones of this formation, see note, page 68.

936. On the next two pages is presented a table of geological equivalents, prepared by Dr. A. Winchell, of Ann Arbor, Michigan. It is mainly confined to the subdivisions of the Lower Carboniferous Formation.

TABLE OF GEOLOGICAL EQUIVALENTS. (By A. Winchell.)

New York.	Ontario.	Michigan.	Ohio.	Indiana.	Illinois.
(Wanting?)	(Wanting.)	Parma Conglomerate.	Conglomerate.	Conglomerate.	Conglomerate.
(Wanting.)	(Wanting.)		False Coal Measures.	?	False Coal Measures.
(Wanting.)	(Wanting.)	Carboniferous Limest'e. Michigan Salt Group.	(Wanting.)	(Wanting.)	Chester Limestone.
				St. Louis Limestone.	St. Louis Limestone.
				Warsaw Limestone.	Warsaw Limestone.
				Keokuk Limestone. Gray Limestone. Brown Shale. Knobstones.	Keokuk Limestone.
					Burlington Limestone.
Catskill Group, including "Carboniferous Cong." and Chemung Cong.	(Wanting.)	Marshall Group.	Waverly Series, in part.	Rockford Limestone and Williamsport Gritstone.	Kinderhook Group.
Chemung Group. Portage Group, embracing the Cashaqua Shale.	Portage Shales.	Huron Group. embracing Micaceous Schists and Flags, Argillaceous Shale, Green Shale,	Chocolate Shale Series. (Base of Waverley Series.)	(Wanting.)	(Wanting.)
Genesee Shale.	Hamilton Shale.	Black Shale.	Black Shale.	Black Shale.	Black Shale.
Hamilton Group.	Hamilton Group.	Hamilton Group.	Hamilton Group.	Hamilton Group.	Hamilton Group.

Iowa.	Missouri.	Kentucky.	Tennessee.	Europe.
?	?	Conglomerate.	Conglomerate.	Millstone Grit.
Kaskaskia ?	?	False Coal Measures.	False Coal Measures.	?
Kaskaskia Limestone.		Kaskaskia Limestone.	Mountain Limestone.	Mountain Limestone.
St. Louis Limestone.	St. Louis Limestone.	St. Louis Limestone.	Upper Siliceous, (b.)	
Warsaw Limestone.	Warsaw Limestone.	?		
Keokuk Limestone.	Keokuk Limestone.	Keokuk Limestone. Knobstones.	Lower Siliceous, (a.)	
Burlington Limestone.	Burlington Limestone.			
Yellow Sandstone Series.	Chouteau Limestone. Vermicular Sandstone and Shale. Lithographic Limestone.	(Wanting.)	(Wanting.)	Old red Sandstone, (Scotland.) Yellow Sandstone, (Ireland.) Westphalian Schists.
Perhaps lower part of Yellow Sandstone Series.	Bluish Shales.	Argillaceous Beds.	(Wanting.)	Cypridinenschiefer.
		Black Shale.	Black Shale.	
Hamilton Group.	Hamilton Group.	Hamilton Group.	(Wanting.)	Orthoceras Schiefer. Speriferen Sandstein, (Nassau.)

CHAPTER XII.

THE COAL MEASURES; FORMATION IX.

TYPICAL TOPOGRAPHY AND STRATA.—(A) THE SEWANEE DIVISION.—(B) THE RACCOON AND WALDEN'S RIDGE DIVISION.—(C) THE NORTHERN DIVISION.—(D) THE NORTHEASTERN DIVISION; ROCKS OF SPECIAL USE, MINERALS, AND AGRICULTURAL FEATURES.

937. We come, now, to the great depository of our *Stone-coal*, the *Coal Measures*, the most important contributor of all the formations, to the mineral formations of the State. This is a series of alternating strata of sandstone, conglomerate, shale, (rarely limestone,) and coal. (§ 319.) It is the last, or uppermost, of the *older* formations occurring in Tennessee.

938. The Coal Measures occupy, topographically, a high position for the most part. They form the top of the Cumberland Table-land, and rest upon the Mountain Limestone described in the last chapter. The hard, weather-resisting conglomerates and sandstones of the formation, appear in great cliffs, around the margin of the Table-land, giving to it sharpness of outline, and protecting the limestones and shales below from denudation. (§ 175.) The *area* occupied by the Coal Measures is co-extensive with that of the Table land. (§§ 172–184.) The two go together. The latter owes its existence, in part, and its preservation as a plâteau, to the former.

939. The hard rocks of the formation, when elevated and approximately horizontal, are plateau-making. Had they been otherwise than hard, or had they been common limestones or shales, rocks that air, water and frost, can, with comparative ease, disintegrate and dissolve, the Table-land region would have been long since reduced to the general level of the valleys and plains around it.

The principles are the same as those involved in the formation of the Highlands out of the "crust" of the Siliceous Group spoken of in §§ 899 and 900, although the latter is a much less marked example of their application.

940. *Typical Topography and Strata.*—The surface of the Table-land may, in general, be described as a *great plain*, or

floor, upon which rests, at a greater or less distance from the bluff-margin overhanging the slopes, (§ 175,) an upper plateau, or on narrow sections of the Table-land, plateau-ridges, from 200 to 300 feet in height, and usually forming a prominent *back bench*.*

941. The plain or floor is underlaid by a heavy stratum, often full of small quartz pebbles, which geologists call, technically, *The Conglomerate*. This rock usually appears in the cliffs around the crested edges of the table-land. Occasionally it thins out before quite reaching the edge, the cliff being formed of some of the lower sandstones. It is, however, sufficiently near the truth, to say, that, the area of the Conglomerate is co-extensive with that of the Table-land.

It must be remarked here, that, on some parts of the Table-land there are two strata, each of which is spoken of as *The Conglomerate*. These may, however, be regarded as one; in fact, at some points, they actually become one, the intermediate layers separating them, running out. (§ 995.)

942. With this premised, the following may be taken as typical, for the most part, of the Coal Measures in Tennessee; as we shall see, however, there are important exceptions :

(c) *Upper Coal Measures*, embraces generally one or two principal sandstones, (one of which may be a conglomerate,) and as many *coal-horizons*, in which one or more beds of coal may be looked for.

These strata make up the upper plateau, or back bench, spoken of above, and have, consequently, a thickness of from 200 to 300 feet.

To the *Northeastern Division* of the Coal Measures, this typical character, as we shall see, will not apply.

(b) *Conglomerate*, making the floor upon which rests the division above, generally abounding in small white quartz pebbles, but occasionally without them.† This sometimes is a double stratum, including an unimportant coal horizon. See last paragraph.

* Sometimes a terrace, or an intermediate bench is met with in passing from the first floor of the Table-land to the top of the upper plateau.

† The Conglomerate at Altamont, in Grundy County, contains a local bed of hard, gray, crinoidal limestone, a rare circumstance in Tennessee. This bed is from three to four feet in thickness. I obtained from it a fine specimen of a species of *Hemipronites* which Mr. Worthen pronounces to be *H. radialis* of Phillips.

(a) *Lower Coal Measures*, often called, without good reason, *False Coal Measures*, by geologists; a series of sandstones and shales with from one to three or four coal horizons. This is an important division of the Coal Measures in Tennessee, and the only one in some regions available as a source of coal. The thickness ranges (not including the *Cliff Rock* of the sections below) from a few feet to 300.

943. The typical character given, applies to the southern, western, and northwestern portions of the Table-land.

The principal exceptions to it are to be found on the eastern side, and especially in the northeastern portion, lying in the counties of Claiborne, Scott, Campbell, Anderson and Morgan. (§§ 185–187.) In some ridges within this area, as in Cross Mountain, the *Upper Measures* are more than 2000 feet thick.

944. It will be seen from the general statements made, that, in Tennessee the portion of the Coal Measures above the Conglomerate have, over large areas, been much denuded. This is more especially the case on the western side of the Table-land, and in sections where the formation is most elevated. Where the base of the latter is low, the denudation has been much less. In the section presenting the greatest thickness of Coal Measures, the Conglomerate is depressed to or below the base of the Table-land, or of the mountains.

The waste caused by denudation is, to some extent, compensated for by the greater development, at many points, of the Lower Coal Measures.

945. It has been stated that the Coal Measures are co-extensive with the Table-land, (§ 938;) this makes their outcrop in Tennessee occupy an area of 5100 square miles. Thus nearly *one-eighth* of the surface of the State is underlaid by the coal-bearing rocks. (§ 178.)

946. With this preliminary notice of the general features of the Coal Formation, we pass to the more detailed description. The Coal Formation, or, what amounts to the same thing, the Table-land, is made up of several portions, or subdivisions, more or less natural. My plan will be to consider these separately, commencing with the more southern, and proceeding northward. The relations that these subdivisions sustain to each other, and to the whole, will also, as we progress, be pointed out, so far, at least, as the data at hand will admit.

947. (A) *The Sewanee Division.*—This includes that part of the Table-land lying west of Sequatchee Valley, and reaching from the Alabama line to the southern boundaries of White

and Cumberland counties. It embraces parts of Franklin, Marion, Sequatchee, Grundy, Warren, Bledsoe, and Van Buren. (See Map.) In this the strata are, approximately, horizontal.

948. The *Sewanee Coal Banks*, at Tracy City, in Grundy County, very near the Marion line, are a well-known point in this division. These banks have a railroad connection with the Nashville and Chattanooga road, and coal from them is taken directly to Nashville. (See page 74, (7).) The section of the Coal Measures to be seen in this vicinity, may be taken as an illustration of the general character of the Formation throughout the division, or, rather, of its character in those parts of the division holding the beds, both above and below the Conglomerate.

949. This section is given below. Its lowest beds outcrop about two miles south of Tracy City, in the "gulf" of the Little Fiery Gizzard, a small creek rising on the plateau in the region of the mines, and tributary to Battle Creek. The overlying beds are met with in succession in ascending this stream, some of them forming cascades, until the plateau or top of the Conglomerate is reached. Proceeding then some distance, and passing Tracy City and the railroad depot, the foot of the *back bench*, or upper plateau, is met with, and the section completed by ascending its slope to the top.

Upper Measures; 290 feet.		
(13)	Conglomerate; cap rock of the upper plateau, and the uppermost stratum in this region,	50 feet.
(12)	**Coal,** a few inches,	
(11)	*Shale,*	23 feet.
(10)	**Coal,** outcrop,	½ foot.
(9)	*Dark Clayey Shale,*	1 foot.
(8)	*Sandy Shale,*	25 feet.
(7)	Sandstone,	86 feet.
(6)	*Shale,* more or less sandy,	45 feet.
(5)	**Coal,** *Main Sewanee,* from	3 to 7 ft.
(4)	*Shale,* some of it sandy,	33 feet.
(3)	**Coal,** outcrop,	1 foot.
(2)	*Shale,*	3 feet.
(1)	*Sandstone,*	17 feet

CONGLOMERATE, ... 70 feet.

LOWER MEASURES; (*Gizzard Portion;*) 228 feet.

(10) **Coal,** outcrop, from.................................... ½ to 1 ft.

(9) *Shale,* with clay at top,.................................... 10 feet.

(8) SANDSTONE, *Cliff Rock,* (*Lower Cong.* of Ætna Mines,) .... 65 feet.

(7) **Coal,** outcrop, from.................................... ½ to 1½ ft.

(6) *Shale,* with a few inches of indurated clay at top,... 8 feet.

(5) *Sandy Shale,*.................................... 22 feet.

(4) SANDSTONE, hard,.................................... 78 feet.

(3) **Coal,** has occasionally shale above and below it; the Coal, from.................................... 1 to 3 ft.

(2) *Hard Sandstone,* local,.................................... 20 feet.

(1) *Shale,* including a thin sandstone,.................................... 20 feet.

MOUNTAIN LIMESTONE; the uppermost bed a limestone containing *Archimedes,* &c., followed below by calcareous shale; the limestone,.................................... 20 feet.

950. The upper and lower parts of the section above, may be taken respectively as types of the upper and lower Coal Measures in the division under consideration. They will serve as starting points in the descriptions below.

951. *The Lower Coal Measures in the Sewanee Division.*—The lower part of the section above presents a phase, and approximately not an uncommon one, of the strata embracing the lower coals. This series, taking it in general, is, to some extent, variable; yet it has, nearly throughout, certain common features. The coal beds are almost always present, if not in workable volume, at least in seams or traces of some kind. In the eastern or southeastern part of the division, there are generally four coal seams below the Conglomerate. Going to the west side of the Table-land in Franklin, and in the southern part of Grundy, one of these is lost, and the number is reduced to three. Going northwest, into the northern part of Grundy, and in Warren, and but two of the seams are left. And the volume of the Measures is reduced, correspondingly, from 360 feet (not including Conglomerate) to 50.

The coal beds are very irregular in thickness. They are most frequently too thin to work with profit, but often swell out locally to thicknesses of three, four, five, and even nine feet. The amount of available coal they contain, notwithstanding the features mentioned, is very great.

The quality of the coal is generally good, but varies with the localities. It is not, as a general thing, highly bituminous; much of it is a solid, cubic, free-burning coal.

952. The lateral extent of this portion of the Coal Formation is very great, its area being the same as that of the entire Sewanee Division of the Table-land. The Conglomerate which overlies it, ought, perhaps, to be included in it, as the upper stratum. The Conglomerate is the principal plateau-making rock of the Table-land, as well as the protecting cover of the lower coal series, and has determined the area of both.*

953. Below are banks which have been opened in the coals below the Conglomerate. Sections and notices of the strata at different points are also given. These examples will serve to show the character of the series at different localities, the changes it undergoes, and approximately the amount of coal it holds.

954. None of the coals of the Lower Measures have been opened in the vicinity of Tracy City. It is their natural outcrops in the gulf of the Little Fiery Gizzard which are given in the section. The lower one (3) is well presented beneath a bluff of sandstone. It is seen to be variable in thickness, ranging from a foot, or even less, to three. If followed or drifted into, it would doubtless be found to swell out, now and then, to a greater thickness, and then, on the other hand, sink to practically nothing

955. Between Tracy City and the Alabama line, on the slopes of the Table-land, and beneath the conglomerate and sandstone cliffs overhanging the valleys of the streams emptying into the Tennessee and Sequatchee rivers, of which Crow, Battle, and Little Sequatchee creeks are the most important, are many outcrops of the lower coals. These often present local, and not unfrequently extensive, developments of the beds. There are many points where no coal of practical importance exists; and there are many others where the coal-horizons are so covered with debris as to make it impossible, without much work, to know what they do contain. More or less of these would show the coal beds thick enough to be made available, and contribute to the known aggregate.

* The part of the Conglomerate in the Sewanee Division of the Table-land is referred to here. This stratum corresponds, let it be noted, with the Upper Conglomerate of the Ætna Section, given on a following page; and the *Cliff Rock* is the Lower. See § 941.

956. In the *Valley of Crow Creek*, near Anderson Depot, on the Nashville and Chattanooga road, the Coal Measures present, at the margin of the Table-land, the following section:

(12) **CONGLOMERATE,** coming in back of the top of the cliff formed by the sandstone below.

(11) **Coal** *and Shale;* coal, so far as seen, only eight or ten inches,.. 40 feet.

(10) SANDSTONE, heavy, makes the *cliff;* thickness (estimated,)..120 feet.

(9) **Coal,** from 2 to 5 feet of lustrous, black, good coal, more or less laminated by thin leaves of mineral charcoal, contains some pyrite occasionally in seams. Several thousand bushels have been taken from the bank at this point. The coal will, perhaps, average,.............. 3 feet.

(8) *Fire Clay,*.. 3 feet.

(7) *Shale,*.. 8 feet.

(6) *Sandstone,*.. 10 feet.

(5) **Coal?** *and Shale,*.. 10 feet.

(4) SANDSTONE *and Sandy Shale,*.. 55 feet.

(3) *Shale,*.. 1 to 6 ft.

(2) **Coal,** has been opened, a laminated, cubic coal, without pyrite, will average, so far as seen, from,..................2½ to 3 ft.

(1) *Shale,* with clay iron-stones, followed below by rocks not seen.

957. In its general features, this section resembles the Gizzard part of the Tracy City section.

The second *Coal* below the Conglomerate (bed 9) has been, and perhaps is now, worked at several points below Anderson. Its average thickness is considerably less than three feet Occasionally it is above this, and at one point in Alabama, not far below the Tennessee line, it measured *seven* feet, soon, however, running down to two.

958. I do not know that the lowest coal of the section above, (bed 2,) has been opened at any other point in this part of the Crow Creek Valley. At the head of Little Crow, where it is nearly two feet thick, some coal has been taken out of it.

959. In § 925, a section of the Lower Coal Measures at the top of the steep slope of the Sewanee Railroad, is given. The uppermost sandstone (4) of the section, is that lying next below the Conglomerate. Following the track of the road

back from the brow, a bed of shale is met with, containing a trace of coal; then comes the *Conglomerate*.

In this region the lower coals are absent, or exist only in traces.

960. On the western brow of the Table-land, in Franklin County, near the Grundy line, and about four miles northwest from the track of the Sewanee road, is the old *Logan Bank*. The section at this point is as follows:

CONGLOMERATE, forming slope back from the crest.

LOWER COAL MEASURES; 202 feet.	(8) *Shale*, perhaps including a thin *coal*, estimated,......	40 feet.
	(7) SANDSTONE, forming cliff,......	74 feet.
	(6) **Coal**,......	1 foot.
	(5) *Fire Clay*,......	1 foot.
	(4) *Shale*,......	8 feet.
	(3) SANDSTONES and Sandy Shales; at lower part, clay shales holding clay iron-stones,......	50 feet.
	(2) **Coal**, of Logan Bank; coal good, variable in thickness, from......	1 to 3 ft.
	(1) *Shale*,......	38 feet.
Limestone, bluish-gray, crinoidal,......		68 feet.

The coal above (3) has also been worked at another point not far off. Other sections of the strata on this part of the Table-land might be given, but they would not vary much from this. At some points the coal is thicker, at others not workable, and might not appear at all.

961. We pass now, in further illustration of the Lower Coals of the *Sewanee Division*, (§ 947,) to the *Valley of Battle Creek and vicinity*, in Marion County.

The following is a section of the Lower Measures at what was once known as *Rice's Bank*. The point is near the lower end of Battle Creek Valley, and on the mountain slope on its northern side:

(15) **CONGLOMERATE,** seen back of the brow of the mountain.

(14) *Shale*, with trace of *coal* (?) a few feet.

(13) *Sandstone*...... 50 feet.

(12) *Shale*, (*coal?*)...... 10 feet.

(11) SANDSTONE, *Cliff Rock*, hard,...... 90 feet.

(10) **Coal,** outcrop,.. 2 feet.
(9) *Shale,* .... 10 feet.
(8) SANDSTONE, even-bedded,.. 40 feet.
(7) **Coal,** Rice's Bank; considerable coal has been taken from this bank; is laminated, more or less, by seams of mineral charcoal; thickness ranges from 2 to 6 feet, so far as penetrated, (1858,) averages about...... .... 4 feet.
(6) *Fire Clay,*.. 2 feet.
(5) *Shale,*... 15 feet.
(4) *Sandy Shale,*.. 38 feet.
(3) *Shale,*... 12 feet.
(2) **Coal,** a trace of coal, with Stigmaria below.
(1) *Sandstone,* rough, concretionary, weathering into shaly matter, ... 12 feet

962. The section below was taken at a point about a mile in an easterly direction from the last, and on the slope of the Table-land facing Sequatchee Valley. It embraces a bank, formerly worked by Rice and others, which may be designated as the *More Bank.* Both this and the Rice bank are at the southern point of the arm of the Table-land separating the Battle Creek and Sequatchee Valleys. The top of the mountain above the More Bank is in sight of Jasper.

(18) **CONGLOMERATE,** heavy, at the top of the mountain, not measured.
(17) **Coal,** outcrops, from...½ to 1 foot.
(16) *Shale,*.. 10 feet.
(15) *Sandstone,* .... 15 feet.
(14) *Sandy Shale (?)* with bluish shale below,........................ 28 feet.
(13) *Shale,*.. 15 feet.
(12) SANDSTONE, *Cliff Rock (Lower Cong. of Ætna Mines,)*... 105 feet.
(11) **Coal,** outcrop, a few inches.
(10) *Shale,* .... 8 feet.
(9) SANDSTONE, ... 45 feet.
(8) *Shale,* upper part sandy, ... 6 feet.
(7) **Coal** same as bed 7, last section; the *More Bank* is in this; bed irregular, ranging from...................................1 to 4 feet.
(6) *Fire Clay,*..3 to 5 feet.
(5) *Shale,*... 5 feet.
(4) *Sandy Shale* and thin sandstones,..................................... 20 feet.

(3) *Slope;* (including a **Coal?**) rocks concealed,................ 25 feet.
(2) *Sandstone*, thin-bedded,.. 33 feet.
(1) *Rocks* below covered, but at another point to *Mountain Limestone* strata.. 30 feet.
Thickness in all below the conglomerate,...............355 feet.

963. Sections taken at other localities on the mountain slopes, bounding, and in the vicinity of, the Battle Creek Valley, might be given, but they would present no essential differences. Banks might be opened at many points where the coal beds, especially 7, of the sections, *swell out locally* to three or four feet. Most work has been done at available localities near the Tennessee River. The railroad will add new vigor to coal mining in this section, and, doubtless, lead to new developments.

964. It is to be noted that, the gulf of the Little Fiery Gizzard, affording the lower part of the section in § 949, is at the head, or, rather, at one of the heads, of the Battle Creek Valley. Comparing the sections just given, with the corresponding part of the one in the paragraph referred to, it will be seen that the series has increased in thickness, in a southeasterly direction, about 125 feet. Comparing them with the section in § 960, and with the top of Sewanee Railroad section, (§§ 925 and 959,) the increase is still greater.. Moreover, a sandstone (apparently 13, of the Rice Bank section) and a coal seam (perhaps bed 7, of the same section) appear to have been interpolated.

965. The margin of the Table-land west of Jasper is generally high and bold. The sections its strata present are, in general features, much the same as those given.

The Conglomerate sometimes appears at the brow of the mountain, making, with the sandstones below, stupendous cliffs, but usually comes in a little back of the crest.

966. Passing to the deep, narrow, cliff-bound *Valley* of *Little Sequatchee Creek*, in the northern part of Marion County, we find the lower coals and sandstones presenting themselves much as in the Battle Creek region. There are many dark, wild gulfs leading into this valley, around which the *Cliff Sandstone*, (12 of the last section,) and often the Conglomerate above, appear in bold faces. In one of the gulfs, at the head of the valley, that of *Cave Creek*, there is a heavy local development of the coal under the Cliff Sandstone. At one point it is nine feet thick, and is exposed for 40 feet in a horizontal direc-

tion. In another gulf, called the *Pocket*, southeast of the latter, the coal beneath certain cliffs, known as the "*Chimneys*," shows itself in an exposure five feet thick.

967. At the head of Indian Creek, a tributary of Little Sequatchee, at a point only about five miles southeast of Tracy City, is the *Parmley Bank*, from which, blacksmiths, years ago, before the opening of the Sewanee Banks, obtained much of their coal, and by whom it was much esteemed. This coal is below the Cliff Sandstone (or 8 of the Gizzard portion of the section in § 949.) The bed here, is from 7 to 9 feet in thickness. It is, however, in a sort of pocket, and is soon reduced, on one side at least, to one foot.

968. Going northward, from Tracy City towards Collins' River, the *Lower Measures* become much reduced in volume, and present generally but two thin seams of coal. The sections below, taken in the vicinity of the Beersheba Springs, a few miles from Altamont, in Grundy County, will serve as illustrations of the character of the Coal Formation in this region. The coals are generally too thin to be of much value, but occasionally swell out in workable thickness.

969. With the Beersheba sections, one is also given, taken on the ridge near Ben Lomond, the well known mountain within a few miles of McMinnville. (page 75, (8).) This mountain is the terminus of the arm of the Table-land dividing the waters of Collins' River and Hickory Creek. In it, the Lower Measures are poorly developed; but at a few points the coal may be mined.

970. The following is a section at the mill, three miles south of Beersheba Springs:

	CONGLOMERATE,	130 feet.
LOWER MEASURES, 78 ft.	(4) **Coal,** a few inches in a bed of shale; all	25 feet.
	(3) *Sandy Shale*	50 feet.
	(2) *Black Band Iron Ore*	½ to 1 foot.
	(1) **Coal,** six inches in shale; all	2 feet.
	Shales and Limestones of the Mountain Limestone Formation	35 feet.

The upper coal of this section swells to a thickness of three or four feet at points not far off.

971. Below is a section at the Falls of the Laurel, a little over a mile from the Springs:

CONGLOMERATE, very heavy.

LOWER MEASURES, 56 ft.		
	(8) *Shale*, abounding in clay iron-stones,....................	8 feet.
	(7) **Coal**, a few inches.	
	6 *Shale*, ...	20 feet.
	(5) *Sandy Shale*,..	10 feet.
	4 *Shale*,...	6 feet.
	(3) **Coal**, good but thin,..	1 to 2 feet.
	(2) *Sandstone*, or indurated shale, ...	4 feet.
	(1) *Shale*, exposed,..	6 feet.

972. The following section occurs on a spur running out from the narrow neck which connects Ben Lomond with the main arm of the Table-land. The locality is about a mile south of Ben Lomond. At many points in this region no coal occurs.

CONGLOMERATE, the same that caps Ben Lomond, shows but few pebbles.

Coal,..10 inchs.

Slaty Clay,...6 to 8 "

Coal,..10 "

Shale, and other rocks below, but the Mountain Limestone soon appearing.

Such a pair of coals might be worked as a single bed, by removing the intermediate layer.

973. The Lower Measures of the western part of Van Buren County, are much like those in Warren and Grundy. Going eastward, into Bledsoe, they become thicker. The character of the Coal Measures in Van Buren will be further illustrated by sections, taken on the Caney Fork, to be given on following pages.

McMinnville was formerly supplied with coal from banks eighteen or twenty miles distant, but the locality of these, and as to whether they are in beds above or below the Conglomerate, I know not.

974. *The Upper Coal Measures in the Sewanee Division.*—The limits of the Sewanee Division have been given in § 947. Having considered the lower coals of this area, that is to say, those below the Conglomerate, we now pass to the upper ones, or those above this rock.

And now, the *upper* part of the section in § 949, will be our starting point, (§ 950.) This, as already stated, may be taken as the type of the Upper Coal Measures in the Sewanee Division, and wherever an upper plateau, or bench, occurs above the Conglomerate, (§§ 940–942,) their strata may be looked for.

975. The area occupied by the plateau-ridges of the upper bench of this division is, in the aggregate, much less than that underlaid by the Conglomerate, or by the Lower Measures. The Conglomerate is almost wholly the surface rock of the Table-land from Tracy City, in a southerly and southwesterly direction, as far as the Alabama line. There is, in fact, nothing more than a few knolls to be met with in that direction, containing strata of the Upper Measures.

976. Some of the most important of these knolls are the following:

1st. One about two miles west of Tracy City, in which is the *Thompson Bank.*

2d. Another at the "Lower Mines," about half way between Tracy City and the Nashville and Chattanooga Tunnel. The best coal has been taken out of this by the Sewanee Company. It was first opened by Porter and Logan.

3d. The knoll in which is the old *Jackson Bank,* about a mile and a half south of the "Lower Mines."

977. From Tracy City, in southeasterly, easterly, and northeasterly directions, the bench-ridges, on the other hand, are often met with. In many cases they are long, serpentine, flat-topped ranges, lying as dividing belts between the extreme head-waters of creeks. They occur extensively on the Table-land around the waters of the Little Sequatchee, and from this region extend northward, between Sequatchee Valley and the waters of Caney Fork, to Cumberland County.

In passing from Tracy City to Altamont, the bench and bench-hills are met with for about eight miles, when the Conglomerate becomes, in the main, the surface rock, and continues so to Altamont, and also from this point on to Beersheba Springs.

978. There having been no regular topographical surveys, the comparative area underlaid by the bench ridges can only be estimated. Perhaps it will be near the truth to say, that they occupy, in the aggregate, about one-fourth of the area of this division of the Table-land.

979. Recurring to the section in § 949, the *Main Sewanee Coal,* (originally called the *Wooten Vein,*) is the only one of the coals in the vicinity of Tracy City that has been mined, (unless done

recently,) to any note-worthy extent. The coal here is of good quality, semi-bituminous, and contains but little pyrite. Perhaps no purer coal is brought to the Nashville market. It is objected to on account of its being more or less fragile, and its tendency to become *fine*; but, if properly handled and screened, it is a very desirable coal. Its fragile character is due to its peculiar *spumous* structure, which has been attributed by some to a sort of crystalization, but which, I think, is attributable to a lateral crushing movement of the strata in the vicinity. It is but a few miles to points where the rocks have been greatly disturbed. This structure is mainly confined to the Sewanee Mines. The thickness of the bed at the mines varies from two and a half to seven feet; it may be regarded here as a four or five foot bed.*

980. The Main Sewanee is a valuable bed of coal, and the most reliable one west of the Sequatchee Valley. It appears to be the southern extension of the Pennsylvania bed (B.)† A list of fossil plants occurring at the Sewanee Mines, in the shales associated with this bed, and its "satellite" below, will be given at the end of the Chapter.

981. This bed is to be looked for at all points on the Table-land where its proper geological horizon is presented, which is generally within 50 or 75 feet of the Conglomerate. It has been seen at quite a number of localities within the division of the Table-land under consideration, outside of the vicinity of Tracy City. Some of these are enumerated below, and the special features of the bed at each, given.

982. (a) The knoll two miles west of Tracy City, may be mentioned. In this a bank was opened many years ago, the coal showing, at the time of my visit, a clear face of 12 feet, and the bottom not seen at that. This thickness, however, was quite local.

983. (b) The "*Lower Mines*" (§ 976) are another point. Here the bed averaged three feet. The coal was cubic in structure. The section at this place is as follows:

* The facts upon which these statements are made, were observed before the war. What the new drifts and rooms would average, I am not informed.

† See page 95, of J. P. Lesley's Manual of Coal and its Topography; 1856, Philadelphia, Lippincott & Co. Also, Dana's Manual of Geology, page 331.

(8) SANDSTONE, more or less shaly, and capping the knoll,... 16 feet.
(7) *Shale*,.. 12 feet.
(6) **Coal,** (*Main Sewanee*,) removed,........................ 3 feet.
(5) *Fire Clay*,.. 1½ feet.
(4) *Sandstone and Sandy Shale*,........................ 16 feet.
(3) *Shale*,.. 15 feet.
(2) **Coal,**.. 1½ to 3 ft.
(1) *Shale*, sandy,.. 10 feet.
CONGLOMERATE, a few feet at top sandstone.

984. (c) A third point is about five miles southeast of Tracy City, a mile and a half from the Parmley Bank, mentioned in § 967, and is near one of the gulfs of the Little Sequatchee. At this place is *Stone's Bank*. The Main Sewanee coal shows well here. It is a good solid coal, from four to five feet in thickness. The plateau-ridge, in which this bank occurs, extends, with but a few breaks, to the Sewanee Mines. The secti .n at Stone's Bank is as follows, thickness estimated:

(9) SANDSTONE, seen,.. 20 feet.
(8) *Space*, doubtful, most likely sandstone above and shale below,.. 60 feet?
(7) *Shale*,.. 2 to 3 ft.
(6) *Sandy Shale*, or *Sandstone*,........................ 3 feet.
(5) **Coal,** (*Main Sewanee*,)........................ 4 to 5 ft.
(4) *Fire Clay*,.. 1 foot.
(3) *Shale*,.. 15 to 20 ft.
(2) *Sandstone*, exposed,.. 2 or 3 ft.
(1) *Space*, rocks not seen,.. 25 feet?
CONGLOMERATE.

985. (d) Outcrops of coal in the Main Sewanee horizon have been observed on the slopes of the plateau, or bench, ridges, around the upper part of the Little Sequatchee Valley, (§ 977,) but as no excavations have been seen, the character of the bed in this region cannot be given.

986. It is to be noted that the two last sections are capped with the sandstone next above the *Main Sewanee* Coal. This, indeed, often forms terraces and tables subordinate to the plateau-ridges.

987. Between the *Main Sewanee* and the Conglomerate, there is very generally a coal bed, or seam, which, for reasons that

will appear, may be called the *Jackson Coal*. (A of Lesley's Manual, page 45.) This is (3) of the section in § 949. At Tracy City, up to the time of my last visit, no developments of interest to a miner had been made in this bed. It is generally too thin to work. There is but one point where it has, to my knowledge, been mined, and that is at the knoll referred to in § 976, containing the old Jackson Bank. The latter bank is in this bed, and hence the name I have given to it. The coal at this point is tolerably good, would be quite so, but for the presence of pyrite. It ranges in thickness from two to three feet, and is separated from the Conglomerate by 12 feet of sandy shale. A considerable amount of coal has been taken out of this bed up to the time the Sewanee Mining Company commenced their operations.*

988. The Jackson Coal can also be seen at the "Lower Mines;" it is 2 of the section in § 983. A drift was run into the bed at this point by the Sewanee Company, but the coal was found to contain so much pyrite and shaly matter as not to be worth the mining.

989. (B) *The Raccoon and Walden's Ridge Division.*—Having considered the Sewanee Division of the Table-land with reference to the Coal Formation, we pass, now, to a second division. (See §§ 946, 947.) This embraces the portion of the Table-land east of Sequatchee Valley and the Crab Orchard Range of Mountains, (§ 188,) and extends longitudinally from the Alabama line to the Emery River, in Morgan County. It includes parts of Marion, Sequatchee, Hamilton, Bledsoe, Rhea, Cumberland, Roane, and Morgan.

990. The topography of this belt has been given in sections 141, 142, and 182. In the diagram on page 139, the part C E is a section of the southern end of the division. It shows how the Coal Measures (X) rest upon the Mountain Limestone (IX.) The elevation of the former is also to be noted. The formations are seen to dip in such a manner as to form a very shallow trough, the strata, however, in the central part being approximately horizontal.

991. In the part of the division east of the head of Sequatchee Valley

* This bank, with others on this section of the Table-land, and among them the Porter and Logan Banks, was first opened by Abram Van Vleck, a working man, but an intelligent one, having no occasion to cloak his ignorance by calling himself a "practical miner."

and Crab Orchard Mountain, this trough-like feature of the strata is more marked. Here, also, and indeed at points further south, the eastern edge of the division is thrown up in a crested ridge, the Conglomerate and sandstones of the Coal Formation entering largely into its structure, and being often tilted at high angles. In the southern part of the division this feature is not prominent, although the strata, as shown at E in the diagram run up, to some extent, as they come to the surface in Lookout Valley.

992. It is to be noted, as stated in § 141, that Walden's Ridge and the Raccoon Mountains appertain to the same belt. The range runs southwesterly, a long distance into Georgia and Alabama.

993. The completion of the Nashville and Chattanooga Railroad through the Raccoon Mountains, has been followed by the building up of a great mining interest in a region once wild, desolate and unproductive. We can learn here a lesson, as to what railroads will do for us when made to traverse mineral ground.* We trust that others will soon be built across our great coal field.

994. We take the region of the *Ætna Mines*, as our starting point in the consideration of the Coal Measures of the division before us. At no other point have the coals been so thoroughly explored as here. The following general section, of the strata in the Ætna region, will illustrate the character of the Coal Formation over a large area. The survey was made in 1858, and in years antecedent. As to whether any essentially new developments have been made since the war, I am not informed. The mountain, at the Ætna Mines, has the typical character described in §§ 940–942, that is to say, it is a table with a plateau-ridge, or back bench, upon it. The latter, on the mountain between the railroad and the Tennessee River, covers a considerable area, but it is often narrow, more or less broken, and much less in extent than the floor upon which it rests.

995. The *Upper Conglomerate* of the section forms a terrace around the plateau-ridges. The *Lower Conglomerate*, which, in the sections west of Sequatchee Valley I have called the *Cliff Rock*, makes, in many portions of the Raccoon Mountains, outside of the Ætna region, the cap-rock of the Table-lands. In fact, at some points, the two rocks appear to come together and form a single stratum.

*Much credit is due to the enterprise of Col. J. A. Whiteside (now deceased) and Robert Cravens, Esq., of Chattanooga, for the developments made in the Raccoon Mountains.

UPPER MEASURES, 220 feet.

(8) SANDSTONE, cap-rock of plateau-ridge above the Ætna Mines,.. 75 feet.

(7) *Shale*,.. 48 feet.

(6) **Coal,** "*Walker Coal;*" uniform, good, cubic......... 4 feet.

(5) *Shale*, including sometimes a thin *coal*, (Cravens,) from..30 to 40 feet.

(4) **Coal,** "*Slate Vein;*" including a layer eighteen inches thick, of shale and coal mixed,...............5 to 6 feet.

(3) *Shale*,.. 44 feet.

(2) **Coal,** "*Kelly Coal;*" good, cubical coal, from.........2 to 3 feet.

(1) *Fire Clay*, from ....1 to 2 feet.

UPPER CONGLOMERATE, simply a sandstone here,...... 75 feet.

(4) **Coal**, seam, a few inches.

(3) *Shale*,..30 to 40 feet.

(2) **Coal**, seam, ten inches.

(1) *Sandy Shale*, from...100 to 130 feet.

LOWER CONGLOMERATE, *Cliff Rock* of the sections east of Sequatchee Valley, in which it is included in the *Lower Measures;* becomes a well-characterized *Conglomerate* over the upper coal (Main Ætna or Cliff Vein) at Gordan's Mines, in Georgia, doubtless coalesce at some points with the Upper Conglomerate, the intervening layers thinning out, from......................70 to 100 feet.

LOWER MEASURES, (not including *Lower Cong.*,) average, 288 feet.

(14) *Shale*, sometimes wanting, the rock above making the roof of the coal from............................0 to 12 feet.

(13) **Coal,** *Main Ætna*, or *Cliff Vein;* the most important bed in the Raccoon Mountains, and has been mined at numerous points by different parties; has a wide spread under the *Lower Conglomerate*, or *Cliff Rock*, of the mountains; is irregular in thickness, ranging generally from eighteen inches to four feet, but occasionally sinking to a few inches, or rising in a swell six, seven, or more feet in thickness; structure of coal often peculiar, is in laminæ from the fraction of an inch to two inches in thickness, the laminæ separated by the seams of mineral charcoal, and each one made up of small, irregular, vertical prisms; the coal is of good quality, and in demand, not highly bituminous, contains but little pyrite, and makes good coke; will average, perhaps,............................ 3 feet.

(12) *Fire Clay*, indurated, contains *Stigmaria*, often with rootlets attached; has been made into good fire-brick,...1 to 3 feet.

LOWER MEASURES, (not including *Lower Cong.*) average, 288 feet.

(11) *Shale?* .... 5 to 20 feet.
(10) **Coal,** thin, ... ½ to 1 foot.
(9) SANDSTONE and *Sandy Shale,* .... 80 to 120 feet.
(8) *Shale,* .... 0 to 5 feet.
(7) **Coal,** of good quality, usually too thin to be mined, from .... ½ to 3 feet.
(6) *Fire Clay,* .... 0 to 2 feet.
(5) *Sandy Shale,* or *Sandstone,* .... 20 to 25 feet.
(4) *Shale,* .... 15 to 20 feet.
(3) **Coal,** lowest bed like the last, and banks have been opened in both; Mr. E. Alley opened a bank in this bed, at one point in the Raccoon region, where it was at first six feet, then nine, but soon fell to three, ... ½ to 3 feet.
(2) *Fire Clay,* .... 0 to 3 feet.
(1) *Shales and Shaly Sandstones,* .... 80 to 150 feet.

MOUNTAIN LIMESTONE FORMATION.
Variegated Shales and Limestones in the Valley of Running Water.

996. The above section presents a fair analysis of the Coal Measures of the Raccoon Mountain Region. There are seen to be *four* coal beds below the Lower Conglomerate, one more than generally occurs below the corresponding rock in the slopes on the west side of Sequatchee Valley. Extending the comparisons made in § 964, to this section, and we see a still further increase, going eastward, in the volume and in the number of coal beds of the Lower Measures.

997. The plateau-ridges, or the Upper Measures, of the Raccoon Region, is, considering the thickness of the strata, very rich in coal. I know not the aggregate area they occupy; it is much less than that of the main floor they rest upon. They are most conspicuous on the part of the mountain between the railroad and the Tennessee River.* The elevation of one point of these above tide, is given on page 74, (6.)

998. The trio of coals, the *Kelly*, *Slate* and *Walker*, appertain doubtless to the horizon of the *Jackson* (3) and *Main Sewanee,* of the section in § 949. (See §§ 980, 964.) Their paleontological features have not been much studied. It is likely that

* In the Ætna Region "they are contained in two ridges, together equal to 1500 acres." (E. Alley.)

the *Kelly* and the *Jackson* are the same, and that the *Slate* and the *Walker* represent the *Sewanee*.

999. I add, here, before passing northward, the section presented at the point of *Lookout Mountain*. (§ 189, and 194, (5).) This is the last of a series of sections taken at intervals in a belt extending from the extreme western to the extreme eastern slopes of the Table-land, including in the latter, the great outlier above. They constitute, in fact, a complete section, running quite across the southern end of our Coal Measures.

The coals at the northern end of Lookout are poorly presented; in fact, the outcrops of most of them do not appear at all. Following the mountain into Georgia, however, several of them become workable beds. A special feature of this section is the great development of the Conglomerate at the top of Lookout.

UPPER CONGLOMERATE, very heavy, makes the great cliffs around the brow of *Lookout;* most of it contains pebbles; thickness estimated by Col. Whiteside and myself,..250 feet.

(3) **Coal,** a trace at the *Point* of mountain.

(2) *Fire Clay,* was used by Mr. Cravens at the old "Bluff Furnace," and obtained from an outcrop below the *Hotel,* answered a good purpose..1 to 9 feet.

(1) *Sandy Shale,* ....10 to 30 feet.

(This space between the two conglomerates, is, at some points, as near the Hotel, reduced to 9 or 10 feet, the *Sandy Shale* thinning out.)

CONGLOMERATE, middle part containing pebbles, on the road down the mountain, from the Hotel, is 25 feet thick, not well developed, contains 5 or 6 feet of shale in its middle part; at the *Point,*......................... 37 feet.

LOWER MEASURES, from 350 to 375 feet.

( ) *Shale* running up into *Sandy Shale,*...................... 15 feet.
( ) *Shale,* dark,... .... 8 feet.
( ) **Coal?**
( ) *Fire Clay,* sandy,.. 5 feet.
( ) *Shale,* ....6 to 8 feet.
( ) *Sandy Shale*.. 15 feet.
( ) SANDSTONE,..15 to 23 feet.
( ) *Sandy Shale,* running up into thin sandstone,.....60 to 70 feet.
( ) *Shale,* heavy, (at the point,) becoming sandy in ascending, ...220 feet.
( ) *Sandstone,* .... 10 feet.

MOUNTAIN LIMESTONE. The sandstone above is immediaetly, or very soon, followed by the variegated shales of this formation; from the sandstone to the first limestone seen, is.. 50 feet.

1000. Passing northward, from the Ætna Mines, we soon get into the narrow valley, or gorge, in which the Tennessee River finds a passage through the Walden's Ridge Range. (§ 149.) The strata of the Lower Coal Measures are here boldly presented in the slopes on both sides of the river. The coals have about the same general features as in the Ætna Region. They have not, however, been so fully explored, and hence, are not as well known. I have seen, however, the four coals below the Lower Conglomerate (or Cliff Rock) on the north side of the river. The Main Ætna is here in place, and has been mined to some extent. One of the lower beds has also been worked. Before the completion of the Nashville and Chattanooga Railroad, coal was taken out of these beds and sent down the river to towns in Alabama. I am not informed as to what has been done with them in late years.

1001. From the Tennessee, northward, through the division, to the Emery River, the Coal Measures have not been, as yet, sufficiently studied. Enough has been done, however, to inform us as to their general character.

The two principal sections given, the Sewanee (§ 949) and the Raccoon, (§ 994, 995,) may be taken in general as types of this portion of the series. Both the Upper and Lower Measures are often present. In the trough of the Walden's Ridge Range (§ 990) there may be, at some points, a few strata higher in the series than the topmost of the Sewanee Section. The *Main Sewanee* is, most likely, the principal coal. The upper bench feature is not as marked as it is south of the Tennessee River, or west of the Sequatchie Valley. Below will be presented a section of the strata in the vicinity of Crab Orchard Mountain, which will serve to illustrate the general features of the *Coal Series* in the northern part of the Division under consideration.

1002. At many points along the eastern slope of the Tableland, from the vicinity of Chattanooga to the Emery River, the coal beds outcrop, and numerous banks have been opened in them. The beds outcropping, are, doubtless, both those below and above the Conglomerate, or conglomerates, as the case may be. Northward, the principal bed in which the banks occur, is, with little doubt, the *Main Sewanee*, or *Coal B*, of Lesley. (§ 980.) But further investigations are required before this can be asserted positively.

1003. The strata along the eastern slope are often much disturbed. (§ 991.) At a few points the Coal Measures are brought down to the valley; at others, detached blocks of the Measures containing coal, lie against the slopes as if they had been pitched over from above.

1004. The following are some of the banks that have been opened on the eastern slope. I quote, in part, from Col. W. B. Gaw's able Report to the officers of the proposed Chattanooga and Kentucky Railroad:

(a) First, may be mentioned here, a bank about six miles from Chattanooga, near the *Suck* in Tennessee River, and a little to the left of Col. Gaw's line; "worked by the Government during the war, and much coal taken out; the opening of the bed about 300 feet above the valley, and 400 feet above the river."

I have not seen this bank, but suppose it to be in the Main Ætna. Thickness variable, from one to eight feet. (§ 1000.)

(b) "At *North Chicamauga Creek*, on the left slope, about three-fourths of a mile to the left of the line of road, and about twelve and a half miles from Chattanooga, mines were worked before the war;" beds "are found upon the top and edge of the ridge," and of good thickness.

(c) *Clift and McRhea's Mines*, on Soddy Creek, about 22 miles from Chattanooga, and near the foot of the mountain. At this point the Coal Measures are brought down into the valley, the mines being in the latter. This depression commences a few miles south of the mines, and is continued to about the Rhea County line. The beds are from two to five feet, rarely swelling out to seven or eight. "The coal from these mines has been consumed in Chattanooga for years."

(d) The next mines are in the vicinity of *Pearson's, on Rocky, or Sale Creek*, and about 28 miles from Chattanooga; "have been worked for a long time; coal known in Chattanooga and Atlanta as the Sale Creek Coal; mines now worked by a company of energetic Welsh."

(e) "*Jack's Bank*" is in the same vicinity. The coal bed at this point is in the knee of a synclinal fold. When I visited this bank, (1855,) there were rooms in the knee 10 to 15 feet high; thickness of bed from 4 to 6 feet; coal crushed, of spumous structure, but comparatively pure and excellent.

(f) "*Maj. Day's Mines*, some forty miles from Chattanooga, in Rhea

County, and about three-fourths of a mile from the proposed railroad. These have not been much worked, but I regard the coal as of superior quality; the beds are of considerable thickness."

(g) "*Miller's Farm*, about 55 miles from Chattanooga. These mines have an especial value, from the fact that the opening of the bed is scarcely fifteen feet above the level of our road, and not more than a quarter of a mile from it." The coal is hard, cubic, and will bear transportation well.

(h) Then follows *Roddy's Mines*, about 62 miles from Chattanooga, and still further north, the banks on *White's Creek*.

(i) *Kimbrough's Mines*, in Roane County. "They are the most reliable and richest along the whole route. They are not worked at present, but before the death of the proprietor, were among the most prominent mines in the country." The bed of coal at Kimbrough's, is, most likely, the same as the *Haley*, (*Main Sewanee*,) in the section below. The bank is in a tilted block of measures, resting against the slope of the mountain. It affords a hard, lustrous, cubic coal. At the top of the mountain, just beyond the crest, there is an outcrop of coal appertaining, most likely, to the same bed.

(j) On *Big Emery* are several banks of coal, most of which, doubtless, like the Kimbrough Bank, are in the Main Sewanee. Four feet, or, perhaps, in a few localities, five feet, is a maximum average for them.

(k) The De Armond Banks, on the Little Emery, although belonging to another division, may be noted here. These are worked to a considerable extent. I have not seen them, but suppose them to be in the same bed as that to which the last mentioned banks have been referred.

1005. I close the description of this Division of the Coal Measures with the following section, which will serve to illustrate the character of the Coal Series, not only in the area to which our attention has been confined, but also in that which will succeed.

The section presents the strata as seen in intersecting, in Cumberland County, the *Crab Orchard Range*, (§ 188,) along the Sparta, or Crossville and Kingston road. It has already been stated that this range is the back of an anticlinal fold. (See § 346 and on.) The strata of the Coal Measures were raised in a great arch by this fold. The topmost of them, however, have since been, in good part, removed by denudation. The Conglomerate now forms the cap rock of Crab Orchard Mountain. The strata dip away from the range on both sides.

The thickness of the strata given, were, in most cases, estimated, and are but approximately true.

UPPER MEASURES, *Approximately 500 feet.*

(9) SANDSTONE, heavy; forms a wide, synclinal trough, in which is the bed of Daddy's Creek; (upon this rests, on the west side of the creek mentioned, a knoll of shale, 40 feet high;) thickness doubtful, say, ... 100 feet.

(8) *Shale*, (**Coal?**) perhaps, ... 25 to 50 ft.

(7) SANDSTONE, heavy; forms, on the east side of the range, the cascade at McNare's, from .... 100 to 150 ft.

(6) *Shale*, (**Coal?**) perhaps, ... 60 feet.

(5) *Sandstone*, including some shale in its middle part, say, ... 60 feet.

(4) *Shale*, (includes a thin sandstone, one or two feet thick, with indications of coal below it,) about .... 50 feet.

(3) **Coal,** *Haley's*, (*Main Sewanee*,) seen west of the mountain, near the road, of good quality .... 4 feet.

(2) *Fire Clay*, ... 1 foot.

(1) *Shale*, ... 30 to 40 ft.

CONGLOMERATE, heavy, much of it coarse, caps the mountain; seen also at a low level on both sides of the range, ... 100 to 150 ft.

LOWER MEASURES, 228 feet.

(5) *Slope*, (*shale with coal?*) .... 15 feet.

(4) *Sandstone* .... 33 feet.

(3) *Slope*, (perhaps mostly *shale*, with one or two *coal seams*,) .... 110 feet.

(2) *Sandstone*, thin bedded, ... 50 feet.

(1) *Shale, coal shale*, ... 20 feet.

MOUNTAIN LIMESTONE, runs up several hundred feet above the base of the mountain.

1006. (C) *The Northern Division.*—This embraces the part of the Table-land lying north of Van Buren and Bledsoe counties, and west of the Crab Orchard Range, (§ 188,) and a line running through Montgomery and Huntsville. Within its limits are parts of White, Cumberland, Morgan, Putnam, Overton, Fentress and Scott counties.

1007. The top of the Table-land is, in this portion, wide and without high mountains, presenting a flat surface, varied by valleys of moderate depth. In passing back from the margin of the slopes an upper plateau, or bench, is often met with, as in the Sewanee Division. (§ 940.)

1008. The maximum thickness of the Coal Measures presented in this area, is about equal to that of the series in the Crab Orchard Section, (§ 1005,) which may be taken as typical of the eastern portion of the area, or, at least, of that part of it adjacent to the Crab Orchard Range. In much of the area, however, especially westward and northward, the thickness is less.

1009. I present, first, a section taken in the vicinity of the old "*Eastland Stand*," on Clifty Creek, in White County, and near the Caney Fork Gulf:

UPPER MEASURES, 308 feet.	(13) SANDSTONE AND CONGLOMERATE, contains small pebbles at some points,	65 feet.
	(12) *Shale*,	0 to 12 ft.
	(11) **Coal**, irregular,	½ to 2 ft.
	(10) *Fire Clay*,	0 to 2 ft.
	(9) *Shale*, mostly, with two or three beds of sandy shale,	60 feet.
	(8) *Fire Clay*, (**Coal?**)	1 foot.
	(7) SANDSTONE, forms cliffs around the head of the gulf,	40 feet.
	(6) *Shale*,	20 feet.
	(5) *Fire Clay*, (**Coal?**)	1 foot.
	(4) *Sandy Shale, or Sandstone*,	25 feet.
	(3) *Shale*,	52 feet.
	(2) **Coal**, at bottom of *Eastland's Well*,	3 feet.
	(1) *Shale*,	25 feet.
	CONGLOMERATE, bottom, with several lenticular masses of *coal* in it; pebbles numerous at some points, at others rare,	60 feet.
L. M. 15 ft.	*Shale*, with one (occasionally two) seams of **Coal**, varying from 0 to 18 inches, in all,	15 feet.

MOUNTAIN LIMESTONE; *limestone*, 40 feet thick, forming a cliff with *Calcareous Shale* below it.

1010. The following is a section of the strata in the region of *Scarbrough's Mill and Coal Bank*, the two being about half a mile apart. The mill is on Caney Fork, just above the head of the Gulf, and at the crossing of the old Ross Road, and about four miles from the Eastland Stand:

Upper Measures, 324 feet.		
	(9) Sandstone,	50 feet.
	(8) *Space*, rocks not seen,	30 feet.
	(7) *Shale*, outcrop not good,	62 feet.
	(6) *Shale*,	38 feet.
	(5) **Coal**, *Scarbrough's*, (may be *Main Sewanee;*) a fine bed; place appears to be above No. 7 (Sandstone) of the Eastern Section. The pits were half filled with water at the time of my visit; could see but the upper part; thickness, according to Scarbrough, from 4 to 6 feet, averaging,	5 feet.
	(4) *Fire Clay*,	2 to 3 ft.
	(3) *Shale*,	18 feet.
	(2) Sandstone,	40 feet.
	(1) *Shale*, (**Coal?**) with a thin sandstone in its middle part,	78 feet.

CONGLOMERATE, forming the rapids.

1011. In the hills south of Scarbrough's Mill, there is another stratum of shale, with a sandstone above, resting upon the upper bed of the last section.

1012. It will be observed that the *Lower Measures* in the Eastland Section are very poorly developed. At many points, however, west of this, in White County, they are of considerable importance. This part of the series occurs beneath the brow of the Table-land at all points, facing the valleys of Caney Fork and Calf Killer, and is sometimes 100, or more, feet in thickness, though usually under this. It generally contains two or three (occasionally four) seams of coal, which frequently are too thin to work. Here and there, however, some one of them will swell out to three, four, or five, (or even, though very rarely, to seven or eight,) feet, affording a valuable local body of coal.

1013. The Measures below the Conglomerate on this part of the Table-land, are much like what they are on the western slope in the Sewanee Division. And it may be stated here in general, although no reference has yet been made to the series in Fentress and Overton, that the *Lower Measures* present similar features throughout, on the western slopes, from Kentucky to Alabama. They consist of shales and sandstones, the latter sometimes absent, and range in thickness from a few feet to about 200. They contain two, sometimes three, rarely more, seams of Coal. These are often too thin for mining, but locally swell out, and form valuable deposits from two and a half to four or five (rarely more) feet in thickness. The Poplar Mountain and Upper Cumberland Coal Banks in Kentucky, are in the northern extension of this same series.

1014. Returning to White County, and the valley of the Calf Killer, the head of which is in Putnam County, we find several banks in the coals below the Conglomerate. Most of these are enumerated below. A few sections are also given, illustrating the character of the Measures.

1015. (a) *Little's Bank*, near the brow of the Table-land overlooking the valley of Calf Killer, about two miles and a half, direct, from Bon Air, and five or six from Sparta; has been opened for many years, the coal being used in Sparta. The following is the section at this point:

CONGLOMERATE, heavy, cap-rock of mountain.

Shale, may have thin seams of *coal*, contains *clay iron-stones*,... 80 feet.

Sandstone,.. 13 feet.

Coal, thin seam, with fire clay,..................................1 to 2 feet.

Shale, lower part blackish,...12 feet.

Coal, *Little's Bank;* coal cubical, of good quality, from 2 to 4 feet in thickness, and averaging,..................................3½ feet.

Under-clay,..1 to 2 feet.

Space, down to the first limestone seen,......... .... 30 feet.

1016. (b) *Lance's Bank*, about half a mile from Littles, on the Bon Air side; bed same as that of Little's; coal three feet; section similar to that just given.

1017. (c) From Lance's Bank, around the mountain to Bon Air, thin outcrops of the seams occur at numerous points. On the old road, leading to the top of the mountain, in the vicinity of the latter place, the Measures below the Conglomerate, which is here 90 feet thick, consist of shales 100 feet in thickness, in which are four thin seams of coal, several of which have under-clays. (§ 923.)

1018. (d) *Rodgers' Bank;* in Dog, or Lost Cove, between two and three miles from Bon-Air, in an easterly or southeasterly direction; opened by Gen. Rodgers; bed two and a half feet at outcrop, may be three or four feet within. In this region are, at some points, four seams, the bank above being in the third below Conglomerate. An outcrop of four feet in one of the seams of this cove is reported to exist at a point not visited.

1019. (e) Passing back to the cliffs overlooking the valley of Calf Killer, we find, at the head of Blue Spring Cove, northeast of Little's Bank, and about four miles north of Bon Air, *Trowbridge's Bank*. The section here is as follows:

CONGLOMERATE, heavy, making the cliff.

Shale, (may have a *coal* seam,) .... 15 feet.

Sandstone, from .... 3 to 6 feet.

Shale, ... 2 feet.

Coal, ... $2\frac{1}{2}$ to 3 feet.

Sandstone, rough, eight or ten feet seen.

1020. (f) North of the last, and on the point of the Table-land about opposite the mouth of Cherry Creek, is *Officers' Bank*, which has afforded considerable coal. Not having visited it, I cannot give its character.

1021. (g) Several fine outcrops are reported in the head of England's Cove, beneath the Conglomerate; one, I was told, is "15 feet thick;" I cannot vouch for the truth of the statement.

1022. (h) At the extreme head of the Calf Killer gorge, in Putnam County, and about a mile south of Whitaker's, on the Walton road, the following section was seen:

CONGLOMERATE, capping the Table-land here .... 100 feet

Shale, ... 4 to 6 feet.

Coal, at least .... 2 feet.

Space, doubtful, ... 5 feet.

Sandstone, ... 35 to 40 feet.

Shale, at top, with lower part doubtful, ... 15 feet.

LIMESTONE.

1023. (i) Other similar sections occur in this region. At Brady's Mill, in the same vicinity, the following is the section, no coal appearing:

CONGLOMERATE, ... 100 feet.

Shelly Sandstone, ... 25 feet.

Sandstone, ... 15 feet.

Shale, with iron-stones, ... 15 feet.

Space, rocks not seen, in which there might be *coal*. The limestone soon follows.

1024. (j) *Horn's Bank*, at the top of the mountain, on the west side of the Calf Killer Valley, in Putnam, near the White County line; a bed six feet thick in the bank; lies immediately below the Conglomerate, or with but a little shale intervening; has a heavy sandstone below it, the Mountain Limestone soon following.

1025. In none of the banks enumerated, has there been anything like extensive mining done. They are little else than openings made in the beds for the purpose of obtaining a little coal for local use. The stimulus of a railroad is needed, to bring out the mineral resources of this region.

1026. Returning to the sections in §§ 1009 and 1010, we see that the *Upper Measures* in these embrace several coals. The two principal ones appear to be the *Eastland* and the *Scarbrough*. The later may be the *Main Sewanee*, or *Coal B*. (§ 980.) Of this I cannot, at present, be certain, though I think it probable. In the sections I have referred the portions above the main Conglomerate to the *Upper Measures*, thus making them equivalent, in general, to the upper portion of the Sewanee Section. (949.) This reference, as in the case of the Scarbrough Coal, is provisional. The plants have not been studied. The underlying Conglomerate is a well defined stratum, and, doubtless, equivalent to that of the Crab Orchard Section. (§ 1005.)

1027. The belt of the Table-land in White and Cumberland counties, west of the Crab Orchard Range, embraces in the most of its area, the upper plateau-ridges, which are usually capped with the topmost stratum of the Eastland Section. They, therefore, may contain the coals of this, and of the section at Scarbrough's. Very few natural outcrops are met with, and it remains for future enterprise to see how far the beds are developed.

1028. The sections taken on the slopes overlooking the Calf Killer, the two just referred to, and that of § 1005, taken together, will enable the reader to appreciate the general character of the Coal Formation across the middle parts of the Table-land.

1029. Before leaving this belt, *Davis' Bank*, in Cumberland County, must be mentioned. This is located about five miles in a southeasterly direction, from Crossville, and about a mile from the old Lowry Stand. The bank is on a branch of Meadow Creek. The coal is near the surface, has no covering but the soil, and is obtained from open pits. The bed is at least six feet thick. The coal is of excellent quality, lustrous, has the structure of the first-mined Sewanee coal, and is used by blacksmiths in Crossville, and at other points.

This coal, with the *Scarbrough* and the *Haley*, may belong to the Main Sewanee. Future investigations must settle this point. The strata in the vincinity of the Davis' Bank are much disturbed West of it, for half a mile or more, is a belt of tilted strata, sandstones and conglomerates out cropping in parallel ledges, which run in a northeasterly and southwesterly course. Following this belt of disturbance on the northwest, is a fault beyond which the rocks are horizontal. This is the first line of marked disturbance met with in traveling southeastward, across this part of the Table-land.

1030. We now pass to the part of the division under consideration, lying in Putnam, Overton, Fentress, Morgan and Scott counties.

1031. The Coal Measures in this area present the same general features that they do in the portion just considered, and it will not be necessary for us to dwell at length upon them.

The *Lower Measures* of the area have been characterized in common with those of the whole western escarpment, in § 1013. The lower coals have been most worked, are best known, and, at many points, are the most available on this portion of the Table-land.

1032. The remarks made in §§ 1026 and 1027, apply as well to what I name here *provisionally*, the *Upper Measures*. The uppermost rock of the Eastland Section (§ 1009) appears to extend northeastward, through Cumberland, into the eastern end of Putnam, the southern parts of Overton and Fentress, the western part of Morgan, and further northward. It becomes at some points, a well defined and heavy conglomerate. It is the cap-rock of the greater part of the region indicated, appearing as the top-rock of the plateau belts between the valleys of the mountin streams. The high, level roads of the Table-land, often run for miles upon it.

1033. The *Main Conglomerate*, separating the Lower and "Upper" Measures, in the Eastland Section, is also well characterized, is often 100 feet, and is the cap-rock of much of the Table-land in Putnam, Overton, Fentress, and the western part of Scott. Jamestown, and much of the surrounding country are based upon it. On the parts of the Table-land capped by the upper Eastland rock, the valleys cut down into the shales underlying the latter, and often through them, to the Main Conglomerate. The Measures between these rocks are thinner in Putnam, and in the northwestern part of Cumberland, than further south, and do not appear to contain as much coal.

1034. It may be found, hereafter, that the two conglomerates above mentioned, go together, like the pair in the Ætna Section, (§§ 994, 995,) although the features of the Eastland and Scarbrough sections point to Sewanee for their parallel. In the Crab Orchard Section, the upper one does not appear as a conglomerate.

1035. I present on next page a few typical sections, and an enumeration of a number of the coal outcrops and banks in this part of the Northern Division.

First is a section taken at the mouth of *Big Hurricane*, in the southwestern part of Fentress County.

Upper Measures, 214 ft.

(6) **CONGLOMERATE,** forms cliffs overlooking the deep, wild gulfs of this region. The upper plateaus crowd in closely here,............................ 40 feet.

(5) *Shale* (**Coal?**) .... 51 feet.

(4) *Sandstone,*.. 6 feet.

(3) *Shale* (**Coal?**) .... 21 feet.

(2) *Sandstone,*.. 46 feet.

(1) *Shale* (**Coal?**) *and Sandy Shale,*.................................. 50 feet.

CONGLOMERATE, mostly without pebbles here, forms a lower terrace of bold cliffs,.. 90 feet.

Lower Measures, 35 feet.

(3) **Coal,** with a sandstone roof, very irregular, varies from 0 to 3 feet, is seen at several different points under the cliffs in the Hurricane gulf, coal cubic, apparently of good quality, from....................0 to 3 feet.

(2) *Fire Clay, Shale, and thin Sandstone,*......................... 4 feet.

(1) *Shale,* with six or eight layers of thin *clay ironstones,*..25 to 30 feet.

Mountain Limestone; limestone 15 feet; followed below by 100 feet of variegated, marly shales.

1036. The following was taken, in the southeastern part of Overton County, on the east side of the East Fork of Obey River, and near the road leading from Bledsoe's old stand to the "Three Forks" of the West Fork. It exhibits one of the coals in the *Upper Measures :*

Upper Measures, 208 feet.

Conglomerate,.. 40 feet.

Shales (**Coals?**) and some thin *sandstones*.................. 80 feet.

Sandstone, shelly,.. 25 feet.

Shale,.. 5 feet.

Coal, has been mined, but the opening mostly closed at the time of my visit; coal cubical, of excellent quality; bed, I was assured, at least,.................. 4 feet.

Shales? .... 54 feet.

CONGLOMERATE, heavy, but not measured; below it are Shales and Sandstones, and below these again, the *Mountain Limestone Formation.*

1037. The sections above present sufficiently well, the general structure of the Coal Formation in this region. The Main Conglomerate has always a coal horizon, made up of shales and sandstones, below it, and, when the cap-rock of the higher plateaus is present, one above it. Both horizons are variable in thickness, and, also, as to number and quality of their coals.

1038. The following are examples of banks opened in the *Lower Measures*, and of some of the natural coal outcrops occurring. Two additional sections are also given, which will further illustrate the character of the series.

1039. (a) *Whitaker's Coal*, in Putnam County. In §§ 1022 and 1023, are sections at the head of the Calf Killer Gulf. From a mile and a half to two miles north of these, on the breaks of Sinking Cane, are Whitaker's Banks. There are two of these, half a mile apart, both under the Conglomerate, a bed of shale intervening. One was six feet thick when first opened, soon, however becoming less; the other is from three to three and a half feet, affording a good, cubic coal, highly esteemed by blacksmiths. At the latter bank there are nearly 100 feet of measures below the Conglomerate.

1040. (b) *Taylor's Bank*, at the head of Buffalo Cove, in Fentress County, and about four miles from Jamestown. The following is an approximate section at this point:

CONGLOMERATE, very heavy, caps the Table-land in this region.

LOWER MEASURES, 130 ft.	*Shelly Sandstone*,	15 to 20 feet.
	Shale and *Sandy Shales*	60 feet.
	Sandstone.	12 feet.
	Shale,	10 feet.
	Coal, lustrous, cubic, excellent coal. About half a mile from this point is another *bank* (*Little's*) in the same bed,	3 to 4 feet.
	Space, rocks not seen,	4 feet.
	Sandstone,	20 feet.

Space, rocks not seen, ... 30 feet.

MOUNTAIN LIMESTONE.

1041. (c) *Poplar Cove Banks*, about three miles west of Jamestown, approximately the same position as the last. These are old banks, worked many years. Two boat loads were taken down the Obey to the Cumberland, and then to Nashville. Bed three to four feet.

1042. (d) On the White Oak, east of Jamestown, are several promising outcrops of coal. One of these is about six miles from Jamestown, at which point the following section is seen, the thickness of the heavier strata being estimated:

CONGLOMERATE, about....................................100 feet.

Lower Measures, 76 feet.		
	Space, rocks covered....................................	25 feet.
	Shelly Sandstone, ...	15 feet.
	Coal, outcrop; a little shale above.....................	1 foot.
	Shales, ...	20 feet.
	Coal, main outcrop, fine natural show of good coal; from two to three feet seen, may be..................	4 to 5 feet.
	Shale and Sandstone,..	10 feet.

Bed of White Oak.

1043. (e) *Stepp's Bank*, on White Oak, at the mouth of Yellow Creek, three miles, air line, from Jamestown. The bed has about the same position below the Conglomerate as the lower coal above; shows at the surface three feet of bright, good-looking coal, and is, doubtless, at least, a four-foot bed.

1044. (f) *Gen. Rodgers' Banks*, in Double-top Mountain, in the western part of Fentress. Double-top is an outlier, situated between the East Fork of Obey and Wolf River. I have not seen these banks, but am informed that the coal is excellent, the bed averaging nearly four feet. The banks are very near Obey's River, and boats, in high water, can be carried out to the Cumberland.

1045. (g) Returning to the head-waters of the East Fork of Obey, we find a fine natural outcrop of coal in Cumberland County, about a mile south of the old Emery road, and on *Dripping Spring Creek*, a tributary of Meadow Creek. This coal is immediately below the Conglomerate, and shows a clear face above the water of four feet, the bottom not being seen. The same coal also appears below, on Meadow Creek.

1046. (h) In the gulf of the *Big South Fork*, there are several outcrops of the lower coals of good thickness, but I cannot, at present, specify them At Beaty's old salt-works, on the Big South Fork, in Kentucky, is a fine show of good coal. It measured, near the surface, from three to four feet; the bed is, doubtless, four or five feet thick.

1047. Outcrops of the *upper coals* are not so numerous as of those below the Main Conglomerate. There, are, at some points, three coal seams in this horizon, at others, two, and occasionally but one. A promising opening in one of these has been given in § 1036. Below are others:

1048. (a) On *Little Laurel*, in Overton County, and very near the Fentress line, is a fine natural exposure of solid, regular, cubical coal. The point is about southeast from Livingston, and a little north of east from the Oil Wells on Spring Creek. The bed is full four and a half feet thick. Coal has been taken from this place for special purposes. My guide (Mr. L. W. Hoover) stated at the time of my visit, that "this coal had made half the game guns in Overton County, besides many that have gone West." The following is the section at this point:

Upper Measure, 240 feet.		
	Upper Conglomerate,	55 feet.
	Shale? (**Coal?**)	60 feet.
	Shelly Sandstone	15 feet.
	Shale?	88 feet.
	Sandstone, seen,	2 feet.
	Shale,	15 feet.
	Coal,	4¼ feet.

Water of a branch emptying into Little Laurel.

1049. (b) At *Hoover's, on Little Hurricane*, (a point just within Overton, and about four miles west of the old Bledsoe Stand,) a bank was opened several years ago, apparently in the same stratum as that above. The coal is of good quality, three feet thick, and has half a foot of slaty cannel above it. The same bed is seen in the valley of the Big Hurricane, about a mile east of Hoover's. The following is the section on Little Hurricane. An upper seam also appears.

Upper Measures, 213 feet.		
	Cap Rock, or Upper Conglomerate	30 feet.
	Shales and thin Sandstones,	90 feet.
	Shale,	5 feet.
	Coal, promising outcrop,	1 to 2 ft.
	Shale and some thin Sandstones,	68 feet.
	Black Slaty Cannel, six inches.	
	Coal, *Hoover's Bank;* may be a four-foot bed; has a good bed of shale above it; near the surface,	3 feet.
	Space, down to Little Hurricane,	15 feet.

This is followed, not far below, by the *Main Conglomerate.*

1050. (c) One of the upper coals occurs at a point near the Putnam County line, about three miles north of the Emery road, and in a direction a little east of north from *Officer's*. It has much shale above it, and appears to have the relative position of the Hoover Coal.

1051. (d) Above the *Whitaker Bank*, containing the bed of coal three and a half feet thick, (§ 1039,) is an upper bed, two feet in thickness. This appears to be above the Main Conglomerate, which is here greatly reduced in thickness, and has, both above and below it, an unusual development of shale.

1052. (e) *Johnson's Bank*, in Cumberland County, on Clear Creek, at a point about two miles northeast of the old Johnson Stand. But little coal has been taken from this. Said to be a four-foot bed. At the time of my visit, the pit was partly filled with water; above the water it showed two feet of excellent coal. Resting upon the bed are fifteen inches of cannel slate, above which are indications of still more coal. This opening promises well. The coal lies but little below the Upper Conglomerate, which is quite heavy here.

This bed shows, at another point about three-fourths of a mile below, on the opposite side of the creek.

1053. An outcrop of one of the upper coals, four feet in thickness, is reported a few miles west of Johnson's, towards the head of England's Cove, and not far above the sub-conglomerate *fifteen-foot* bed spoken of on a previous page.

1054. On the old stock road leading south from the Bledsoe Stand, the two Conglomerates, with the shales between, are well seen. Below the upper one is a thin outcrop of coal, which appears to have the place of the Johnson Bed.

1055. (D) *The Northeastern Division.*—This, the remaining division of the Tennessee Coal Field, embraces parts of the counties of Morgan, Anderson, Scott, Campbell and Claiborne. Within it are numerous high ridges, or mountains, that rise above the general level of the Table-land, and in which is found a *great* development of the Coal Measures. In these ridges the shales, coals, and sandstones, generally horizontal, or nearly so, are piled up in alternating series to a great height above the Conglomerate. Altogether, the Coal Formation in this part of the State has a thickness not far from 2500 feet. Nowhere else in Tennessee does the formation present anything like this volume; nowhere else are there so many coal beds, or such an aggregate mass of coal.

1056. The topography of this area has been noticed in the First Part of this Report. The high ridges referred to are mostly included in the New River Group, (§§ 185–187.) They lie, for the most part, east of a line running through Montgomery and Huntsville, and occur, in general, as great water-sheds around the mountain-hemmed valleys of the upper tributaries of New River. They thus divide the waters of this river from those of the Emery on the south, those of the Clinch on the east, and those of Clear Fork and Telfico creeks of the Cumberland, on the north. From the main water-sheds great fingers run in, and interlock with the ramifying tributaries of New River.

The "*detached block*" of the Table-land, or nearly detached, as well as the remarkable skirting ridge, called here *Walden's Ridge*, are to be noticed. (See §§ 179–184.)

1057. The character presented in §§ 940–942 as typical of the Coal Field in general, is nearly lost in this division. The *Lower Measures* occur below the Conglomerate, but the *Upper*

Measures, as seen in that type, have piled upon them many superior strata. By *Upper Measures*, however, I mean here, as elsewhere, all above the *Main Conglomerate.*

1058. It is not in my power to present, at this time, a complete analysis of this rich portion of the Coal Field. There has not been time enough granted for that. I will be able, however, to give my readers its general features, which will enable them to appreciate its great mineral resources.

1059. I present, first, a section of the *Upper Measures* as seen in *Cross Mountain.* (§ 186.) This was taken in 1859, across the great ridge, at a point opposite Col. R. D. Wheeler's residence, in Campbell County, and about four miles in a southwesterly direction from Jacksboro.' My instrument was a pocket-level. The thicknesses are approximations. The section begins near the base of the mountain, at *Wheeler's Coal Bank*, and ascends to one of the highest points, the elevation of which is about 3,370 feet above the sea, and 2,329 feet above *Cove Creek.* (See page 73, (2).) The strata are nearly horizontal, excepting at the base, where they dip at a small angle into the mountain.

(45) SANDSTONE, caps the highest points of the mountain,.........100 feet.
(44) *Shales and Shaly Sandstones*,.. 55 feet.
(43) *Sandstone*,.. 15 feet.
(42) *Shales and thin Sandstones*,...165 feet.
(41) *Shale*,... 14 feet.
(40) **Coal,** *a fine exposure*, contains a six-inch seam of black shale, but otherwise pure cubic coal,.. 6 feet.
(39) *Shale*,... 40 feet.
(38) *Thin Sandstones and Shales;* these rocks are in the gap through which the path leads from Wheeler's across to Beech Creek,...155 feet.
(37) *Shale*,... 45 feet.
(36) SANDSTONE,... 37 feet.
(35) *Shale and Sandy Shale*,.. 74 feet.
(34) **Coal,** fine outcrop, (may be 6 feet,)................................ 4 feet.
(33) *Shale and thin Sandstones*,...40 to 60 ft.
(32) *Sandstone*...60 to 80 ft.
(31) *Shale*,... 50 feet.
(30) **Coal**, *outcrop*,.. 1 foot.
(29) *Fire Clay*,...1 or 2 ft.

(28) *Shale,* .... 50 to 80 ft.
(27) SANDSTONE, ... 60 to 90 ft.
(26) *Shales,* .... 130 feet.
(25) *Shales,* with *clay ironstones,* .... 20 feet.
(24) **Coal,** *outcrop,* .... 1 foot.
(23) *Shale,* .... 6 feet.
(22) **Coal,** *outcrop* at a large "lick" on Beech Creek side, may be a five or six-foot coal, ... 3 feet.
(21) *Shale,* .... 50 to 80 ft.
(20) *Sandstone,* .... 50 feet.
(19) *Shales, mostly,* .... 100 to 120 ft.
(18) SANDSTONE, ... 75 to 100 ft.
(17) *Shale,* .... 45 feet.
(16) **Coal,** *outcrop,* with shaly parting of three inches, ... 3 feet.
(15) *Shale and Sandstones,* shales predominating, ... 190 feet.
(14) SANDSTONE, ... 50 to 80 ft.
(13) *Shale,* .... 20 feet.
(12) **Coal,** .... 3 feet.
(11) *Shale,* with *clay ironstones,* .... 25 feet.
(10) *Sandstone,* .... 25 feet.
(9) *Shale,* heavy, thickness uncertain, say, ... 110 feet.

WHEELER'S BANK.
(8) *Shale and "black slate,"* .... 10 feet.
(7) **Coal,** *outcrop,* .... 1 foot.
(6) *Shale and Fire Clay,* .... 4 feet.
(5) *Shale,* .... 5 feet.
(4) **Coal,** with a three-inch parting in upper portion, ... 5 feet.
(3) *"Black Slate,"* contains *Stigmaria,* with rootlets, ... 3 feet.
(2) *Shale and Fire Clay,* with *Stigmaria,* .... 6 feet.

(1) *Sandy Shale,* (foot of mountain,) .... 30 feet.

1060. The entire thickness of the strata in the section above, is about 2,100 feet. At no point, except in Wheeler's Bank, has any work been done to lay open the *coal seams,* yet we have, known only by their natural outcrop, no less than *nine* of them, six of which show not less than three feet of coal each. The aggregate amount of outcropping coal is 27 feet. This promises well for the Measures when they shall have been thoroughly examined. Many seams, doubtless, do not appear at the surface, and the aggregate of the coal, when fully made out, will be found to be more than double that given.

1061. Below is a section of *Tellico Mountain*, lying on the northwestern side of the Elk Fork Valley, (§ 354.) This valley is divided longitudinally by a great fault running through it. To the northwest of this fault lie the Coal Measures, the Conglomerate being the lowest stratum seen in the valley; immediately to the southeast, as shown in the section, are much lower formations, while the Conglomerate is raised to the very top of Pine Mountain.

This section was taken by F. G. Chavannes, Civil Engineer, in a survey of the Elk Fork Valley. It indicates, like the last, great richness in *coal*. The thicknesses are approximate.

MEASURES OF TELLICO MOUNTAIN, 1620 feet, (approximately.)

(11) *Shales, Slate, etc.*, a portion not defined; contains a bed of **Coal** not located; a heavy series at the top of *Tellico Mountain*, with a maximum thickness, according to Chavannes' sections, of not less than.......600 feet.

(10) SANDSTONE, compact, forms cliffs, about....... 90 feet.

(9) *Shales and Flaggy Sandstones;* "contains, I think, a three and a half feet **Coal Seam,**"....... 50 feet.

(8) *Micaceous Flaggy Sandstones, Shales, Flaggy Sandstone,* .... 80 feet.

(7) *Shales and Slate,* and very probably a valuable **Coal Bed,**.......100 feet.

(6) *Flaggy Sandstone, Shales, Flaggy Sandstone;* contains **Coal Seams,**.......250 feet.

(5) *Slate,* **Coal** one and a half feet thick, *Slate, Sandstone,* **Coal** two feet, *Slate, Grit, Shales, Slate, Grit,* 120 feet.

(4) *Coarse Micaceous Sandstone,*.......200 feet.

(3) *Slaty Grit* on top, *Shales, Slate, Yellow Shales,*....... 80 feet.

(2) *Slaty Grit* on top, *Shales* eight feet, *Slate,* probably a four feet **Coal Bed,** Shales,....... 50 feet.

(1) **CONGLOMERATE,** quartzose, thickness unknown. This outcrops in the Elk Fork Valley on the northwest side of the Fault. Mr. Chavannes, without giving any especial reason, says: "This rock is evidently higher in the series than the Conglomerate on the top of Pine Mountain." I know of no reason why it may not, provisionally, at least, be regarded as the same.

1062. Below is a section of the *Lower Measures*, as presented in the upper part of *Pine Mountain*. The *Conglomerate* of this is most likely a detached part of that at the base of the last section, and will serve to unite the two sections.

No outcrops of the lower coals have been observed on the face of Pine Mountain that I know of, but the seams are doubtless present. This section, with the exception of the parts within parentheses, is Mr. Chavannes'. As before, the thicknesses are approximate:

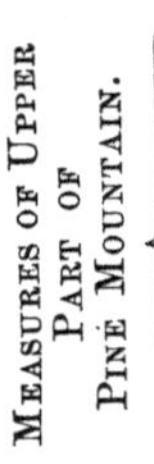

(4) **CONGLOMERATE,** at the summit of *Pine Mountain*, thickness unknown; has *Slate* and *Shales* below.

(3) *Flaggy Micaceous Sandstone* on top; *Slate* and *Shales* below, (contains, doubtless, a **Coal** or two, S.).....220 feet.

(2) *Compact Grit on top*, Slate, Shales, (**Coal?** S.,).........120 feet.

(1) *Coarse Sandstone* on top, *Clay*, *Slate*, *Shales*, (**Coal,** S.,) ....100 feet.

Then follows below the Mountain Limestone, forming the lower part of Pine Mountain.

1063. The sections above may be taken as typical of the character of the Coal Measures in the mountain ridges of the Northeastern Division. The high mountains in Anderson County, the *American Ridge* back of the Saltworks, (Winter's Gap,) present sections similar to that of the Cross Mountain, opposite Col. Wheeler's. The aggregate thickness of the natural coal *outcrops* on the side of the American Ridge, was estimated at 35 feet.

The mountains northeast of Montgomery and Wartburg belong to the same group as those mentioned, and have the same features as to Coal, and the Coal Formation.

1064. The parts of the division not presenting high mountains, have the character of the Coal Field in general, and a geological structure corresponding more or less nearly to that of the type given in § 942; at some points, one or more coal horizons are added above.

1065. In the Cross Mountain Section, (§ 1059,) I have included *Wheeler's Coal Bank*. This is in a very valuable bed of coal that appears to lie at the base of Cross Mountain, from the vicinity of Elk Gap to Coal Creek, and, indeed, at the base of the main mountain, as far down as the Saltworks. It doubtless extends southwest from this point, and may be the bed worked in some of the banks on the waters of the Emery. This bed has been the main source of the coal used in Anderson and Campbell counties. It is of excellent quality, and highly esteemed. The features of Col. Wheeler's Bank are given in the section. Below are other banks in this bed.

1066. *Morrow's Bank*, near Elk Gap. I saw this in 1859. It was an opening made for the purpose of showing the coal, and the thickness of the bed. The presentation was about as follows:

Shale, heavy bed above.

Coal, *ten feet* exposed in the bank, but somewhat contorted; a six-foot bed at least indicated.

Black Slate, highly bituminous, approaching cannel coal, two and a half feet thick.

Fire Clay and *Sandy Shale*, below.

The Shale upon this coal is followed above by sandstone, above which again, is another *coal bed*, said to be three feet thick.

1067. *Wiley's Bank*, about half a mile to the right of the *Coal Creek* Gap, in Anderson County. The following is the section:

Shale.

Coal,	1 foot.
Clay Seam	2 to 3 inchs.
Coal,	3½ feet.
Black Slate, with *Stigmaria*	6 inches.
Coal,	1 foot.
Fire Clay,	1 to 2 feet.
Sandy Shale,	4 feet.
Thin Sandstones	10 to 15 feet.
Sandy Shales,	40 feet.
Shale, with *Clay Ironstones*, running down to the creek,	55 feet.

1068. *Bank* in the vicinity of the *Salt-works* (Winter's Gap,) in Anderson. Bank (1854) about one mile from the Gap, and about 60 feet above the branch; the coal of first quality, and from six to seven feet in thickness. Knoxville has obtained the most of its coal here. It is a solid, bituminous, gas-making coal.

I do not assert positively, that the bed here is the same as that of the three banks mentioned above, though I think it is. This is a point to be definitely settled hereafter. Its general topographical and stratigraphical relations are about the same.

1069. This great bed, which we may call throughout, the *Wheeler Coal*, presents, to say nothing of other beds, an amount of fuel which many generations will not exhaust. Being near the base of the mountain, it is easily approached, and will be extensively mined when the Knoxville and Kentucky Railroad is completed.

1070. I am not prepared to say, as yet, what bed of Lesley's classification the Wheeler Coal is to be referred to. If called upon to fix it *provisionally*, I would make it Bed B, the *Sewanee*. (§ 980.) How far it may be above the Conglomerate I know not. The Gap in Walden's Ridge,* (§§ 183, 184,) through which Coal Creek runs, presents a section which, if there be no fault, would throw it more than 600 feet above the Conglomerate, but this is hardly admissible.

1071. About Montgomery and Wartburg, there are three beds of *coal*. One, opposite Montgomery, appears to be a four-foot bed of good quality. As to the character of the others, I am not informed. These beds doubtless occur at numerous points in the slopes and hills bounding the valley of the Emery River. Scores of banks might be opened along this stream.

1072. *Rocks of Special Use, Minerals, and Agricultural Features of the Coal Measures.* The great mineral product of this formation, is, of course, *Stone-coal.* This is incomparably more important than all of the other mineral substances of the formation, susceptible of application to special use, taken together.

1073. Outside of coal, *Iron-ore* may be mentioned. This is at some points, quite abundant in the shales of the formation. It occurs in nodules, balls, and in flattened concretions arranged in layers in the shales, or scattered through them, and forming what are called *clay-ironstones.* This ore is quite different from anything worked in Tennessee. It consists of *carbonate of iron*, more or less mixed with clay or sand. It is an important ore in Pennsylvania and Ohio, and is extensively used in those States in making iron. The clay-ironstones are mentioned in a number of the sections given on previous pages. They are

* It may be remarked that the skirting Walden's Ridge in Anderson, and in counties further north, is mostly made up of strata belonging to the lower part of the Coal Formation. Some of the lower Sandstones, and the Conglomerate itself, are seen in this ridge, as great, highly inclined, or sometimes vertical, plates, between which are shales and sometimes coal. These strata come out from under the main mountain, and turn abruptly up, at a high angle.

quite abundant in the lowest bed of shale in the Wiley Bank Section. (§ 1067.)

1074. *Flag-stones* of good quality may be obtained at many points in this formation. Near Wartburg, in Morgan, are good quarries.

1074 a. The sandstones of the Coal Formation are often an excellent building material. When these are white, and of good grain, they make a handsome building. The name *free-stone* is given to some sandstones, on account of the ease with which they may be cut in any direction.

1075. The topographical features of the area underlaid by the Coal Measures, or, in other words, of the Table-land, have been given in the first part of the Report. (See page 66, and on.) The surface of the Table-land has many attractions; its clear, pure water; its comparatively mild and salubrious climate; and in many parts, its wild, native scenery, make it an inviting region. Its soils, however, are light, and not comparable with those of the great limestone valleys and areas of the lower portions of the State. They are derived from sandstones and shales, interstratified with which are no limestones, and are, therefore, sandy loams, without calcareous matter. The soils are usually of fine texture and easily tilled, and with proper manipulation, are productive. The addition of composts with lime, will make them highly so.

1076. As we have seen, the surface of the Table-land is more or less cut up into valleys of moderate depth, and wide, flat-topped ridges. Arable land occurs both in the valleys and on the ridges, though the latter are sometimes too poor for cultivation. The native growth is mostly made up of oaks, chestnuts and hickories.

At some points yellow pine abounds. Along some of the streams, or on slopes richer than usual, poplars, maples, and walnuts, are met with. Some of the slopes of the high mountain-ridges in the Northeastern Division are covered with a heavy growth of timber, and are among the most fertile parts of the Table-land.

1077. As stated in § 171, this portion of the State is, as yet, thinly settled. The towns located upon it are *Huntsville*, *Jamestown*, *Montgomery*, *Crossville*, *Spencer* and *Altamont*. In addition, *Wartburg*, near Montgomery, and *Tracy City*, might be mentioned.

The agricultural features of the Table-land will be further noticed hereafter.

1078. *Fossil Plants of the Main Sewanee and Jackson Coal Horizon.*—This is the list referred to in § 980. The specimens have been seen by Prof. *L. Lesquereux*, and were labelled by him.

(1) *Neuropteris heterophylla*, Brgt. *Main Sewanee*, Tracy City; *Jackson*, R. R. cut near "Lower Mines," (Porter and Logan Banks.)

(2) *Neuropteris Loschii*, Brgt. *Jackson*, R. R. cut near Lower Mines.

(3) *Hymenophyllites giganteus*, Lsqx. *Main Sewanee*, Tracy City.

(4) *Alethopteris Serlii*, Gopp. *Jackson*, R. R. cut near Lower Mines.

(5) *Alethopteris lomchitidis*, Sternb. *Main Sewanee*, Tracy City.

(6) *Asterophyllites grandis*, Sternb. *Jackson*, R. R. cut near Lower Mines.

(7) *Calamites cruciatus*, Sternb. *Main Sewanee*, Tracy City.

(8) *Stigmaria ficoides*, Brgt. *Main Sewanee* in under-clay, Tracy City.

(9) *Sigillaria Brardii?* Brgt. *Main Sewanee*, Tracy City.

(10) *Sigillaria Menardi?* Brgt. *Main Sewanee*, Tracy City.

(11) *Sigillaria tessellata*, Brgt. *Main Sewanee*, Tracy City.

(12) *Sigillaria elegans*, Brgt. *Main Sewanee*, Tracy City.

(13) *Sigillaria attenuata*, Lsqx. *Main Sewanee*, same locality as the last.

(14) *Sigillaria alveolaris*, Brgt. *Main Sewanee*, Tracy City. (This and the last species may be the same.)

(15) *Syrigodendron cyclostegium*, Brgt. *Main Sewanee*, locality as the last.

(16) *Syrigodendron pachyderma*, Brgt. *Main Sewanee*, locality as above.

(17) *Lepidodendron obovatum*, Sternb. *Main Sewanee*, Tracy City.

(18) *Lepidodendron aculeatum*, Sternb. *Main Sewanee*, located as above.

(19) *Lepidodendron elegans*, Brgt. *Main Sewanee*, located as above.

(20) *Lepidodendron vestitum*, Lsqx. *Main Sewanee*, Tracy City.

(21) *Lepidodendron rimosum*, Sternb. *Main Sewanee*, locality as above.

(22) *Lepidostrobus ornatus*, Lind. & Hutt. *Jackson*, R. R. cut near Lower Mines, and *Main Sewanee*, Tracy City.

(23) *Trigonocarpum. Main Sewanee*, Tracy City.

(24) *Rhabdocarpus venosus*, Lsqx. *Main Sewanee*, located as last.

1079. Specimens of the following species have been obtained at the *Ætna Mines*, from the *Main Ætna* or *Cliff-Vein Horizon:*

(1) *Sphenopteris tridactilites?*

(2) *Hymenophyllites Hildreti*, Lsqx.

(3) *Lepidodendron rugosum*, Sternb.

(4) *Lepidodendron rimosum*, Sternb.

(5) *Lepidodendron modulatum*. Lsqx.

1980. The following are the fossil *nuts* found at the base of the Coal Measures on the Sewanee Railroad. (See section in § 925.)

(1) *Trigonocarpon Saffordi*, Lsqx.

(2) *Trigonocarpon olivæformis*, Lind. & Hutt

(3) *Trigonocarpon Nœggerathii*, Brgt.

CHAPTER XIII.

THE CRETACEOUS FORMATIONS; SERIES X.

1081. We come now to the comparatively unconsolidated strata of West Tennessee. (§ 272.) The formations hitherto considered are made up of solid rocks, and belong to the second great division of geological time, the *Paleozoic*. (See page 156.) The formations to be described in this and in the three following chapters, appertain to the *Mesozoic and Cenozoic* divisions, and some of the recent alluvial beds, to the *Age of Man*.

1082. The place of the *Cretaceous formations* in the complete geological column, (see pages 154 and 155,) is some distance above that of the *Coal Measures*, the interval being occupied by several heavy formations. In Tennessee, however, this interval is vacant, and we pass abruptly from the Coal Formation to the Cretaceous, no strata of the *Permian*, *Triassic* and *Jurassic* formations, appearing.

1083. In traveling westward from Middle Tennessee, we, very soon after passing the Tennessee River, meet with a line along which the older formations are suddenly and deeply beveled off. This has been already spoken of in §§ 272 and 832. This slope was perhaps the shore of the arm of the Atlantic mentioned in § 331. It is now, for the most part, the eastern rocky side of a deep trough, in which lie the stratified sands, clays, marls and loams of Western Tennessee and Eastern Arkansas. See also § 326, and the paragraphs referred to.

1084. The topographical features of West Tennessee have been given in the First Part of the Report. §§ 272—294. The reader is also referred to the Map and the section at its base, as well as to the diagram following.

1085. The *Cretaceous Series* includes in Tennessee, the following formations:

10,c. *Ripley Group*, (provisional.)
10,b. *Green Sand*, or the *Shell Bed.*
10,a. *Coffee Sand.*

Each of these, commencing with the lowest, will be the subject of a separate section.

SECTION I.

THE COFFEE SAND; FORMATION 10,*a*.

1086. This is the oldest member of the Cretaceous Series, outcrops in Hardin and Decatur Counties, and overlaps the western beveled edge of the older rocks. Its outcrop occupies a belt of territory varying from about two to eight miles in width, and running more than half way through the State.* (See 10,a. upon the Map.) The diagram on page 413 exhibits the relation this formation sustains to the older rocks and to the *Green Sand* above it.

1087. By referring to the Map it will be seen that the Tennessee River is, with the exception of *a single break in Hardin County*, bordered throughout on the west by a belt of Paleozoic rocks. Along this break the river comes in contact with the strata of the *Coffee Sand*, and washes them for eighteen or twenty miles, presenting, at intervals, several bluffs that exhibit interesting sections.

1088. These bluffs are much alike; they vary from 80 to 100 feet in height, and are capped with a layer of gravel belonging to one of the gravel beds to be described. The principal ones are given on the Map, and are *Coffee Bluff* (sometimes strangely called "*Chalk Bluff*") at *Coffee Landing*, that at *Crump's Landing*, and the one at *Pittsburgh Landing*. The first, which gives name to the bed under consideration, is nearly two miles long. One of its sections will be given below.

*There is some doubt in regard to the northern limits of this and of the succeeding formation. Their limits, as given on the Map north of Beech River, are provisional. The outline given is probably not far from the correct one.

1089. The Coffee Sand consists mostly of stratified sands usually containing scales of mica. Thin leaves of dark clay are often interstratified with the sand, the clay leaves occasionally predominating. Sometimes beds of dark laminated or slaty clay of considerable thickness—from one to twenty feet or more—are met with in the series. It very generally contains woody fragments and leaves, converted more or less into *lignite.* Silicified trunks of trees are not uncommon. The maximum thickness of the series in Tennessee is not known; it is probably not far from 200 feet.

1090. A section of the bluff at Coffee may be taken as a type of the materials and stratification of this group.

(4) *On top;* gravel and ferruginous conglomerate.

(3) *Sands,* with thin laminæ of slaty clay; much like No. 1 below.. 10 feet.

(2) *Slaty clay,* with but little sand; contains fragments of wood and leaves.. 20 feet.

(1) *Gray and Yellow Sands,* interstratified with numerous thin laminæ and some thicker layers of slaty clay; strata of sand occasionally from three to six feet, without clay. Leaves, in fragments, and pieces of lignitic wood abundant. Projecting from the mass are the ends of two large trunks, their bark converted into lignite, and their wood silicified.

Contains pyrite and yields proto-salts of iron and ferruginous waters.

Extending to the water's edge.................................. 65 feet.

1091. The following is a section seen at one point of the *Bluff at Pittsburg Landing.*

(2) *Gravel,* on top,... 30 feet.

(1) *Yellow, Red* and *Orange Sands,* much interstratified with thin *laminæ of Clay;* beds of sand occur, three or four feet thick without the clay laminæ, then a bed as thick, or thicker, is full of them. The sands contain occasionally, a thin seam of ferruginous sandstone. But little vegetable matter is seen in this bluff,...................60 to 70 ft.

1092. In low sheltered places the sands in the exposures of this formation are generally dark gray, and contain pyrite. In exposed situations, however, as in old washes or near the surface, their contents become peroxydized, their lignitic matter is removed, (consumed,) and the sands assume brighter colors, becoming white, yellow, red or orange, as the case may be.

1093. Although fragments of leaves are abundant at some localities, yet it is difficult to obtain good specimens. None that I know of have been described. Within the limits of Tennessee I have not found any animal remains in this group. Along the Memphis and Charleston Railroad, in Mississippi, I have seen many imperfect casts of shells in its southern equivalent, the *Tombigbee sand* of Hilgard, which, perhaps, ought to be included in his *Eutaw Group*. One of these was forwarded, with other Cretaceous fossils, to Mr. Wm. M. Gabb, of Philadelphia, who described it as *Volutilithes Saffordi*, giving "Tennessee," by mistake, as the locality. (*Jour. Acad. Nat. Sci.*, [2,] iv, 299.) The specimen was obtained from a cut about three miles and a half west of Burnsville.

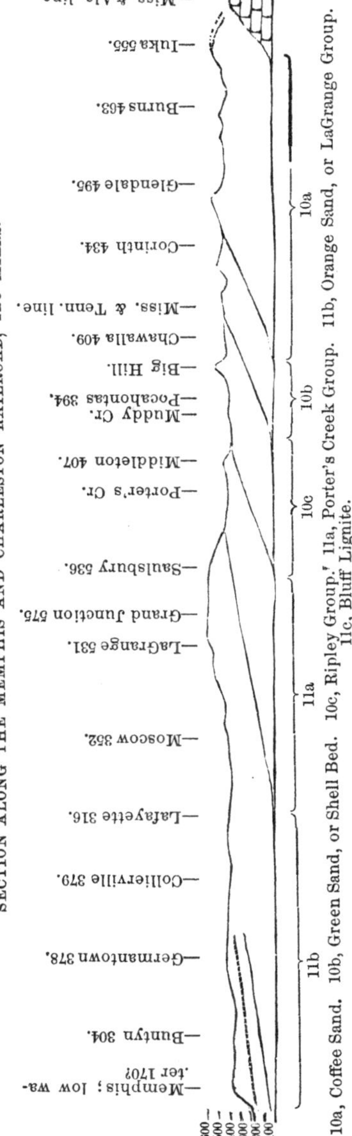

SECTION ALONG THE MEMPHIS AND CHARLESTON RAILROAD, 120 MILES.

10a, Coffee Sand. 10b, Green Sand, or Shell Bed. 10c, Ripley Group.' 11a, Porter's Creek Group. 11b, Orange Sand, or LaGrange Group. 11c, Bluff Lignite.

1094. Away from the streams there are few characteristic exposures of this formation to be met with. At many points where its strata would otherwise outcrop, everything is covered with *gravel*. Decaturville is located upon its feather edge, and west of this place its sands and clays are met with, resting upon the Silurian limestones.

1095. It is the formation at *Scott's Hill*, on the road from Lexington to Clifton, and sections of it may be seen in this vicinity.

1096. Following it westward, it runs under the Green Sand, and it is the reservoir yielding water, when the formation mentioned is pierced by the well-borers. (§§ 269–270.)

SECTION 11.

THE GREEN SAND, OR SHELL BED; FORMATION 10,*b*.

1097. This is an interesting formation, and has long attracted attention on account of the great number of fossil shells it contains. These occur by cart-loads at some points, and are gathered and burned into lime. It is through this formation that the semi-artesian wells of Hardin, McNairy and Henderson counties are bored. And again, this bed contains grains of a soft greenish mineral, called *glauconite*, which give the mass a greenish color, and hence the name *green sand*. The material of the layers in which grains of glauconite are abundant, is a valuable fertilizer, and is applied like a marl to the lands. Such material, in fact, is often called *marl*.

1098. With reference to the *conspicuous shells*, the "*bald hills*," and the *bored wells* of this formation, see §§ 263 and 264, and also §§ 269 and 270.

1099. At many points along its eastern edge, this formation is seen to rest upon the *Coffee Sand*. Its mass consists generally of fine quartzose sand mixed with clay, forming a clayey sand, which is more or less calcareous. It contains *green grains* throughout, though not abundantly, and fine scales of mica. Owing to the clay present, and a certain degree of induration, the mass is generally firm enough to form the walls of the "bored wells," tubing being dispensed with. When dry, the material of the formation has a greenish gray color, which becomes much darker when wet. It has much uniformity in character. That of different layers, however, differs to some extent in hardness, and in the proportional amount of green grains Some of the harder layers are called "rocks" by the well-borers. There is such a layer very generally at the bottom of the series.

1100. Below the soil, for ten or twenty feet from the surface, the green sand is usually converted, by atmospheric agencies, into a grayish or dirty-buff tenacious material, locally called "*joint clay*," from its tendency to cleave, when losing moisture, in irregular, block-like masses.

1101. It abounds in shells. *Exogyra costata*, *Gryphæa vesicularis*, *Ostrea larva* and *Anomiæ*, are found at nearly all exposures. Individuals of these species are plentifully strewed over the "*bald hills*," (§ 263,) the large shells being very conspicuous. This formation is pre-eminently the *shell-bed* of the Post-paleozoic beds of West Tennessee. A list of species collected will be given below. It also contains wood and leaves, but not as abundantly as the Coffee Sand.

1102. This bed is the northern extension of the *Rotten* limestone of Mississippi and Alabama. Its outcrop in Tennessee occupies a belt of the surface averaging about eight miles in width for at least half way through the State. (See Map, 10b, and also the diagram just given.) Further north it becomes inconspicuous. Its limits in this direction have not been satisfactorily made out. (See note under § 1086.) The thickness of the formation is known from data supplied by the well-borers. Along the western margin of its outcrop it varies from 200 to 350 feet, the maximum being in the southern part of the State.

1103. The list below contains the species collected by myself from this bed. These, together with the species collected from the succeeding group, were submitted to the examination of Messrs. Conrad and Gabb. The new forms were described by them in the *Jour. Acad. Nat. Sci.*, vol. iv, 2d series. In their descriptions some are referred to wrong localities. The principal and correct localities are indicated upon the Map by small crosses, and will be designated in the list by letters. They are as follows:

(*a.*) The first, at the very bottom of the bed, in a cut in the Memphis and Charleston Railroad, about 2½ miles east of Corinth, Mississippi.

(*b.*) The "Bald Hills," 14 or 15 miles north of *a*, in Tennessee, and 3 miles northwest of Monterey, in McNairy county.

(*c.*) A bank about 2⅓ miles east of Purdy, Tenn., and very near the top of the bed.

(*d.*) A cut in the Memphis and Charleston Railroad, very near the point where the railroad crosses the Mississippi and Tennessee line.

1. *Platytrochus speciosus*, Gabb and Horn,.......... .... *d.*
2. *Corbula crassiplica*, Gabb,.. *d.*
3. *Crassatella vadosa* Mort., (Syn. *C. Ripleyana*, Con.,)......... *a, c.*
4. *Astarte crinulirata*, Con.,.. *d.*
5. *Venilia Conradi*, Mort.,.. *a, c.*
6. *Cardium abruptum*, Gabb,........... .... *c.*
7. *Cardium*. n. sp., casts. ("Common in New Jersey,")...... *a, c.*
8. *Trigonia thoracica*, Mort.,.. *a, c.*
9. *Arca Saffordi*, Gabb,.. *d.*
10. *Nucula distorta*, Gabb,.. *d.*
11. *Cucullæa Tippana*, Con.,.. *c.*
12. *Ctenoides* (*Lima*) *pelagica*, Mort.,.. *a.*
13. *C. reticulata*, Lyell and Forbes,.. *a.*
14. *Pecten virgatus*, Nilsson,.......... .... *a.*
15. *Neithea occidentalis*, Con.,.. *a, b, c.*
    (Syn. *P. quadricostata*, Rœmer, and perhaps *quinquecostata* of Mort.)
16. *Ostrea larva*, Lam., (Syn. *O. Falcata*, Mort., not Sow.,)..... *a, b, c, d.*
17. *O. plumosa*, Mort.,.. *a, b.*
18. *O. tecticosta*, Gabb,.. *a, b, c, d.*
    (I think this must be *O. crenulata*, Tuomey.)
19. *Exogyra costata*, Say,.. *a, b, c, d.*
20. *Graphæa vesicularis*, Lam.,.. *a, b, c.*
    (Syn. *O. convexa*, Say, and *G. mutabilis*, Mort.)
21. *G. Vomer*, Mort.,.. *a, b.*
22. *Anomia tellinoides*, Mort.,.. *a, b.*
23. *A. Argentaria*, Mort.,.. *a, b. c, d.*
24. *Placunanomia Saffordi*, Con.. *a, b, c, d.*
    (Syn. *P. lineata*, Con. *P. lineata* can be connected with *P. Saffordi* by intermediate forms. The species is an abundant and variable one. Its individ-

uals are often much larger than those figured. Figure 21, pl. 46, (*Jour. Acad.*, vol. iv,) shows the appearance of the tooth after the *enamel*, that coats the inside of the valves, has been removed. Since the species was described, a few perfect valves have been found. The tooth is a prominent, nearly rhombic boss, the inner angle longer than the one behind and longitudinally striated. One muscular impression nearly central; another nearer the tooth from which the ossified plug appears to start.)

25. *Scalaria Sillimani*, Mort., ... *a.*
26. *Natica rectilabrum*, Con., ... *c.*
27. *Volutilithes Texana*, Con., ... *a.*
28. *Rapa* (*Pyrula*) *Richardsonii?* Tuomey, ... *a.*
29. *R. trochiformis*, Tuomey, ... *a.*
30. *Anchura abrupta*, Con., ... *c.*
31. *Baculites compressus*, Say, ... *a, c.*
32. *Enchodus ferox*, Leidy, ... *b.*
33. *Sphyræna*, sp.? .... *a, b.*
34. *Ischyrhiza mira*, ... *b.*

Besides these, I have in my collection from this bed, uncertain species of *Teredo*, *Serpula*, *Rostellaria*, *Fusus*, *Turritella* and *Delphinula*.

Section III.

THE RIPLEY GROUP; FORMATION 10,*c*.

1104. This is a provisional series, and is mostly based upon observations made along and in the vicinity of the Memphis and Charleston Railroad. It is only in this region that determinable species have been found, although search has been made elsewhere for them. Its northern extension has been inferred from the general bearings and relations of its strata and of those of the adjacent groups.

Its outcrop occupies a belt of the surface, (10c, 10c, on the Map,) extending through the State, and being, along the railroad, about fifteen miles wide, but having a less average width.

This belt is, in general, rough and hilly. The high ridges dividing the waters of the Tennessee and Mississippi rivers lie mostly within its area. (§§ 276–278.)

1105. The formation must be of considerable thickness, not less than 400 or 500 feet. It is mostly made up of stratified sands. Occasionally an interstratified bed of dark slaty clay, ten to thirty feet thick, is met with, but more frequently a sandy bed laminated with clayey leaves. In its lithological character, the group is much like the *Coffee Sand.* Its sandy mass, as seen at the surface, is very generally yellow, brown or orange, its contents being peroxydized; occasionally, however, in partially protected or in fresh exposures, its material is dark colored, abounding more or less in fragmentary lignitic matter.

1106. The outcrop of the group very commonly presents layers or masses of ferruginous sandstone, locally indurated by oxyd of iron. This sandstone often occurs in plates, scrolls, tubes and other curious shapes. At some points, especially upon high knobs and ridges, it is found in heavy massive blocks from two or three to fifteen feet in thickness. The occurrence of such sandstone is, however, common to all the sand-formations of West Tennessee. In this group it appears to be especially abundant.

1107. An interesting section of this formation, nearly 100 feet thick, is to be seen at the cut in the Big Hill, a few miles east of Pocahontas, through which the Memphis and Charleston Railroad passes.* The hills about Purdy, in McNairy, and about Lexington, in Henderson, show these rocks well.

1108. In the vicinity of the Memphis and Charleston Railroad, in Hardeman County, there are in the upper part of the series, two local beds, interesting on account of the fossils they contain. The first is a bed of buff gray, impure *limestone,* from two to six feet thick. It is found on both sides of the railroad, near Muddy Creek.† It abounds in two or three species of *Turritella, (T. Saffordi, and pumilla* of Gabb,) *Ostrea Vomer,*

* This section is noticed by Dr. Hilgard in his Mississippi Report, (p. 16,) who refers its strata to his superficial *Orange Sand Formation.* I cannot agree with my learned friend in this reference. Indeed, I think that much of his Orange Sand is nothing more than the peroxidized outcrops of formations lower than he makes this. I do not deny, however, that within certain limits, there is such a formation.

† On the Map Muddy Creek is the first stream represented east of Middleton.

Mort., claws of a *Calianassa?* (for which I propose the name of *C. Gwyni*,*) and other species. The position of the *limestone* is indicated on the Map by the short, heavy lines near Muddy Creek. It is doubtless the "Turritella" and "Bored" limestone of Hilgard's sections, Nos. 12, 13 and 14; pp. 86–88.

1109. The second is a bed of clayey sand with *green grains.* This has been seen west of the limestone at two exposures; one in a small cut on the railroad, about two miles east of Middleton, the other about two miles south or southeast of Middleton, on a branch of Cypress Creek, (of Hardeman,) and near the "old stage road." Each point is indicated upon the Map by a small cross.

1110. The following is a list of species from the two beds, to which, it will be seen, quite a number of the forms are common. Most of them are described in the *Jour. Acad. Nat. Sci. of Phila.*, vol. iv., 2d series. The localities are (a.) *limestone*; (b.) *sand-bed.*

1. *Corbula subcompressa*, Gabb, ... *b.*
2. *Venus Ripleyana*, Gabb, ... *a, b.*
3. *Crassatella pteropsis*, Gabb, ... *a, b.*
   (Conrad had previously given this name to a species of *Crassatella; Jour. Acad.*, iv, 279. I therefore propose *C. Gabbi*, for it.)
4. *C. Monmouthensis?* Gabb, ... *b.*
5. *Cardita subquadrata?* Gabb, ... *b.*
6. *Leda protexta*, Gabb, ... *b.*
7. *Modiola Saffordi*, Gabb, ... *a, b.*
8. *Ostrea denticulifera*, Con. .... *a, b.*
9. *O. crenulimarginata*, Gabb, ... *b.*
   (If No. 8 is referred to the proper species, then *O. crenulimarginata*, Gabb, is, I think, its lower or larger valve.)
10. *Gryphœa Vomer*, Mort., ... *a.*
11. *Turritella Tennesseensis*, Gabb, ... *b.*
12. *T. Saffordi*, Gabb, ... *a, b.*
13. *T. Hardemanensis*, Gabb, ... *b.*
14. *T. pumila*, Gabb, ... *a, b.*
15. *Natica rectilabrum*, Con., ... *b.*
16. *Fasciolaria Saffordi*, Gabb, ... *b.*

* Dedicated to Prof. H. A. Gwyn, of Saulsbury, Tennessee.

17. *Neptunea impressa*, Gabb,.. *b.*
18. *Callianassa? Gwyni*, Safford ....*a, b.*
19. *Lamna gracilis?* Ag.,.. *b.*
20. *Crocodilus?* (Tooth.).. *b.*

It will be seen that but two species of those given, *Gryphæa Vomer* and *Natica rectilabrum*, are common to this group and the Green Sand. Localities in Mississippi, however, furnish series of fossils which unite the groups more intimately. It will be found, perhaps, that the two form, paleontologically, but one formation.

1111. The group also contains wood and leaves. The leaves are generally found in an imperfect condition, and have received but little attention. As the age of the beds containing them are known, their study would be very interesting in connection with that of the leaves of the formation further west, which are of uncertain age.

1112. *Minerals, Materials of Special Use, and Agricultural Features of the Cretaceous Formations.* But few minerals of interest occur in these rocks. The *glauconite* in the Green Sand, is prominent among those that do occur. This is a compound of *silica*, *oxide of iron*, *alumina*, more or less, *potash* and *water*. The fertilizing effects of the *green marl* are, doubtless, due in good part, to the potash, and its commercial value as a fertilizer, depends upon the relative proportion of glauconite it contains. In samples, containing fragments of shells, or decomposing shells, a part of the effect is to be attributed to carbonate of lime. In such cases, the substance becomes, in good part, a true calcareous marl.

1113. Much of the Green Sand is too poor in glauconite to bear transportation. The richest beds are known by their dark green color. The formation is intersected by the Mobile and Ohio, and the Memphis and Charleston Railroads, which renders it accessible. But little use has been made, as yet, of the Tennessee Green Sand. Some experiments were made with it before the war with satisfactory results; and others on a larger scale had been commenced. The matter is worthy of attention. It will be referred to again.

1114. *Pyrite*, in small quantity, is a common mineral in the beds of all the Cretaceous formations, especially at points where their materials have not been weathered. It is the source of the iron of many chalybeate springs.

1115. *Lignite* is also often met with, generally, however, as carbonized fragments of wood, sticks, pieces of bark, and leaves. I have not met with any considerable beds of this mineral in these rocks.

1116. A considerable belt of West Tennessee, including nearly all of McNairy, the western part of Hardin, much of Henderson, the western parts of Decatur and Benton, and the eastern parts of Carroll and Henry, is underlaid by the Creta ceous strata. Many sections of this area, both upland and valley, present good farming lands, the soil being generally a mellow siliceous loam, with a more or less clayey basis, and adapted to the growth of cotton and corn, and some parts to wheat and allied crops. In many of the valleys where the soils are stiffer, grasses find congenial conditions, and meadows might be established more extensively than they are.

1117. This belt, however, is the roughest part of West Tennessee, and not a few of its ridges are poor. It includes the "Tennessee Ridge" and its ramifications, mentioned in the First Part of the Report. (See §§ 276 to 278, inclusive.)

CHAPTER XIV.

THE TERTIARY GROUP; SERIES XI.

1118. This, from an agricultural point of view, is a very important series of formations. It underlies, as may be seen by reference to the Map, a wide central belt in West Tennessee, which includes within its outcrop a very large portion of the most desirable lands of this section of the State. The geological age of its formations is, as yet, not fully settled. It is not even certain that all of them are Tertiary, though with the data before us, this is the best disposition we can, at present, make of them.

1119. The series includes the following formations, or subgroups:

11,c. *Bluff Lignite*, (provisional.)
11,b. *Orange Sand*, or *LaGrange Group.*
11,a. *Porter's Creek Group*, (provisional.)

SECTION I.

THE PORTER'S CREEK GROUP; FORMATION 11,*a.* (*Provisional.*)

1120. I have heretofore included this division in the *Orange Sand*. It may be well, however, to keep it separate, until its age is more satisfactorily ascertained. There is no marked distinction between this and the adjacent groups, except that it contains proportionally much more *laminated or slaty clay.* The clay has the usual characters, contains mica scales, is dark when wet, and whitish gray, when dry. The thickness of the series is, perhaps, 200 or 300 feet. In this are usually several beds of slaty clay from five to fifty feet in thickness. In

Hardeman County, on Porter's Creek,* is a heavy bed, said to be 100 feet thick. I have seen as much as 50 or 60 feet of it exposed.

1121. Along the Memphis and Charleston Railroad, the belt of surface occupied by the group is about eight miles wide. It becomes narrower as we follow it northward. (11a, 11a, on the Map.) The belt appears to be the northern extension of Hilgard's "Flatwoods" region, the group, itself, forming the lower part of his "*Northern Lignitic.*"

1122. An interesting section of the beds included in this division, may be seen on the road from Bolivar to Purdy, commencing about seven miles from the former place, and extending to, or beyond Wade's Creek. In this region are alternating beds of *slaty clays*, ("*soap-stones*,") hard, argillaceous *sandy rocks*, *orange sand*, and at some points, *white clays*. The wells of the region are mostly in "soapstone." The sandy rocks above contain casts of shells.

1123. At *Paris*, in Henry County, the following section occurs, the lower part of which, is referred to the Porter's Creek Group:

(6) *Soil and Sub-soil* at the top of the plateau on which Paris is located.

(5) *Orange Sand*,.. 30 feet.

(4) *Light Yellow Sand*, with numerous thin leaves of *Sand stone* and "*Soapstone*,".. 5 feet.

(3) *Light Yellow Sand*,.. 12 feet.

(2) *Thin Sandstones and Slaty Clay*,................................ 1 foot.

(1) *Slaty Clay*, (*Soapstone*,) the lowest stratum seen,............ 20 feet.

1124. At *Huntingdon*, and at many other points within the belt in which this group outcrops, beds of the laminated clays occur.

1125. I have not as yet, met with rocks in this formation containing determinable shells. In several of the cuts along the Memphis and Charleston Railroad, specimens of leaves are found in the clays, and sometimes in thin local sandstones. The leaves in my collection from this group, which are not many,

* The first creek on the Map, west of Middleton, on the Memphis and Charleston Railroad.

have not been examined. One is much like *Quercus Saffordi*, Lsqx., of the succeeding group, and may be that species; the others are unknown to me.

Section II.

ORANGE SAND, OR La GRANGE GROUP; FORMATION 11*b*.

1126. The outcrop of the *Orange Sand** or *La Grange Group*, forms more than a third of the entire surface of West Tennessee. It occupies a belt about 40 miles wide, which runs in a northeasterly direction through nearly the central portion of this division of the State. (See Map and section 11b, 11b.) As seen in bluffs, railroad cuts, gullies, and in nearly all exposures, it is generally a great stratified mass of yellow, orange, red, or brown and white sands, presenting occasionally an interstratified bed of white, gray, or variegated clay. The sand-beds are usually more or less argillaceous; sometimes but little or not at all so. Like the Ripley Group, it contains occasionally, patches, plates, and thin layers of ferruginous, sometimes argillaceous, sandstone, and, as in that group, presents, locally, massive blocks of sandstone on high points. At La Grange, a fine section of the group, more than a hundred feet in thickness, is exposed.

If penetrated to some depth, the beds of the Orange Sand would lose their bright colors, and become gray or dark.

1127. In deep wells, dark beds of sand, with occasionally one of clay, are met with. These often contain vegetable matter. Now and then, the trunk of a tree is encountered, much to the annoyance of well diggers. I have seen but one bed of lignite in the group, and that a limited one, near its southeastern margin.

* The name, *Orange Sand*, was originally applied by me (Reconnoisance, 1856,) to a series of strata of which the formation now thus designated was the principal member. It then included the *Cretaceous* beds; these have been excluded, but the name has not been dropped. Since my first use of the name, Drs. Harper and Hilgard, in their respective Reports, have applied it to a superficial formation occurring in Mississippi, quite different from anything it was intended to include.

1128. It is difficult to estimate the thickness of this group. It doubtless dips, though at a small angle, to the west. Its thickness may be assumed to be about 600 feet.

1129. The Orange Sand includes within its outcrop, nearly all of the following counties: Fayette, Haywood, Madison, Gibson and Weakley; the larger parts of Hardeman, Carroll and Henry; and small parts of Shelby, Tipton, Henderson, Dyer and Obion.

1130. At the bottom of a railroad cut three miles south of Somerville, in Fayette County, I collected, a number of years ago, from a thin, local sandstone in place, a series of fossil leaves, beautifully presented. These were described by Prof. Leo Lesquereux, in 1859,* but the figures were not given. They may now be found figured on plate K, of this volume.

In addition to these, several leaves, or rather, the impressions of leaves, have been collected by Prof. Meigs, from the clays at La Grange, three of which, Prof. Lesquereux has described.

1131. Below is a list, including all the species described from both localities. Nos. 12, 13, and 14, are the LaGrange species; all the others are from near Somerville. At the end of this section is added the descriptions of the species from the latter locality.

1. *Quercus crassinervis*, Ung.
2. *Quercus Saffordi*, Lsqx.
3. *Quercus myrtifolia?* Willd.
4. *Quercus Lyelli*, Heer.
5. *Prudus Caroliniana*, Michx.
6. *Fagus ferruginea*, Michx. (Fruit.)
7. *Elœagnus inœqualis*, Lsqx.
8. *Andromeda vaccinifoliœ affinis.*
9. *Andromeda dubia*, Lsqx.
10. *Sapotacites Americanus*, Lsqx.
11. *Salix? densinervis*, Lsqx.
12. *Salix Worthenii*, Lsqx.
13. *Ceanothus Meigsii*, Lesqx.
14. *Juglans Saffordiana*, Lsqx.

1132. Of the species above, No. 3, 5, and 6 are living; the others are only known as extinct forms.

In regard to the age of the Orange Sand and its equivalent, in Mississippi, it is the opinion of Prof. Lesquerux, that the leaves make it "most intimately related to the Miocene of Europe." He adds, however, the following:

"Still, I do not consider the question as solved. It can only be satisfactorily settled by recognized differences, or identity of species collected in

* American Jour. Sci. [2,] XXVII, p. 363.

these strata of American formations. For it may be, that, as we have in our Upper Cretaceous dicotyledonous plants of genera still represented in our living Flora, like some of the Miocene of Europe, we may have Eocenic deposits with species still more nearly related to our present vegetation; thus bearing a character approaching that of the European Miocene. Under the uniform development of the formations of the Mississippi Valley, the typical forms may have escaped changes from disturbing influences similar to those which have evidently modified, by repeated cataclysms, the recent formations of Central Europe."

1133. I must confess that I cannot rid myself of the impression that this group is at least *Eocene*. I do not know that I can assign a good reason for this *impression*. I have seen, however, imperfect specimens of leaves in older beds, even in known *Cretaceous clays*, much like some of those of this group, although I could not say they were absolutely identical, on account of their unsatisfactory condition. I see too, that Dr. Hilgard is inclined to place his "*Northern Lignitic*," which includes my *Porter's Creek* and *Orange Sand* groups, at the very bottom of the *Eocene*. (See his Report, page 108, and on.)

I have not been able to find even the cast of a shell in this formation. The discovery of a few known species, if such exist, is a desideratum.

APPENDIX.

1134. "*Species of Fossil Plants collected near Somerville, Fayette County, Tennessee, by Dr. J. M. Safford, State Geologist of Tennessee. Described and Figured by L. Lesquereux.*" The following short description of these fossil leaves has already beenpublished in Silliman's Journal, (May, 1859.) Though, since that time, I have had opportunity to examine other specimens of some of these species, I do not find any reason to change my opinion about their relation or their identity. It is, nevertheless, necessary to remark, that if many species of living plants or trees may be easily identified from their leaves only, the determination of fossil leaves is always more or less hypothetical, at least, so far as specific identification is concerned. This is not a reason to prevent the publication of fossil plants, and to deny the value of the indication which they give concerning the age of the strata in which they are found. Peculiar genera or groups of plants are peculiar to each formation, and these groups are, generally, well characterized enough to show, even without identification of species, to what geological epoch the leaves belong.

The species are figured on Plate K, of this volume:

1. *Laurus Caroliniensis.** Michx. (Red-bay,) *Fig.* 10, grows now in the swamps from south Delaware and south Virginia, to the two Floridas, in

*Since this paper was written, Prof. Lesquereux has identified this species with *Quercus Lyellii*, Heer.

pine barrens. Good and entire specimens collected from the same Geological horizon, and belonging to the cabinet of the Mississippi University of Oxford, show an identity of form between the fossil leaves and the living species.

2. *Prunus Caroliniana*, (Michx.) (Wild Orange tree.) *Fig.* 6. The species is now confined to the islands, and near the coasts of Carolina, Georgia, etc., and in the Bahama islands, where it is at its true latitude.

Michaux remarks that this species is not found on the main land at a distance of two to ten miles from the shores, where the temperature is five to six degrees colder in the winter, and proportionally milder in the summer.

3. *Quercus myrtifolia*, (Willd.) *Fig.* 3. Inhabits now the islands south of Georgia and along the coasts of Florida. Comparison of living specimens with this fossil leaf shows a perfect identity of form and venation.

4. Fruit of *Fagus ferruginea*, (Michx.) (Red Beech.) *Fig.* 11. This fruit is somewhat more distinctly ribbed on the sides and margins than in our living species; but the characters are not marked enough to permit a separation. Though the range of the American beech is indicated as rather northern, the tree is found most abundant, and of the most remarkable growth, on the Tertiary, and even Cretaceous formations of the south, even in Louisiana.

The following species are either new, that is extinct or undescribed species, or unknown to me:

5. *Salix? densinervis*, (Lsqx.) *Fig* 9. Leaves narrow, one and-a-half to two inches long, lanceolate or tapering at both ends, entire. Medial nerve scarcely inflated at the base. Secondary nerves very close, anastomosing as in the leaflets of a fern or of a *Trifolium*. This nervation is quite peculiar for a Salix, and probably when better specimens are found the plant will be referred to another genus.

6. *Quercus crassinervis*, (Ung.) *Fig.* 1. The specimen is broken, and shows only the middle part of a large, sharply dentate leaf, apparently oval-lanceolate in outline The broad nerves, and the running of the secondary nerves to the point of the teeth, as the form of the acute teeth would refer this species to *Quercus crassinervis*, Ung., a species found in the Upper Miocene of Europe.

7. *Quercus Saffordi*, (Lsqx.) *Fig.* 2, *a. b, c.* Leaves nearly linear, rarely an inch broad, four to six inches long, gradually tapering to a point. Margins regularly and distinctly mucronate-serrate, entire near the base, and decurrent in a broad petiole or enlarged nerve. Medial nerve, broad and flat, secondary nerve, oblique, straight, running to the point of the teeth, and alternating with shorter and slender ones. There is not any published fossil species that might be compared with this. It is distantly related to living species of southern Texas and Mexico; but among the leaves kindly furnished to me for comparison by Dr. Asa Gray, there were none of these new species to which it could be referred.

8. *Andromeda dubia*, (Lsqx.) *Fig.* 5. A thick, smooth, roui d-elliptical, obtusely pointed, leaf, with entire, wavy, somewhat reflexed margins and obsolete nervation. It is related to *Andromeda ferruginea*, Michx. of the pine barrens of the south.

9. *Andromeda vaccinifoliæ affinis*, (Lsqx.) *Fig.* 4, *a*, *b*. Thick, oval-lanceolate, pointed or obtuse leaves, with perfectly the same size, outline and nervation as the *Andromeda vaccinifolia*, (Heer.,) a plant of the Upper Miocene of Europe. Its nearest relative in America, is, I think, *Andromeda acuminata*, Michx.

10. *Elœagnus inœqualis*, (Lsqx.) *Fig.* 7. Leaf long-elliptical, obtuse, with entire wavy margin, rounded near the base on one side, and about one inch longer, and decurrent on the other side of the short petiole. Secondary nerves well marked, thick near the base, emerging in acute angle, with a camptodrome much divided nervation. I do not know of any living species to which this could be compared. Among the fossil plants published till now, its nearest relative is *Elœagnus acuminatus*, (Web.,) of the Miocene of Europe.

11. *Sapotacites Americanus*, (Lsqx.) *Fig.* 8. Though the specimen shows only the upper part of the leaf, the form and the nervation agree well with that of the species of this genus found in the Miocene of Europe. I have not seen any other specimen but the one figured here.

SECTION III.

THE BLUFF LIGNITE; FORMATION 11,*c*. (*Provisional.*)

1135. This is a provisional group, and consists, especially in the middle and southern parts of the State, of a series of stratified sands with more or less sandy, slaty clay, characterized by the presence of well-marked beds of *lignite*.* I have sometimes included it in the Orange Sand. It will be best, however, to keep it separate until the questions of age are definitely settled. The upper part of the series is generally well exposed below the *Gravel* of the *Mississippi Bluffs*. (§§ 279–283.) At Memphis, however, it scarcely appears above low water. About one hundred feet of the series has been seen. In this

*In the northern part of the State, its upper portion is frequently more or less indurated, presenting layers of soft sandstone; and here, too, the lignite is not as well seen.

thickness it contains from one to three beds of *lignite*, which are from half a foot to four feet in thickness.

1136. The *Bluff Lignite* appears to have no marked eastern outcrop, and may thin out in an easterly direction beneath the Gravel; at least, the beds of lignite by which it is characterized do not appear to extend very far east from the range of the bluffs. (See section on the Map, Form. 11c.)

1137. Below is a section of the bluff at Randolph, (§§ 280, 282,) which will serve to illustrate not only the character of this division, but also that of the overlying formations to be described.

(3) BLUFF LOAM, 68 *feet.*

Fine siliceous earthy matter of a light ashen or a light buff color, containing land shells.

(2) BLUFF GRAVEL, 24 *feet.*

Chert Pebbles, and coarse yellow and orange sand, with a bed six feet thick of variegated plastic clay beneath.

(1) BLUFF LIGNITE, 90 *feet.*

A mass of dark grayish laminated micaceous sand, with lignitic woody fragments, leaves, &c. Laminæ of sand alternate with other laminæ, containing more or less clay. Interstratified with this are *two beds of lignite*; the upper one six feet from the top, and from six inches to two feet thick; the other twelve feet lower, and about eight inches thick. Some thin laminæ of *lignite* occur below this bed.

This portion in all,..48 ft.

A portion not exposed in place where the section was taken, but seen in part at another point; consists of laminated sand, like that above.

Down to the water's edge,..42 ft.

1138. The following section, taken at "*Old River*," (§ 280,) in the southern part of Tipton County, exhibits the different strata which at that point compose the Bluff.* The entire thickness is 168 feet.

*I am under especial obligations to Dr. C. W. Dickson, of Portersville, for kindly guiding me to this point—a distance of sixteen miles from his residence—and for his assistance otherwise.

I take this occasion, also, to express my thanks to Dr. Oldham, of Ripley, who, notwithstanding his engagements at home, traveled with me to and from the lignite localities near Fulton, a distance of fifty miles in all.

(3) BLUFF LOAM, 45 *feet.* (Caps the Bluff.)

Bed of light-yellow ashen earth or loam, more or less calcareous; contains land-shells, (*helix*, *cyclostoma*, etc.

The lower part becomes more yellow and sandy.

(2) BLUFF GRAVEL, 39 *feet.*

(*d*) Layers of orange and yellow sand, with thin seams of red· sandstone, three and a half feet.

(*c*) Bed of coarse *gravel* and sand, sixteen feet.

(*b*) Reddish and white potter's clay, in seams with sand, one foot and a half.

(*a*) Bright yellow sand, with occasional seams of clay, eighteen feet.

(1) BLUFF LIGNITE, 84 *feet.*

(*h*) Thin seams of gray or white sand and clay, interstratified with some vegetable matter—fifteen feet.

(*g*) Bed of *lignite*, from three to four feet.

(*f*) Dark clay and *lignite* interstratified—two feet.

(*e*) Seams of gray and white sand, interstratified with layers of lignite—five and a half feet.

(*d*) Bed of *lignite*, six inches—becoming, a few hundred yards to the left, along the Bluff, four feet thick.

(*c*) Gray sand in thin layers, with numerous seams of dark clay and layers of *lignite*, some of which are from three to six inches thick—thirty-two feet.

(*b*) Same as above mostly; one bed of *lignite*, (leaves, etc.,) two feet thick—fifteen feet.

(*a*) Beds of dark laminated clay. The base of the Bluff is concealed mostly by a talus of materials from above—ten feet.

Level of alluvial plain.

1139. I add here the section of the bluff at Raleigh on Wolf River, in Shelby County:

(3) BLUFF LOAM, 34 *feet.* (Top of the bluff.)

Light-yellow ashen siliceous earth or loam.

(2) BLUFF GRAVEL, 47 *feet.*

Yellow and orange sands containing more or less gravel throughout, some layers mostly gravel; a few clay seams near the top; presents a few mosses of ferruginous conglomerate; has a chalybeate spring at its base.

(1) BLUFF LIGNITE, 20 *feet.*

(*b*) *Bed of Lignite*, has been mined, and was used one winter,

(1855-6,) by Dr. D. Coleman; from ten inches to three feet in thickness; has an under-clay a few inches thick.

(*a*) A laminated gray mass of thin clay and sand seams; contains leaves and sticks, layers of which occasionally make black lines in outcropping on the face of the exposure; runs down to the bed of the Wolf.

1139. Leaves from the Bluff Lignite, at least from the portion in Tennessee, have not, so far as I know, been examined. The series may be synchronous with that at the *Chalk Banks*, near Columbus, Ky., some of the leaves of which have been described by Mr. Lesquereux. (*Am. Jour. Sci.*, [2], XXVII, 364.)

1140. *Minerals, Useful Material, and Agricultural Features of the Tertiary Group.*—This Group, like the others peculiar to West Tennessee, contains but few minerals. *Lignite* is a note-worthy one in this. In small pieces, it may be said to be common in all the divisions of the Group. It is met with in the bottoms of wells, and in exposures where the strata have not been weathered. A bed of it in the Orange Sand has been mentioned in § 1118. It is in the *Bluff Lignite*, however, that the beds of this substance are the most conspicuous. The sections just given present some of these, and exhibit their relations to the other strata. The beds may be traced in some cases for long distances, in a horizontal direction.

1141. Beds of pipe and potter's clay occur at numerous points in this formation. At a few localities, potteries have been established, but the manufacture of stone-ware has not been carried to the extent that it might well be.

1142. The agricultural features of the territory underlaid by these formations, and especially by the Orange Sand, are often very good. Much of the best cotton land of West Tennessee rests upon the Orange Sand. The soil is a mellow siliceous loam, and, where the ground lies well, presents us with very desirable farming regions. But as the soil is easily tilled, so it is easily washed away. Special attention, proper draining, and good farming, are required to keep it up, and to improve it. (See §§ 274 and 286.)

CHAPTER XV.

THE BLUFF GROUP, AND THE ALLUVIUM; SERIES XII AND XIII.

1143. In this Chapter are embraced the remaining formations of the State. Two of these appertain to the Mississippi Bluff, or rather to a belt of country which terminates on the west with the Bluff; two of the others include superficial gravel beds occurring in different parts of Tennessee; and the last groups together the alluvial bottoms and beds of the rivers. They will be briefly considered, and are as follows:

(2) ALLUVIUM, SERIES 13.
- (c) *Bottoms, and Alluvial Beds.*
- (b) *The Eastern Gravel.*
- (a) *Ore-Region Gravel.*

(1) BLUFF GROUP, SERIES 12.
- (b) *Bluff Loam.*
- (a) *Bluff Gravel.*

SECTION I.

THE BLUFF GRAVEL. (12,*a*.)

1144. This bed varies in thickness from ten to fifty feet. It consists generally of coarse yellow and orange sands, with everywhere more or less coarse gravel, and has usually, a layer of white or variegated clay at its base. The gravel is generally the most conspicuous portion. This is sometimes cemented by oxyd of iron (occasionally by calcareous matter) into great blocks of coarse conglomerate. It consists of water-worn pebbles, from the size of a man's fist down to that of a pigeon's egg. The pebbles have been derived mostly from Carboniferous chert.

1145. The Bluff Gravel is remarkable for its extent in a general direction parallel with the river. It is seen along the face of the *Mississippi Bluff*, (§ 279,) from the Mississippi line to Kentucky, and both ways much beyond these limits.

Its eastern outcrop is not well marked. It appears to extend from 15 to 20 miles eastward from a straight line drawn through the most westerly parts of the bluff. The bed is represented on the Map and in the section by a dotted line. It will be seen that the narrow river-valleys of West Tennessee cut this and the Bluff Loam into sections.

1146. The general character of the formation, and its relations to other groups, are exhibited in sections already given, and to these the reader is referred. (§§ 1137, 1138 and 1139.) At Memphis the highest part of the Bluff is about 100 feet above low water. The lower half of the section at this point belongs to the *Bluff Gravel*, and consists of alternating layers of yellow, orange, and white sands, containing towards its base, more or less gravel. It also contains a few seams of whitish clay. At some points also masses of ferruginous conglomerate occur, as well as thin plates and scrolls of red sandstone. In a branch back from the river a bed of coarse gravel was observed.

Section II.

THE BLUFF LOAM. (12,*b*.)

1147. This, the topmost of the Bluff formations, is generally a mass of siliceous loam, somewhat calcareous, and usually of a light ashen yellowish or buff color, but sometimes lacking the yellow tinge. It is indistinctly stratified; contains land and fresh water shells, and frequently oddly shaped calcareous concretions. It has in Tennessee, a maximum thickness of about 100 feet, ranging generally, however, from 30 to 80. In the Bluff at Memphis, it is from 40 to 60 feet thick, and presents in its lower part, along a well-marked horizon, and in a vertical position, earthy ferruginous casts or moulds of what may have been the long tapering tap-roots of some tree.

1148. The Loam rests directly upon the Bluff Gravel, and its range and extent are shown upon the Map by the spaces included within the dotted lines representing the outcrops of the Gravel. Its eastern limit, like the eastern outcrop of the underlying bed, is with difficulty defined; both alike are given approximately.

See also sections in §§ 1137, 1138 and 1139.

1149. This formation is seen to underlie large parts of the following counties, the first tier east of the Mississippi River: Shelby, Tipton, Lauderdale, Dyer and Obion. Its agricultural features are interesting and important; they have been spoken of in § 287, to which the reader is referred.

1150. The following species of shells have been collected from this formation:

1. *Helix appressa*, Memphis.	6. *Planorbis bicarinatus*, Memphis.
2. *H. hirsuta*, "	7. *Cyclas*, sp.? "
3. *H. monodon*, "	8. *Amnicola lapidaria*, "
4. *H. solitaria*, Dyer County.	9. *Lymnea*, sp.? "
5. *H. profunda*, Hickman, Ky.	10. *Succinea*, sp.? "

1151. Dr. Wyman has published a "Notice of Fossil Bones from the neighborhood of Memphis," which he states are representatives of the genera *Mastodon*, *Megalonyx*, *Castor* and *Castoroides*, and that they are "from, as is supposed, the diluvium of the Mississippi."* The geological position, as given here, is very indefinite. I think it, however, more than probable that the bones come from the *Bluff Loam*.

Section III.

ORE-REGION GRAVEL. (13,*a*.)

1152. It would have been better, perhaps, if this description had been placed as an Appendix after that of the *Bluff Gravel*. The age of this formation is only known approximately. It is certainly of later date than the Cretaceous beds in the Western Valley.† (Page 104.) It may b

* Amer. Jour. Sci., [2,] X, 56.

† At no point in Tennessee have I seen Gravel running under the Cretaceous beds. In northeastern Mississippi I have observed some doubtful evidences of this. Should such beds be found, it will make the Gravel of different ages. In the latter case, a portion of the deposits might be the remains of the ancient shingle of the Cretaceous sea, or estuary. So far, however, as my observations have extended, I am compelled to refer all the deposits, in Tennessee at least, to the same epoch.

synchronous with the Gravel of the Bluff; but of this I have no satisfactory proof. The formation is not indicated upon the Map.

1153. This is a wide-spreading, superficial formation. It is most conspicuous in the *Western Valley;* but its pebbles, sometimes in considerable beds, sometimes thinly strewed over the surface, are found on nearly all the high ridges lying between the Western Valley and the *Central Basin;* they occur, as will be seen, at the ore-banks, and are often a part of the matrix in which the ore is found.

1154. This gravel formation is by no means continuous. It occurs in patches, or detached beds, depending much, in this respect, upon the nature of the surface on which it rests, and upon the extent to which it has been denuded. The beds, however, in the Western Valley especially, cover locally large areas, the observer traveling upon them without a break for many miles. Their thickness is not great, rarely exceeding fifty or sixty feet, and being generally much less.

The gravel beds overlying the *Coffee Sand,* and forming the cap strata in the sections taken at Pittsburg and Coffee Landings, and given on previous pages, belong to this formation.

1155. The material of the formation was doubtless deposited after the Valley of the Tennessee had received, for the most part, its present general form. Its beds are found upon the bluffs of the river, upon the uplands back of the bottoms, on the western as well as the eastern side. Its extension westward is eight or ten miles. In a northerly and southerly direction, it skirts the river on both sides, from Alabama and Mississippi to the Kentucky line.

1156. The materials of the formation are water-worn siliceous pebbles, with more or less sand, the latter, however, not prominent. The pebbles have been derived mostly from Carboniferous rocks. The worn pebbles are sometimes locally mingled with angular cherty fragments; but in such cases the beds are in the vicinity of Paleozoic rocks, the known source of the angular chert. Not unfrequently masses of the gravel may be seen cemented, usually by oxyd of iron, into heavy blocks of coarse conglomerate. At the iron-ore banks, sections present mingled masses of worn pebbles, angular chert, and limonite, in irregular forms and in "pots," the masses occasionally cemented into solid blocks.

1157. The *Western Iron Region* may be noticed here, as its ores are often associated with the gravel of this formation, and may be, as already suggested, of the same age. (§ 910.)

This is a large belt of the State in which "banks," or accumulations of iron-ore, occur at intervals. The area includes, in Tennessee, all or parts of the following counties: Lawrence, Wayne, Hardin, Lewis, Perry, Decatur, Hickman, Humphreys, Benton, Dickson, Montgomery and Stewart. It also extends further north into Kentucky. Over this whole region more or less ore occurs. At *certain centres*, which are called *banks*, it is found accumulated in deposits, many of which are of great extent and highly valuable.

1158. The *banks* generally have a high position, being located, with rare exceptions, on the tops or edges, of the plateau-ridges, which, in good part, make up this section of the State. To appreciate their geological relations, it must be recollected that these ridges are capped with the leached remains, the debris of the strata of the Siliceous Group, consisting of angular fragments of half-decomposed, and often bleached, chert, and of soft sandstones, imbedded in clay, with which there is often more or less sand. To this, matter is very frequently added above the water-worn gravel of the formation just described. Among the cherty masses, specimens of *Lithostrotion Canadense*, and other fossils, are often found. (Compare §§ 888, 889 and 910–912.

1159. This bed of debris is from a few feet to 100 feet in thickness, and has no special stratification, excepting that here and there traces of the original bedding are left. In this bed, as a matrix, the iron ore, at certain centres, as stated, has accumulated and given us the "banks."

1160. The ore is *Limonite*.* Its source, I am inclined to be-

* There is but one exception to this, and that is found in the Red Ore Bank of Marion Furnace, near Clifton, in Wayne County, which is mostly *Hematite*. The ore occurs here in irregular layers, and presents features different from those of the other banks.

lieve, as I have already stated, (§§ 888 and 912,) has been the ferruginous chert of the Lithostrotion Bed.

1161. It occurs in irregular lumps or in hollow concretions called "pots," scattered through the matrix. These are often amassed in bodies of greater or less size, which present frequently the appearance of very irregular veins winding through the bank in different directions, and then again are mere shapeless masses. These bodies are often congeries of small pots; but sometimes have an open, spongy, or "honey-comb" structure throughout. The ore masses, both large and small, not unusually contain imbedded fragments of chert, from the size of a grain of corn to that of a man's head, or larger.

The principal varieties of ore are the *compact*, *"honey-comb," pot, and pipe ores* and *ochre.* The first three are common, and are found at nearly all the banks. "Pots" often occur, filled with decomposing chert, frequently with water, and a few have been observed enclosing splendid crystals of selenite. I have one in my cabinet enclosing a specimen of *Lithostrotion Canadense.* The pots vary in size from that of an orange, or smaller, to rough hollow spheres two feet in diameter. Pipe ore, in workable quantity, occurs at some localities in Stewart County.

1162. It is difficult to determine how much of the mass of matter in any one bank is ore. The banks differ very much in richness. It may be near the truth to say, that the best of them afford on an average from one fourth to one third ore out of the material removed. The mode of occurrence of the ore in the banks is very irregular. It is found aggregated in bunches, or pockets, in irregular veins or beds, and columns, imbedded in, or traversing the matrix in different directions. These are of all dimensions up to masses twenty or more feet through. Or it occurs in isolated lumps of small size, scattered through the matrix. The large masses sometimes supply scores of tons of ore before they run out. In the excavations a mass is struck and followed until it disappears, when another is sought for. In a following chapter, other facts with reference to this iron region will be given.

I omitted to state in the proper place, that it is a rare circumstance to meet with beds of gravel or sand outside of the reach of the water courses in the *Central Basin.* In Wilson County, however, a belt of sand and gravel of this kind, several miles in length, lies between Lebanon and the Cumberland River. From one point of this, Lebanon is supplied with sand for building purposes.

Section IV.

THE EASTERN GRAVEL; RIVER BOTTOMS AND ALLUVIAL BEDS.

1163. A. *The Eastern Gravel.*—As in the western part of the State the Tennessee River is bordered with gravel on high points, so in the Valley of East Tennessee, nearly all the rivers, and especially those that flow into the State through the gaps of the Unaka Chain, (§ 6,) have belts of similar material skirting them. Approaching within two or three miles of these rivers, the traveler very often meets with coarse gravel, (coarser than that of the Ore-Region Gravel,) on the ridges, and often at a height of 300 or 400 feet above the level of the streams. The appearance of such material has more than once been to the writer the first intimation of the proximity of a river.

1164. These pebbles, of all sizes below that of a man's head, have doubtless been brought from the Unakas, and from the mountains in North Carolina. Some of them are from *Chilhowee Sandstone* mountains, (§§ 479–485,) and show the characteristic Scolithus-rods. They are found back from the rivers, as far as from one to three or four miles. The fact is an interesting one, but I do not propose, at present, to inquire how or when they got there, or, as to what changes have occurred since that time.

1164. B. *River Bottoms, and Alluvial Beds.*—From an agricultural point of view, the river bottoms are full of interest. They contribute to the State many thousands of acres of first class lands. Many of them have one drawback, and that is their exposure to overflow; but many of them are above ordinary high-water mark, and most of those that are not, are free from water the greater part of the year, and permit of the raising of splendid crops of corn.

As yet but little attention has been given to the geology

of our river beds, and alluvial bottoms. This remains to be done.

By far the most important alluvial area in Tennessee, is the *Mississippi Bottom.* The topographical features of this area have been given in the First Part of the Report, (page 119,) and to this the reader is referred.

SUPPLEMENT TO SILICEOUS GROUP. (*Page* 338.)

1165. In 1866, Dr. A. Winchell, of Ann Arbor, Michigan, and myself, agreed to prepare, jointly, a paper on the *Siliceous Group.* With a view to this, I was to put into his hands such species as I might have, or might collect, for examination and comparison. The same year I discovered what was, to me, a *new fauna*, and one that interested me much, and to which, as well as to the calcareo-siliceous, fetid shale in which the species occur, I have referred in §§ 883 and 884. A series of the fossils of this fauna, as well as others, from the base of the Siliceous Group, was sent to Dr. Winchell.

1166. After this, both of us being much engaged in other matters, nothing was done towards the carrying out of our mutual project, excepting that the fossils from near Manchester, and the Orthis, from White's Creek, were examined, and the results communicated to me. But so far as the others were concerned, nothing was done with them until within a few weeks; and since the section on the *Siliceous Group* has been in print, I have received the following paper.

1167. It will be seen that Dr. Winchell has described a number of species. This was done in accordance with my wish. It is to be noted, that he makes the shale of the age of the Kinderhook Formation of the northwestern States. This, to my mind, makes the Kinderhook Carboniferous; for it does appear to me, that the fetid (fragrant) shale is inseparably connected with the main mass of the "*Protean Member.*" Of this, however, more hereafter.

NOTES ON FOSSILS FROM TENNESSEE, COLLECTED FROM STRATA IMMEDIATELY OVERLYING THE BLACK SHALE, AND TRANSMITTED FOR EXAMINATION BY DR. J. M. SAFFORD.

These fossils, so far as I know, are the only ones which have been discovered in Tennessee, in strata immediately above the *Black Shale;* and I entered upon the study of them with a great degree of interest. This interest had been enhanced by the opportunity of making personal examinations in Tennessee, in the winter and spring of 1866, along a line from Nashville, through Lebanon and Sparta, to the Cumberland Table-land. On this tour, I was enabled to verify the statements made in the "Geological Reconnoisance of Tennessee," and in Part First of "The Geology of Tennessee," in reference to the physical geography and geology of a remarkable portion of the earth's surface. I satisfied myself then, and so announced in a Report, which I afterwards made to a private company, that the "Siliceous Group" is, strictly, the prolongation of the "Knob Formation," of Kentucky and Indiana, and that it corresponds to some of the lower members of the Mountain Limestone series of America. It was still more apparent, that the St. Louis Limestone, in a siliceous condition, is spread out over most of the "Highland Rim" on the northern and eastern sides of the "Central Basin;" while the great mass of Limestone beneath the "False Coal Measures" of the Cumberland Table-land, is the Kaskaskia.

The fossils which I have now submitted to a careful investigation, were obtained from three different localities on the borders of the Highland Rim—one upon the eastern border of the Central Basin, one upon the northern, and one upon the western. Their stratigraphical position in each case, is such, that their identification must determine the age of the formation reposing directly upon the Black Shale. The fossils from the eastern and northern borders are:

1. *Spirifera Logani?** Hall, a Keokuk Limestone species.

2. *Producta semireticulata*, Martin, sp., which ranges through the Carboniferous rocks.

3. *Orthis Michelini*, L'Eveille, also a Carboniferous species, and found in the "Knobs" of Kentucky.

Higher up in the Siliceous Group, I have heretofore identified *Rhynchonella Verneuilana*, a Chester Limestone species; and still higher, numerous species of the St. Louis Limestone, such as *Lithostrotion Canadense*, *Producta semireticulata*, *Streptorhynchus umbraculum*, *Spirifera Keokuk*, Var., and *S. perinflata?*

It is probable, therefore, that, in these portions of the State, the Siliceous Group embraces representations of the Keokuk, Chester and St. Louis Limestones.

* Better specimens than those in the hands of Dr. Winchell show this, in my opinion, to be *S. imbrex* of the *Burlington Limestone*. See page 342.—Safford.

Greatly to my surprise, the collection of fossils from Hickman and Maury counties, on the western side of the "Highland Rim," discloses the existence of a formation hitherto unknown in Tennessee—the representative of the Kinderhook Group, of Illinois, and its equivalents. The following identifications have been made:

1. *Spirifera hirta*? White and Whitfield, from the Yellow Sandstones of Iowa.

2. *Rhynchonella Sageriana*, Win., from the Marshall Group, of Michigan and Ohio.

3. *Chonetes multicosta*, Win., from the Yellow Sandstones of Iowa.

4. *Chonetes pulchella*? Win., from the Marshall Group, of Michigan and Ohio

5. *Producta concentrica*, Hall, from the Yellow Sandstones of Iowa, and the same horizon in Michigan, Ohio and Indiana.

6. *Chonetes Fischeri*, Nor. and Prat., from the Yellow Sandstones of Iowa.

7. *Lingula subspatulata*? Meek and Wor., from the Black Slate, of Illinois, and a black shale embraced in the Waverly, of Ohio.

8 *Zaphrentis Ida*? Win., from the Rockford Goniatite Beds.

9. *Conularia byblis*, White, from the Yellow Sandstones of Iowa.

10. *Leda bellistriata*? Stevens, from the Marshall Group, of Michigan.

11. *Solen scalpriformis*, Win., from the Marshall Group, of Michigan.

This is a list of identifications from a collection of 18 species; of which two others are more doubtfully identified with known species. Unexpected as this result may be, and questionable as two or three of the identifications may be, I feel constrained to state, that the indications of a majority of the specimens point conclusively to the existence in Tennessee, of a feeble representation of those beds in the horizon of the Marshall group, whose geological age has been the subject of so much discussion.

On studying the matrix in which these fossils are imbedded, I find that those marked "c," are from a rock almost identical with the yellowish-brown, calcareo-argillaceous beds of Rockford, Ind., (not the limestone in which the Goniatites are imbedded,) while those marked "b," are from calcareo-siliceous shales extremely similar to those of the Kinderhook group in southern Illinois, and finally, those marked "a," are from dark bituminous shales identical with those embraced in the Waverly of Ohio, at various places, and at Vanceburg, Ky.

The siliceous shales of the Kinderhook group of Illinois, reach to the southern extremity of the State. It is not at all improbable that they should extend along the western border of the Carboniferous area across the narrow end of Kentucky, into Tennessee. It may be pronounced probable that some representation of this formation will yet be traced from the eastern border of the Carboniferous area in Indiana, southward into central and southern Kentucky.

I append a more particular notice of the fossils embraced in these investigations, including diagnoses of four, which seem to be undescribed species:

NOTES ON THE SPECIES.

I. *Fossils from near Manchester, Cannon County, Tennessee, "immediately above the Black Shale."*

1. SPIRIFERA LOGANI?* Hall, Io. Geol. Rep., p. 647, pl. xx, fig. 7, and xxi, figs 1.a, b, and 2.

The collection embraces eight *silicified* specimens of a large Spirifera, which nearly agrees with specimens of this species from above Alton, Ill., and above St. Genevieve, Mo. They are, however, of smaller size—the largest measuring three inches along the hinge line.

2. PRODUCTA SEMIRETICULATA, Martin, sp.

Four specimens of a Producta agreeing in all respects with forms usually referred, in this country, to the above species. I have collected this species throughout the north-western States, in the horizon of the Marshall group, and thence through the Mountain Limestone, into the Coal Measures.

3. ZAPHRENTIS CANNONENSIS, n. sp.

Coral strongly curved, having the diameter of the cup, to the length along the outside of the curvature, as 1 to 3. Exterior somewhat smooth, impressed by numerous medium-sized wrinkles of growth. Fossette narrow and deep. Number of lamellæ, 28, in seven groups—besides the three in the fossette. The group on each side of the fossette contains 5 lamellæ; next is a pair of groups, each with 3 lamellæ, then a pair, each with 4 lamellæ, and lastly an azygos group, with 3 or 4 lamellæ. The lamellæ are not perceptibly twisted toward the center.

This species approaches nearest to an undescribed Zaphrentis from the Keokuk Limestone, near Burlington, Io.; but the latter species, besides being somewhat larger, is much more tapering below, less strongly curved, and has a deeper cup. It agrees nearly as well with *Z. elliptica*, white, which has an elliptic transverse section instead of a circular one.

II. *A Fossil from White's Creek, Davidson County, Tennessee, found three feet above the Black Shale.*

4. ORTHIS MICHELINI, L'Eveille.

This Orthis is absolutely identical with forms from the Carboniferous rocks of the north-west, which have been generally referred to *O. Michelini*—though, sometimes to *O. Vanuxemi*, Hall, a closely related species. It is said by Prof. Safford to occur in the "Knobs," near Louisville, Ky.

III. *Fossils from "shales just above the Black Shale, in Hickman County, and the adjoining edge of Maury County, Tennessee."*

5. SPIRIFERA HIRTA? White and Whitefield, Proc. Bos., Soc. Nat. Hist. [Labeled 4.b.]

The single specimen referred to this species, is considerably larger than

*See Note on page 440.

specimens from Burlington, Iowa, the typical locality; and perhaps, the area is a little more extended latterly, but I can scarcely doubt that the species is the same.

Types from the "Yellow Sandstone," Burlington, Iowa.

6. RHYNCHONELLA SAGERIANA, Win., Proc. Acad. Nat. Sci., Phil., Sep., 1862, p. 407. [Labeled 1, and 1a, and 6a.]

Six specimens, showing both valves, and agreeing well with this species. *R. Sageriana* has a wide geographical distribution, being hitherto known by me in remote parts of Michigan, and from Medina, Trumbull, Cuyahoga, Summit, Knox and Licking Counties, Ohio.

Types from the "Marshall Group," Michigan.

7. CHONETES MULTICOSTA, Win., Proc. Acad. Nat. Sci., Phil., Jan., 1863, p. 5. [Labeled 3.c and 3 a.]

The two dorsal valves in the collection agree in all respects with this species, except that the striæ are considerably more obscure than even in the typical specimens, and the exterior surface is minutely granulated.

Types from the base of the "Yellow Sandstones" at Burlington, Io., and into the base of the "Burlington Limestone,"

8. CHONETES PULCHELLA? Win., Proc. Acad. Nat. Sci., Phil., Sep., 1862. [Labeled 5. c.]

The single ventral valve of this species, shows only the inside, and hence, the number of ribs cannot be satisfactorily ascertained. There is a slightly divergent spine at each extremity of the hinge-line.

Types from the Marshall Group, of Michigan. This species occurs, also, in the Waverly, of Ohio.

9. PRODUCTA CONCENTRICA, Hall, Io. Geo. Rep., p. 517, pl. vii, fig. 3; Rep. N. Y. Regents, p. 180. See also, Winchell Proc. Acad. Nat. Sci., Phil., July, 1865, p. 115. [Labeled 2.c and 2.b.]

The agreement in this case is all that could be desired. The collection contains one specimen showing both valves, one showing the ventral, and one, both sides of the dorsal valve.

Types from the "Yellow Sandstones," Iowa. This species occurs also in the same horizon, in Indiana, and in northern and southern Michigan.

10. Another specimen, marked 2.a, exhibits the exterior of a ventral valve resembling the forms named *P. Shumardiana*, by Prof. Hall, but this species is probably only a form of *P. concentrica*.

11. CHONETES FISCHERI, Norwood and Pratten, Jour. Acad. Nat. Sci., Phil., [2] Vol. III, p. 25, pl. ii, fig. 3. [Labeled 2 a.]

A single exterior of a ventral valve. The inner surface is less finely pustulose than in the Burlington specimens, and the exterior is a little more distinctly striate.

Types from the "Yellow Sandstones," of Burlington, Iowa.

12. DISCINA SAFFORDI, n.sp. [Labeled 6,a.]

Shell rather small, outline nearly circular, but generally a little flattened, posteriorly, and also on each of the postero-lateral boundaries.

Upper valve rather depressed-conical, with the beak midway between the centre and the posterior side; under surface presenting a faint, but distinct linear ridge, extending anteriorly from the beak, one-fourth the diameter of the shell. Lower valve very depressed convex, with an apical pyriform indentation, having a blunt spur projecting from its broad anterior end. *No perforation visible.* Exterior of both valves ornamented with numerous fine, unequal, concentric striæ; interiors smooth, except the faint vascular markings near the borders.

This curious species most resembles in general appearance, *Discina Lodensis*, Hall, from the Genesee Shale; but the pyriform indentation of the ventral valve, the finer exterior striæ, and the unconspicuous foramen, will serve to distinguish it.

13. LINGULA SUBSPATULATA? Meek and Worthen, Ill. Geol. Rep., Vol. III, p. 437, pl. xiii, fig. 1. [Labeled 5.c]

The single specimen, showing inside of (apparently) the ventral valve, is not over one-third the length of the specimen figured in the Illinois Report; but it otherwise agrees with the description in outline, markings, position of the beak, and faint, radiating lines along the middle.

L. subspatulata was described from the "Black Slate," of Union County, Illinois. At Vanceburg, Kentucky, and other localities near the Ohio River, and also in northern Ohio, is a black shale, embraced within the Waverly series, which contains a small Lingula closely resembling this specimen from Tennessee. If the Kentucky and Tennessee specimens are really *L. subspatulata*, it is singular that this species should be found in Illinois, in a shale occupying a position so much lower.

14. *Zaphrentis Ida?* Win., Proc. Acad. Nat. Sci., Phil., July, 1865. [Labeled 12.b, 12.c.]

The three specimens in the collection are all without epitheca, and lack the profound wrinkles of growth, which belong to the types of this species, from Rockford, Indiana. They also enlarge, upward, somewhat more rapidly.

15. CONULARIA BYBLIS, White, Proc. Bos. Soc. Nat. Hist., Feb. 1862, p. 22. [Labeled 8.a.]

I feel no doubt of the identity of this species. It possesses the small, isolated eminences or granulations ranged in a line along the crests of the ridges, which characterize well preserved specimens from Burlington, Iowa.* From 60 to 75 of these eminences may be counted in the space of an inch.

Types from the "Yellow Sandstones," Burlington, Iowa.

16. LEDA BELLISTRIATA? Stevens, Amer. Jour. Sci. [2] Vol. XXV, p. 261. [Labeled 10.a.]

* Dr. White does not mention these, and only says: "Spaces between the ridges finely crenulate." This condition appears on worn specimens. Compare with this, *C. Gervillei*, d'Arch. et Verneuil, Mem. Foss. Rhen. Prov. in Trans. Geol. Soc., Lond., Vol. VI, p. 351.

These five specimens are thus referred solely on account of external resemblances. The Tennessee specimens are a little over an inch in length, but do not, in this, exceed specimens from Michigan. At the same time, no indication of hinge structure has been observed; and the shell seems to have been thinner than usual, for species of this family. Should further discovery demonstrate that these specimens do not belong to Leda, they will probably fall into the genus *Sedgwickia*; but I do not consider it allowable, to propose a specific name to be based on the discoveries of some future investigator.

Types from the Marshall Group, Battle Creek, Michigan.

17. SOLEN SCALPRIFORMIS, Win. Proc. Acad. Nat. Sci., Phil., Sep. 1862, p. 423. [Labeled 9.a.]

Shell, like the foregoing unusually thin and delicate.

Types from the Marshall Group, Marshall, Michigan.

18. PLEUROTOMARIA HICKMANENSIS, n. sp. [Labeled 7.a.]

Globose shells in an incomplete state of preservation, showing regularly convex whorls, ornamented with numerous delicately raised and finely beaded revolving striæ, and a well defined band without distinct carina. The striæ limiting the band are not beaded, but all the others on both sides bear 50 to 60 granulations to the inch. The striæ are quite unequal in number and distribution, since they increase by implantation, with the growth of the shell. The base of the shell is about an inch in diameter, and seems to be perforated by a small umbilicus.

I am unacquainted with any species, in any formation, which presents the above combination of characters.

19. PHILLIPSIA TENNESSEENSIS, n. sp [Labeled 13.b, 13.c.]

Glabella prominent, indented by a small, round, depressed, postero-lateral lobe, and isolated by a deep occipital furrow, from a prominent occipital ring which extends, narrowing in width and curving backwards, entirely across the border, fading out toward the short, acute, genal angle. Border concave, bounded by a prominent ridge, outside of which is a linear groove limited peripherally by a sharply elevated, delicate linear margin. Surface of glabella, accessory lobe and neck-ring covered with fine, unequal granulations; a row of granules along the ridge of the border.

Pygidium broadly rounded, nearly twice as long as broad, apparently depressed; axis with 8 or 9 rings, tapering to the posterior end, which is somewhat abruptly rounded off, one tenth of an inch from the extremity of the pygidium; lateral lobes with 8 or 9 segments, becoming obscure posteriorly. Border about one sixteenth of an inch broad, marked on the under side by nine rigid, sharply impressed, parallel striæ. Exterior of the crust very finely and obscurely granulated. Length about three eighths—breadth five eighths of an inch.

Other characters of this species are unknown. It seems to approach nearest to *Phillipsia articulata*, Hall, sp.; (xv. Rep., N. Y. Regents,) from the Waverly of Ohio, but is destitute of the anterior and middle furrows of the glabella. Neither does the description of that species give the surface characters, though comparison is made with *Proetus Missouriensis*, Shum., from the Lithographic Limestone of Mo., which is granulated like this. It differs from *Proetus* (*Phillipsia?*) *elliptica*, Meek and Worthen, (Ill. Geol. Rep., Vol. III, p. 460, pl. 14, fig. 8,) from the Kinderhook Group, in the characters of the cephalic border, in the absence of glabella furrows, and in the border of the pygidium.

20. Has the appearance of a minute *Spirifera peculiaris*, Shum., from the Choutean limestone, Mo., and the Yellow Sandstones of Iowa. [Labeled 5.c.]

21. Resembles *Spirifera Urei*, Fleming, (*Ambocœlia gemmula*, McChesney, &c.,) a carboniferous species. [Labeled 2.b.]

22. Portion of the test of a crustacean or dermal plate of a fish. Indeterminable. [Labeled 11.d.]

A. WINCHELL.

University of Michigan, *Ann Arbor*, 19*th March*, 1869.

PART THIRD.

THE MINERALS AND ROCKS OF SPECIAL USE.

1168. In the Part of the Report just finished, the principal purpose has been to describe the structure and the great rocky formations of the State, (§ 315,) the notices of the minerals, and especially useful mineral substances, although in many cases full, being subordinate. In this Part the latter are classified, and constitute the principal subject. Much, however, having been already written that properly belongs here, this division of the Report will be, to a considerable extent, an *annotated index* of the minerals and mineral substances already described. The whole is an outline of our mineral resources. There is yet much filling up to be done.

1169. The most important elements in the mineral resources of Tennessee are *iron-ore* and *stone-coal,* and this is as we would have it, for to these, above all other minerals, are the vigor, the thrift, and the wealth of civilized nations to be attributed. Our, *gold, zinc, lead, marble, petroleum,* and even *copper,* although constituting, in the aggregate, a very important general interest, are individually quite subordinate. These have a local interest. The *copper mines* have been a rich boon to Polk County, and neighboring parts of East Tennessee, and have, moreover, contributed to the revenue of the State; but the *iron-ore* involves an interest which is directly State-wide, and one which has added, and is adding, vastly more to the wealth of Tennessee. So the *stone-coal,* stored in a great field that lies between two of the most extensive sections of the State, that includes parts of many counties within its area, and has an extent of more than 5000 square miles, is something that we are all interested in individually and as citizens.

1170. It becomes us to look to these interests, and especially to the coal-interest, for the development of this is far behind what it ought to be. We need not send money to Kentucky or Pittsburg for coal. We must have a railroad across our coal field and make the very heart of it accessible. Nashville and Knoxville are the important points, respectively, of two great sections of the State, and approximately on the same parallel, and one, moreover, north of the middle of the State, yet to pass from one point to the other, it is necessary to go out of the State into Georgia and Alabama, and go round our coal-field. Rather a severe commentary on our enterprise, especially when it is recollected that a direct road would pay for itself in the opening out of our buried resources. But it is gratifying to know that this state of things will soon be rectified. The Nashville and Chattanooga Road has done much, as we have seen, (§ 993,) towards the development of the coal interests of Tennessee; the Knoxville and Kentucky Road will do much; but the Tennessee and Pacific Road will do more.

CHAPTER XVI.

THE ORES AND METALS.

1171. In this chapter are considered the minerals used as ores, and such metals as occur native, like gold.

The chapter that follows will embrace minerals not used as ores, of which coal is an example, and rock-products, like marble and buhr-stone.

SECTION I.

IRON. (1.)

1172. The variety and the aggregate amount of *iron-ore* in Tennessee, its excellent quality, its favorable association with the necessary conditions for the economical manufacture of iron, place the State among the best as an iron-producing region.

1173. The localities and outcrops of the iron-ore of Tennessee, including all its varieties, whether in local deposits or in regular beds, are found in *three* belts of the State, which are quite distinct, and differ, more or less, in geological and mineral character. These belts, or iron-regions, as I shall call them, are as follows:

(A.) THE EASTERN IRON-REGION. Extends through the State, lies along with and in front of the *Unaka Range*. (§ 41.)

(B.) THE DYESTONE-REGION. Skirts the eastern base of the Cumberland Table-land, or of Walden's Ridge, from Virginia to Georgia; extends out laterally into the Valley of East Tennessee from ten to twenty miles; the Sequatchee and Elk Valleys are included.

(C.) THE WESTERN IRON-REGION. Occupies a belt of the Highlands contiguous to the Western Valley, (§§ 250 to 252,) and a part of this valley itself; the belt runs through the State, from Kentucky to Alabama.

A.—THE EASTERN IRON-REGION.

1174. This region includes the counties of Johnson, Carter, Sullivan, Washington, Greene, Cocke, Sevier, Blount, Monroe, Polk, and the eastern part of McMinn, or, in other words, those counties in which the Unaka Range, with its outliers and included valleys and coves, is found. (§§ 41, and 124–137.) It is in these valleys and coves that most of the ore-deposits occur. As, for example, in the picturesque valleys of Johnson, in the Valley of Stony Creek, of Carter, Bompass and Greasy Coves, of Washington, the coves of Greene, those back of Chilhowee, in Sevier and Blount, and in those back of the outliers, in Monroe, and Star's Mountain further south. The valleys which skirt the outliers (§ 46) on the west are to be included. In all of these ore is found, and is to be looked for. No doubt numerous deposits remain to be discovered, notwithstanding the number known. Many of these valleys and coves are from ten to twenty miles long, and from one to five miles wide. Those in Johnson and Carter, especially, are remarkable for their extent, and for the numerous deposits, or banks, of ore occurring in them.

1175. The typical geological structure of many of the iron-bearing valleys and coves, is illustrated by the diagram on page 202. The bottoms of the valleys are occupied generally by variegated shales and slates, and magnesian limestones of the *Knox Group*. At many points these rocks have been greatly leached or weathered, and have left ridges or knolls of *debris*, consisting of clay, sand, chert and shaly fragments, or where the rock is mainly limestone, or dolomite, little else than clay. In these leached masses the ore, at certain places, has accumulated, and thus the banks have been formed. See, also, §§ 562 and 563, and compare, in addition, § 1182.

1176. In the diagram referred to, the valleys (A and B) are flanked by a sandstone mountain on each side. Many of the iron-bearing valleys or coves, however, have a mountain on but one side. In a few cases, extensive banks, as those in Sullivan and one in McMinn, are entirely detached from the main mountains, and sustain no particular relation to them. These are exceptions, and are thrown into the eastern region on account of their proximity, and for convenience.

1177. The Eastern Iron-Region affords three species of ore, as follows:

(1) *Limonite;* contains, when pure, 60 (59.92) per cent. of metallic iron; powder brownish or *yellow;* by far the most abundant ore.

(2) *Hematite;* has, when *pure*, 70 per cent. of iron; powder *red;* includes two varieties, as follows: (a) *Hard Solid Ore*, and (b) *Dyestone*, or stratified ore.

(3) *Magnetite;* contains, when *pure*, 72 (72.4) per cent of iron; powder *black;* the richest and the rarest ore in Tennessee.

1178. (1.) *Limonite.* This is the great ore of this Iron-Region, and will always be meant unless the others are specified. When pure, it consists of

Iron,..	59.92
Oxygen,..	25.68
Water,..	14.40
	100.00

It never, therefore, contains more than 59.92 lbs. of iron in one hundred of ore. Practically, it never contains this amount, owing to impurities.

1179. In the field before us, it occurs both as "honeycomb" and hard solid ore—occasionally in grains, and called shot-ore—sometimes in ochreous and earthy forms. It exists in the banks in masses of all sizes, from small lumps up to blocks and beds, sometimes ten or fifteen feet in diameter. It is found, too, in contorted layers, from a few inches to two or three feet in thickness, partially stratified with seams of earthy matter, and, in some cases, more or less parallel to the irregular surface of limestone rocks below. The ores generally are excellent, yielding iron of first quality.

1180. The knolls, hills and ridges, which generally afford the most important banks, though some of them are in low grounds, are from fifty to two hundred feet high, and often several miles long. The deposits occur upon these at intervals, and sometimes the ore can be traced for half a mile or more.

1181. Considerable of the superior ore of Johnson, Carter, and Washington contains *lead* and *zinc*. The ore of Bompass Cove, in Washington, and that used at Carter's Furnace, in Carter county, are of this character. The iron made from both is excellent. Often, after blowing out, several hundred pounds of lead have been obtained in the crevices of the stacks. The zinc collects in a hard incrustation around the mouth of the furnace.

1182. It is an interesting fact pointing to the origin of the limonite in these banks, that localities are met with in the coves, in which the banks occur, where the limestones and dolomites contain disseminated grains of *pyrite*, *blende* and *galena*, (*galenite.*) Such is the case in Bompass Cove, and at one point the galena is so abundant as to have attracted notice as a "*lead mine.*" (§ 566.) We are led to infer from such facts that the limonite of the ore-bank, at another point in this cove, and the *lead and zinc ores* associated with it, are oxidized portions of the leached remains of limestones, which, like those above, originally contained pyrite, blende and galena.

1183. The data on hand are not sufficient for the making out of a complete list of the limonite banks of the Eastern Iron-Region. The deposits are very numerous, and there is scarcely a cove or valley in which note-worthy accumulations of ore do not occur. The most of these, however, are of limited extent. The number of first class banks, that is to say, deposits upon which a furnace, or set of furnaces, could depend for an abundant supply of ore for years, or such as would justify the erection of extensive works, will average, perhaps, including the hematite banks of Sullivan, three or four to the county.

1184. The great caps of *limonite*, or "*gossan*," over the Ducktown Copper Veins, may be enumerated here. The geological relations of these masses are different from those of the deposits we have discussed, and will be referred to under "Copper.

1185. (2.) *Hematite.* This includes, as stated, the *Dyestone;* some of its varieties are known as *Specular Iron.* It contains, when pure,

Iron,...	70
Oxygen,...	30
	100

Hence, one hundred pounds of this ore might afford seventy pounds of iron. In practice, however, as in the case of the ores mentioned, the maximum per centage, on account of impurities, is never reached.

1186. As before stated, there are two varieties of it in the iron-region under consideration.

(*a.*) *Hard Solid Ore.* I know of but three or four localities of this ore in Tennessee, excepting those of the small cabinet specimens of specular iron that occasionally occur in the older formations.

1187. The first is the *Cannon Bank*, seven miles from Elizabethton, in the valley of Stony Creek. The ore occurs here in a regular and solid bed. It rests upon a thin stratum of conglomerate, of pea-like quartz pebbles, while above and below the rocks are sandy slate, or shale, all having a gentle dip. There is some doubt in regard to its exact geological position. See § 511, where also this bank is noticed. It is worked at Nave's Forge, (1856,) and yields a good iron.

1188. The other localities which have come under my observation are in the eastern part of Sullivan, a mile or two west of the Holston, and near the residence of Mr. James Cowan.

One, known as the "*Crockett Bank*," half a mile southwest of Cowan's, is an extensive bank or ridge of red earth, with numerous small blocks of solid hematite scattered through it. Near the surface, it is associated with more or less "honeycomb" brown ore. There is another locality about a mile and a half in the same range to the northeast, not as yet opened, which, from external appearances, promises to be valuable.

1189. About one and a half miles northwest or north of Cowan's, at the *Sharp Bank*, is an interesting vein-like mass of the same compact ore. This has been noticed in § 564. It appears to dip with the dolomites of the Knox Group. It is capable of affording much good ore.

1190. The neighboring localities, before spoken of, are doubtless associated with the same dolomite. It may be that the loose blocks have been derived from a vein like the last, which has not yet been exposed. Some of the small blocks were seen with imbedded crystals of quartz.

At all of these localities the ore is more or less magnetic. They have been worked to considerable extent by the furnaces and forges of Sullivan.

1191. These Sullivan ores are hardly true hematite; they occupy rather an intermediate position between this and limonite, or are mixed ores.

1192. (*b.*) *Dyestone.*—There is one interesting and extensive deposit of this ore, which, on account of its proximity to the Unaka Range, it has been found convenient to throw into this iron region. Its character, however, connects it with that next to be described. It is Hill's Bank, in the eastern part of McMinn. The ore is a stratified, fossiliferous, iron-rock. The main deposit is a third of a mile or more in length, and at some points fifty or sixty feet wide. For three or four miles, along its range, traces of the ore occur, and at several points it swells out into other important deposits.

The ore is composed, in good part, of flattened oölitic or rounded grains, and frequently contains impressions of crinoidal buttons. Owing to its separating into small blocks, it is sometimes styled "block ore." A small bloomary, five miles distant, uses this ore, and makes good iron—said to be "hard and tough."

The geological relations of this bed are spoken of in § 657.

1193. (3.) *Magnetite.*—This is also known as Magnetic Iron ore. When pure, its composition is:

Iron,	72.4
Oxygen,	27.6
	100.0

One hundred pounds of *pure* ore contains therefore 72.4 pounds of iron.

1194. Magnetite is a rare ore in Tennessee. I only know of one locality affording it in workable quantity. A locality in Cocke County is barely mentioned by Dr. Troost. The first referred to—which I have visited—is in Crab Orchard, Carter

County (§ 389.) It is about six or seven miles from the summit of the Roan, (§ 55,) and lies at its base. The ore is associated with a greenish crystalline mineral, called *sahlite*, and occurs with this, and with the decomposing gneissoid rocks around it, in irregular layers, patches, and wedge-shaped masses, often several feet or yards in length. No well determined vein has been exposed, though the ore and sahlite are found along a certain range for some distance.

1195. The masses taken out and used are composed of grains of ore, mixed, more or less, with quartz, sahlite and other foreign matter. This ore occurs in the Metamorphic Group. (See also, § 414.)

The ore is worked at Hampton's bloomary, near the locality, and yields a most excellent iron. Several miles farther east, in North Carolina, are the Cranberry Iron Works, which makes use of the same kind of ore.

1196. The occurrence of cabinet specimens of magnetite in the semi-metamorphic strip in Union County, may be mentioned here. (See § 399.)

1197. Previous to the war there was considerable activity in the Eastern Iron Region in the business of making iron. But the grievous war prostrated all interests of this kind. How far these interests have been revived, how many forges have rekindled their fires, how many furnaces are under the blast, I know not. It is difficult to get reliable information as to such matters without traveling over, in person, most of the ground, and that has been out of the question.

1198. As to one county, however, *Greene*, I have partial information. This county has done well. Since the war two large furnaces have been erected within its limits, and are now in operation. The following letter from Gen. E. L. Hayes, describes one of them:

Office Greene County Iron Co.,
Hayesville, Tenn., Feb. 22, 1869.

Dr. J. M. Safford,
State Geologist, Lebanon, Tenn.:

Dear Sir:—We submit the following information in regard to our Works, and hope it may be of service to you:

The *Greene County Iron Company* was organized in the City of New York, in September, 1867, in compliance with the laws of the State of New York, for the purpose of making iron in the State of Tennessee, with a capital stock of one hundred thousand dollars. The land purchased by the Company comprises 5,564 acres, mostly timbered mountain land lying in nearly a southern direction from Greeneville, and eleven miles distant from that place, on a small mountain stream known as Back Creek, a tributary of the Nolichucky River. The ore is found in great abundance on the right bank of the creek, and at the base of the mountains known as part of the Smoky Range [Unaka Range] which separates the States of Tennessee and North Carolina. The furnace erected by the Company is double hot blast, built of limestone, and said to be one of the finest in the United States. The capacity is from ten to twelve tons per day of charcoal iron. The ore is a brown hematite, (limonite,) yielding from 40 to 50 per cent. of tough gray iron. Both ore and charcoal are very accessible to the furnace. A town has been laid out, and named *Hayesville;* some forty buildings have been erected; a post-office has been established; a school district organized; and a school house and church are in process of erection.

Very respectfully, yours,

E. L. HAYES, *Supt.*

1199. In order that the reader may know what was once the extent of the iron-making business in the region under consideration, the statistics of 1854 bearing upon this business, (collected by the author,) will be given. Similar statistics will also be given for the remaining iron regions. These will be found presented in the tables at the end of this section.

1200. It will be seen, by referring to the tables that there were, in the Eastern Iron Region, in 1854, *nine furnaces*, and all but one, Tellico, cold blast; of these, five were in operation that year, and produced 1855 tons of cast iron—Tellico and Pleasant Valley producing by far the greater part.

The forges were much more numerous, thirty-nine in all; of which thirty-two were bloomaries, and seven, refineries; making, altogether, in 1854, 912 tons of bar-iron, and 480 tons of blooms.

In addition, the Rolling Mill in connection with Pleasant Valley Furnace, is to be noted.

1201. We now pass to the western side of the Valley of East Tennessee. The middle part—that included between the iron regions—does not afford any very extensive banks of iron ore. Small deposits of limonite, however, are very numerous. They can be found upon most of the cherty ridges of the Knox Limestones. The ore occurs, within limited areas, scattered through the soil. At some points, enough could be obtained to supply a bloomery for several years. No forges, however, nor furnaces, are located in this part of the valley.

B.—The Dyestone Region.

1202. This iron region differs from the eastern, in its geographical position, in its geological relations, and in its ores.

It occupies a belt of the State skirting the base of the Cumberland Table-land, or of Walden's ridge, as stated in § 1173. All of some of the following counties, and parts of the others, are included in its area: Hancock, Claiborne, Grainger, Campbell, Anderson, Roane, Rhea, Meigs and Hamilton. It embraces the Sequatchee and the Elk Fork Valleys; this places, also, parts of Marion, Sequatchee and Bledsoe counties, within its area.

1203. The great ore of this region is the stratified red ironstone, called at many points, *dyestone*, being sometimes used for dying purposes. It is a variety of hematite, as stated in § 1177. It generally soils the fingers readily. At most points the ore is hard enough to be quarried out in blocks; at others it is soft, and easily crushed, as at Kimbrough's, in Roane County. Sometimes the soft variety presents the appearance of a true, scaly, specular ore. The dyestone is further described in § 777, to which the reader is referred.

The impurities contained in the dyestone are sandy and argillaceous matters, and carbonate of lime. The presence of the latter is, in certain proportion, no defect, as it can be made to act the part of a flux.

1204. The iron produced from this ore is excellent, both the pig-metal of the furnaces, and the bars of the bloomaries. Occasionally the bar inclines to be *cold-short.*

1205. In addition to the dyestone, limonite is found on the ridges within this iron-region, under circumstances similar to those mentioned with reference to the middle part of the Valley. The two are sometimes mixed in working, with good results.

1206. In the description of the group or formation containing the dyestone beds, (page 302,) the geological relations of the ore have been sufficiently presented.

The ridges, or ranges, called *Dyestone Ridges*, in which the ore-beds occur, have also been enumerated. See § 784, and on. The outcrops of the ore-beds lie in the red lines on the Map.

1207. The first of these, the *Mountain Ridge*, is one of the most important. (See § 785.) The *bed of ore* in this skirting ridge extends, with but few interruptions, from Virginia to Georgia, a distance of nearly 160 miles. There are not more than three or four interruptions, averaging in length from two to three miles each; so that in this range, we have, what may be regarded, as a continuous band of ore 150 miles in length.*

At Cumberland Gap the ore is, as stated, (§ 756,) from 24 to 30 inches thick, and of excellent quality. I visited a locality in Roane, belonging to Gen. G. L. Gillespie, formerly of Kingston, where the ore appears to be seven or eight feet in thickness, though no excavation had been made. At other points near by, which could not be visited at the time, it is said to be much thicker. In the southern part of the State it is less heavy. The entire average thickness of the bed must be at least 20 inches; perhaps it is more.

At numerous points its quantity is greatly increased by the folding of the strata, giving often three or four parallel bands within a few hundred yards.

The soft ore at Kimbrough's is in this range.

1208. Col. W. B. Gaw, in a Report already referred to, (§ 1004,) has the following notes on *iron-ore*. The localities referred to belong mainly to the *Mountain Ridge or Range*.

"The first bed of ore upon our line, occurs in Hamilton County, across the river from Chattanooga. The beds are from one to four feet in thickness, and were formerly worked by the East Tennessee Iron Manufacturing Company, producing a good quality of iron. The ore is the dyestone.

"This ore is found in all the 'valley ridges' along the entire length of road, and in close proximity to it, but we will only mention the points where it has been, or is now worked.

"The next point where the ore has been worked, is at Smith's Cross Roads,

* In speaking of the occurrence of the dyestone, or, as it is often called, the lenticular argillaceous ore, I have confined myself to Tennessee. It has, however, a wonderful range beyond the limits of this State. It is a member of the Clinton Group, of the north, and reaches from Tennessee, through Virginia, Pennsylvania, into New York, and even into Canada. It has been traced out over a good part of this entire range. At numerous points in the states mentioned, it supplies furnaces and forges with ore. Southward, it reaches many miles into Alabama, where it finally disappears beneath more recent formations. This extent, considering that the beds are very seldom more than three feet thick, and often but a few inches, is truly wonderful.

We appear to have in Tennessee our full share of this valuable ore. So far as we have been able to ascertain, it occurs nowhere in beds thicker or more plentiful.

in Rhea County, where several bloomaries were in operation some years ago.

"There are two bloomaries at White's Creek, in Roane County, the ore used, being the same as that already mentioned.

"At Kimbrough's, extensive beds are found, and a bloomary was worked during the war.

"Ore is found in large quantities at D'Armond's Gap, but is not now worked."

1209. The other Dyestone Ranges, with notices of the beds of ore included in them, are described in §§ 788 to 799, to which the reader is referred. The ore of the Elk Fork and Sequatchee valleys is mentioned in §§ 804 to 806.

1210. As in the case of the Eastern Iron-Region, the facts in reference to the production of iron in this region, in 1854, may be found tabulated at the end of the section.

There were, it will be seen, five furnaces—two having steam power and hot blast. Only two were in operation in 1854, producing 1168 tons of cast iron. Of the five furnaces, two—the *Cumberland*, at Cumberland Gap, and the *Bluff*, at Chattanooga, were destroyed during the war. How it has fared with the others I know not.

The forges, which were fifteen in number, were all bloomaries, and produced in 1854, 257 tons of bar-iron.

APPENDIX.

1211. *The Cumberland Iron-Region.*—As an Appendix to the Dyestone Region, I bring in the Table-land as an *iron-field.* In the course of my investigations I have met with many beds of shales in the Coal Measures, containing *clay iron-stones.* These are quite plentiful in the shales below the Wheeler coal, as at Wiley's Bank, on Coal Creek. (§ 1067.) Their occurrence is also noted in many of the sections given in chapter XII. See pages 372, 373, 396, &c.

1212. The *clay iron-stone* is an ore quite different, in appearance and in composition, from any worked at present within Tennessee.

It is an impure carbonate of iron. An analysis before us, by Professor ROGERS, of one of the best specimens found in Pennsylvania, is, in 100 parts of ore:*

* Overman's Manufacture of Iron; p. 30.

Protoxyd of Iron,	53.03
Carbonic Acid,	35.17
Lime,	3.33
Magnesia,	1.77
Silica,	1.40
Alumina,	0.63
Peroxyd of Iron,	0.23
Bitumen,	3.03
Water,	1.41
	100.00

Throwing it into another form, we have, in 100 parts:

Metallic Iron,	41.25
Oxygen of the Protoxyd above	11.78
Carbonic Acid,	35.17
Impurities and Water,	11.80
	100.00

The best ores, therefore, contain a little more than 40 per cent. of pure iron; practically, they yield 30 or 33—sometimes, however, approaching 40.

1213. This ore occurs in nodules and balls, or in flattened concretions, disposed in layers, and interstratified with the shales of the Coal Measures. These balls, or concretions, run up in size from small pebbles to masses weighing a ton or more.

The clay iron-stones are a variety of the crystalline carbonate of iron called *siderite*. Though not as rich as some ores, they are, nevertheless, highly valued, and partly on account of their association with stone-coal.

1214. Whitney, in his "Metallic Wealth of the United States, says:

"This is, perhaps, the most important ore of iron; not generally in its sparry state, but as a mixture with clay and the hydrated oxyd which results from its decomposition, and as constituting a part of the great Carboniferous Formation; hence, occurring with the coal required for its reduction, it becomes of great importance."

"It is to the abundance of her coal-measure iron-stones that England is indebted for her vastly preponderating production of this metal; and it is thus that she has been able to supply the rapidly increasing demand for railway iron, which the discovery of a new means of national intercommunication rendered necessary. The coal-fields of North and South Wales, North and South Staffordshire, etc., while they furnished fuel to smelt the ore, furnished the ore itself, and the necessary flux from the same shaft, with hardly any increased expense beyond what it would have cost to raise the coal alone."

1215. Below the Wiley Coal Bank, in Anderson County, there is a bluff of shale 55 feet thick, with numerous layers of the balls, and flattened masses of this ore in it. Doubtless, along the base of the great ridge, at the foot of which the Wheeler Coal Bed outcrops, as well as at higher levels in this mountain, much clay iron-stone could be obtained. There are, also, other points within the area of the Table-land at which this ore deserves attention.

1216. There is another ore of iron which has, of late years, attracted much attention in Scotland and other countries. It is a *coaly* impure carbonate of iron, peculiar to the coal series, and called the *black-band* or *Mushet iron-stone.* Indications of this have also been discovered in our Coal Measures. A layer of it, from 6 to 12 inches thick, is seen in the section taken three miles south of Beersheba Springs. (§ 970.)

Finally, in addition to the ores mentioned, more or less *limonite* is scattered over the Table-land; but, as yet, I have not met with any very considerable deposit.

C.—The Western Iron-Region.

1217. The counties embraced within this Iron-Region have been given. It occupies a belt, about 50 miles wide, running directly through the State. See §§ 1157, 1158, and 1173. Within this area the banks are met with, at greater or less intervals.

1218. The mode of occurrence of the ore in the banks, as well as its varieties, have been spoken of in §§ 1157 to 1162. It may be added, here, that some localities do not abound in chert; a few afford ore, in red clay alone. The ore is raised from excavations, made either in the tops of the ridges, or in their sides—all being open to the day.

1219. It is not in my power to give a complete catalogue of all the noteworthy banks in this iron-field. As an illustration of their number and value, I will refer to those of Hickman County. It must be observed, however, that this, as an ore-producing county, is *much above* the average of the counties embraced within the iron-region.

1220. In Hickman, at least *twenty banks* occur, upon nearly all of which a furnace could depend for a supply of ore. These lie on both sides of Duck River, and are thus located:

On the waters of the Beaver Dam—six; these, with those on Swan Creek, include the Ætna Furnace banks.
On the waters of Swan Creek—seven.
On Jerry's and Ore branches, north of Duck River—*one*, the *Brown Bank*, an excellent and extensive deposit of ore.
On *Haley's Creek*, the *Cantrell Bank.*
On *Defeated Creek*, the *Puckett Bank.*
On *Piny*, near Vernon, *Lee's Bank.*
On *Mill Creek*, also near Vernon, the *Extra Oakland* No. 1, and *Oakland* No. 2.
On *Garner's Creek*, the *Garner's Creek Bank.*

The localities of the most of these banks are indicated on the Map by groups of small dots.

1221. The greatest of these banks is one belonging to the Ætna Furnace property. We present it as an example of one of the most extensive banks, if not the most extensive, in the whole iron region.

It lies between two tributaries of Beaver Dam Creek—the Brushy and Piney forks. It is from two to three miles long, and will average nearly or quite a mile in width.

Here we have more than two square miles of ore ground, with a depth of from 10 to 100 feet. At scores of points over this area the ore presents itself in natural exposures, or proves its presence in quantity by the fragments scattered over the surface.

1222. It must not be understood that all this ground presents ore which it will be profitable to raise; by no means: it is rather a group of numerous rich deposits of ore. But there is no estimating the amount of mineral it can yield. Ætna Furnace has obtained its ore from the north-western end of this bank—that nearest the stack—and, although the furnace has made over 20,000 tons of metal, this end even is not fairly opened. Several large excavations have been made in the margin of the bank, in which large houses might be put, but they are as nothing—mere notches in the edge of the great plateau of ore.

The bank can feed as many furnaces as can be conveniently located around it. But the great quantity is not the only desirable feature of this bank; its mineral is of excellent quality, and the iron made from it is of superior character.

1223. The mineral resources of Hickman County have not been adequately developed, more on account of the want of the means of transportation than anything else. Next to Hickman, Dickson and Stewart take rank as iron counties, but some of the others are not much behind them.

1224. The property of the Cumberland Iron Works, in Stewart County, is one of great extent and value. It embraces not less than 111.5 square miles of territory, much of which is good arable land. It has many exposures of ore upon it. Its two principal banks are the old *Bear Spring*, and the *Morgan Bank*. The first of these has afforded a great amount of ore. Several furnaces have been supplied from it. The Morgan Bank is comparatively a fresh one. The Cumberland Rolling Mill was formerly an important part of this property, but is now in ruins. One furnace is in blast, another on the property (Bellwood) was burnt during the war, and has not been rebuilt. A bed of fire-clay on this property has been spoken of in § 907.

The *La Grange* is another excellent bank in Stewart county.

1225. We have confined our attention to the western side of the Highland Rim; but this iron field has, in fact, a counterpart, though of much less extent and importance, on the eastern side of the Rim, lying in the range of counties along the base of the Table land, including White, Warren, Coffee, etc. These counties have afforded some ore; and one bloomary is now in operation on Rocky River, in Warren. We look forward with interest for greater developments in this detached section.

1226. The ores of the Western Iron-Region are generally of good quality, and make excellent iron. The following analyses were made by Dr. Troost:

No.	Peroxyd of iron.	Oxyd of Manganese.	Water.	Earthy matter and loss.	Per cent. of pure iron.	Locality.
1	83.0	1,0	14.0	2.0	58.1	Perry county. (?)
2	63.0	2.0	15.0	20.0	44.1	Hickman county.
3	80.0		12.0	8.0	56.0	Brownsport.
4	80.0	1.0	15.0	4.0	56.0	Bear Spring.
5	76.5	5.0	12.0	6.5	53.5	" "

1227. The ore that has been used at Marion Furnace is Hematite, as has been stated. (§1159, note.) It is related to the dyestone ore. It is a fine granular ore, at some points hard and compact, at others soft, unctuous, and staining a deep red. It occurs in several knobs in the region, and is irregularly arranged in layers, with red clay and shaly matter. The ore is highly esteemed, and yields an excellent iron.

1228. There were in the Western Iron-Region, before the war, 35 furnaces, the blast of all but two being made by steam power. Many of them were extensive and elegant establishments. Thirty-one were in operation in 1854, and made 37,283 tons of iron.

Four bloomaries were in operation, making the same year, 91 tons of iron.

The refineries, thirteen in number, were generally efficient establishments, having about fifty-nine fires. They made in 1854, 6,808 tons of blooms, and a few tons of bar-iron. Further statistics are given in the tables.

1229. We add a word in regard to the *fuel* used by our furnaces and forges. As yet, it is throughout the State wholly *charcoal*. Wood in the iron fields is cheap and abundant, and and will be for many years. When it becomes indispensable, we have ample supplies of stone-coal in the bosom of our Table-land, and by that time railroads, as well as our rivers, will bring it to the mouths of our furnaces.

1230. TABLE OF THE TENNESSEE FURNACES, INCLUDING THEIR PRODUCTS, ORES USED, ETC. (1854.)

(a) *Eastern Iron-Region.*

* Blast created by *steam*-power; that of the others by *water*-power. Nos. 8, 13 and 14, are *hot blast;* the others *cold blast.*

No.	Name.	Owners.	County.	PRODUCTS OF 1854.			Kind of Ore.	REMARKS.
				Pig Metal and Castings.	Cas'gs alone.	Mo's in bl'st		
1	Union, ...	Carter & Co.	Carter.	250	....	....	Limonite.	....
2	O'Brien's, ...	....	"	....	....	....	....	Out of blast since 1840.
3	Bushong's, ...	William Bushong.	Sullivan.	105	25	....	Hematite.	....
4	Welcker's, ...	Welcker, Beidleman & Co.	"	....	....	....	"	In blast during 1855.
5	Pleasant Val'y	R. L. Blair & Brothers.	Washington.	700	100	6	Limonite.	Con. with ref. & r. mill.
6	Clark's Creek, ..	" "	"	....	....	....	"	Out of blast since 1844.
7	Bright Hope...	John Shields.	Greene.	....	....	....	....	Out of blast for sev'l yrs.
8	Tellico, ...	Welch, Harris & Co.	Monroe.	730	....	7	Limonite.	....
9	Ball Play, ...	S. S. Glenn & Co.	"	70	....	2	"	....

(b) *Dyestone Region.*

No.	Name.	Owners.	County.	Pig Metal and Castings.	Cas'gs alone.	Mo's in bl'st	Kind of Ore.	REMARKS.
10	Cumb'lnd Gap	John G. Newlee.	Claiborne.	238	38	4	Dyestone.	Now extinct, (1869.)
11	Crockett's, ...	Rose & Fugate.	"	....	....	....	D. and L. ?	In blast in 1855.
12	Sharp's, ...	....	Grainger.	....	....	....	Dyestone.	Repairing.
13	Eagle,*	T. T. Iron Manufac'g Co	Roane.	930	....	7	"	....
14	Bluff,*	" "	Hamilton.	....	....	....	"	Now extinct, (1869.)

15	Brownsport*..	Ewing, Dick & Co.	Decatur.	2109	....	11 5	Limonite.	....
16	Decatur*.......	Golladay, Cheatham & Co	"	....	....	....	"	Started Jan 55, c. 2000t
17	Marion*.........	J. J. H. & J. K. Walker.	Hardin.	915	?	6	Hematite.	Made some sugar ket'ls.
18	Forty-eight*....	F. & S. Pointer.	Wayne.	2445	....	12	Limonite.	Uses two stacks alter'ly
19	....	....	Lawrence.	....	....	....	"	Out of blast sev'l years.
20	Cedar Grove*..	Wm. Bradley & Co.	Perry.	1500	?	....	"	Uses 2 stacks alter'ly.
21	Ætna*.........	Goodrich, Fell & Hillman.	Hickman.	1509	....	9	"	....
22	Oakland*.......	Studdurt, Foulkes & Brat'	"	385	....	3	"	....
23	Worley*.........	Jas. L. Bell.	Dickson.	950	....	....	"	Has a refining fire.
24	Jackson	Estate of M. Bell.	"	50	....	....	"	In blast but a few w'ks
25	Piney*...........	Napier & Holt.	"	1731	70	....	"	.........[of '54.
26	Laurel*.........	William C Napier.	"	257	....	4.5	"	Has a refining fire.
27	Cumberland*..	Anthony Vanleer.	"	1926	....	....	"	....
28	Carroll*.........	Robert Baxter.	"	1050	....	9	"	....
29	Louisa*	Jackson, McKerman & Co	Montgomery	2154	....	....	"	....
30	Sailor's Rest*..	Isaac D. West.	"	600	....	7	"	In '54 wat'r-power now
31	Yellow Creek*	Robert Steele.	"	600	....	....	"	Same as last. [steam.
32	O. K.*...........	Caldwell, Vanleer & Co.	"	1160	....	....	"	....
33	Phœnix*........	....	"	1500	....	11 5	"	....
34	Montgomery*.	Russell, Robertson & Co.	"	1000	....	....	"	....
35	Poplar Sping*	John H. Jones & Co.	"	1175	....	....	"	.... [kettles.
36	Saline*..........	Lewis Irwin & Co.	Stewart.	1200	1200	....	"	Iron made into sugar
37	Great West'n*	Newell & Prichett.	"	....	....	....	"	Started in 1855, of large
38	Iron Mount'n*	Brien, Ledbetter & Co.	"	1015	....	4	"	New furnace. [capacity
39	Peytona*	Thomas Kirkman.	"	1220	....	7	"	....
40	Bellwood*	Woods, Lewis & Co.	"	2006	....	....	"	....
41	Cross Creek*	Newell, Irvine & Co.	"	1905	....	11.5	"	....
42	Rough & Ready*	Barksdale, Cook & Co.	"	1050	....	11.5	"	....
43	Bear Spring	Woods, Lewis & Co.	"	885	....	....	"	This furnace now ext'ct
44	Dover No. 2*	" "	"	....	....	....	"	New, old site; blast '55
45	Union*	Standfield & Kimble.	"	550	....	....	"	New furnace.

TABLE OF FURNACES, ETC.—*Continued.*

(*c*) *Western Iron-Region.*

No.	Name.	Owners.	County.	PRODUCTS OF 1854.			Kind of Ore.	Remarks.
				Pig Metal and Castings.	Cas'gs alone.	Mo's in bl'st		
46	Ashland*	....	Stewart.	1200	....	....	Limonite.	....
47	La Grange* ...	Cobb, Phillips & Co.	"	1910	....	....	"	....
48	Eclipse*	" "	"	641	....	4	"	New furnace.
49	Clark*	Broaddus, Vaughn & Co.	"	585	....	4	"	New furnace.

The whole amount of cast iron produced in 1854, was 40,306 tons, (2268 lbs. to the ton,) of which 1433 were castings. At a few of the furnaces, other castings, to a limited extent, were made for local use; such are included with the pig-metal.

The production of the furnaces for 1855, would be considerably over the above amount.

1231. TABLE OF THE BLOOMARIES, INCLUDING THE NUMBER OF FIRES, PRODUCTS, ETC. (1854.)

(a) *Eastern Iron-Region.*

County.	No. of forges.	No. of fires.	1854. Fires used.	1854. Tons of bar iron made.	Remarks.
Johnson......	14	26	26	367	All use Limonite.
Carter........	5	10	10	168	Limo. mostly; also Magn. & H.
Sullivan......	2?	4 ?	4 ?	30 ?	Hem. See table refin'res & note
Washington	2	4 ?	4 ?	55	One, cin. and Lim.; other, Lim
Greene.......	6	9 ?	7 ?	95	Limonite.
Sevier........	1	1	1	2	"
Blount........	1	1 ?	1 ?	12	"
McMinn.....	1	1	1	13	Dyestone (See § 1192.)
(b) *Dyestone Region.*					
Hancock.....	1	1	....	....	When operating uses Dyestone
Claiborne ...	3	5	4	90	Dyestone, sometimes with Lim
Campbell....	5	10	5	105	" " " "
Anderson ...	?	?	....	....	Sev'ral old forges not operating
Roane.........	1	1	1	5	Dyestone.
Rhea	5	10 ?	10 ?	55 ?	"
(c) *Western Iron-Region.*					
Lawrence ...	3	3	3	80	
Warren......	1	1	1	11	
Total..... ..	51	87	78	1090	2240 lbs. to the ton.

So far as I was able to ascertain, this table included all the *working bloomaries* in the State. There were other old blooming forges which had gone partly or entirely down. Some of them in the Western Region had been converted into refineries.

It is proper to state that most of the bloomaries in the table were not in operation more than half of 1854, owing to the unusually low stage of water in the streams—all of them deriving their blast from water-power.

1232. TABLE OF THE REFINERIES, INCLUDING FIRES, PRODUCTS, ETC. (1854.)

(a) *Eastern Region.*

COUNTY.	No. of forges.	No. of fires.	OPERATIONS OF 1854. Fires used.	Tons blo'ms made.	Tons bar-iron.	REMARKS.
Carter*........	3	5?	2?	....	20?	Most likely more iron [made.
Sullivan†.....	2?	8?	6?	....	75?	
Washington.	1	5	5	480	....	Pleasant Valley W'ks.
Monroe........	1	2	2	....	75	In '55, wk'g old cinder
(b) *Western Region.*						
Davidson‡	2	10	5	600	....	1 not operating in '54.
Dickson‖	1	6	4	140	20	1 run-out fire besides.
Montgom'y§	5	23	17	2900	....	Three steam forges.
Stewart........	2	14	14?	3068	....	Both steam forges.
Humphreys¶	1	4?	4?	100?		
Hickman......	2	2?	....	....	....	Formerly bloomaries.
Total,.	20	79	59	7288	190	

A ton of blooms in the Western Iron-Region is 2464 lbs. It may be that the 480 tons made at the Pleasant Valley Works were estimated at 2240 lbs. per ton; if so, the *total amount* will be reduced to 7244 *bloom* tons. The bar-iron is estimated at 2240 lbs. to the ton.

The table gives *less* than the actual production of 1854. It was almost impossible to get the necessary information from some of the forges.

Between 2000 and 3000 tons of the blooms were converted

* Product of one small forge not included.

† There were *four* forges altogether in Sullivan, making in 1854 about 105 tons of bar-iron. My information was not sufficiently definite to enable me to separate satisfactorily the *refineries* and *bloomaries;* in fact, some of them had both refining and blooming fires.

‡ One did not operate in 1854.

‖ Operated but part of the year.

§ Having no statistics from the Tennessee forge, in Montgomery, its fires, products, etc., were not included.

¶ This forge did some work in 1854. We have not been able to procure the necessary items in regard to it.

into manufactured iron by the Cumberland Rolling-Mill in 1854; the remainder was mostly sold in Cincinnati—some in Pittsburgh.

TENNESSEE ROLLING-MILLS—THEIR PRODUCTION, ETC. (1854.)

1233. There were in 1854 *three* rolling-mills in the State; two in East and one in Middle Tennessee; the last two are now extinct.

1*st*. *Pleasant Valley Rolling-Mill*, in Washington—R. L. Blair & Brothers. Manufactured, in 1854, 480 tons of blooms into nails. This rolling-mill, as before stated, was, and perhaps is now, connected with a furnace and forge, all located at the same point on the Nolichucky, which supplies a splendid water-power.

2*d*. *The Rolling-Mill at Loudon*, in Roane—Samuel M. Johnson & Co. Operated on a limited scale in 1854. Amount of products not known.

3*d*. *Cumberland Rolling-Mill*, in Stewart—Woods, Lewis & Co. Product in one year, from October, 1853, to October, 1854, 2223½ tons of manufactured iron, which was distributed about as follows: 1000 tons to Memphis, Vicksburg, and New Orleans; 800 tons sold in Nashville; 423 tons sold at the works, and consumed in Kentucky and Western Tennessee.

Two furnaces—Bellwood and Bear Spring—and a refinery, with eight fires—all steam-power establishments—were connected with this rolling-mill. Their respective products, for the time specified above, were: pig-metal, 3241½; blooms, 2068½ tons; manufactured iron, 2223½ tons. (see § 1254.)

The entire value of all the iron produced in 1854, including pig-metal, castings, blooms, and manufactured iron, was but little short of *two millions of dollars*.

SECTION II.

COPPER. (2.)

1234. The Ducktown Region is the only locality in Tennessee yielding *copper-ore* in note-worthy quantity.

1235. Two points have been met with, one in Monroe, and another in Grainger, between Clinch Mountain and Copper Ridge, where very small quantities of carbonate of copper, *malachite*, occur in limestone. At the latter place also a little sulphuret is found associated with pyrite.

Some green carbonate has been found on the waters of the Tellico River and of Cane Creek, in Monroe.

At many points within the Unaka region, traces of copper are met with, but no locality of any importance has come under my observation.

1236. The history of the developments at Ducktown, is full of interest. Previous to 1860, Polk County had attracted no attention, and was simply known as an out-of-the-way, mostly mountainous section. But the discovery of the copper deposits at Ducktown, and the great developments made there, soon placed this county among the highest tax-paying counties of the State. Bradley County also, and the town of Cleveland, as well as the whole southern part of East Tennessee, felt the influence of this new interest, partook of its life, and were not a little benefited.

1237. It is not proposed to give a full account of the mines at Ducktown. What is presented is mainly an outline of the history of the developments made, and of the character of the deposits.

1238. The *Ducktown Region,* or simply *Ducktown,* is part of a mountain basin belonging *physically* to North Carolina and Georgia. Accidentally, as it were, the south-eastern corner of Tennessee was thrown beyond its normal place, and the State made to include the area of the mines. See §§ 68, and 396, and also, Map.

1239. The surface of the country about the mines is rolling —cut into ridegs by rather deep valleys and ravines. The general elevation is about 1,000 feet above the valley of East Tennessee, and not far from 2,000 above the sea. (§§ 419 and 428.)

1240. The region is intersected by the *Ocoee River*, the course of which, after entering Tennessee, conforms successively to the character of this area, and to that of the mountain ranges through which it afterwards breaks. Flowing out of Georgia, this stream (passing in the meantime through the southern part of the mining district) flows *quietly* north-westward for five or six miles, until it strikes the main Unaka Range. It then begins to descend *in rapids* through the wild *narrows* of the mountains. For twelve or thirteen miles in its tortuous course, it rolls along over the rocks, while high and grand cliffs of *slate and conglomerate* come down to the water's edge on both sides, scarcely affording, at any point, space enough for a garden spot. After leaving the narrows, the river flows for four or five miles through a more open valley, and then escapes entirely from the mountains into the great Valley below.

Along the river, through the narrows, a good road running

but little above the water's edge, has been cut out of the cliffs, a work originating with Mr. John Caldwell, one of the pioneers in the Ducktown developments. The magnificent scenery along this road, enlivened by the constantly roaring rapids, will itself repay the amateur on a visit to the copper mines, even before he reaches his destination. See also §§ 423 to 428.

1241. *Historical Sketch.**—In 1836, Dr. Troost passed through the Ducktown Region, and in his subsequent Report, (the Fourth,) has the following brief statement:

> "Continuing my reconnoissance in a northwest direction between the Hiwassee and Ocoee Rivers, I came altogether on grauwacke and grauwacke slate to near the junction of the Ocoee and Hiwassee rivers. At several places in the mountains between these two rivers, I saw hydroxide of iron, similar to the ore used in Middle Tennessee in the blast furnaces."

1242. For several years previous to the discovery of the Copper mines, much excitement had existed through the country on account of the discovery of gold on Coqua Creek.

In 1843, a Mr. Semmons, one of the gold-hunters, struck with the appearance of things at the point where the Hiwassee mine is now located, began to wash in the branch for gold. At first he thought himself highly successful, finding an abundance of what he took to be the precious metal. Upon a second examination, however, it proved to be crystals of *red copper ore.* This discovery led to no important results. "Some further work was done by Mr. Grant, who found several rich specimens of native copper."

1243. Some time afterwards, it appears, the property got into the hands of others, who discovered the "*black oxide,*" which has been, so far, the most important ore of the mines. Its nature and value, however, were unknown to them. The company forwarded a quantity of "samples" found in their work, and in the vicinity, to New York, for examination, but, regarding the *black ore* as worthless, they did not, with perhaps

*The following facts bearing upon the history of the mines were, for the most part, published in my Reconnoissance in 1856. They were collected from a variety of sources; some of them from gentlemen directly concerned. We are especially under obligations to Dr. Charles A. Proctor, and formerly of the mines, not only for the tables included in this article, but also for several maps and sections relative to Ducktown. Valuable facts, too, have been obtained, and quotations made, from an article on the "Copper District," in The Southern Journal of the Medical and Physical Sciences.

the exception of a single fragment, include it. The report received, as might have been anticipated, was unfavorable, and resulted in the winding up of operations for that season.

1244. In April, 1847, Mr. Weber, a German, informed the company of the value of the black oxide, and, securing a lease from them, commenced mining operations. The result of this work was the shipment of ninety casks of ore "to the Revere Smelting Works," near Boston, the value of which was thus reported: Three casks were very poor, so that they were not sold. The balance were put up in two lots. No. 1, of 18,750 lbs., deducting water, was worth 32.5 per cent.; No. 2, 12,460 lbs., was worth 14.5 per cent. copper." Meanwhile, Weber left, and operations were suspended.

1245. There is another circumstance bearing upon the discovery of copper at other points in Ducktown, which is in place here.

The same year, 1847, Mr. B. C. Duggar, attracted by the high price of iron in this region, and the immense masses of iron-ore, or "*gossan*," which occur along the outcrops of many of the veins, commenced building a forge for the manufacture of iron, on property now belonging to the Cherokee Mine. In 1848, the forge was completed; but this enterprising gentleman was doomed to disappointment. The iron produced was *red-short*, and of but little value. "If heated to a white color, and immersed in water until cold, it would show a very thin copper precipitate on the surface. Sometimes the forge flame had a green tinge." After fully trying the "*gossan*" of Ducktown, Mr. Dugger was finally compelled to get his ore from a distant locality. The facts thus developed had their effects ultimately upon the copper interests.

1246. In May, 1849, the property which Weaver had leased was secured by another person, who let it remain undeveloped until 1850, when general attention began to be called to the mines.

1247. In order to show the spirit which animated and the circumstances which surrounded some of the pioneers in the development of this copper region, I take the liberty of quoting the following interesting letter, written by Mr. John Caldwell, at the request of Dr. Proctor:*—

"GENTLEMEN:—I came to Ducktown in 1849, scouting for copper, and found some five or six tons in a cabin, ten feet square, on the property now known as the Hiwassee. I found the country unexplored—the school section, a property now worth a million of dollars, attracting little or no

*Southern Journal, vol. iii., page 43.

attention. Sat down in the woods for three hours, to mature a plan to control and open the section. I owned, at the time, one twenty dollar bill. After three hours' reflection, resolved to call a meeting of the citizens of the township, and make a speech explanatory of the value of the school section, and of the importance of leasing it for mining purposes. Told the people that as soon as the mines could be opened, their condition would be improved, and that civilization, intelligence, comfort and wealth, would be the inevitable results. At the conclusion of this remark, a speaker arose in the crowd, and informed me that a large portion of the inhabitants had come here to get away from civilization, and if it followed them, they would run again.

"After the speech was made, drew up a memorial to the Legislature, praying the passage of a law authorizing the commissioners to give a mining lease on the school section. The memorial was signed by a majority of the citizens, and, on personal application, the law was passed, and under it the lease was taken.

"In May, 1850, commenced mining in the woods. In the same year sunk two shafts, and obtained copper from both of them. The excavations made did not exceed twelve feet—at that depth the copper being found. Commenced mining at the Hiwassee Mine in 1851, in connection with S. Congdon, the agent of the Tennessee Mining Company. Built a double cabin, and taught Sabbath-school in the kitchen end of the establishment, aided by young Mr. Walter Congdon."

In regard to the road down the Ocoee, of which I have already spoken, (§ 1240,) he says: "While this same miner"—one who had spoken irreverently of their laudable Sabbath-school efforts—"was planning a way to pack the copper ore out of the mountains on mules, I surveyed the Ocoee River, and determined to make a road eighteen miles through an impassable desert. I had no means, but a strong determination to surmount every obstacle. Going to a Methodist camp-meeting, I obtained permission to make a road speech in the recess of Divine service. The speech over, we took up a collection, principally on a credit and payable in trade. This, however, served the purpose; and on the 6th of October, 1851, the work was commenced. On the first day, three hands worked; on the second, two; and the third, worked *alone*—public opinion, strong and powerful, being against the enterprise. On the fourth day, hired a dozen Cherokees.

Thus began one of the most important projects in the State, which was consummated in two years, at an expense of about $22,000. The Tennessee Company came early to help in the enterprise, but the Hiwassee held back till fourteen miles of the road were passable for wagons. At the close of the first year, Robert McCampbell was employed as the engineer of the road, after which I again turned my attention to mining."

1248. As a continuation of this historical sketch, I give on the next page, a table of the mines, made out the last of September, 1855.

No.	Name of Mine.	When opened.	By whom.
1	Hiwassee	August, 1850.	T. H. Callaway.
2	Cocheco.............	October, "	J. V. Symons.
3	Tennessee..........	October, 1851.	John Caldwell.
4	Polk County........	November, 1852.	" "
5	Cherokee............	December, "	Samuel Congdon.
6	Eureka...............	April, 1853.	John M. Dow.
7	East Tennessee...	June, "	Capt. J. Tonkin.
8	Isabella..............	July, "	C. A. Proctor.
9	London...............	Sept., "	Capt. J. R. Pill.
10	Mary's................	" "	C. A. Proctor.
11	Callaway............	Nov, "	" "
12	Culchote............	February, 1854.	William Bunter.
13	United States......	August, "	Capt. Williams.
14	Biggs.................	" "	William Mayfield.

1249. The last table, together with the one immediately following, both of which are from my Reconnoissance in 1856, exhibits the progress already made. The one below gives the product and the condition of the mines for the month mentioned above, (September, 1855;) also, the per centage of the ore sold, and the points where sold.

No.	Name.	Lbs. produced in Sept., 1855.	Value per cent. of ore last sold.	Where sold.
1	Hiwassse	269,174	24	New York.
2	Cocheco	....	....	....
3	Tennessee...........	217,641	26	Baltimore.
4	Polk County.......	254,172	29½	London.
5	Cherokee...........	....	....	....
6	Eureka...............	281,714	3¾	Boston.
7	East Tennessee...	....	....	....
8	Isabella..............	279,614	29	London.
9	London..............	239,716	41	"
10	Mary's................	267,146	36	"
11	Callaway............	....	....	....
12	Culchote............	....	....	....
13	United States......	....	....	....
14	Biggs.................	....	....	....

According to the table, seven of the mines produced in September, 1855, 1,809,177 lbs., or a little more than 807½ tons. Though I have not the facts necessary to determine accurately, yet the value of this ore is, perhaps, about $80,000.

1250. I add below another table, showing the extent of operations, and the entire amount of ore shipped from the mines up to the last of September, 1855.

No.	Name.	Tons shipped.	Feet of shafts.	Drivage in ft.
1	Hiwassee	4156	641	2784
2	Cocheco	......	98	74
3	Tennessee	} 7355	472	1161
4	Polk County		347	1341
5	Cherokee		335	1147
6	Isabella		217	711
7	Mary's		189	197
8	Eureka	1100	180	872
9	London	1680	264	742
10	East Tennessee	......	191	640
11	Callaway	......	100	147
12	Culchote	......	207	289
13	United States	......	114	100
14	Biggs	......	70	14

It will be seen that eight mines produced and shipped 14,291 tons, worth more than a million of dollars. The Hiwassee alone shipped 4156 tons—about two-sevenths of the whole.

1251. To bring this sketch down to later years, I add the following, from a Report published in 1866 for the Union Consolidated Mining Company of Tennessee.*

"In 1854, a couple of blast furnaces had been erected at the Tennessee Mine, but were afterwards abandoned for want of competent persons to smelt the ores. In June, 1855, smelting-works on the Welsh (Swansea) plan, were commenced at the Eureka Mine, and soon after put in operation, with complete success, shipping regulus of an average quality of 54 per cent. In the following year, smelting was successfully recommenced at the Tennessee Works. Another similar establishment was built at the Hiwassee, and additional works constructed at the Eureka Mine.

In the progress of this industry, it was soon discovered that considerable quantities of copper could be produced from the mine-waters; and in 1859, the Hiwassee, Eureka, and Isabella obtained monthly more than 40,000 lbs. of copper from that source alone.

The smelting-works at the Isabella and Cocheco Mines were erected in the same year; and, after some experiments, it was found that ingot copper, and that of a superior quality, could be produced in the metallurgical establishments.

* This Report was published by the American Bureau of Mines, in New York, October, 1866.

Upon the basis afforded by these facts, and in view of the great advantage of uniting isolated interests, a consolidation of some of the most productive mines was effected in 1858, including the East Tennessee, Mary's, Callaway, Isabella, Cherokee, and others. This combined property is now owned by the Union Consolidated Company. It comprises the following areas:—

East Tennessee	480	acres.
Mary's	160	"
Callaway	320	"
Maria	80	"
Isabella	240	"
McCoy	140	"
Buena Vista	240	"
Johnson	315	"
Beaver	40	"
Cherokee	320	"
Ocoee	240	"
Total	2,575	acres

In 1860, it was resolved by this and other companies, to construct refining-works in common. These works were finished in the same year, and, except during the greater part of the late rebellion, have been ever since in most successful operation, producing refined copper of excellent quality, and eagerly sought in the market.

Another proof of the confidence placed in these copper mines was furnished in the erection, by a new company, of an excellent copper rolling-mill, together with wire-works, at Cleveland Tennessee. This establishment produced sheets and wire of good quality, but was unfortunately destroyed during the war.

The interruption of mining operations during the greater part of the war rendered their resumption peculiarly difficult at its close. In view of the dispersion of skilled workmen. and the inevitable effects of so protracted a suspension in the mines themselves, it is not a little surprising to find the underground operations of the Union Consolidated Company, as well as the smelting-works, again in full activity, amply provided with all the necessary supplies, and running according to a well-organized working system. There appears to be no reason why these mines should not continue to be largely productive. The refining-works have yielded since the war more than 1,000,000 lbs. of ingot copper, of which some 600,000 lbs. were for the Union Consolidated Company,

These remarkable results, as well as the great success of the Ducktown mines and furnaces before the war, are due in large measure, to the ability and energy of Mr. Julius E. Raht, who still holds the position which he has so long and so creditably occupied, as General Superintendent and Agent of most of the companies actively at work in the district. This gentleman is efficiently supported by assistants, among whom Capt. John

Tonkin, one of the oldest mining officers in Ducktown, deserves especial mention."

1252. *The Veins and their Geological Relations.*—The rocks of the Ducktown area are, for the most part, as already stated, (§ 405,) talcose, chloritic, and mica slates. The strata generally dip at high angles to the southeast, and consequently, outcrop in lines having a northeasterly and southwesterly direction. The age of these rocks is spoken of in § 408, to which the reader is referred.

1253. The *ore-deposits* are not true *fissure-veins*, yet I see no reason why, they may not be called *veins*. They are great lenticular masses of ore and gangue-material, lying conformably between strata of the country rock. These lenticular masses, or veins, occur, for the most part, in long ranges, or belts, one succeeding another longitudinally, in approximately the same line; sometimes their feather-edges overlap though thrown apart by intervening rock.

1254. The walls of the veins are not well defined, for the reason that the ore, away from the centres of the masses, is seen in the slates, and disappears gradually. Hence the deposits are said to be *impregnations*. This may be such, but it does not necessarily follow; for, as Mr. Dana says: "Such a blending of a vein with the walls, is a natural result, when its formation in a fissure takes place at a high temperature during the metamorphism, or crystallization of the containing rock."*

1255. I quote further from the able report above mentioned, with reference to the *belts* and the *deposits* included in them.

"The hitherto discovered deposits of Ducktown are in three series, or belts, which have been erroneously regarded as three great veins. It is probable that the progress of mining operations will eventually expose other deposits, so that they will appear, not confined within particular limits, but scattered with less regularity over a wide area. The discovery of those deposits only, which lie in certain lines, is explained by the fact that the miners have always supposed them to be veins, and have, therefore, conducted explorations mainly, or wholly, on the course of mines already opened.

The Ducktown deposits all have the same course as the country rock, viz.: N. E.—S. W., and the same steep dip to the S. E.

The first and most westerly of the three series, or so-called "veins," con-

* Manual, page 714.

tains the deposits of the Burra-Burra, (*i. e.*, Hiwassee and Cocheco,) the London, and the East Tennessee Mines.

The second and middle series includes the Cherokee, Tennessee, Culchote, Eureka and Isabella.

The third comprises the Polk County, Mary's and Callaway deposits.

Of these properties, the Mary's, Callaway, Isabella, Cherokee and East Tennessee, belong to the Union Consolidated Company, in fee simple.

In the following, the Ducktown deposits from the outcrop downward, four entirely different zones or stories are passed through, which are generally sharply distinguished from each other. Their depth, their specific character, and their distance from the surface vary in the several deposits; but the following order of succession is common to all:

1. Upper part of the "vein," consisting of "Gossan," *i. e.*, sandy, porous, massive or reniform ore, mixed with streaks of reddish-brown slate. In this zone, and especially in its lower portion, occur malachite, azurite, cuprite, in grains, masses, and threads, and native copper in foliated and dendritic forms. Cuprite, (the red oxyd of copper,) and the so-called black oxyd, become more and more abundant, and gradually form

2. The second zone, the transition to which occupies generally, not more than ten feet on the dip of the vein. This may be called the zone of the black copper ores. It branches upward, somewhat into the Gossan. It varies in depth from two to eight feet, and appears to follow with its upper limit, the contour of the surface above. In it are found layers, nodules and pockets of cuprite, and granular admixtures of iron and copper pyrites. This division is abruptly cut off below by

3. The third zone—that of iron pyrites, and pyrrhotite (magnetic pyrites,) containing but little disseminated copper pyrites, and, on the other hand, a large proportion of tremolite and actinolite, of radial, fibrous structure, and wine-yellow to brown, color. The disseminated copper pyrites grow more abundant in depth, until they form

4. The fourth zone—that of copper pyrites. In the centre of the deposit this mineral is almost pure and solid, containing some 30 per cent. of copper. Towards the walls, where it is mixed with pyrrhotite, iron pyrites, tremolite, and actinolite, the average contents of copper in the whole mass is 8–10 per cent.

In almost all the Ducktown mines, operations have been confined to the rich zones of black and red copper ore. These have been followed and wrought, and abandoned as soon as the pyrites was reached. Only in one mine—the East Tennessee—a shaft has been sunk through the valueless pyritic zone, and mining is now carried on with profit in the yellow copper ore below, of which, more hereafter.

The decomposition of the Ducktown deposits, from the outcrop to the water-line, (which, as has been said, is not a horizontal line, but follows the depressions and elevations of the surface,) is the result of penetrating waters and atmospheric influences. A slow and gradual process of decomposition, reduction, oxydation, and mutual chemical reaction, has been going on, producing new mineral combinations. Among the results of this secondary process, must be included the formation of the whole zone of oxydized copper ores."

A list of the ores and minerals of the Copper Mines will be found on page 179 of this Report.

1256. The following diagram will illustrate, in a general way, the character of the Ducktown deposits. It represents the section of a ridge supposed to contain one of the veins:

SECTION OF A DUCKTOWN COPPER "VEIN."

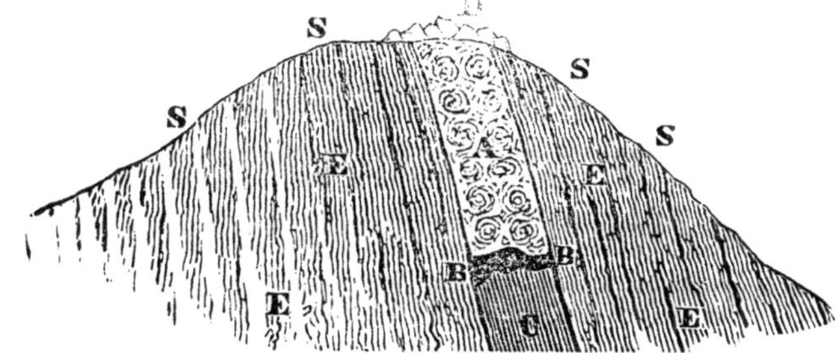

S, S, S, S, surface of the ridge intersected. E, E, E, E, talcose and micaceous slates. A, C, the vein. D, "gossan" on the surface.

1257. It will be seen that the "vein" is composed of three distinct portions, as follows:

(1) The part A. This is the upper zone (1) of page 478, consisting of "Gossan," etc.

(2) The portion B, B, corresponding to 2, on the same page.

(3) The part C. This includes zones 3 and 4, mentioned above. I doubt the propriety of dividing this.

1258. Below are examples of some of the principal mines. The extent and volume of the deposits are illustrated by them.

"I. *The East Tennessee Mine.* This is the northern mine of the western Ducktown belt. It is wrought upon an impregnation of ore, with massive lenticular centre, which has been exposed in a longitudinal extent of 600 feet, and has a maximum thickness of 60 feet, contracting at both ends to a few feet. * * * * * * * *

The zone of pyrites in this mine consists of pyrites and pyrrhotite, with more or less copper pyrites, hornblendes, (tremolite, actinolite,) and now and then, a little galena or zinc-blende. The various proportions of these different minerals, and the degree of their predominance over the slates which they impregnate, give to this zone some variety of appearance.

As has already been stated, a shaft was sunk in the Tennessee Mine through the pyritic zone, which is too poor in copper to be worked. An improvement was soon observable; the copper ore began to concentrate and become more abundant; and at 130–140 feet depth, the shaft entered a massive body of copper ore, almost free from iron and hornblende, into which it has now penetrated for 55 feet. This ore contains about 30 per cent. of copper. It has been explored by drifts for a length of 100 feet or more, and the thickness of the massive central body is about 20 feet, so that a mass of 100,000 cubic feet, or about 10,000 tons of rich copper ore is exposed. This estimate, as appears from the foregoing description of the character of the deposit, is only a rough one, and certainly far below the truth; since, outside of the massive center of the deposit, and gradually passing into the wall-rock, stands a considerable thickness of ore, which, although not so rich, may still be worked with profit. * * * *

II. *The Isabella Mine.*—This is situated on the northernmost deposit of the middle belt, which comprises the Cherokee, Tennessee, Calchote, Eureka and Isabella properties. This deposit has an enormous outcrop of gossan, which appears in a thickness of about 350 feet on the right bank of Potato Creek, on the precipitous side of that valley. (Fig. 3.) During the war, the ferruginous quartzite and the iron ore of this outcrop were used in the production of iron at the neighboring Eureka Furnace, which was altered for the purpose. An adit from the valley bottom has been driven through this deposit, exposing a thickness of nearly 400 feet. The gossan zone extends to about the level of the adit, below which the black ore suddenly appears, carrying however, an average proportion of only 5 per cent. of copper, and having a depth of but 3 or 4 feet. It is not horizontal in upper or lower limit, but follows more or less closely the rise of the hillside above. Below, it is cut off suddenly by the zone of pyrites.

Hitherto only the black ores have been mined at the Isabella. The zone containing these has been followed, and the sulphuretted ores in depth are entirely untouched. The analogy of the East Tennessee Mine, and the occurrence of rich yellow copper at the bottom of the neighboring Eureka shaft, on the same deposit, leave no doubt that deeper workings on the Isabella will open a large and profitable mining ground. This course is urgently recommended.

At present, water is conducted through the old workings, so as to dissolve the efflorescing salts of copper; and from this solution about 9,000 lbs. of cement-copper, containing 75–90 per cent. of pure metal, are produced monthly.

III. *The Cherokee Property.*—This contains several deposits, belonging to the same belt as the foregoing. Two of these have been developed by small openings, now in ruins. They have no gossan, and almost no black ore; both these zones having probably been rendered friable by atmospheric influences, precipitated down the steep hillside, and carried entirely away by the mountain brook. One of these deposits is 10 feet, and the other 4 feet, in thickness; they consist of predominating iron pyrites, showing some yellow copper, which, judging from analogy, is likely to be more abundant in depth. Their character is certainly promising, although they are not sufficiently developed to be thoroughly studied.

"IV. *The Mary's Mine, (including the Callaway Property.)*—This comprises a number of deposits belonging to the southeastern belt. Their lenticular form is most clearly seen in Mary's Mine. They lie in such a relative position that one commences where another ends, without being in exactly the same line; so that if the series were considered as a vein, that vein would appear to have suffered a number of dislocations. The real explanation of this phenomenon has been repeatedly given in the present Report.

The operations in this mine have been confined to the black ores. It presents an inviting field for enterprise, since the deposits attain a thickness of 75 feet, and their whole character, as well as the analogy they bear to the East Tennessee, justifies the belief that in depth they will pass into copper pyrites."

1259. Aside from the refining works mentioned above, the Union Consolidated Company has *smelting works* of its own, as follows:

1. At the Isabella Mine. Three blast-furnaces, with ample blast-apparatus, having as motor a water power, which also drives the pumps of the mine; one calcining-furnace of large size; a new roasting-kiln; and a number of substantial sheds for heap-roasting and storage of charcoal, ore, and other material. There are two furnaces always in operation while one is undergoing repairs.

2. On the Tennessee School Land, (leased by the Company:) Four blast-furnaces, with two sets of blast-apparatus and water-wheels, and all necessary ore, coal, and roasting sheds.

The smelting capacity of the furnaces of both works is at least one thousand tons per month. The production is estimated at about 400 tons of matte, of which nearly half is re-smelted after roasting, so that there could be delivered monthly at the United Refining Works, from 280 to 300 tons of copper-matte.

The United Refining Works comprise four blast-furnaces, a calcining-furnace, three reverberatories, a 45-horse-power steam-engine, with blast-apparatus, crusher, stamps, and all necessary sheds for coal, ore, and roasting the matte. Connected with the establishment are blacksmiths' and carpenters' shops, an office, and a well-arranged chemical laboratory, fitted up with all the apparatus required for copper assays and complete mineral analyses.

The capacity of this establishment will allow a production of 14,000 lbs. of refined copper, daily, provided the three companies now furnishing it with matte for refining, deliver their product of an average quality, not below 30 per cent. of copper.

The present monthly production of the Union Consolidated Company's mines is from 350 to 400 tons of ore, yielding 10–12 per cent. of copper.

It is intended to raise the production to 1,000 tons per month, and to introduce at the same time extensive dressing machinery, by means of which the average quality of the ores will be considerably improved; so that the increased production will not necessitate any additional furnaces or machinery.

Section III.

LEAD AND ZINC. (3 *and* 4.)

1260. Ores of both these metals occur at numerous points in East and Middle Tennessee, but most frequently in unimportant quantity. The two metals are often associated. They occur as sulphurets, (*galenite and blende,*) in veins; in centres in limestone or dolomite, points at which the rock is more or less richly impregnated with the ores; or sparsely disseminated (*galenite*) in grains and buttons through the mass of extensive strata.

1261. The following are the ores occurring, the second and third being of little importance:

(1) *Galenite,* often named *galena* and *sulphuret* of lead; when pure, contains in 100 parts,

Lead	86.6
Sulphur	13.4
	100.0

This ore is recognized, generally by its metallic lustre and *lead* color. An important ore.

(2) *Cerussite: White Lead ore, or Carbonate of Lead.* It is composed, when pure, in 100 parts of

Lead	77.7
Oxygen	5.9
Carbonic Acid	16.4
	100.0

In small quantity; results from the decomposition and oxidation of galenite.

(3) *Sphalerite,* or *Zinc Blende;* named also *Sulphuret of Zinc,* and "*Black Jack,*" has the following composition:

Zinc	67
Sulphur	33
	100

This is a brittle mineral with a resinous lustre, and generally brownish yellow, though sometimes of other colors.

(4) *Smithsonite; a Carbonate of Zinc; Dry Bone* of the miners; is composed of

Oxide of Zinc	64.8
Carbonic Acid	35.2
	100.0

Color usually white or gray, sometimes brownish; effervesces with acids.

(5) *Calamine*, or *Silicate of Zinc*, with a composition of

Oxide of Zinc	67.5
Silica	25.0
Water	7.5
	100.0

Color, white, also yellowish or brown. Smithsonite and Calamine are usually associated, and are sometimes mixed in the same mass.

1261a. The last two minerals have little of the aspect of ores, and would escape the attention of one not acquainted with them. They occur massive or incrusting: sometimes in mammillated or stalactitic forms; often as earthy or stony masses of yellowish-gray colors. As a general thing, masses, supposed to be these ores, may be tested by pulverizing them, and throwing the powder on glowing charcoal. If zinc be present, a white cloud of oxide will arise, and may be collected on a cold plate of iron over the fire. The weight will sometimes give a useful hint as to their nature.

1262. *Lead in East Tennessee.* There is scarcely a county in East Tennessee in which *galenite*, in small quantities, may not be found. It occurs, for the most part, in strata of the Knox Dolomite. (§ 535.) Its modes of occurrence are given in § 566, as well as in § 1260 above.

1263. In Claiborne and Union Counties, there are numerous localities of this ore, which have attracted attention, and at several of which, a little work has been done. These localities are, generally, near Powell's River, on the back of the great anticlinal, spoken of in §§ 544 and 550.

There is an extensive region herein which the sparry dolomites contain, generally, much galenite. But it is thinly scattered through the rocks, and is not available. The principal stratum of this kind, has been mentioned in § 567. Most of the localities of ore referred to above, are nothing more than centres, where small masses of galenite have accumulated in the dolomites. At some of them, however, veins do exist.

1264. Of all that I have seen, there is but one that I regard as promising, and that is the *Caldwell Mine* on Powell's River. (§ 566.) This is in Union County, at a point on the river between Tazewell and Jacksboro', and about sixteen miles from the former place. The vein fills a nearly vertical fissure, about twenty inches wide, in nearly horizontal rocks. It can be traced for nearly a mile. At the time of my visit, (July, 1855,) very little had been done towards its development, but its character, in one place on the surface, could be distinctly seen. The galenite, associated with blende, and some pyrite, occurs in several sheets, with an aggregate thickness of about five inches. The sheets are separated by a gray vein-stone. There is reason to believe that the character of the lode will improve farther down. The property belongs to Messrs. Caldwell, Birdseye, and others.

Since the above observations were made, Mr. Caldwell has sunk a shaft on this vein. He states the results to be as follows:

"Went down 24 feet to the vein, and then into it five feet; vein at first, two feet thick, increased slowly in descending; the galena at the bottom of the shaft, in two sheets, averaging, in the aggregate, 12 or 16 inches; outside of the sheets, the galena diffused through the gangue."

The vein crosses Powell's River, and runs in a nearly east and west direction.*

The gangue rock appears to be a breccia made up of fragments of dolomite and chert, the former most abundant.

1265. In Johnson County, south of the Watauga, on the Duggar property, there appears to be a vein of galena with blende. It was not sufficiently exposed, however, at the time of my visit, to enable me to form an opinion, of its character.

1266. In the valley-range west of the line of *red knobs* that extend from Strawberry Plains to Georgia, (§§ 112 and 615,) thereare in Bradley and Monroe counties, three points at which considerable lead mining has been done. The most southerly

* N. 75° W., and S. 75° E.

of these is in *Chatata Valley*, in Bradley, which is one section of the valley-range referred to. This locality belongs to Mr. John Hambright. The others are in Monroe, and are known, respectively, as the Carter and Montgomery Mines.

1267. (1) *Hambright's Mine* is about four miles south of Charleston, near the middle of the Chatata Valley. It is in the Knox Dolomite, (§ 535,) but near the junction of this with the Maclurea Limestone. (§ 590.) I have been at this point several times, but never found the excavations open. The following information was given me by Mr. Hambright: "The *lead vein*, when worked, showed a layer averaging eight inches in thickness, and dipping with the rocks [about at an angle of 15°] to the southeast. The gangue was heavy spar. The *galena* exposed was a continuous layer, ranging from one to four inches in thickness, and associated with more or less blende, and other ores of zinc. Where the layer of galena was thin, the enclosing rocks held more or less of the ore in grains.

"Masses of galena have been found in the neighborhood of the vein, weighing from 200 to 300 pounds. A flat mass, weighing 53 pounds, was taken from the vein Two or three tons have been dug out of the earth near the vein since 1850."

At this locality are old and quite extensive "diggins," about which the oldest inhabitants, and the Indians before them, knew nothing. They were, doubtless, made for loose pieces of galenite in the soil.

1268. (2) The *Carter Mine* is three miles directly east from Sweetwater. It is in the same valley-range, as stated, as the Hambright Mine, and has about the same geological relations. I visited this point in 1859, and received the following items: The mine was worked in 1826 by John Carter and others, under the name of Bell & Co. They worked ten negroes for a year, sunk a shaft 25 or 30 feet deep, and raised enough ore to pay expenses, and perhaps something over.

After that, and nearly up to the time of my visit, nothing had been done. In 1859, John Smith & Co., had an engine on the ground, and were preparing to resume operations. What they did I am not informed.

I am not able to give the features of this deposit; when there, the shaft was full of water. The galenite, both at this and the mine mentioned below, is associated with barite, fluor, blende, and pyrite.

1269. (3) *The Montgomery Mine* is about two miles northeast of the last. It was also held under lease by Smith & Co. An engine had been placed at this mine also. I have never seen this point. Its features are, doubtless, like those of the Carter Mine.

1270 The lead of ore of *Bompass Cove* has been spoken of in connection with the origin of the iron-ore occurring in the same cove, (§ 1182,) and also in § 566. Some work has been done here, but the developments made are not promising.

1271. Many years ago some lead-ore was raised in Jefferson County, but I know nothing of its mode of occurrence.

1272. The presence of *cerussite* in the soil, at a point in the valley between Greeneville and and the Warm Springs, is mentioned in § 568.

1273. Galenite also occurs in Grainger, six miles north of Rutledge, in Roane, in Bradley, a few miles southwest of Cleveland, and, as I have said, in most of the counties of East Tennessee, but generally in quantities too small to be of special interest.

1274. The limestone constituting the base of the Cumberland Table-land, which lies both in East and Middle Tennessee, affords lead-ore at several points. A vein occurs in Marion County; other localities are on the sides of the mountain above Sequatchee Valley; lead, too, has been found in White, in the "Gulf of Caney Fork." (§ 932.)

1275. *Lead in Middle and West Tennessee.*—Veins of galenite, generally associated, as in the Eastern Division, with blende, occur in many counties in Middle Tennessee. Most of them are of no practical importance. See §§ 700, 701, 740, 824, and 932.

1276. In regard to a "large vein" in Davidson, in the vicinity of Haysborough, Dr. Troost, in his seventh report, says:

> "It is very probable that this vein is very extensive and rich, and the ore is good. It has been penetrated about ten or twelve feet, and has already, at this inconsiderable depth, produced about 1000 lbs. of lead. This vein being situated near a rivulet, the work was impeded by the water, and the operation abandoned. By an accurate search, the same vein may be found at a more convenient place; or by erecting pumps, the vein may, perhaps, be worked with advantage. It is very probable, as I mentioned above, that this vein is extensive; traces of it are found on the bank of the Cumberland River in several places."

This galenite, associated with some blende, occurs in a *gangue of barite.* It is not at present in a condition to admit of examination.

1277. Some lead ore has been reported as occurring in the limestones of West Tennessee. Loose fragments or pebbles of galena have occasionally been noticed in the gravel-beds of this part of the State.

1278. *The Zinc of East Tennessee.*—I have already had occasion to speak of the occurrence of blende in connection with galenite. The two important ores of zinc, however, are smithsonite and calamine. (See §§ 1261 and 1261a.) They occur in deposits, and in irregular veins, in the dolomites of the Knox Group, (see § 1260, and also § 569,) at numerous localities, the most important of which are in Union, Claiborne and Jefferson counties.

1279. The zinc ores of Claiborne and Union have been long known.* They occur at intervals, with more or less galenite, on the back of the anticlinal referred to in § 1263, and described in previous sections. Many of these, however, are too limited to be worthy of special mention.

1280. The *Stiner* locality is the most important that I have met with in this region, and it is certainly an interesting one. This locality is in Union County, near one of the roads leading from Tazewell to Jacksboro', and about three-fourths of a mile from Powell's River, and is, moreover, from three to four miles, in a southwesterly direction, from the Caldwell Lead Vein.

1281. The ore outcrops here in a belt or zone, which is from 50 to 60 feet wide, and runs, in an east-northeasterly direction, across a low ridge. This zone has always been marked out by the absence of trees. Over the area, six or seven pits, (at the time of my last visit, 1865, mostly filled up,) were dug many years ago, and a dozen tons of ore thrown out. Some of this was taken down the river, but the most of it has been lying on the ground ever since. So far as could be seen, the ore, *smithsonite* and *calamine*, with here and there buttons, and small masses of galenite, and occasionally of blende, occurs, with much siliceous matter, in irregular "veins," or in a network of veins. The veins *apparently* run vertically into the rocks, are from a few inches, to several feet, in thickness, and with the enclosed matter, make up the zone above mentioned.

The rocks of the vicinity are dark and blue magnesian limestones, of the lower part of the Knox Dolomite. (§ 535.) Some of them are oolitic, and a few thin beds of Knox variegated shale are met with. The strata, in general, are approximately horizontal.

The masses of ore thrown out are rough, heavy, and generally more or less open.

1282. There are doubtless a number of localities in the Lead and Zinc Region of Powell's River, that will, hereafter, prove themselves to be valuable, notwithstanding the failures thus far, to open remunerative mines. The region is away from the

* To Dr. Troost is due the credit of having first called attention to the zinc of East Tennessee.

means of transportation, the river amounting to but little, and this has embarrassed and retarded mining operations.

1283. Five or six miles from Tazewell, in the vicinity of Mr. John Fulps, on Straight Creek, are deposits of ore, both of lead and zinc. Some digging has been done, and ore taken out, but the extent of the deposits remains to be determined.

1284. At several points in Jefferson County, ores of zinc occur. The most important appears to be at Mossy Creek. At this locality, numerous irregular "veins," in rocks nearly horizontal, and of the Knox Dolomite Formation, occur on a hill-side within an area of several acres. The ore is smithsonite and calamine, with more or less blende.

1285. Within a few years, works have been erected at Mossy Creek, for working the zinc ores, and especially, as I understand, for the manufacture of the white oxide used like white lead in painting. For a few months after the completion of the works, the proprietors succeeded in making considerable quantities of the oxide, ("zinc paint;") but after that, for reasons that I do not understand, operations were suspended, and the works have been idle ever since. I have not had occasion to visit Mossy Creek since the operations above mentioned commenced, and know not what developments were made. I am told that the ore proved abundant, and of good quality.

1286. Some ore has been found in the vicinity of Dandridge. From Mossy Creek, down, through the New Market Valley, and in a southwesterly direction, through Knox, as far as Loudon, zinc ores, smithsonite, etc., are found in small quantity, at numerous points.

Localities also exist in Cocke County.

In Middle Tennessee, there are no noteworthy localities of zinc ore, that I know of. The occurrence of blende, with galenite, in this part of the State, has been referred to.

APPENDIX.

1287. *Note on Silver.*—In Dr. Troost's Fifth Report, as well as in my *Reconnoissance*, (1856,) mention is made of the finding of "*Sulphuret of Silver*" in Cumberland Mountain and Calf-killer River. After further investigation, I have satisfied myself that the specimens in question were *not* of Tennessee origin. I have reason to believe that the specimen found in the Calf-killer, by Troost, was purposely placed there by some unknown person. It is time the whole matter was expunged from Tennessee Reports.

1288. *Silver in Lead—Indian Stories.*—Some silver, though generally in mere traces, is found in our lead ores. I know, as yet, of no locality of such ore, of any importance, though such may be looked for. A lead ore containing five or six per cent. of silver, would be a silver ore.

The *numerous* old Indian stories about silver mines, which are so common in East and Middle Tennessee, there being at least one, perhaps two, on an average, for every county, are entitled to no credit. To give a specific amount of them, would require a volume, which, when written, would be worth practically nothing.

SECTION IV.

GOLD. (5.)

1289. During the last thirty-eight years gold, in limited quantity, has been obtained in Tennessee. The region which affords it lies in the south-eastern part of the State. From my own observations, I would give greater limits to this region than those hitherto assigned it.

1290. More or less gold could doubtless be found in the mountain parts of all the eastern counties, from the French Broad to Georgia, wherever the semi-metamorphic slates of the Ocoee Group are to be met with.

In many parts of this region lenticular conformable veins of quarts abound, and some of them will doubtless prove to be rich enough to work. (See § 475.)

1291. There are numerous localities where gold has been found. At most of them it occurs in small quantity. In all cases, with but a few exceptions, it has been washed out of the gravel and sands of branches, creeks or rivers.

The following are some of the localities: In Blount County, a few miles east of Montvale Springs, and back of Chilhowee Mountain; in Monroe, at several points, as follows—on the waters of Citico Creek, in the bed of Cane Creek, on the head-waters of Tellico River, and on those of Coca or Coqua Creek; in Polk County, also, it has been found.

1292. *Coca Creek and Vicinity.*—The localities which have afforded most of or nearly all the gold, are those of *Coca Creek and vicinity*, embracing a strip of country perhaps eight or ten miles long, and two or three wide. This region is a part of the depression or mountain trough spoken of in § 437. It is intersected by the Tellico, and supplies some of the important tributaries of that river. Coca Creek, a tributary of the Hiwassee, flows through the southern part.

1293. The first gold was discovered in 1831. So soon as the fact became generally known, hundreds of persons flocked to the golden field, and engaged in working the debris of all the low places and streams, small and great, in the region. Every year since, more or less work has been done, and gold to the value of many thousand dollars has been collected and carried off.

At first, in the richest localities, an *industrious* man could average two dollars a day, which was then, when wages were low, considered an excellent business. In a short time, the average was reduced to a dollar and a half, and then to one dollar, and lower.

At present some washing is occasionally done. About fifty cents a day to the hand can be depended upon, with the additional prospect of greater yields at intervals.

1294. The following table shows the amount of Tennessee gold deposited at the United States Mint, and branches, from 1831 to 1853, inclusive:*

VALUE OF TENNESSEE GOLD DEPOSITED AT THE UNITED STATES MINT, ETC.

Years.	Value.	Years.	Value.	Years.	Value.
1831	$1,000	1839	$300	1847	$2,511
1832	1,000	1840	104	1848	7,161
1833	7,000	1841	1,212	1849	5,180
1834	3,000	1842		1850	1,507
1835	100	1843	2,788	1851	2,377
1836	300	1844	2,240	1852	750
1837		1845	3,202	1853	149
1838	1,500	1846	2,642	1854	
					$46,023

The largest *piece* of native gold that I have heard of, found

*The part of the table from 1831 to 1847, inclusive, has been taken from Dana's Manual of Mineralogy; the remainder, from 1848 to 1853, from Whitney's Metallic Wealth of the United States.

In the latter work, the amount deposited from 1838 to 1847, inclusive, is given in the aggregate at $50,446; while in the former, the amount for the same time is but $16,499, making a difference of $33,947. As the product of each year is specified in Dana's Manual, we adopt $16,499 as being most likely correct. Whitney gives $79,970 as the entire yield for the period included in the table above.

at any time in the Coca region, weighed twenty-one penny-weights; a smaller peice weighed eleven.*

1295. *Source of the Gold—the Whippoorwill Vein.*—The gold found in Tennessee has been derived mainly from *quartz veins.* Liberated by the disintegration of these, the rains and the streams have washed it, together with gravel, sand and earth, into the low places. This view has been confirmed, within a few years, by the discovery of a *gold-bearing quartz vein* in the Coca Creek Region. This has been found on a small branch called *Whippoorwill*, the waters of which find their way into the Tellico. The place is near a low ridge, dividing the Coca Creek and Tellico waters, and is about six miles east of the Tellico Iron-works.

1296. Through the kindness of Austin Fry, Esq., I had the opportunity of seeing and examining this locality.

The "vein" lies *between* the strata, not intersecting, but dipping with them to the south-east at an angle of about forty-five degrees. It is composed of brittle quartz, rather compact, but occasionally affording cavities, some of which are rhombohedral or cubic (pyrite) in outline, and filled with brownish or yellowish ferruginous matter. This vein or sheet of quartz, has an average thickness of about six inches; its surfaces have a wavy or rolling character like those of the adjoining slates.

The outcrop was exposed for many yards, and ran up the side of the hill. The gold occurs in grains and scales through the quartz, and also occasionally in the ferruginous matter mentioned above. I saw many fragments of quartz, taken from the vein along its outcrop, containing visible particles. Some very fair cabinet specimens have been obtained.

1297. A company was formed some years ago, under the style of the Whippoorwill Mining Company, that proposed to ascertain the richness of the quarts, and the extent of the vein. What they have done, if anything, I am not advised.

This vein we regard as but one of many auriferous veins like it, some of them perhaps much more extensive, that may be found at different points in the region specified in the beginning of this section.

The geological character of the Coca Creek Region is given in §§ 437 and 438, to which the reader can refer.

*A pennyweight of native American gold is usually worth from ninety-five cents to one dollar.

CHAPTER XVII.

MINERALS NOT CONSIDERED ORES, AND ROCKS OF SPECIAL USE.

1298. Having considered the ores and metals, we take up now the minerals not used as ores, and the rock-material of the formations susceptible of useful application. Many of these substances have been described, and will be but little more than enumerated here.

SECTION I.

STONE COAL. (1.)

1299. In considering the *Coal Measures*, the coal was necessarily included. The reader is, therefore, referred to chapter XII, where this formation is described, for the principal facts as to the coal, and coal beds. What is added here, is supplementary.

1300. *Amount of Coal.*—It is a difficult matter to make a reliable estimate of the aggregate amount of coal in Tennessee. The superficial area of the coal-field is 5,100 square miles, as given in § 945. I once estimated the amount of coal to be equal to a solid stratum eight feet thick, and co-extensive with the Table-land.* This would be equal in volume to a solid block, 8 feet high, 51 miles wide, and 100 long. As to how this approximates to the truth, the reader can form some idea by studying chapter XII., and its sections. It is, perhaps, a maximum estimate.

1301. *Quality.*—All the Tennessee coals are bituminous; but, as such, they present many varieties. Some are highly

* Reconnoissance, page 95.

bituminous, gas-making coals; others, are semi-bituminous; some, open, free-burning, while others are coking coals. The coals beneath the Conglomerate appear to be as variable in quality as they are in volume. I am inclined to think that the Tennessee coals, in general, contain less pyrite than usual. Of this, however, I cannot be certain, until further observations are made.

1302. I will not attempt any classification of the coals, as to quality. The data are not yet sufficient for this. Below, are a number of analyses of Tennessee coals, collected from a variety of sources:

ANALYSES OF TENNESSEE COALS.

No.	County.	Name of bank.	Specific gravity.	ANALYSES.		
				Carbon.	Volatile matter.	Ashes.
1	Roane	Kimbrough's	1.45	71.00	17.00	12.00
2	Rhea	Gillenwater's	"	69.00	14.00	17.00
3	?			76.00	17.00	7.00
4	Grundy	Sewanee		65.50	29.00	5.50
5	"	"		59.38	34.50	6.12
6	Marion	"Upper Seam."		59.50	38.00	2.50
7	"	" "		56 50	41.50	2.50
8	"	"Lower Seam."		49.50	43.00	7.50
9	"	Ætna		65.00	32.50	2.50
10	"	"		74.20	21.39	4.41
11	Hamilton	§ 1004 (a)		63.90	26.80	9.30
12	"	Sale Creek		56.75	40.75	2.50
13	Anderson	Coal Creek		55.00	40.00	5.00

Nos. 1. 2 and 3, are by Dr. Troost.

No. 4, is by F. Zwickl, of New York.

Nos. 5, 6, 7, 8, 9, 12 and 13, are by Prof. W. M. Stewart, of Glenwood, near Clarksville.

No. 10, is by Dr. Julius J. Pohle.

No. 11, is by T. Sterry Hunt, of Canada.

Ashes of 6 and 7, light drab; of 8, dark gray; of 10, fawn-colored; of 11 and 12, reddish gray; of 13, light gray.

The ashes of 10 are made to include: moisture, 1.30; sulphur, 0.71; and ashes, 2.40.

Nos. 6 and 7, above, are from the region in which the sections §§ 961 and 962 were taken. Considerable work has been done recently in this vicinity by Lewis & Co., but as to the developments, I am not informed.

1303. The following statement from Mr. J. H. Kendrick, Secretary of the Nashville Gas Light Company, is interesting with reference to Tennessee gas coals:

Gas Coals.—The old Sewanee coal is now being used in large quantities for gas at Nashville. This coal gives the very *best coke*, and gives a fair yield of gas, the quality of which is made to equal to *Pittsburg coal gas*, by using, say, two and a half pounds of crude resin to every bushel of coal.

The Anderson County coal, is the best *gas coal* in the eastern portion of the State; it compares well with Pittsburg coal.

The New Coal, from the mines of Lewis & Co., on the Jasper Branch Railroad, shows itself by experiments so far, to be equal to any thing in the State, and if they improve as the mines are opened the coal may equal any Pittsburg coal for any use.

1304. *Production, etc.*—At this time the principal points at which coal-mining is done in Tennessee, are *Tracy City*, in Grundy, and the *Ætna Mines*, in Marion. There are many other points at which Coal is mined, a large aggregate amount being thus produced; but by far the greater part of the Coal taken to market comes from the two localities mentioned.

The Ætna Mines are active, but I have no statements from them.

1305. The following letter from A. S. Colyar, Esq., President of the Tennessee Coal and Railroad Company, gives us satisfactory information in reference to the condition and operations of the *Sewanee Mines*.

An analysis by Mr. Yaryan is also added, which makes three in all, that we have of this Coal.

NASHVILLE, March 22, 1869.

DR. SAFFORD:

Dear Sir:—In answer to your inquiry, I have to state that the Sewanee Mines, now being worked by the Tennessee Coal and Railroad Company, have been gradually improving in appearance and quality since they were opened. The mine is thoroughly opened, there being now about 4½ miles of railroad track under the ground. The openings are by three main entries from the outside; one extending over 700 yards, the others about 300 yards each. These entries, and the crossings, penetrate enough of the hills on both sides of the railroad to demonstrate, that this single bed of coal has an extent of at least 1500 acres. The entire vein is level, being about 15 feet above the railroad.

The work of this Company for three years, has been to increase the facilities for shipping coal, and it is now shipping about 6000 bushels per day. The next year's work will amount to 80,000 tons, or 2,000,000 bushels. The demand for coal is increasing to such an extent that this Company lacks more of supplying the demand, shipping 25 cars per day, than it did 3 years ago, shipping 5 cars per day.

The coal is usually 4 feet 8 or 10 inches; but there is much coal 7 feet thick. Since penetrating the mountain, however, a considerable distance, the vein is quite uniform at from 4½ to 5 feet. This coal is much harder, and in every way superior to the coal taken out for several years after the mine was opened.

A remarkable fact has occurred in the use of this coal in engines. The argument against burning coal instead of wood in engines is, generally, that it burns out the fire-box. This Company is now using two engines which have been in constant use 12 years. They have both been rebuilt in the last two years, having run ten years with the same fire-boxes. The machinist in rebuilding one of these engines would have put back the same fire-box, but that it was broken in taking the engine to pieces. Mechanics say there is scarcely such another instance recorded.

The composition of this coal, by the analysis lately made by Mr. Yaryan, of this city, is

Fixed Carbon	63.5
Volatile Matter	29.9
Ash	6.6
	100.0

Specific gravity............1.312. Coke....................... 70.1

After considerable tests, it is pretty well settled, that this coal will make iron without coking. It is now used in preference to any other tried at the *Vulcan Works* at Chattanooga, and at the large Rolling Mill of Scofield & Gray, at Atlanta.

The mining of this coal costs about 3 cents per bushel; and all the railroads South have reduced the freight on coal until it can now be shipped over any of the roads south of Nashville, including the Nashville & Chattanooga Railroad, at prices as low as those the roads in Pennsylvania are charging.

Truly,

A. S. COLYAR, *President.*

1306. As a part of the history of the mining and consumption of coal in Tennessee, I add the following table. The facts embraced were obtained in 1855, by the author, in most cases from the proprietors of the banks themselves.

The entire amount of coal mined in 1854, is seen by the table to have been 247,400 bushels, or 8,836 tons:*

* In Tennessee a bushel of coal is 80 pounds; a ton, therefore is 28 bushels.

PRODUCTION AND CONSUMPTION OF TENNESSEE COAL IN 1854.

COUNTY.	BUSHELS RAISED.	REMARKS.
CLAIBORNE	500	Used by blacksmiths mostly. Two thousand bushels in addition were brought from Kentucky.
CAMPBELL............	4000	Consumed by blacksmiths mostly. Fine banks occur, from 4 to 6 feet thick.
ANDERSON.		
(*a*) Coal Creek.....	3000	Used by blacksmiths mostly.
(*b*) Poplar Creek...	35,000	Coal consumed for manufacturing and domestic purposes in Knoxville, North Alabama, and by blacksmiths of the county. Excellent banks, 6 and 7 feet thick. Fifty thousand bushels estimated production of 1855. Coal in Knoxville is worth from 18 to 25 cents per bushel.
ROANE.		
Kimbrough's Bank.	83,000*	One-third made into coke, and sent to Knoxville, Georgia and Alabama. Sold near the bank at 15 and 12½ cents per 40 lbs. The remainder consumed in Loudon and Knoxville for manufacturing and domestic purposes. Sold near the bank at 12½ and 10 cents per each 70 lbs.
HAMILTON & MARION		
(*a*) Jack's Bank.......	1000	In 1853, raised 15,500 bushels. Sold at 7 cents at the bank.
(*b*) Clift & McCree's	25,000?	Perhaps more.
(*c*) Tennessee River.	14,000	Two or three banks where the river breaks through Walden's Ridge. Coal delivered on the bank at about 10 cents, and consumed mostly in North Alabama.
(*d*) Raccoon Mou'tn.	24,500	Banks near the railroad. Coal sent to Nashville, Chattanooga and Georgia. Consumed as above. Estimated production of 1855, 300,000 bushels.†
(*e*) Battle Creek......	11,000	Two or three banks.

* A larger amount was given us, but estimated at seventy pounds to the bushel.

† Not having the exact amount, we have estimated the production of these banks, in 1855, at 9009 tons.

COUNTY.	BUSHELS RAISED.	REMARKS.
RHEA. Roddy's Bank*......	2000	Used in the vicinity. In 1853, about 20,000 bushels were raised at this bank, and consumed at Eagle Furnace, Chattanooga, and in Georgia, for purposes as above.
FRANKLIN	15,000?	Used mostly in Winchester for domestic purposes, and by blacksmiths, etc.
GRUNDY.............., WARREN.............., VAN BUREN.........	8500	Used in the counties mostly by blacksmiths. Coal delivered in McMinnville costs about 20 cents.
WHITE..................	15,000	Used within the county, mostly in Sparta, both by blacksmiths and for domestic purposes. In great part obtained from two banks, from 3½ to 4½ feet thick.
PUTNAM.............., OVERTON ...., FENTRESS...........	1400	Used by blacksmiths. Considerable coal was sent, a few years ago, from Fentress to the Nashville market.
SCOTT.................., MORGAN..............., BLEDSOE..............	4500	Used by blacksmiths mostly. Numerous exposures of coal, from 1 to 6 feet, many of them of excellent quality.

1307. In 1855 there was a great increase in the quantity of coal mined. This was due,

First, to the greater activity of operations at the Raccoon banks;

Secondly, to the beginning of coal-mining by the *Sewanee Company*.

1308. The estimated production of the Raccoon banks during this year, (1855,) was 9000 tons, an increase of 8125 over the yield of 1854.

1309. The Sewanee Mining Company was organized in January, 1854. At the start, they took the coal out of the hill at the "*Lower Mines*." (See §§ 976 (2), and 983,) and sent the first

* Or, Gillenwater's. (See table, § 1302.)

car-load of coal to Nashville in June, 1855. Up to the last of December, of the same year, 3823 tons had been delivered at the city depot.

1310. The production of 1855 will, therefore, stand in tons, as follows:

Increase over last year at Raccoon banks,	8125
Sewanee banks,	3823
Production of last year,	8836
Total production of last year,	20,784

In this we allow nothing for the increased quantity of coal raised at other banks, which would swell the total amount to 21,000 or 22,000 tons. The aggregates for succeeding years have not been made out.

Section II.

LIGNITE OR BROWN COAL. (2.)

1311. Lignite presents itself as a half-made stone coal. It occurs in the beds much like coal, and has analogous geological relations, the strata of sand corresponding to sandstones, and the laminated clays to shales. The lignite beds at several localities in the Mississippi Bluff, (§ 279,) are a conspicuous feature. They occur at numerous points, and often have a volume of three or four feet, rarely swelling out to five and six.

I have already spoken of the Lignite of the Mississippi Bluff, and of the formation containing it. See §§ 1135 to 1140.

1312. In Carter County, lignite occurs with clay in an isolated deposit, a few miles north of Elizabethton, at the termination of the Holston Mountain. Its lateral extent appears to be limited. A pit has been sunk through the clay into the lignite, penetrating the latter, as I was informed, nine feet. At the time of my visit, the excavations were partly filled with water, which prevented as thorough an examination as I desired.

1313. So long as coal is cheap, and wood plenty, there will be no demand for lignite. As fuel, it is much inferior to either of the former.

Section III.

PETROLEUM AND ALLIED SUBSTANCES. (3.)

1314. These substances are mixtures, and not simple minerals. The more fluid kinds, like ordinary naphtha and petroleum, consist, generally, of a number of simple hydrocarbons; the viscid and solid kinds contain oxygenated hydrocarbons.* They may be conveniently classified as follows:

(1) *Petroleum;* liquids or oils; characteristic constituents, (though the ethylenes and paraffines are most abundant,) hydrocarbons of the Marsh-gas series.

(2) *Pittasphalts*; viscid oils, mineral tar; characteristic ingredients, hydrocarbons of the Ethylene Series.

(3) *Asphalts*; mostly solid; mineral pitch; contain oxygenated and nitrogenous hydrocarbons.

These substances run into each other through a multitude of gradations.

1315. The occurrence of *Petroleum* is mentioned on pages 268, 284, 319, 334, 336, 350, and 363.

Since the paragraph on page 350 was written, I have received the following communication from Col. C. H. Irvin, with reference to the Spring Creek oil wells, and also, as to the well on Jones' Creek, in Dickson County, and others on Eagle Creek in Overton.

NASHVILLE, TENN., April 14, 1869.

DR. J. M. SAFFORD:

Dear Sir:—Wells have been sunk on Spring Creek for oil, as follows:

The *Jackson Company's Well*, 600 feet deep; no oil.

The *Newman Well* struck oil of 32° gravity, at 19 feet, in 1866. About 2,000 barrels were pumped at this depth. This well failed, and was then bored to a depth of 52 feet, when about 2,000 barrels more were taken out. The well was abandoned in 1867, on account of the difficulty of transportation. In 1868, it was pumped again, and gave every indication of pro-

*See system of Mineralogy; J. D. Dana; Fifth Ed., pp. 720 to 752.

ducing at least 100 barrels per day. The pump valves got foul, and it was necessary to take up the tubing, since which no oil has been obtained from this well. Mr. Pedrick is now engaged in boring it deeper.

The *Douglass Well*, which is about 75 feet from the Newman Well, produced at the rate of about 30 barrels per day, at a depth of 22 feet, and ceased producing at the same time the Newman Well first failed. This well has never been operated since.

The *Hoosier Well*, about 250 feet from the last named well, got oil, in 1867, at a depth of 35 feet. It is operated by the Tennessee Oil Refining Company. They have obtained 5,000 barrels of oil from this well, at the rate of 50 barrels per day. The well failed in the fall of 1868, and has since been bored to the depths of about 70 feet. Three weeks ago oil was struck again, and the well is now pumping at the rate of 50 barrels per day. The last report from the well is that the quantity is daily increasing.

The oil, to be refined, is now brought to Nashville, by wagons 50 miles to McMinnville, and thence by rail to Nashville, 104 miles.

The South-Western Railroad, now in course of construction, will pass within one mile of these wells, and the Tennessee & Pacific Railroad will pass not further than 15 miles from them.

The same parties are boring who first commenced explorations in 1865, and are still firm in the belief that the Spring Creek oil field will prove as good as any in Pennsylvania.

The well owned by Messrs. Hudson & Co., on Jones' Creek, in Dickson County, produced about 100 barrels in the fall of 1867, at a depth of 132 feet. The well has since been sunk to the depth of 340 feet. Mr. Hudson has lately procured new machinery, and intends boring 1,000 feet, unless oil is met with at a less depth. The indications are very favorable.

Three wells have been bored on Eagle Creek, and some oil obtained from all of them, but the difficulty of access, and low price of oil, caused them to be abandoned in the latter part of 1866.

Your obedient servant,

CHARLES H. IRVIN.

1316. *Pittasphalt* is mentioned on pages 268 and 284. There is a locality of this in Hickman County, on a fork of Blue Buck Creek, called Ugly. Blue Buck is a tributary of Swan Creek. The locality is at Perry's. The pittasphalt, or asphalt, for the substance appears to be intermediate in character, occurs tolerably plentifully in thin, vertical seams, running through a thick layer of limestone, lying about twelve feet below the Black Shale. The formation is *Nashville*, upon which the Black Shale in this region rests.

1317. *Asphalt* is enumerated, with other minerals, on pages 284 and 334.

SECTION IV.

SALT, NITRE, ALUM, EPSOMITE, GYPSUM, BARITE, COPPERAS, CHALCANTHITE, PYRITE AND BLACK MANGANESE.

SALT. (4.)

1318. Some salt was formerly manufactured in Tennessee, and there are a dozen or more old "saltworks" in the State. But of late years, little has been done in the way of making salt. Within two or three years, an establishment has been built, and put in operation on Obey River, the *brine* being obtained from the wells bored for petroleum. I have not learned what success has attended the enterprise.

The manufacture, hitherto, has been mostly confined to White and Anderson counties.

1319. About the year 1820, Mr. William Simpson, as I am informed, made fifty bushels of salt per day, for months, at the old saltworks on the Calf-killer, in White, three and a half miles northeast of Sparta. After a few months of successful work, the property became involved in a law suit, which embarrassed, and finally stopped operations. The well, 386 feet deep, has been sunk through the *Siliceous Group*, and appears to terminate in the *Black Shale*. When this depth was first reached, large quantities of gas and salt-water were blown out. In about ninety days the gas, in good part, ceased; after this the water was obtained by pumping.

1320. The saltworks of Anderson are situated immediately at the eastern base of the Cumberland Table-land. The well, which is now about one thousand feet in depth, passes through nearly horizontal strata of sandstones, shales, and coal, very near the line of an immense dislocation, (§ 786,) which has brought the *Coal Measures* down to the level of the Valley, and in contact with the Shale of the Knox Group. Such a location is certainly favorable. The water obtained, is, however, weak.

The works were once in the possession of Capt. M. Winters, but afterwards came under the control of Mr. Joseph Estabrook, now deceased, who, with characteristic energy, labored to make them productive. Had Mr. Estabrook been permitted to carry out his plans, he would have probably succeeded.

1321. In Middle Tennessee, salt water was met with in most of the borings made since the war, for petroleum. Brine was thus obtained in Warren, Van Buren, Overton and Jackson. In many cases it was strong, and so far as quality is concerned, would have done well for boiling. With the exception of the water from some of the wells on Obey, it has not been made use of. The principal trouble in the manufacture of salt in Middle Tennessee, has been the failure of the brine after a few years.

NITRE. (5.)

1322. There are hundreds of caves in the limestone formations of Tennessee, and especially in the limestones of the Cumberland Table-land, which afford *nitrous earth* for the manfacture of *nitre.* During the first part of this century, (in the years 1812–1814 especially,) these caves were well ransacked, and the most accessible parts of the earth raised and leached. It is surprising to see how much work was done. In many of the larger caves remains of the old hoppers and troughs are still to be seen. The marks of the picks and shovels upon the parts of the walls of the caves laid bare by the removal of earth, are as fresh as if done yesterday. (See also § 932 (6).)

1323. In some of the caves the earth first worked has acquired considerable strength again, though nothing like that of the original earth, much of which was exceedingly sharp to the tongue. Since 1860, and during the war, some work was done in these caves, but in no case did it amount to much.

1324. The nitrous matter in the earth of the caves is mainly a *lime-saltpeter*, (*nitrocalcite.*) This is leached out, concentrated by boiling, and while in solution, converted into *potash-saltpeter*, or common *nitre*, by the introduction of potash.

Most of the nitre of commerce comes from India ; some from Spain and Egypt.

ALUM. (6.)

1325. The principal source of native alum in the State, is the Black Shale. The mineral has been spoken of in connection with this formation on pages 334 and 335, to which the reader is referred.

See, also, paragraphs 450, 473 and 474.

EPSOMITE. (7.)

1326. *Epsomite*, or *Epsom Salt*, is one of the products of oxidation, found with *alum*, *copperas*, and *nitrocalite*, in caves and "rockhouses." Alum Cave, in Sevier County, is an interesting locality. (See § 473, and also § 932.)

GYPSUM. (8.)

1327. I know of no beds of gypsum in Tennessee extensive enough to be of practical importance. It is to be hoped that such beds may yet be discovered.

Localities, affording elegant cabinet specimens, are numerous. At "Gray's Cave," in the north part of Sumner County, fine specimens of transparent cleavable gypsum (*selenite*) are found, some of it in crystals, as well as masses of snowy gypsum, and elegant rosettes.

See, also, pages 254, 283, 357, and 362. In addition, the occasional occurrence of elegant crystals of gypsum, in the limonite pots of the Western Iron-Region, has been mentioned.

BARITE. (9.)

1328. This mineral is sometimes called *heavy spar*, on account of its weight. Other names are, *barytes* and *sulphate of baryta*. It occurs in veins, as a part of the gangue, or matrix, of the ore. It is often the matrix of lead ore.

The white varieties are ground up and used as a substitute for white lead, in paint.

Barite is met with at numerous points in Tennessee. The formations in which it occurs, and a few localities, are mentioned on pages 224, 254, 268, 283, and 362. In Roane County, it is the gangue of the vein containing galenite.

COPPERAS. (10.)

1329. *Copperas* (*melanterite*) is composed of suphuric acid, protoxide of iron, and water. It results, generally, from the decomposition of pyrite, and it is common to meet with it in sheltered places, where the rocks contain this mineral.

Large quantities of copperas were manufactured, during the war, from the heaps of pyrite and rubbish which had accumulated around the openings of the Ducktown Copper Mines.

See, also, pages 179, 196, 197, 334, and 335. As an appendix to § 871, I will add, that at the locality of pittasphalt, mentioned in § 1316, I saw, a few years ago, a stone-fence, and the half-built walls of a new house, constructed out of slabs of the Black Shale. The fence, at several points, was crumbling down into heaps, like those at Blount Springs, and the house was getting ready to follow, showing at once the folly of using such material for building purposes, and its availability as an alum and copperas-producing rock.

CHALCANTHITE. (11.)

1330. This is commonly known as *blue vitriol*, or *blue stone*. It is a *sulphate of copper*. The mineral occurs as one of the oxidized ores, in the upper portions of the Ducktown veins. It is also found in solution in the waters which flow from the mines, constituting an item of considerable importance. The blue stone is decomposed, and the copper precipitated, by causing the water holding the sulphate in solution to pass through a very long and continuous line of troughs, which are half filled with scrap iron. The iron and copper exchange places; the latter is precipitated in the metallic form, while the iron flows off with the water held in solution as copperas. See the section, in the last chapter, on copper.

PYRITE. (12.)

1331. *Pyrite*, also called *pyrites*, is composed of *sulphur* and *iron*. It occurs, associated with another mineral, composed of the same elements, and called *magnetic pyrites*, (*pyrrhotite*,) in large quantities, in the Ducktown veins.

This mineral has been frequently mentioned. See pages 179, 196, 197, 223, 254, 268, 284, 319, and 329; also, the notice of the Eastern Iron-Region. Pyrite is also mentioned in connection with the Cretaceous Formation. The locality spoken of on page 223, is on the land of Mr. James Lowrey, and about three miles a little west of south, from Greeneville.

BLACK MANGANESE. (13.)

1332. *Black Manganese*, including several oxides of Manganese (*pyrolusite*, *psilomelane* and *wad*) occurs, associated with limonite, at numerous localities. At most of the ore banks both in the Eastern and Western iron-regions, more or less of it is found.

A little metallic manganese in cast-iron makes the latter all the better fitted for making some kinds of steel; and iron is now manufactured in Greene County for this purpose, from limonite, containing more or less oxide of manganese.

1333. This mineral is easily distinguished, as a general thing, from iron-ores, by the black, sometimes earthy black, color of its powder. It is not used as an ore, excepting in the way above mentioned, metallic manganese, as such, not being employed in the arts. The oxides are used extensively for decomposing muriatic acid and furnishing chlorine; as a cheap source of oxygen; as a coloring material in the manufacture of glass and enamels; as a flux in the preparation of cast-steel; and as the source of a useful mordant in calico printing.

As to the occurrence of this mineral, or rather of this group of minerals, in the Knox Dolomite, see page 224.

Dr. Troost, in his Fifth Report, says, "There is," in the northern part of Cocke, near Stone's Creek, "a vein of excellent black oxyd of manganese, which appears to be abundant." By "vein," I suppose the Doctor means deposit, like others occurring with limonite.

1334. For the notices of other minerals naturally classified with those given in this section, but of less practical importance, such as *quartz*, *calcite*, *fluorite*, *native sulphur*, etc., the reader is referred to Part Second. The pages on which they are mentioned can be found by referring to the Index.

SECTION V.

MARBLE. (14.)

1335. Great interest and importance are attached to the marble of Tennessee. It is now, in the columns and balustrades which, within, adorn the building, one of the chief ornaments of our own noble Capitol, as it is also, and in a much greater degree, of the National Capitol, at Washington.

1336. The principal varieties of marble* in Tennessee, are as follows:

1. REDDISH VARIEGATED FOSSILIFEROUS MARBLE; most abundant and most important.
2. WHITISH VARIEGATED FOSSILIFEROUS MARBLE; runs by gradations into that above.
3. DULL VARIEGATED MAGNESIAN MARBLE; often an excellent and available building material.
4. BLACK AND DARK-BLUE MARBLES; sometimes having white reticulating calcite veins.
5. BRECCIA AND CONGLOMERATE MARBLES, of the Unaka coves and valleys.

1. REDDISH VARIEGATED MARBLE.

1337. This, the most important variety, occurs in East, Middle and West Tennessee, but is most abundant and of the finest quality, in the first mentioned division of the State.

1338. In West Tennessee there are beds of this marble, which are rendered the more valuable, from the circumstance of their presenting almost the last outcrop of limestone seen in going west towards the Mississippi. In Henry County there is a quarry from which considerable marble, for building purposes and for tombstones, has been taken. Some of it has been carried to Paris, more than twelve miles distant, and used in the construction of the foundation of the Court House, and for other purposes.

In Benton, as for instance, a few miles from Rockport, on the Tennessee, the residence of Col. A. P. Hall, the same rock occurs. It is also seen farther south, in Decatur. See §§ 811 and 822.

1339. In Middle Tennessee, in Franklin County, there are

* A *marble* may be defined to be a durable limestone, pure or impure, susceptible of a good polish, and presenting a pleasing appearance when polished.

many localities of marble, and several extensive beds. It was worked here, to a limited extent, for several years. See § 737; and, also, § 738.

The upper part of the Mountain Limestone at Bon Air, in White, affords a clouded white, from which a few tombstones have been taken.

1340. In the Valley of East Tennessee, the Reddish Variegated Marble occurs in the following counties: *Hawkins*, Hancock, Grainger, Jefferson, Knox, Roane, Blount, Monroe, McMinn and Bradley. Some of it also occurs in Meigs, Anderson, Union and Campbell. Its presentations and characters have been already given in the Second Part of the Report, and to this reference must be made. It will be seen that there are two distinct beds of this marble. One of these, the lower part of which is sometimes whitish marble, is described on pages 236–239; the other on pages 244 and 245. Both of them are confined to the belts on the Map colored blue.* Each of them outcrops in several long narrow ranges.

1341. The lithological character of these marbles is given in §§ 606 and 633. The marble of Middle and West Tennessee is of the same nature and equal to much of that of East Tennessee, but inferior to the best.

1342. In the Eastern Valley this variety appertains to the Trenton and Nashville Series; in Franklin County it is *Nashville*, and in the Western Valley *Meniscus*, or *Niagara*.

1143. *Production.*—This marble has been extensively quarried at several points in East Tennessee. *Sloan's Quarry*, in Knox County, is mentioned in § 608, and the *National Quarry* in Hawkins, in § 609.

I have very recently been informed that a quarry has been opened on the farm of Dr. James Blair, in the vicinity of Loudon, and that variegated marble is now being shipped north from this point.

There is no limit to the quantity, and Tennessee could supply the world.

1344. The systematic working of marble appears to have been commenced in Hawkins County. The marble in this

* To two of these blue belts I have given special names; the *wide* one running through Knox County is the *Red Belt*, (§ 610;) the greater one. the course of which lies east of the last, is the *Gray Belt*, (§ 640.) It must not be understood that all of the Red Belt is marble. Its area is made up for the most part, of other rocks, interstratified with which are the marble beds.

county outcrops in a line which is about twelve miles long, and runs in a northeasterly and southwesterly course, through a portion of the valley next west of that in which Rogersville is located. It is not represented on the Map, but the *belt of Trenton and Nashville rocks*, of which it is one of the members, is, (§ 613.) This belt is the blue band next west of Rogersville, and in this the marble lies. (See section in § 751.) Several quarries, at distant points, were opened on this line many years ago, and furnished marble of the first quality.

1345. In April, 1838, the "Rogersville Marble Company" was formed, by gentlemen in and near Rogersville, for the purpose of "sawing marble, and establishing a marble factory in the vicinity of Rogersville."* Orville Rice, Esq., was elected President, and S. D. Mitchell, Secretary. The company operated to a limited extent, for several years, erected a mill, and sold several thousand dollars' worth of marble annually, which was mostly distributed in East Tennessee.

In 1844, the company sold out to Mr. Rice, who, on a moderate scale, has perseveringly and successfully carried on the business ever since.†

1346. Mr. R. sent a block of the "light mottled strawberry variety" to the Washington Monument. This was called the "*Hawkins County Block*," and bears the inscription, "*From Hawkins County, Tennessee.*" Another block of one of the best varieties, was sent by act of the Legislature, which was called the "*State Block.*"

1347. These blocks attracted the attention of the Building Committee of the National Capitol, who, although they had numerous specimens from all parts of the Union before them, decided in favor of the East Tennessee marble.

An agent was soon after sent by them to ascertain whether or not it could be obtained in quantity, who, when on the ground, had no difficulty in satisfying himself as to that point.

1348. As the result of these circumstances, an extensive quarry affording an excellent material, was opened at a point about nine miles southwest of Rogersville, where the Holston

*It appears that attention, resulting in anything practical, was first called to the Hawkins marble by the favorable opinion expressed with reference to it by Dr. Troost.

†The elegant residence, "Marble Hall," four miles below Rogersville, and built by Mr. Rice, is really a museum of the finest marble East Tennessee affords.

River intersects the marble range. The rock here is in good part, massive, and several hundred feet in width. The location of the quarry is excellent, and admits of the easy transportation of the blocks to the boats. Many thousand cubic feet of marble was sent off. It was taken down the river, and then by railroad to Charleston or Savannah, where it was shipped for Washington.

1349. A good use has been made of this marble in the Capitol at Washington. The balustrades and columns of the stairs leading up to the House and Senate galleries, the walls of the Marble Room, and other parts of the building, are of Tennessee marble. It doubtless forms half the ornamental marble there. As an ornamental material, it has few superiors of its kind.

1350. Mr. James Sloan opened his quarry (§ 608) in 1852. The range is intersected by the East Tennessee & Virginia Railroad, and also by the Holston River. It has been stated that the variegated marble of the Capitol, at Nashville, came from this point. Mr. S. also furnished marble from the same quarry for the State Capitol of Ohio.

In 1856, manufactured marble sold in Knoxville at an average price of $3.00 per cubic foot, and in Nashville at $4.50.

2. WHITISH VARIEGATED MARBLE.

1351. This variety forms the lower part of the *Red and Gray Marble Bed* already referred to on page 236, and is particularly spoken of in § 607.

It is a coralline, sparry, and as stated, a grayish white rock. The white ground of much of it is mottled with pink or reddish spots; it is then called *Strawberry Marble.* The reddish variegated, sometimes presents the same character. The two varieties, indeed, run into each other, there being no essential difference between them.

1352. I have already mentioned Col. Williams' quarry, near Knoxville. (See § 607, and note at the bottom of page 237.)

A large amount of marble has been taken from this quarry. Several factories in Knoxville have worked it extensively. There is no superior building rock in the State.

1343. Five miles east of Knoxville, at Mecklenburg, a beautiful bluff of the same marble is boldly exposed on the French Broad River, near its mouth. This has already been mentioned. The upper part is variegated with light flesh-colored points and patches.

Similar gray marble occurs about a mile east of Athens, in McMinn, and at many other points.

3. DULL VARIEGATED MAGNESIAN MARBLE.

1354. The extreme upper part of the Knox Dolomite is often a gray and dull reddish-brown, mottled rock, which makes a good building material, and, sometimes, a fair marble. This has, however, been sufficiently described. (See §§ 539 and 554.)

1355. At Chattanooga, associated with the marble above, are layers highly argillaceous, which, when weathered, form a variegated material, easily cut, and worked into fancy objects. The Union soldiers, during the war, amused themselves by cutting, or turning, ink-stands, pipes, paper-weights, boxes, picture-frames, etc., out of this material. These were sent home as memorials, and as specimens of "Chattanooga Marble." There were two or three workshops where the manufacture of these articles was carried on in a business like way.

4. BLACK AND DARK BLUE MARBLES.

1356. At many points in East Tennessee, are black or dark-blue limestones, especially in the extreme eastern counties, which are susceptible of a good polish, and would make handsome marble slabs. At many points, moreover, these rocks are traversed by white veins of calcite, and in such cases, particularly if of the proper grain, might be worked up into desirable marble. I have, however, spoken of these already. See §§ 555 and 556. In some parts of the Valley, especially, eastward and southward, the Maclurea Limestone, (page 232,) is compact and almost black, and would make a fair marble. Much of it also is traversed by a net-work of white veins.

5. BRECCIA AND CONGLOMERATE MARBLES.

1357. A *breccia* is any rock composed of angular fragments, or at most, of fragments but little rounded, firmly cemented in a solid mass. A limestone of this character, if made up of fragments of different colors, or of different shades of color, and susceptible at the same time, of a good polish, constitutes a marble which is often very beautiful. A slab of it is, in fact, a *native mosaic*, the component pieces of which, are irregular in outline, and promiscuously arranged.

1358. Marbles of this sort occur in the valleys and coves among and bordering the Unaka ridges. They have been referred to in §§ 476 and 557.

Dr. Troost, in his Fourth Report, referring to the marbles of East Tennessee generally, says: "I have seen there, breccia marble, which surpasses any thing I know." He doubtless refers to those of the Unaka region.

1359. A locality of *conglomerate marble*—a rock in which the component fragments are rounded and a polished section of which presents a variety of circular, instead of angular patches—has been observed at the end of Star's Mountain in McMinn. Another occurs in Greene County. Such marble is also seen on the Little Tennessee, in Blount and Monroe counties, and at other points.

These breccia and conglomerate dolomites and limestones, are comparatively of limited extent.

SECTION VI.

MILLSTONES, ROOFING SLATES, FLAGSTONES, AND BUILDING MATERIALS.

MILLSTONES. (15.)

1360. Several of the Tennessee formations supply millstones, some of which are of excellent quality.

The *gneissoid* and *white quartz* millstones, of the Metamorphic Group, are spoken of in § 411.

The *chert* of the Knox Dolomite supplies excellent millstones. (See § 559.) This has been made into millstones at a number of points in East Tennessee. At Big Spring, in Claiborne County, Col. Hugh Jones manufactured, during his life time, not many less than 100 pairs of stones from this chert. They were quite in demand, and were considered to be equal to the French buhrstone.

The Nashville Formation furnishes a bed of millstone-grit in Sumner County. (See § 739.)

Millstones for grinding corn have frequently been made from the conglomerate of the Coal Measures.

Dr. Troost, in his Third Report, speaks of a superior kind of "siliceous millstone" near Harpeth River. I have not seen this, but suppose it to be some layer of chert, in the Siliceous Group.

The chert of the Knox Dolomite, where used as above, is a true *buhrstone.*

ROOFING SLATES. (16.)

1361. The roofing slates of Tennessee are confined to the Ocoee Group. They may be found in the counties of Polk, McMinn, Monroe, Blount, Sevier, and Cocke. See §§ 436, 472. (Compare § 871.)

The great presentation of slate on the West Fork of Little Pigeon, in Sevier County, is unusual. See §§ 448 and 449.

1362. Dr. Troost, in his Sixth Report, thus speaks of one of the bands of roofing-slate found in the southeastern part of Sevier: "This is a very extensive tract of slate, and from the superficial examination to which I could subject it, no quarries having yet been made in it, seems to be of an excellent quality. I have seen slabs of it, which have been detached by some natural cause, from ten to twelve feet square, and of uniform thickness, perfectly level and sonorous."

1363. Slate used for roofing is generally of a dark-bluish or purplish color. The color is not, however, important. "To be a good material for roofing, it should split easily into even slates, and admit of being pierced for nails without fracturing. Moreover, it should not be absorbent of water, either by the surface or edges, which may be tested by weighing, after immersion for a while in water. It should also be free from pyrites, and every thing that can undergo decomposition on exposure."*

FLAGSTONES. (17.)

1364. When rocks split readily into thin tough layers, or slabs, they are called flagstones, and are used for paving purposes.

Such slabs, of good quality, are greatly in demand in cities and large towns, and a quarry of them, favorably located for transportation, is often valuable. As an evidence of this, I refer to the fact that in Nashville now, as a substitute, masses of limestone are slowly *sawed*, at comparatively great expense, into paving stones.

1365. Excellent sandstone flags occur in Morgan County, not far from Montgomery.

Many of the roofing slates of the Unaka region might be used as flagstones. They could, also, be manufactured into

* Dana's Manual of Mineralogy.

mantles, slabs for tables, and other similar articles. Slate has been used of late years to a considerable extent, as a substitute for marble.

See, also, with reference to flagstones, §§ 622, 699, 735, and 934.

BUILDING MATERIALS. (18.)

1366. It may appear superfluous to speak of the building materials of a State in which limestones and sandstones are so abundant; nevertheless, much might be said with reference even to our common rocks, that would be suggestive, and have a direct practical bearing. It is not proposed, however, to enter upon a general consideration of these materials, but simply to bring together the paragraphs of the Report in which special rocks have been mentioned.

Tennessee "*granite*," as a building material, has been spoken of in § 410. For notices of other materials, see §§ 554, 665, 698, 726,* 735, 822, 884, 934 and the last of Chapter XII. The section on marble might be included with these references. (Compare § 871.)

SECTION VII.

HYDRAULIC LIMESTONES, CLAYS, GREEN SAND, AND MINERAL WATERS.

HYDRAULIC LIMESTONES. (19.)

1367. The fact has been mentioned that the blue limestone flags exposed at many points on and in the vicinity of the Tennessee River, in Hardin, Wayne, Perry and Decatur counties, will, when burnt, yield *hydraulic cement*. See §§ 716 to 718. But little attention has been paid to the manufacture of this material outside of the region specified.

Near Knoxville, hydraulic cement has been made from the Brown Shale. See § 638.

Large quantities of cement are used in Tennessee. It comes

* With reference to the rock out of which the Capitol, at Nashville, is built, see (2) under this paragraph, on pages 277 and 278.

mostly from abroad. We ought, and it is hoped soon will, manufacture every pound we use.

1368. The following is from the "Geology of Canada," p. 804. It is a good presentation of the character of cement-making limestone:

"Certain impure limestones yield by calcination, a substance which, instead of slaking with water, like ordinary lime, forms with it a paste, which after a greater or less lapse of time, sets or becomes hard, even under water. This property is now known to depend upon an admixture of clay or silicate of alumina, containing an alkali; and artificial mixtures are prepared by mingling chalk, or any other carbonate of lime, with a proper quantity of clay, and calcining the mixture. In this way the so-called *Portland Cement*, and many other similar compositions, are prepared, both in England and in France. The *pozzuolana* of the Italians, and the trass of the Germans, are argillaceous materials of volcanic origin, which, when mingled with pure lime, yield hydraulic cements; and these substances may also be imitated by calcining ordinary clays, and then grinding them to powder. When, however, natural admixtures of clay and carbonate of lime can be obtained in abundance, it is more advantageous to employ them than to resort to artificial preparations. When a limestone contains ten or fifteen per cent. of clay, it yields a mortar which hardens almost immediately under water. The proportion of clay may even rise to sixty per cent., without destroying this property. Magnesian limes yield hydraulic cements equally good with those of pure lime; and, as already noticed, a mixture of magnesia with pozzuolana or with calcined clay, forms a valuable water cement."

CLAYS. (20.)

1369. The *under-clays* of the coal beds at very many points, are a good *fire-clay*. Most of the coal seams have such under-clays. See pages, 370, 372, 373, 374 and 380; also, Ætna Section, page 383; and Lookout Mountain Section, page 385; as well as most of the remaining sections of the Coal Measures, in Chapter XII. See, also, notices of clay in §§ 907, 908 and 1141.

1370. At many points in Hickman, Perry, and the counties in the vicinity of the Tennessee River, the shales of the Meniscus Formation, (§§ 807 and 811,) yield by weathering, *potter's clay*. On the Sulphur Fork of Beaver Dam, in Hickman, such clay is used by Mr. Adam Coble for making a brick red stone-ware. Mr. C. colors some of his ware with black manganese obtained in the vicinity. The clay is obtained from beneath the Black Shale.

I also call attention here to the *siliceous*, chalky material of Wayne, in § 885.

GREEN SAND, OR GREEN MARL. (21.)

1371. This substance, and the use to which it may be applied, have been noticed in §§ 1097, 1112 and 1113.*

The following are analyses of the green sand of McNairy County, by Troost. Phosphoric acid, which is doubtless present in the marl, does not appear to have been separated:

No.	Silica.	Alumina.	Protoxyd of Iron.	Potash.	Carbonate of Lime.	Water.	Loss
1	48.00	7.00	20.70	10.10	5.70	8.00	.50
2	45.30	6.20	18.00	10.40	10.80	8.50	.80
3	51.70	6.50	21.20	11.30	2.00	7.30	.00

1372. In the State of New Jersey green-sand similar to that of West Tennessee, has been extensively used as a fertilizer. The following are analyses of some of the best samples of the green-sand, or marl, raised and sold in that State.†

	1	2	3	4	5	6
Phosphoric acid	0.38	1.12	1.70	3.73	4.54	2.69
Sulphuric acid	0.20	1.54	....	2.44	0.43	0.26
Silicic acid	53.10	48.86	51.20	49.68	51.16	49.40
Carbonic acid	....	....	....	....	....	....
Potash	3.78	6.24	2.96	4.98	4.27	6.31
Lime	....	1.81	1.51	4.14	3.48	2.52
Carbonate of lime	12.10	....	....	....	....	....
Magnesia	0.70	2.13	1.50	0.47	2.04	3.25
Oxide of iron	15.39 ‡	17.78 ‡	23.67	} 28.71 {	17.67	18.66
Alumina	6.30	7.16	11.90		6.10	8.90
Water	8.64	12.03	5.53	5.54	9.13	7.55
	100.59	98.67	99.97	99.69	98.82	99.54

1373. It is stated in § 1097, that Green Sand contains grains of a soft greenish mineral, called *glauconite*. The following

*Dr. Troost mentions the marl of West Tennessee in his Third Report, as far back as 1835; as well as in several of his succeeding reports.

†From the "Geology of New Jersey," by George H. Cook, State Geologist, 1868.

‡ Protoxide.

analyses of the *pure* mineral are taken from the New Jersey Report, page 281:

	A	B	C	D	E	F
Silica	42.643	48.639	49.152	51.110	48.977	50.923
Peroxide of iron	23.223	19.802	18.481	18.231	20.466	19.353
Alumina	7.093	6.842	8.519	6.214	8.566	7.503
Protoxide of iron	4.718	4.236	3.219	4.033	4.135	3.909
Magnesia	2.366	2.326	2.790	3.134	2.647	2.918
Potash	9.071	9.087	8.730	7.607	7.262	7.505
Water lost at 212 degrees	6.668	4.629	3.527	5.165 }	7.947	7.889
Water lost above 212 "	4.218	4.439	5.222	4.506 }		
	100.000	100.000	100.000	100.000	100.000	100 000

1374. It is seen from this table, that glauconite, when pure, does not contain *phosphoric acid*, the most important constituent of Green Sand. The value of the marl as a fertilizer, does not depend upon the relative proportion of glauconite, as stated in § 1112, unless we include with this the phosphoric acid.

1375. The constituents which give value to the Green Sand are *phosphoric acid*, *potash*, *sulphuric acid* in combination with lime as *gypsum*, *soluble silica*, *oxide of iron*, and, perhaps, *magnesia*.—COOK. To these must be added, in calcareous marls, *carbonate of lime*. Prof. Cook, in order to supply data for the determination of the value of any sample of marl to the farmer, estimates the most important ingredients to be worth (in the marl) as follows:

Phosphoric Acid	$12.50	per	100	lbs.
Sulphuric Acid	80	"	"	"
Potash	1.00	"	"	"
Carbonate of Lime	40	"	"	"

That is to say, a quantity of marl containing as much as 100 pounds of phosphoric acid, will be worth $12.50 for this ingredient alone, and if it contain also 200 lbs. of potash, it will be worth $2 more, making $14.50 for both ingredients, and so with the rest, each adding something to the value.

1376. About *one million* tons of Green Sand are used annually, as marl, in New Jersey. It sells for from 35 to 75 cents a ton at the pits, according to quality.

1377. These facts are stated, in order to call the attention of enterprising farmers in West Tennessee to the value of this substance as a fertilizer. I quote further from the Geology of New Jersey.

"The marl which has been described in the preceding pages has been of incalculable value to the country in which it is found. It has raised it from the lowest stage of agricultural exhaustation to a high state of improvement. Found in places where no capital and but little labor were needed to get it, the poorest have been able to avail themselves of its benefits. Lands which, in the old style of cultivation, had to lie fallow, by the use of marl produce heavy crops of clover, and grow rich while resting. Thousands of acres of land, which had been worn out and left in commons, are now, by the use of this fertilizer, yielding crops of the finest quality. Instances are pointed out everywhere in the marl district of farms, which, in former times, would not support a family, but are now making their owners rich from their productiveness. Bare sands by the application of marl are made to grow clover, and then crops of corn, potatoes and wheat. What are supposed to be pine barrens, by the use of marl are made into fruitful land. The price of land in this region was considerably below that in the northern part of the State forty years ago; now that the lands are improved their prices are higher than those in the northern part of the State, though even there they are higher than any where else in the United States. In 1830, Thomas Gordon said of these lands:

'It would be difficult to calculate the advantages which the State has gained, and will yet derive from the use of marl. It has already saved some districts from depopulation, and increased the inhabitants of others, and may, one day contribute to convert the sandy and pine deserts into regions of agricultural wealth.'"—*Gordon's History and Gazetteer of New Jersey—Part* 2, *p.* 5.

This prediction is fast being fulfilled.

* * * * * * * *

"The marl is in the form of an earth, and is dugwith spades, or, if very compact, is loosened by grubbing hoes; and, when fairly crumbled, as it soon is by the sun and air, it is as easily handled as sand. It can then be spread evenly over the surface of the ground. The quantity used varies with the quality of the marl, and the crop to which it is applied. In Eastern Monmouth, where the Lower Marl Bed is largely developed, and is rich in powdered carbonate of lime and poor in phosphoric acid, it is used in enormous quantities, and never injures crops, but on the contrary is of the greatest utility. From one hundred to two hundred tons to the acre are not uncommon. Marls of any kind, which are acid from containing sulphate of iron or sulphate of alumina, are applied sparingly and with care. If put on potatoes in the hill the sprouts are killed by them, and a dressing of fifty tons to the acre has sometimes destroyed all vegetation. The safe way of using such marls is found to be upon well limed lands, or else in dressings of from ten to twenty tons per acre, or else composted with lime. Those marls which contain no carbonate of lime, but are rich in phosphoric acid, are used in quantities of from five to twenty tons per acre.

"In some places the marl is so strongly acid that it is not used, the labor of composting it with lime being more than it is thought worth. It cannot, however, be too strongly insisted upon, that lime will certainly correct the injurious effects of such marls, and no cases can probably be found but what one bushel of slaked lime to ten bushels of marl will be sufficient for the purpose, and generally a half, or even a quarter of that amount, will be enough. The effect of the lime is to decompose the sulphate of iron or alumina and form sulphate of lime (plaster,) which is a valuable fertilizer, and would greatly improve the quality and effects of the marls, so that these *poison* or *black* marls, when properly corrected, are more valuable than those which are not poisonous. This is abundantly verified by the experience of good farmers."

1378. Professor Cook, after giving many details and facts bearing upon the application of the marls in New Jersey, draws the following practical conclusions:

1. That the most valuable marls, and those which will best pay the cost of long transportation, are those which contain the largest percentage of phosphoric acid.

2. That the most durable marls are those containing carbonate of lime, the more the better.

3. That greensands containing but little of either phosphoric acid or carbonate of lime, become active fertilizers when composted with quick-lime.

4. That marls which are acid and burning from containing sulphate of iron, can be rendered mild in properties and useful as fertilizers, by composting them with lime.

5. That crops particularly improved by it are all forage crops, grass, clover, etc.; for these the green marl may be spread upon the surface to the amount of from one hundred to four hundred bushels per acre. The crop is generally doubled, and in some cases quadrupled, by this application. Other marls must be used in larger quantities, but will produce good results.

Potatoes. For this crop marl seems to be a specific. It does not materially increase the growth of vines, and the yield is not much greater, but the potatoes are smoother and fairer in the skin and dryer, and of better quality when boiled. The marl is put on the potatoes in the hill at planting; if not acid, it is thrown directly on the tuber; if acid, the potato is first covered by earth and the marl thrown on or beside that. From five to thirty tons may be used on an acre.

Buckwheat. Most remarkable effects upon this crop are produced by marl. Two and a half tons or fifty bushels to the acre, spread on after sowing, have caused an equal amount of buckwheat to grow on land which otherwise was not worth cultivating.

Wheat, rye, oats and corn, are improved by the use of marl, though not with the striking results seen on the crops before mentioned. It is applied as a top-dressing on the prepared ground, is spread on the surface before plowing, is worked in the hill or drill, or is composted with barnyard manure and spread on the ground according to the farmer's judgment. From five to thirty tons and even more, may be used upon an acre.

With any kind of garden or field-crop it may be used, and will be beneficial both to the crop and soil. It is free from the seeds of weeds, is dry, and convenient to handle—all of which recommend it to any snug farmer."

1379. *Bat Manure.*—It may be well to mention in this place, the fact of the occurrence of heaps and beds of bat excrements in many of the limestone caves of Tennessee. This substance is in considerable quantity in the parts of the caves that have not been disturbed by the nitre-makers. The heaps met with are the accumulations of scores of years. This manure is valuable as a fertilizer, and has been used locally with good effect. I have recently received the following information:

Dr. I. W. Sparks, of Baltimore, is now manufacturing a fertilizer which he terms "nitro-ammoniated guano," at the Hebeling Cave, in Warren County, Tennessee. It is composed of bat manure, nitrous earth, and the leached ashes which have been used in the manufacture of saltpetre. Dr. Sparks claims that there are at least 30,000 tons of bat manure in the portion of the cave he has explored, and that the nitrous earth is inexhaustible. He ships this material to Baltimore. The trials made with it last year have demonstrated its value as a fertilizer for tobacco and all root crops.

MINERAL WATERS. (22)

1380. Mineral springs in Tennessee are very numerous, and of many varieties. A full account of them would make a volume in itself. No thorough investigation of these springs has been made, and but few complete analyses.

1. *Sulphur Springs* abound in all divisions of the State. They flow often from limestone formations; as, for example, in the Western Valley. (See §§ 265–268.) The well known Sulphur Spring, at Nashville, is also an example. The *Black Shale* is, however, most prolific in springs of this character. (See § 873a.) The sulphur springs mentioned in § 419 have their origin in this formation.

2. *Chalybeate Springs* also, are plentiful, and are found in all the divisions of the State. The cool, inviting summer-retreats of the Cumberland Table-land, like Beersheba and Bon Air, look to these mainly, for their supply of mineral water. (See

§ 197.) Chalybeate waters are especially characteristic of the Coal Measures.

3. *Epsom Salt,* and *Alum Springs,* occasionally occur. Of the first class is the water of Montvale Springs in Blount County, (§ 801, and diagram, page 190.) The water of the sulphur springs frequently contains Epsom Salt, or epsomite. The sulphur springs at Bon Aqua, for example, west of Nashville, contain more or less of this salt. There is also, a chalybeate spring at this watering place.

The Alum Well in Hawkins, is mentioned in § 864.

Section VIII.

METEORITES. (23.)

1381. The following notice of a meteorite, which was seen to fall in this State, was published in 1856, in my Reconnoissance:

The Lincoln Meteorite.—Within a few months, another small meteoric mass has been added to the list of those extra-terrestrial bodies which have fallen within the limits of Tennessee. This recent visitor is a stone, weighing, when first obtained, three pounds.

An esteemed friend, the Rev. T. C. Blake, of Cumberland University,* to whose zeal we owe a knowledge of this interesting specimen, has furnished the following particulars in regard to its history.

It fell two miles west of Petersburg, and fifteen northwest of Fayetteville, in Lincoln County, about half-past three o'clock, P. M., August 5, 1855, during, or just before, a severe rain-storm. Its fall was preceded by a loud report, resembling that of a large cannon, followed by four or five less reports; these were heard by many persons in the surrounding country. Immediately after, the mass or fragment, was seen by James B. Dooley, Esq., to fall to the ground. It approached him from the east, appeared, while falling, to be surrounded by a "milky" halo, two feet in diameter, and fell one hundred and fifty or two hundred yards from him, burying itself about eighteen inches in the soil. When first dug out, it was too hot to be handled.

This specimen, which now lies before us, has an edge broken off, revealing the character of the interior. Within it is of an ashen-gray color, varied by patches of white, yellowish, and dark minerals.

* Now, T. C. Blake. D. D., of the *Banner of Peace,* at Nashville.

With the exception of the broken edge, it is covered, and when first obtained was entirely covered, as most meteorites of this kind are, with a very thin "black, shining crust, as if it had been coated with pitch;" this was doubtless formed by the fusion of its outer surface in its rapid passage through the air.

One end or face, which may be regarded as the base, has an irregular rhomboidal outline, averaging 2¾ by 2½ inches. Placing the stone upon this end, the body of it presents the form of an irregular, slightly oblique, rhomboidal prism. The upper end, however, is not well defined, but runs up to one side in a flattened protuberance, giving the entire specimen a form approaching roughly, an oblique pyramid. The length from the base to the apex is 4½ inches.

Three adjacent sides are rough, being covered with cavities and pits. It is likely that the stone has been torn off from a larger mass, or from other fragments, along these faces.

The other sides are smoother and rounded, and appear to have constituted a portion of the surface of the larger mass.

The specimen acts upon the needle; fragments of it readily yield particles of nickeliferous iron by trituration in a mortar. The specific gravity of the entire specimen is 3.20. Its weight, in its present condition, 3.83 lbs.

Professor J. Lawrence Smith, of the Medical Department of the University of Louisville, has analyzed fragments of this meteorite, and has kindly furnished us with a copy of the result.

The minerals found in the meteorite are:—

"Pyroxene—principal portion of the mass;

Olivine and Orthoclase, }—disseminated through the mass;

Nickeliferous iron—forming about one half per cent. of the mass.

In addition to these, there are specks of a black, shining mineral, not yet examined.

The general analysis is as follows:—

Silica	49.21
Alumina	11.05
Protoxyd of Iron	20.41
Lime	9.01
Magnesia	8.13
Manganese	.04
Iron	.50
Nickel	trace
Phosphorus	trace
Sulphur	.06
Soda	.82
	99.23

1382. *Tennessee Meteorites in General*.—There are *three* different Tennessee meteorites the time of the falling of which is known. Besides these, many others have been discovered, which are known, from their character, to be of the same origin. Our State has proved itself rich in these wonderful messengers from the sky.

For the benefit of those who may desire such information, a table is added including all, so far as I know, that have been described.

TABLE OF TENNESSEE METEORITES.

No.	County in which found.	General Character	Weight.	Time of falling.	By whom and when described	Through whom made known.
1	Sumner	Stony.	11 lbs.	May ,9 '27	Seybert.	
2	Cocke	Malleable iron.	2000 "	Unknown	Troost, 1840.	Hon. Jacob Peck.
3	Dickson	"	9 "	July or Aug. 1835	" 1845.	J. Voorhies, Esq.,
4	Greene	"	20 "	Unknown	" 1845.	Mr. Jos. Estabrook & Hon. Jacob Peck.
5	DeKalb	"	36 "	"	" 1845.	
6	Jackson	"	15 oz.	"	" 1846.	Col. S. D. Morgan.
7	Smith	"	280 lbs.	"	" 1846.	Col. S. D. Morgan.
8	Rutherford	"	19 "	"	" 1848.	
9 ?	Jefferson	"	2½ lbs	"	Shepherd, 1854	Hon. Jacob Peck.
10	Claiborne	"	60 lbs.	"	Smith, 1854.	Prof. J. B. Mitchell..
11	Campbell	"	4½ oz.	"	" 1855.	Prof. J. B. Mitchell.
12	Lincoln	Stony.	3 lbs.	Aug. 5, '55	Safford, 1856, & Smith, 1856.	Dr. T. C. Blake.
13	Robertson	Iron.	37 "	Unknown	Smith, 1861.	Dr. J. B. Lindsley.

PART FOURTH.

SOILS AND AGRICULTURAL FEATURES.

1383. This is a brief part of the Report, and, like the one just ended, is to a great extent, an annotated index. In the Second Part, I have noticed generally, the soils and agricultural features presented by each formation within the area, or the areas of its outcrop. It is proposed here, to group these soils and their areas, and to bring together the scattered notices.

Much remains to be done, before the subject of the soils of Tennessee, their kinds, the excellencies and deficiencies of each, to what best adapted, the special treatment each requires, and what they, in general, need, to bring them up to a maximum fertility, can be presented in a full and satisfactory way. What follows is nothing more than a contribution to such a presentation. It is in good part, an outline of a classification of the soils, or of the areas containing them, from a geological point of view.

1384. At the last is added a supplementary chapter, on climate, consisting mainly of tables prepared by Prof. W. M. Stewart, of Glenwood, near Clarksville, from his own observations. The State is greatly indebted to this learned, accurate and indefatigable observer. Prof. S. has kept a full and unbroken record of the weather, for the last twenty years. These tables are supplementary to the article on the climate of the State, in chapter I, which was written before the war.*

* The following note from Prof. Stewart, bearing on periodic oscillations in the annual quantities of rain falling, will be found interesting. It is introduced here as a matter of convenience. "In looking over my records, I think I can trace an ascending line (in the tables of precipitation,) in the advancing years; very much zigzagged by the oscillations from year to year, but still *generally* ascending. Taking the year 1851, as the minimum, there is a general increase in the annual quantities of rain which culminates in a maximum in 1865. The tables give, it is true, a double curve, but the general mean line is unmistakable. It would appear, therefore, that the period of these observations covers a little more than half a curve of oscillation, (15 years,) and that a whole oscillation, from maximum to maximum, would require thirty years. The tables appear to show that for 1866 and 1867, the curve makes a start towards another maximum. Whether this will be realized or not, will remain to be determined by future observations. As it seems almost certain, that, in other meteorological phenomena, there are such periodical oscillations, it would be highly interesting to determine whether this is the case with the aqueous meteors."—W. M. S.

CHAPTER XVIII.

SOILS AND AGRICULTURAL FEATURES: CLIMATIC TABLES.

1385. Of all the interests in any way growing out of the natural resources of the State, the agricultural are by far the most important. We have, it is true, mines of iron and copper, beds of coal, quarries of superior marble, and many other resources of the kind, all in the aggregate, constituting a source of wealth of which we may justly be proud. Yet these, compared with our soils, contribute little to the productive capital of the State, and comparatively as little to the thrift of the people. The soils are everywhere. Every man has an interest in them, and they are not less universal in their distribution than they are essential to the prosperity and happiness of all.

1386. It has been stated in § 23, that *variety* in natural features is a characteristic of Tennessee. This holds good in the soils as well as in the rocks, topography and climate of the State. It holds good, also, in agricultural character, for this depends upon the soil, the topography, and the climate, and varies with them.

1387. The climate controls the soil, to a considerable extent, and says what shall spring from it and thrive, and what shall not. It permits cotton in the southwestern part of the State, and forbids it in the northeastern. In certain regions it prematurely opens flower buds, and exposes tender germs to late killing frosts, while in others, the buds are not forced, and escape the frosts. A knowledge of the general character, as well as of the whims of the climate, is desirable, in order that we may control our work accordingly. For that reason, such facts bearing upon the climate of the State, as were accessible, have been incorporated in this Report.

1388. In the latter part of paragraph 315, (which see,) it is stated, that the soils are derived from the rocks which underlie them, and that to these rocks, for the most part, they owe their characteristics. This is true, and hence it follows, that a geological map is a map of the soils. The only practicable way to map the soils, is to map the formations beneath them. The geological map which goes with this Report, is an agricultural one in so far as the boundaries and areas of the several classes of soils are concerned. Any one desiring information as to where are limestone soils, sandstone and shale soils, can generally find it by *studying* this map and the text which goes with it.

1389. The map presents to the eye the several great agricultural districts of the State, exhibits their relative importance as to the areas they occupy, and brings them prominently before us for consideration and discussion. A larger map, going still more into detail, would be proportionally more useful, but this is highly suggestive, and in connection with the text, can be used to good purpose. See, for example, what it teaches with reference to the Central Basin and the Cumberland Table-land.

1390. Below, the principal classes of soils are given, with more or less of detail. The notices of these are mostly in the paragraphs given, and to these the reader is expected to refer. The alluvial soils are not included here. (See § 1164.)

(1.) CALCAREOUS SOILS.

1391. The soils coming from the disintegration of limestone, dolomites and calcareous shales, are the best in the State. These present many varieties, depending upon the impurities contained in the rock. Sandy, argillaceous, fossiliferous, limestones, like those of the Nashville Formation, yield, perhaps, the very best soils we have. Clayey limestones and dolomites give a strong and excellent soil, especially if the latter contain fine gravelly chert in due proportion. Calcareous sandy shales are often overlaid by rich arable land.

1392. The areas on the Map colored blue, (formations 3 and 4;) light pink, (form. 2*c*;) red, (form. 5*d*;) and the areas 6, the upper part, (Lithostrotion Bed,) of 8*a*, and of 8*b*, are underlaid by calcareous rocks, and are the most desirable agricultural regions of Middle and East Tennessee.

1393. With reference to the *Central Basin*, see §§ 227–249; also, §§ 694 to 697.

As to the Valley of East Tennessee, §§ 90–168; also, §§ 658 to 660, §§ 527 to 534, and §§ 572 to 576.

As fo the Western Valley, §§ 250–271; also, §§ 827 and 870. See in addition, § 217 and §§ 890 to 893.

Also, as to the slopes of the Table-land, § 935.

(2.) SOILS OF WEST TENNESSEE.

1394. These are, in general, underlaid by unconsolidated strata of sands and clays. See § 1081.

In reference to the topography of West Tennessee, see 272–294.

The soils of the different formations are spoken of in §§ 1116, 1142, 287 and 288.

(3.) SOIL OF THE CUMBERLAND TABLE-LAND.

1395. The area of the Cumberland Table land is presented prominently on the Map. The topography and climatic features of this region are given in §§ 169 to 205.

This is a large portion of the State, and deserves more study than there has been time to give to it. The general character of its soils are spoken of in §§ 1075 to 1077; and I wish it to be understood that I do not represent them as by any means equal to our limestone soils, or to those of West Tennessee. Nevertheless, there are many reasons why a home on this Table-land is very desirable. With good management, its lands may be made very productive.

1396. The following communication will be read with interest. It is from the pen of an accomplished gentlemen and farmer, who has resided on the Table-land for many years, and whose name has already appeared in our pages. (§ 198.)

"So much has been written about the Table-land of Tennessee, by interested parties, that any one stating the plain truth will be said by them to be an enemy to the progress of the State. Such persons have, in my opinion, been a real drawback upon the prosperity and settlement of the Table-land. It is true of a country, as Washington Irving has said of a man: 'The public will forgive a man any thing sooner than being overpraised.' So of a country, if it be praised for that to which it is not entitled, emigrants on being disappointed, will not give credit for its real merits.

But many things belonging to the Table-lands of this State can scarcely be overpraised. The water, the climate and the health, have not been fully valued in the estimate of this part of our State. On the great plateau of Tennessee the soft, limpid, purity of the water is admired by all observing travelers. The climate, equally exempt from the frigid rigor of the North and the debilitating heat of the South, is no where excelled for the comfort a population. Here may be enjoyed the clearness and brightness of an Italian atmosphere, without the baleful influence of the Maremma marsh, or the debilitating effects of the African sirocco. Here Hygeia's reign is undisputed. Neither cholera, consumption, nor fever, ever pretend to dispute her salutary sway. Emigrants from the frozen shores of the St. Lawrence, or from the fenny bogs of the Carolinas here meet the invigorating breeze; and if health is to be found upon earth, they may hope for it here.

The extent of the Cumberland Table-land within this State, makes it important that its value in an agricultural point of view should be well understood. Reaching across the State from north to south, it is, on the road from Kingston to Sparta, at least forty miles wide from east to west. Most of this large surface is beautifully level, and generally well covered with timber, consisting of various kinds of oak, chestnut and hickory, with other kinds along streams. The soil is a sandy loam, easy of culture, and though not so fertile as other portions of the State, may be made by the application of lime, which is within reach, and proper tillage, very productive at moderate expense.

The Table-land is the genial and appropriate home for all the delicious fruits of a temperate climate. The apple, when raised here, will keep longer than when raised upon a lower level in the same latitude. The same facts are observed here which have been demonstrated elsewhere, that all Alpine productions are superior for their kind. Though the soil will not produce so many bushels of wheat per acre, yet the bushel is heavier than that raised upon richer land. So of other cerealia and the grasses.

At no distant day, these highlands will be much prized, not only for the production of all kinds of fruits, but for the production of stock. For seven or eight months in the year cattle here require no expense from the owner, except salting. Sheep are as healthy as the deer which roam over the forests; no rot or foot-rot ever attacks them; old age appears to be the only malady the flock-master need fear. The natural productions of the soil furnish a copious pasturage for two thirds of the year, and improved meadows of blue-grass, red top, or other perennial grasses, would supply the balance. Here swine live from year to year, and increase without care, upon the natural range. Here the sportsman may find the wild boar as fierce and with tusks as long as any that ever honored the chase in the Hercynian forest."

1397. Mr. J. W. Dodge, who formerly resided in Cumberland County on the Table-land, and who made himself and the mountain famous, by raising and bringing to market, superb apples, related the following circumstance to me: "While I was at the Hermitage, painting Gen. Jackson's picture, the old General one day said to me, in his emphatic way, Mr. Dodge, I have traveled over the Table of the Cumberland Mountain, frequently, and it is my opinion that it is destined to become the garden spot of the Union."

(4.) SOILS OF THE UNAKA MOUNTAINS.

1398. The topographical and climatic features of the Unaka Ranges have been considered in §§ 40 to 89, and their agricultural features in §§ 416 to 420, 477, 478 and 496.

It is as pasture, or range ground, that these mountain areas are at present interesting. A rich spot here and there, may be found in cultivation. At these, heavy crops of wheat and other cereals are sometimes raised. I recollect of seeing, at one point near the "Cold Spring," (see p. 32,) buckwheat high enough to completely hide a man riding through it on horseback. The soil and position of these rich spots appear to be well adapted to the raising of Irish potatoes.

(5.) SOILS OF THE BARRENS AROUND THE CENTRAL BASIN.

1399. These have a siliceous basis, and may be compared with those of the Table-land. See §§ 208, 216 and 890.

CHAPTER XIX.

CLIMATE: SUPPLEMENTARY.

1400. The following tables are introduced as a supplement to Chapter I. See § 1384. In the chapter referred to, the weather tables embrace observations taken previous to 1860. In this, the observations at one station, Glenwood, (page 14,) are brought down to 1868.

1401. APPENDIX TO § 30.

"*Tabular Abstract of monthly Mean Temperature, for the years* 1861 *to* 1868 *inclusive, observed at Glenwood, Montgomery County, Tennessee.*"

The figures show the temperature to hundredths of a degree.

	1861.	1862.	1863.	1864.	1865.	1866.	1867.	1868.
January	°37.55	°42.11	°40.91	°32.91	°31.39	°38.11	°31.74	°31.00
February	44.55	39.53	41.62	38.80	41.61	37.36	45.26	39.91
March	48.49	47.83	47.38	42.10	50.88	47.28	39.86	55.04
April	57.65	58.57	57.69	52.80	58.67	61.54	57.58	55.44
May,	63.53	65.63	63.88	63.00	65.70	62.86	61.40	65.30
June,	74.61	69.58	67.84	72.30	74.61	71.33	73.82	71.93
July,	73.24	75.19	73.22	75.87	75.72	77.44	74.67	79.42
August,	73.21	76.33	73.03	73.92	74.25	72.24	74 54	72.98
September,	68.19	70.33	65.20	68.94	74.13	67.95	71.90	65.76
October,	57.64	57.05	50.60	52.70	55.91	58.09	69.59	55.99
November,	49.96	45.73	46.89	47.37	47.54	48.88	49.57	44.71
December,	43.75	42.49	40.57	37.87	40.40	37.43	42.07	33.37
Mean,	57.69	57.53	55.73	54.88	57.57	56.71	57.67	55.90

Annual Mean for 8 years, 56.71.

1402. APPENDIX TO § 34.

Tabular Statement of the occurrence of Frost, during the period from 1861 *to* 1868, *inclusive.*

	Last frost in Spring.	First light frost in Autumn.	First killing frost or skim ice.	No. of days free from frost.	No. of days free from killing frost.
1861	April 20	September 21	October 24	153	186
1862	April 26	October 18	October 20	174	176
1863	April 9	September 19	October 6	162	178
1864	April 18	October 10	October 14	174	177
1865	March 26	October 5	October 16	192	202
1866	April 10	October 21	October 24	193	195
1867	May 8	October 1	October 31	145	175
1868	April 8	....	October 9	184	......
			Mean of 8 years,	172	184

1403. The following is one of the most interesting Tables of the Series, from an agricultural point of view. It shows the vicissitudes of temperature to which vegetation is exposed—an important consideration. It is, also, highly interesting in other respects, which will be appreciated by the intelligent reader.

CLIMATICAL TABLE,

SHOWING THE MONTHLY EXTREMES, AND RANGE OF TEMPERATURE, FOR THE YEARS 1851 TO 1868, INCLUSIVE.

MONTHS.	1851.			1852.			1853.			1854.			1855.			1856.			1857.			1858.			1859.		
	Max.	Min.	Range.	Max.	Min.	Range.	Max.	Min.	Range.	Max.	Min.	Range.	Max.	Min.	Range.	Max.	Min.	Range.	Max.	Min.	Range.	Max.	Min.	Range.	Max.	Min.	Range.
January	68°	11°	57°	67°	—7°	74°	59°	17°	42°	70°	5°	65°	66°	9°	57°	57°	—1°	58°	48°	—8°	56°	62°	28°	34°	58°	8°	50°
February	72	25	47	74	25	49	67	14	53	70	21	49	62	7	54	45	—3	48	77	16	61	68	8	60	74	13	61
March	76	26	50	84	23	61	76	24	52	80	31	49	75	17	58	67	16	51	80	18	62	79	17	62	75	34	41
April	76	35	41	82	37	45	85	40	45	86	30	56	90	36	54	85	32	53	71	22	49	80	34	46	83	31	52
May	91	34	57	87	46	41	84	51	33	86	42	44	93	43	50	86	46	40	84	45	39	85	45	40	84	54	30
June	92	56	36	89	50	39	93	60	33	92	54	38	89	50	39	92	54	38	88	57	31	89	53	36	87	48	39
July	98	57	41	95	63	32	91	59	32	95	68	27	90	64	26	93	62	31	89	59	30	89	65	24	95	56	39
August	96	65	31	88	58	30	91	56	35	98	65	33	88	66	22	91	60	31	87	56	31	90	54	36	86	57	29
September	96	42	54	88	49	39	86	46	40	98	52	46	88	51	37	89	37	52	86	42	44	86	52	34	86	55	31
October	83	26	57	84	37	47	78	31	47	85	38	47	75	32	43	83	35	48	73	31	42	87	38	49	84	25	59
November	81	24	57	76	25	51	74	27	47	68	26	42	72	27	45	71	22	49	75	30	45	63	21	42	73	15	58
December	69	6	63	73	25	48	65	20	35	62	15	47	62	3	59	70	6	64	69	28	41	70	17	53	72	3	69
ANNUAL MEANS	83°	34°	49°	82°	36°	46°	79°	37°	41°	82°	37°	45°	79°	34°	45°	77°	30°	47°	77°	33°	44°	79°	36°	43°	79°	33°	46°

Months.	1860.			1861.			1862.			1863.			1864.			1865.			1866.			1867.			1868.		
	Max.	Min.	Range.	Max.	Min.	Range.	Max.	Min.	Range.	Max.	Min.	Range.	Max.	Min.	Range.	Max.	Min.	Range.	Max.	Min.	Range.	Max.	Min.	Range.	Max.	Min.	Range.
January	67°	5°	62°	60°	18°	42°	70°	16°	54°	67°	15°	52°	72°	—8°	80°	53°	8°	45°	73°	12°	61°	62°	4°	58°	66°	11°	55°
February	69	—1	70	73	22	51	68	11	57	68	9	59	73	9	64	63	22	41	66	0	66	69	—4	73	67	18	49
March	80	27	53	77	25	52	77	22	55	74	28	46	73	15	58	75	16	59	71	24	47	74	11	63	78	21	57
April	86	35	51	78	38	40	80	40	40	85	32	53	76	37	39	80	39	41	89	37	52	84	40	44	80	31	59
May	87	42	45	87	45	42	84	47	37	81	47	34	85	42	43	83	41	42	84	44	41	81	40	41	86	51	35
June	89	57	32	90	57	33	88	52	36	85	54	31	90	56	34	90	62	28	88	55	33	87	63	24	91	59	32
July	99	61	38	90	58	32	90	63	27	86	57	29	91	57	34	90	64	26	90	60	30	89	63	26	94	70	24
August	98	60	38	90	62	28	91	59	32	87	53	34	87	60	27	89	63	26	93	51	42	88	62	26	88	61	27
September	90	44	46	86	43	43	88	51	37	90	42	48	90	47	43	88	56	32	91	44	47	91	52	49	87	43	44
October	82	31	51	78	33	45	87	24	63	74	33	41	76	35	41	76	38	38	78	32	46	87	33	54	77	33	44
November	68	13	55	77	25	52	74	25	49	77	16	61	69	18	51	70	27	43	77	28	49	75	29	46	74	25	49
December	62	15	47	75	19	56	70	9	61	62	15	47	71	3	68	74	8	66	64	13	51	73	21	52	62	1	61
Annual Means	81°	32°	49°	80°	37°	43°	80°	35°	45°	78°	33°	45°	79°	31°	48°	77°	37°	40°	80°	33°	47°	80°	34°	46°	79°	35°	44°

Note.—In the above Table, the minus sign (—) indicates temperatures below zero. The thermometers employed in these observations, are of the most careful construction; are provided with adjusting arrangements at the top of the tube, and are, at least verified once during the year, by reference to the freezing point. They are free from reflected heat, and exposed to an open circulation of air, on a northern aspect.

It will be observed, by an inspection of the Table, that during the period over which these observations extend, the temperature has never reached 100° Fahrenheit, during the warmest terms; a temperature which is frequently attained in the Northern States and Canada. In July, 1860, the mercury rose to to 99°, which is the highest range. During the same period, it will appear, the temperature has fallen below zero; on several occasions, the lowest being minus 8°, in January, 1857 and 1864, respectively, making the range for the period, 107°. Our coldest days occur in January; the warmest, in July, with very few exceptions. The mean maximum temperature, is 79°.5; the minimum, 34°.3; the range, 45°.2.

1404. Appendix to § 38.

Quantity of Rain, (including melted snow,) fallen, monthly, during the years 1861 *to* 1868, *inclusive, given in inches and thousandths, observed at Glenwood, Montgomery County, Tennessee.*

The figures show the depth of rain fallen, supposing the water to have remained when it fell, without running off or evaporating.

	1861.	1862.	1863.	1864.	1865.	1866.	1867.	1868.
	In.	In.	In.	In.	In.	In.	In.	In.
January,	2.210	5.136	8.582	2.428	2.378	4.365	1.612	5.030
February,	2.701	8.230	6.456	1.127	3.970	4.145	8.988	1.310
March,	2.151	4.767	5.032	3.911	7.983	5.067	8.282	5.519
April,	5.440	8.015	3.271	3.567	11.330	4.396	4.897	7.605
May,	5.838	2.457	2.744	1.880	3.386	2.110	4.555	3.217
June,	2,488	4.971	8.865	2.979	2.675	2.843	2.533	1.915
July,	7.026	5.751	2.243	1.757	5.153	4.929	4.052	4.410
August,	7.850	1.204	1.758	6.207	4.923	0.675	1.300	3.018
September,	3.230	2.489	1.997	2.056	6.186	5.601	0.545	3.802
October,	2.090	0.666	6.041	3.904	1.034	2.240	1.975	1.556
November,	5.082	2.675	2.598	7.627	1.223	4.722	5.935	2.024
December,	1.941	3.280	4.762	3.867	9.763	3.712	4.249	5.371
Annual Amount,	48.047	49.641	54.349	41.310	60.004	44.805	48.923	44.777

Annual Mean for 8 years, ... 48.982 inches.

1405. Barometric Observations.

Tabular abstract of monthly mean pressure, corrected for temperature and capillarity, (but not for altitude above sea level,) for the years 1861 *to* 1868, *inclusive, observed at Glenwood, Montgomery County, Tennessee.*

	1861.	1862.	1863.	1864.	1865.	1866.	1867.	1868.
	In.	In.	In.	In.	In.	In.	In.	In.
January	29.640	29.578	29.616	29.701	29.657	29.728	29.584	29.666
February	29.574	29.576	29.647	29.630	29.585	29.766	29.590	29.715
March	29.629	29.385	29.566	29.450	29.553	29.668	29.572	29.538
April	29·466	29.528	29.531	29.450	29.590	29.527	29.512	29.510
May	29.485	29.499	29.527	29.464	29.475	29.471	29.461	29.406
June	29.524	29.508	29.540	29.547	29.572	29.534	29.512	29.585
July	29.553	29.515	29.530	29.578	29.578	29.579	29.536	29.519
August	29.542	29.572	29.615	29.506	29.581	29.542	29.535	29.583
September	29.597	29.588	29.649	29.544	29.608	29.554	29.606	29.590
October	29.572	29.649	29.596	29.553	29.585	29.653	29.652	29.657
November	29.504	29.628	28.672	29.571	29.655	29.616	29.944	29.682
December	29.751	29.720	29.651	29.569	29.629	29.622	29.593	29.662
Mean	29.569	29.562	29.595	29.447	29.589	29.605	29·566	29.593

Annual Mean for 8 years, ... 29.578.

APPENDIX A.

PALEONTOLOGY.

1406. In the course of this work quite a number of new species have been named, and some briefly described; and at the end of the volume the figures of several of them are presented on the plates. It was my purpose to describe them in full in this Report, but it is found to be impracticable. The descriptions will appear hereafter in the Journal of Science.

1407. I add a few notes with reference to certain species:

(1.) *Carinaropsis carinata* in the table on page 289 has been described by Mr Hall as *Carinaropsis* (*Phragmostoma*) *cunulæ*, in the Fourteenth Regent's Report.

(2.) Mr. Hall suggests, in a letter received since page 328 was printed, that *Orthis Halli*, in the table on the page referred to, is his *O. strophomenoides*, of Vol. III, of Pal. N. Y. Two of the Tennessee specimens were sent to him. They do not, however, show the internal structure. The point can be determined so soon as specimens showing this are met with.

(3.) The substance of the following remarks and descriptions were communicated by the author, many years ago, to the American Journal of Science. In the original paper the varieties of *Tetradium fibratum*, *apertum* and *minus*, were considered species.

The genus *Tetradium*, has been characterized by Prof. Dana in his great work on Zoophytes.* His description and remarks are as follows:

"Coralla massive, consisting of 4-sided tubes, and cells with very thin septa or parietes; cells stellate with four narrow laminæ.

"This genus is near Receptaculites, but differs in having very thin parietes and four distinct rays within the cells, one to each side. The specimen answering to the description, is a fossil of uncertain locality, in the collections of Yale College, New Haven. The cells are about half a line in breadth. The name, from the Greek, τετρας, *four*, alludes to the quadrate structure."

To us this genus is of great interest, from the fact that it is a common form in the limestones of the *Central Basin.*

* United States Exploring Expedition during the years 1838, 1839, 1840, 1841, 1842, under the command of Charles Wilkes, U. S. N. Vol. 8th, page 701.

In addition to the characters given above, we add the following: The *tubes*, in the different species, vary from $\frac{1}{4}$ of a line to nearly a line in breadth; they are very long, and are most frequently united throughout laterally, forming massive coralla resembling more or less those of Favosites and Chætetes; sometimes, however, they are united in single intersecting series, as in *Halysites catenulatus*, Linn.; not unfrequently, too, the tubes are isolated, or only united at irregular intervals, thus forming loose fasciculated coralla resembling certain forms of Syringopora.

The *isolated tubes* are nearly quadrangular, the edges being more or less rounded. A slight linear depression down the middle of each side externally, opposite the lamellæ. Fig. 1 will serve to give an idea of the transverse, or horizontal section of one of these tubes. In the massive specimens, the horizontal sections of the tubes are square, or nearly so. In all of the species, the walls are more or less rugose.

1.

Separately growing tube of Tetradium; transverse section, magnified 3 or 4 times linear.

The increase appears to be by the division of the tubes, the latter splitting sometimes into two cell-tubes, not unfrequently, perhaps, into four; opposite laminæ unite and form the new walls of the young cells, each of which is, in the mean time, supplied with its four rays.

Among the numerous specimens of this genus seen, I have met with but one which shows clearly the presence of transverse septa. This is a fragmentary specimen of the first species described below. In it, the septa are distant about twice the breadth of a tube; but few, however, are seen, and these are confined to one end of the mass.

This group is regarded as being allied, in some respects, to the *Favositidæ*, while on the other hand, the cruciform arrangement of the lamellæ unite with the *Zoantharia rugosa* of MM. Milne Edwards and Haime; in fact, it appears to afford an interesting type of the quadripartite character of the lamellæ, first pointed out by these distinguished authors, in many palæozoic corals.

I give the following species, which, as well as the genus itself, so far as I know, are confined to Lower Silurean rocks.

1. *Tetradium fibratum*, Safford, *variety A.* (Fig. 2.) Coralla massive, hemispherical, or flattened hemispherical, composed of diverging tubes. Cell-tubes four-sided, with thin, and slightly rugose walls; the four lamellæ distinct, nearly reaching the centre of the tubes; breadth of full grown tubes usually about, or but little more, than half a line, varying occasionally from one-third to three-fourth of a line. Transverse septa usually absent. A few have been seen in one specimen, which were about twice the breadth of a tube apart.

2.

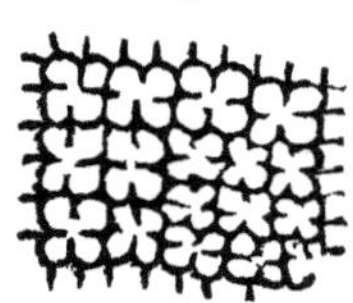

Transverse section of a few tubes of T. fibratum, magnified.

This species occurs abundantly throughout the upper half of the Lower Silurean rocks of Middle Tennessee, associated with *Columnaria stellata*,

Hall, *Ambonychia radiata*, Hall, and other Hudson River species. Large masses, a foot or two in diameter, are met with. The calcareous specimens often resemble, in a weathered longitudinal section, a fossilized, but previously somewhat macerated mass of woody fibre, and hence the name of the species.

Variety B, apertum—Tubes isolated or fasciculated, or else united in linear series which often intersect, forming irregular reticulations; breadth of tubes about half a line; lamellæ as in variety A.

This includes certain open, loosely constructed corals. Two sub-varieties may be designated. These run into each other in some specimens.

(*a*) Masses composed of separate tubes, occasionally united by their sides. These forms often resemble *Syringopora.*

(*b*) Masses composed of tubes arranged in linear series, the latter intersecting, and forming masses like those of *Halysites catenulatus*, Linn.

The first sub-variety is abundant in the middle part of the Lower Silurean Series of the Basin. The second is found in the upper half, as well as near the base. I have observed the same species in Kentucky.

Variety C, minus.—I include here, massive specimens, (generally small,) the tubes of which are only from one-fourth to one-third of a line in breadth. The tubes in some specimens, are quite regular, in others, though generally four-sided, are more or less irregular, and have the aspect on the upper surface of Chætetes. Lamellæ as in variety A.

I have occasionally seen this variety in the upper division of the Lower Silurean in Middle Tennessee, as well as in Kentucky.

2. *T. columnare*, Hall; Syn. *Chœtetes columnaris*, Hall. Pal. of N. Y., vol. I, p. 68, Pl. XXIII, Figs. 4, 4a—Mr. Hall's species, we think referable to this genus. It differs from *T. fibratum* in the following particulars: The tubes are not as uniformly four-sided, nor are they arranged with equal regularity; the walls are more strongly rugose; the lamellæ appear to have been more delicate, and are generally not to be seen; traces of them, however, can, in most instances, be found upon close examination. The four-sided character of the tubes is sufficiently well marked to justify this refence, in connection with the fact that traces of the lamellæ can often be detected.

This species is associated with the last, and occurs, in addition, lower in the series, with *Columnaria alveolata* Hall. It is a common fossil in our Central Basin.

INDEX.

[NOTE.—In making out the formations and soils of the Counties, the Map must be used in connection with the Text.]

ERRATA.

Page 8, 10th line from bottom, for "latterly," read *laterally*.

Page 68, the note in reference to Sequatchee County was written before war, and is to be disregarded.

Page 132, 9th line from top, for "lawyer," read *layer*.

" 175, 19th line from bottom, for "chorite," read *chlorite*.

" 179, 7th line from bottom, expunge "chalcotrichite, unimportant."

" 190, 5000 at end of the diagram, should be one division higher.

" 200, 18th line from top, insert *of*, before "Johnson."

" 251 and 252, about the middle of the pages, for "Grainger and Union," read *Claiborne and Union*.

Page 254, 4th line, for "hydraulei," read *hydraulic*.

" 256, for "Section III," read *Section II*.

" 263, 268, for "Silurean," read *Silurian*.

" 264, 7th line from bottom, for "usual," read *unusual*.

" 289, in regard to species 104, see page 533.

" 329, 3d line, for "shale," read *slate*.

" 329, 12th line, for "coperas," read *copperas*.

" 340, in ¿ 881, for "comminuted shells," read *comminuted crinoidal remains and shells*.

Page 343, in ¿ 888, for *Upper Lithostrotion*," read *Upper*, or *Lithostrotion*.

PLATE 1. (E.)

Fig. 1, *a–h*. CYRTODONTA GANTII, *n. sp.* (Page 287.)

Fig. 2, *a–i*. CYRTODONTA WINCHELLI, *n. sp.* (Page 287.)

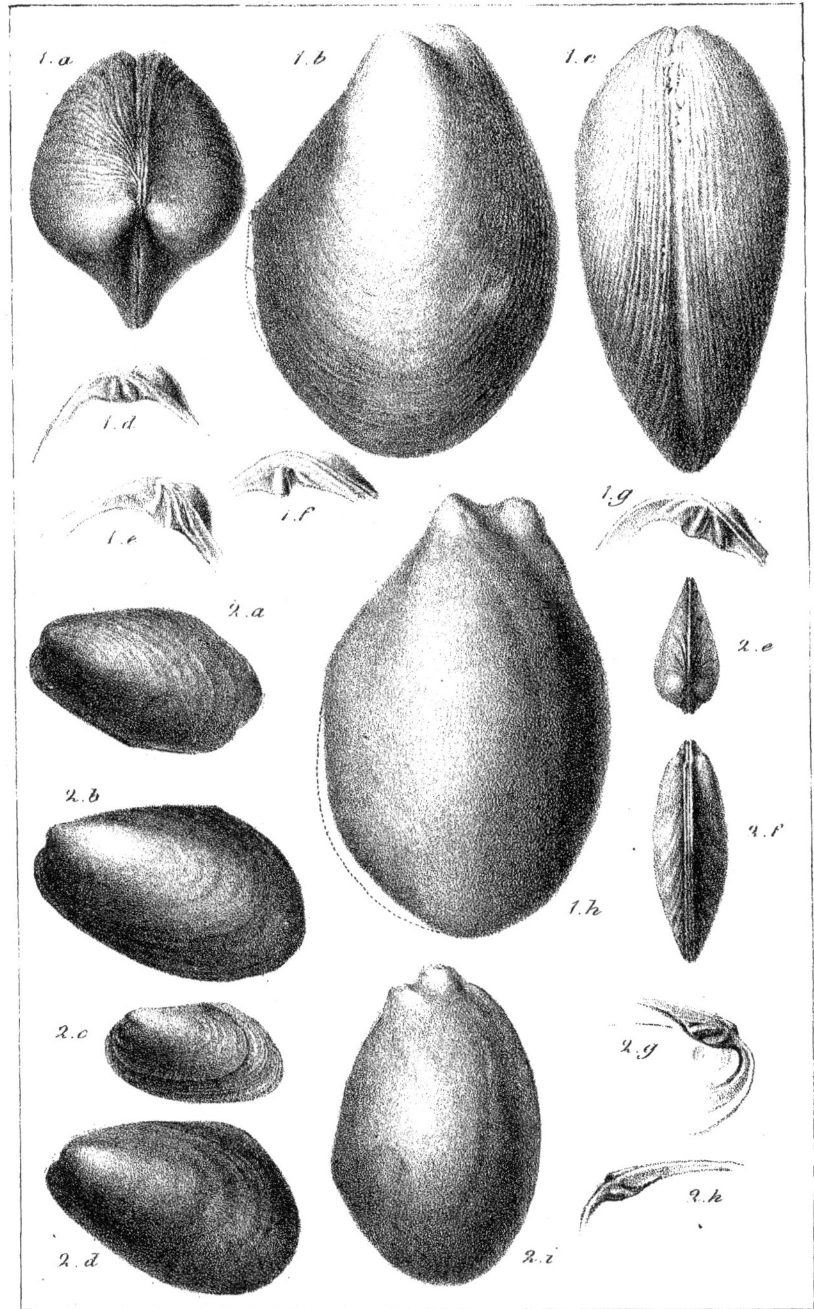
1.a
1.b
1.c
1.d
1.e
1.f
1.g
2.a
2.e
2.b
2.f
1.h
2.c
2.g
2.h
2.d
2.i

PLATE II. (F.)

Fig. 1, *a–e.* CYRTODONTA HAYNIANA, *n. sp.* (Page 287.)

Fig. 2, *a–g.* CYRTODONTA SAFFORDI, Hall. (Page 287.)

Fig. 3, *a–f.* CTENODONTA HARTSVILLENSIS, *n. sp.* (Page 287.)

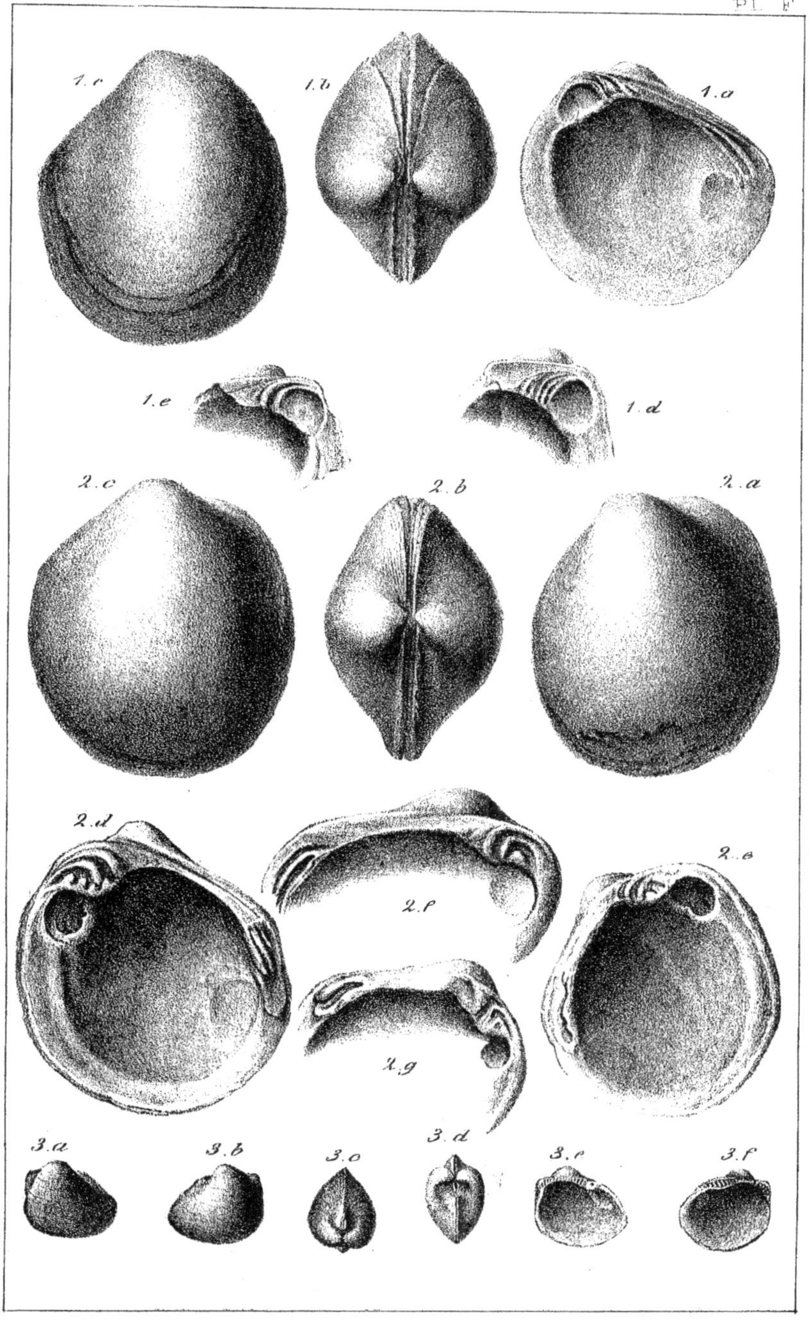
1.c
1.b
1.a
1.e
1.d
2.c
2.b
2.a
2.d
2.f
2.e
2.g
3.a
3.b
3.c
3.d
3.e
3.f

PLATE III. (G.)

Fig. 1, *a–f.* Murchisonia Sumnerensis, *n. sp.* (Page 288.)

Fig. 2, *a–c.* Murchisonia Bowdeni, *n. sp.* (Page 288.)

Fig. 3, *a–d.* Bellerophon Lindsleyi, *n. sp.* (Page 289.)
(On the page referred to the reference is erroneously Fig. 4.
It should be Fig. 3.)

Fig. 4, *a–d.* Bellerophon Troosti? *D'Orb.* (Page 289.)
(On same page as above, the reference should be Fig. 4.)

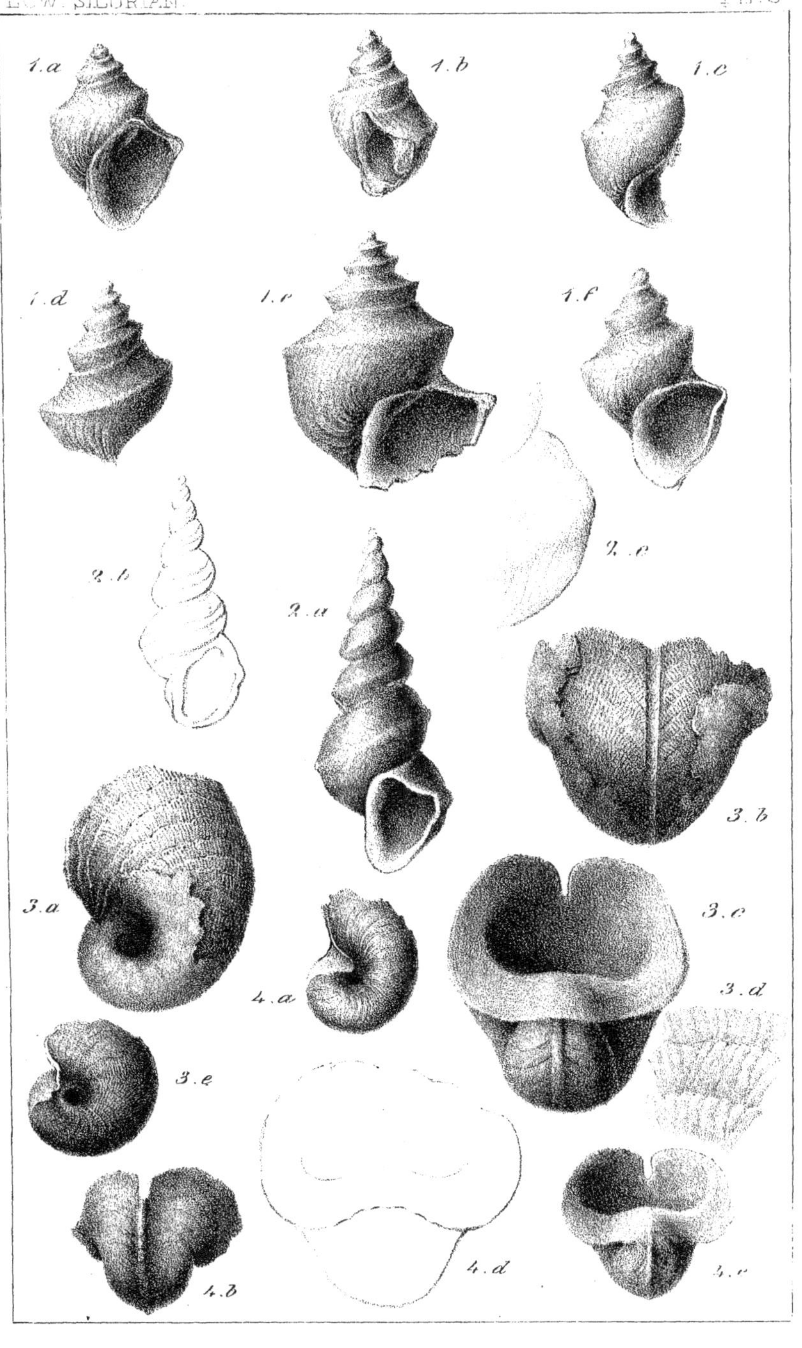
1.a
1.b
1.c
1.d
1.e
1.f
2.a
2.b
2.c
3.a
3.b
3.c
3.d
3.e
4.a
4.b
4.c
4.d

PLATE IV. (G.3.)

Fig. 1, *a–b.* ORTHOCERAS CAPITOLINUM, *n. sp.* (Page 290.)

Fig. 2, *a–c.* CYRTOCERAS? STONENSE, *n. sp.* (Page 290.)

Fig. 3, *a–d.* CYRTOCERAS BONDI, *n. sp.* (Page 290.)

Fig. 4, *a–b.* CYRTOCERAS MASSIENSE, *n. sp.* (Page 290.)

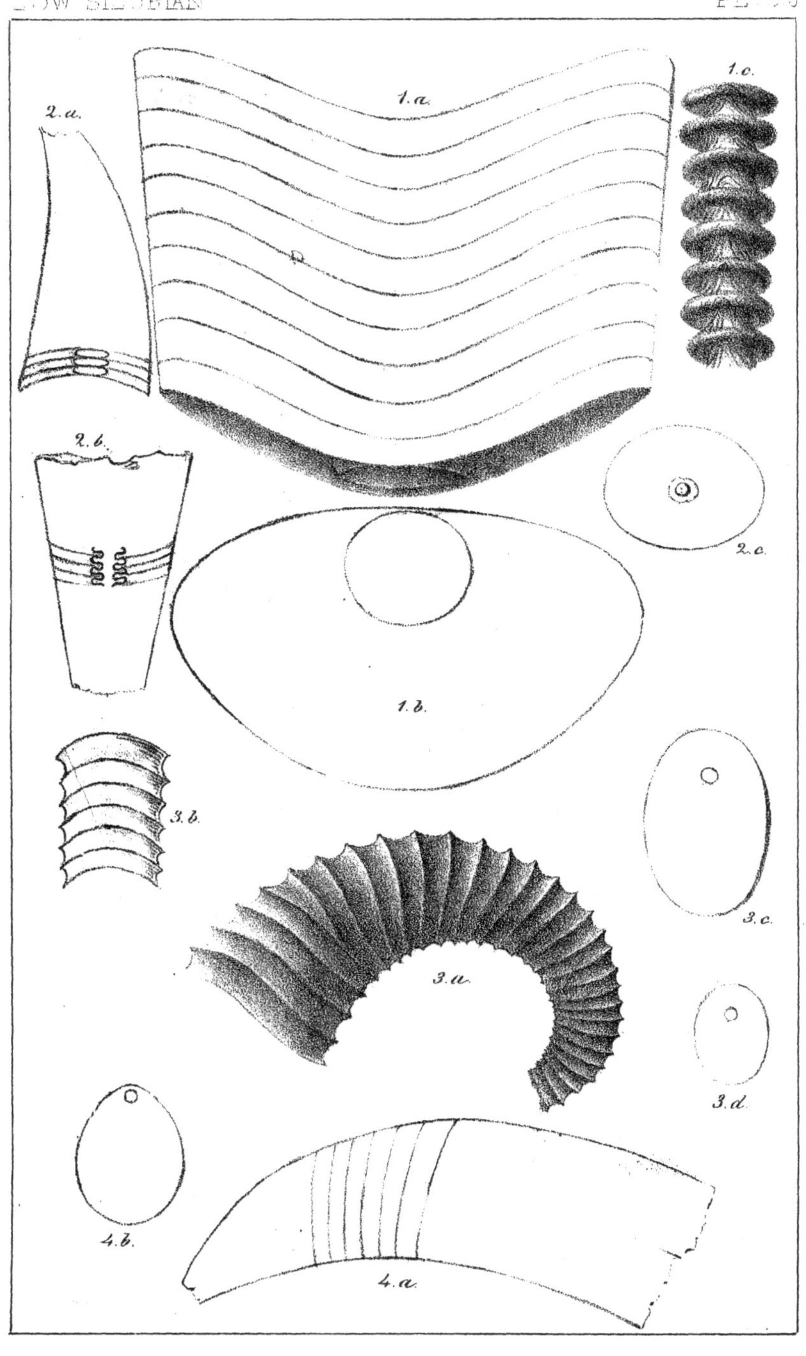
1.a.
1.b.
1.c.
2.a.
2.b.
2.c.
3.a.
3.b.
3.c.
3.d.
4.a.
4.b.

PLATE V. (H.)

Fig. 2, *a–e*. ASTRÆOSPONGIA MENISCUS, *Roemer*. (Page 311 and 320.)

(Figs. 1e and 1d, are sections of individuals of this fossil. The shading in these does not represent internal structure.)

Fig. 2, *a–h*. PETRAIA WAYNENSIS, *n. sp*. (Pages 314 and 320.)

Fig. 3, *a–g*. PETRAIA FANNINGANA, *n. sp*. (Page 320.)

Figs. 4, *a–e*. CALCEOLA TENNESSEENSIS, *Roemer*. (Page 321.)

UP SILURIAN PL. H

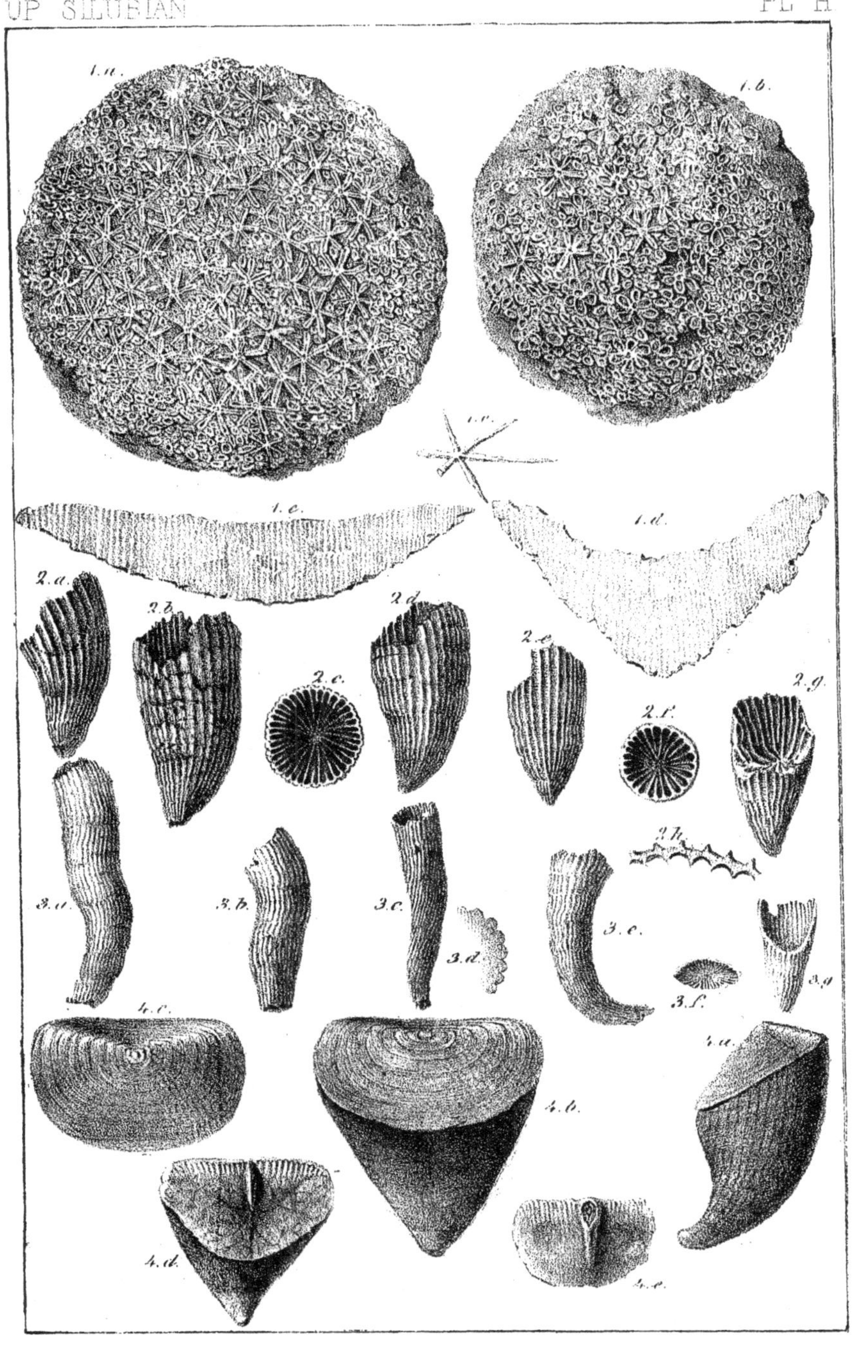

PLATE VI. (I.)

Fig. 1, *a–d.* MELONITES STEWARTII, *n. sp.* (Page 346.)

Fig. 2, *a–d.* PENTREMITES OBLIQUATUS? *Roemer.* (Page 346.)

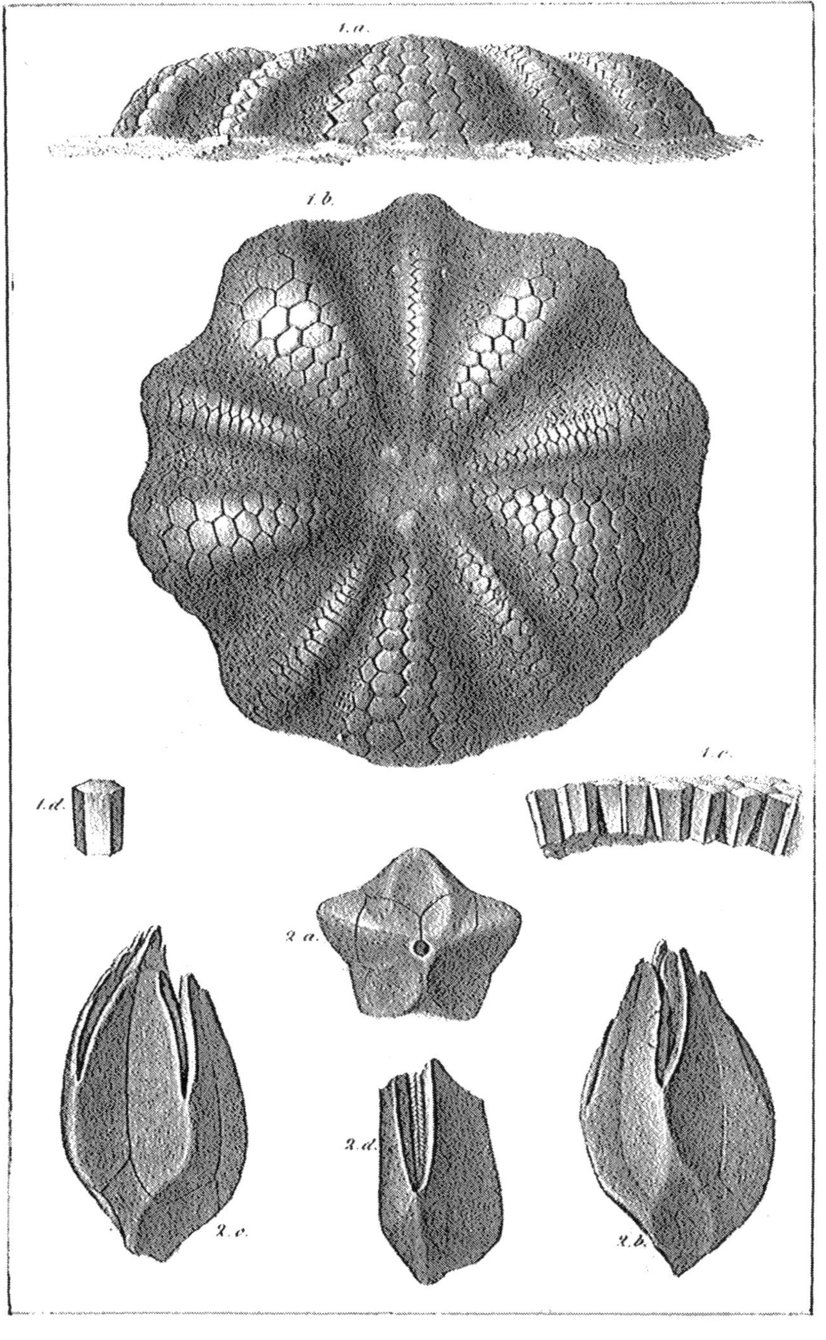
1.a.
1.b.
1.c.
1.d.
2.a.
2.b.
2.c.
2.d.

PLATE VII. (K.)

Fig. 1. QUERCUS CRASSINERVIS, *Ung.* (Page 427.)

Fig. 2, *a–c.* QUERCUS SAFFORDI, *Lsqr.* (Page 427.)

Fig. 3. QUERCUS MYRTIFOLIÆ, *Willd.* (Page 427.)

Fig 4, *a–b.* ANDROMEDA VACCINIFOLIÆ AFFINIS, *Lsqx.* (P. 428.)

Fig. 5. ANDROMEDA DUBIA, *Lsqx.* (Page 428.)

Fig. 6. PRUNUS CAROLINIANA, *Michx.* (Page 427.)

Fig. 7. ELÆAGNUS INÆQUALIS, *Lsqx.* (Page 428.)

Fig. 8. SAPOTACITES AMERICANUS, *Lsqx.* (Page 428.)

Fig. 9. SALIX? DENSINERVIS, *Lsxx.* (Page 427.)

Fig. 10. QUERCUS LYELLII, *Heer.* (Page 426, note.)

Fig. 11. FAGUS FERRUGINEA, *Michx.* (Page 427.)

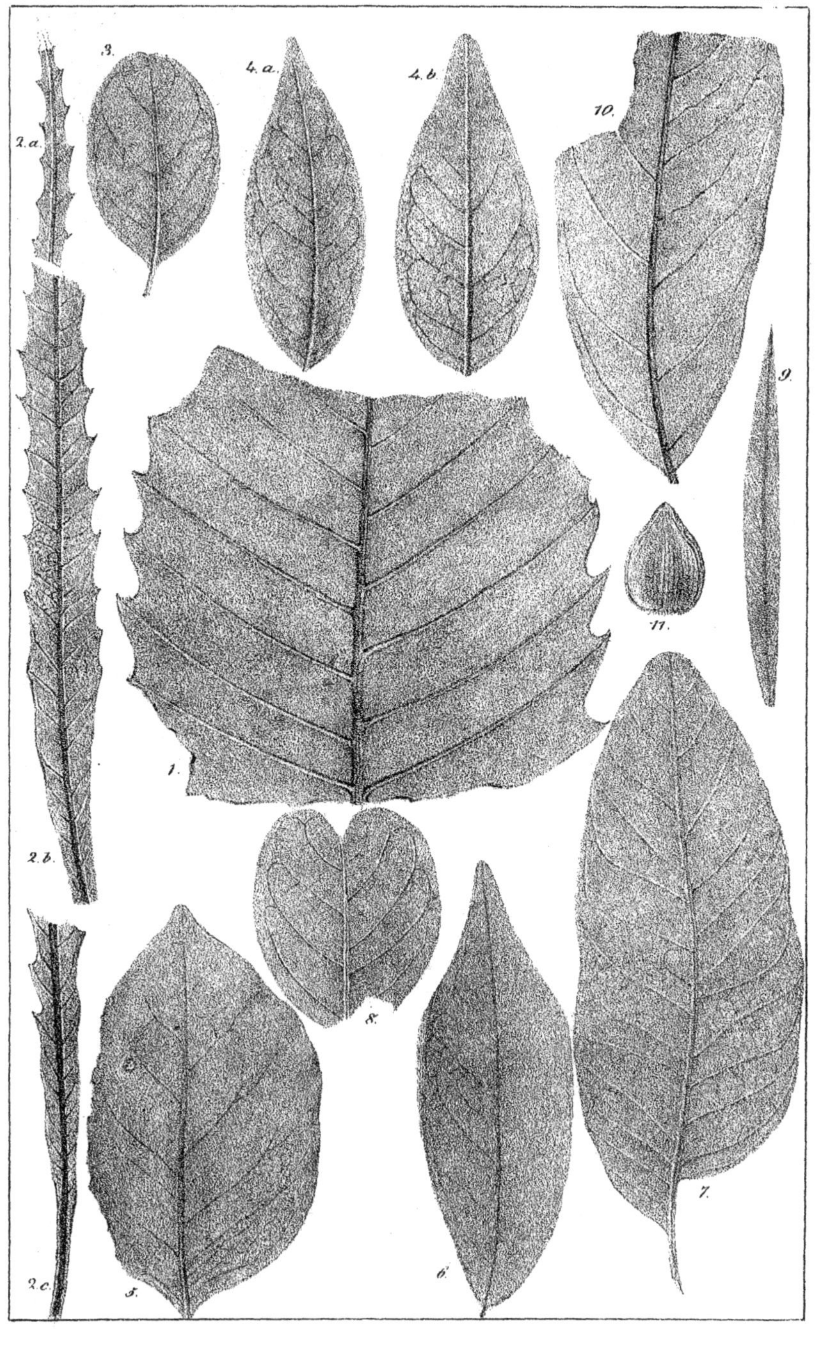
2.a.
3.
4.a.
4.b.
10.
9.
2.b.
1.
11.
8.
7.
2.c.
5.
6.

www.ingramcontent.com/pod-product-compliance
Lightning Source LLC
LaVergne TN
LVHW021223110826
845150LV00002B/233